International Business

International Business
Challenges and Choices

Alan Sitkin and Nick Bowen

OXFORD
UNIVERSITY PRESS

OXFORD
UNIVERSITY PRESS

Great Clarendon Street, Oxford ox2 6DP

Oxford University Press is a department of the University of Oxford.
It furthers the University's objective of excellence in research, scholarship,
and education by publishing worldwide in

Oxford New York

Auckland Cape Town Dar es Salaam Hong Kong Karachi
Kuala Lumpur Madrid Melbourne Mexico City Nairobi
New Delhi Shanghai Taipei Toronto

With offices in

Argentina Austria Brazil Chile Czech Republic France Greece
Guatemala Hungary Italy Japan Poland Portugal Singapore
South Korea Switzerland Thailand Turkey Ukraine Vietnam

Oxford is a registered trade mark of Oxford University Press
in the UK and in certain other countries

Published in the United States
by Oxford University Press Inc., New York

© Oxford University Press 2010

The moral rights of the author have been asserted
Database right Oxford University Press (maker)

First published 2010

British Library Cataloguing in Publication Data

Data available

Library of Congress Cataloging-in-Publication Data

Data available

Typeset by MPS Limited, A Macmillan Company
Printed in Italy
on acid free paper by
LEGO SpA — Lavis, TN

ISBN 978–0–19–953391–6

1 3 5 7 9 10 8 6 4 2

Preface

International Business: Challenges and Choices has been written to offer readers a number of added benefits. This textbook is a unique learning tool, since it

- is shorter and more concise than its rivals;
- avoids business school jargon by focusing exclusively on the crucial challenges and choices that international managers face in their day-to-day activities—an orientation exemplified, for instance, in each chapter's unique practitioner interviews;
- is a fully integrated package, with close links between the textbook and a comprehensive online resource centre; in addition to case studies, activities, and learning resources that are available online, students seeking thematic extension will find material enabling them to explore advanced theories and dilemmas, making the package suitable for both a final-year undergraduate student and a masters student;
- features extensive use of up-to-date international case examples from all across the world, demonstrating both good and bad practice;
- considers companies of varying sizes, helping readers to prepare for their future roles in international business.

The book also stands out because of the particular philosophy guiding its writing. In general, academics can be divided into those who search for a single solution to a specific set of problems, and those who want learners to develop a wide set of skills, allowing them to cope, under constraint, with an unspecified set of problems. A rarity in international business studies, the book is firmly set within the latter tradition.

This approach reflects the authors' belief that the key competency for any successful international career is cultural self-awareness and a healthily sceptical attitude towards any and all value systems. In other words, to gain a full picture of international business, it is crucial to listen not only to its supporters but also to the voices that the economist Joseph Stiglitz has called the 'discontents of globalization'. Thus, unlike many of its rivals, this book positively invites controversy. It believes that animated debate is a useful academic tool for promoting constructive classroom polemics and generating real passion among students for this most dynamic of management disciplines. Furthermore, it is only by giving a fair hearing to globalization's critics, who are more widespread in society as a whole than in most management schools or international business texts, that students can gain a real understanding of the context in which they will be pursuing their career upon graduation.

Uniquely, this book is also written from the perspective that there is nothing 'irreversible' about certain major trends that have prevailed since the 1980s, such as the declining power of states or the increasing interconnection of markets. International business has existed in many shapes and forms, and it is inaccurate to suggest that further openness is inevitable. Future business practitioners are better served by the realization, first, that there are many different ways to transact across borders, and, secondly, that international business is actually very difficult. The enormous challenges and choices facing international practitioners today—such as the ongoing ecological crisis and the 2008–9 credit crunch, themes that run throughout this textbook—are often experienced in very different ways across the world. A checklist approach to business education will not prepare learners sufficiently for the diversity of the human experience. On the other hand, the multi-disciplinary and critical approach that this book embodies will equip readers with the necessary tools to navigate their way through international business.

The main audiences for this book are

- undergraduate students across the globe taking their first module in international business and looking for a refreshingly critical approach to the subject;
- postgraduate students taking MA and MBA courses in international business; the extensive online material allows readers to tackle more advanced and challenging material.

Acknowledgements

General Acknowledgements

We would like to thank our colleagues within the Faculty of Business and Management at Regent's College who have seen, read and/or commented on one or more of the chapters:

Asif Ali Khan
Azam Ali
Richard Cawley
Paul Coldwell
John Diamondopoulos
John Harrison
Dominic Laffy
Amparo Lallana
Richard Mannix
Katie Morris
Josef Mueller
Assia Rolls
Noemi Sadowska
Ibrahim Sirkecki
John Thorp
Lorna Walker

Thanks are also due to Tim Harrison at Regent's College for filming the interviews for 'Inside Business'.

Thanks to the European Business School London and the Faculty of Business and Management, Regent's College, for some research funding for costs of filming, travel expenses, and other sundry items. Our thanks for support from Michael Scriven, Martin Timbrell, Peter Green and Tommie Anderson-Jacquest.

Thanks to the team at OUP, especially Sarah Lodge (Senior Development Editor) and Nicki Sneath (Commissioning Editor).

We would also like to express a special thanks to all the interviewees who contributed to the Inside Business boxes and accompanying DVD, and to James Tomalin for his excellent editing work.

Thanks also to those reviewers who chose to remain anonymous. The publishers would be pleased to clear permission with any copyright holders that we have in advertently failed, or been unable to, contact.

Nick Bowen's Acknowledgements

I would like to thank previous teachers, professors, and colleagues at LSE, Lehigh University, Kent State University, Cambridge University, and EBS London for their guidance and encouragement at various times.

I would also like to thank my three sons who have seen or read one or more chapters:

Chris, Alex, and Phil Bowen. They are constructively critical supporters and a great source of joy to me.

My enduring and undying debt is, as ever, to my wife Joan.

Alan Sitkin's Acknowledgements

In line with the book's international theme, the many people who have supported me so handsomely during this project come from all across the world. My deepest thanks to them and apologies to anyone there is no room to mention here.

Domecqs, Yann, Philippe, Rémi et Richard Zizou, *c'est une belle aventure*. Rainer (und Rolf), *immer dabei*. Drew, Matthew, Jeff and Gentleman Jack, Barbara and Achilleas-reh, *audere est facere*. Also in England, a great thanks to our wonderful OUP friends, *amica* Nicki Sneath and especially development editor Sarah Lodge, a great help at all levels, smart, friendly, fun, and just plain good. A great career beckons—she's a star!

Lastly, a special mention for beloved family members who have shaped my values and vision for this book. Dear Dolans. Patty and Roger and all of my *pueblo unido*, past and future, from the ranch. Helga and Larry, to whom I owe everything. Sue Sue and Jim, whom I am so lucky to have by me, always. Above all, sf Lea and Dani, who have made my life so blessed; and Verena, who is the best.

Brief Contents

Detailed Contents

Abbreviations

ABB	Asea Brown Boveri		EU	European Union
ACP	African, Caribbean, Pacific		FAO	Food and Agriculture Organization
ADB	Asian Development Bank		FCO	Foreign and Commonwealth Office
ADR	American depository receipt		FDA	Food and Drug Administration
AEC	African Economic Community		FDI	foreign direct investment
AIA	Academy of International Business		FOB	free on board
APEC	Asian Pacific Economic Cooperation		FX	foreign exchange
ASEAN	Association of Southeast Asian Nations		GATS	General Agreement on Trade in Services
B2B	business-to-business		GATT	General Agreement on Trade and Tariffs
B2C	business-to-consumer		GDP	gross domestic product
BA	British Airways		GIA	Global International Assignments
BBC	British Broadcasting Corporation		GM	General Motors
BEA	British European Airlines		GM	genetically modified
BIS	Bank for International Settlements		GRI	Global Reporting Initiative
BOAC	British Overseas Airways Corporation		GSP	General System of Preferences
BRICs	Brazil, Russia, India, and China		HCN	host country national
BRP	Bombardier Recreational Products		HIPC	highly indebted poor country
CAP	Common Agricultural Policy		HR	human resource
CARICOM	Caribbean Community		HRM	human resource management
CCT	cross-cultural training		IADB	Inter-American Development Bank
CEO	chief executive officer		*IBR*	*International Business Review*
CI	competitive intelligence		IBRD	International Bank for Reconstruction and Development (the World Bank)
CIF	cost, insurance, and freight			
CR	corporate responsibility		ICA	International Cocoa Association
CSR	corporate social responsibility		ICT	information and communication technology
CTT	currency transaction tax			
EBRD	European Bank for Reconstruction and Development		IEA	International Energy Agency
			IFF	International Fisher Effect
EC	European Commission		IFI	international financial institution
ECOWAS	Economic Community of West African States		IHRM	international human resource management
			IJV	international joint venture
EEC	European Economic Community		ILO	International Labour Organization
EDF	Electricité de France		IMF	International Monetary Fund
EDI	electronic data interchanges		IO	international organization
EFTA	European Free Trade Association		IPCC	Intergovernmental Panel on Climate Change
EIBA	European International Business Academy			
			ISO	International Organization for Standardization
ERM	Environmental Resources Management			

IT	information technology	RFID	radio frequency identification technology
ITO	international trade organization	ROE	return on equity
JIBS	*Journal of International Business Studies*	SBU	strategic business unit
JV	joint venture	SCM	supply chain management
KM	knowledge management	SITS	Single IT Solution
LDC	less developed country	SME	small and medium-sized enterprise
LIBOR	London Interbank Offered Rate	SOE	state-owned enterprise
M&A	mergers and acquisitions	SWF	sovereign wealth fund
MAI	Multilateral Agreement on Investment	TCN	third-country national
MFN	most-favoured nation	TNC	transnational corporation
MNC	multinational corporation	TQM	Total Quality Management
MNE	multinational enterprise	TRIM	Trade Related Investment Measure
NAFTA	North American Free Trade Agreement	TRIPS	Trade Related Aspects of Intellectual Property Rights
NGO	non-governmental organization		
NIB	Nordic Investment Bank	UKTI	UK Trade and Investment
NTB	non-tariff barrier	UN	United Nations
OECD	Organization for Economic Cooperation and Development	UNCAC	United Nations Convention against Corruption
OPEC	Organization for Petroleum Exporting Countries	UNCTAD	UN Conference on Trade and Development
OTC	over the counter	USD	US dollar
P&C	People and Culture	UNESCO	UN Educational, Scientific and Cultural Organization
PC	personal computer	USP	unique selling proposition
PCN	parent country national	USSR	Union of Soviet Socialist Republics
PLC	product life cycle	VAR	Value-at-Risk
ppm	parts per million	VER	voluntary export restraints
PWN	Professional Women's Network	VW	Volkswagen
QR	quantitative restriction	WBCSD	World Business Council for Sustainable Development
R&D	research and development		
RA	regional agreements	WoW	ways of working
RATP	Régie Autonome des Transports Parisiens (the Paris Transport Authority)	WHO	World Health Organization
		WTO	World Trade Organization

List of Case Studies

List of Inside Business

Guided Tour of the Textbook Features

Chapter-opening features

Overview

The chapter overview provides a clear outline of thechapter's contents.

Learning outcomes

Each chapter contains a bulleted list of the main concepts and ideas. These serve as helpful indicators of what you can expect to learn in the chapter.

Opening case study

A case study at the beginning of each chapter provides you with an introduction to the subject and helps to set the scene.

In text features

Inside business

Practitioners provide a short summary of their experiences in the world of business and how the theories and concepts discussed within the chapter are used in practice.

Case study

The book is packed full of examples to help link business theory and concepts to the real business world.

Online resource centre references

Specific links to extension material hosted on the Online Resource Centre (ORC) allow you to expand and stretch your knowledge and understanding.

Challenges and choices

This feature highlights the challenges and choices that business practitioners face in each particular subject area.

Key terms and glossary

Key terms are highlighted and defined where they first appear. They are also defined in the glossary.

End-of-chapter features

Chapter summary

Chapters conclude with a brief summary of the key concepts and points made within the chapter.

Closing case study and questions

At the end of each chapter is a case study accompanied by questions, which enables you to test your knowledge.

Discussion questions

These stimulating questions are designed to help you to engage with and reflect upon the chapter.

Further research

Suggestions for further reading are contained at the end of each chapter.

Guided Tour of the Online Resource Centre

www.oxfordtextbooks.co.uk/orc/sitkin_bowen/

The Online Resource Centre (ORC) comprises resources for both lecturers and students.

For students

Free and open-access material available to students:

Extension material

A vast amount of material with specific links to the textbook enabling you to expand your knowledge.

Multiple choice questions

These provide a quick and easy way to test your understanding, with instant feedback.

Key references

Includes a list of key texts and websites where you can learn more about a particular topic.

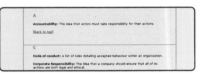

Glossary

A searchable glossary helps you to quickly locate key terms.

Critical skills activity

Scenarios or activities are provided to encourage you to think critically about an aspect of business, enabling you to understand alternative viewpoints and arguments.

Revision tips

Each chapter is accompanied by revision tips, which help sum up the key points from each chapter.

For lecturers

Free for all registered adopters of the textbook:

PowerPoint lecture slides

A suite of customizable PowerPoint slides has been provided to use in your lecture presentations.

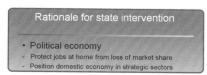

Running a seminar

The authors have provided suggestions and ideas for how to structure a seminar and integrate the textbook and its resources in your teaching.

Seminar discussion questions

These can be used to help spark debate amongst students during seminars.

Case study questions and indicative answers

Questions and answers are provided for each case study for use in class or to set as home work.

Oral presentation

Ideas for individual and group oral presentations are provided.

Project task

Suggestions for various projects that students can embark on are provided for use in tutorial work.

Additional case study

An additional case study accompanies every chapter and can be used to provide students with a further example of how theory is applied in practice.

Test bank

A ready-made electronic testing resource, which is fully customizable and contains feedback for students, will help you to save time creating assessments. There are 20 questions per chapter, each with feedback.

Guided Tour of the DVD Resources

The lecturer's DVD contains short videoed interviews with practitioners who talk about their experience in relation to the chapter subject area. There is one per chapter and each interview is summarised within the textbook through the 'Inside Business' feature. These clips provide students with a real insight into a variety of organizations, including large multinational corporations, small and medium sixed companies, and government organizations. Below are just six examples of the companies featured in the book.

Denitza Roussinova
Formerly Managing Director, Portfolio Manager Eastern Europe Middle East Africa Fund, Black River Asset Management

Emil Gigov
Partner, Albion Ventures LLP

Johnny Akerholm
President and CEO, Nordic Investment Bank

Robert Dennis
Advisory Board Member, Zafesoft

Arve Thorvik
Formerly Vice President for European Affairs, StatoilHydro

Tom Glocer
CEO, Thomson Reuters

Introduction to International Business

Overview

The chapter begins with an explanation of the philosophical distinction between 'international' and 'global' approaches to business. This is followed by a justification of the book's core belief that it is more useful for international managers to develop an ability to respond to varying international circumstances than to seek a 'one-best-way' solution applicable everywhere and always. Significant statistics are provided, demonstrating the growing importance of international business in the modern world. The final section reviews some of the many different reasons why companies engage in cross-border transactions, highlighting the specific difficulties that they will face in international as opposed to domestic dealings.

Introduction

Section I: Visions of international business

    Definitions and philosophy

    Key statistics

Section II: The international business framework

    Activity drivers

    Challenges and choices

Learning Objectives

After reading this chapter, you will be able to:

+ compare the concepts of international and global business;
+ determine the value for international managers of developing a flexible mindset;
+ understand the main terminology used in international business studies;
+ perceive the link between politics, economics, and international business;
+ analyse the internal and external drivers of international business.

Case Study 1.1

When American cars fall behind international standards

The first foreign producers to gain a significant share of the US automotive market were the Japanese in the 1970s, led by Toyota, Honda, and Nissan (or Datsun, as it was known). Offering fuel-efficient models that were better adapted to the high oil prices of the time, the Japanese helped to build a new market niche in a country where low fuel prices had always been taken for granted. The American carmakers, led by the 'Big 3' (General Motors, Ford, and Chrysler), reacted to this competition in their home market by lobbying Washington to place restrictions on Japanese imports. This seemed a cheaper option than redesigning their product ranges away from the big gas-guzzlers that American consumers had traditionally favoured.

The counter-oil shock of 1986, which led to a dramatic fall in fuel prices, appeared to justify the Big 3's strategy. Indeed, with energy inflation seemingly under control, the American carmakers decided to invest massively in the light truck segment, promoting household purchases of minivans, 4x4s, pick-ups, and sport utility vehicles. These vehicles were anything but efficient, and, despite a great deal of technological progress, fuel consumption averages actually rose in the USA between the 1980s and the 2000s. At the same time, strong light truck sales, which by 2008 accounted for 54 per cent of all new vehicle purchases in the USA versus 22 per cent in the 1980s, helped to restore the Big 3's profitability temporarily. This strategic decision came with a heavy cost, however, since it lulled US auto executives into believing that they still did not have to incorporate long-term global trends into their planning.

The energy crisis of 2006–7 shook up the global economic environment, with oil prices hitting new records and peaking US consumers' interest in fuel-efficient cars. This was a great opportunity for Toyota, which had concentrated more on global energy trends and used the years since the 1980s to develop a hybrid model (the Prius) that consumed less oil and emitted less carbon dioxide (a key contributor to global warming). This positioning gave the Japanese carmaker a tremendous edge and revealed serious flaws in the Big 3's strategic outlook. The 2008 credit crunch, which caused new model sales to crash worldwide, added to the pressure on the American carmakers. Not only were the Big 3 unable to count on export markets to offset falling demand at home; the recession meant that even in their domestic market it was also harder for them to sell the big

The credit crunch affected large American pick-up trucks more than it did fuel-efficient Japanese vehicles (© iStockphoto).

expensive vehicles in which they had specialized. The American carmakers' product range is especially unfortunate given the likelihood that much future growth in the world automotive markets will occur in emerging economies, where households can afford only modest vehicles, like the small cars that companies such as Romania's Dacia or India's Tata are developing.

With hindsight, the decision taken by America's Big 3 carmakers during the 1980s and 1990s to remain focused on domestic conditions and consumer preferences undermined their chances of survival in what has become an increasingly globalized business. Things got so bad that by summer 2009 General Motors had declared bankruptcy and Italian carmaker Fiat had taken over Chrysler. This could be contrasted with the promising outlook for new producers like China's BYD, a battery specialist that was having great success in applying its technology to new kinds of passenger vehicles. One of the first rules of international business is that, with very few exceptions, global trends tend to have a greater impact than domestic ones.

Introduction

The simplest definition for international business is 'cross-border economic activity'. This has existed in various forms ever since human communities began interacting with one another. When human tribes first started trading beads or minerals like flint more than ten thousand years ago, they were engaging in prehistoric forms of international business (Watson 2005). Of course, trade has become slightly more complicated since then. Nowadays, international business refers to the exchange not only of physical goods but also of services, capital, technology, and human resources. The first point to make about this field is that it covers a very broad spectrum of activities.

Just as important is to recognize what makes international business distinct from other areas of study, and where it overlaps with them. Many aspects of domestic business are also found in international business, but they are treated differently because of the latter field's emphasis on cross-border aspects. Similarly, international business covers most if not all of the same topics as international management but goes much further. Where international management focuses mainly on decisions made by individuals operating within a corporate setting, international business also incorporates the broader political, economic, social, technological, philosophical, and environmental contexts within which firms operate. It is a very broad discipline with connections to many if not most of the issues affecting people in their daily lives. The best international business students and practitioners can analyse on many different levels and tend not to recognize artificial borders between business, economics, and politics (White 2001). Indeed, the ability and desire to embrace diversity give this discipline its distinct philosophy and enduring attraction.

Section I: Visions of international business

+ **Globalization**
Process whereby the world becomes increasingly interconnected at an economic, political and social level.

A good starting point for this book is to distinguish between the concept of international business and the neighbouring notion of globalization, with which it is often confused (Hirst and Thompson 1999). Every discipline has its own vocabulary, and it will be useful to introduce certain key terms early on. Subsequently there will be a brief look at the philosophies underlying international business. Lastly, analysis of current statistics will give readers a sense of its characteristics today.

Definitions and philosophy

+ **Home/host country**
People/companies originate from a 'home country'. When they operate abroad, they are working in a 'host country'.

International business, if only because of its cross-border nature, raises several specific challenges that business practitioners and academics ignore at their peril. It can be a very difficult adjustment for companies or individuals leaving a home country with which they are familiar to operate in a host country where the environment and people are foreign to them. There is no doubt that the world has shrunk over human history and that globalization has been a key factor in this process (MacGillivray 2006). At the same time, it is unrealistic and even dangerous to assume that societies worldwide are converging to such an extent that there is no longer any need to study their economic, political, and cultural differences. This recognition that the world remains a complex and diverse place is best expressed through the distinction made between the terms 'global' and 'international'.

The word 'global' is associated with the idea of a single world and therefore stresses similarities between different communities. The word 'international', on the other hand, starts with an emphasis on the lack of similarity. There is a strong argument that this latter approach is more useful, since it acknowledges the specific obstacles that arise when people from different nations and cultures come together. It also prepares practitioners to develop

Thinking point

Which has a bigger effect on the business environment, national differences or global similarities?

the insiderization strategies that are necessary to overcome the many barriers that people face when they cross borders (Ohmae 1999). In an ideal world, no such barriers would exist. Unfortunately, humankind does not live in such a world, if only because of xenophobia and the feelings of 'animosity' that some populations have towards others (Amine 2008). This is not to deny growing similarities between many societies at certain levels, or that some sectors of activity operate along global instead of national lines (see Chapters 5 and 6). Indeed, there is little doubt that greater global interconnectedness has had a very deep effect on business and individuals, and some sociologists have identified what should be greeted as a positive trend towards greater cosmopolitanism and tolerance amongst many citizens of the world (Giddens 2002). By the same token, other observers doubt how long this new religion of 'globalism' will last, preferring to highlight the enduring and even resurgent nature of national awareness (Saul 2006). As shown by rising sentiments of protectionism in the wake of the 2008 credit crunch, when times are hard, many people's first concern is still for the welfare of their local community. Indeed, as the crisis worsened, fears arose that the world might 'retreat to narrow nationalism' (*Guardian* 2009). In our opinion, there is nothing inevitable about globalization or, indeed, any other socio-economic or cultural trend.

What is clear is that most people have an identity that reflects, at least in part, the specificities of their culture of origin and/or the paradigm they use to make sense of the world (see Chapters 2 and 10). An 'international' approach embodies this principle more completely than a 'global' one does, if only because it starts with an acknowledgement of individuality. Philosophically, it is not a neutral choice to stress diversity as opposed to oneness. It is an attitude that leads to the expectation that the international business strategies and behaviour that apply in one situation may not be appropriate in another—there is no 'one best way' of doing business. This may seem obvious to people whose culture of origin emphasizes the need to seek multiple solutions to any one problem, but it can be a difficult adjustment for people from a culture where the emphasis is on discovering a single optimal solution to a problem. A prime example from the early 1990s was when academics, impressed by Toyota's successful industrial methods, published an analysis that some observers took as proof that one particular way of working can be superior to all others at a given moment in time (Womack et al. 1991). This caused a storm in university circles. It is best to state openly that the present book is based on the idea that international business students are better served by an approach aimed at helping them to develop a flexible mindset instead of trying to help them find the 'right answer'.

Companies doing international business

Now that we have outlined how the term 'international' will be used here, the next task is to define what kind of business is actually involved. It could be argued that 'international business' is already occurring any time an individual engages in a cross-border transaction. Indeed, private parties play an important role in the world economy: investors purchasing currencies or shares in foreign companies (see Chapters 13 and 14); or local agents acting as representatives and providing firms with information on countries with which they are unfamiliar (see Chapter 8). Unsurprisingly, however, most international business is done by companies, ranging from huge firms to small and medium-sized enterprises (SMEs) to micro-firms that may or may not be 'born global' from the very outset. It is impossible to generalize why firms might want to seek their fortune abroad. In general, the main motivation used to be the acquisition of resources, whereas nowadays it tends to be the development of knowledge and markets (Aharoni and Ramamurti 2008). Paradigms vary strongly over time, however. As Chapters 4 and 5 demonstrate, history is another discipline that has much to offer the international business student.

The general terminology that this book uses to refer to companies that have regular dealings outside their home country is multinational enterprise (MNE). Other international business books will often use other terms, such as multinational corporation (MNC),

---

+ Insiderization
When people or companies are so deeply integrated into a local society that their foreign origins are forgotten.

+ Xenophobia
Fear of things that are foreign.

+ Protectionism
General policy where a national government adopts policies restricting foreign producers' access to its domestic market.

+ Paradigm
A worldview—that is, a vision of how things are and/or should be organized.

+ Small and medium-sized enterprises
'Enterprises which employ fewer than 250 persons and which have an annual turnover not exceeding 50 million euros, and/or an annual balance sheet total not exceeding 43 million euros' (European Commission 2003).

+ Multinational enterprises
Firms whose regular activities cause them to engage with and/or operate in more than one country at a time.

transnational corporation (TNC), and global firm. The problem with these other expressions is that each designates a specific kind of company and is therefore not general enough. For instance, talking about MNCs neglects the fact that not all actors playing a role in international business are corporations or even privately owned enterprises. Similarly, terms such as TNCs and above all global firms do not sufficiently communicate the connections that continue to tie most companies with international interests to their country of origin. MNE is a more neutral term to describe the broad category of firms that, according to some statistics, account for more than 70 per cent of world trade (Steger 2003). Thus, for the rest of this book, the term MNE (which can include SMEs engaged in foreign transactions) will be the basic unit of analysis.

MNE configurations

A firm that owns facilities in a single country but carries out transactions regularly outside its borders may qualify as an MNE, but a far more typical and informative figure is the firm whose international configuration is comprised of a head office and subsidiaries located in different parts of the world. It has been estimated that MNEs' foreign subsidiaries are responsible for slightly more than 10 per cent of global economic activity (Serfati 2006). The significance of such units' activities can vary widely between countries like France or the UK, where they account for up to 30 per cent of national sales, and others like Japan, where they play almost no role at all in key areas like manufacturing employment. In general, however, there is a trend towards MNEs expanding their international presence through foreign subsidiaries. Alongside trade, companies' foreign direct investment (FDI) is the second main pillar of international business and constitutes a key focus in this field

The tendency has been for MNEs to try to integrate units' functional activities. This has often been in application of theories that different locations should specialize in activities where they have a competitive advantage (see Chapter 4). One consequence is that an increasing proportion of international business involves MNE subsidiaries trading with one another and/or with subcontractors (Coleman and Underhill 1998). This is one reason why it is so important to understand the different ways in which MNE head offices organize their relational networks (see Chapter 9).

International value chains

The most useful way of picturing MNEs' work organization is to imagine the production and sale of a good or service as a series of acts adding to the item's value as it is transformed from a raw material into a semi-processed stage before ending up as a finished good or service (see Figure 1.1). This series of acts is called the value chain. It is divided into production-related upstream activities (see Chapter 11) and marketing-related downstream activities (see Chapter 12). One of the main features of international business today is that many firms do not perform by themselves all of the activities comprising the value chain in which they are involved. Instead, they might ask external partners to take responsibility for certain phases. As such, it is more accurate to represent international value chains as the sum of several intermediary value chains. A good example is provided by blue jeans, which should be analysed not just as a finished product but as the sum of many lower-level generic products. One of these is the zip, which is the culmination of several intermediary businesses, starting with extraction of minerals, the processing of basic metals, and their subsequent transformation into zips. It is important to understand that the end product of one company's international value chain (for example, zip-makers) is just an intermediate phase in the value chain of another company (the jeans-maker).

This portrayal of international business as a series of cross-border value chains raises questions about the rate at which value accumulates while a service or good is being transformed into its final form. For presentation's sake, Figure 1.1 shows value accumulating at a linear rate. This is not entirely realistic, since, depending on the sector in question, value

Margin glossary

+ **Global firm**
Company that is conceived of as serving a unified world market rather than differentiated national markets.

+ **Configuration**
How a company designs and locates different corporate functions such as research, production, marketing, and finance.

+ **Subsidiary**
(Foreign) unit belonging to a company's head office.

+ **Foreign direct investment (FDI)**
Where a firm funds a permanent or semi-permanent physical unit abroad. One definition is that this involves a company taking a minimum 10 per cent stake in a foreign entity.

+ **Value chain**
Succession of acts that successfully add value to an item as it is transformed from a raw material or input stage to a finished product or service.

+ **Upstream**
Early value chain activities undertaken when processing or transforming a product or service.

+ **Downstream**
Later value chain activities relating to the interface between a company and its customers.

+ **Generic**
Item that is not differentiated for a specific use but has a variety of applications.

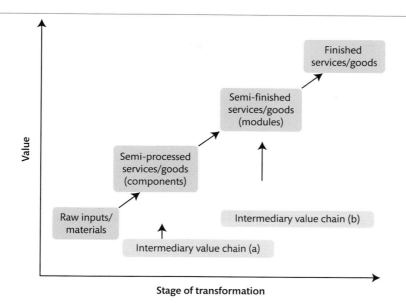

Figure 1.1
Visualizing the
transformation of
a good or service:
each level adds value
and also has its own
intermediary value
chains.

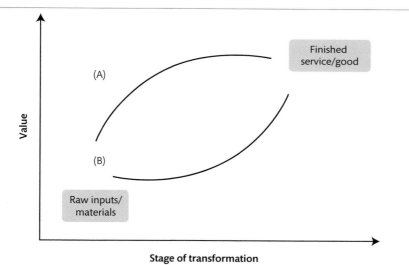

Figure 1.2
Value tends not to
increase in a straight
line. Curve (A) indicates
a product or service
where the upstream
side accumulates
a greater share of the
value added than the
downstream. Curve (B)
indicates the opposite.

will tend to accumulate more or less quickly when the good or service is more towards the upstream or downstream side of the value chain. For instance, in the coffee business, a tiny percentage of what consumers pay for a cup at Starbucks goes to upstream bean-growers, possibly reflecting producers' lack of bargaining power when dealing with powerful MNEs whose main area of operations is further downstream, closer to consumers. Inversely, in a sellers' market (like oil) marked by less competition amongst producers, value will tend to accumulate in the hands of upstream producers. Figure 1.2 offers a more realistic picture of (international) value chain curves.

Clearly it is more efficient to operate at that part of the value chain where value accumulates most intensively (i.e. where the value-added curve is steepest). This is just as true for national economies as for companies. Those countries whose firms specialize in high value-added production are clearly at an advantage over those that specialize in low value-added goods—or, as economists would put it, they enjoy better terms of trade. For example, if US firms are global champions in computers and Sri Lankan companies lead the world in the tea business, the USA is clearly at an advantage, since the markets where it dominates create greater value than the markets where Sri Lanka dominates. National governments are

+ Terms of trade
Relationship between
the value added
inherent to the goods/
services that a country
imports, on one hand,
and that it exports, on
the other.

Photo 1.1
Jeans are the culmination of many lower-level value chains, including zips, buttons, and pockets (© iStockphoto).

+ Offshore
Transactions or actors over which national regulators have no authority.

Thinking point

To what extent can international business be discussed without considering politics?

+ Shareholder value
Idea that the purpose of a company is to maximize returns to shareholders.

+ Technology transfer
Where technology belonging to one country or company is shared with another under a formal partnership arrangement.

+ Triad/OECD countries
World's more affluent and industrialized nations. Triad refers to the three regions of Western Europe, North America, and Japan/Oceania. The Organization for Economic Cooperation and Development (OECD) is a Paris-based association whose membership is comprised of the world's leading economies.

very aware of this factor and will often take measures to improve their country's competitive position. Such efforts are part of the political environment within which MNEs operate—as are the measures enacted by global bodies (see Chapter 6) to control the actions that states might wish to take in the marketplace. When devising their value chain strategies, companies need to be aware of all relevant political and legislative frameworks, if only because they must obey the laws of the different countries where they will be operating. The problem is that many firms operate today on an offshore basis outside a single government's control. Further confusion is caused by the fact that many of the government regulations affecting international business (such as import taxes or export subsidies) vary significantly in time and place. In international business, political considerations are a key aspect of corporate strategizing.

Who benefits from globalization?

One source of political tension in international business is widespread disagreement about the distribution of the costs and benefits associated with this activity. This debate is crucial because of the way it impacts public policy and therefore the general environment. MNEs are affected by political tensions but will in turn also influence the political sphere. Ethical conflicts that arise within a domestic context, such as whether a company exists to maximize shareholder value or to serve the wider community, are aggravated when they extend across borders (see Chapter 3). As demonstrated in the statistics below, MNEs play a crucial role in most of the world's national economies, distributing wealth through their capital allocation and technology transfer decisions. At the same time, wealth distribution has become increasingly uneven (Milanovic 2005). MNEs representing the interests of the world's more affluent nations, alternatively called Triad or OECD countries, are blamed by some observers (Scholte 2005) for the problems faced by poorer nations, broadly described as less developed countries (LDCs). Inversely, others view globalization as the best hope of ending poverty (Samuelson 2008). Indeed, there is a growing sense that international business, alongside disciplines such as economics, sociology, or political sciences, is a key element of the development trajectories in which many poor countries are engaged (Lévy 2007). As such, it is logical that this book be divided between a 'macro' section describing national frameworks, and a 'micro' section focusing on how companies organize themselves to gain advantage.

Key statistics

International business is very much a living subject, rooted in the relationship between actions and outcomes. For this reason, it is crucial that practitioners and students develop the ability to analyse the basic concepts of this discipline in terms of what happens in the real world. Viewing international business in context means, among other talents, being able to link theory to front-page news.

International trade data

The 2008 credit crunch was devastating to world trade and investment. A complete set of statistics for early 2009 was not yet available by the time of this book's publication. (Go to the Online Resource Centre, extension material 1.1, to learn more about indicative post-crisis performance in a few leading trading nations.) However, the first indications are that trade and FDI had crashed much more quickly than the global economy had as a whole. One noteworthy figure is the 46 per cent fall that Japanese exports recorded between January 2008 and January 2009. A second is the estimation made two months later by the World Trade Organization (WTO), a leading body of global governance (see Chapter 6), that international trade was destined to suffer a 9 per cent fall over the course of 2009—much greater than the 1 or 2 per cent shrinkage that another major organization, the International Monetary Fund (IMF), was predicting for the global economy. This disproportionate fall in cross-border activity is unsurprising, since during a recession national governments tend to provide 'stabilizer' financial resources (paying welfare benefits or running budget deficits) that will be spent mainly on domestic activities like services. At the same time, it is very significant that many if not most economies react to crises by becoming more inwardly focused, at least temporarily. In a sense, the 'de-globalization' fears associated with the crisis of the late 2000s have revealed the limitations of international business.

Nonetheless, longer-term statistics have clearly shown a trend towards increased cross-border activity, and there is every chance that this will resume once the effects of the credit crunch have faded. Arguably it is a poorly designed global financial system that is to blame for the crisis, not international business *per se*. Analytically, there is a clear need to distinguish between open product and service markets, on the one hand, and open capital markets, on the other (see Chapter 14). The two do not necessarily go hand-in-hand, and there is little reason to think that the likely future reregulation of the international banking and finance systems will seriously hamper trade and FDI in other sectors of activity. At the same time, it is also in international managers' interest to keep track of any decisions made regarding the global financial framework at meetings like the April 2000 G20 summit in London. The financial markets may be separate from the product or service markets, but the two spheres do interact.

Figure 1.3 shows how, in the decade preceding the credit crunch, world trade had risen by an annual average of around 5.5 per cent, or about 2 per cent faster than the global economy as a whole. The result of this trend is that international business had become a dominant aspect of many people's lives. Just one generation ago, trade accounted for around 10 per cent of the US gross domestic product (GDP); from 25 to 30 per cent of GDP in medium-sized industrial exporting nations such as Germany, France, and Japan; and around 50 per cent of GDP in some smaller open economies like the Netherlands. By 2008, the openness to trade in most of these countries, measured as the sum of imports and exports divided by GDP, had at least doubled (see Figure 5.5). Even more dramatically, in countries such as China, Russia, and India, which for political reasons had engaged in very little trade before the 1990s, the sum total of imports and exports amounted by the late 2000s to between 45 and 65 per cent of GDP. Of course, it could be argued that simply adding imports and exports overstates an economy's degree of openness. Admittedly, this is an inadequate way of accounting for certain situations, like temporary imports of components assembled in final goods destined for export markets. Similarly, in the wake of the 2008 credit crunch, some observers were predicting that, within a few short years, global trade would fall from an early 2008 peak of around two-thirds of global GDP to a more sustainable figure of 40–50 per cent (Munchau 2009). This is still very high, however. Even after the 2008 recession, there is no doubt that international trade will continue to account for a large proportion of all business today—justifying an in-depth study of this topic.

+ **Less developed countries (LDCs)** Countries where the industrial base and general level of human welfare do not enable most citizens to achieve a decent living standard. This is an umbrella term covering a vast range of economic, social, and demographic situations, ranging from 'emerging' or 'newly industrialized' countries that are on a clear industrialization trajectory to 'failed states' with very poor growth prospects.

> Go to the ORC

+ **Gross domestic product (GDP)** Country's income, defined by national consumption ± investment ± government spending ± trade balance.

> Go to the ORC

Figure 1.3
Average export growth
has been much faster
than average economic
growth for at least
a decade now (WTO
2009).

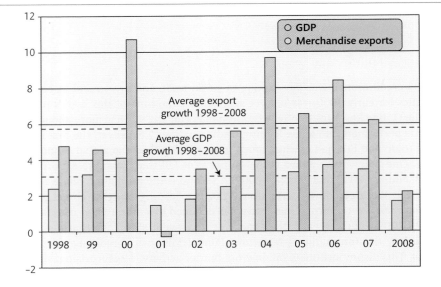

Within the overall trend towards increased world trade, Figure 1.4 shows variations among different regions of the world. The uneven breakdown of trade has clear implications for the politics of international business.

Figure 1.4 is interesting for both historical and current reasons. First, compared with the global breakdown in 1990, exports from North America and Western Europe have fallen in relative terms, compared to exports from the ex-Soviet Union, Africa, the Middle East, and above all Asia. For the first three regions, the change is largely explained by higher commodity prices. For Asia, it reflects the region's growing role as the world's manufacturing centre. (Go to the Online Resource Centre, extension material 1.2, for statistics concerning some aspects of the breakdown of trade between the primary sector (raw materials and agricultural products), the secondary sector (manufactured goods) and the tertiary sector (services).)

All these trends are driven largely by MNEs' behaviour—before shaping, in turn, the contexts to which MNEs are forced to adapt.

Further study of Figure 1.4 reveals an enormous and rising gap between US imports and exports. As exemplified by the financial crisis of late 2008, there are serious questions about the sustainability of a global trading system in which the lead economy runs a huge deficit. Certainly this imbalance cannot help but affect different regions' growth prospects in the years to come. Despite the size of its economy, the USA is not even the world's leading exporter at present—Germany holds that title, a remarkable performance given Western Europe's generally lower share of world exports. Conversely, exports from China, the ex-Soviet Union, and India have risen at an impressive pace. For the first two countries, export growth has been accompanied by an equally rapid rise in imports, an unsurprising outcome given the huge development needs that these continent-sized nations face. The shifting geography of international business is one of the key features of the modern era (see Chapter 16). It has an enormous impact on MNEs' structure and the global distribution of capital and will affect managers' decisions at many different levels.

LDCs accounted for 37.6 per cent of total world exports in 2008 but only 33.5 per cent of imports. Some observers might analyse this as a sign that globalization offers poorer nations greater market opportunities, especially considering that, as recently as 1990, LDCs accounted for only around 25 per cent of world trade. This view is encapsulated in the body of theory supporting the idea that, one way or another, all countries stand to gain from international trade (see Chapter 4). Yet there is another side to this argument. First, countries that rely excessively on foreign demand to fuel their development trajectories are most at risk in case of a global slowdown—one example being the particularly devastating

	Value exports 2008	Total global exports 2008 %	Total global exports 1990 %	Value imports 2008	Total global imports 2008 %
World	**16,127**			**16,415**	
North America	**1,757**	**10.9**	**16.6**	**2,584**	**15.7**
USA	1,301			2,166	
South and Central America	**602**	**3.7**	**3.1**	**595**	**3.6**
Mercosur (*)	279			259	
Europe	**6,456**	**40.0**	**49.6**	**6,833**	**41.6**
European Union (27)	5,913			6,268	
Germany	1,465			1,206	
France	609			708	
UK	458			632	
CIS (ex-Soviet Union)	**703**	**4.4**	**1.7**	**493**	**3.0**
Africa	**561**	**3.5**	**3.1**	**466**	**2.8**
Middle East	**1,047**	**6.5**	**4.1**	**575**	**3.5**
Asia	**4,355**	**27.0**	**21.8**	**4,247**	**25.9**
China	1,428			1,133	
Japan	782			762	
India	179			24	
Asian NICs (†)	1,033			1,093	
ASEAN (‡)	990			936	
Developing economies	6,025	37.6		5,494	33.5
Least Developed Economies	176	1.1		157	0.9

Figure 1.4
World merchandise trade, by region and selected country, in US$ billion and percentages; exports accounted for FOB (free on board), imports on CIF (cost insurance freight) basis (derived from WTO 2006, 2008).

(*) Argentina, Brazil, Paraguay, Uruguay
(†) Hong Kong; Republic of Korea; Singapore and Chinese Taipei
(‡) Brunei, Cambodia, Indonesia, Laos, Malaysia, Myanmar, Philippines, Singapore, Thailand, Vietnam

effects that the 2008–9 crisis had on the exporter nations of South East Asia. Secondly, just as there are great disparities within the developing world between those countries that are emerging and those that are not, even within those countries where overall and average income has risen substantially, some segments of the population have benefited more than others. International business does not affect all parts of every society in the same way. Indeed, as shown by Figure 1.5, in recent years FDI has risen even more quickly than trade. Chapter 7 discusses the various ways in which FDI impacts home and host country populations. Long-term FDI trends, including the potential effects of the 2008 credit crunch (see Online Resource Centre, extension material 1.3), constitutes another key topic in international business.

> Go to the ORC 🌐

Introduction to foreign direct investment

Recent FDI data should be handled with care due to statistical categorization problems and because the events of 2001 (the 9/11 attacks on New York's World Trade Center and the bursting of the 'dot.com' stockmarket bubble) made annual FDI flows plunge to levels from which it would take them years to recover. This explains the decision to analyse 2007 using a more distant benchmark like 1997. Excluding adjustments for inflation, the global stock of inward FDI increased more than fourfold over the decade in question, with only minor variations in the breakdown between developed countries (accounting for about two-thirds of all FDI stock) and LDCs. On the other hand, in terms of annual flows of inward investment, LDCs accounted for a mere 27 per cent of total FDI in 2007, down from 39 per cent a decade earlier. These statistics offer further proof of the Triad countries' ongoing domination of international business. They also raise questions about why LDCs have experienced faster growth in trade than in FDI. Chapter 8 will offer some insight into the reasons why MNEs' sense of comfort causes them to enter different foreign markets in different ways.

At the same time, trends explored in Chapter 7 indicate the possibility that FDI flows might even out in the future between the developed and developing worlds. Recent years have witnessed an increase in capital flows to poor countries, especially FDI, which amounted to more than 3 per cent of LDCs' gross domestic product in 2006, versus only 0.2 per cent in the early 1980s (Dorsey 2008). Whereas the developing world had an accumulated current account deficit equal to 3 per cent of GDP in the mid-1990s, by 2006 this measure was more or less in balance. The change is a positive one, all the more so because an increasing proportion of flows to LDCs now involve equity transfers (like FDI) as opposed to loans that must be reimbursed later. A major topic in international business discussions (see Online Resource Centre, extension material 1.4) is determining to what extent modern globalization has been helpful or harmful to the world's poorer nations. This is another of the many levels where 'micro' discussions of business strategies link to more political 'macro' analyses of national interest.

Chapter 16 explores several examples of how international managers might incorporate major macro-level trends (such as the growing ecological constraint or the emergence of new economic powers) into their strategic thinking. A notable case in point was the 2008 credit crunch and subsequent recession. Clearly this downturn will have significant effects on cross-border trade and FDI patterns for years to come. What is unknown, however, is exactly what shape these effects will take. Some observers predict that the credit crunch will go so far as to reverse the trends of the previous half-century and spark a return towards renewed protectionism by national governments—that is, 'de-globalization'. Others forecast

---

+ Current account
Country's 'balance of trade' (exports minus imports) plus or minus its financial flows from abroad (interest or dividend payments, cash transfers).

+ Outsourcing
Where a company buys supplies that it needs for its products or services from an outside company instead of making them itself.

> Go to the ORC

Thinking point
What are the chances of de-globalization occurring in the wake of the credit crunch?

Figure 1.5		1997	2007
Major FDI indicators in US$ billion (UNCTAD 2007).	Global stock of inward FDI	3,502	15,211
	Global inward flows	486	1,833
	Developed economies		
	• Stock of inward FDI	2,351	10,459
	• inward flows	285	1,248
	• outward flows	400	1,692
	(balance)	(−115)	(−444)
	Developing economies		
	• Stock of inward FDI	1,122	4,248
	• inward flows	191	500
	• outward flows	74	253
	(balance)	(+117)	(+247)

that the recession will force companies to accelerate their cost-cutting efforts, renewing the decades-old trend towards international outsourcing. The only thing that is clear is that international business cannot be analysed in isolation from broader circumstances and must therefore always be studied in context.

Case Study 1.2

The *Fortune* Global 500

Fortune, an American business magazine that has been ranking the largest US corporations for more than fifty years, started a similar listing for multinational enterprises in 2005 (see Figure 1.6). In the years following the Second World War, the US economy dominated the rest of the world to such an extent that domestic performance was considered sufficient in and of itself. One sign of the rise of globalization is the central role that foreign markets now play in most large corporations' outlook. Fewer and fewer companies nowadays are isolated behind national borders.

Within a few short decades, Walmart grew from this small store in Bentonville (Arkansas) to become the biggest MNE in the world (reproduced with kind permission of Walmart).

Rank	Company (Headquarters)	Main sector	Revenues	Profits
1	Walmart (USA)	Retail	378.8	12.7
2	Exxon Mobil (USA)	Oil refining	372.8	40.6
3	Royal Dutch Shell (UK)	Oil refining	355.8	31.3
4	BP (UK)	Oil refining	291.4	20.8
5	Toyota Motor (Japan)	Automobile	230.2	15.0
6	Chevron (USA)	Automobile	210.8	18.7

Figure 1.6
World's twenty leading MNEs in 2008, by sector; data in US$ billion (*Fortune* 2008).

Figure 1.6 (continued)

Rank	Company (Headquarters)	Main sector	Revenues	Profits
7	ING Group (Netherlands)	Banking	201.5	12.6
8	Total (France)	Oil refining	187.3	18.0
9	General Motors (USA)	Automobile	182.3	–38.7
10	ConocoPhillips (USA)	Oil refining	178.6	11.9
11	Daimler (Germany)	Automobile	177.2	5.4
12	General Electric (USA)	Electronics	176.7	22.2
13	Ford Motor (USA)	Automobile	172.5	-2.7
14	Fortis (Belgium/Netherlands)	Banking	164.9	5.5
15	Axa (France)	Insurance	162.8	7.8
16	Sinopec (China)	Oil refining	159.3	4.2
17	Citigroup (USA)	Banking	159.2	3.6
18	Volkswagen (Germany)	Automobile	149.1	5.6
19	Dexia Group (Belgium)	Banking	147.7	3.5
20	HSBC Holdings (UK)	Banking	145.5	19.1

The *Fortune* list of the world's 500 largest MNEs is notable in this respect because of the domination of just a few sectors. The sector with the largest number of representatives is banking, followed by the oil-refining and automotive sectors, followed at a distance by food/drug retailers, telecommunications, insurance, and electronics. Different factors explain the rise of global MNEs in these sectors. First and foremost has been firms' perceived need to consolidate their international operations—that is, to merge with rivals in order to achieve economies of scale and gain competitive advantage. There is also the fact that different paradigms dominate different sectors of activity, with more cultural fields like food or clothing tending to emphasize national differentiation, whereas hi-tech fields focus more on the efficiency of global operations (see the discussion of MNEs' 'push' or 'pull' orientations in Chapter 9). It is important to remember that international business is not a science but involves trying to understand managers' highly informed yet ultimately subjective appreciation of their circumstances. Lastly, there is the fact that the relative importance of different sectors will vary over time. For instance, the 2008 credit crunch was particularly damaging to companies in the banking sector, but also to airliners, because of the general fall in consumer spending on leisure pursuits. There is every chance that in years to come, the number of MNEs from sectors like these will diminish, replaced by firms from new growth areas like clean technology.

The *Fortune* rankings are also interesting for the information they offer on which countries host the most MNE headquarters. As Figure 1.7 shows, since the magazine started compiling figures worldwide in 2005, the share of US and Japanese companies in the Global 500 has fallen, whereas companies from the Far East have increased their representation.

+ Economies of scale
When a company increases output using the same equipment, its per unit production costs fall.

	Number of *Fortune* 500 MNE headquarters in 2005	Number of *Fortune* 500 MNE headquarters in 2008
USA	176	153
Japan	81	64
France	39	39
Germany	37	37
UK	35	34
China	16	29
South Korea	11	15

Figure 1.7
Number of *Fortune* 500 companies with headquarters in world's seven leading home countries, 2005 and 2008 (*Fortune* 2008).

This is partially the result of currency movements—the US dollar declined over the period in question, reducing on paper the size of companies whose accounts are in dollars. Above all, it reflects a shift in global economic power. Without underestimating the ongoing strength of the US and indeed the Japanese and European economies, companies from newly industrialized Asian economies are now big players on the international business scene.

Some observers would point to this trend as indicative of a world in which power is starting to spread. Others might emphasize the fact that the vast majority of the biggest MNEs hail from OECD countries. Indeed, with most high tech production activities also situated in the developed world, global economic power is still divided very unevenly (Mann 2004). MNEs' role in aggravating or reducing income inequalities, on a national but also a global scale, is another major topic of debate in international business.

> **Thinking point**
> Can MNEs be criticized for becoming 'too big'?

Section II: The international business framework

A range of motivations, largely discussed in Chapters 8 and 9, explains why and where companies operate internationally. Some reasons for going abroad are timeless in so far as they involve strategic thinking unrelated to the circumstances that a company faces at a given moment in time. Others are more specific and involve corporate attempts to respond to a temporary context (see Chapter 5). This section offers an overview of both general and time-specific rationales for international business.

Activity drivers

Some of the motivations for international business are 'micro' in nature and mainly relate to firms' profit-seeking initiatives and strategic intent. Others involve companies' reactions to external 'macro' trends such as political, governmental, macro-economic, and socio-cultural factors over which they have little control (Yip 1989). Of course, 'micro' and 'macro' motivations are often interrelated. One example of this linkage can be found in the corporate philosophy of internalization. This is the idea that, when markets function poorly (for example, where market participants do not receive a fair reward for their efforts), companies may wish to run their international value chain operations themselves, if only because they wish to maintain in-house any knowledge that they may possess (Buckley and Casson 1976). In this view, firms will not need external partners to lead their internationalization drive as long as they have high-quality managers capable of assuming responsibilities abroad, and as long as the host countries are not too different from the ones to which the company and its managers are accustomed. This is a case where international business springs from the interface between a company's internal attributes (managers' qualities) and the characteristics (foreignness and/or market mechanisms) of the host

+ **Internalization**
When a company decides to run a particular function itself (using its own employees) instead of delegating it to an external partner.

Figure 1.8
Summary of main
factors driving
international business
today.

Internal drivers

- Expand sales
- Leverage existing competencies
- Use extra capacities
- Spread risks
- Avoid saturation
- Internalize competencies
- Acquire resources
- Access more efficient inputs

External drivers

- Technology
- Liberalized regulatory framework
- Free trade friendly institutions
- Global competitive paradigm
- Deregulated finance

country where it is hoping to move. Another example of the interconnection between some micro- and macro-drivers of international business is when an MNE calculates that the costs of going abroad are lower than the potential gains it might achieve by operating in a regulatory, labour, or tax system where it is well placed to put pressure on the government (Ietto-Gillies 2003). This is because a company's cross-border success will depend not only on how suitable its behaviour is to the market(s) where it is operating (Porter 1986) but also on how effectively it deals with non-business actors such as politicians or regulators. In short, separating micro- and macro-drivers of international business may be a useful categorization (see Figure 1.8) but it is necessarily an artificial one.

Internal drivers of international business

Companies often operate outside their borders because they are in a sector shaped by international rather than domestic factors. At the same time, it is rare to find companies launched as multinationals from the very outset. The vast majority of MNEs throughout history—with the exception of 'born-globals' (see Chapter 9)—have started in their home markets and then moved abroad, expanding downstream to increase sales, upstream to acquire resources, or in both directions to diversify risk. Each of these actions is based on a different logic.

Expand sales

+ **Leverage**
Organizing operations in a way that maximizes output without increasing inputs.

Once a firm has built a system allowing it to produce and market a product or service efficiently, it will usually want to leverage this competency by selling the finished good, with or without modification, into a new market. Thus, on the downstream side, the expansion of sales is the main driver of international business. There are countless examples of this rationale being put to use. For instance, Dutch vegetable farmers have developed the greenhouse technology to grow tomatoes and peppers even during cold North European winters. Because consumer demand for these products from neighbouring countries such as Germany and the UK remains strong all year long, doing business across borders is a natural step for Dutch agribusiness companies like The Greenery, which sources fresh produce and sells it to foreign retailers. A related example is the trade between Japan, a dynamic but

mineral poor industrial giant whose factories require enormous amounts of raw materials, and Australia, which has an abundance of minerals as well as an industrial sector capable of refining ore (like bauxite) into usable production inputs (like aluminium). For Australian mining or refining companies, exporting to Japan is a logical extension of what started out as a domestic activity. A third example from the service sector is the way that huge international banks such as Citigroup in New York or Barclays in London leverage their expensive trading infrastructure to sell financial products to customers located outside their national borders. Expanding sales worldwide is a quick way of paying for the enormous costs that they incurred building their trading rooms in the first place. Lastly, cross-border sales can also be a natural move for SMEs operating in sectors that are by their very nature international in scope. One example is IdeaCarbon, a UK-based consultancy that offers advice on carbon finance worldwide and which in 2008 signed a carbon instrument co-development agreement with India's MCX exchange. In all these instances, international business is as relevant to the company's mission as the work that it does in its home market. This is especially true when the company is looking to move into a foreign country that is similar in political, economic, and/or cultural terms, not to mention close geographically. Without minimizing the real differences that exist between the USA and Canada, when McDonald's first began expanding across America, setting up outlets across its northern border must have seemed a relatively easy step. The skills developed selling in one country can sometimes be transplanted seamlessly to another.

There are also strategic reasons why companies organize their commercial functions to embrace international sales as a matter of course. As mentioned above, a basic principle of modern production is that selling large volumes is beneficial because it creates economies of scale. In a similar vein, the greater the experience that a company has acquired in producing something, the better it becomes at this activity. This is because it appropriates skills that will allow it to achieve productivity gains. As a result, many companies size their production operations to obtain critical mass. To justify these investments and avoid surplus capacities, they often need to sell more than they would if they were simply serving domestic customers. This is especially true if the firm comes from a small country. For example, discount airliner Ryanair would have been at a disadvantage using its Dublin home as its only hub. With so many more passengers travelling through the UK, it made sense for this Irish company to run its main

+ Critical mass
Minimum threshold beyond which positive, size-related benefits arise.

operations out of London Stansted Airport, which is, after all, a foreign location. Another way of looking at the size factor is in financial terms. In the mid-2000s, the cost of building a new automotive factory was roughly $1 billion. To have any hope of recovering such a large upfront investment, a car company would have to make sure that its new plant produced enough cars to justify the expense. This is not possible if the plant is located either in a small country (Luxembourg does not have a car plant serving its domestic market alone, for instance) or in one where demand is already saturated due to competition. In both cases, the production scale must be international or else the investment becomes impracticable.

Risk diversification

Another strategic driver of international business is the desire to spread risk by working in more than one country at a time. In and of itself, spreading risk is generally seen as a safe business principle, in part because it helps to avoid over-dependence on a single location or market. One way of looking at this is from an upstream, production perspective. If a firm had all its industrial assets in northern Turkey and another terrible earthquake were to hit the region, its chances of continuing manufacturing operations would be worse than if it also had plants in zones not affected by the earthquake. That is why so many firms have disaster plans allowing them to continue functioning in case a catastrophe affects one of their main locations. The same logic can be applied on the downstream, sales side. A company that is selling into only one market runs the risk that the market might collapse for whatever reason (natural disaster, bad policy, war) without there being any other customers to compensate for lost sales. Any firm whose entire business revolved around exports to Iraq at the time of the 2003 invasion would, for instance, have had difficulties surviving. The adversity that a company experiences in one location has less of an effect when it has interests in many others.

Spreading risk through international operations can be done in different ways. Commercially, there is something called the 'product life cycle' (PLC), which from an international marketing perspective is the idea that a product or service that is on an upward trend in some countries may be in decline elsewhere (see Chapter 12). Clearly, it is advantageous for firms to sell goods in markets where demand is on the rise, since they will be able to command higher prices. One example from the 1970s and 1980s is the way that jeans were so much more expensive in Western Europe, where they were new and fashionable, than in California, where they had long been a commodity product. The PLC variation enabled San Francisco firm Levi Strauss to offset lower revenues in its home market via exports to Europe. International business can be used to diversify other risks as well. Foreign sales can offset the foreign exchange risk of accumulating revenues (or liabilities) in just one currency (see Chapter 13). In a sense and despite the challenges of operating in a foreign environment, diversification means that international business can actually be a way for a company to reduce risk.

Thinking point
Is international risk automatically more dangerous than domestic risk?

Acquire inputs

The final internal driver of international business is the acquisition of resources (materials and labour but also capital and technology) used during a firm's production process. Sometimes this involves inputs that are unavailable at home. One example is the way that non-oil-producing countries such as Japan, Germany, and France must look abroad to source this commodity. At other times, the cost of an input might be so much lower overseas that a company would be at a competitive disadvantage if, unlike its rivals, it did not source the factor where it can be acquired most cheaply. As discussed in Chapter 8, this can be done via FDI or trade. UK vacuum cleaner manufacturer Dyson provides one example of a firm engaging in FDI to reduce input costs. Portrayed as the symbol of the rebirth of British manufacturing in the 1990s, by 2002 Dyson had decided that its new priority was to lower its cost base. Accordingly, it moved almost all its production activities to Malaysia, where workers' wages were a fraction of those paid to British production staff. As for reducing input costs through trade, the solar energy business is a good case in point. Builders worldwide seeking to enter this fast-growing sector need to source solar panels competitively. However, few countries can make these components as cheaply as Germany, where SMEs like Ritter Solar have already achieved critical mass. Thus, it is in the interest of energy system installers worldwide to import from Germany if they want to acquire resources cheaply. In short, international business is often driven by firms focusing more on the advantages inherent to a given production location and less on whether this site is in their country of origin or not.

External drivers of international business

Technology

It is not always easy to determine which drivers a company can control, and which it cannot. One case in point is technology, a key factor in today's global economy. This is an umbrella term that refers to companies' internal innovation efforts (see Chapter 11's section on knowledge management) but also to the technological advances that a particular society achieves as a whole. Thus, technology affects the international business environment at many different levels. On the upstream side, for instance, improved telecommunications enable companies to stretch their value chains to distant locations offering competitive advantages. One example is when hospitals in the West use remote diagnostics facilities to get advice from doctors located, for instance, in India. Out of a service that was once as localized as medical treatment is, modern technology has created an opportunity for an international work organization. The same applies to downstream activities, for instance, where company–customer relationships extend worldwide due to technological advances like the Internet. When consumers worldwide purchase their books through Amazon instead of at their local bookstore, they are cementing technology's role as a key organizing principle in international business. Indeed, given the positive impact that technology-related transportation improvements have traditionally had on trade, it can be argued that technology is one of the main causes of today's shrinking world. It is rare that a community chooses to remain completely isolated once the means exist for it to interact with other communities. Google's rapid rise in China, despite the obstacles raised by the Beijing government, is a good case in point. Before China had any exposure to Western consumption goods (or ideas), its population was much less focused on such items. People's outlooks and desires often change when they see how foreigners live. Cross-border comparison has always been a significant driver of international business.

Regulatory framework

+ Barriers to entry
Regulatory, competitive, financial, and other obstacles that make it difficult for a firm to enter a particular market.

However, just because a technology exists enabling something to happen does not mean that it will necessarily occur—even if it were to create an advantage for someone. For international business to happen, there must be a general regulatory framework enabling it. After all, the leading responsibility of any national government is to ensure the well-being of its population in the face of danger from abroad. The main threat is clearly war, but, in so far as foreign economic competition can be damaging to certain parts of a local economy (even as it benefits others), states will also come to a judgement as to what kind of international business they find acceptable. Chapters 4 and 5 look at the issue of state intervention in greater depth. For the moment, it is worth stating that the general paradigm in many countries since the early 1980s has been to accept and indeed promote cross-border flows by allowing foreign actors to enter domestic marketplaces. The effect of this deregulation (also known as 'liberalization') trend has been to reduce barriers to entry, making it easier for companies to operate on an international scale.

Thinking point

What would international business be like in a protectionist world?

A liberalization philosophy has affected the trade and FDI regulations of most if not all of the world's nation-states, but, as Chapter 6 details, it has also led to the creation of a global framework that is conducive to international business. One aspect is the rise of regional trading arrangements like the European Union (EU). These are groups of neighbouring countries that have signed agreements enabling easier access to one another's markets. Their degree of integration can vary, but in general such arrangements promote free trade among members. The same philosophy has also led to the creation of trade-friendly international institutions like the WTO, whose laws create a framework in which countries are positively discouraged from adopting isolationist policies. The idea is to create a world where cross-border transactions are no longer considered unusual.

Global competition

In terms of corporate strategy, a whole new vision has arisen regarding what it means to compete. Before the arrival of a world of free trade, companies would position themselves in terms of local and/or national rivals, competing for a share of their domestic markets. Today, with increasingly penetrable national borders, economic rivals might come from anywhere, deriving competitive advantages derived from whatever experiences they have accumulated at home or abroad. This means that some companies that have worked very hard over the years to improve productivity or quality, and that would be very competitive in a purely domestic framework, might suddenly lose market share because of the arrival of hyper-competitive foreign companies. For example, where Bordeaux wineries used to compete successfully with domestic rivals from France's Burgundy region, they must now face challenges from New World winemakers from Australia, Chile, and South Africa. With rivals achieving economies of scale because they already operate globally, Bordeaux winemakers can no longer afford to think in domestic terms alone. Furthermore, the profits that global groups make in one market can be used to fund their activities in another, which is why it is sometimes just as important to go abroad specifically to limit rivals' profitability as it is to turn a profit oneself. This explains the outcry when companies, like US aircraft-maker Boeing and its European rival Airbus, suspect one another of receiving different kinds of preferential treatment at home, enabling them to subsidize lower prices to foreign customers, thereby gaining global market share to their rivals' detriment. The new competition involves fighting not just in rivals' home markets but also in markets all across the world—which is why business has become so much tougher in many sectors today.

Thinking point

How meaningful is purely domestic competition nowadays?

The main consequence of the new competitive paradigm is that producers are no longer able to rely on the comfortable positions they used to hold in their domestic markets. Consumers' greater awareness of possible foreign alternatives to domestic products, and their ability to access rival products at competitive prices, has given buyers greater power over sellers. For example, in the mid to late twentieth century, when German consumers could buy their television sets only from local companies AEG Telefunken and Grundig (or Dutch rival Philips), these proud old firms were in a position to sell their high-quality products at a good profit. Once the market began to be flooded with equally good but cheaper Japanese alternatives, the two Germans were forced to compete at a level to which they were unaccustomed. Today both survive only as brand names listed in other firms' product portfolios. Given the partial convergence of consumer behaviour and demand patterns worldwide (see Chapter 12), companies have come to realize that, regardless of how directly or indirectly they operate outside their national borders, international business will affect them at one level or the other. As Chapter 9 discusses, MNEs running worldwide operations increasingly look to integrate their units' management, in a bid for greater coherency (Held et al. 1999). Everyone's playing field has become bigger.

International finance

Corporate finance has also been affected by the trend towards a more globalized world. To source the capital needed to run vast multinational empires, MNEs often have to rely on different funding sources, many of which operate offshore, thus free from domestic controls. The deregulation of the finance industry since the 1980s (see Chapter 14), part of an overall 'liberalization' paradigm, has led to an explosion in cross-border capital flows. Much of this money is free floating—that is, not directly associated with the production of goods and services. This partial separation of finance from real business activity, one of the causes of the 2008 credit crunch, has added to pressures weighing on MNE managers today. On the one hand, financial asset prices are becoming increasingly volatile and difficult to predict, adding to the uncertainty of international business. On the other, whereas many MNEs used to be owned by 'passive shareholders' mainly interested in the safety of their investments, in the new 'shareholder value' paradigm international managers are under pressure to maximize short-term financial returns by running tighter operations and/or taking greater risks. In a similar vein, the deregulation of the world's financial markets means that problems first affecting just one country, like the 2007 subprime crisis in the USA, have become more contagious and are therefore more likely to affect other economies. A more globalized world has advantages but also creates particular challenges.

Challenges and choices

The demanding and constantly evolving nature of modern international business is the final point to be made in this introductory chapter. Some textbooks adopt what seems at times to be a checklist approach to international business, giving readers the impression that they will necessarily succeed in their foreign endeavours if they simply tick certain action boxes. In the opinion of the authors of this book and based on their personal experience and research, this is wrong, and books transmitting such an idea do a great disservice. If readers are led to believe that international business is a mere subcategory of domestic business, they will not develop the varied world view characterizing the vast majority of successful international practitioners. Thinking internationally is something new for many people.

It is true that international business is capable of creating the greatest opportunities for profit maximization—as proven by the fact that most if not all the wealthiest companies (and people) in the world operate on a cross-border basis. At the same time, operating internationally requires an ability to cope with challenges that do not arise at the domestic level. Politically, despite the trend towards more internationalist thinking, resistance to foreign competition for markets, resources, and jobs remains very widespread. Economically, many foreign operations (like technological transfers or global funding) are associated with distinct sets of problems. Socially, there is widespread condemnation of the unequal distribution of globalization's costs and benefits. Environmentally, there is the extra usage of resources and generation of waste caused by the organization of trade over long distances. Last but not least, psychologically there is the obstacle of xenophobia. Despite the authors' personal rejection of this attitude, the academic value of the present book would be undermined if its impact on international business relationships were underplayed. Now, some might argue that globalization stems from (and/or causes) lesser xenophobia. Conversely, others would argue that increased contact with foreigners sparks, at least in certain communities, greater dislike of the outside world (Huntingdon 2002; Barber 2003). If an international business book overestimates the cross-border obstacles that managers face, then at worst it is guilty of advocating excessive caution. If, on the other hand, it underestimates these obstacles, then it is guilty of leaving readers totally unprepared for the situations that they will face in the future. The consequences of the latter error would be much more severe than the former.

For this reason, the chapters in this book will include special sections highlighting different challenges inherent to international business, as well as choices that managers might make to overcome them. Each of these choices—how to allocate resources, target markets and customers, relate to foreign individuals or governments—should be grounded in managers' ability to provide an appropriate response to a specific set of circumstances. To repeat, the fundamental philosophy of this book is that it is more important to help readers learn how to make choices than to dictate to them what choices they should be making.

Chapter Summary

This brief introduction set the scene by identifying the differences between global and international approaches, and asking whether it is more effective to seek a 'one-best-way' approach that can be applied in all circumstances or to develop an ability to respond flexibly to different environments. In both cases, an argument was made in support of the second alternative. This is justified in part by the chapter's statistical analysis of the recent rise in world trade and FDI. Depending on their personal and national interests, people will react in different ways to the presence of foreign companies. Successful international managers will therefore be those whose thinking incorporates a range of views. Business is, after all, a social science.

The second section studied in greater depth the drivers of modern international business, categorizing them as macro-factors external to a firm's internal workings and micro-factors reflecting the policies it chooses to adopt. A distinction was made between factors that might be applicable irrespective of the circumstance and others that are directly linked to modern globalization. The chapter's final section stated the importance for future practitioners of respecting the challenges associated with international business.

Case Study 1.3

What powers Electricité de France?

Nationalized in 1946 by a post-war government seeking to exert state control over a strategic power sector, for a long time Electricité de France (EDF) enjoyed a monopoly status in France. This protection from market competition had several consequences, the main one being that EDF could always count on state support and therefore did not have to worry about funding and profitability constraints to the same extent as a private company would have done. As such, it was in a position to act quickly on any strategic opportunity it saw, whether or not the venture took a long time to turn a profit. In this atmosphere, EDF executives were quick to develop major ambitions, largely because they had a shareholder (the French state) with pockets that were deep enough to fund whatever expansion plans they concocted. By the 1980s, however, many observers were criticizing the company's structure as bloated and mismanaged, doubting whether support for EDF constituted a good use of French taxpayers' funds. Alongside this, as the European Union (EU)

moved towards a Single Market in the 1990s and began promoting deregulation, France's politicians came under increasing pressure to privatize EDF and open up the domestic market to foreign competition. It is true that the French state dragged its feet in this respect, and at year end 2007 it still maintained a 84.8 per cent interest in EDF. There was also some reluctance to open up the French domestic utilities market as widely as the EU would have liked. Nevertheless, sensing changes in the competitive environment, EDF executives turned their attention to the expansion possibilities that international business offers. Their actions exemplify some of the approaches found in international business today.

Clearly, an imbalance exists when a company from a country like France, characterized by a particularly state-oriented business culture, engages with companies from countries like Britain, where the state has traditionally had much less of a presence in the economy. During 1999–2002, EDF embarked on acquisitions of £6.2 billion in the UK, merging companies such as London Electricity, the Southwest Electricity Board, and SEEBOARD to form EDF Energy, which became one of the UK's largest utilities. Under normal circumstances, a company with such enormous debts as EDF was carrying at the time would never have been able to fund this kind of programme. Clearly the investment was made possible only because EDF had political support for its projects back in France, and because it lacked any real opposition in the UK. The company's strategic interest was to establish a foothold in the UK, where there were plans to increase national capacities for producing nuclear power—an area where EDF benefited from a great deal of technological competence, largely because of the years of research assistance it had received from the French government. In September 2008 this strategy culminated in EDF's £12.4 billion acquisition of British Energy, whose power stations were responsible for more than 20 per cent of all electricity generated in the UK. Dominating a neighbour's domestic energy market in this way was quite an achievement for a state sector company.

Not all foreign markets were so welcoming to the French utilities giant, however. In early 2008, for instance, EDF expressed an interest in taking over the Spanish energy firm Iberdrola. The target company reacted by lodging several complaints against EDF with the European Union, specifically because the French predator's quasi-government status would have given it an unfair advantage in the event of a stockmarket battle. This was

The UK's need to replace existing nuclear plants has attracted the attention of foreign utilities like EDF (Photodisc).

not the first time that a company sought legal protection against a foreign competitor accused of not respecting the rules of capitalism, and it probably will not be the last. It is notable that EDF's main interest in Iberdrola related to the Spanish company's position as world leader in the growing wind power sector. Whereas growth in the UK had been aimed at leveraging EDF's existing technologies, growth in Spain was aimed at accessing new ones.

This also seemed to be EDF's motivation when it signed a photovoltaic solar panel supply master agreement in 2008 with a privately owned Californian 'start-up' called Nanosolar. The potential scope of the American deal was very different from the Spanish one, however, if only because of Nanosolar's ownership structure. Whereas publicly listed firms are increasingly being required by demanding shareholders to maximize short-term returns, unlisted firms are often given more time by their owners to develop a new technology. This explains the success of the venture capital model implemented by many computer companies that started in Silicon Valley—where Nanosolar, coincidentally enough, was also located. EDF may have wanted to purchase Nanosolar much like it acquired British Energy and tried to buy Iberdrola, but this option was never really possible. Instead, the French company had to resort to a more modest outsourcing and cooperation arrangement. These activities would be added to the portfolio that EDF lodged in a new subsidiary called 'EDF Energies Nouvelles'. By definition, the French utilities giant was committed to raising its profile in the global market for renewable energies. The diverse nature of the international business environment meant that it would need different methods to fulfil this commitment.

Case study questions

1. Electricité de France is virtually a state-owned company. What other examples exist of public sector organizations pursuing a direct interest in international business?

2. How does the French business culture vary from the British, Spanish, or American? What about your own country of origin?

3. What are some of the reasons motivating companies to engage in international business?

Discussion questions

1. Is globalization inevitable?

2. Is nationality an important factor in the way people do business?

3. To what extent is international business beneficial to wealthy and/or poor countries?

4. How would international business work if national regulatory environments were stricter?

5. To what extent is international business based on objective science versus human psychology?

References

Aharoni, Y., and Ramamurti, R. (2008). 'The Internationalization of Multinationals', *Research in Global Strategic Management*, 14 (June).

Amine, L. (2008). 'Country-of-Origin, Animosity and Consumer Response: Marketing Implications of Anti-Americanism and Francophobia', *International Business Review*, 17/4 (Aug.).

Barber, B. (2003). *Jihad vs. McWorld: Terrorism's Challenge to Democracy*. London: Corgi Books.

Buckley, P., and Casson, M. (1976). *The Future of the Multinational Enterprise*. New York: Holmes and Meier Publishers.

Coleman, W., and Underhill, G. (1998) (eds.). *Regional and Global Economic Integration*. London: Routledge.

Dorsey, T. (2008). 'A Capital Story', *IMF: Finance and Development*, 45/2 (June).

EDF Energy (2008). www.edfenergy.com (accessed 15 July 2008).

European Commission (2003). 'The New SME Definition', http://ec.europa.eu (accessed 2 July 2009).

Fortune (2008). 'Global 500 ... Ranking of the World's Largest Corporations', http://money.cnn.com (accessed 13 July 2009).

Freyssenet, M. (forthcoming). *The Second Automobile Revolution*. London and New York: Palgrave Macmillan.

Giddens, A. (2002). *Runaway World: How Globalization is Shaping our Lives*. New York: Routledge.

Greentech Media (2008). 'EDF Energies Nouvelles Enters Strategic Partnership with California-Based Nanosolar', 3 Apr., www.greentechmedia.com (accessed 15 July 2008).

Guardian (2009). 'Globalisation: Parallel Worlds', 31 Jan., p. 34.

Held, D., McGrew, A., Goldblatt, D., and Perraton, J. (1999). *Global Transformations: Politics, Economics and Culture*. Stanford, CA: Stanford University Press.

Hirst, P., and Thompson, G. (1999). *Globalization in Question*. 2nd edn. Cambridge: Polity Press.

Hollinger, P., and Mulligan, R. (2008). 'EDF Plays a Political Game in its Attempt at International Expansion', 7 Apr., www.ft.com (accessed 14 July 2008).

Huntingdon, S. (2002). *The Clash of Civilizations: And the Remaking of World Order*. London: Simon & Schuster.

Ietto-Gillies, G. (2003). 'The Nation-State and the Theory of the Transnational Corporation', www.econ.cam.ac.uk (accessed 6 July 2007).

Lévy, B. (2007). 'The Interface between Globalization, Trade and Development: Theoretical Issues for International Business Studies', *International Business Review*, 16/5 (Oct.).

MacGillivray, A. (2006). *A Brief History of Globalization: The Untold Story of our Incredible Shrinking Planet*. London: Robinson.

Mann, M. (2004). 'Has Globalization Ended the Rise and Rise of the Nation-State', in D. Held and A. McGrew (eds.), *The Global Transformations Reader: An Introduction to the Globalization Debate*. Cambridge: Polity.

Milanovic, B. (2005). *Worlds Apart: Measuring International and Global Inequality*. Princeton: Princeton University Press.

Mulligan, M. (2008). 'Iberdrola Lodges Complaint against EDF', 28 Feb., www.ft.com (accessed 14 July 2008).

Munchau, W. (2009). ICES European Business School London conference, discussion with the author, 17 Feb.

Ohmae, K. (1999). *The Borderless World: Power and Strategy in the Interlinked Economy*. New York: Harper Business Publications.

Porter, M. (1986). *Competition in Global Industries*. Boston, MA: Harvard Business School Press.

Samuelson, R. (2008). 'The Moral Challenge of Globalization', 28 May, www.realclearpolitics.com (accessed 12 July 2008).

Saul, J. (2006). *The Collapse of Globalism and the Reinvention of the World*. London: Atlantic Books.

Scholte, J. A. (2005). *Globalization: A Critical Introduction*. Basingstoke: Palgrave MacMillan.

Serfati, C. (2006). 'Quelques enjeux autour de la notion de nationalité des firmes', in S. Matelly and S. Nies (eds.), *La Revue internationale et stratégique*. Paris: Dalloz.

Steger, M. (2003). *Globalization: A Very Short Introduction*. Oxford: Oxford University Press.

UNCTAD (2007). 'FDI Stat', http://stats.unctad.org/FDI (accessed 27 Feb. 2009).

Watson, P. (2005). *Ideas: A History of Thought and Invention, from Fire to Freud*. New York: HarperCollins.

White, H. (2001). *Markets from Networks: Socioeconomic Models of Production*. Princeton: Princeton University Press.

Womack, J., Jones, D. T., and Roos, D. (1991). *The Machine that Changed the World: The Story of Lean Production*. New York: Harper Perennial.

WTO (2006). 'World Merchandise Exports by Regions, 2005', www.wto.org (accessed 12 July 2008).

WTO (2008). 'World Trade 2007, Prospects for 2008', www.wto.org (accessed 12 July 2008).

WTO (2009). 'World Trade 2008, Prospects for 2009', www.wto.org (accessed 28 Apr. 2009).

Yip, G. (1989). 'Global Strategy ... in a World of Nations?', *MIT Sloan Management Review*, 31/1.

Further research

Mattoo, A., Stern, R. M., and Zanini, G. (2007). *A Handbook of International Trade in Services*. Oxford: Oxford University Press.

Propelled by ongoing improvements in information technologies, the service sector has become a crucial part of international business. Companies working out of central locations are increasingly in a position to offer foreign customers a variety of services, ranging from computer advice to insurance policies, banking, and tourism. Furthermore, many cross-border investments involve projects whose industrial element is associated with the local delivery of a service. This is particularly true in sectors like telecommunications, transportation, or energy, many of which used to be at least partially nationalized but are now subject to the rules of international competition. Given the expansion in other international service sectors such as education and medical diagnostics, it is no surprise that international trade and FDI in services have outpaced the total growth in goods since the mid-1990s.

At the same time, the investments and individuals that providing cross-border services still face many barriers to entry. Unlike the trade in goods, which really start to affect an economy only once products have crossed the national border, services usually materialize at the very heart of a society, if only because of the growing number of individuals employed in many economies in service-sector activities. This explains ongoing resistance in some corners to the liberalization of services. All in all, trade and investment in services have become a very specific and interesting subcategory of international business.

Online Resource Centre

Visit the Online Resource Centre that accompanies this book to read more information relating to international business: www.oxfordtextbooks.co.uk/orc/sitkin_bowen/

part

1

International Contexts

2 National Cultures

Overview

This chapter explores the concepts and manifestations of culture, focusing particularly on the variety of national cultures. It starts with definitions and discussions of what is meant by the term and then considers the various forms that it takes, ranging from concepts of a single world culture to the many models for understanding its impact on international business. Some of the key models explored are those of Hofstede, Trompenaars and Hampden-Turner, Hall, Maslow, and Lechner and Boli. The main focus of the chapter is the application of models and concepts to people's ability to understand each other's cultures and to the way that business is done across the world. Not only do people need to have sympathy with other cultures; they also need to devise strategies for conducting business successfully within the constraints of the organization for which they work.

Section I: Interpretations of culture

Religions and languages

World demography

Section II: Models of national culture and the conduct of international business

Models of national culture

The impacts of culture on international business

Learning Objectives

By the end of this chapter, you should be able to:

✦ understand definitions and uses of the concept of national cultures

✦ recognize and understand the different models of culture, particularly as applied to international business

✦ evaluate the implications of national cultures on business and employment relationships

✦ understand the relationship between cultural attitudes and business behaviour

✦ assess the abilities required by managers to navigate their way through a world of different cultures

Case Study 2.1

Food courts and the globalization of national tastes

Hawaiian pizza with pineapple? Lasagne with the flavours of Mexican tortilla or chicken tikka masala? Lattes not café au lait in French patisseries? Le Big Mac and a Royale with cheese? Black pudding mousse au chocolat? Sherry with ice? Brazilian sushi?

The development towards a world culture has introduced global food to consumers, but there are many difficulties with the globalization of food and drink. These include whether people are eating the genuine or original form of the food or drink. It is also of concern as to how far companies can afford to alter the 'pure' form of the food and drink before it can really no longer be sold as belonging to that culture. Above all, if the item that consumers eat or drink is not authentic, will they have an incorrect impression of the country of its supposed origin?

The food court acts as a telling microcosm of the globalization and homogenization of food. Originating in the shopping malls of the USA, food courts are now widespread throughout the world. The food court offers many different types of food and drink provided by specialist outlets—noodles from Asia, pizza from Italy, burgers from America, sushi from Japan, curry from India, doughnuts and pretzels. Commercial logic has resulted in single sites providing an international range of food. Often located in international airports, food courts have also been established in shopping areas and universities in many countries throughout the world.

A regular feature in food courts and in other internationalized eating and shopping locations is pizza. Originally an Italian dish, pizza has been spread throughout the world as an international food, available for home consumption and for eating out in restaurants. Much of the development of pizza as a world food has come from the creations of Italian immigrants to the USA and, indeed, from Greek immigrants and their version—the Greek pizza. Among the international industry leaders are Pizza Hut and Dominos.

One of the most unusual pizza offerings comes from a US-based company called California Pizza Kitchen (CPK), founded in 1985 by two former lawyers. The company had revenues of nearly $165 million in 2008, with just over 10 per cent growth compared to 2007. CPK has over 200 outlets in 29 states in the USA and in other countries—China, including Hong Kong, Japan, South Korea, Indonesia, Singapore, Malaysia, the Philippines, and Mexico (California Pizza Kitchen 2008). CPK's menu now includes many other items, but the pizzas offered cover such non-Italian varieties as mango tandoori chicken pizza, Jamaican jerk chicken pizza, and Thai chicken pizza. Is this the ultimate departure from an original national food into an internationalized commodity designed to appeal to a universal set of customers?

The combination of the pizza outlet and the range of other drink and food provided in a food court is a striking expression of the globalization of eating and drinking. Food courts are simultaneously evidence of the international market for restaurants and showcases for national tastes in food and drink. They are a fascinating illustration of both the clash of national cultures and the possibilities of a new world culture.

Canal Walk Shopping Centre, Cape Town. Food courts reflect the globalization of eating and drinking (Canal Walk Shopping Centre, Cape Town, South Africa).

Figure 2.1
Layers of culture
(adapted from
Trompenaars and
Hampden-Turner
1997).

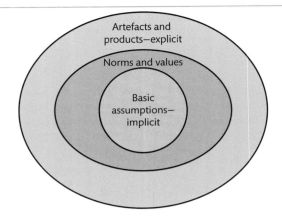

Introduction: What is culture?

+ Culture
Broad term that covers
many patterns of
human activity that
exemplify the ways
of life of a certain
population.

Most successful international business relies on factors such as clear strategy, cost control, pricing, product quality, meeting customer needs, and an understanding of national cultures. Each multinational enterprise (MNE) operates within internal and external contexts, and one of the most significant aspects of the external environment is national culture. The simplest international form of the impact of national culture is when the MNE comes from one country, is 100 per cent staffed by people from that country, and operates in only one foreign country. Although this might have been true of international activities many decades ago, it is now far more common that any MNE is staffed by nationals of many different countries, that it operates throughout the world, and that its 'original' country of origin may be hidden behind the international image that it projects to its worldwide customers.

Thinking point

To what extent
are some national
cultures dominated
by the impact of
the American way
of life?

An accepted view of culture is that it is like an onion with several different layers that can be peeled back to reveal deep meanings and core values, as noted in Figure 2.1. The outside layers feature explicit manifestations of the culture—products, artefacts, food, language, shrines, markets, houses, monuments, art, and so on. The intermediate layers, contain the norms and values of the individual culture; these include the mutual and agreed sense of what is meant by 'right' and 'wrong', whether these are expressed as formal laws and/or as informal social control, and what is understood to be 'good' or 'bad'. For Trompenaars, the difference between norms and values is that norms 'give us a feeling of "this is how I normally should behave"' whereas values 'give us a feeling of "this is how I aspire or desire to behave"' (Trompenaars and Hampden-Turner 1997).

Section I: Interpretations of culture

+ Hierarchy of needs
Maslow's concept sets
out a pyramid of layers
of human need, from
basic needs such as
food, water and shelter
to the realization of
personal potential and
self-fulfilment.

As noted above, one of the interpretations of culture, as indicated in Figure 2.1, is that it consists of different layers, with the centre containing the fundamental aspects of human culture and human existence. At their most basic, these are survival in the face of natural elements, security from hunger and want, and provision of people's basic and physical needs, such as shelter. At the higher end of the spectrum, human beings have aspirations towards greater self-fulfilment. The many variations in human values, needs, and wants have also been explored by other writers (e.g. Kluckhohn and Strodtbeck 1961). All these layers of culture can also be expressed in Maslow's hierarchy of needs—an attempted gradation of human needs from the most ordinary (at the bottom of the pyramid) to the most extraordinary (at the top of the pyramid).

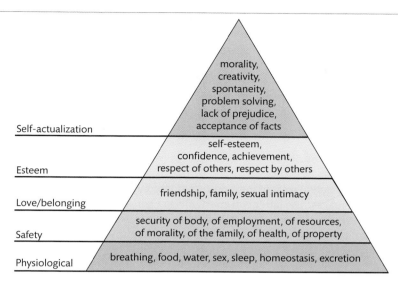

Figure 2.2
Maslow's 'Hierarchy
of Needs' (adapted
from Maslow 1943;
reprinted with the kind
permission of APA).

In the 1940s and 1950s, Abraham Maslow set out an approach for understanding the full range of human needs. He originally stressed that each person is motivated by needs, starting from the most basic, which are innate, having evolved over tens of thousands of years. Maslow's 'Hierarchy of Needs' is designed to help explain how these needs motivate all humans. It states that people must satisfy each need in turn, starting with the first, which deals with survival itself. Only when the lower-order needs of physical and emotional well-being are satisfied are people concerned with the higher-order needs of influence and personal development. Conversely, if the factors that guarantee the satisfaction of lower-order needs are removed, people are no longer concerned about the maintenance of the higher-order needs.

Over time the model of the 'Hierarchy of Needs' has developed from an original set of five needs, as illustrated in Figure 2.2, to seven needs, with the addition of cognitive (knowledge and meaning) and aesthetic (appreciation and search for beauty, balance, and form). For people engaged in business, whether domestic or international, there can be real applications of Maslow's concepts and the models of the hierarchy.

The highest concept of self-actualization relates directly to the present-day challenges and opportunities for employers and organizations—that is, the need to provide real meaning, purpose, and true personal development for employees. This confirms the view that people in employment need to have a true life–work balance; their key needs relate to their whole life, not just to the time and effort that is devoted to work. For some companies, typically in Scandinavian business cultures, strenuous efforts are made to ensure that staff efficiency comes from a combination of working hard while taking regular work breaks and holidays. Similarly, but in a different national and business context, a company such as Mont Blanc (luxury pens, watches, jewellery, and other products) requires staff to take a certain number of holiday weeks and cultural breaks, such as visits to the theatre and concerts (private information).

Maslow noted the fact that employees at all levels of the company have a basic human need and right to strive for self-actualization, just as much as corporate directors and owners do. Increasingly, the successful organizations and employers in many cultures will be those that genuinely care about, understand, encourage, and enable their people's personal growth towards self-actualization. This means that MNEs, and other firms engaged in international business, realize that they need to go beyond traditional work-related training and development, and abandon the concepts and behaviour of old-style autocratic management. Modern business employers have learnt that ongoing and sustainable success is built on a serious commitment to helping people identify, pursue, and reach their own

Thinking point

For most successful business people, such as chief executive officers (CEOs) of MNEs, what level of needs are most appropriate? Why?

+ Autocratic management
Management style that is domineering and dictatorial, sometimes with the exercise of unrestricted authority.

unique potential. The assumption is that, when people are encouraged to grow, they automatically become more effective and valuable as employees. Most personal growth is seen as producing new skills, attributes, behaviour, and wisdom that are directly, or indirectly, transferable to any sort of job or employment role. In the most effective national and corporate cultures, the best modern employers recognize the importance of personal growth and offer development support to their members of staff so that the person seeks to grow and become more fulfilled (see Chapter 15).

Religions and languages

As noted above, the outer layers of the culture 'onion' contain factors such as art, literature, religions, and languages. The latter two are significant constituents and main determinants of national cultures, thus forming the backdrop to countries, and indeed to other entities, such as communities or regions. As can be seen from Figures 2.3–2.6, the variety of religious adherence and faith, and of languages, contributes massively to the kaleidoscope that contains all the coloured pieces that constitute the culture of a nation or a society.

Figure 2.3 demonstrates that the main global religions of the world are clearly Christianity and Islam, but, as is evident from many of the social and political disputes in the world, some of the main divisions are within these broad religious categories. The separation in terms of belief, faith, and values between Shiite and Sunni Islam or between Catholic and Protestant Christianity are often greater than between the two main religions. Each of these world religions is really a classification of multiple distinct movements, sects, divisions, and denominations. None of these world religions is a single, unified, monolithic organization, but the diversity within these groupings varies. Hinduism, for example, is sometimes

Figure 2.3
Religions of the world in percentages, 2005 (taken from www. adherents.com).

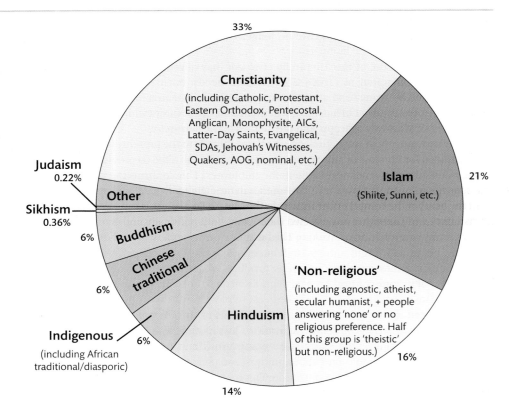

Note: Total adds up to more than 100% because of rounding and because upper band estimates were used for each group.

Branch	Number of adherents
Christianity	
Catholic	968,000,000
Protestant	395,867,000
Other Christians	275,583,000
Orthodox	217,948,000
Anglicans	70,530,000
Islam	
Sunni	940,000,000
Shiite	120,000,000
Ahmadiyya	10,000,000
Druze	450,000

Figure 2.4
Major groups within Christianity and Islam by number (taken from www.adherents.com).

described as a collection of very different traditions, bound by a geographical and national identity—that is, within the Indian subcontinent. At the other extreme, and in contrast to complex religious groupings such as Christianity and Hinduism, there is the Babi and Baha'i tradition, which is probably the most unified of the classical world religions. The Baha'i Faith, based in Haifa, Israel, is almost entirely contained within one highly organized and very hierarchical denomination.

Most adherents of a single religion usually share at least some commonalities, such as a common historical heritage and some shared doctrines or practices. But these common factors are often limited by the many exceptions. A listing of doctrinally and organizationally meaningful divisions or denominational branches for all religions would be much more complex. Figure 2.4 summarizes the main divisions of the world's two largest religions, Christianity and Islam.

From these figures, it can be seen that the largest single groupings are Catholics and Sunnis at 968 million and 940 million respectively. Within these two massive sections of the world's population, there is sometimes little direct contact. The most significant considerations for understanding of national cultures come not from these raw figures and listings but from a more detailed analysis of the role of religions within geopolitical regions. The impact of religion has often affected the conduct of international business, whether in the days of Venetian maritime trade, the difficulties of commerce along the silk route, or the triangular trade involving the transportation of African slaves to North America in the eighteenth and nineteenth centuries.

At the heart of the complex conflict within the Middle East, there is the separation between Christianity and Islam that has affected the region, both politically and economically, since the rise of Islam over 1,200 years ago. The battle for Jerusalem, which is a holy site for both religions, as well as for Judaism, has exemplified the bitter nature of the religious (and other) differences that have arisen. A further cultural complication within the Middle East is the division of the region into the Sunni and Shiite branches of Islam. However, even when two of the major countries in the region are dominated by Shiites—Iran (89 per cent) and Iraq (65 per cent)—it does not prevent them from engaging in conflict, including the long war of 1980–8, which cost well over a million lives (Global Security 2009). The differences of language (Farsi in Iran and Arabic in Iraq) and the differences of politics, economics, and society overrode the similarities of religion.

Another major determinant of national cultures is the language (or languages) spoken in each nation state and in different parts of the world (see Figure 2.5). As with religion, it is sometimes the divisions created by languages that have most impact on the world and on the interplay between national cultures. The understanding and mastery of another language is often a great advantage for managers in their conduct of international business.

Thinking point

How might religious differences complicate the conduct of international business?

Figure 2.5
Major language groups in the world (numbers of people) (adapted from Gordon 2005; Ethnologue. Used with permission).

Language	Family	Number of people (2005 estimate)
Mandarin	Sino-Tibetan, Chinese	873,000,000
Hindustani	Indo-European, Indo-Iranian, Indo-Aryan	366,000,000
Spanish	Indo-European, Italic, Romance	322,300,000
English	Indo-European, Germanic, West	309,350,000
Arabic	Afro-Asiatic, Semitic	206,000,000
Portuguese	Indo-European, Italic, Romance	177,500,000
Bengali	Indo-European, Indo-Iranian, Indo-Aryan	171,000,000
Russian	Indo-European, Slavic, East	145,000,000
Japanese	Japanese–Ryukyuan	122,400,000
German	Indo-European, Germanic, West	95,400,000

The period from the seventeenth to the nineteenth centuries witnessed the spread of European languages around the world as part of the expansion of various empires, especially those of Spain, Portugal, the Netherlands, France, and Great Britain. This accounts for the continued spread of European languages (see Figure 2.5). In particular, the nineteenth and twentieth centuries saw the increasing dominance of English as the language of business and culture, as Anglicization and then Americanization spread throughout the world. Accordingly, English is usually ranked as the most commonly learnt and spoken second language, with possibly nearly two billion speakers using it as either first or second language (Crystal 1997, 2003).

Figure 2.6
World map depicting predominant religions. Adapted from (CIA World Factbook, 2008).

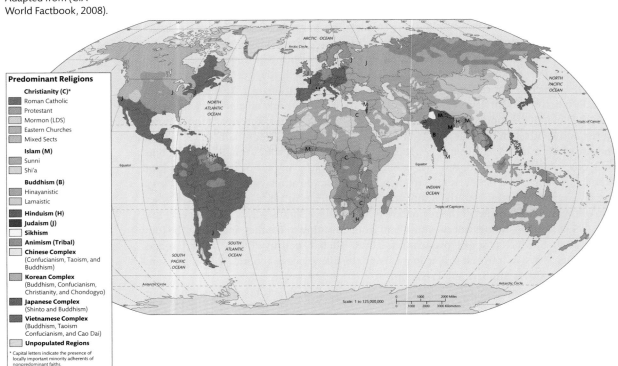

Predominant Religions

Christianity (C)*
- Roman Catholic
- Protestant
- Mormon (LDS)
- Eastern Churches
- Mixed Sects

Islam (M)
- Sunni
- Shi'a

Buddhism (B)
- Hinayanistic
- Lamaistic

Hinduism (H)
Judaism (J)
Sikhism
Animism (Tribal)
Chinese Complex (Confucianism, Taoism, and Buddhism)
Korean Complex (Buddhism, Confucianism, Christianity, and Chondogyo)
Japanese Complex (Shinto and Buddhism)
Vietnamese Complex (Buddhism, Taoism Confucianism, and Cao Dai)
Unpopulated Regions

* Capital letters indicate the presence of locally important minority adherents of nonpredominant faiths.

Within the large families of language (see Figure 2.5), it is evident that the proximity of some languages, both geographically and linguistically, can sometimes lead to conflict. Within the medium-sized country of Spain (total population of about 40 million in 2008), there is harmony of religion (94 per cent Roman Catholic) but divisions arising from several different languages: Castilian Spanish (74 per cent), Catalan (17 per cent), Galician (7 per cent), and Basque (2 per cent) (CIA 2008). The linguistic and cultural divisions have led to political and armed campaigns opposed to control by Madrid from the Basques and Euskadi Ta Askatasuna (ETA—Basque for 'Homeland and Freedom'), to the creation of more autonomous regions (such as Catalonia), and to regular cultural rivalries such as football-club allegiances (including Real Madrid versus Barcelona).

Religion and language can be sources of both friction and stability for a national culture, or for a region within the world. The tendency towards friction and conflict arises from the apparently small differences that communities can magnify. As shown above, conflicts within the Christian or the Islamic worlds can stem from differences of belief such as those between Catholics and Protestants, or Sunnis and Shiites. The best international managers and their companies have strategies for overcoming these barriers.

Unity of language, culture, and religion can lead to greater political and economic harmony and the development of successful international commerce. The linkages between some of the predominantly Christian and English-speaking countries of the Commonwealth, such as Canada, Australia, New Zealand, and the UK, have led to major migrations of people and considerably eased cross-border transactions between those who share language and culture. In the same way, the influence of Spanish, Portuguese, and Italian companies in Latin America is partially a product of cultural and linguistic similarity, as well as historical and commercial ties.

Inside business

Denitza Roussinova, Former Managing Director, Portfolio Manager Eastern Europe Middle East Africa Fund, Black River Asset Management
(speaking in a personal capacity)

Black River Asset Management is an alternative asset management company operating in global financial markets. It was created in 2003 as an independently managed subsidiary of Cargill Incorporated, which is an international provider of food, agricultural, and risk management product and services operating in sixty-seven countries and is privately owned. Black River operates out of fourteen offices in twelve countries.

I am responsible for local markets trading in Central Europe, the Middle East, and Africa. The mandate covers a broad range of products—currencies, local currency debt, derivatives, and equities. At present I focus mainly on Hungary, Poland, Czech Republic, Slovakia, and Bulgaria in Europe, as well as South Africa, Israel, Egypt, and Nigeria.

Speaking different languages (Bulgarian, English, Russian, Italian, and Spanish) has been extremely important for me. It gave me the opportunity to come and study in London, Italy, and Spain in my year of study abroad; and it allowed me to start my professional life in the UK. In the sphere of finance, English has undoubtedly been the most essential language. This is partially due to the fact that there are specific terms in finance that people know mainly in English. I am surrounded by people who are fluent in two or three languages, which now has become more of a norm than an exception.

In my interaction with colleagues and counterparts, I have not experienced specific differences coming from religious beliefs. Certain markets can be closed for longer periods because of religious holidays, but ultimately people everywhere are looking for an attractive return on their investment, regardless of their religion.

Most people in my profession, regardless of nationality or cultural background, seek higher returns and are willing to tolerate a higher level of risk. However, if we look at individual retail investors, you can see differences in their investment behaviour. For example, in my opinion, Polish people stand out as more entrepreneurial and they manage their financial investments pretty actively. This is different from Bulgaria, where most people keep their savings in deposits. People in the Czech Republic also come across as more prudent and conservative.

My job has given me many opportunities for professional and personal development, which has been encouraged and supported by my employer. Throughout my job, my areas of responsibility have evolved and broadened and I have certainly not experienced a 'glass ceiling'. Financial markets recognize and reward good performance, and from this point of view if you do a good job there are no career limitations. I think the main challenge for women is in achieving the appropriate balance of work and family.

World demography

+ **Demography**
Statistical study of all populations and the specific features of such populations related to their size, structure, and distribution.

Another fundamental factor in the development of national cultures—and their changes over time—is demography. For the world as a whole, the possible developments in age demography are dramatic. The key drivers of the move towards an ageing world population are the combination of rising life expectancy and low or falling fertility. As Magnus (2008) has indicated, there are four main characteristics to the ageing population. The first is that the proportion of people over 60 worldwide is 'going to more than double to 22 per cent by 2050'; the second is that the under-15 age group is 'going to shrink or stagnate'; the third is that 'the number of people of working age will also decline'—by 16 per cent in the EU and by nearly 40 per cent in Japan; finally 'the welfare and prospects of older, economically inactive people will become increasingly dependent on a falling, or slowly growing, population of working age' (Magnus 2008: 14–15).

Demography covers the key elements of the structure of each country. These include socio-economic level, age distribution and life expectancy, gender distribution, and literacy and education levels. Even among a selection of major countries there can be some large variations. Figure 2.7 supplies details for 2007–8, showing, for example, the high life expectancy in Japan and France (over 80 years) compared not only with South Africa (49 years) but also with India (69 years) and Russia (66 years). Similarly, the male–female ratio ranges from Russia, where it is 0.8 male to 1.2 female, to China and India, where it is the reverse (1.04 and 1.03 male to 0.96 and 0.97 respectively). The largest discrepancy in Figure 2.7 is, of course, per capita income (GDP per head at purchasing power parity): the world average is $10,000, the lowest is India with $2,700, and the highest is the USA with $45,800.

The demographics of nations throughout the world have major impacts on the kinds of products and services that MNEs will decide to provide in each country. Products for elderly people will clearly have a larger market, both in real terms and in proportion to the population, in Japan than in South Africa. Attempts to reach a literate public will be different in India from what they are in European countries.

Caution must be exercised about some of the statistics cited in Figure 2.7 and in any comparable listing of figures drawn from a variety of national and international sources. Literacy figures, for example, are surprisingly similar, with six countries, ranging from Russia to the USA, all claiming that 99 per cent of the population are 'literate'. They are also suspiciously high for certain countries, and it is clear that the national determination of what is meant by the ability to 'read and write' has differed considerably.

As noted above, at the heart of the successful conduct of international business is a full understanding of the key determinants of the market, especially its demographic structure. The size of the market as a whole—as specified by factors such as population, age group, and income level—is vital information for any business, and successful international companies research demographic basics very carefully.

	Population	GDP	Life	Literacy	Gender
World	6.7bn.	10,000	66	82	0.92
China	1.3bn.	5,300	73	91	1.04
India	1.1bn.	2,700	69	61	1.03
USA	303m.	45,800	78	99	0.94
Indonesia	237m.	3,700	70	90	0.96
Brazil	196m.	9,700	71	89	0.9
Russia	141m.	14,700	66	99	0.8
Japan	127m.	33,600	82	99	0.94
Germany	82m.	34,200	79	99	0.95
France	64m.	33,200	81	99	0.93
UK	61m.	35,100	79	99	0.95
South Africa	49m.	9,800	66	99	0.8

Figure 2.7
Selected demographic statistics (adapted from CIA 2008).

Pop = Population in millions (m) or billions (bn)
GDP = GDP per capita in $ at purchasing power parity
Life = life expectancy at birth (in years, total population)
Literacy = percentage of those over 15 who can read & write
Gender = sex ratio of males (total population)

Section II: Models of national culture and the conduct of international business

Models of national culture

When national, or regional and local cultures are considered, the concern is with the extent to which these cultures differ and how this might affect the conduct of international business. For managers and others engaged in the practicalities of business, one of the key questions is: 'What sort of accommodation do "we" have to make to "you"?' For the purposes of understanding culture and national cultures within international business, the emphasis is on certain limited aspects of this exceptionally broad topic.

The focus in this book is, therefore, on Hall's notions of high and low context, on the categories established by Hofstede and Trompenaars, and on the experiences of business people in the ways in which they have confronted these varieties of culture. As the Chinese philosopher Confucius has been quoted: 'All people are the same. It's only their habits that are so different.' Business people can optimize their activities and those of their companies only when they understand the vital differences in national habits.

High-context and low-context cultures

A key insight into understanding national cultures is Edward Hall's identification of countries (1976) that have 'high-context' or 'low-context cultures'. The broad distinction that was made by Hall is that low-context cultures require explicit communication through language and specific signals. This means that low-context cultures value verbal abilities, logic, and reasoning. By contrast, high-context cultures are identified by the fact that physical context and the nature of the people are key means by which communication is made. Hall set out

+ **Cultural context (high and low)**
Definition of the situational framework by which it is possible to distinguish the degree a special code is needed to understand the signals and communications of a culture.

Figure 2.8
Level of context,
identified by culture
(adapted from Jandt
2007).

High	Low
China	Switzerland
Japan	Germany
Korea	USA and Canada
Latin America (most countries)	Nordic/Scandinavian countries
Arab countries (most)	

a view that high-context cultures make greater distinction between insiders and outsiders than do low-context cultures. He also commented that people raised in high-context systems expect more of others than do the participants in low-context systems. When talking about something that he has on his mind, a high-context individual will expect his interlocutor to know what is bothering him, so that he does not have to be specific.

As can be seen in Figure 2.8, there are countries where important information and messages—for example, about whether a deal can be done—are going to be communicated very clearly and directly (low context). The opposite way of communicating (high context) is done more subtly and indirectly; much of the business will be done because the people know each other or get on well. In both cases, it is assumed that the basic features of the deal (product, quantity, quality, costs, time scale) make it feasible. The high-context social and business culture is reflected very clearly among the Chinese, expressed by the concept of *guanxi*. This is a concept that promotes personal relationships and mutual trust. It also stresses family and personal relationships and the hierarchy of age and experience over youth and inexperience. *Guanxi* emphasizes the importance of reciprocal ties and personal relationships for the successful conduct of business. It can also be seen as a system that appears difficult to understand and impenetrable for outsiders (that is, non-Chinese).

+ *Guanxi*
Chinese concept
in which personal
relations and the
establishment of
mutual trust and
obligations are seen
as essential for the
conduct of business.

What does high- and low-context actually mean for the conduct of business in specific situations? Take the hypothetical case of a Saudi Arabian business person trying to work with a company in North America; assume, too, that the Saudi is male. The Saudi will assume that there should be social courtesies before any discussions take place; that a considerable amount of time will be required to conduct the business; that any exchange of information with his counterparts does not imply any agreement to the deal; that he will need to refer major decisions and certainly the final decision back to his superiors in Saudi Arabia; and that the final deal will have to be agreed and signed in a relatively formal ceremony, probably accompanied by some lavish hospitality. The difference in context and formality may lead to all sorts of misunderstandings: feeling downgraded because there has been no ceremony (the Saudi); feeling insulted (the Saudi) by the forceful, direct approach (of the North American); thinking (the North American) that discussions are proceeding too slowly; feeling misled because the information given (by the North American) has not been fully passed on to his own superiors (by the Saudi); possibly feeling uncomfortable if he (the Saudi) has to deal with a woman (North American) who is at a higher level; feeling 'tricked' (the North American) by the politeness (of the Saudi) when no agreement is reached; and, by contrast, feeling 'tricked' (the Saudi) by the degree to which his counterpart (the North American) had assumed that everything was going very well. In so many instances, the business arrangement between the two has been harmed by cultural misunderstandings and the inability to communicate on the same level or with the same objectives.

This gap between the 'high-context' Saudi and the 'low-context' North American may not be so wide if they know each other from other social or business connections; for example, if they went to the same university or have done business with each other for decades. In such circumstances, there would be a level of contact and personal relationship that would overcome the gap in the contexts.

Dimensions of Culture: Hampden-Turner, Trompenaars, Hofstede and others

Among the other main aspects of national culture that are relevant to international business, there are a number of factors identified by Fons Trompenaars and his collaborators. The principal finding from Trompenaars and Hampden-Turner is that 'foreign cultures are not arbitrarily or randomly different from one another. They are instead mirror images of one another's values …' (Hampden-Turner and Trompenaars 2000). This finding derives from 'eighteen years of cross-cultural research' and is reflected in the posing of opposites such as 'universalism–particularism', 'individualism–communitarianism', and 'specificity–diffuseness' (see Online Resource Centre, extension material 2.1). In addition, their research uncovered three other opposites or dilemmas: 'achieved status–ascribed status', 'inner direction–outer direction', and 'sequential time–synchronous time' (Hampden-Turner and Trompenaars 2000).

> Go to the ORC

These six factors have been identified through extensive, longitudinal studies, originally conducted by the Centre for International Business Studies, established by Trompenaars. These studies were based on a series of questionnaires designed to discover the values of managers around the world.

As far as business is concerned, the general meaning of these pairs of opposed dimensions are explained briefly below, with some business cultures cited as examples:

- *Universalism–particularism*. People in a universalist culture respect rules and often value them more highly than relationships. Universalist people (Americans and northern Europeans) are less likely to do business with others simply because of a personal contact. For particularists (Asians and people from the Middle East), it seems very strange not to base their business dealings around the people they know and trust.
- *Individualism–communitarianism.* The most important values for individualists are competition, self-reliance, self-interest, personal growth, and fulfilment. These give them a view of business where individuals need to compete and struggle. By contrast, the business principles within a communitarian society (Chinese, Japanese, Arab cultures) are cooperation, social concern, altruism, public service, and societal legacy. These encourage connections between business, education, finance, labour, and government, so that the society as a whole benefits from shared knowledge.
- *Specificity–diffuseness*. Cultures that tend towards specificity in business value analysis, action research, measurement of results, and feedback on performance. By contrast, diffuse business cultures emphasize work as a process, complex interactions, and the sharing of commitment to quality.
- *Achieved status–ascribed status*. The culture that values achieved status puts emphasis on what people have actually done in business—their track record (Northern Europeans, North Americans). The other side of this dimension values people's potential and connections—*who* people are, rather than *what* they are (Southern Europeans, Latin Americans).
- *Inner direction–outer direction*. This dimension focuses on the origin of people's convictions and beliefs. The inner-direction culture looks at people's inner convictions and conscience, while the outer-direction cultures stress that the most important influences and examples come from outside the self.
- *Sequential time–synchronous time*. The time dimension is quite a stark contrast between those people who think that time is a race along a set course (sequential) and those who see it as a matter of precise coordination (synchronous). Those people in the synchronous category are likely to be able to multi-task better than others. (Men are thought to be sequential and women synchronous.)

It is surely no coincidence that, like Trompenaars, one of the other main experts in the area of cross-cultural research, Geert Hofstede, is Dutch. Perhaps the special position of the

Dutch within Europe explains the prominence of Trompenaars and Hofstede in this field. They come from a relatively small country with an open culture, a trading and imperial heritage, a gift for other languages, a multi-ethnic society, and a capacity to survive while surrounded by more powerful neighbours. Like Trompenaars, Hofstede has undertaken a lifetime of research on national cultures in business, much of it based on original studies of employees in IBM.

Stephan Dahl, a commentator on intercultural research, has indicated the similarities between the main factors identified by Trompenaars and Hofstede. He has suggested that over half of the different factors are closely related and claimed that some of Trompenaars and Hampden-Turner's 'value orientations can be regarded as nearly identical to Hofstede's dimensions' (Dahl 2006). (Go to the Online Resource Centre, extension material 2.2, to learn more about cross-cultural studies.)

> Go to the ORC

There are five key dimensions identified by Gert Hofstede.

Power distance

The concept of power distance is an attempt to measure 'the extent to which the less powerful members of institutions and organizations within a country expect and accept that power is distributed unequally' (Hofstede and Hofstede 2005: 46). This represents a view of inequality, of more versus less, that is shared and supported by the followers as much as by the leaders.

The variations of power distance in its simplest form are demonstrated by the national societies with the highest measures (Malaysia, Slovakia, Guatemala, and Panama) and the lowest ones (Austria, Israel, Denmark, and New Zealand) (Hofstede and Hofstede 2005: 43–4). The implication for the conduct of international business is that people from the lowest power-distance countries, such as Scandinavians and Israelis, tend to be more informal and relaxed in their attitude to approaching their counterparts, carrying out negotiations, and making deals.

Individualism–collectivism

Individualism is a measure of the extent to which individuals are integrated into groups within society or business. On the individualist side, there are 'societies in which the ties between individuals are loose: everyone is expected to look after himself or herself and his or her immediate family' (Hofstede and Hofstede 2005: 76). By contrast, on the collectivist side, there are 'societies in which people from birth onward are integrated into strong, cohesive in-groups which, throughout people's lifetimes, continue to protect them in exchange for unquestioning loyalty' (Hofstede and Hofstede 2005: 76). The idea of 'collectivism' in this sense has no political meaning because it refers to the group, rather than to the state.

In the general measures that Hofstede has developed for these five factors, the most contrasting cultures in terms of individualism and collectivism are the USA, Australia, Great Britain, Canada, Hungary, and the Netherlands as the most individualist, and, on the collectivist side, a group of Latin American countries (Guatemala, Ecuador, Panama, Venezuela, and Colombia), and Pakistan and Indonesia (Hofstede and Hofstede 2005: 78–9). The international business implication is that more individualist people, such as the North Americans and the British, are inclined to work independently, to take decisions on their own, and lead a team or group 'from the front'. They are less likely to seek consensus or wait for their team to come up with solutions.

Masculinity–femininity

The third of Hofstede's measures is perhaps the one that is most puzzlingly named, masculinity–femininity. The measure refers to the distribution of roles between the genders, which can be regarded as another fundamental issue for any society.

One of the main sources of evidence within Hofstede's research has been the two phases of studies based on employees at IBM, the large IT company. These studies revealed that women's values differed less among societies than did men's values, which tended to contain a dimension that was very assertive and competitive and very different from women's values. The assertive pole was called 'masculine' and the modest, caring pole 'feminine'. A feminine society is one where 'emotional gender roles overlap', so that both men and women are perceived to be 'modest, tender, and concerned with the quality of life' (Hofstede and Hofstede 2005: 120). In masculine societies, 'gender roles are clearly distinct: men are supposed to be assertive, tough and focussed on material success'. These countries thus show a gap between men's and women's values (Hofstede and Hofstede 2005: 120).

On this measure, the national cultures at the extremes are the most 'masculine': Slovakia, Japan, Hungary, Austria, Venezuela, Switzerland (German part), and Italy; the most 'feminine' are the Scandinavian/Nordic countries (Sweden, Norway, Denmark, Finland), the Netherlands, Slovenia, Costa Rica, and Chile (Hofstede and Hofstede 2005: 120–2). The consequence for the conduct of international business is that the Scandinavians and the Dutch tend to be less impressed with outward status symbols and are inclined to work cooperatively with both their fellow-workers and their opposite numbers in other companies.

Uncertainty avoidance (risk aversion)

The fourth of Hofstede's factors is called either uncertainty avoidance or risk aversion. In general, it deals with a society's tolerance for uncertainty and ambiguity and indicates 'the extent to which the members of a culture feel threatened by ambiguous or unknown situations' (Hofstede and Hofstede 2005: 167). Cultures that tend towards 'uncertainty avoidance' try to minimize the possibility of such situations by strict laws and rules, by safety and security measures, and, on the philosophical and religious level, by a belief in absolute Truth. Hofstede also draws the conclusion that people in uncertainty-avoiding countries are generally more emotional, and motivated by inner nervous energy. By contrast, his research suggests that the opposite cultures —those that accept uncertainty—are more likely to be tolerant of different opinions. It is claimed that these cultures try to have as few rules as possible. People within them are more phlegmatic and contemplative and less likely to express emotions.

The national cultures at the extreme ends of this measure are Greece, Portugal, Guatemala, Uruguay, Belgium (Flemish part), Malta and Russia (most risk averse), contrasting with Singapore, Jamaica, Denmark, Sweden, and Hong Kong (least risk averse) (Hofstede and Hofstede 2005: 168–70). As with the conclusions from the other measures cited above, the business and management implications of uncertainty avoidance/risk aversion is that the nationals of such countries as Singapore and Hong Kong are most likely to take business risks, and that these countries are the ones that have created a risk-welcoming business environment.

Long-term orientation (time)

The final factor in the Hofstede scheme—and one that is common to most other views of national cultural differences—relates to time. This fifth dimension was originally found in a study among students from twenty-three countries around the world, the Chinese Value Survey. This was then expanded by Hofstede into a further survey covering a total of thirty-nine societies. Values associated with long-term orientation are thrift and perseverance; whereas values associated with short-term orientation are respecting tradition, fulfilling social obligations, and protecting one's 'face'. Both the positively and negatively rated values of this dimension are found in the teachings of Confucius, but 'the dimension also applies to countries without a Confucian heritage'. There are other interesting measures related to time that are especially important for international business, such as a concern for the start, duration, and finish (let alone the purpose) of meetings, attitudes towards punctuality, and emphasis on deadlines.

As far as this factor is concerned, the countries with the greatest long-term orientations are almost all Asian (China, Hong Kong, Taiwan, Japan, Vietnam, South Korea) and Brazil;

at the other end of the spectrum, the short-term cultures are Pakistan, Czech Republic, Nigeria, Spain, Philippines, Canada, Zimbabwe, Great Britain, and the United States (Hofstede and Hofstede 2005: 210–12).

On his website and in his many books, Hofstede and his collaborators have provided interesting three-dimensional maps of the combinations of these characteristics in the national cultures of over 100 countries. They have also managed to ensure the updating of this information, as, for example, Russia has emerged from the Soviet Union or South Africa has moved on from the apartheid era of white domination. Some early tables and figures provided by Hofstede (and by Trompenaars and others) have proved to be very fixed in time and place. As the societies have changed, so have their orientations and, consequently, what the indicators have been measuring.

For the immediate purposes of this book and as a rough guide to understanding the relative measures for eleven major countries, Figure 2.9 measures their rankings in relation to each other for all five of the Hofstede dimensions.

It can be seen from the rankings in Figure 2.9, that even among these eleven countries there are significant differences of approach to business, so that the conduct of commerce and trade is complex. Looking at the relationship between two of the Asian giants, China and Japan, the greatest gulf is the factor of uncertainty avoidance (a ranking difference of 9). Not only does this suggest that the business environment in China is more attuned to and welcoming of taking risks, whether in investments or trading, but it also provides evidence to confirm the stereotype that Chinese business people are more adventurous than their Japanese counterparts. Doing business in Japan takes place within a more cautious environment in which long-term planning plays a large part, decisions are made more slowly, and the prevailing attitude is a conservatism rejecting outside influences that the Japanese perceive as designed to change the system.

There is an equally large difference between Russia and Germany (a ranking difference of 9) on the factor of power distance. This confirms the experience of those who have carried out business in or between these two countries. For Russians, there is still a view that the gulf between the top and bottom of the business world, let alone in society as a whole, is wide. This confirms the new oligarchs' view of themselves as superior creatures and that their new-found wealth requires them to be aloof in their business dealings.

Thinking point

What kind of business ventures are likely to be most successful in risk-friendly cultures? Why?

+ Stereotype Simplified and/ or standardized conception or image with specific meaning, often held in common by people about another group.

Figure 2.9
Summary of selected countries, ranked against each other for each category (ranking of 1 for PDI = most distance; I–C = most individual; M–F = most masculine; Uncertainty= most keen to avoid uncertainty; Time = most long-term orientation) (derived from Hofstede and Hofstede 2005; produced with the kind permission of Geerte Hofstede).

Rank	PDI	I–C	M–F	Uncertainty	Time
Brazil	4	10	9	4	3
Canada	9	3	8	7	10
China	2	11	3	11	1
France	5	5	10	3	5
Germany	10	6	4	6	7
India	3	7	7	9	4
Italy	7	4	2	5	6
Japan	6	8	1	2	2
Russia	1	9	11	1	n.a.
UK	11	2	5	10	9
USA	8	1	6	8	8

As with the demographic figures cited above, these ranking differences are very broad and mask the complexities of the mapping that the detailed Hofstede system can uncover. The implications of and the conclusions drawn from these indicators should be regarded with some degree of scepticism.

Stereotyping and 'World Culture'

There are inherent difficulties in ascribing certain characteristics to specific cultures as though such cultures are homogeneous. It is usually only an average characteristic that is being described. This is the false currency of stereotypes.

A possible advantage of stereotypes and stereotyping is being able to make some general comments about peoples, rather than having to keep stating that general types do not exist. The view that all Germans or all Indonesians, or even all Bavarians and all Javanese, think, behave, or act in a certain way is clearly erroneous, but, used carefully, there can be a valid possibility of stating that, in general, when doing business with Germans, Bavarians, Indonesians, or Javanese, certain things may be true and distinctive.

A modern view, sometimes hotly debated, suggests that it is possible to abandon the use of stereotypes and to rise above the focus on national cultures; this view is associated with the development of the concept of a world culture.

Some writers have argued that world culture is 'a global, distinct, complex, and dynamic phenomenon' (Lechner and Boli 2005). Some of the examples of a world culture include the Olympic movement and the Olympic Games, the worldwide rituals and experiences of the United Nations organization (and its many agencies), and the various worldwide activities of non-governmental organizations and social movements. The central argument behind the idea of world culture is that 'it concerns the routine realities of everyday life. Most directly involved are people of the relatively affluent countries and social classes but increasingly we find world culture influencing the lives of even the most remote places and poorest people' (Lechner and Boli 2005).

+ World culture
Growing concept of a universal culture that rises above national cultures and emphasizes global events and world organizations.

Photo 2.1
The opening ceremony of the Beijing 2008 Olympic Games at the National Stadium, also known as the 'Bird's Nest', Beijing, China, 8 August 2008 (© ALLESANDRO DELLA BELLA/epa/ Corbis).

Case Study 2.2

Visuals and graphics: Do you see what I see?

A common form of communication in international business is through visual displays and graphic representations. This is done on the assumption that businesses are thereby avoiding the difficulties of communication through language. Recent research has indicated, however, that 'communicating with diagrams can be problematic'.

The general view among international managers is that graphic formats (pie charts, bar charts, matrices, decision trees, Venn diagrams, flow charts) are intuitively understood by employees who have different levels of qualification and experience. Similarly, it is expected that this understanding is extended across cultural, national, and linguistic boundaries. In the modern world, too, the presentation of facts and figures is increasingly fast, instant, and changing. It is sufficient to look at the scrolling of such data in onscreen displays (OSDs) across split screens, the use of graphical user interfaces (GUIs), and straplines by financial media producers such as Bloomberg, Thomson Reuters, CNBC, and CNN to acknowledge the danger of the assumption that all people might interpret this information in the same way. MNEs regularly use 'standardized graphic formats' in corporate newsletters, annual reports, video screen displays, team meetings, strategy workshops, and Powerpoint presentations. MNE managers assume that they know what is the most crucial information to be cascaded down to staff, and the best format for its graphic representations.

There has been some specific analysis of cultural differences in the interpretation of data, figures, and graphic representations. Eppler and Gee's study (2008) examined the perception of business graphics by over 100 Chinese and British business students in Beijing and Cambridge. They asked the students (58 men and 43 women) to categorize a number of typical business visualizations. Accepting that their findings are tentative and limited, Eppler and Gee note a number of significant differences in the interpretation of figures. These are:

1. 'diagram understanding is neither intuitive nor cross-cultural';

2. there may be 'considerable differences among male and female groupings';

3. Asians are generally less keen strictly to 'group or classify elements based on their attributes compared to people from the West';

4. Asians are more likely to 'emphasize the context in which something is used'.

These points confirm some of the assumptions made about Eastern and Western differences and the need for inter-cultural sensitivity. The lesson for European and Asian MNEs working together is 'that Europeans should be especially careful when using visual means of communication in China, as Chinese employees may not be highly familiar with these formats or interpret them differently (i.e. as with regard to quantitative vs. qualitative charts)'.

The evidence is clear: not only do people not necessarily hear the same thing; they do not always see the same thing. The cultural differences of the world are very deep, and this is a key lesson for international business people to learn and understand.

It can be dangerous to assume that everybody interprets data in the same way (reproduced with the kind permission of Thomson Reuters).

The impacts of culture on international business

As business people navigate their way through the complexities of culture within international business, they acknowledge that cultures will have varying effects. This section deals, therefore, with these different aspects.

Culture and the regulatory framework

Around the world, the variance in national cultures forms (or reflects) different attitudes towards rights of ownership and property. In more highly regulated and legalistic cultures (such as the Northern European or Northern American), the legal rights and obligations of landowners, tenants, lease holders, and so on are clearly defined. Any disputes to the title of lands are governed by the legal and court system, and, in the vast majority of cases, the judgments and rulings of the court authorities are accepted by participants in the case. This is not always so in the less legalistic cultures where the 'rule of law' is regarded less highly.

Firms engaged in international business need to know the status of the land that they occupy—whether it is an office, a factory or processing plant, agricultural land, or land for hotel and leisure facilities. Not only can companies not afford doubts about their right to carry out business on a particular piece of land, they must have certainty over other legal issues as well, such as laws relating to ecology and environment, health and safety, insurance, and security. For MNEs, the legal culture of nation-states is also revealed in the rules and customs surrounding competition law—an essential element for the successful conduct of international business (see Online Resource Centre, extension material 2.3).   > Go to the ORC

Companies must also be aware of the prevailing philosophy underlying the regulatory framework. The national culture sometimes plays a key role in determining the nature of the economic system operated by the state. There are three key systems that can be operated by different countries: laissez-faire, interventionism, and command economy and central planning. The political philosophies that underlie these different systems are explored more fully in Chapter 4. As far as the cultural implications are concerned, those countries with the greatest degree of laissez-faire, such as Singapore and the USA, tend to permit business to operate with as little involvement of the government as possible. At the other end of the spectrum, there used to be countries, such as the old communist bloc, where the governments dictated the central elements of the economy and the business environment.

There are many other forms of national culture that can affect business operations. These include a system often called 'cronyism' in which the majority of business decisions are made on the basis of economic and political calculation, which favours friends or 'cronies' of those in power. There is also the possibility of a business system that can be classified as 'theocracy'. In this system, the culture is based on some form of religious rule, and the regulation of business stems from the fundamental beliefs and tenets of that religion. Modern examples of theocratic states are those where Islam is the dominant religion and where banking and other forms of business are governed by Muslim principles, such as the Islamic Republic of Iran. Rather different from a theocratic state are countries such as Saudi Arabia and many of the Gulf states, such as Dubai and Bahrain, which combine modern capitalism in its laissez-faire manifestation with strong social and economic policies derived from Islam.

Culture and the employment relationship

The relationships between employees and the MNEs that employ them can be characterized by different forms of behaviour and attitude that may be reflective of national cultures. In some cases, these relationships can be viewed through the models of Hofstede or Trompenaars. These observations of culture and the employment relationship are gathered under the headings of identification with the job, attitudes towards technology, education and training, culture's effect on demand and consumption, and business leadership and national culture.

Identification with the job

One of the main aspects of employees' identification with the job is their approach towards working collectively or individually. This aspect can be connected to the second of Hofstede's dimensions (individualism–collectivism) and is very observable in the approach that different cultures have towards teamwork or individual efforts. In a BBC TV programme *Working with the French* (2008), there are some excellent examples of the attitudes of British people working in France towards the French view of teamwork. They observe that, although French people in the various companies illustrated work in teams, they are really working for themselves rather than in and for the team. The ways in which this is exemplified are that the French employees are reluctant to share with other members of the team the knowledge and the skills that they have. As Luan Greenwood, International Communications Manager at Ondeo, noted: 'in France you can say there is a team and a team set-up, but each member of that team will work separately' (BBC Languages 2008).

A further example of the individualist end of this working spectrum is revealed in the American approach towards what they would call 'rugged individualism'. This implies that people stand or fall on their own efforts. Each employee has to take responsibility for his or her own actions, and there can be no possibility of hiding behind others' efforts. This view of employment is strongly reflected in those societies that, as pointed out by Hofstede, are at the individualist end of the individualism–collectivism spectrum: USA, Australia, Hungary, Netherlands, UK, Canada, Italy.

In addition to the view of the individual or the team in international business, there are also different attitudes towards hierarchy (reflected by Hofstede's concept of power distance), labour mobility in general, flexibility of working, and the work ethic itself. Within these aspects of employment relations, there is a fundamental difference between those societies and national cultures in which work is seen as an expression of self and those in which it is viewed as an obligation imposed on the individual by outside forces. For the latter societies, there is a tendency to take work more lightly; to be happy with a job that is completed though not perhaps to the highest quality; to resist moving from one job to another, let alone from one part of the country (or the world) to another; and to hide behind the function of the job and the hierarchy of the company that has imposed it.

Attitudes towards technology

As far as culture and attitudes towards technology are concerned, there is often a direct connection to the behaviours and attitudes attributed to the national cultures commented upon above. The key aspects of international attitudes towards technology in business are (1) Luddism, (2) views of education and training, embracing the attitude towards learning and change and the willingness to share and spread knowledge, and (3) the view of whether industrial and scientific research should be applied or theoretical.

The complexity of cultural attitudes towards technology is affected by economic issues facing different countries and groups of people, and by individual and specific national and personal responses to changes in the external environment. It is impossible to say that certain cultures are intrinsically in favour of or hostile to technology. For example, in the Gulf states (United Arab Emirates, Qatar, Bahrain, and so on), the wealth of the top sectors of society has inspired people to embrace many aspects of the new technologies. There is an abundance of advanced communications (mobile phones, MP3 players, satellite navigation systems, and so on) and an extraordinary development of modern architecture and construction, such as the Burj Dubai—set to be the world's tallest building and scheduled for completion in September 2009. Side by side with this impressive encouragement of high technology, the society remains rooted in its conservative and traditional socio-cultural ways and its adherence to old-fashioned courtesies.

Thinking point

How and why might multinational teams in a company hinder the successful conduct of business?

+ Luddism
Term used to characterize any resistance to change and innovation in technology. It is derived from the actions of the Luddites, who campaigned against the introduction of textile machinery in the early nineteenth century.

Thinking point

Why do some people resist changes in technology or innovations in the organization of work?

Photo 2.2
The Burj Dubai in the UAE—already the tallest man-made structure on earth even before its completion (© iStockphoto).

Education and training

Different cultures' views on the value of education and training can also impact on business. The cultural attitudes towards education, training, and research are conditioned by a country's relative wealth, but there can also be a strong aspirational element where importance is placed on education by the family, or the society as a whole, and is disproportionate to the per capita GDP of the country.

In relation to population and investment in education, Figure 2.10 shows the immense focus of the USA on the need for public investment in the sector. Within the UNESCO figures, also noteworthy is the relatively high attainment of regions such as South and West Asia and Latin America and the Caribbean, where the investment in education is 6.9 per cent and 7.6 per cent of the world total, respectively. Although well behind the industrialized and developed countries of North America and Western Europe (55.1 per cent) and the region of East Asia and the Pacific (17.9 per cent), these are the parts of the world where most attention is paid to education (UIS 2007).

Country	Percentage of world total (international PPPs (percentage purchasing power))
Brazil	2.7
Italy	3.1
France	4.2
UK	4.1
Germany	4.4
India	5.2
Japan	5.5
China	5.9
USA	28.0

Figure 2.10
Global distribution of public expenditure on education for selected countries, 2004 (adapted from UIS 2007).

Culture's effect on demand and consumption

From another perspective, socio-economic conditions can affect people's relationship to spending and buying. In line with the ideas of Maslow's hierarchy (see above), some historical periods of economic development of economies and certain socio-economic classes have lead to the phenomenon of conspicuous consumption.

The theories of conspicuous consumption suggest that certain classes of people (or sectors of society) like to consume goods and services almost as a function of their status and ability to show that their level of consumption is higher than other people. The main proponent of this theory was Thorstein Veblen, who wrote in the late nineteenth century about the growth of a leisure class that engaged in extravagant consumption of expensive goods and services in order to demonstrate status and wealth (Bullock et al. 2000). There are many contemporary examples of this kind of consumption—the new Russian (and other former Soviet Union) elites since the fall of communism and the wealthy Gulf state elites—that demonstrate very clearly that it is not particular to any national culture. It is also reflected in the purchase of football clubs (both Chelsea FC by Roman Abramovich and Manchester City FC by Sheikh Mansour Bin Zayed Al-Nahyan's Abu Dhabi United Group within the English Premier League), in the use of large yachts and personal aeroplanes, in the development of extensive art collections, and through the ownership of many very expensive houses around the world (Kane 2008).

Associated with the melding of cultures and consumption is the notion that the wealth of certain elites allows them to consider instant rather than delayed gratification; they can have what they want immediately rather than having to wait for it. At certain socio-economic levels below the elites, this kind of behaviour can also be enjoyed. As people move up through the classes, it is often possible for them to buy goods and services at a more expensive level or more rapidly than was possible before. Examples of this form of consumption can be found in many advanced industrialized societies in the expansion of exclusive shopping outlets, the growth of luxury advertising, and a mass desire to own sophisticated products and services.

A further consideration within the bounds of demand and consumption is the different perceptions of value that exist. The tension between aesthetic beauty and functionality, so often dependent on one's socio-economic level and national culture, means that consumers can indulge in more aesthetic and less functional purchases. This can be seen in everyday

+ **Conspicuous consumption**
Extravagant purchase and use of expensive goods and services, usually by a leisure class, in order to demonstrate status and wealth.

Photo 2.3
Designer outfits for pampered pets illustrate consumers' indulgence in luxury items (© iStock photo).

life, as purchasing decisions are made whether to buy a device for boiling water (a pot or a kettle priced purely for its function) or an extravagant and expensive piece of equipment that does the same thing but costs a great deal more.

Business leadership and national culture

A further aspect of the expression of national culture can be seen in the function of the chief executive officer (CEO) of leading companies in the world of international business. There have been some recent extensive studies of the relationship between organizations, leaders, and cultures, especially in the work of Mansour Javidan, Robert House, and others: the GLOBE study of many societies across the world (House et al. 2004). The more specific aspects of corporate culture are explored in Chapter 10, but the following example is useful for understanding the differences in national cultures.

Within three of the key countries in the EU, there are some significant areas of agreement among the views of 200 CEOs surveyed about the best and worst things they perceived about leading companies. As Figure 2.11 indicates, there is very strong agreement about the lack of personal time. Similarly, about seven other factors are close enough to indicate that North European chief executives agree on their major items of concern. However, it is also most striking that there is a fundamental difference in the category that suggests that the French and German CEOs are much more affected by conflict within their management team than British ones.

The more qualitative aspects of the MORI–DDI survey used for Figure 2.11 revealed various other key differences between the national characteristics of the 200 chief executives. The research labelled 'French captains of industry as "autocrats", Germans as "democrats" and British as "meritocrats"' (Maitland 2006). While this may seem a sweeping generalization and typical stereotyping, the survey revealed that 'fewer than three in 10 French bosses are happy to be challenged about the decisions they make, compared with half of Germans and more than nine out of 10 business leaders in the UK' (Maitland 2006).

The managing director of DDI noted that executives of international companies need to be able to adapt to the corporate and national culture in which they work, without forsaking their

	UK	France	Germany
Keeping pace with legislation	1	8	4=
Lack of personal time	2	1	1
Having to make tough decisions affecting people's future	3	7	2
Addressing corporate governance issues	4	6	11=
Concerns about having the right talent/best people	5	3	4=
Knowing that failure at this level is big failure	6	4=	3
The loneliness of knowing the buck stops with me	7	4=	7
Dealing with the press	8	10=	10
Conflict/warring egos within the management team	9	2	4=
Keeping ahead of the competition	10	9	9
Dealing with financial stakeholders, such as analysts	11=	10=	8
Public view of company directors/directors' pay	11=	10=	11=

Figure 2.11
Ranking the worst things about being a leader (adapted from Maitland 2006, and DDI 2006).

individualism. He stressed: 'The danger for any leader is only being able to operate within one of these styles. If you take an autocratic style into a culture that expects more democratic or meritocratic style, the chances are that you will trip up' (Maitland 2006).

Success in international business comes, therefore, from an ability to adapt as need be to different national cultures and to know the limits of action and operation for the MNE in its conduct of international deals. This applies at the personal level for directors and managers, as well as for the company as a whole.

Challenges and choices

→ Understanding cultures is very important for managers in international companies wanting to do business successfully. Whether managers need to be able to comprehend and manipulate such complex systems as Chinese *guanxi* or simply accept the impact of cultural differences on commercial deals, there is no doubt that cross-cultural awareness and perspectives are essential. The challenge for each manager is to know the best ways of making the right choices in selecting overseas business partners, in committing his/her own company to the best investment, and in enjoying productive business relationships around the world.

→ In the late twentieth and early twenty-first centuries, the trend towards a globalized world suggested that cultures were becoming increasingly homogenized and that a world culture might become a reality. The cultural, financial, and economic challenges of the early 2000s have subsequently revealed that cultural differences remain strong at a national level. The business that needs to be conducted over the next few decades will still require business people to develop and maintain awareness and sensitivity to the particular nature of the foreign companies and organizations with which they have to deal.

Chapter Summary

The points to be drawn from this chapter are the importance of an awareness and understanding of the complexity of national cultures, and the models that have been devised as a means of assisting managers to comprehend this complexity and carry out international business successfully.

The first section outlined the global variations in factors such as demography, culture, religion, and language. Not only is there is a massive diversity among the 200 national cultures that exist, but their subsets—that is, local and regional cultures—add immeasurably to the difficulties of drawing sensible and solid conclusions on which to base business activity and MNE policies, decisions, and actions. In addition to all of this, there is the growth of some aspects of a 'world culture' and the global manifestations of other cultural attitudes and activities.

The many aspects of culture that are relevant to conducting business successfully include understanding languages, fostering awareness of other people's cultures, developing sensitivity to counterparts, and recognizing what is appropriate in different business settings and cultures. This means that the culture of a nation or a society could be viewed as a kaleidoscope containing the colours of language, literature, art, customs, religion, attitudes, and patterns of behaviour.

The second section of the chapter explored the impact of national cultures on factors such as the employment relationships within MNEs, attitudes towards technology, education and training, culture's effect on demand and consumption, and business leadership.

Case Study 2.3

Taking medicine

The pharmaceutical industry, featuring some of the world's major MNEs, including Johnson & Johnson, Pfizer, Bayer, GlaxoSmithKline, Sanofi Aventis, Astrazeneca, Roche, and Novartis, is ranked as one of the key industries in the world. The leading company in the field, Johnson & Johnson, had total revenues of $53.3 billion, net income of $11 billion, and 138,000 employees in 2006. Many of the features of the pharmaceutical business are exactly what would be expected of such a massive industry: international production, a complex supply chain, extensive research and development (R&D), multiple locations, and complicated structure and control systems. However, one of the surprising aspects of the industry is how 'national' it can be, and perhaps has to be, when it comes to the delivery of medicine to the patient. It seems that people in many different countries like to take their medicine in different ways, such that the major MNEs have to manufacture and sell their end product in many different forms.

From the patients' perspective, there is only one imperative: when they are ill, they want only to be cured. But how best to administer the medicine? In general, it seems that the 'Latins' within Europe, such as the French, Italians, and Spanish, generally like to take their medicine by means of suppository, the Germans by injection/vaccine, the British and the Americans by tablet, and the rest of the world in powder or liquid form. This is a reflection of personal preferences on a large scale and thus an aspect of national culture. As John Barrable, leader of a pharmaceutical marketing survey in the 1990s, noted: 'What's fascinating is that what we've learnt seems to reflect what one thinks of as national characteristics ... Different nations seem preoccupied with different parts of the body.' In relation to medicine-taking in the UK, he commented that 'there is a positive advantage ... to making something taste nasty because [British] people then think it must be doing them good' (Gill 1991).

However, it is also a major cost item for the pharmaceutical companies. They need to establish the special compound for a particular treatment and then produce it, if possible, in a range of delivery modes, depending on where it is to be sold. In some cases, this is relatively simple, but in others it takes time and effort to convert one successful delivery mode into another. The extent of the technical work usually requires the deployment of a multidisciplinary team, with chemists for synthesis and structure determination, biochemists and pharmacologists for testing and biological investigation including toxicology studies, and clinicians for evaluation of drug efficacy. To be effective in the pharmaceutical industry, the team requires people with experience in synthetic organic chemistry, with ability to carry out structural characterization by spectroscopic techniques, and with familiarity in chromatography. All these skills are required for the testing and trialling of different compounds and for bringing the products to market.

When a new formulation is developed by a pharmaceutical company, it is initially produced in tablet (pill) form, especially when the primary method of administering the drug is by the patient at home. Capsules have also become a popular method of delivery, although, in certain markets, such as Islamic countries and Jewish communities, it is not possible to sell capsules as they are made with gelatin, derived from pigs and thus unacceptable to religions that prohibit the eating of pork. Liquid preparations, in the form of syrups or powders to be dissolved in water, are generally acceptable throughout the world. There has recently been a tendency to move away from syrups, which were heavily based on sugar, to lighter liquids or to other forms of treatment.

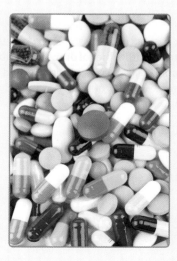

Tablets are just one of the many different ways in which different cultures prefer to have their medicine administered (© iStockphoto).

It is thought that one of the simpler modes of delivery for the future may turn out to be the patch, since it may be culture neutral. The patch has proved to be very successful in getting people in many different cultures to reduce or stop smoking—the use of nicotine patches—and there are various companies, including smaller ones such as Novosis, which has been part of Schweizerhall since spring 2008, working on the application of patches and other forms of pharmaceutical treatment. The work of Novosis ('A success story that gets under your skin') is primarily in taking drugs that are already patent protected and devising new dosage formats; the company is particularly involved in transdermal therapeutic treatments—that is, patches that deliver the drug through the skin. It is anticipated that such transdermal treatments, as well as being more effective for the patient, may be more applicable to all cultures and thus a universal way of delivering treatments.

People around the world have differing access to health and medicine. In some countries, people have virtually no access to basic health care, whereas in others people can be treated in the most modern and sophisticated ways. Regardless of these disparities, there appear to be some basic and possibly innate differences in the ways in which people like to take their medicine. National cultures have an impact all the way down to the methods by which people prefer to take their medicines.

Case study questions

1. What is the impact on international pharmaceutical companies of having to make products sold in different markets?
2. What methods of medicine taking are most common in different parts of the world? Why may new methods, like patches, become more acceptable?
3. Assess the importance of multidisciplinary teams in the design and delivery of pharmaceutical products.

Discussion questions

1. How far are the key determinants of national culture likely to vary from one country to another?
2. What is the relevance of Hofstede's work on companies' ability to do business in different countries?
3. How much do different religions affect commercial and business relationships?
4. Does a world culture exist? If so, what are its advantages and disadvantages?
5. What benefits would a universal language have on international business?

References

Al-Khatib, J. A., Malshe, A., and AbdulKader, M. (2008). 'Perception of Unethical Negotiation Tactics: A Comparative Study of US and Saudi Managers', *International Business Review*, 17/1 (Feb.).

American Food Courts (2008). www.afcbrands.com (accessed 26 Sept. 2008).

Archer, C. (2008). *The European Union*. Abingdon: Routledge.

Bangkok Food Courts (2008). www.bangkok.com (accessed 26 Sept. 2008).

BBC Languages (2008). 'Working with the French', www.bbc.co.uk/languages (accessed Aug. 2008).

Bullock, A., Stallybrass, O., and Trombley, S. (2000). *The New Fontana Dictionary of Modern Thought*. 3rd rev. edn. London: Fontana Press.

California Pizza Kitchen (2008). www.cpk.com (accessed 26 Sept. 2008).

Chapman, M., Gajewska-De Mattos, H., Clegg, J., and Buckley, P. J.

(2008). 'Close Neighbours and Distant Friends: Perceptions of Cultural Distance', *International Business Review*, 17/3 (June).

CIA (2008). 'The World Factbook', www.cia.gov (accessed Oct. 2008).

Clark, T., and Pugh, D. S. (2001). 'Foreign Country Priorities in the Internationalization Process: A Measure and an Exploratory Test on British Firms', *International Business Review*, 10/3 (June).

Crystal, D. (1997). *English as a Global Language*. Cambridge: Cambridge University Press.

Crystal, D. (2003). *The Cambridge Encyclopedia of the English Language*. 2nd edn. Cambridge: Cambridge University Press.

Cuervo-Cazurra, A. (2007). 'The Effectiveness of Laws against Bribery Abroad', *Journal of International Business Studies* (Dec.).

Dahl, S. (2004). 'Intercultural Research: The Current State of Knowledge', Middlesex University Discussion Paper, No. 26 (Jan.).

Dahl, S. (2006). 'Trompenaars and Hampden-Turner', http://stephan.dahl.at (accessed 31 Aug. 2008).

DDI (2006). Development Dimensions International, *Leaders on Leadership*, MORI–DDI survey.

Eppler, M. J., and Gee, J. (2008). 'Communicating with Diagrams: How Intuitive and Cross-Cultural Are Business Graphics?' *Euro Asia Journal of Management*, 18/1 (June).

Galloway, D. (1994). *Mapping Work Processes*. Milwaukee, WI: ASQC Quality Press.

Gill, L. (1991). 'Uncommon Market: What is Medicine for one European can often be Poison for Another', *The Times*, 10 Oct.

Global Security (2009). 'Iran–Iraq War, 1980–1988', www.globalsecurity.org (accessed 6 July 2009).

Gordon, R. G. (2005). *Ethnologue: Languages of the World*. 15th edn. SIL International.

GSK (2008). Meetings and email messages with GSK employees (Aug.–Sept.)

Guegen, D. (2007). *European Lobbying*. 2nd edn. Brussels: European Politics.

Hagen, S. (2005). *Language and Culture in British Business*. London: CILT.

Hall, E. T. (1976). *Beyond Culture*. New York: Anchor.

Hampden-Turner, C., and Trompenaars, F. (2000). *Building Cross-Cultural Competence: How to Create Wealth from Conflicting Values*. Chichester: Wiley.

Harris, S., and Carr, C. (2008). 'National Cultural Values and the Purposes of Businesses', *International Business Review*, 17/3 (Feb.).

Helmreich, R. L., and Merritt, A. C. (2001). *Culture at Work in Aviation and Medicine: National, Organizational and Professional Influences*. 2nd edn. Aldershot: Ashgate.

Hofstede, G. (1980). *Culture's Consequences: International Differences in Work-Related Values*. London: Sage.

Hofstede, G. (2001) *Culture's Consequences: Comparing Values, Behaviors, Institutions and Organizations across Nations*. London: Sage.

Hofstede, G., and Hofstede, G. J. (2005). *Cultures and Organizations: Software of the Mind*. 2nd edn. London: McGraw-Hill.

House, R. J., et al. (2004). *The GLOBE Study of 62 Societies: Culture, Leadership and Organizations*. Thousand Oaks, CA: Sage.

Huff, A. (1990) (ed.). *Mapping Strategic Thought*. New York: Wiley.

Jandt, F. E. (2007). *An Introduction to Intercultural Communication: Identities in a Global Community*. 5th edn. London: Sage.

Kane, F. (2008). 'The Gulf's New Bling Kings', *Observer*, 7 Sept.

Kluckhohn, F. R., and Strodtbeck, F. L. (1961). *Variations in Value Orientation*. Evanston, IL: Row Peterson.

Kurlansky, M. (2000). *The Basque History of the World*. London: Vintage Books.

Lechner, F. J., and Boli, J. (2005). *World Culture: Origins and Consequences*. Oxford: Blackwell.

McSweeney, B. (2002). 'Hofstede's Model of National Cultural Differences and their Consequences: A Triumph of Faith—a Failure of Analysis', *Human Relations*, 55: 89–118.

Magnus, G. (2008). 'Financial Crisis and Ageing', *World Today*, 64/12.

Maitland, A. (2006). 'Le Patron, der Chef and the Boss', *Financial Times*. 9 Jan.

Maslow, A. H. (1943). 'A Theory of Human Motivation', *Psychological Review*, 50: 370–96, http://psychclassics.yorku.ca (accessed 6 Sept. 2008).

Mole, J. (1995). *Mind Your Manners: Managing Business Cultures in Europe*. London: Nicholas Brealey.

Novosis (2009). www.novosis.de (accessed 26 Apr. 2009).

Schneider, S. C., and Barsoux, J.-L. (2003). *Managing across Cultures*. 2nd edn. Harlow: FT Prentice Hall.

Transparency International (UK) (2003). 'Freed from Corruption: The Next Steps', *TI (UK) Strategic Plan 2004–2006*. Transparency International (UK).

Trompenaars, F. (1993). *Riding the Waves of Culture: Understanding Cultural Diversity in Business*. London: Nicholas Brealey.

Trompenaars, F., and Hampden-Turner, C. (1997). *Riding the Waves of Culture: Understanding Cultural Diversity in Business*. 2nd edn. London: Nicholas Brealey.

UIS (2004). UNESCO Institute of Statistics, 'A Decade of Investment in Research and Development (R&D)', *UIS Bulletin on Science and Technology Statistics*, 1 (Apr.).

UIS (2007). UNESCO Institute of Statistics, 'Global Education Spending Concentrated in a Handful of Countries', *UIS Factsheet*, 03 (Oct.).

Walsh, J. (2009). 'A Fusion too Far', *Independent*, 28 Jan.

Further research

Hofstede and Trompenaars' extensive and complex work. It has also been the subject of considerable commentary, criticism and discussion. Some key participants in this discussion include Jean-Louis Barsoux (INSEAD, Fontainebleau, France), Stephan Dahl (Middlesex University, UK), J. Patrick Gray (University of Wisconsin-Milwaukee, USA), Brendan McSweeney (University of Essex, UK), and Susan Schneider (HEC University of Geneva and INSEAD). The cross-cultural research undertaken by these academics and others has emphasized the complexities of understanding different cultures and the difficulties of applying this in a meaningful way to the conduct of international business.

It is worth consulting any of the texts by the authors cited above as well as the following journals:

Journal of International and Cross-Cultural Studies
Communal/Plural: Journal of Transnational and Cross-Cultural Studies
World Cultures eJournal

Online Resource Centre

Visit the Online Resource Centre that accompanies this book to read more information relating to national cultures: www.oxfordtextbooks.co.uk/orc/sitkin_bowen/

International Corporate Responsibility

Overview

The chapter opens with a brief introduction to the concept of business ethics, noting their variations in time and space. The first section offers a theoretical discussion of whether firms should be expected to commit to an explicit corporate responsibility (CR) policy, before analysing CR in specifically international settings. The second section explores this topic from a more practical perspective, starting with the main CR issues faced by multinational enterprises (MNEs). This is followed by analysis of the different ways in which CR is codified across the world and the different problems of enforcement.

For clarity's sake, the chapter uses the term 'ethical' in the traditionally 'moral' sense applied in philosophy to refer to the kind of behaviour that produces a positive or negative outcome. 'Corporate responsibility' is the term that will be used to refer to companies whose explicit policy is to act ethically. Note that this term replaces the older but narrower term of 'corporate social responsibility' (CSR), which does not necessarily cover all of today's ethical priorities, in particular environmental concerns.

Section I: The foundations of international corporate responsibility

How ethics vary in time and space

For and against corporate responsibility approaches in business

Corporate responsibility in specifically international contexts

Section II: The practicalities of international corporate responsibility

The main ethical dilemmas that multinationals face

International codes

Enforcing international corporate responsibility

Learning Objectives

After reading this chapter, you will be able to:

+ weigh up (international) ethical considerations versus self-interest
+ apply ethics in (international) business frameworks
+ evaluate corporate responsibility issues
+ discuss international efforts to codify ethical behaviour
+ highlight the difficulties faced in enforcing international corporate responsibility

Case Study 3.1

Ethics and marketing: Nestlé and the milk of human kindness

In the past, Nestlé, like other food sector MNEs, has promoted formula milk in less-developed countries (LDCs) in a way that some critics have considered inappropriate. Many poor families lack access to the clean water and sterilized equipment that they need to ensure that infants can drink formula milk safely. Moreover, some parents in LDCs have limited reading skills and rely heavily on visual signals. Nestlé has also been criticized for allegedly enlisting the help of health-care professionals to influence Bangladeshi mothers to buy Nestlé's formula, despite its commitment to avoid such aggressive forms of marketing. It has also been accused of using advertisements to communicate the wrong impression that powdered milk is better for babies than breastfeeding (Moorhead 2007; Baby Milk Action 2008; International Baby Food Action Network 2009). The end result has been a series of conflicts pitting Nestlé against local health authorities and international critics.

In 1981, against a backdrop of public outcry, the World Health Assembly brought food sector companies and their critics together to discuss a mutually agreeable code of standards. The initiative was successful and for a while things seemed to settle down. In 1988, however, the International Baby Food Action Network accused the baby milk companies of again trying to build excessive market share by flooding LDC health facilities with cheap goods (Baby Milk Action 2008). Nestlé countered that there was nothing unethical about this, since its product labels offered clear instructions and relevant advice. Not everyone accepted the MNE's argument, however, with Nestlé products suffering occasional consumer boycotts throughout the 1990s as a result.

In 2000 Nestlé signed up to the United Nations (UN) Global Compact, a voluntary policy initiative whose signatories commit to a set of ethical principles. This helped the MNE's reputation, and criticism faded somewhat in the years that followed. Then, in May 2007, a non-governmental organization (NGO) called Save the Children investigated the Bangladeshi baby milk market and found that only 20 per cent of local children were being breastfed until the World Health Organization's recommended age of 6 months. Western baby food companies again came

under the spotlight for showing pictures of wealthy white mothers sitting with rosy-cheeked babies in doctors' waiting rooms. Save the Children drew a direct connection between these advertisements and the large numbers of bottle-fed babies needing admission to the main diarrhoea hospital in Bangladesh's capital city of Dhaka. The implication was that some MNEs were breaking the standards that they themselves had set in the 1980s. This revelation caused surprisingly little outcry, however, either because expectations of corporate ethical standards today are generally lower than they used to be, or because MNEs have become better at public relations. In general, consumer protests in the early twenty-first century appear to be less of a feature on the international business landscape than they were just ten or fifteen years previously—a change that has major implications for the future of corporate responsibility.

Products requiring safe drinking water may not be appropriate in poor countries (© iStockphoto).

Introduction

International business ethics involves the definition and cross-border transfer of value systems. For people to interact peacefully, including in a business context, they must have some values in common. What is problematic is determining which values should govern cross-border dealings in a world where economic, political, social, and legal cultures are so varied (see Chapter 2). After all, when people come from very different backgrounds, there is every chance that they will have divergent views of which ethical values should be applied in a given situation.

Ethics can create confusion at several levels. One is whether the benefits of an MNE's presence offset the damage that it might cause due to some of its practices (for example, child labour) or the outcomes that it produces (for example, pollution). This is especially hard to calculate, because actions considered appropriate in some societies may be deemed unsuitable in others this variability makes it difficult for companies to devise codes of conduct that will be relevant in all circumstances. There is also a debate about whether firms should be free to define their own corporate responsibility or whether this should be imposed on them, and, if so, by whom. Lastly, in the wake of the 2008 credit crunch, there is much debate about the ethics of actions that, although legal, lead to an uneven distribution of risks and rewards between a particular company or sector, on the one hand, and the rest of society, on the other. A prime example is the way a select group of investment bankers received enormous bonuses for creating poorly understood products whose ultimate disintegration created real economic hardship for billions of people worldwide. This contradiction between micro- and macro-level interests causes a great deal of ethical confusion.

Section I: The foundations of international corporate responsibility

> Go to the ORC

Moral philosophy, which is the cornerstone of modern business ethics, is an ancient field of study. (Go to the Online Resource Centre, extension material 3.1. for a brief historical overview.) One starting point for analysing its application in a purely business context is to look at the factors guiding individual managers' conduct. In a sense, people are 'moral navigators' balancing their values against those of the firm for which they work (Morgan 1998). As demonstrated by Figure 3.1, a dilemma arises if the two value systems clash. This

Figure 3.1
The 'ethical fit' can vary between personal, company, and societal values.

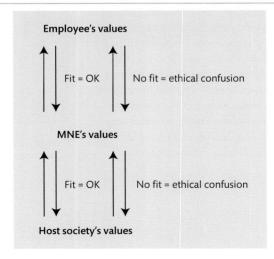

may occur if an employer's code of conduct is too vague, as is often the case in decentralized management structures (see Chapter 9) or if executives provide contradictory signals. In short, the first obstacle to ethical business behaviour arises when employees are not clear about what is expected of them—a situation that might be called 'ethical confusion'.

It is true that people often join a firm specifically because they identify with its stated values. At some point, however, many if not most employees can be made to feel pressures that will affect the decisions they take, whether consciously or otherwise. This means that individual ethics cannot be understood without considering the values of the company for which a person works (see Chapter 10)—as well as the interface between these values and the ones typifying the host country at large.

How ethics vary in time and space

Ethical behaviour must always be analysed in context. Slave traders, 'robber barons', and 'imperial corporations' are universally condemned today, but in many societies they were once highly praised figures (Schwartz 1999). Practices like child labour that are widely criticized in Europe at present were widespread before nineteenth-century reformers such as the UK's Charles Dickens or France's Émile Zola first began to denounce them. A country that is desperate for industrialization might accept higher levels of corruption or pollution than it will when it reaches a more comfortable level of socio-economic development (see Chapter 16). Many of the politicians who blamed investment bankers for the 2008 credit crisis had previously glorified the same individuals as creators of wealth. Indeed most actions are considered unethical only once their uglier sides are revealed.

> **Thinking point**
>
> If ethics are entirely relative, does this mean that they have no innate meaning?

A watershed moment for business ethics came in the early twentieth century, when the birth of large, multi-divisional firms (see Chapter 9) led to a split between the roles of owners and managers. The significance of this shift lies in the opposition between managers' allegedly greater sense of responsibility to the wider community and owners' greater focus on profits (Vogel 2006). By the 1960s, influential thinkers like J. K. Galbraith

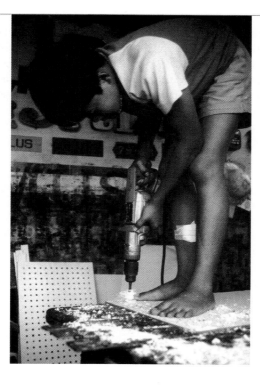

Photo 3.1
Child labour in developing countries: balancing ethics versus poverty
(© International Labour Organization).

were saying that, above and beyond any direct business aims, a manager's role in a company was to promote the overall welfare of a society. Some leading executives of the time, like Chase Manhattan Bank's David Rockefeller, understood this to mean that companies should engage in philanthropy. Despite constituting a form of ethical behaviour, this approach was not particularly effective at addressing the social problems associated with business activities. In large part, this was due to the fact that charity giving of this kind is rarely systematic. There is also the more recent revelation that nearly 90 per cent of all companies who engage in philanthropy are in actual fact looking for something in return (Bonini and Chênevert 2008). This too may limit the effectiveness of charitable actions.

+ Philanthropy
Long-term charitable donations to worthy causes.

The philanthropic model remains dominant in certain parts of the world (mainly Asia and Africa) (Hopkins 2007). In the USA and other affluent nations, however, the general paradigm has moved on. Noting how and why moral behaviour diverges is an important topic in international business. Many factors are involved, one being countries' different stages of socio-economic development. Another relevant factor in moral relativity is culture, with recent studies having indicated, for instance, that cultural attitudes towards 'collectivism' and 'power distance' (see Chapter 2) help predict executive attitudes towards social responsibility (Waldman et al. 2006). In a sense, the best proof of the relativity of ethics is the fact that people can act differently and be driven by varying motivations yet all be seen as behaving ethically.

The concept of externalities

Reversing the trend witnessed in the mid-twentieth century, since the 1980s managers and shareholders' interests have become increasingly aligned in a number of industrialized countries. This is largely due to the rise of profit-sharing bonus schemes motivating managers to focus on their firm's earnings alone, to the exclusion of broader societal considerations. A prime example is the way that the 2008 credit crunch was sparked by the actions of certain UK and US bankers trying to maximize their personal bonuses by aggressively selling overvalued mortgages (see Chapter 14). This practice was less common in other business cultures, in part because limitations on open-ended bonus schemes in places like Japan and Germany meant that bankers there had fewer incentives to create such risks. The first rule of business ethics is that abuses are less likely to occur in a system where no one stands to benefit from actions that might harm the rest of society (see Figure 3.2). Conversely, when someone can benefit from an unethical action, it becomes more likely.

+ Externalities
When an economic action affects parties not directly involved in it. This effect can be positive or negative.

The turn of the twenty-first century offers many examples of societies suffering the negative externalities of some company's short-term, profit-seeking actions—behaviour that, according to the definitions provided, can be unethical whether or not it is legal. Global warming (and resource depletion) have accelerated because of the decision by carmakers GM, Ford, Nissan, and Land Rover to produce petrol-guzzling sports utility vehicles instead of promoting energy-efficient alternatives. Tens of millions of peasants in inland China have lost their livelihood as farmland has been paved over by property developers with little regard for local needs. A few major Asian and Latin American clothing manufacturers have made an excellent living employing untold numbers of workers in terrible sweatshop conditions. There are countless other examples as well.

Some eminent economists, like Nobel Prize winner and ex-World Bank economist Joseph Stiglitz (2006: 190–5), criticize the 'misalignment of economic incentives when corporations do not bear the downside costs [of their actions]: social welfare is not maximized if corporations single-mindedly maximize profits'. In other words, the current debate over international ethics should also look at the distribution of benefits and costs. If just a few persons within a society enjoy positive externalities, versus a huge number who suffer from negative externalities, there is a good case for considering that the activity is unethical, regardless of its legality.

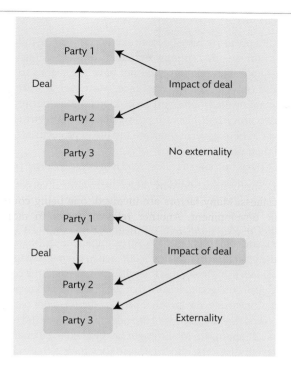

Figure 3.2
Externalities can either help or hurt someone who is not party to a deal.

For and against corporate responsibility approaches in business

The growing demand for ethics in business has led generally to wider support for the CR agenda, which can encompass a range of objectives. Yet not everyone agrees with this approach. The argument is ongoing between free market enthusiasts, who feel that CR is wrong because businesses should focus on profitability alone; cynics, who see CR as a way of diverting people's attention from corporate misconduct; and supporters, who think that it provides a remedy to the failure of the market to address the negative side effects of business activities.

Photo 3.2
Starbucks helps fund health clinics and other projects to support communities from which it buys coffee (reprinted with the kind permission of Starbucks).

For corporate responsibility

Generally, opposition to CR appears to have become a minority view. In today's world, MNEs control such a large share of the world economy that many observers consider CR no longer a luxury but a necessity—nation-states simply do not have the means to attend to all the social, environmental, and other problems they face. Moreover, governments often fail to enact much needed social or environmental protections, either because lobbyists have manipulated the legislative process or because politicians are ineffective, corrupt, and/or can be misled (Frost 2004). Where governments are unable to protect stakeholder interests, companies need to act in their place.

One of the reasons why CR has become so widespread is because so many people are affected by the externalities of business. Besides, there is no moral justification why shareholders should be exempted from the kinds of burdens that society as a whole faces. An infamous example from the year 1986 was when 3,000 citizens in the Indian town of Bhopal died because of leaks at Union Carbide's local chemicals plant. The company paid reparations, in part because it would have been unthinkable for shareholders not to do so. An example from 2006 was the death of ten Ivory Coast citizens, and the poisoning of a further 9,000, when chemical waste was discharged from a ship chartered by a Dutch firm, Trafigura (Russell 2006). Because the company benefited from the activity, it was ethically obliged to ensure that the general Ivoirian population did not suffer ill effects as a result. Conversely, the fact that people who were not party to the contract did in fact suffer from it showed that at least one of the sides in to the deal did not fulfil its ethical duties. In the absence of a CR approach, MNEs might be tempted to calculate that they need not do their utmost to prevent disasters, either because they have a free rider mentality and expect governments to compensate victims on their behalf, or because the profits from their activities exceed any penalties they might have to pay. This irresponsible attitude would lead to a repetition of disasters—clearly an unsatisfactory outcome for international business.

Some observers who regret the shift in power from the public to the private sector (see Chapter 5) have welcomed CR as a way of getting corporations to give something back to society. MNEs such as Starbucks, Rio Tinto, BP, and Vodafone have invested sizable sums worldwide in community education, a sector that in many countries has traditionally been the responsibility of the state. These MNEs are concerned with their image and use CR to prove their good faith. Living in a 24/7 news world has increased general awareness of good and bad corporate behaviour. This is one of the main reasons why companies like Body Shop, with its overt attachment to ethical values, have succeeded in winning customers' affection. By giving business to ethical companies, many baby boomers can maintain their 1960s social conscience even as they pursue the more material values that typified the 1980s (Vogel 2006). After all, CR and profit-making are not mutually exclusive.

In sum, a strong business case exists for CR. Triple bottom line performance, a key component of CR, can help companies in terms of reputation, access to ethical investor funds, recruitment, staff motivation, risk management, and relationships with stakeholders, especially consumers (Hopkins 2007). If consumers do not trust a company and/or do not want to support its social, environmental, or other policies by buying its products and services, they will probably take their business elsewhere. Business schools training tomorrow's executives understand how important CR has become, as witnessed by the increasingly widespread injection of sustainability into their curriculum. In the early twenty-first century, CR has clearly gone mainstream.

Against corporate responsibility

In the late 1980s, one of the authors of this book suggested launching a corporate recycling scheme, only to be criticized for 'wasting time' by a boss who argued that an employee's only concern should be how to make money. It is fair to say that CR has not always been a popular topic in some executive circles.

+ Stakeholder
Anyone affected, however indirectly, by an organization's actions. The term is often understood to include employees, local governments, suppliers, consumers, and host communities.

+ Triple bottom line
Idea that firms should report not only financial but also social and environmental outcomes.

Thinking point

How real is CR? Is it a fad or a durable trend?

+ Sustainability
Search for societal solutions providing long-term human and environmental benefits.

At a theoretical level, the free market economist and Nobel laureate Milton Friedman (2002) has equated corporate payments made in the name of CR with forcing shareholders to accept lower dividends, workers to accept lower wages, and/or customers to pay higher prices. In this view, as long as a firm acts legally, it is 'subversive' to force it to divert its attention from the profit-maximization principle. In a similar vein, the Cato Institute has accused CR supporters of unfairly

Case Study 3.2

Lenovo and its Greenpeace rankings

China's industrial expansion has raised living standards for tens of millions of citizens. This welcome boom has had a less positive effect on the environment, however. Not only do the country's rising CO_2 emissions contribute to climate change, but China faces many other problems, including groundwater pollution and lethal air pollution ('killer smog').

Hence the general delight in March 2007 when Chinese computer-maker Lenovo came top of Greenpeace's list of the world's most environmentally friendly electronics company (Thurrott 2007), based on criteria like the elimination of hazardous substances and the organization of a take-back/recycling programme. This was a significant achievement, given the huge volumes that the company had been trading ever since it had acquired IBM's Personal Computing Department in 2005. Lenovo had been conscientiously developing a green strategy for a number of years, having, for instance, taken part in the Hong Kong Rechargeable Battery Recycling Program in 2006. It continued in a similar vein after heading the Greenpeace table, with the establishment of a division called Lenovo Asset Recovery Services (ARS) aimed at helping customers to 'manage their end-of-life technology equipment by providing computer take-back, data destruction, refurbishment and recycling' (Lenovo 2008). The company's green reputation seemed secure, despite some criticism of the use of toxic substances during its manufacturing processes. Lenovo's subsequent announcement that it would work towards eliminating PVCs and brominated flame retardants (BFRs) within a few short years was meant to consolidate its Greenpeace ranking. The future seemed bright for Lenovo's brand image as an environmental champion.

Lenovo's commitment to recycling old computers is a key aspect of its CR approach (© iStockphoto).

Just two years later, things looked different. Lenovo dropped to fourteenth place in the rankings (Greenpeace 2009), having been assessed a penalty point for backtracking on its commitment to eliminate PVCs, and BFRs in all its products by the end of 2009. Its toxic chemical scores were better than its recycling activities, which were penalized for unclear data. Above all, Lenovo scored poorly in terms of the two criteria that Greenpeace has added to its poll in recent years: specifically carbon footprint; and energy consumption (since compliance with Energy Star standards was not standard on all Lenovo models). Having created expectations that it could sell itself as one of the global electronics sector's greenest representatives, Lenovo was discovering that brand image is a double-edged sword, since it forces companies to remain vigilant to maintain their status. As the years go by, standards in the environmental and other areas tend to become more demanding, and, with competitors constantly fighting to improve their own ranking, companies cannot rest on their laurels. Like most areas of international business, green marketing is a battle that can never be won.

+ Free riders
Parties who benefit
more from an
economic activity than
their contribution to it
entitles them to.

Thinking point

Is CR a luxury of
the rich?

+ Regime shopping
Decision to locate an
MNE's activities based
on the relative laxness
of a host country's
requirements (taxes,
regulations).

Thinking point

Can MNEs ever be
morally justified in
trying to negotiate
better terms
with poor host
countries?

portraying firms as free riders enriching themselves to local communities' detriment. The idea here is that firms do not receive sufficient credit for the taxes and wages that they pay into the general economy. Instead, it is CR that should be condemned, because it discourages equity investment and risk-taking, brings 'interest-group politics into the boardroom', and imposes excessive accountability on managers—especially ones operating in legal systems that hold them personally liable for their company's conduct (Marcoux 2000). Along these same lines, former Czech President Vaclav Klaus (2007) has criticized the 'opportunity costs of ... wasteful environmentalist policies ... adopted to the detriment of other policies, thus neglecting many other important needs of millions of people all over the world'. Here the debate is whether LDCs can afford to require multinationals to engage in CR if this gets in the way of other priorities.

It is also worth noting that some critics of CR are also highly dubious about free market capitalism. The idea in this group is that corporate responsibility is a 'sham ... bamboozling an increasingly sceptical public' (Hopkins 2007: 122–8). This suggests a sense that many companies use CR as a marketing tool to hide other misdeeds they might commit—the 'greenwashing' accusation that is reviewed in further depth below.

Corporate responsibility in specifically international contexts

The section above shows that the divide between shareholder and stakeholder perspectives is a key issue in all business ethics. In cross-border situations, however, it can become particularly poignant. Great resentment arises when 'the sound of business ... [drowns] out the voices of other interest groups' (Hertz 2001: 3). One such situation is when a powerful MNE tries to bully an LDC into lowering its taxes and/or regulatory standards, threatening to take its much needed investment elsewhere if the country does not offer advantageous market entry conditions. Regime shopping of this sort (also called 'regulatory arbitrage') puts pressure on impoverished host governments to abandon one crucial need (for example, a clean environment or workers' health and safety) in the hope of satisfying another (jobs from the new investor). Forcing countries into these kinds of trade-off is ethically dubious.

MNEs could respond, with some truthfulness, that global competition forces them to run tight operations, which can among other things involve pressuring workers to perform. In this kind of context, adopting overt CR policies can improve perceptions of the company. Examples include Anglo American's contribution to the fight against AIDS in Africa, in what can be viewed as a conscious effort to overcome the region's general mistrust of Western mining companies' intentions (Cronin 2006). Some of Chiquita's past CR initiatives in Central America, detailed in Case Study 3.3, appear to have had a similar purpose. International CR is sometimes a vehicle for regaining trust.

Local cultural attitudes towards the profit motive can also determine whether a foreign MNE will be accepted if its conduct diverges from local norms. For instance, Germany's long-standing support for worker rights and traditional resistance to 'Anglo-Saxon capitalism' meant that there was a great uproar in the 1990s when American retailer Walmart tried to force local employees to work overtime. This put the MNE under much pressure to find other ways of demonstrating its good faith. Note that resentment can also be fuelled if the local society is ethnically or politically divided, and if the MNE is seen as siding with one constituency over another. One example is the way that Shell's dealings with Nigeria's central government during the 1990s worsened its relations with the Ogoni population, the ethnic group inhabiting the region where the company had its oil-drilling platforms. If a legal system hides certain unethical outcomes, then it is hard to argue that obeying the law constitutes moral behaviour in and of itself.

This is an important distinction, since it undermines the argument of some CR opponents like Milton Friedman that the only thing that companies need to do to be ethical is to act

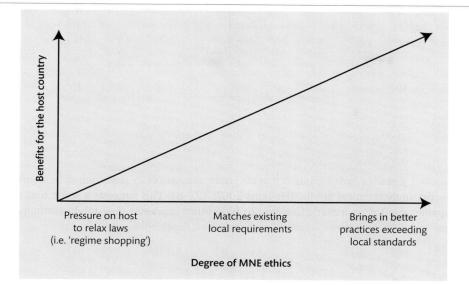

legally. The reality is much more complicated (see Figure 3.3). Laws reflect the balance of power in a society at a particular moment in time. A much more meaningful measurement of international CR is 'ethical compliance', or the idea that MNEs might be held to similar minimum standards wherever they operate, regardless of local legislation.

Donaldson's ethical algorithm

In the absence of explicit CR, MNEs might have problems deciding where their minimum or maximum ethical duties lie (Kline 2005). In 1989, Thomas Donaldson, a seminal thinker in the field of international business ethics, devised a model that managers can apply to the practical ethical dilemmas they face abroad. Noting that the 'stakeholder' concept offers little real guidance about how to juggle different constituencies' interests, Donaldson built an alternative that starts by contrasting the 'fundamental (basic) duties' that are part of a person's social contract with society from lesser 'derivative (non-basic) duties' like the ones a manager owes to shareholders. He determined that to get the social contract to work in different countries, agreed standards of justice are needed, since these are better indicators of fairness than contracts, which strong parties can force on weaker ones. The idea here is that MNEs have a minimum (thus mandatory) duty to respect basic rights, and a maximum (thus voluntary) duty to respect non-basic rights. For Donaldson, examples of basic rights included human rights like freedom from torture, with a clean environment being, in his opinion, an example of a non-basic right. Others might have had different priorities but would agree with his principle that there is such a thing as a hierarchy of rights.

+ Social contract
Idea that people will hand some of their rights over to an authority that offers them order in return.

Donaldson went on to ask what managers should do if a conflict arises between the norms found in the home and host countries—that is, whether an MNE can apply standards abroad that are not acceptable at home. As shown in Figure 3.4, he used the 'no harm' principle first advocated by philosopher J. S. Mill to construct an 'ethical algorithm' for international managers' usage.

The end result is a 'social contract model' that distinguishes between MNEs' minimum duty of not depriving people of their rights and their maximum duty of actively 'aiding the deprived'. This has the positive effect of offering managers a concrete tool they can use to decide when it is appropriate to apply their own value systems in a foreign context. By so doing, it helps firms to satisfy their 'same duty to be ethical in [both] mature and emerging markets' (Mellahi and Wood 2003: 68).

Figure 3.4
Donaldson's 'ethical
algorithm': juggling
different value systems.

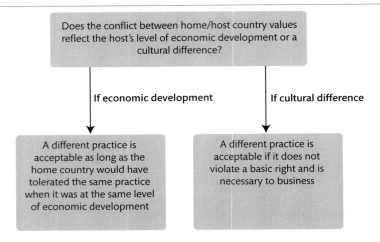

Section II: The practicalities of international corporate responsibility

+ Environmental
footprint
Ecological impact of
a human activity.

> Go to the ORC

As mentioned, above, the difference between modern CR and the older CSR construct is that CR is broader and includes companies' environmental footprint. In fact, in recent years, there has been a tendency to widen the scope of CR to include any and all ethical issues affecting MNEs (see Figure 3.5). (Go to the Online Resource Centre, extension material 3.2, for an exploration of a broad range of CR issues.) The section below studies the main international issues facing companies today.

The main ethical dilemmas faced by multinationals

Human rights

> Go to the ORC

A serious dilemma for MNEs is whether they should refuse to do business with countries that violate the principles of liberty and humanity put forth by the United Nations in its 1948 Declaration of Human Rights (reproduced in the Online Resource Centre, extension material 3.3). This question arises, for example, when extractive industries need to access assets in countries run by non-democratic regimes. Examples include 'blood diamonds' sourced in war-torn Sierra Leone, or mines run by companies like Anglo American in Robert

Figure 3.5
CR covers a
growing number of
international issues.

Leading CR issues for multinationals

   Human Rights

   Labour relations / supply chain management

   Corruption

   Environment / sustainability

Other CR issues

   Cultural imperialism

   Socially responsible investing

   Corporate governance

   Corporate philanthropy and community service

   Product and process safety

Mugabe's distressed Zimbabwe. In a similar vein, there are cases of MNEs outsourcing or offshoring manufacturing activities to countries where union rights are restricted and/or acts of violence committed against labour leaders. A number of sources, including an activist non-governmental organization (NGO) called War on Want (2006), have tried to associate Coca Cola with anti-union violence across the world. In 2001, for example, a lawsuit was lodged in a US court accusing the company of complicity in the murders of union members employed by FEMSA, the franchise bottler with whom Coca Cola works in Columbia. The company was also criticized following the alleged beating of trade unionists by the police in Turkey. Coca Cola has responded that it is deeply concerned for workers' safety everywhere and takes protective measures to ensure their well-being. What is clear, in any event, is that being even remotely associated with these kinds of human rights violations is of no benefit to any MNE's reputation.

> **+ Non-governmental organizations (NGOs)** Associations created by members of the general public to deal with specific issues or to promote an overall ethos or policy. International NGOs usually focus on cross-border problems.

Other examples highlight similar dilemmas. Despite Indonesia's disturbing reputation for harassing union representatives, exemplified by the widely denounced imprisonment of labour leader Dita Sari in 1997 (Jordan 1998), Western companies have continued to do business with suppliers from this country. This has had the ironic effect of causing garment workers from Indonesia to call for the boycott of locally made clothing products sold by giant MNEs like Gap, accused of tolerating union harassment in subcontractor factories and/or poor health and safety conditions (*Associated Press* 2002). Gap protested that it was aware of these problems and deeply committed to improving welfare for workers throughout its supply chain. This may not always be enforceable, however. The general challenge is to determine the net effect of MNEs doing any business at all in countries where abuses are rampant.

On the one hand, MNEs refusing to work with a regime because of its anti-democratic or corrupt government might be starving the local economy of much needed capital, jobs, and technology. Yet engaging with an unethical state may directly worsen the local population's situation. For example, US and French oil companies Unocal and Total have both suffered criticism because of the human rights violations that the military regime in Myanmar (ex-Burma, South East Asia) committed during the construction and protection of two pipelines built to bring the MNEs' output to market (Kaneva 2006). As part of this project, entire villages were destroyed with little or no attention being paid to inhabitants' welfare. Accusations of forced labour were also made. The MNEs could correctly claim that they were not responsible for this oppressive regime, and that, had they not invested in Myanmar, other companies would have done so.

According to Kline (2005), MNEs' responsibilities in countries where human rights are flaunted depend on their intentions, awareness of the situation, and proximity to the problems. By itself, business cannot be expected to solve all the world's political problems. However, MNEs should at the very least avoid making things worse for victims of human rights abuses. They can do this by considering which sections of a host country are likely to benefit from their actions—and which are not.

Labour relations and supply chain management

The labour relations category of ethical practices includes the 'hiring and firing' of employees, wage policies, overtime, health and safety, the treatment of female workers, child labour, union relations, and fair trade considerations. It rivals the environment today as the main focus for ethics in international business.

> **+ Fair trade** Trade where profits are distributed fairly along the value chain so that upstream producers receive a decent 'living' wage.

As discussed throughout this book, one of the main drivers behind modern globalization is the way that so many companies move upstream production activities to low-cost countries, either through outsourcing or via foreign direct investment (FDI). These actions all have major political and strategic implications. They also raise a number of ethical challenges.

Many people worldwide have benefited from the internationalization of supply chain operations. In home countries, consumers enjoy lower prices and shareholders receive higher profits; in host countries, workers get jobs and governments collect tax revenues. In countries like South Korea and Singapore, an entire development trajectory has been based on MNEs' outsourcing contracts or FDI actions. Yet the internationalization of production has also hurt many people, and it is here that an ethical dilemma arises. When MNEs offshore or outsource jobs to lower-wage countries, the home country workers who get fired will easily fall victim to a 'spectre of uselessness' if they do not find new employment quickly (Sennett 2006). Conversely, host countries (often LDCs) are often forced to compete with one another to attract the new business. This can lead to a 'race to the bottom', with jobs being allocated only to those countries whose desperately poor citizens, lacking union representation, are forced to accept wages that are hard to survive on. One example is Cambodia, whose workers' rising standard of living has been endangered by competition from China following the January 2005 lifting of the Multi Fibre Agreement on textile quotas (Bradshaw 2005). Today, poor Cambodian workers must choose between wage cuts or job losses. This is certainly not the development model that the country had hoped to follow.

> **+ Race to the bottom**
> Where competition among disadvantaged producers forces them to accept lower remuneration for their services.

It seems obvious that MNEs are a force for good when they pay above-average wages to their LDC workers or pressure local subcontractors to improve their labour standards. Yet even such ethical behaviour can cause problems, as witnessed by the dilemma of child labour. On one hand, children must be put in a position where they can receive an education—this is a basic human right and a necessity for any society's development. The press is full of terrible images of very young children—in India and Pakistan, for instance—spending long days sewing cheap clothes for major Western brand names instead of going to school. By 2008, most leading MNEs like Gap and Primark had implemented social audit systems to detect subcontractors using child labour and prohibit this practice. However, local contractors are often adept at tricking inspectors. This means that, despite being condemned by many if not most MNEs, the practice of child labour remains widespread, stretching from South Asian sweatshops to Egyptian cotton fields or El Salvadoran sugar plantations. The background to this tragedy is the fact that countless families worldwide are so desperately poor that they need whatever income their children can provide. Indeed, LDCs themselves have often been the strongest opponents of efforts to prohibit child labour. The ethical dilemma for MNEs is that boycotting a country's suppliers because of disgust with their practices (for example, child labour) often leads to greater unemployment for the local population, making things worse for the very people who were supposed to receive help (Kline 2005). Indeed, most activists today encourage MNEs to work with suppliers to improve conditions, rather than abandoning a particular supply chain.

Corruption

Corruption has long been an area of concern for international bodies, in part because bribery, in its different forms, is so widespread. There have been many noteworthy examples of systematic corruption at the corporate level, one recent headline case being the condemnation of giant German engineering MNE Siemens for €1.3 billion worth of suspicious international payments made between 2000 and 2006 (Crawford and Esterl 2007). At a more personal level, MNEs grapple day in day out with the question of how large a gift it is ethical to offer a counterpart. The problem is determining when such low-level presents turn into fully-fledged bribery, which is rarely a victimless crime. In a case denounced most famously by Indian novelist Arundhati Roy, former US energy company Enron allegedly paid a small sum to an official in Maharashtra state, who then awarded the MNE a power plant generation contract despite receiving lower bids from rival companies like Deutsche Babcock. In the end, local residents found that they had to pay much higher utilities bills than they should have done (Hamilton 2002). Corruption skews market transactions to the benefit of the few and the detriment of the many.

Note that accusations of corruption can be very hypocritical. No one calls for a boycott of the European Union (EU) or the USA, yet some consider political lobbying in Brussels and Washington (see Chapter 7) as tantamount to corruption, materializing in the cosy relationship that exists between big business and 'political stakeholders' (Holtbrügge et al. 2007). A very topical debate is the morality of non-corrupt countries enabling MNEs' tax avoidance through the use of questionable transfer pricing practices (see Chapter 14). At a certain level, corruption discussions can easily spill over into debates about political ideology.

Rank	Country	Score	Rank	Country	Score
1	Denmark	9.3	40	South Korea	5.6
1	New Zealand	9.3	54	South Africa	4.9
1	Sweden	9.3	55	Italy	4.8
4	Singapore	9.2	72	China	3.6
5	Finland	9.0	72	Mexico	3.6
5	Switzerland	9.0	80	Brazil	3.5
7	Iceland	8.9	80	Saudi Arabia	3.5
7	Netherlands	8.9	85	India	3.4
9	Australia	8.7	109	Argentina	2.9
9	Canada	8.7	115	Egypt	2.8
14	Germany	7.9	121	Nigeria	2.7
16	UK	7.7	126	Indonesia	2.6
18	Japan	7.3	134	Pakistan	2.5
18	USA	7.3	147	Russia	2.1
23	France	6.9	178	Iraq	1.3
33	Isreal	6.0	178	Myanmar	1.3
35	United Arab Emirates	5.9	180	Somalia	1.0

Figure 3.6
Selected countries and their corruption levels (reprinted from Global Corruption Perceptions Index. ©2008. Transparency International: the global coalition against corruption. Used with kind permission. For more information visit http://www.transparency.org).

As Figure 3.6 shows, perceived levels of corruption clearly vary internationally. Depending on a country's cultural heritage, however, practices considered corrupt in some environments may be acceptable (and even normal) in others—one example being the Arab practice of *bakshish*, which can be analysed as a bribe or, alternatively, as something as harmless as a finder's fee or a tip. Logically, the deeper a form of corruption is embedded in a culture, the harder it is to remove (Gichure 2006). Similarly, other studies have demonstrated links between certain religions and levels of perceived corruption (Beets 2007). Classifying an act as corrupt is less straightforward than it first seems. An added complication is that firms or individuals who act ethically most of the time may be capable of acting unethically on a few specific occasions. This inconsistency makes it very hard to audit corruption, either internally by MNEs' compliance departments, or externally by national authorities. It also explains why a number of major global initiatives have been devised (notably by the UN or the OECD) to deal with this problem.

Environment and sustainability

With few exceptions (as when British Petroleum changed its advertising strapline in 1998 to 'Beyond Petroleum' to highlight its interest in renewable energies), until recently green issues were less central to multinationals' CR image than labour standards or human rights. Things have changed as the extent of the planet's ecological problems has become more apparent—and, more cynically, possibly because environmental problems affect industrialized countries, whereas labour ethics mainly involve LDCs (Vogel 2006).

Chapter 16 takes an in-depth look at the environment's impact on the future of international business. From an ethical perspective, the main issue is how to allocate responsibility for today's ecological problems. One widespread explanation is that the world suffers from a 'tragedy of the commons' (Hardin 1968). In this metaphor, shepherds let their flock over-graze a pasture because it is free, without considering how everyone will suffer from over-consumption in the

Photo 3.3
Ecological catastrophes occur when firms cut corners (Photodisc).

long run. Humankind, including and especially the business sector, has consumed inputs and emitted waste for centuries, acting as if the earth's ability to provide resources and accommodate pollution were unlimited. There is growing realization that this is not the case. The damage being caused to many millions today, and to future generations, makes ecology an ethical topic.

Where problems are limited to one country, the national government can apply a 'polluter-pays' principle to try to induce sustainable behaviour. Unfortunately, environmental damage often knows no borders, and the absence of an all-powerful international authority makes it easier for polluters, or resource wasters, to commit 'enviro-crimes'. The UN has tried to lead from the front in this area, but, as discussed below, its lack of enforcement powers means that it can do little better than develop idealistic codes. A further complication is the fact that some countries view sustainability as a global governance issue (see Chapter 6) whereas others do not—many LDCs justifiably consider it unfair to curtail their development simply because the industrialized countries have already exhausted the world's ecological possibilities. Many consumers are also unwilling or unable to pay for the true environmental costs of the products they buy. Identifying an ethical issue in international business is usually much easier than finding a consensus about how to resolve it.

International codes

There have been many attempts over the years to codify ethical behaviour on an international scale. The two main categories are efforts made by the United Nations and voluntary codes drafted by companies.

United Nations conventions

The UN is the closest thing that the world has to a global government. It falls far short of fulfilling this role, however, because of its lack of policing abilities and because its decisions require consensus agreement from members whose interests often differ. This means that UN declarations tend to be weak compromises or mere statements of intent.

Nevertheless, the UN's output is still worth reviewing in detail, if only because it signals policies that are likely to promote values acceptable to a broad cross section of today's global community. The particular declarations and conferences summarized below are of special interest to international managers because of their relevance to the main business ethics debates discussed in this chapter. Topics typically covered by the UN, such as the environment, corruption, human rights, and development, usually concern firms and non-corporate interests alike. CR topics like corporate governance, which are more specific to the business sphere alone, will tend to be addressed by bodies like the OECD, whose governance ambitions are less extensive than those of the UN.

1948 UN Declaration of Human Rights

Adopted in the wake of the Second World War, this document specifies minimum freedoms that governments must afford citizens (like the 'right to life, liberty and security of person'). It is often a basis for international human rights complaints.

1992 UN Rio de Janeiro Conference on Environment and Development

This was the famous 'Earth Summit' where the UN brought together leaders from across the world to 'rethink economic development and find ways to halt the destruction of irreplaceable natural resources and pollution of the planet'.

1997 UN Kyoto Framework Convention on Climate Change

This convention set 'an overall framework for intergovernmental efforts to tackle the challenge posed by climate change'. Its effectiveness was undermined when several major polluter countries, notably the USA and Australia, refused to ratify it. A follow-up conference in Bali in 2007 was somewhat more successful.

2000 UN Global Compact

Members sign up to indicate their support for the Compact's principles (see Figure 3.7). Probably the world's largest voluntary network, with 4,300 business subscribers in June 2008, this is a purely voluntary norm of corporate citizenship. The aims are to 'mainstream [the] ten principles in business activities across the world' and 'catalyse actions in support of UN goals'.

Human rights		
Principle 1	Businesses should support and respect the protection of internationally proclaimed human rights; and	
Principle 2	Make sure that they are not complicit in human rights abuses.	
Labour standards		
Principle 3	Businesses should uphold the freedom of association and the effective recognition of the right to collective bargaining;	
Principle 4	The elimination of all forms of forced and compulsory labour;	
Principle 5	The effective abolition of child labour; and	
Principle 6	The elimination of discrimination in respect of employment and occupation.	
Environment		
Principle 7	Businesses should support a precautionary approach to environmental challenges;	
Principle 8	Undertake initiatives to promote greater environmental responsibility; and	
Principle 9	Encourage the development and diffusion of environmentally friendly technologies.	
Anti-corruption		
Principle 10	Businesses should work against all forms of corruption, including extortion and bribery.	

Figure 3.7
UN Global Compact (2009).

This compact has rapidly become the cornerstone of international corporate responsibility, but not everyone is convinced of its effectiveness. Shortly after its enactment, the compact came under sharp criticism at the Porto Alegre World Social Forum, mainly because it allows MNEs to pick and choose which principles they want to support and legitimizes their image while ignoring the more 'structural' factors involved in corporate responsibility (Utting 2002). Doubts have also been expressed about its enforceability—a problem that afflicts many UN decisions.

2001 UN Johannesburg World Summit on Sustainable Development

Disappointing progress since the 1992 Rio summit underlined how hard it is to move towards sustainable development. This led to the organization of a second development conference in 2001. One of the main topics was whether the codes of conduct that international firms adopt to promote ethical behaviour should be mandatory (Type I) or voluntary and self-enforced (Type II).

2005 United Nations Convention against Corruption (UNCAC)

This agreement expanded upon its main predecessor, the 1997 OECD Convention on Combating Bribery of Foreign Public Officials, by including pure private sector dealings. The problem is that the only authorities with real power to punish corrupt companies are national governments applying domestic legislation (US Foreign Corrupt Practices Act). In the absence of sanctions, international codes lack power.

Voluntary codes

Companies like to publicize the fact that they have drafted a code of ethical conduct, or signed up to an existing one, since this improves their reputation and defuses possible criticisms.

+ Ethical reporting group
Associations of companies and other organizations promising to respect certain ethical standards.

Two of the largest ethical reporting groups, after the UN Global Compact, are the Global Reporting Initiative (GRI) and the SA8000. The GRI is a large, 'multi-stakeholder network' of experts promoting triple bottom line disclosure within a 'Sustainability Reporting Framework'. The purpose is to give the public a full and transparent vision of the actions of its more than 1,000 members (companies but also state agencies and NGOs). The SA8000 is a 'Social Accountability Standard' and verification system aimed at 'assuring humane workplaces'. According to ethicmatch.com statistics, 881 facilities worldwide, representing a total of 507,736 workers, had been SA8000 certified by 31 December 2005.

Many branches of business have devised their own codes of conduct. Examples include the International Council of Toy Industries and the International Code of Conduct on the Distribution and Use of Pesticides. Branch level codes focus as much on labour practices and product safety as on environmental standards.

Also noteworthy is the rise of environmental and social ratings agencies that provide similar functions as Standard and Poor's or Moody's ratings do in regards to financial performance (see Chapter 14). Examples include Environmental Resources Management (ERM) in the USA/UK or BMJ Ratings in France.

Lastly, a fast-growing area of ethical codification is the fair trade branch, where certification is largely overseen by FLO International (Fairtrade 2009), with an oversight including '20 labelling initiatives in 21 countries and producer networks representing Fairtrade Certified Producer Organizations in Central and South America, Africa and Asia'. The fair trade sector started with attempts to create products (such as Fair Trade Coffee and Rugmark carpets), whose entire branding revolves around the use of ethical business practices, mainly ensuring living wages for upstream producers by paying them above-market prices. As such, it constitutes the purest example of CR turned into profit strategy.

Inside business

Rakhil Hirdaramani, Director, Hirdaramani Group

The Hirdaramani Group is a family-run business with interests primarily in the manufacture of clothing, as well as property investment and IT consultancy. The operations are based in South Asia, most notably in Sri Lanka, Bangladesh, and Vietnam. I work with one of the members of the older generation in running the mixed production units, catering predominantly for Marks & Spencer.

The company has two different strategies for its supply chain and sourcing. For the European business, Hirdaramani primarily sources from South Asian countries, particularly as we benefit from GSP+ (Generalized System of Preferences), which is a duty-free concession for importing into the European Union. For US-based customers, the company sources most of its raw materials from the Far East, mainly China but also Taiwan and Korea. To facilitate the sourcing operations, the company has offices throughout Asia that help to find and develop new suppliers.

Hirdaramani has signed up to the Ethical Trading Initiative, which supports fair and safe working practices for employees. The company pays above the minimum wage in all the countries where it operates. For the 15,000 employees worldwide, the majority of whom are women and often the primary breadwinners, relative job security is essential. As far as Hirdaramani is concerned, any cost savings must come from efficiency rather than from sacrificing ethical or moral standards. The concept and practice of corporate social responsibility (CSR) varies in different countries, depending on perceived local needs and on the marketing requirements of the organization. Conducting ethical business is a combination of moral behaviour, together with fair and safe working practices. Major international companies and brands, such as Tesco, Marks & Spencer, Nike, Adidas, Abercrombie and Fitch, and Levis have strict guidelines for being an approved supplier and also take compliance very seriously.

The relationship between the company and the governments of the countries where Hirdaramani operates is very important. In particular, the company's relationship with the government of Sri Lanka is mutually beneficial, so that we have the ability to discuss various development targets for the country. Hirdaramani's continued growth in Sri Lanka has been supported by the government.

For a developing economy such as Sri Lanka, ecological sustainability is a new concept. However, Hirdaramani has recently launched its own Green Initiative, whose motto is 'Reduce, Reuse or Recycle'. The company has also started operations at its Green Factory, Mihila; this is a low-cost, forward-looking factory that is very 'green'. Mihila has also just been awarded the Gold Award by LEED and is also the first custom-built eco-friendly apparel-manufacturing facility in the world.

Fairtrade remains a marginal market, accounting for less than 1 per cent of all retail sales in the OECD countries. It is on the rise, however, as exemplified by the sector's 47 per cent growth rate in the UK in 2008, where a number of household brand names, including Cadbury's or Tate & Lyle, have entered a market that was previously occupied by a few specialist small and medium-sized enterprises (SMEs) alone (Wiggins 2009). It is true that this expansion mainly occurred before consumers began to feel the full effects of the 2009 recession. Indeed, one risk is that people will be less willing to pay more for ethical goods in times of recession. A second concern for the fair trade sector, and for CR as a whole, is the credibility of ethical business. A number of MNEs highlighting their ethical activities through advertising are in actual fact overstating the extent of their ethical involvement. This practice is called 'greenwashing' when it involves firms exaggerating their environmental credentials. The codes of conduct developed by MNEs guilty of such practices could be seen as providing them with cover to mislead the general public, and thus as instruments of unethical behaviour.

Take the famous example of Nike, which, along with other clothing giants like Adidas, came under enormous pressure in the 1990s when it was accused of looking the other way while its suppliers committed serious human rights abuses against workers operating in sweatshop conditions. After first protesting its lack of responsibility for other firms' bad labour practices, Nike changed tack and openly embraced an ethical auditing regime. Proud of its new image, the MNE then advertised how well workers in its supply chain were being treated—claims denied by a Californian activist named Marc Kasky, who in April 2002 launched a lawsuit that Nike ultimately settled out of court.

There is no doubt that Nike did take concrete measures to improve workers' conditions. It signed an Apparel Industry Partnership code, set up a Labour Practices Department, and implemented a tight and transparent supplier audit system. It also received favourable reviews from the World Business Council for Sustainable Development (WBCSD), an association of around 200 companies working to develop the link between business and sustainable development. Yet, fairly or unfairly, some mistrust of Nike persists to this day. It is very hard for MNEs to regain an ethical reputation once this has been damaged—especially when, as is often the case, local and global approaches to CR are not of the same standard (Husted and Allen 2006).

Enforcing international corporate responsibility

It is one thing to specify the ethical standards that MNEs should adopt. It is another to ensure that they actually implement them. Many actors are directly or indirectly involved in enforcing CR worldwide. Altogether, they constitute a sphere of 'civil regulation [filling] the gap between law and market' (Zadek, in Vogel 2006: 9).

Because ethical behaviour is easier to identify within a national framework where everyone answers to a single authority (the government), enforcement is also more straightforward at this level. International organizations like the EU or World Trade Organization (WTO) may be able to sanction wrongdoers in a few limited areas (see Chapter 6), but they generally lack the power to enforce global codes covering basic ethical dilemmas like relative poverty and inequality (Eckert 2008). Yet there is a strong argument that it is in the world's interests to unify its 'fragmented legal systems [since] making firms pay for the damage they inflict [gives them] greater incentive to act more responsibly and ensure their employees do' (Stiglitz 2006: 205–7). One step in this direction would be to let companies be sanctioned in one country for actions elsewhere (for example, the suit launched against Unocal in California for its conduct in Myanmar). MNEs can also be held accountable for unethical actions they have committed in the past—as in the lawsuit that human rights group Khulamani launched against MNEs accused of supporting South Africa's oppressive former apartheid regime (Evans 2008). For the foreseeable future, however, with the exception of global NGO campaigns aimed at raising consumers' global ethical awareness, CR is mainly enforced within the boundaries of the nation-state.

National traditions of CR enforcement

Corporate responsibility materializes across the world in different forms. According to one school of thought, stringent European legislation ensures that companies acting legally in this part of the world are already acting ethically (Matten and Moon 2004). In the USA, on the other hand, firms may feel greater pressure to prove that they are ethical. This can be partly explained by the fact that, before the Sarbanes-Oxley corporate governance bill became law in 2002, US executives could often avoid personal responsibility for their actions at work by 'hiding behind the corporate veil' of limited liability (Stiglitz 2006). One example of overt CR efforts made by US companies to overcome doubts about their ethics is McDonald's publication of ingredient quality standards that go well beyond US Food and Drug Administration minimum requirements. In an environment where accountability is less formalized, overt CR reassures the public and becomes a competitive tool. US firms Ben and Jerry's and American Apparel are aware of this factor and have long sought to turn it to their advantage, strengthening customer loyalty by highlighting their progressive

+ **Accountability**
Idea that actors must take responsibility for their actions.

values and commitment to sustainability. CR has provided a new market niche for a whole range of companies.

In Europe, on the other hand, there is a 'long tradition of business/government cooperation' (Vogel 2006: 10), reflected in strong philosophical traditions like Germany's legal concept of *Eigentum verpflichtet* (loosely translated as the idea that 'ownership implies duties' and not just benefits). More recently, there has also been the appearance of triple bottom line legislation, like France's 2001 *Nouvelles Régulations Economiques,* which require most local firms to publish environmental and social accounts alongside their financial statements. Some analysts have come to the opinion that Europe 'outshines' the USA in CR matters (Maitland 2002). Others have a different opinion, based on the fact that many large US companies are leading signatories of global ethical reporting initiatives. It is risky generalizing about whether one business culture is more ethical than another.

Thinking point
Are some cultures fundamentally more ethical than others?

Japan's CR profile resembles Europe's to the extent that this is a collective culture where the search for social harmony, an Asian cultural value enshrined in the writings of the philosopher Confucius, takes precedence over self-interest. Unsurprisingly, there are also exceptions to this rule, one being the health crisis provoked in the mid-1950s by the Chisso Corporation's dumping of mercury into Minimata Bay (Schwartz 1999). Moreover, many countries in Asia share similar values without CR being as prevalent as it is in Japan. This is further proof that a society's attitudes towards ethics in business is conditioned by factors aside from culture (like its stage of economic development).

Hopkins's study (2007: 170–87) of CR in the developing world reveals a mixed picture. The topic has attracted increased interest, particularly in countries like India, where a vibrant civil society coexists with MNEs (like Tata) that act on a global stage and therefore need to bolster their image in much the same way as Western MNEs do. In China, income inequality and poor working conditions have caused serious industrial unrest, meaning that MNEs operating here are increasingly obliged to accommodate local labour needs. One example is the way that Walmart, famous for its confrontations with organized labour at home in the USA, was forced by the Chinese government in 2004 to accept the unionization of its local workforce. Note that the union in question was state run, exemplifying the fact that stakeholder relations in LDCs generally differ from those in the industrialized world. Some developing regions (like the Middle East but also India) have a long tradition of philanthropy—but, as discussed above, charity is not the same thing as CR. Indeed, Hopkins criticizes philanthropy in Africa because firms use it 'as a respectable means of buying off stakeholders to accept their operating practices'. Brazilian society is also known for its long-standing 'concern with social issues in business', but here too CR has had only limited applications. This may be changing, however, because of the efforts of President Lula, a former trade unionist, to make CR part of a 'broader agenda that aims to reinstate universal public policies at the centre of the Brazilian model of socio-economic development' (Cappellin and Giuliani 2004). It is worth recalling that national CR efforts almost always vary over time.

Historically, LDCs' main priority has been to create jobs and spark growth by attracting inward FDI. Moreover, many LDCs do not have sufficiently strong civil institutions to exert moral pressure on companies. Corruption is rife, often because living standards are so low that potential recipients of bribes (understandably) cannot afford to turn their backs on any sources of extra income. In some areas of the world, CR does seem a luxury. At the same time, it is patently unfair that the world's poor should benefit from a lesser degree of CR than anyone else.

Protest NGOs and consumers

A rapidly expanding feature of the international ethics landscape is NGOs' use of high-profile communications (media, conferences, demonstrations, and Internet magazines such as *Ethical Corporation* or *Corpwatch*) to influence how the general public views MNEs. Much of the time, this involves denouncing some MNEs' refusal to accept responsibility for the direct costs of their activities (as well as a number of indirect ones like resource depletion and subcontractors' unethical labour practices). NGOs' public exposure of corporate behaviour is intended to attract the attention of politicians and legislators (in the hope that they will intervene) and consumers (in the hope that they will threaten commercial boycotts). Chapter 6 explores NGOs' world view in further detail and asks whether growing activism reflects civil society's fear of giant corporations dominating weakened state authorities. If so, NGOs should be categorized as a new international power base helping to define today's ethical framework.

The NGO protests' effectiveness as a vehicle for enforcing CR remains to be seen. MNEs may wish to avoid the 'social blowback when stakeholders perceive that they have breached their deal with society' (Donaldson, in Webb 2006) but this does not mean that they are going to agree to any and all protestor demands. First, there is a perception in many boardrooms that NGO campaigners lack legitimacy (Logister 2007). Above all, the benefits of unethical behaviour may be higher than the costs of compliance with legal and/or CR standards—especially when the misbehaviour occurs in some remote location and is invisible to most consumers. Empirical studies have found, for instance, that some companies will select a level of CR compliance depending on their perception of the extent to which customers are likely to sanction them in case of non-compliance (Christmann and Taylor 2006). In some boardrooms, CR is analysed more in cost/benefit terms and less as an ethical issue.

On the other hand, MNEs who fear that a lack of CR would put them at odds with public opinion may also decide that it is in their interest to proactively take the moral high ground. For instance, there had been little specific pressure on the British media company News Corporation to reduce its carbon footprint when it announced on 9 May 2007 that it hoped to achieve carbon neutrality within three years. That same month, Barclays Bank announced that it would be launching a credit card aimed at getting consumers to act in a more environmentally friendly manner—again, without the company having been targeted by any high-profile campaign. The question is the extent to which such volunteer CR steps are a reflection of managers' sincere goodwill (because they do not 'leave their values at home when they arrive at work') or their fear of becoming a target of 'supermarket activism' (Hertz 2001: 179, 113). In all likelihood, it is a combination of the two. Indeed, as MNEs build up their 'community affairs' or 'sustainability' departments and staff them with former public-sector workers whose personal ethos is not necessarily profit-oriented, there is every chance that ethical attitudes will become increasingly widespread in the business world (Murray 2006). The only real question is the extent to which difficult economic circumstances, like the ones associated with the 2008–9 financial crisis, will delay this process.

In sum, most companies are capable of doing both good and bad (Strike et al. 2006). The Swiss pharmaceutical Novartis, for instance, was a trailblazer in eliminating genetically modified ingredients from consumer products yet took the morally questionable step of challenging Indian patent laws aimed at enabling cheaper generic medicine for LDC consumers. Greenpeace alleged in 2006 that McDonald's was co-responsible for the destruction of the Amazon rainforest yet proudly uses its blog to talk about the tonnes of fish that it sources sustainably. Few MNEs are 100 per cent ethical or unethical.

Challenges and choices

→ Corporate responsibility requires significant investment, at least in the early stages of an activity. The challenge for managers is determining whether they are spending enough in the right areas to satisfy their ethical goals without wasting company money. Since there is no certainty in this area, the choice that they constantly have to make is whether to err by spending too much or too little on CR. It is also debatable whether companies should allow a CR ethos to filter into every aspect of their value chain, or whether they should restrict it to certain well-defined functions. The answer often depends on the dominant corporate culture.

→ For society as a whole, the CR challenge is getting the corporate sector to help fund a range of social needs that often extend beyond direct business activities. Placing too heavy a financial or regulatory burden on mobile MNEs is risky, since this could motivate them to move operations elsewhere. On the other hand, letting companies get away with minimal contributions means that most of the burden of ensuring social welfare falls on the state, which may not have the necessary resources. The challenges and choices inherent to CR go to the very heart of the relationship between MNEs and host countries.

Chapter Summary

Despite some remaining opposition to Corporate Responsibility, expectations of ethics in business have become so widespread that CR is likely to be a cornerstone of international business in the future. Indeed, stakeholder opposition to unethical companies means that the latter risk their survival (Singer 2004). The problem, as discussed in the chapter's first section, is defining what constitutes ethical behaviour in cross-border situations that may be characterized by divergent value systems and national interests. The main international CR issues (human rights, labour standards, corruption, and the environment) are viewed differently across the world.

The chapter's second section discussed attempts to codify business ethics, many driven by the United Nations. Since the UN lacks the power to ensure compliance with its codes, and given variations in national CR traditions, enforcement remains patchy. Currently, the main constraints on the behaviour of mobile MNEs are consumers and NGOs. National governments are notable for their absence from international CR enforcement—a situation that will be analysed in further detail in Chapters 4 and 5.

Case Study 3.3

Ethics and politics: Chiquita going bananas

Ethical activists have long had the United Fruit Company in their sights. As far back as the 1920s, the company's domination of poor Central and South American countries laid it open to criticism. Allegedly, it had helped to plan an invasion of Honduras in 1911; bribed officials to gain land concessions detrimental to local farmers; conspired with Costa Rica's government violently to repress a 1928 strike; spearheaded CIA efforts to topple Guatemala's crusading land reform government in 1954; and helped fund the 1961 Bay of Pigs attack on Cuba. United Fruit also used to be severely criticized for draining much needed funds out of poor local economies when it transferred back to the USA what many observers considered excessive dividend payments. Conversely, it was also accused of paying too little tax in the United States, where it was known for cultivating close relationships with some political elites (Chapman 2007).

This is not to say that the company (now known as Chiquita Brands International, www.chiquita.com) did not also engage in a number of beneficial CR actions. From early on, many Chiquita employees and their families enjoyed specially built schools and health centres. Starting in the 1960s, the company began returning some of its surplus

MNEs provide work in many LDCs but conditions can be very hard (© iStockphoto).

land holdings to Central American communities. When a 1972 earthquake devastated Nicaragua, Chiquita played a strong role in funding relief efforts, describing this work as its normal 'social responsibility'. As the years passed, Chiquita's overall CR efforts went further still. Pesticide use fell, labour relations were formalized, and working conditions improved—to such an extent that by 2001 it was given the Rainforest Alliance's first ever Sustainable Standard-Setter Green Globe Award for its promotion of biodiversity and sustainability. By 2005 all Chiquita's Latin American farms were certified SA8000 international labour standard compliant—not the sign of an MNE that forces misery upon host countries.

Yet the picture remains a mixed one. In 1998, for instance, Chiquita (and its tycoon CEO, Carl Lindner) came under fire for trying to pressure the US government to sue the European Commission (EC) due to the banana quota regime that the EC had set up to provide assistance to poor Caribbean producers in countries with historical ties to Europe. Analysts who equated EC policy with aid felt that it was immoral for Chiquita to get US leaders to complain to the WTO about European 'anti-market' practices. The WTO ultimately found in favour of Chiquita, accusing the European Union (EU) of protectionism and authorising punitive retaliation. Not only was this a bad result for many small Caribbean growers but Chiquita continued to attack the EU in following years, filing for damages as late as 2001.

In 2007, Chiquita again made the front page for the wrong reasons, admitting that for several years

it had made payments to right-wing Colombian death squads designated as terrorist organizations by the US government. The morality of this affair is unclear, with Chiquita depicting itself as the victim of a protection racket. The main question is how can a company that is capable of doing so many good things also commit so many dubious acts.

Case study questions

1. To what extent should United Fruit be criticized for its past behaviour in Central America?
2. How should Chiquita have managed its public relations at the time of the EC banana war or Colombian payments scandal?
3. How is it possible to tell whether Chiquita has made a sincere conversion to sustainable development?

Discussion questions

1. What kind of positive and/or negative connection exists between the corporate profit motive and the greater social good?
2. Is Kline right to fear that MNEs might use the pretext of moral relativism to avoid responsibility for ethical behaviour?

3. Do ethical problems necessarily arise when MNEs from the world's wealthier countries interact with LDCs?
4. To what extent are smaller MNEs likely to be more ethically sensitive than larger ones?
5. What should MNEs do if ethical behaviour puts them at a competitive disadvantage?

References

Associated Press (2002). 'Indonesian Workers Ask the West to Boycott Gap', 30 Nov., www.ctv.ca (accessed 9 Oct. 2008).

Baby Milk Action (2008). 'Briefing Paper', www.babymilkaction.org (accessed 8 Oct. 2008).

Beets, S. D. (2007). 'Global Corruption and Religion: An Empirical Examination', *Journal of Global Ethics*, 3/1 (Apr.).

Bonini, S., and Chênevert, S. (2008). 'The State of Corporate Philanthropy: A McKinsey Global Survey', Feb., www.mckinseyquarterly.com (accessed 24 June 2008).

Bradshaw, S. (2005). 'Free Trade, After a Fashion', *Panorama* series, 7 Mar., http://news.bbc.co.uk (accessed 8 Oct. 2008).

Cappellin, P., and Giuliani, G. (2004). 'The Political Economy of Corporate Responsibility in Brazil: Social and Environmental Dimensions', UNRISD Technology, Business and Society Programme Area (2000–5).

Chapman, P. (2007). 'Rotten Fruit', 4 May, www.ft.com (accessed 8 Oct. 2008).

Christmann, P., and Taylor, G. (2006). 'Firm Self-Regulation through International Certifiable Standards: Determinants of Symbolic versus Substantive Implementation', *Journal of International Business Studies*, 37/6 (Nov.).

Crawford, D., and Esterl, M. (2007). 'How Siemens Paid out Bribes across 3 Countries', *Wall Street Journal-Europe*, 16–18 Nov., p. 1.

Cronin, J. (2006). *Let Business Lift Africa out of Poverty*, BBC, 4 July, http://news.bbc.co.uk (accessed 8 Oct. 2008).

Donaldson, T. (1989). *The Ethics of International Business*. Oxford: Oxford University Press.

Eckert, A. (2008). 'Obligations beyond National Borders: International Institutions and Distributive Justice', *Journal of Global Ethics*, 4/1 (Apr.).

Economist (2001). 'Fruit Suit', 1 Feb., www.iimahd.ernet.in (accessed 8 Oct. 2008).

Entine, J. (2007). 'The Contrarian: Chiquita Counts the Cost of Honesty', Ethical Corporation, 7 May, www.ethicalcorp.com (accessed 8 Oct. 2008).

Evans, I. (2008). 'Multinationals Face Damages Claim from Victims of Apartheid', *Observer*, Business and Media section, 18 May, p. 2.

Fairtrade (2009). www.fairtrade.net (accessed 15 July 2009).

Friedman, M. (2002). *Capitalism and Freedom*. 40th edn. Chicago: University of Chicago Press.

Frost, R. (2004). 'Corporate Responsibility and Globalization: A Reassessment', *IABC's Online Newsletter for Communication Management*, 2/2 (Feb.), www.iabc.com (accessed 20 July 2009).

Gichure, C. (2006). 'Towards Instilling Ethics in African Business and Public Service', *Institute of Business Ethics Review*, 8/2.

Greenpeace (2005). 'We're Trashin' it', www.greenpeace.org.uk (accessed 8 Oct. 2008).

Greenpeace (2009). 'Guide to Greener Electronics', Mar., www.greener computing.com/research/report/2009/03/31/greenpeaces-guide-greener-electronics-march-2009

Hamilton, J. (2002). 'How Arundhati Roy Took Back the Power in India', www.commondreams.org (accessed 8 Oct. 2008).

Hardin, G. (1968). 'The Tragedy of the Commons', *Science Magazine*, 162/3859.

Hertz, N. (2001). *The Silent Takeover*. London: Heinemann.

Holtbrügge, D., Berg, N., and Puck, J. F. (2007). 'To Bribe or to Convince? Political Stakeholders and Political Activities in German Multinational Corporations', *International Business Review*, 16/1 (Feb.).

Hopkins, M. (2007). *Corporate Responsibility and International Development: Is Business the Solution?* London: Earthscan.

Husted, B., and Allen, D. (2006). 'Corporate Social Responsibility in the Multinational Enterprise: Strategic and Institutional Approaches', *Journal of International Business Studies*, 37/ 6 (Nov.).

International Baby Food Action Network (2009), www.ibfan.org/site2005/Pages/index2.php?iui=1 (accessed 7 Sept. 2009).

Jordan, B. (1998). *Indonesia: Detention of Dita Sari*, 3 Dec., www.icftu.org (accessed 9 Oct. 2008).

Kaneva, M. (2006). *Total Denial: A Film by Milena Kaneva*.

Klaus, V. (2007). 'Czech President Warns against Global Warming Intolerance', Mar., www.hrad.cz (accessed 8 Oct. 2008).

Kline, J. (2005). *Ethics for International Business*. New York: Routledge.

Lenovo (2008). 'Lenovo Asset Recovery Service Helps Businesses Go Green, Turning Computer Trash into Cash', 17 June, www.lenovo.com (accessed 1 July 2009).

Logister, L. (2007). 'Global Governance and Civil Society: Some Reflections on NGO Legitimacy', *Journal of Global Ethics*, 3/2 (Aug.).

Maitland, A. (2002). 'Europe Outshines US in Corporate Responsibility', *Financial Times*, 13 Feb.

Marcoux, A. (2000). 'Business Ethics Gone Wrong', *Cato Policy Report*, 20/3 (May–June), www.cato.org (accessed 8 Oct. 2008).

Matten, D., and Moon, J. (2004). *Implicit and Explicit CR: A Conceptual Framework for Understanding CR in Europe*, www.nottingham.ac.uk (accessed 8 Oct. 2008).

Mellahi, K., and Wood, G. (2003). *The Ethical Business: Challenges and Controversies*. London: Palgrave-MacMillan.

Moorhead, J. (2007). 'Milking it', *Guardian*, 15 May, www.guardian.co.uk/business/2007/may/15/medicineandhealth.lifeandhealth

Morgan, E. (1998). *Navigating Cross-Cultural Ethics: What Global Managers Do Right to Keep from Going Wrong*. Woburn, MA: Butterworth Heinemann.

Murray, S. (2006). 'Corporate Social Responsibility: A Much More Competitive Market as Public/Private Lines Blur', 16 Nov., www.ft.com (accessed 26 June 2008).

Nestlé (2008). 'Baby Milk Issue Facts', www.babymilk.nestle.com (accessed 8 Oct. 2008).

Russell, J. (2006). 'Ivory Coast Toxic Waste—Dumped on', Ethical Corporation, 12 Oct., www.ethicalcorp.com (accessed 8 Oct. 2008).

Schwartz, P. (1999). *When Good Companies do Bad Things: Responsibility and Risk in the Age of Gobalization*. New York: John Wiley & Son.

Sennett, R. (2006). *The Culture of the New Capitalism*. London: Yale University Press.

Singer, P. (2004). *One World: The Ethics of Globalization*. New Haven: Yale University Press.

Stiglitz, J. (2006). *Making Globalization Work: The Next Steps to Global Justice*. London: Allen Lane.

Strike, V. M., Gao, J., and Bansal, P. (2006). 'Being Good while Being Bad: Social Responsibility and the International Diversification of US Firms', *Journal of International Business Studies*, 37/6 (Nov.).

Taylor, G. (2007). 'Chiquita has Set a High Bar for the Banana Industry', 12 May, www.ft.com (accessed 8 Oct. 2008).

Thurrott, P. (2007). 'Lenovo Tops in Environmental Friendliness', Penton media, www.windowsitpro.com (accessed 10 Oct. 2008).

UN Global Compact (2009). www.unglobalcompact.org (accessed 15 July 2009).

Utting, P. (2002). 'The Global Compact and Civil Society: Averting a Collision Course', *Development in Practice*, 12/5, 5 Nov.

Vogel, D. (2006). *The Market for Virtue*. Washington: Brookings.

Waldman, D., et al. (2006). 'Cultural and Leadership Predictors of Corporate Social Responsibility Values of Top Management: A GLOBE Study of 15 Countries', *Journal of International Business Studies*, 37/6 (Nov.).

War on Want (2006). 'Coca Cola: The Alternative Report', Mar., www.waronwant.org (accessed 9 Oct. 2008).

Webb, T. (2006). 'Business Strategy: Blowback and the Social Contract', 7 Nov., www.ethicalcorp.com (accessed 8 Oct. 2008).

Wiggins, J. (2009). 'Cadbury Wraps up Fairtrade Agreement', *Financial Times*, 4 Mar., p. 4.

Further research

Leisinger, K. (2007). 'Capitalism with a Human Face: The UN Global Compact', *Journal of Corporate Citizenship*, 28 (Winter).

Leisinger sees poverty as today's central social challenge and feels that it cannot be resolved without extensive input from businesses working alongside government and civil society. One problem in getting different categories of stakeholders to cooperate is the cynicism that many NGOs feel towards large companies. In Leisinger's study, 59 per cent of all interviewees expressed the view that global corporations do not work in society's best interests. Conversely, from MNEs' perspective, there is the risk of 'corporate responsibility fatigue'.

Leisinger advocates addressing the conflicts between these two sectors through a renewed spirit of cooperation. Greater collaboration between MNEs and NGOs could accelerate societal development. More broadly, the hope is that joint approaches can generate a more sustainable and inclusive global economy—concretizing the lofty aims of the UN Global Compact.

Brown, D., and Woods, N. (2007) (eds.). *Making Global Self-Regulation Effective in Developing Countries*. Oxford: Oxford University Press.

It is one thing to assert and define MNEs' ethical responsibilities; it is another to enforce them, especially with firms whose operational networks span the globe. Because they need to bolster their ethical reputation and given the absence of international bodies empowered to enforce behaviour, many multinationals have adopted internal codes of labour, environmental, and financial conduct. What is questionable is the effectiveness of such self-regulation, particularly in LDCs, where governance institutions are weak.

Online Resource Centre

Visit the Online Resource Centre that accompanies this book to read more information relating to international corporate responsibility: www.oxfordtextbooks.co.uk/orc/sitkin_bowen/

4 Theories of International Business

Overview

The chapter starts with a brief history of trade, followed by an introduction to the key theories of state economic power. This is a prelude to Chapter 5, which will discuss the role that states play in international business in further depth. The rest of the chapter offers a chronological study of the great trade theories that have guided international business attitudes, and thus policies, over the centuries. This review can roughly be divided into two categories: pre-Second World War theories such as mercantilism, classical economics, and factor proportions theory; and more recent theories containing a greater focus on companies and foreign direct investment (FDI).

Section I: A brief history of trade and FDI
Hopkins's four phases of globalization
Introduction to international political economy

Section II: Theories of international business
Pre-Second World War theories
Post-Second World War theories
Welfare economics

Learning Objectives

After reading this chapter, you will be able to:

✦ **chart a course through international business history**

✦ **compare leading trade and FDI theories**

✦ **determine why countries specialize in certain industries**

✦ **discuss free trade theory in cost/benefit terms**

✦ **distinguish between classical and 'new' trade theories**

Case Study 4.1

Theories and trade policy: South Korea's commercial soul

The general image of South Korea today is that of a thriving manufacturing economy, home to many successful products like Hyundai cars, Samsung mobile phones, and LG refrigerators. South Korea is a member of the Organization for Economic Cooperation and Development (OECD), a body representing the world's advanced economies; its school leavers regularly rank among the world's top performers; and the country is making steady progress up the international GDP per capita charts. Yet, just one century ago, Korea was a nation of poor farmers whose limited relations with the outside world had earned it the name 'The Hermit Kingdom'. The policies that South Korea has implemented during its industrial ascent offer a number of lessons about the real world application of trade theories.

One starting point for studying Korean development is the country's occupation by Japan during the first half of the twentieth century, given that Korea's first real steps towards industrialization were in actual fact forced upon it by its former colonizer. After Japan's defeat in the Second World War, two competing powers, China and America, stepped into the vacuum, triggering a terrible war that split the Korean peninsula in half. After an armistice was signed in 1953, North Korea ended up with a communist regime and closed its borders to international trade. South Korea, on the other hand, joined the capitalist world's open trade regime.

Throughout the 1950s, the South Korean government imitated many newly independent less developed countries (LDCs) that were trying to improve their terms of trade through manufacturing. This involved an 'import substitution policy' aimed at supporting domestic industries capable of producing the goods that South Korea used to import, while protecting these sectors from international competition. The idea was that South Korea's new industries needed time to develop the financial strength and knowledge required to compete successfully with more established foreign rivals.

One of the side effects of excluding efficient foreign producers from the South Korean market was high inflation. The government of General Park Chung Hee therefore decided to change gears in the 1960s by adopting a 'strategic trade policy'. Instead of trying to improve South Korea's trade balance by minimizing imports, the new priority was to increase exports by strengthening high value-added industries through low interest rate loans and above all direct state subsidies. Accompanied by a devaluation of Korea's national currency, the Won, the new policy triggered a period of export-driven growth. At the same time, it also required

major investments in target industries such as shipbuilding, steel, and chemicals. Because of a lack of domestic capital, Korea had to borrow greater sums from abroad. The deficits it accumulated eventually caused a financial crisis—a major factor in the Park regime's demise in 1979.

Partially in reaction to this crisis but also to stay in touch with ideological shifts occurring in the rest of the world, South Korea again changed course in the 1980s, opting for a policy of 'trade liberalization'. Key elements of the new approach included relaxing earlier import restrictions and eliminating many export subsidies. South Korean industry was increasingly expected to compete with foreign rivals without receiving any financial aid from the state. Henceforth, governmental interventions would be mostly limited to two kinds of indirect action: a big investment in workforce education; and government coordination of private economic decisions.

South Korea has expanded rapidly, to the extent that this once-poor developing country is now a fully-fledged industrial economy. Nevertheless, its reliance on Western product markets—and its vulnerability to international financial storms like the 1997 Asian currency crisis (see Chapter 13)—means that it is increasingly dependent on events decided outside its borders. Autonomy, once a key goal for policy-makers, is much less of a factor today.

The three trade policies that South Korea has pursued since the 1950s (import substitution, strategic export promotion, and trade liberalization) all had their own rationales, strengths, and weaknesses. Each served a purpose in getting South Korea to where it is today. The clear conclusion is that no trade policy is appropriate in all circumstances and at all times. The same might be said about the theories underlying these policies.

Korea, an industrial powerhouse today, was a mainly agricultural nation until a few decades ago (Photodisc).

Introduction

'The ideas of economists and political philosophers, both when they are right and when they are wrong, are more powerful than is commonly understood. Indeed, the world is ruled by little else. Practical men, who believe themselves to be quite exempt from intellectual influences, are usually the slaves of some defunct economist …'

(Keynes 1936)

To understand the policy environment in which international business takes place, it is crucial that managers gain awareness of the trade and investment theories underlying policy-makers' decisions. In turn, theories can be fully appreciated only if they are considered in the historical context where they were first developed. Learning how past theorists reacted to the circumstances they faced is useful because of the lessons that can be drawn for today.

The above quotation, famously expressed by the British economist John Maynard Keynes in reference to the power of theories, states that thinkers' attempts to make sense of the world shapes people's beliefs, thus their behaviour. In other words, 'if enough people believe a theory, even a false one, it becomes self-fulfilling and therefore true' (Caulkin 2005). In international business, as in all social sciences, reality and perception influence one another.

Section I: A brief history of trade and FDI

Some analysts consider the history of international business as a never-ending drive towards greater interconnectedness: 'the same forces … traders, preachers, adventurers, and warriors … are at work today in connecting the world ever faster and tighter' (Chanda 2007). If this were true, the consequences would be enormous, since it would mean not only that one day all barriers to trade are destined to disappear but possibly that national identities will also merge into one another.

+ **Import substitution**
Trade policy of supporting the domestic production of goods that would otherwise be imported.

+ **Strategic trade policies**
Trade policy of strengthening local firms' export competitiveness in specific sectors.

+ **Trade liberalization**
Loosening of regulations in a bid to reduce government influence on a country's import/export performance.

The opposite argument—namely, that there is nothing inevitable about globalization—seems more convincing. General satisfaction with open-border policies has ebbed and flowed throughout history. In 1920, for example, Keynes (1920: 11) could write: 'The inhabitant of London could order by telephone, sipping his morning tea in bed, the various products of the whole Earth, in such quantity as he might see fit, and reasonably expect their early delivery upon his doorstep.' By the mid-1930s, however, international trade had already contracted dramatically, after the enactment of protectionist laws such as the 'Imperial Preferences System' in the UK or the 'Smoot–Hawley Tariff Act' in the USA. These were pieces of legislation that reacted to the Great Depression by trying to protect domestic producers from international competition. The evolution in Korean trade policy, from import substitution to strategic trade policies to trade liberalization, indicates a shift over time in national attitudes towards international business. Similar variations remain possible in the twenty-first century. Cross-border activity has exploded since the 1980s but remains subject to events such as international tensions, energy prices, or financial crises. In early 2009, for instance, trade and FDI nosedived in the wake of the credit crunch, a 'de-globalization' trend that could have far-reaching consequences. International business cannot be analysed accurately out of context, since it will occur only if enough nations, companies, and people, at a given moment in time, are convinced that the benefits outweigh the costs.

Hopkins's four phases of globalization

The modern era is not the first time that the world has witnessed globalization— defined in Chapter 1 as the process of increased global economic interconnection. Past versions of

Globalization era	Characteristics
1. Archaic (pre-1600s)	• Global division of labour but only occasional impact on local economies. • Some international coordination but most societies remain independent. • 'Before mass production imposed standardization, difference was an important precondition of globalization'.
2. Proto (1600s–1800)	• Rise of finance, services, and pre-industrial manufacturing. • 'Military fiscalism' – i.e. raising taxes through conquests. • Trade still based on differences.
3. Modern (1800–1950)	• Rise of the nation-state and spread of industrialization. • Decline in small local ownership, progressively replaced by salaried employment in large corporations. • 'Regions producing raw materials integrated with the manufacturing centres of Europe', especially England.
4. Post-colonial (post-1950)	• Trade increasingly based on inter- and intra-industry integration. • Finance, technology, and information are main drivers. • US becomes the world's leading power. • Power of intergovernmental organizations, MNEs.

Figure 4.1
The four phases of globalization (derived from Hopkins 2002: 4–8).

globalization had less impact than the current form, however, mainly because they tended to involve little more than irregular contacts between distant communities. Conversely, modern globalization, marked by ultra-rapid telecommunications, deregulated financial and product markets, cheap logistics, and a generally more global outlook, reaches further into people's lives than past versions did. What is unsure is which of these aspects is destined to last. It is risky predicting the future—but even riskier to assume that nothing will ever change.

Studying the history of globalization is important, because it reveals the different factors that have driven international business in the past; their limitations; and the effects they have had on key economic and political players. One long-term trend that can be detected throughout the four historical eras identified by British historian Anthony G. Hopkins (2002) and summarized in Figure 4.1 is the greater ability of private companies and individuals, and relatively lesser ability of states, to influence international business. At the same time, a more detailed study would reveal that this trend has been interrupted on many occasions, particularly in times of crisis. An example is the general resurgence in state power in reaction to the 2008 financial crisis. History is not a one-way street.

Thinking point

Is globalization a reversible phenomenon?

Archaic era (pre-1600s)

The main driver behind foreign expansion during the Archaic era, which Attali (2006) called the 'time of empires', was the ambition of sovereigns, who were often treated like gods. Nevertheless, some international business during this period was the work of merchants: Phoenician traders sailing the Eastern Mediterranean during Roman times; caravans travelling Central Asia's Silk Route; or Marco Polo's 1215 voyage from Venice to China. General insecurity, poor logistics, and a lack of knowledge of distant markets meant, however, that archaic trade was usually too risky to be financed by private interests—all the more so because states controlled most capital at the time.

Proto era (1600s–1800s)

The rise of sea trade, itself the result of improved navigational technology, is one distinguishing feature of globalization's second era. Exploration increased knowledge of distant lands, which were often targeted for colonial invasion. At the same time, political stability in some regions gave birth to a merchant class and the growing accumulation of private wealth. Examples include Amsterdam and Hamburg, a leading member of the

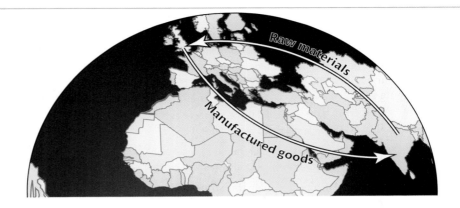

Hanseatic League of North European trading cities. In addition, new forms of joint stock companies like the British East India Company promoted international trade, notably in Asia once Britain, the world's leading economy at the end of this era, had lost its American colonies.

Modern era (1800s–1950)

During the modern era, rapid industrial advances in some parts of the world led to an international division of labour in which some regions specialized in much higher value-added goods than others. An entire ideological framework was developed to justify stronger nations' colonial exploitation of weaker counterparts. Examples include the looting of Africa's natural resources or the way that India was forced to purchase clothing made in Britain from Indian cloth instead of being allowed to manufacture higher-value textiles itself (see Figure 4.2).

The modern era was also a time when national trade paradigms varied more than they do today. An example is the contrast between Japan's 1854 decision to open its borders and Germany's 1879 *Zollverein* decision to erect customs barr iers. Such extreme differences in policy have become less frequent because of the rise of global governance mechanisms (see Chapter 6).

Post-colonial era (post-1950)

It is too early to view the post-colonial era in a historical light, but a few milestones are already identifiable. First, the USA became the world's leading economy, taking over from Britain, which as late as 1900 still accounted for about 50 per cent of global FDI. Secondly, advances in logistics, telecommunications, and international finance mean that much international business today is conducted by huge multinational enterprises (MNEs), many of which organize their supply chains on a cross-border basis. Lastly, national governments' monopoly of political power is being disputed not only by MNEs but also by global governance bodies like the World Trade Organization (WTO). This latest period has been one of great ideological upheaval.

Introduction to international political economy

It is one thing calculating the kinds of economic decisions that a country or company consider useful in different contexts. It is quite another to determine their power to act. At the most basic level, trade theories cannot be addressed without an understanding of one of the basic principles of political economy—the relative power of public and private sectors.

Neo-liberalism

Hopkins's post-colonial era has been dominated, at least until the 2008 credit crunch, by an attitude of neo-liberalism based on the idea that governments should 'allow people to do as they like' (the French translation of this expression, *laissez-faire*, is used in many languages). Neo-liberalism argues that government should run few if any areas of economic activity. It is grounded in a strong belief in personal initiative, market efficiency, and the sanctity of private property.

It is worth noting that, whereas pure neo-liberals believe that a nation's borders should be open to trade, there are many examples of regimes advocating neo-liberal policies in their domestic markets but intervening outside their borders. In 2006, for example, the UK's proudly free market government refused a Russian takeover of the energy company Centrica because it feared losing control in this strategic sector. A similar logic presided over the US government's refusal to allow Chinese state interests to purchase a stake in Unocal, a California oil company. Ideological attitudes as to what constitutes an ideal trading system can be easily overshadowed by a country's sense of its immediate interests.

Critics of neo-liberalism may accept that this orientation helps to create wealth but argue that its cost is social inequality and economic volatility. Many are dismayed by the neo-liberal idea that almost all aspects of life can be reduced to a market transaction (Choonara 2006). There is also a sense that pure neo-liberalism remains more of an idea than a reality. For example, in countries like the USA, where the political culture is dominated by laissez-faire thinking, the state continues to play a larger role than is commonly understood. One example is the willingness of successive US governments to bail out US carmakers in the wake of the 2008 credit crunch, a move that German Chancellor Angela Merkel would later criticize as a 'protectionist' gesture that distorted international competition. As Chapter 5 argues, having less of a state is not the same thing as having no state.

Lastly, general support for a political economic paradigm like neo-liberalism also depends on attitudes towards the leading countries advocating this philosophy. For example, as a global superpower not only in economic and political terms but also academically and culturally, the USA has had an influence on other nations' political views. This indicates that, if the desire to copy US policy were to fade in general, support for its preferred economic philosophy would probably fall off as well (Jacques 2008). The shortcomings of the US economy, revealed during the 2008 credit crunch, along with the rise of China, with its more interventionist and state-oriented world view, have strong implications for future trade and FDI theories.

Interventionism

This philosophy encompasses a range of ideas. These start, at one extreme, with communism and its belief in state ownership of all means of production. There are very few communists any more, however, and modern interventionism is dominated by 'social-democratic' thinking of the kind advocated by Keynes (and implemented by US President Franklin Delano Roosevelt) during their 1930s battle against the Great Depression. Social democrats believe that capitalism is prone to alternating periods of expansion and recession, and that the state needs to correct the markets' occasional but recurring failures. Their solution is state intervention (via fiscal or monetary policy) to smooth out business cycles and to support the vulnerable in society. The emphasis here is as much on the redistribution of wealth as on its creation.

Like neo-liberals, interventionists can also pursue international policies that are at odds with their fundamental domestic approach. Keynes himself supported open borders, although not all modern Keynesians express unconditional support for all aspects of free trade, as exemplified by certain positions taken by Barack Obama during the 2008 US presidential election campaign. Contradictory political philosophies (such as interventionism and neo-liberalism) can combine

+ **Neo-liberalism** Belief in a minimal interference of government in the economy. Often associated with classical economics.

Thinking point
Is it hypocritical to be neo-liberal at home but support interventionism in foreign markets (or vice versa)?

+ **Interventionism** Belief that the state has some role to play in ensuring a fair distribution of wealth and that market mechanisms perform well.

+ **Business cycle** Period during which the economy alternates between boom and bust.

+ **Free trade** Belief that goods and services should be negotiated on foreign markets without any government interference.

in different ways at different times. Many nations pursue mixed economic policies that borrow to varying degrees from both schools.

Critics of interventionism say that it can be 'dysfunctional [and] bad economics', because it distorts market behaviour and causes a poor allocation of resources (Lal 2006). This might happen in several ways. For instance, when a national government intervenes to protect domestic producers from foreign rivals by taxing imports (see Chapter 5), domestic industries have less of an incentive to modernize. Restricting consumers' access to cheap foreign goods also raises their costs. State support for uncompetitive local producers can become a never-ending drain on public funds, when the local producers are 'lame ducks' with no hope of ever being able to survive on their own. This may be acceptable if the beneficiaries are strategically important (for example, Europe's Common Agricultural Policy was originally designed to subsidize farmers to ensure that the region produced enough food), but it is wasteful when the same product can be produced much more efficiently abroad.

The laissez-faire and interventionist philosophies each have their strengths and weaknesses. They also constitute, in their most radical forms, the two extremes of political economic opinions that international managers are likely to encounter in their careers. Most people operate somewhere in the middle of this spectrum. As such, it is good to practise judging opinions in terms of these two opposing visions. They are a useful background to any review of international business theories.

Thinking point

Is there any possibility of overlap between neo-liberal and interventionist thinking?

Section II: Theories of International Business

For centuries, analysts have devised theories to explain why nations produce what they do and how they can improve trade performance. The remainder of this chapter will explore the most famous of these theories in chronological order. The international economic environment at the time each of these theories was devised should be kept in mind, as this demonstrates the links between world views and people's material circumstances. Putting opinions into context is another important skill for international managers.

Pre-Second World War theories

Thinkers have long grappled with trade as a topic, and some old debates still resonate. Many ancient Greeks took a dim view of foreign merchants (Irwin 1996), and, as discussed in Chapter 1, international managers still need strategies to overcome reactions of xenophobia (from the Greek for 'fear', *phobia*, and 'foreign', *xenos*). The philosophers Plato and Xenophon did acknowledge the usefulness of establishing an economic division of labour but applied this to individuals and not to countries. Aristotle accepted the need for imports but thought they should be limited to certain goods only—a forerunner to today's strategic trade policies. In general, resistance to foreign trade and/or traders was the norm.

This general suspicion of merchants continued into the European Middle Ages. Trade's image as a fundamentally immoral activity slowly began to change under the influence of thinkers like Thomas Aquinas. By the sixteenth century, legal experts like Spain's Francisco de Vitoria were writing that it is 'natural' for nations to trade with foreigners as long as this causes no harm to domestic interests. This new vision paved the way for a doctrine that became known as 'the right of nations' to trade. Once this view was legitimized, it was a short step to mercantilism, the first fully-fledged trade theory.

Mercantilism

This school of thought dominated from about 1550 until 1776. Its main driver was the idea that the purpose of a national trade policy should be to ensure higher exports than imports.

This was based on the notion that national wealth materializes not in the economic activities that a country hosts but instead in its accumulation of currency (mainly gold at the time—most of which could only be sourced only via foreign trade) (Reinert 2007). In this regime, trade is seen as a win–lose proposition, with all nations competing, using almost any means, to improve their trade balance.

The proposition may seem logical, but mercantilism has come in for a great deal of criticism over the years. One factor explaining recent scepticism towards this theory is that countries can prosper even when running a trade deficit. Some modern analysts even believe that a country's trade balance no longer matters, and that a more important objective is to ensure domestic firms' profitability. Arguments over (neo-)mercantilism remain highly topical.

Mercantilism is also relevant to contemporary debate about the tools that governments might use to protect domestic producers (see Chapter 5). Thomas Mun (1571–1641), a leading mercantilist, was very aware of the problems created by the standard 'defensive' solution of taxing imports to make them more expensive than goods manufactured domestically. His 'proactive' solution was to propose that countries concentrate on producing better-quality exports. As shown by South Korea's example, there is a difference between countries' proactive and defensive trade policies.

Examples of other mercantilist policy instruments that remain in force include subsidies, 'industrial regulations, state-created monopolies, import and export restrictions [and] price controls' (Lal 2006: 305–19). Many have the same effect as increasing taxes on consumers and importers. To escape these 'distortions', business interests might resort to corruption, tax evasion, and capital flight. This will undermine a state's tax base and reduce the capital available to government—the very problem that mercantilism was supposed to resolve. Mercantilism is an honest philosophy in the sense that it recognizes the reality of national interests. It is also an ineffective one when it distorts economic behaviour.

Classical economics

The father of 'classical' economics is the Scotsman Adam Smith (1723–90), whose seminal work from 1776, *The Wealth of Nations*, laid the foundations for many of the economic and trade principles that are still being discussed and applied today (see Figure 4.3). A keen observer of the changes that Britain experienced during the first Industrial Revolution, Smith took as his starting point a strong opposition to mercantilism, which he accused of falsifying competition and benefiting inefficient domestic producers to consumers' detriment (Yardeni and Moss 1990). Smith believed that governments should stay out of markets, which should be driven by an 'invisible hand of God' and by individuals' pursuit of self-interest (which he called 'utility'). In this conception, economics have their own laws, irrespective of people's political interests. What matters is performance in the marketplace, not which vested interests in society plead their case most loudly, or who has inherited the most wealth.

> **Thinking point**
> How much of a problem is it for a country to run a constant trade deficit?

> **+ Trade balance**
> Relationship between the value of a country's exports and imports. When exports exceed imports, the country has a trade surplus. When imports exceed exports, it has a trade deficit.

> **+ Capital flight**
> A situation when investors or savers transfer large amounts of money out of a country because of fears about local risks or policies.

> **+ Trickle down economics**
> The idea that it is acceptable for those at the top of society to be the prime beneficiaries of certain economic policies if their gains ultimately benefit the rest of society. Often used as a justification for low tax regimes.

Smith's ideas	Modern application	Impacts on modern trade
Maximizing individual outcomes optimizes overall welfare	**Trickle down economics**	WTO rulings discouraging subsidies to weak producers, import tariffs, etc.
The market can organize itself most efficiently without state interference	Market liberalization	Privatization programmes, deregulation
Efficiency derives from specialization	(International) Division of labour	Interdependence between nations focused on different parts of the value chain

Figure 4.3
Adam Smith's classical economics.

Such was the power of Smith's 'classical-liberal' analysis that it continues to dominate trade discussions today.

Classical economics are driven by the idea that when markets are left to their own devices they will tend towards an optimal allocation of resources, called 'equilibrium'. One of the main ways that an economy achieves equilibrium is by allowing uncompetitive industries to die naturally, while remaining focused on sectors with good growth prospects (a process that the economist Joseph Schumpeter called 'creative destruction'). This ties in neatly with Smith's idea that, to enhance overall efficiency, countries should specialize their production in sectors where they have an advantage, and willingly abandon all others, even at the price of temporary, frictional unemployment as workers in the old sectors lose their jobs.

In trade terms, such thinking translates into the view that open borders are beneficial because pressure from foreign industry forces national producers to become efficient. An example from the 1990s was Mexico's willingness to sign the North American Free Trade Agreement (NAFTA) with the USA, a measure that would force poor Mexican corn farmers to compete with more mechanized, thus more efficient, American rivals (Campbell and Hendricks 2006). Another example from the same decade was the newly unified German government's refusal to support the Trabant automotive company, which had a dominant position in the former East Germany's protected market but crumbled when exposed to Western competition. In 2008, more than fifteen years after reunification, joblessness in Germany's eastern provinces still stood at 12.2 per cent versus 7.4 per cent for the country as a whole—a situation that continues to cause numerous social problems. Yet few would disagree that Germany stands a better chance of competing in international markets with BMW, Mercedes, and Volkswagen cars than it could have done trying to sell Trabants—or that using state funds to prop up inefficient firms like this old East German carmaker would have become a never-ending drain on national resources.

Despite this strong logic, classical economists are often guilty of over-confidence in market mechanisms. In a globalized world, there is always a risk that international competition will kill off entire sectors of domestic activity. The improvement in a nation's overall economic efficiency is of little consolation to the many citizens who lose their jobs (Held and McGrew 2007). As Keynes wrote, the problem with classical economists' focus on long-term equilibrium is that, 'in the long-term, we are all dead.'

A distressing example of the contradiction between long-term goals and short-term realities is the explosion of slums in many LDC cities, filled with ex-farming families who have lost their livelihood because of their inability to compete against farming interests from the world's wealthiest nations. Even among supporters of free trade, there are growing fears that millions of once-protected service sector employees might lose their jobs, in part because of the recent arrival on the global labour market of millions of highly educated workers from China, India, and Russia (Blinder 2007). Classical economists may feel that markets have their own laws, but it is difficult to argue that they can exist independently of the politics of human welfare.

+ Frictional
Refers to the problems that can arise when changes like new technology cause an existing economic sector to disappear and a new one to arise. Friction exists when the process of transition between the two sectors is not smooth—that is, where it takes a long time for people who lose their old jobs to find new ones.

Photo 4.1
Communist East Germany's old Trabant cars may have found it difficult to compete in Western markets (© iStockphoto).

Absolute advantage

A theory that seems to work better is Smith's idea that efficiency goes hand in hand with specialization, which can be achieved through a 'division of labour'. The view here is that, when two countries both have absolute advantage in different products (say the British in textiles and the Portuguese in wine), it is in the interest of each to import the other's speciality product instead of making it at home. This is a scenario where trade enables one country to benefit from another's specialization.

This proposition is also substantiated every time a country uses a cheap imported component in its domestic production process instead of manufacturing the same component locally but at a higher cost. It is the reason, for instance, why US carmakers complained so loudly after the Bush administration's 2002 imposition of extra tariffs on steel imports. The added cost of this 'generic' input (see Chapter 11) had a knock-on effect all the way down the automotive value chain. Domestic producers realized that they would either have to accept lower margins or pass the cost on to consumers and become less competitive. Conversely, it is noteworthy how little resistance the WTO faced when it tried to promote global free trade in computer goods in 1997. Manufacturers in many countries were happy to get cheap access to intermediary goods like microprocessors because they could put them to good use in their domestic production processes. The foreign origin of the component was irrelevant—what mattered was the beneficial effect on the value chain.

Despite its strengths, Smith's absolute advantage theory is also insufficient and imperfect. In the real world, advantage is distributed unevenly, with some countries enjoying greater factor endowments (such as land, capital, or natural resources) than others. This may be a question of size—larger countries often benefit from greater access to factors like labour (China) or natural resources (Russia and Australia), and/or from more dynamic market structures (the USA). Whatever the cause, there is no question that some countries are relatively handicapped in the face of international competition. This raises the question of why they would even want to open their borders to foreign rivals. In addition, analysing nations in terms of the 'natural advantages' they inherit from their geographic or demographic situation is a static approach. Countries and/or entrepreneurs

+ **Absolute advantage**
Where one country, offering the same amount of input as another, achieves greater output of a good and therefore can be said to produce it more cheaply.

+ **Factor endowments**
Human, financial, and physical assets that an economic entity (often a country) can use in its production process.

Photo 4.2
Some imports help a country to gain competitive advantage (© European Community).

are capable of acquiring new advantages (especially technology). Japan, for example, has few natural advantages yet is a real economic powerhouse. Smith did not address this possibility.

Another weakness in Smith's theory is that countries lacking absolute advantage—or suffering from poor 'terms of trade', an issue that Smith also did not address—will be too poor to buy the goods that their more competitive counterparts produce. International trade can function only if customer nations are solvent. Western Europe, for example, was able to purchase American goods after the Second World War only because the USA came up with Marshall Plan funding to put money back into European pockets. The same argument is often used today to justify aid to LDCs. To organize a successful market, it is not enough to have efficient producers, as Smith thought; there must also be customers with enough money to spend.

The 2008 credit crunch revealed other ways in which Smith's trade theory is conditioned by solvency considerations. In the years preceding the crisis, substantial trade surpluses had been accumulated by a number of countries whose industrial apparatuses, in line with Smith's reasoning, were geared towards the kinds of production in which each had a real advantage (technology for Germany, cheap labour for China and the South East Asian 'tiger' economies). As global demand dried up, however, output plummeted in these economies, largely because their reliance on global exports meant that their goods had insufficient local or regional outlets once Western buyers retreated (Minder and Olivier 2009). As noted by a senior Taiwan official, a 2 or 3 per cent fall in global consumption can cause a 40 per cent fall in exports—a contraction that can be especially dramatic in small internationalized countries where trade accounts for a disproportionate percentage of total GDP (Bradsher 2009). By spring 2009, regional bodies like the Association for Southeast Asian Nations (see Chapter 6) were meeting to discuss ways of replacing extra-regional business with intra-regional flows, much in the same way that China was counting on domestic infrastructure projects to reduce its dependency on overseas buyers. Smith's theory does not satisfactorily address the need for a balance between domestic and foreign outlets.

Lastly, a Smithian free market can function fully only if it is deeply embedded in a society's political and cultural fabric (Kay 2004) and reflects the social reality of markets as perceived by the people actually participating in them (Aldridge 2005). Discussing the benefits of Smith's vision without reference to local circumstances, customs, and institutions is unrealistic. It is dangerous for international managers to go abroad with the idea that they need not pay attention to the specificities of the different host countries in which they will be operating.

Comparative advantage

David Ricardo's *Principles of Political Economy and Taxation* (1817) created the idea of comparative advantage, which remains the basis of many modern trade models. Ricardo's idea addressed one shortcoming of Smith's theory—namely, how to interest countries lacking any absolute advantage in opening their borders to international trade. The great novelty of Ricardo's work, itself an attack on Britain's protectionist Corn Laws of the era, was its vision of international trading as a 'win–win' proposition that under certain conditions benefits all countries, even less competitive ones. In this view, a country's absolute disadvantage no longer precludes its participation in international trade, since workers in less productive countries can still be gainfully employed, as long as their salaries are adjusted to reflect their lesser efficiency. This was a first step towards resolving the problems associated with Smith's absolute advantage construct.

Like Smith, Ricardo used a wine versus textiles example to prove his theory (see Figure 4.4). Unlike Smith, his starting point was the idea that Portugal produces both goods more cheaply than England does. Ricardo then asked why England should open its borders if it had no absolute advantage in either market.

If both countries were to work in autarky, so that consumers traded only domestic prices, 1 unit of wine and 1 unit of textiles each cost 15 points in England. Domestic prices

+ **Solvent**
Having sufficient funds to pay for goods.

+ **Comparative advantage**
Where one country produces all goods more efficiently than another but agrees not to produce, and therefore to import, the good whose production makes the least efficient use of its resources.

+ **Autarky**
Where an entity operates self-sufficiently and in isolation.

	Wine cost	Textiles cost	Domestic price structure (autarky)	At international price of 1 unit of wine = 0.75 units of textiles
In Portugal	5	10	1 wine = 0.5 textiles (5/10)	Receives an extra 0.25 units of textile when exporting 1 unit of wine
In England	15	15	1 wine = 1 textiles (15/15)	Receives an extra 1.33 units of wine (1 / 0.75) when exporting 1 unit of textile

Figure 4.4
A basic Ricardian model.

in Portugal, on the other hand, mean that in this country 1 unit of wine costs 5 points and 1 unit of textile 10 points—that is, in Portugal wine trades at half the price of textiles. Thus, if the Portuguese could receive more than one half unit of textiles for each unit of wine they sold, exporting wine and importing textiles would be advantageous for them. This condition is met if international prices mean that 1 unit of wine trades at the equivalent of 0.75 units of textiles.

From England's perspective and because wine and textiles sell domestically at the same price, international trade is worthwhile if consumers can buy 1 unit of wine for less than 1 unit of textiles. This condition is also fulfilled at the above international prices, since England needs to produce and export only 0.75 units of textiles to receive 1 unit of wine. It therefore saves 33 per cent (1 unit of wine divided by 0.75 units of wine) by purchasing wine abroad. In short, even if a country has an absolute disadvantage in all goods, it can still benefit from open borders if a certain relationship exists between domestic and international prices.

A simplified explanation for Ricardo's insight comes from an anecdote that some have attributed to US economist Paul Samuelson. Sally is the best solicitor but also the best typist at her firm. Despite being the most productive person at both jobs, it makes more sense to use her for lawyering and to hire someone else as secretary. The opportunity cost of not using a comparatively worse typist to do the administrative work is lower than the opportunity cost of not using a comparatively worse solicitor to do the legal work.

Ricardo's theory is imperfect and has been criticized, for instance, because it ignores factors such as capital mobility and technological transfers. These are important, because they affect the international distribution of comparative advantages. There are many real-life examples of Ricardo's theory at work today. One is the Russian agricultural sector, which produces both cereals and farm equipment less competitively than its French counterpart. Under Smith's theorem, Russia would have to import both goods from France. In actual fact, it imports tractors but exports grains, since its productivity disadvantage in grains costs it less than its disadvantage in tractors. This real-life outcome is perfectly predictable under Ricardo's theorem.

+ **Opportunity cost**
Cost of doing something in a certain way, thus not receiving the benefits of doing it another way.

Infant industries

The English philosopher John Stuart Mill (1806–73) saw three main advantages to free trade. The first two followed on from Smith's and Ricardo's theories about the advantage of specialization and the need for countries to specialize in whatever activities increase global productivity. Mill's third construct (the 'intellectual and moral gains' that a country makes from its contacts with foreigners) was new but remains topical given the debate over whether or not free markets actually strengthen democracy (Cohen 2007). One of the ideas here is that open borders can help to prevent wars, because countries that trade with one another are less likely to fight. This was one of the drivers behind the foundation of the WTO.

Mill's most significant contribution to international trade theory was the infant industry argument that he developed at the same time as a German economist, Friedrich List. In Mill's opinion, the one area where government intervention is justified is when a country needs to protect industries that are brand new and therefore vulnerable to foreign competition. 'The superiority of one country over another in a branch of production often arises only from having begun sooner. There may be no inherent advantage on one part, or disadvantage

Thinking point
Are open economies more conducive to democracy than closed ones?

+ **Infant industry**
Sector of activity that has developed only recently in a particular country and whose prospects for survival are uncertain because the sector lacks the capital and experience to compete with existing (foreign) producers.

on the other, but only a present superiority of acquired skill and experience' (Mill 1848). This idea is relevant to modern concerns about the ability of countries, particularly LDCs, to enter sectors where MNEs are already firmly entrenched. Examples include India's interest in developing its own semiconductor manufacturing capabilities, despite the global overcapacities that have already become apparent in this sector.

Trade as exploitation

Underlying Smith's liberal (or classical) theory is the optimistic idea that a properly functioning market economy benefits society as a whole. Ricardo's opposition to England's early nineteenth-century Corn Laws led him, on the other hand, to the observation that some social classes (industrialists, workers) are more dynamic than others (landowners). In other words, Ricardo's thinking recognized the possibility of an uneven distribution of economic benefits. German philosopher Karl Marx (1818–83) expanded this principle, stating that the starting point for all economic analysis should be capitalism's basis in the exploitation of one social group by another. Marx's critical attitude towards the capitalist system (and, by extension, towards free trade) probably explains his absence from many international business textbooks. Yet Marx's accusations of unfairness, a far cry from Smith's optimism, still resonate today when LDCs accuse wealthy nations of using open-border globalization as a smoke screen for domination—or 're-colonization', as Malaysia's ex-President Mahathir called it (Fuller 1999). It is a mistake to study capitalism without considering the view of capitalism's leading critic. This is especially true in the wake of the 2008–9 global financial crisis.

One Marxian theory with direct relevance to international business today is the 'law of diminishing returns', which holds that firms operating in a closed capitalist economy will, for a number of reasons, suffer from falling profit rates. In this view, to have a hope of surviving, firms have no choice but to internationalize. The theorem is not entirely robust, having been largely disproved by Joseph Schumpeter's 1912 demonstration of how growth within a national economy can be sustained through 'technological progress'—a key factor in modern explanations of corporate location (see the discussion below on 'New Trade Theory'). It remains that many business analysts are unintentionally arguing a Marxian position when they assert that internationalization is a necessary condition for firms' survival.

A twentieth-century variant of Marx's doubts as to the benefits of global free markets can be found in the critical writings of economists like Waldo Bello, or in the 'dependency theories' that Latin American scholars like Raul Prebisch developed. A very interesting school of thought called 'welfare economics' formulates a less political and more economic debate about free markets' degree of fairness. This school will be studied in the chapter's final section.

Case Study 4.2

Theory and economic dependency: Bolivia Cochabamba

After many years as a Spanish colony, Bolivia finally became independent in 1825 but immediately ran into difficulties because of insufficient agricultural output, scarce investment capital, and heavy national debt. The economy improved somewhat in the 1830s after tariffs had been implemented to protect the country's infant textile industry. All in all, however, it remained very poor for most of the nineteenth century.

The turn of the twentieth century saw a brief period of expansion because of a temporary rise in the global price of tin, one of Bolivia's few natural resources. When this market collapsed in the 1920s, Bolivia again started to run up a large debt, mainly to the United States. There was a growing sense during the 1940s that reform was needed, in part because of the widening gulf between Bolivia's rich and poor.

National conservative and socialist parties had very different ideas about how to solve this problem, however, and the country fell victim to decades of political unrest and economic mismanagement. During this time, the USA provided much needed aid but also increased its control over the Bolivian economy. The net effect of these recurrent crises was to leave Bolivia weakened and vulnerable to foreign creditors' dictates. This sparked great resentment, with new Bolivian regimes deciding every now and again to renationalize American assets.

When the country turned to the World Bank in the 1990s for loans to fund a water system near its third largest city, Cochabamba, it was more or less ordered to structure the project as a private initiative run by a consortium comprised mainly of US and Italian firms. Bolivia's financially strapped government agreed, but the ensuing privatization (and abandonment of public subsidies) led to a sharp rise in water bills. Local consumers were supposed to pay not only for the project's production costs but also for foreign shareholders' dividends. Cochabamba's impoverished citizenry could not afford the new rates. The combination of raised prices for

a staple like water, along with long-standing resentment of foreign domination, led to riots of such violence that the water system was ultimately renationalized and a Socialist president elected in 2005. The whole incident led to widespread criticism of global free markets. It will be interesting to see how much of an impact this anger will have in the years to come.

Bolivia: modern water supply systems may be more efficient but they also cost more (© iStockphoto).

Factor proportions (Heckscher–Ohlin)

Swedish economists Eli Heckscher (1879–1952) and Bertil Ohlin (1899–1979) devised a model stating that, when two countries trade, each will export the good that makes the most intensive use of the particular factor input (labour, capital, or material resources) that it has in abundance. This is because each can source the abundant factor cheaply, thereby raising its (export) competitiveness in the sectors where this factor is key. Conversely, a country should import the good that makes the most intensive use of the factor input that is most scarce locally.

Figure 4.5 illustrates the Heckscher–Ohlin (H–O) model. In France, for example, capital is abundant, and the country specializes in the export of factory-made carpets. In Turkey, on the other hand, labour is abundant, so wages are low, making it economically more viable to produce and export handmade rugs. At its simplest level, this elegant model is the core of neo-classical trade theory.

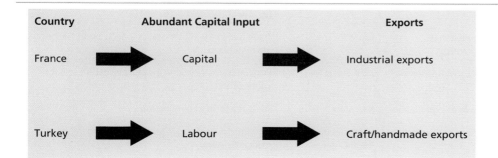

Country	Abundant Capital Input	Exports
France	Capital	Industrial exports
Turkey	Labour	Craft/handmade exports

Figure 4.5
Application of the Heckscher–Ohlin model, which focuses on differences in countries' factor endowments.

The problem is that H–O's power to explain real data is severely limited (Feenstra 2004). The most famous criticism of H–O was formulated in 1953 as Leontief's Paradox, which asked why the USA, the world's most capital-intensive country at the time, imported capital-intensive goods and exported labour-intensive goods—the exact opposite of what H–O would have predicted. Although Leontief's findings have lost weight over time, doubts still remain as to H–O's applicability in its original form. More specifically, H–O seems to really work only when cross-border differences in productivity and technology are introduced. (Go to the Online Resource Centre, extension material 4.1, for several examples of theorems that seek to detect how variations in factor prices affect international trading patterns.)

> Go to the ORC

It is one thing assuming that countries will differ in terms of their aptitudes; it is another explaining why this is so. Ricardo and other classical economists (see Figure 4.6) postulated that national factor inputs remain constant, since to a large extent this was the world they inhabited. Since the mid-twentieth century, however, market liberalization and improved telecommunications have intensified the international mobility of certain factor inputs, such as technology and capital. To reflect the new reality, theory has had to broaden its scope beyond trading nations' characteristics.

Post-Second World War theories

The leading business theories since the mid-twentieth century, summarized in Figure 4.8, focus on company behaviour more than national economies. Recent 'welfare economics' theories (see Figure 4.9), on the other hand, have tended to pass judgement on the benefits of globalization as a whole. The search for an all-encompassing theory of international business, economics, and politics is ongoing.

Product life cycle

In a persuasive article published in 1966, Raymond Vernon linked international manufacturing location decisions to the product life cycle (PLC). Note that the name chosen by Vernon for his theory is the same as one used in a marketing concept developed by the Boston Consulting Group (www.bcg.com). Vernon's concept (see Figure 4.7) covers four phases.

1. *Introduction.* The new good is manufactured in the technologically advanced country where it is invented (often the USA in Vernon's original model). At this early stage, what counts is the MNE headquarters' ability to control the risks involved in a new

Figure 4.6		Key economist(s)	Main points
Most pre-Second World War theories focused on national circumstances.	Mercantilism	Thomas Mun	Trade creates winners and losers Policy aim should be trade surplus
	Classical economics, absolute advantage	Adam Smith	Markets find their own equilibrium Specialization means efficiency (International) division of labour
	Comparative advantage	David Ricardo	Trade is a win–win proposal as long as opportunity costs are minimized
	Infant industries	John Stuart Mill	Protectionism is counter-productive except to help young firms
	Trade as exploitation	Karl Marx	Trade is a form of domination
	Factor proportions	Eli Heckscher/ Bertil Ohlin	Countries export goods using their abundant factor most intensively

product launch. Price competition is not an issue yet, especially if the product is an innovation. Demand may spread rapidly in the home country, but, in other industrialized markets, the item remains a luxury good sold through exports.

2. *Growth*. As demand spreads in the rest of the developed world and foreign rivals set up plants in their home markets, it becomes worthwhile for the original MNE to do the same, especially since it can leverage the manufacturing experience it gained back home. At the same time, foreign production limits the need for exports and the market starts to organize itself on a country-by-country basis.

3. *Maturity*. The technology begins to age and the market saturates in the industrialized world. Prices fall and costs become crucial. This leads to the establishment of manufacturing facilities in low-cost LDCs.

4. *Decline*. In the end, cost pressures are so severe that all plants must shut down in the industrialized world. The remaining manufacturing sites are located in LDCs, with output being re-exported back to the OECD markets.

A prime example of PLC at work is the changing location of Xerox photocopier manufacturing plants. Output began in the USA in the 1940s and 1950s, before moving to Europe within a decade, and finally, as the technology matured, to India in the 1970s and 1980s. The automotive industry offers another useful example, with Ford and GM undertaking their first FDI in Europe in the 1920s before subsequently opening plants in the developing world and shutting more and more sites in the OECD countries.

Vernon's theory is interesting, although it does not apply in all circumstances. Products with a short life span (like microprocessors) may not last long enough to experience the entire PLC. Also, products like luxury goods, whose perceived value can be deeply modified by marketing campaigns, may not age in the way that the model predicts. The idea that a product can at different times find itself in different countries at different stages of the life cycle is a valuable one, however.

New Trade Theory

The starting point for the New Trade Theory is John Dunning's 1977 proposal of an Eclectic Paradigm—itself partially derived from earlier analysis by Stephen Hymer regarding the advantages for a firm of maintaining control over its internal capabilities (Dunning and Pitelis 2007). The idea here is that, because markets often function imperfectly, MNEs are likely to face higher costs in a foreign market than its domestic firms will. In this case, FDI is attractive only if internationalization offers specific incentives.

- *Ownership advantages*. The foreign MNE must have a special product or production process that it can use against rivals operating in their home market. This explains why technologically advanced companies guard their secrets so jealously.

- *Location advantages*. Moving production abroad must offer some advantage, like the possibility of achieving economies of scale.

- *Internalization advantages*. It must be useful for the MNE to exploit the ownership advantage by itself, instead of licensing or selling it to someone else. The company must want to control a larger portion of its total value chain.

Phase	Introduction	Growth	Maturity	Decline
Market dynamics	High-priced new good	Demand spreads	Competition intensifies	Demand declines
Key factors of success	R&D, confidentiality	Market coverage	Rejuvenation via marketing	Low prices
Production location	OECD home country	All OECD countries	OECD and LDC countries	LDC countries only

Figure 4.7

Vernon's PLC theory: production location depends on a product's commercial age.

Carrying on from Dunning, Markusen (2002) started with the observation that most trade and FDI occurs between neighbouring countries with similar levels of industrial development. This finding, which contradicts classical economists' predictions that trade is likely to occur between countries that are very different, is called the 'gravity model' (Krugman 1997a). Markusen researched this discovery and found that, more often than not, FDI involves 'horizontal integration' and a production of similar goods at home and abroad, rather than 'vertical integration' and a production of different goods at different stages of the value chain (see Chapter 7). His conclusion was that the key factor in MNE internationalization is knowledge capital—a finding substantiated by the disproportionate concentration of MNEs in more hi-tech and research-oriented sectors, such as computing or pharmaceuticals, where intangible, firm-specific assets are a key factor of success.

In this new vision, international business has two main drivers. The first is learning effects, or the idea that, because knowledge is easier and cheaper to transfer than other forms of capital, it can be fragmented relatively efficiently between an MNE's research & development (R&D) team, working out of corporate headquarters, and its manufacturing teams, working in its national subsidiaries. The second driver is first mover advantage, or the idea that the first firm to enter a new market and leverage its existing experience there will achieve economies of scale and learning effects, thereby shutting out future rivals.

Unlike Heckscher-Ohlin's emphasis on national factor endowments, the New Trade Theory's main explanation for international success is a company's knowledge, and its ability to apply this worldwide. This introduces the notion that the location of a particular activity may be a simple accident of history and have nothing to do with a country's absolute or comparative advantage. After all, there is nothing that predestines Seattle or Toulouse (respectively centres for Boeing and Airbus operations) to dominate global aircraft manufacturing. The New Trade Theory highlights the consequences of international managers' very human decisions. It is this ability to incorporate human factors (see Online Resource Centre, extension material 4.2) that makes this the most interesting of all post-Second World War theories.

> **+ Learning effects**
> Added production efficiency and lower costs that companies gain from accumulating experience in a particular activity.

> **+ First mover advantage**
> Benefit of being the first party to move into a market segment or location.

> > Go to the ORC 🌐

Competitive advantage

Michael Porter's famous 1990 study, *The Competitive Advantage of Nations*, focused less on FDI than on the connection between countries' relative endowments in capital, natural resources, and labour, on one hand, and MNEs' historical development, on the other. Porter's 'Diamond' identifies four sources of competitive advantage for companies, some relating to external factors and others reflecting corporate actions.

Factor endowments

Porter distinguished between basic inputs (natural resources, climate) and advanced, productivity-enhancing inputs rooted in countries' long-term investments in technology and education. In his opinion, this latter category, largely developed in response to the pressures that countries face to make better use of natural factor endowments, is the main driver of national competitive advantage.

- *Demand conditions*. Variables here are a domestic market's size and buyers' sophistication. MNEs that have flourished in large home markets characterized by demanding consumers are better equipped to succeed abroad.
- *Related and supporting industry*. This was probably Porter's most useful insight. Firms benefit from the proximity of 'clusters' of efficient upstream suppliers that can offer inexpensive components and 'knowledge spillovers' (see Chapter 11).
- *Firm strategy, structure, and rivalry*. A firm's managerial orientation (focus on finance, engineering, and so on) is crucial to its success. Also, companies that hone their skills against tough domestic rivals compete better abroad.

Theory	Key economist(s)	Main points
Product Life Cycle	Raymond Vernon/BCG	Production location depends on phase in product's life
New Trade Theory: Eclectic Paradigm	John Dunning	FDI undertaken to maintain advantages
New Trade Theory: Knowledge Capital	James Markusen	FDI driven by knowledge; first-mover advantage
Competitive advantage	Michael Porter	Diamond model. National circumstances affect MNEs

Figure 4.8
Post-Second World War international business theories have focused on FDI as well as on trade.

Prime examples of Porter's insights are industrial districts, famously exemplified by the cluster of small and medium-sized companies specializing in the production of ceramic roof tiles near Sassuolo in Italy's Modena province. This is a high-performance local economy where information is shared vertically up and down the value chain, and where companies export goods only once they have had a long apprenticeship in their local marketplace. The organization of this 'cluster' of companies fits in with Porter's predictions.

As rational as Porter's theory is, there is the problem that, despite specifying the conditions in which companies can become an international success, it does not explain why failures continue to occur even when these conditions are fulfilled. Clearly other factors are at work as well—one strong possibility being the 'organizational learning' that will be discussed in Chapter 9.

Inside business

David Held, Graham Wallas Professor of Political Science, Co-Director of the Centre for the Study of Global Governance, London School of Economics and Political Science (LSE)

All businesses today—of any size—operate in the context of political economy and operate in complex markets subject to complex regulations. Doing business today requires knowledge of the theory of trade, financial flows, foreign direct investment [and] corporate structures.

In the particular situation of the economic and financial crisis of 2008–9, the costs of banking failure have been externalized onto states. Furthermore, there is the distinct possibility of rising protectionism in a new era of 'managed trade'; or 'the strong hand of the state on the tiller'. Economies that have done well over the last few decades have tended not to be those that the liberal proponents of free and open markets would have predicted but partially state-managed economies such as India, Vietnam, Uganda, and China. This may herald a philosophical move away from the idea that markets know best and can remain relatively unregulated.

We need to move away from the idea that one economic model will solve everybody's problems. Although countries generally get out of crises by trading, there is still a need for the economies of the developing world to have some degree of infant industry protection. In general, trade liberalization has been successful—and, if properly managed, can be the key to global economic prosperity—but the liberalization of financial markets has not been of benefit across the world.

The importance of good relationships between major companies and their host governments should not be underestimated. Virtually all companies are now keen to establish themselves as good corporate citizens and adherents to the notion of corporate social responsibility.

Welfare economics

A flurry of studies has emerged since the 1980s arguing about whether globalization's costs and benefits are distributed efficiently and/or fairly. This debate expands upon notions of 'optimality' developed about a century ago by the Italian economist Vilfredo Pareto (see Online Resource Centre, extension material 4.3). Some texts by the globalization critic and Nobel laureate Joseph Stiglitz also contain welfare aspects. This is a thought-provoking school that operates at the interface between economics and politics.

> Go to the ORC

Paul Krugman

This prolific economist (and 2008 Nobel Prize winner), whose early contributions to New Trade Theory helped advance understanding of the 'gravity model', has focused since the 1980s on globalization's impact on worker welfare. After discovering in the 1990s that real wages reflect productivity across the whole of an economy and not just in sectors exposed to international competition, Krugman initially refused to blame open borders for falling salaries amongst less-skilled US workers. His argument at the time was that 'bad jobs at bad wages are better than no jobs at all' (Krugman 1997b). A decade later, however, following massive job losses in the USA and an unexpectedly rapid rise in the country's imports, he had a change of heart. Concerned that globalization was wreaking havoc on the world's labour markets, Krugman now highlighted the imbalances caused by the faster than expected rise in outsourcing to China, where wages are a fraction of US levels and much lower than they were in earlier outsourcing destinations such as South Korea or Taiwan. Nowadays, Krugman criticizes globalization because 'winners don't compensate the losers' (Stewart 2007). The vision here is that theories of economic efficiency are inoperative if they ignore social realities.

Jagdish Bhagwati

Whereas most theorists would support politicians' efforts to ensure that international trade agreements protect workers' rights, Bhagwati (2007) surprisingly condemns such efforts as counter-productive. In his neo-liberal value system, any attempt to reduce globalization's reach ends up by harming the world's poor and is therefore regressive. Bhagwati's opinion is partially based on his analysis of the way that late-twentieth-century globalization raised living standards in many poor nations—for example, in South East Asia. He contrasts this with the lower standard of living of citizens from African LDCs that have failed to adopt a free market approach.

Amartya Sen

A true Renaissance man active in many fields, Sen is mainly known for his attempts to find a middle ground between interventionist support and neo-liberal criticism of welfare policies (Steele 2001). Instead of expending much energy on a cost/benefit analysis of globalization, Sen has mainly focused on showing that standards of living cannot be assessed using purely numerical indicators like GDP. Hence his creation of what has become the United Nations' Human Development Index (UN 2006) (see Online Resource Centre, extension material 4.3), a measure that has in turn become the cornerstone of international welfare comparisons. The relevancy of Sen's vision to the theories studied in this chapter is his belief that market mechanisms cannot in and of themselves produce Pareto optimality (see Online Resource Centre, extension material 4.4). The benefits of free trade are self-evident—but the world also requires 'countervailing powers' to protect the interests of its 'less assertive citizens'.

> Go to the ORC

> Go to the ORC

Welfare economists	Mainly known as:	Propositions
Paul Krugman	Neo-Keynesian critic of globalization's side effects	Outsourcing of jobs will create misery for workers in industrialized countries.
Jagdish Bhagwati	Author of In *Defence of Globalization*	Focusing on people's short-term interests undermines their long-term prospects. Intervention distorts markets.
Amartya Sen	Economist for Peace and Security – neutral towards free market globalization	Economic success must be measured in qualitative terms, not just quantitative ones. GDP figures do not tell us enough about people's welfare.

Figure 4.9
Welfare economics: a growing branch of theory that looks at the political consequences of trade.

Sen's vision tries to chart a middle course between radically different ideologies to ensure that economics serve humankind and not vice versa. His welfare-seeking aims are commendably ethical. What is questionable is whether his prescriptions are practical in a world where self-interest dominates and power is distributed unequally. As Chapters 5 and 6 will demonstrate, international business cannot be studied without an understanding of political power.

Challenges and choices

→ During the course of their career, international managers are likely to encounter all kinds of national political cultures, many associated with protectionist attitudes that can become major obstacles to cross-border activity. The challenge is learning how to overcome such constraints. Clearly, it is less problematic working in host countries with a strong tradition of open borders. The real question is how much success firms can expect to have in countries where other world views and theories prevail. At a certain point, managers will need to decide whether to invest substantial resources in such environments, or whether the likelihood of being mistrusted as a foreigner is too high a risk.

→ It is difficult for managers to develop a reliable opinion about a location's long-term prospects if they lack information on local decision-makers' preferred policy options. It is almost impossible to judge a host country's political economy without understanding leaders' hidden worldview. A major challenge for many MNEs is determining what steps are needed to develop such an understanding. The choice usually comes down to whether a company should invest more in human resources merely to gain greater knowledge of local politics.

Chapter Summary

A common thread in this chapter is the idea that thinkers are children of their era, and thus that the theories they develop can be understood only within a historical context comprised of political, economic, social, and technological factors. Indeed, with more time, it would be worth analysing why mercantilism dominated early ages of exploration; why liberalism (and socialism) arose during the first Industrial Revolution; and how the rise of modern globalization has coincided with New Trade Theory.

Since the dawn of civilization, people have tried to develop theories to explain trade and, more recently, FDI. The chapter began with a brief review of trade history and the different contexts within which economists' ideas have flourished. After touching on the crucial philosophical divide between the preference for a powerful or weak state, the main trade theories were broadly divided between pre-Second World War theories focused on national policy (and including ideas such as absolute or comparative advantage), and modern theories focused more on company frameworks, product life cycle, FDI, and knowledge management. The chapter concluded with a brief introduction to the welfare theorists whose analyses bear directly on the political framework, which will be explored in greater detail in Chapter 5.

Case Study 4.3

Theory and regime change: Russia from Gorbachev to Putin

The Union of Soviet Socialist Republics (USSR), of which Russia was the key member state, ran a communist regime from 1917 until 1990. One of the most noteworthy features of this system was its command economy, where government bureaucrats made most economic decisions about investment, pricing, incomes, and trade. Communism's worthy goal of social equality paled alongside its other faults, which in the field of economics included its inefficient industrialization processes and terrible consumer shortages. In the end, Mikhail Gorbachev oversaw the dissolution of the Soviet regime, which officially disappeared on 25 December 1991.

The new President, Boris Yeltsin, and his main economic adviser, Yegor Gaidar, were strongly influenced by the radical neo-liberal attitudes of the 1990s. Their policy was to apply a 'shock therapy' of market-oriented reforms, including the phase-out of price controls and subsidies, privatization of national industries, and acceptance of foreign entities like the International Monetary Fund (IMF). The IMF provided much needed loans but also exerted a strong influence over Yeltsin's budgetary and monetary policies. The mid-1990s were a period of extreme inflation and fiscal deficits, with the new state seemingly incapable of raising enough tax revenue to meet its budgetary needs. Soaring interest rates, reflecting in part the 'stabilization' policies demanded by foreign creditors, made it difficult for Russian industry to fund its ambitious modernization investments. National GDP fell by an estimated 50 per cent as the economy restructured. The Russian

The Kremlin, under new management (© iStockphoto).

currency suffered from volatility, culminating in a 1998 financial crisis when the Rouble's value was halved and many financial institutions went bankrupt, destroying the savings of millions of households. Such was the lack of confidence in Russia's future that the country recorded an estimated annual net capital outflow of $20 billion during the 1990s.

By 2007, net private capital inflows in Russia were around $35 billion, a phenomenal turnaround. The 1998 crisis had been the low point, as Russia's unique endowment in natural resources such as gas, coal, and minerals meant that it was well placed to benefit from the sharp rise in world commodity prices that began in the late 1990s. Whereas in 1998 Russia's balance of payments was more or less zero, by 2006 it had a massive surplus of $94.5 billion. The annualized interbank lending rate, which had reached 140 per cent in September 1998, was down to 3.3 per cent in 2007. Russia had experienced uninterrupted strong GDP growth since 1999, with annual rises averaging around 6 per cent over this period.

Some observers analyse the improvement in Russia's economic fortunes as the by-product of its conversion to a market economy. There is no doubt that the new regime has eliminated many distortions found in the old one, but it would be wrong to assume that Russia embraced free trade wholeheartedly. By 2008, the country had still not joined the WTO and continued to levy high tariffs on imports. As unpopular as this policy was among Russian importers and consumers, it did indicate ongoing mercantilist attitudes in many parts of government.

Russia's strength in the early to mid-2000s is partially explained by the world's thirst for its natural resources, meaning that it could put strong pressure on trading partners without fearing a loss of business. Using economic language, the country has benefited from the relatively high price of its factor endowments. Another factor was Russia's centralized political culture. Many Kremlin leaders felt unhappy with the dictates that foreign creditors had imposed on this proud country during the Yeltsin years. On 31 December 1999, Vladimir Putin came to power and not only proceeded to restore the central state's internal authority but also began wielding Russian power in the international arena. One instrument implemented towards this end was greater state control over national energy giants like Gazprom. Foreign MNEs like BP and Shell were made to understand that Russia intended to reign supreme over its domestic economy, with both companies being strong-armed into selling their stakes in local projects they had with Gazprom. Many analysts have come to consider Gazprom, along with other leading Russian energy companies, as quasi-nationalized firms run by an inner circle of Kremlin leaders. Clearly, although Russia has adopted many capitalist attributes, it has chosen a direction quite distinct from the one imagined by the free market prophets who flocked to Moscow at the end of the communist era.

Case study questions

1. To what extent did Russia benefit from, or was damaged by, the neo-liberal policies it applied in the 1990s?
2. How justifiable is Russia's pursuit of its perceived national interest?
3. How sustainable is Russia's current mercantilist policy?

Discussion questions

1. Adam Smith's theory views the international division of labour favourably. How does this approach fit the needs of the modern world?

2. Citing current examples, how well does Ricardo's comparative advantage theory explain countries' varying fortunes?

3. Are there any limitations to the idea that countries should be allowed to protect infant industries?

4. Give examples of industries where Vernon's Product Life Cycle theory does or does not apply.

5. The economist Jagdish Bhagwati believes that it is by allowing capitalism to operate freely that welfare can be maximized, including for the poorer members of society. Is this a robust argument? Why?

6. Paul Krugman disagrees with the idea 'that the people who lose from free trade tend to be small, well-organized groups and the winners are more widely spread'. He thinks that it may be the other way around. Comment.

References

Aldridge, A. (2005). *The Market*. Cambridge: Polity Press.

Attali, J. (2006). *Une brève histoire de l'avenir*. Paris: Fayard.

Bank of Russia (2008). 'Monetary Statistics', www.cbr.ru (accessed 15 Oct. 2008).

Bhagwati, J. (2004). *In Defence of Globalization*. Oxford: Oxford University Press.

Bhagwati, J. (2007). 'Foes of Free Trade Get Foot in the Door', *Financial Times*, Comment section, 22 May, p. 15.

Blinder, A. (2007). 'Free Trade's Great but Offshoring Rattles Me', 6 May, www.washingtonpost.com (accessed 29 June 2008).

Blomfield, A. (2006). 'Kremlin Inc.: Putin Runs Gazprom In-House', 12 Dec., www.telegraph.co.uk (accessed 15 Oct. 2008).

Bradsher, K. (2009). 'East Asia Rethinking Reliance on Exports', *International Herald Tribune*, 5 Mar., p. 9.

Campbell, M., and Hendricks, T. (2006). 'Mexico's Corn Farmers See their Livelihood Wither away', 31 July, www.sfgate.com (accessed 29 June 2008).

Caulkin, S. (2005). 'That's the Theory, and it Matters', 2 Oct., http://observer.guardian.co.uk (accessed 29 June 2008).

Chanda, N. (2007). *Bound Together: How Traders, Preachers, Adventurers, and Warriors Shaped Globalization*. New Haven: Yale University Press.

Choonara, J. (2006). 'Interview with David Harvey', www.socialistreview.org.uk (accessed 29 June 2008).

Cohen, P. (2007). 'An Unexpected Odd Couple: Free Markets and Freedom', *Observer*, 14 June.

Dunning, J., and Pitelis, C. (2007). 'Stephen Hymer's Contribution to International Business Scholarship: An Assessment and Extension', *Journal of International Business*, www.palgrave-journals.com (accessed 29 June 2008).

Ethier, W. (1995). *Modern International Economics*. London: W. W. Norton & Co.

FAO (2001). Food and Agriculture Organization, *The State of Food and Agriculture 2001*, www.fao.org (accessed 15 Oct. 2008).

Feenstra, R. (2004). *Advanced International Trade: Theory and Evidence*. Woodstock: Princeton University Press.

Fuller, T. (1999). 'Mahathir Discerns Threat from "Ethnic European" Colonizers: A Fiery Warning in Malaysia', 19 June, http://iht.com (accessed 14 Oct. 2008).

Held, D., and McGrew, A. (2007) (eds.). *Globalization Theory: Approaches and Controversies*. Cambridge: Polity.

Hopkins, A. (2002) (ed.). *Globalization in World History*. London: Pimlico.

Irwin, D. (1996). *Against the Tide: An Intellectual History of Free Trade*. Chichester: Princeton University Press.

Jacques, M. (2008). 'Northern Rock's Rescue is Part of a Geopolitical Sea Change', *Guardian*, 18 Feb., p. 29.

Kay, J. (2004). *Culture and Prosperity*. New York: HarperCollins.

Keynes, J. M. (1920). *The Economic Consequences of the Peace*. New York: Harcourt Brace Jovanovich.

Keynes, J. M. (1936). *The General Theory of Employment, Interest and Money*. London: Macmillan.

Klaus, E. (2005). 'Bolivia National History', 5 Dec., www.aeroflight.co.uk (accessed 15 Oct. 2008).

Krugman, P. (1997a). *Pop Internationalism*. Boston: MIT Press.

Krugman, P. (1997b), 'In Praise of Cheap Labour', www.pkarchive.org (accessed 29 June 2008).

Lal, D. (2006). 'The Contemporary Relevance of Heckscher's Mercantilism', in R. Findlay, R. Henriksson, H. Lindgren, and M. R. Lundahl (eds.), *Eli Heckscher, International Trade, and Economic History*. Cambridge, MA: MIT Press.

Lee, J. (1996). 'Economic Growth and Human Development in the Republic of Korea 1945–1992', UNDP, http://hdr.undp.org (accessed 15 Oct. 2008).

Lobina, E. (2000). 'Cochabamba—Water War', University of Greenwich, www.psiru.org (accessed 15 Oct. 2008).

Markusen, J. (2002). *Multinational Firms and the Theory of International Trade*. London: MIT Press.

Mill, J. S. (1848). *Principles of Political Economy*. London: Prometheus Books.

Minder, R., and Olivier, C. (2009). 'Asia Trade Suffers as Chinese Imports Fall', *Financial Times*, 2 Mar., p. 6.

Porter, M. (1990). *The Competitive Advantage of Nations*. London: Palgrave Macmillan.

Reinert, K. (2007). 'Analyzing Trade', 5 Mar., http://mason.gmu.edu (accessed 15 Oct. 2008).

Ricardo, D. (1817). *Principles of Political Economy and Taxation*. Oxford World's Classics. Oxford: Oxford University Press.

Sen, A. (2001). *Development as Freedom*. Oxford Paperbacks. Oxford: Oxford University Press.

Smith, A. (1776). *The Wealth of Nations*. Oxford Paperback. Oxford: Oxford University Press.

Steele, J. (2001). 'Food for Thought', 31 Mar., www.guardian.co.uk (accessed 29 June 2008).

Stewart, H. (2007). 'He has an American Dream', *Observer*, Business and Media section, 17 June, p. 9.

Stones, M. (2007). 'French Machinery Exports Take off', 8 Mar., www.fwi.co.uk (accessed 15 Oct. 2008).

UN (2006). United Nations, 'Beyond Scarcity: Power, Poverty, and the Global Water Crisis', *Human Development Report*, http://hrd.undp.org (accessed 15 Oct. 2008).

Vernon, R. (1966). 'International Investment and International Trade in the Product Cycle', *Quarterly Journal of Economics*, 80/2.

Yardeni, E., and Moss, D. (1990). 'The Triumph of Adam Smith', www.adamsmith.org (accessed 29 June 2008).

Further research

Harvey, D. (2005). *A Brief History of Neo-Liberalism*. Oxford: Oxford University Press.
Neo-liberalism, with its vision of minimal state economic intervention and lesser state responsibility for social welfare, has dominated thought and practice in much of the world since the 1970s, at least until the 2008 credit crunch. This book tells the political-economic story of where neo-liberalization came from and how it spread. While Thatcher and Reagan are often cited as the leading drivers behind this paradigm, Harvey shows how a complex combination of forces, from Chile to China and New York City to Mexico City, also played its part. He explores continuities and contrasts between the avenues explored by so-called Third Way politicians like Bill Clinton or Tony Blair and the neo-conservatism of George W. Bush. A critical analysis of what the author sees as neo-liberalism's political and economic dangers assesses the prospects for the different alternatives that many oppositional movements are starting to advocate. Regardless of readers' fundamental support for or rejection of neo-liberalism, the book makes for very relevant reading in the wake of the 2008 financial crisis.

Online Resource Centre

Visit the Online Resource Centre that accompanies this book to read more information relating to theories of international business: www.oxfordtextbooks.co.uk/orc/sitkin_bowen/

International Actors

5 Actors in International Business: States

Overview

This chapter, the first in a trilogy about the actors driving international business, is divided into three sections. The first analyses the tools available to states if they want to influence patterns of trade and for eign direct investment (FDI). The second examines the argument that nation-states are much weaker today than they used to be, focusing on the cyclical nature of political economic thinking; the spread of neo-liberalism; and the specific impact of globalization on state power. The final section explores the counter-argument that states remain major players in international business, based on the continued importance of domestic business; economic patriotism; and states' ongoing usefulness as tools of national competitiveness.

Section I: State intervention in trade and FDI

    Reasons for state intervention

    Tools of state intervention

Section II: The argument that states have lost power to affect international business

    Paradigm shifts

    The international diffusion of the neo-liberal paradigm

    Globalization as a factor that has undermined state power

Section III: The argument that states have retained power to affect international business

    The continuing importance of domestic business

    Economic patriotism

    States as tools of international competition

Learning Objectives

After reading this chapter, you will be able to:

- ✦ assess the rationale for and against government intervention
- ✦ identify the different tools that states use to control trade and FDI
- ✦ trace historical shifts in state paradigms and their diffusion worldwide
- ✦ analyse globalization's impact on nation-states
- ✦ judge the political constraints weighing on international business

Case Study 5.1

States and their regulatory role: Medicine in China

Since the early 1990s, there have been at least eight episodes of mass poisoning cau sed by companies selling pharmaceutical products in which expensive medical ingredients had been replaced by cheap toxic substances (Bogdanich and Hooker 2007). Experts calculate that these actions have resulted in thousands of deaths, including scores of children in Panama who died in 2006 after their parents unwittingly gave them poisoned medicine. This is criminal fraud on a massive scale, and a prime example of failure in government regulation.

Several incidents involved items sold by chemical firms located near China's Yangtze River delta. These companies (or traders marketing their output) would falsify certificates of origin to hide the fact that they were not licensed to make pharmaceutical substances. This kind of deceit is always a possibility in international business and can be prevented only if the supervisory system in the country where it occurs is sufficiently strong, with enough inspectors to check samples regularly and enforce regulations. China has evolved from a country featuring a dominant state apparatus to one where government struggles to keep up with the private sector. The new China has created space

for a whole population of dynamic new Chinese entrepreneurs, most of whom operate within the law. However, there are always a few exceptions.

The best way to stop criminal activities is to hunt down the perpetrators in their country of origin—something that China started doing in 2006, closing 440 counterfeiting operations and arresting two regulators accused of taking bribes. A second-best solution is to inspect products in their destination country and trace any counterfeit substances back to the manufacturer by investigating every step of the supply chain. However, this kind of control would require full-scale cooperation between the regulatory authorities in all the countries through which the goods transit. Where regulators cannot or do not coordinate, it becomes almost impossible to police criminal activities. Thus, cooperation between the US Food and Drug Administration (the FDA) and their Chinese counterparts is more than a political courtesy; it is a crucial public health issue. Unfortunately, joint inspection regimes are unlikely, if only because of divergences in the two countries' political and economic interests. Discussions about state power often include sovereignty considerations.

The safety of medicinal products requires a strict enforcement of regulations (© iStockphoto).

Introduction

Companies do not operate in a vacuum but exist in a framework defined by laws, regulations, and institutions that states create to achieve a number of non-market goals. These include protecting domestic producers from foreign competition; improving national terms of trade; raising tax revenues; and pursuing strategic opportunities. As demonstrated in Section 2, the neo-liberal thinking that dominated international policy-making for the thirty years preceding the 2008 credit crunch largely meant that most countries chose not to wield the tools that were available to them to achieve these goals. This does not mean, however, that states never intervened in international business over this period. After all, one of the prime functions of government is to monitor the activities of foreigners operating on national soil. Thus, regardless of ideology, nation-states always retain an arsenal of weapons that they can use to shape trade and FDI in their national interest. As stated in Chapter 4, neo-liberalism and interventionism are theoretical extremes on the scale of political economic behaviour, with most countries (and individuals) operating somewhere in the middle. It is almost impossible to conceive of a political regime so opposed to the concept of state authority that it refuses to wield any of the powers at its disposal.

Section I: State intervention in trade and FDI

State intervention in trade often means supporting local producers' interests to the detriment of foreign producers and/or local consumers. Chapter 4 showed that supporting local industry can be politically smart but economically sub-optimal. Conversely, organizing 'efficient' markets (where participants are left free to succeed but also to fail) can be economically advantageous but politically damaging. These tensions are reflected in the political economic choices that governments routinely make.

Reasons for state intervention

Some state interventions are meant to have an economic effect, while others are geared towards international relations. The former category mainly involves protecting the domestic population's welfare, while the latter is more oriented towards active competition with foreign interests.

Intervention for economic reasons

Domestic employment

Employment becomes a major concern if foreign producers take a big share of a domestic market. Until the 1970s, national governments tended to address this problem through import substitution policies (see Chapter 4), but since then there has been a generally greater focus on competitiveness. A leading issue in many elections in Organization for Economic Cooperation and Development (OECD) countries during the first decade of the 2000s was the link between open borders and the outsourcing of jobs. In 2008, for example, a key aspect of Democratic candidate Barack Obama's economic platform was a modification of the US tax system to penalize those American companies that ship jobs abroad, while offering tax credits to firms employing workers at home. Notwithstanding the benefits of 'free trade', politicians are very aware of the danger for their careers if constituents suffer too many job losses.

Strategic positioning

Open borders can damage countries that, because of their structures and economic history, tend to export low value-added goods and import high value-added goods. To improve their countries' terms of trade (see Chapter 1), governments intervene by pursuing long-term industrialization policies and/or supporting growing 'infant industries' in certain strategic sectors. Similar actions involve protecting sectors that the government consider crucial to the national identity, such as rice in Japan or wine in France. Many such interventions are funded through higher taxes, a key lever in the exercise of state power.

Safety/security

One area where governments often intervene to protect citizens' welfare is public health. Another is national security, with governments often keeping a close eye on the trade of arms or hi-tech computer systems. For example, the United States Department of Commerce's Bureau of Industry and Security (www.bis.doc.gov) restricts trade in items that potentially hostile countries (or individuals) might use for military purposes. Such controls, often leading to the establishment of export licensing systems, are prime examples of government intervention in trade.

Interventions for reasons of international relations

Reciprocity

Nation-states are not in the business of handing out favours without getting something in return. For instance, a government will expect a foreign market to be as open to its national producers as the domestic market is to foreign producers. Things can degenerate where people sense that reciprocity is lacking. In extreme cases, this leads to trade wars. Note, for instance, the US/EU dispute over genetically modified (GM) food. A US multinational, Monsanto, developed a seed technology that resulted in higher crop yields. This was poorly received in Europe, because EU citizens are less comfortable with artificial agricultural processes. In addition, the technology would force European farmers to order new seeds from Monsanto every year. In American eyes, EU resistance to GM imports was a pretext for refusing American companies access to European markets. In 2003 the USA therefore filed a complaint against the EU with the World Trade Organization (WTO)—which provisionally ruled in favour of the European position.

Influence

During the 2000s, several partners (including the EU) signed preferential trade agreements with Afghanistan in a bid to offer its farmers incentives to grow crops other than poppy seeds for opium. This exemplifies a proactive use of trade as a tool for influencing a foreign country's behaviour. It can be contrasted with a more defensive approach that involves limiting relations with certain partners to try to convince them to change direction. This was exemplified in 2007 when the Democrat majority in the US Congress got the Bush administration to introduce minimum enforceable standards into free trade treaties being negotiated with certain Latin American countries to force them to improve labour and environmental standards.

Sanctions

Governments are apt to restrict trade with governments, investment funds, or MNEs from countries with which they have a hostile relationship. Examples include many Arab countries' boycott of Israeli goods because of political tensions in the Middle East; the US government's blockade of Cuba; or EU and US threats against Iran because of its nuclear enrichment programme.

Industrialization policies Concerted state efforts to increase manufacturing's proportion of national economic output, or to support industrial sectors considered strategic.

Thinking point Are trade wars an acceptable tool of foreign policy?

Tools of state intervention

States can influence international business through many tools that have a direct effect on market conditions (see Figure 5.1). Some tools, like import quotas and anti-dumping provisions, specifically target trade. Others, like ownership restrictions, apply only to FDI. Lastly, some intervention tools, such as subsidies and macro-economic policies, are more general in nature, since they affect the economy as a whole.

Trade tools

The main distinction for government intervention in trade is whether the foreign partner must pay a sum of money or undergo administrative controls.

Tariffs

+ Tariffs
Taxes that governments levy on goods (usually imports) when they cross national borders.

Tariffs (or customs duties) are usually assessed as a percentage of a shipment's value—that is, on a so-called *ad valorem* basis. However, they can also be 'specific' and represent a lump sum for a given physical quantity. National governments often use tariffs to try and modify international trade patterns and ensure that the home economy focuses on higher value-added activities. To avoid penalizing domestic industries that import basic goods, tariffs tend to be higher on more processed products—that is, on goods whose transformation has advanced further along the international value chain. This means, for example, that tariffs on finished goods like shoes are usually higher than on raw materials like leather.

By artificially raising the price of foreign goods, import tariffs affect consumer product preferences. These are some of the main tools that governments use when intervening in trade and are therefore a topic of debate during most trade negotiations. A good example in 2007 was India's imposition of heavy duties on liquor imports, a measure that angered both the USA and the EU. Threatened with a WTO Dispute Resolution procedure (see Chapter 6), India ultimately dropped this idea.

Non-tariff barriers

Higher oil prices in 1973 raised national energy import costs worldwide and sparked a wave of protectionist sentiment. Obliged by their commitments as signatories of the General Agreement on Trade and Tariffs (GATT) to keep import tariffs low, many countries started looking for other trade intervention tools. The end result was a series of non-tariff barriers (NTBs), led by quantitative restrictions (QRs), standards, and anti-dumping provisions.

QRs.   There are two main variants of QRs: voluntary export restraints (VERs); and import quotas. VERs refer to one country's agreement to limit the volume and/or value of its exports to another country, usually to avoid the kind of hostile response that can occur when one country has a dominant share of another trading partner's domestic market. Famously, this tool was used in the 1970s when Japan was persuaded to limit its available exports to

Figure 5.1
Summary of some of the ways that governments intervene in trade and FDI.

Government tool	Examples
Tariffs	*Ad valorem* or specific duties
Non-tariff barriers	Quantitative restrictions, standards
Anti-dumping	Retaliatory measures
Performance requirements	Local contents, dividend repatriation
Ownership restrictions	Joint ventures, (re-)nationalizations
Subsidies	Cash payments, preferential terms
Macro-economic policy	Fiscal, monetary, and currency actions

the USA. Japanese companies' growing share of the American car market had destroyed jobs in the USA and created much resentment. Japan's VER policy was one way to prevent Washington from taking more drastic measures. A similar case from April 2007 was when China voluntarily cut steel exports to the USA.

Quotas specify the maximum quantity of a good that a country is prepared to import (or occasionally to export). These quantities are usually agreed through licensing arrangements that, under WTO regulations, must be transparent and non-discriminatory. Note that under the GATT rules that used to apply before the WTO's foundation in 1995, less-developed countries (LDCs) were permitted to apply QRs or other non-tariff measures if they needed this to protect infant industries (Hoekman and Kostecki 2001). The special treatment accorded to the developing world remains a leading topic in the debate on state intervention in trade.

By restricting the supply of foreign goods, both VERs and import quotas increase their price to domestic consumers. A higher price means extra revenue for the foreign producer selling the goods. On the other hand, when import tariffs are applied, it is the domestic government that pockets the surcharge, in the form of taxes collected as the goods enter the country. In this sense, tariffs are a more effective way of protecting national interests than quotas.

Standards. Where consumer health is at stake, governments often require scientific evidence of a product's safety. Problems arise when one country accuses another of misusing controls to disguise protectionist intentions. One example is the EU–US dispute over GM food. Similarly, there has been much disagreement about whether countries with tough environmental legislation should be allowed to restrict imports of goods produced to a lower standard. In 1998, for example, the WTO rejected a US ban on the import of shrimp caught in nets that could harm sea turtles. Attitudes have changed since then, however, and it is increasingly acceptable to the WTO for countries to prohibit products manufactured in a less environmentally-friendly manner. A fundamental question for states is how much priority should be given to economic priorities as opposed to other concerns.

Governments sometimes apply technical standards that have no health implications but reflect national specificities. One example that will be discussed in further detail in Chapter 12 is a German law (*Reinheitsgebot*) that was used to prevent foreign breweries from calling their exports to Germany 'beer' until a 2004 EU ruling that this constituted disguised protectionism. Along these lines, the Geneva-based International Organization for Standardization (ISO) tries to harmonize national quality regimes by providing guidelines that companies worldwide use to audit internal performance (see Chapter 11). It is sometimes difficult to say whether a country's import standards are a protectionist tool or an honest attempt to ensure quality and/or public health.

Anti-dumping provisions. Businesses sometimes try to gain market share by **dumping** goods at artificially low prices. The problem is determining whether imports are cheap because foreign producers are manipulating prices or because they are manufactured more competitively. Governments that accuse foreign producers of dumping will usually fine them—one example being the additional tariffs that the EU levies on subsidized biodiesel imports from the USA (Chaffin and Tighe 2009). The frequency with which both OECD countries and LDCs accuse one another of dumping raises suspicions that many fines are hidden protectionism.

Lastly, note that a number of NTBs are more administrative in nature. These include product labelling or rules of origin requirements, as well as assorted bureaucratic controls.

> **Thinking point**
> Are standards a hidden form of protectionism?

> **+ Dumping**
> When exporters sell goods at a loss or below the normal price specifically to gain market share and put rivals out of business.

FDI tools

Some tools of intervention specifically involve controls on MNE subsidiaries. This has become necessary because of the growing role that FDI plays in total global economic activity.

Thinking point

Is it acceptable for national governments to place extra demands on foreign MNEs' subsidiaries?

Performance requirements

Governments impose conditions on local subsidiaries of MNEs for different reasons. Sometimes the purpose is to monitor the use of state aid. At other times it is to control MNE subsidiaries' behaviour, often (especially in LDCs) to ensure that their actions improve the host country's balance of trade. These are the main performance requirements.

- *Local contents ratios.* Companies must ensure that a minimum percentage of the value of the goods they are selling comes from components sourced from local manufacturers. For example, to benefit from preferential tariffs, at least 40 per cent of the value of goods (re-)exported from the Association of Southeast Asian Nations (ASEAN) free trade area must have been manufactured in a member state.
- *Dividend repatriation restrictions.* Limits are sometimes placed on the quantity of money that an MNE can take out of a country in the form of dividends.
- *Technology transfers.* Here the goal is to ensure that MNEs bring knowledge into the host country and/or undertake a certain amount of research locally.
- *Employment measures.* These are initiatives aimed at accelerating recruitment, improving pay scales, or enhancing worker training (see Chapter 15).

Neo-liberals dislike performance requirements, which they accuse of being an interventionist vehicle for politicizing FDI decisions that they believe the market should determine. One notable effort to disband performance requirements during the 1990s was the OECD's controversial Multilateral Agreement on Investment (MAI), which would have harmonized the global deregulation of FDI and allowed MNEs to sue any state whose intervention had cost them earnings. Many non-governmental organizations (NGOs) perceived MAI as a direct attack by global business interests on the sovereignty of nation-states, and the proposal was ultimately shelved in 2000. Subsequently, the WTO developed a similar proposal called Trade Related Investment Measures (TRIMs), although this also encountered serious opposition (see Chapter 6). Performance requirements are strongly supported by those who argue that, without such protections, the gains from FDI would benefit MNEs more than host countries. Because FDI penetrates host economies more deeply than trade does, it causes greater suspicion.

Ownership restrictions

As Chapter 8 will discuss, national governments have good reason to try to ensure that domestic interests take an equity stake in MNEs' local units—studies show that strong local ownership helps to ensure that FDI-related productivity spreads more widely through the host economy (Marcin 2008). Ownership restrictions can range from limiting MNEs' stake in local ventures to the outright nationalization of foreign companies' local units. More widely, in many countries the FDI environment is strongly influenced by competition regulators whose role is to ensure that foreign interests do not abuse their power. One example is the Irish government's decision in 2008 to oppose Heineken's attempt to acquire home drinks company Beamish, in principle to prevent the Dutch MNE from dominating the local market. Policies of this sort are usually justified by a desire to protect domestic competition. Often enough, however, their real purpose is to protect domestic competitors.

General intervention tools

This category, referring to actions affecting the economic environment within a particular host country, is comprised of domestic initiatives that have international repercussions.

Subsidies

The most common variety of trade-related government subsidies involves direct payments to domestic exporters and/or producers operating in sectors that suffer from foreign competition. Examples include sums paid to US farmers to help them compete against agricultural imports from Mexico (Tobar 2008). A second category is comprised of loans or insurance offered to exporters at a preferential rate.

Subsidies enabling uncompetitive companies to stay alive are deemed to distort the market and cause much conflict in international business—as exemplified by the angry reaction of German carmaker BMW's chief executive when General Motors (GM) tried to convince EU governments to provide aid to keep GM's European subsidiaries Opel and Vauxhall alive in the wake of the 2008 credit crunch (Schäfer and Milne 2009). BMW stood to benefit from the two companies' probable disappearance in the absence of state assistance. From an EU perspective, this had to be weighed against the spectre of job losses. Subsidies are a key tool in many governments' employment policy.

In situations where producers in one country lose market share to a subsidized foreign rival, their government will often try to offset this advantage by fining the company in question. Penalties of this kind, called 'countervailing duties', are supposed to restore a semblance of fairness to the market. The complication is that in certain situations—for example, where infant industries are involved (see Chapter 4)—it is actually the subsidies that re-establish a level playing field.

Thinking point

Why should a state subsidize an industry that has no hope of ever becoming competitive?

Macro-economic policy

A country's trading position is also affected by its government's general economic policies. Thus tax systems can be used to shift domestic demand towards home-made products (for example, by raising VAT on goods that the country traditionally imports). Special 'free trade zones' can be set up, enabling companies to import on a tax-free basis, components destined for re-exportation (see Chapter 11). Interest rates can be raised or lowered, respectively, to reduce demand when a country has a trade deficit and needs to cut consumption, or to increase demand when it has a trade surplus and can afford to consume more. Countries can sometimes keep their currency rates artificially low to facilitate exports, or set them too high to reduce the price of imports (see Chapter 13). Many national economic decisions are taken with a view towards achieving certain international outcomes.

Lastly, governments also have a number of targeted competitiveness schemes at their disposal. Examples include state-sponsored workforce training programmes; payroll tax relief for export companies; preferential treatment for domestic companies bidding on public procurement contracts; and export assistance packages specifically targeting local small and medium-sized enterprises (SMEs). Governments can also try to alter domestic consumer behaviour through 'buy-local' campaigns. Few countries in the world ignore the effects that international business has on their national economy.

It is one thing for states to have reasons and tools for intervening in international business. It is another for them actually to use these tools—or to be allowed to do so. Some observers argue that there is a long-term trend towards reduced state power. Others think that state power has not shrunk but merely changed in nature. The remainder of this chapter will explore these two opposing arguments.

Section II: The argument that states have lost power to affect international business

The argument over the ideal role of the state is crucial to understanding the framework within which international business operates. The 'global economic order is not founded on state power and rules alone, but also on sets of policy ideas and beliefs' (Woods 2004: 467). Few topics are as hotly debated in business, and all social sciences, as state power.

Paradigm shifts

Chapter 4 discussed how theorists have been concerned for centuries with the question of which of society's economic functions (such as infrastructure, security, health, or education) should be run by government and which should be left to private enterprise. It defined the two main schools of thought in this area (neo-liberalism and interventionism) and analysed the philosophical foundations for each. What remains to discuss is how the implementation of each approach has varied in time and place (Hibou 2004).

In the early twentieth century, many politicians in the world's leading power of the day, the UK, believed in minimal government intervention. This attitude applied not only to international trade but also to the domestic business cycle, viewed by classical economists at the time as a natural phenomenon best left untouched.

Such passivity came under widespread criticism when the 1929 Wall Street Crash was followed by the Great Depression. The crisis led to calls for a new kind of economic policy, one in which the capitalist state would be empowered to manage the business cycle proactively. The end result was the rise of interventionism, largely based on the views of the British economist John Maynard Keynes, who believed that government's first priority is to address any short-term human needs that the market does not always satisfy (see Chapter 4).

By the mid-twentieth century, Keynesianism had become the dominant economic paradigm in much of the capitalist world. The new consensus was that states could and should control many domestic sectors; develop welfare systems; engage in economic planning; and even manage entire industrial sectors, such as aviation, steel, and communications. State involvement often went far beyond Keynes's original advice, but criticisms remained muffled as long as economies boomed—as many did for the thirty years following the Second World War.

Once again, it was an economic crisis that changed dominant thinking about the ideal state (see Figure 5.3). The global economy slumped in the 1970s, suffering from high oil prices, budget deficits, inflation, unemployment, and saturated markets. There was widespread disenchantment with Keynesianism and renewed support for classical economics, renamed neo-liberalism. This led in 1979 and 1980 to the elections of UK Prime Minister Margaret Thatcher and US President Ronald Reagan, supporters of a monetarist economist, Milton Friedman, who thought that a state's main priority was to ensure stable prices and not to promote welfare directly. Laissez-faire ideology was back in fashion.

After communism crumbled in Eastern Europe in 1989, influential thinkers floated the idea that nation-states had arrived at the 'end of history', with the superiority of free market capitalism having been proved once and for all (Fukuyama 1993). Associated with this vision was a package of policies that all states were advised to implement. This new paradigm was called the 'Washington Consensus' (see Figure 5.4)—or, more humorously, the 'Golden Straitjacket' (Friedman 2000). Its basic concept was that states exist for three reasons: to help markets function by producing whatever necessary goods the markets cannot provide by themselves; to remedy market failure (see OnlineResource Centre, extension material 5.1);

+ Welfare systems
Provisions made alongside the productive economy to support vulnerable members of society. Usually government-sponsored.

+ Market failure
Where a market performs inefficiently by not allocating resources optimally. Reasons include non-transparent price formation, insufficient competition or rampant externalities.

> Go to the ORC

Figure 5.2
Government intervention smoothes out the highs and lows of the business cycle.

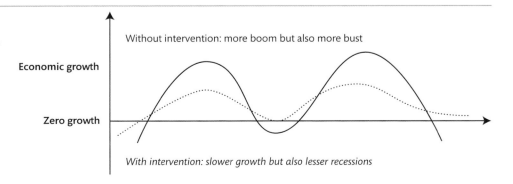

Without intervention: more boom but also more bust

Economic growth

Zero growth

With intervention: slower growth but also lesser recessions

Laissez-faire	Crisis = shift	Interventionism	Crisis = shift	Laissez-faire
First wave of globalization	Depression, Second World War	Keynesianism, post-war boom	Oil shocks, stagflation	Neo-liberalism, second era of globalization
c.1880s–1929	1929–1945	1945–1973	1973–1979	1979–ongoing

Figure 5.3
Crisis-related paradigm changes during the twentieth century in the world's dominant economies (UK then USA).

and to help society's most vulnerable members (Wolf 2004). The strong expectation now was that, except in extreme cases, politics should take a back seat to business.

The question is how long this approach will dominate. History teaches that paradigms last for only as long as enough people believe in them. If neo-liberalism were to prove incapable of resolving a major crisis like the 2008 credit crunch, there is every chance that it will lose popularity. Indeed, by early 2009, governments worldwide were intervening massively, with a mounting tide of voices demanding the re-empowerment of the state. Examples included China, where there is a long tradition of governmental authority (Anderlini 2009), but also the UK, where many normally neo-liberal observers began arguing in favour of such interventionist measures as the nationalization of banks (Wolf 2009) or the adoption of a proactive 'Gaullist' French government model (Davies 2009). Attitudes towards state power have always varied depending on circumstances, and it is very risky for an international manager to attempt long-term predictions in this area.

Thinking point

Can future paradigm shifts be expected, and, if so, when?

The international diffusion of the neo-liberal paradigm

It is important to remember that the world is capable of accommodating different paradigms at the same time, and that a given approach can vary from one country to another. For example, one explanation for East Asia's excellent trade performance since the mid-1990s is the region's market orientation. Yet national governments in this part of the world have also retained a very strong role. Moreover, the East Asian form of neo-liberalism comes in many different shapes, ranging from China's special market zones to Singapore's hi-tech government-aided research centres (Ong 2006). There is no single model of free market capitalism.

The international diffusion of a particular paradigm also depends on broader political factors. For most of the twentieth century, two ideological blocs (communism and capitalism) vied for world dominance, with each trying to bring as many countries as possible under its wing. The fall of communism removed a major obstacle to global integration. Paradigms tend to spread more easily in the absence of geo-political tensions.

One consequence of the end of the cold war was that many LDCs that used to be strongly opposed to the neo-liberal model began embracing it to varying degrees. After gaining independence in the mid-twentieth century, many former colonies had opted for interventionist policies that they felt better reflected their newfound sovereignty. By the end

- Private sector becomes the main engine of economic growth; subsidies must be slashed and state-owned enterprises privatized
- Budget deficits, taxes, and public spending have to be minimized
- Price stability becomes a priority; interest rates are set by the market
- Deregulation becomes a priority; property rights are paramount
- Financial markets are deregulated and pension schemes privatized
- Exchange rates become competitive and completely convertible
- Trade is liberalized: no barriers to entry; export orientation
- Foreign direct investment and ownership must be accepted and domestic monopolies discouraged

Figure 5.4
The Washington Consensus principles that became the hallmark of modern neo-liberal economic management (adapted from Williamson 2002).

of the century, however, many of these governments were being criticized as 'predatory' and corrupt bureaucracies (Lal 2003). Tellingly, a neo-liberal approach began to take root in places that used to be hotbeds of interventionism, like once socialist Tanzania in Africa, or the Indian state of Kerala, which had famously prioritized state-run education and health programmes over business-oriented growth policies. With increasing numbers of LDC elites being educated in Western business schools, it is no surprise that many began to favour market economics.

This is not to say that the neo-liberal agenda ever gained unanimous approval across the developing world. In some places, the philosophy was only imposed through violence—a terrible example being Chile, where Salvador Allende's democratically elected socialist government was overthrown on 11 September 1973 by a US-supported military dictatorship that soon became a laboratory for Milton Friedman's free market ideas (Perkins 2004). Ongoing Latin American resentment following this episode is one reason why the region ended up rejecting the initiative of the Free Trade Area of the Americas that George W. Bush's US administration tried to implement in the early 2000s. Similarly, the world's largest LDCs joined forces later in the decade to reject the WTO's efforts during the 'Doha Round' to force open their service sectors (see Chapter 6). Nevertheless, despite such headline resistance to certain aspects of liberalization, there is little doubt that the main feature of economic policy in most of the world's leading emerging nations over the past two decades has been their adoption of an increasingly market-friendly stance.

The same phenomenon could be witnessed in Europe, despite this region's historic acceptance of state power, viewed by many citizens as a protective shield and instrument of popular will. A prime example of Europe's traditional attitude was the famous 1966 dictum by France's ex-President Charles De Gaulle that *La politique de la France ne se fait pas à la corbeille* ('The stock market does not dictate French policy'). There would be nothing surprising about this anti-market statement except for the fact that De Gaulle was a democratic conservative who defined himself in opposition to communism. In the European tradition, opposition to laissez-faire economics has deep roots.

European attachment to state-driven solutions faded somewhat in the 1990s and 2000s, with some analysts blaming the region's generous welfare systems for the relative under-performance of its economies ('Euro-sclerosis'). Evidence of newfound interest in market mechanisms appeared not just in Eastern European transition countries rejecting their communist past but also in Western social democracies like Germany, France, the Netherlands, and Sweden, where parties calling for less state interventionism won several elections over the period 2005–7.

It remains to be seen whether this trend will survive the 2008 credit crunch, widely attributed in Europe (as elsewhere) to insufficient government regulation of the banking sector. Certainly, January 2009 riots in Greece, Italy, France, and elsewhere demonstrate that Europeans still tend to look to the state when things go bad.

Thinking point

How will the 2009 recession affect the spread of neo-liberal convictions?

Photo 5.1
The international business environment changed dramatically when the Berlin Wall came down in 1989 (© iStockphoto).

Globalization as a factor that has undermined state power

Trade and FDI are widely viewed as important wealth drivers in today's increasingly globalized world. Politicians are acutely aware that getting MNEs to trade and invest in their country helps to create jobs and enhance economic prosperity, thereby improving their chances of re-election. Thus, in so far as governments are forced to compete with one another to attract MNEs, and since companies tend to prefer deregulated environments, there is a strong argument that free-market globalization itself has been a factor in undermining state power.

Clearly, MNEs' willingness to do business in a country depends on more than the regime's political philosophy alone. Companies are understandably most attracted to dynamic, fast-growing markets, even when these are located in interventionist states like China. Conversely, large and/or wealthy countries are in a better position to drive a hard bargain with potential foreign investors. A fuller analysis of this aspect of state–company relations features in Chapter 7's discussion on international 'lobbying'.

The aspects of modern globalization that have tended to erode state power include the way technology has brought about a greater decentralization of power; the fact that companies are more mobile than governments; the rise of alternative forms of governance; and the power invested in the global financial markets. It is worth remembering, however, that none of these factors will remain constant over time. Much like international business itself, state power varies in time and place.

Technology

Advances in telecommunications enable individuals to 'act on the world stage directly— unmediated by a state' (Friedman 2000: 14). Among other effects, the democratization of information via the Internet has empowered consumers to shop across borders. This weakens the position of national producers, who are no longer free to determine their prices based on local market conditions alone. In turn, this contributes to the retreat of the state, since it is easier for governments to affect the behaviour of national industries with roots in the local economy than to control consumers who can spend their money abroad.

> **Thinking point**
> Does global consumerism undermine national sovereignty?

In addition, with the exception of state-funded research programmes, today it is private companies, and mainly large MNEs, that dominate the development of new technology (see Chapter 11). Understandably enough, companies will try to derive competitive advantage from the technologies they control. This often leads to a minimal diffusion of knowledge—a serious problem for LDCs whose national development trajectories are dependent on greater learning (Loveridge 2002). In a similar vein, where an MNE's technological capabilities exceed a government's ability to monitor its activities, it becomes very easy and therefore tempting for the company to try to hide its transactions from public scrutiny. This imbalance of power was particularly evident as the 2008 financial crisis unfolded.

MNE mobility

MNEs generally have an advantage over states since they are not bound to any particular territory and have a choice of locations where they can operate. As discussed in Chapter 3, MNEs that practise 'regime shopping' often play countries off against one another to get the best deal for themselves. For example, despite the negative effect on fiscal revenues, in 2007 Bulgaria came to the conclusion that the only way to attract much needed FDI was to cut corporation tax rates to a minuscule 10 per cent. The fear was that MNEs would otherwise move operations to nearby Slovakia or Lithuania, where tax rates were just as low. Of course, government attempts to attract companies through low tax rates can also be portrayed in a more positive light as 'regime competition'. There is nothing controversial, for instance, about national investment or marketing agencies advertising their country's charms. Such competition becomes problematic only when it breaches international agreements, like when EU member states try to attract FDI away from fellow members by watering down agreed European labour laws. An intermediate example is when countries offer mobile MNEs tax holidays, grants, and/or infrastructure investments. The common point in all these situations is that MNEs' mobility gives them a bargaining chip to use against national governments.

Global governance

For reasons that Chapter 6 will explore in further detail, most countries worldwide have joined regional associations and/or intergovernmental organizations (IGOs), all of which impose rules on member states. In some analysts' view, this trend has narrowed the scope of national policy-making and contributed to the 'retreat of the state' (Strange 1997). One of the main IGOs affecting international business is the WTO, whose purpose is to promote a free trade regime. One of the WTO's guiding principles is non-discrimination, or the idea that a country's trade policies should not benefit national producers to the detriment of fellow WTO members. This takes away sovereign states' traditional prerogative of being able to favour domestic interests. By joining the WTO, they accept that they will no longer have a monopoly over all domestic political economic decisions (see Online Resource Centre, extension material 5.2). In essence, this kind of structure means swapping a dominant role in a smaller framework (the nation-state) for a smaller role in a larger entity (the WTO). It is true that many states would like to have the best of both worlds, maintaining absolute sovereignty at home while having a greater say on the global stage. This tends to be easier for larger countries, which find it easier to dominate IGO proceedings. Such attitudes may be hypocritical, but they are unsurprising—international studies teach that most countries tend to use any and all means at their disposal to expand their sphere of influence. Indeed, one of the reasons behind the rise of IGOs was to restrict such behaviour.

> Go to the ORC

Finance

The gigantic sums traded in today's deregulated financial markets match and often exceed the funds available to national governments, whose ability to raise money is constrained by international tax competition—and by the fact that the countries with the greatest capital needs are often those with the lowest savings. Because of this imbalance between public and private wealth, states are often forced to cater to the 'electronic herd' of global investors who prefer to invest in those countries whose governments have accepted neo-liberalism's 'Golden Straitjacket' (Friedman 2000: 86–7)—whether or not such policies are suitable to local circumstances. The problem here is that countries pursuing domestically oriented policies may be out of tune with offshore investors' demands. For example, if a government tries to accelerate national growth through lower interest rates, international investors might decide to withdraw their money and invest it in another currency offering higher interest. In the worst-case scenario, this can cause capital flight and a currency crisis (see Chapter 13). The lesson is clear—in countries where the government depends on foreign sources of funding (as has increasingly been the case over the past twenty-five years of financial globalization), politicians cannot exercise power without taking investors' judgements into account.

+ **International tax competition**
Where a country tries to attract offshore funds by offering investors lower tax rates than they can find elsewhere.

+ **Financial globalization**
Deregulation of world capital markets and the associated acceleration in cross-border capital movements of funds.

The political domination of global finance has been aggravated by the concentration of capital in relatively few hands. In 2004, for instance, the world's 300 top pension funds owned up to 15.8 per cent of the 1,000 largest corporations (Monks 2005). This uneven distribution of power, along with the difficulties that national authorities face in monitoring and taxing capital held offshore, have long been criticized as the worst aspects of modern globalization's attack on the nation-state (see Online Resource Centre, extension material 5.3). By spring 2009, given the visible flaws in the world's existing financial system, a consensus began to grow among most if not all governments worldwide that the time had come to reassert control over the global markets. Whether or not politicians will succeed in this effort, what is clear for more and more people is that the trend towards reduced state power has already met its limits.

> Go to the ORC

Photo 5.2
Government policies are often under scrutiny from international financial markets (© iStockphoto).

Section III: The argument that states have retained power to affect international business

Many analysts argue that news of the death of the state is very premature. Three ideas are at work here: domestic frameworks remain crucial to economic activity; most people still feel emotionally attached to their country of origin; and states continue to operate as tools of international competition. Instead of viewing international business as being run entirely by de-territorialized global entities such as MNEs or IGOs, the view here is that independent and sovereign states still play a very significant role—as exemplified by massive interventions by governments everywhere in response to the crisis that began in 2008.

The continuing importance of domestic business

Notwithstanding the expansion of international business, the fact remains that 'all economic and financial activity, from production, R&D [research & development] to trading and consumption, occurs in geographical not virtual space' (Held and McGrew 2002: 42)—a space that is usually subject to the authority of a nation state. Governments continue to raise corporation and personal taxes, set macro-economic targets, operate welfare and educational programmes, invest in infrastructure, and determine immigration policies (El-Ojeili and Hayden 2006)—this last factor offering clear proof that the world is not entirely 'borderless', as some globalization enthusiasts would have it (Ohmae 2005). Moreover, despite talk about global companies, statistics show that most MNEs' primary operations are still in their home regions (see Chapter 9). When companies go abroad, they face a whole range of barriers to entry: foreign accounting rules and legal systems; a different language and culture. At home, on the other hand, they benefit from experience in managing their assets; tried and trusted supplier networks; superior knowledge of human resources; and, above all, brand loyalty. It should never be forgotten that, despite all its attractions, international business is a daunting prospect, and that many companies tend to be most comfortable dealing in their domestic market—an environment that is subject to the unrivalled authority of a national government.

> **Thinking point**
>
> To what extent can an economy ignore offshore interests?

Figure 5.5 shows international trade as a percentage of GDP in the world's leading economies. As discussed in Chapter 1, since the late 1980s the trend of this (imperfect) measurement has been upwards. Just as striking is the high proportion of GDP that continues to be realized on a purely domestic basis. The calculation is complicated, due to

Figure 5.5
Total 2006 trade in goods and services, in US$ billion and as percentage of gross domestic product (WTO 2007; IMF 2007; reprinted with the kind permission of the WTO and the IMF).

	Exports	Imports	Total trade goods/ services	GDP	Trade/GDP (%)
USA	1,038	1,919	2,957	13,245	22.4
Mexico	250	268	518	840	61.7
Brazil	138	96	234	1,068	21.9
France	490	535	1,025	2,232	45.9
Germany	1,112	909	2,021	2,897	69.8
Netherlands	462	416	878	663	132.4
UK	448	619	1,067	2,374	44.9
Russia	305	164	469	979	47.9
South Africa	58	77	135	255	52.9
India	120	175	295	887	33.6
China	969	792	1,761	2,630	70.0
Japan	650	580	1,230	4,367	28.2
Korea	326	309	635	888	71.5

> Go to the ORC

the fact that there is no obvious link between country size and international penetration. Also, the statistics do not reflect national differences in sectorial specialization, or the fact that some sectors (like the trade in medical products) lend themselves to cross-border operations, whereas others (like healthcare administration) are by definition organized on a more local basis. Still the statistics preceded the collapse in cross-border trade as a percentage of total economic activity following the 2008 credit crunch (see Online Resource Centre, extension material 1.1). At the very least, domestic business, conducted in a setting subject to the authority of a national government, continues to coexist with international business.

At a more personal level, despite the existence of a few 'cosmopolitan' citizens of the world, most people worldwide continue to live near where they were born, consuming domestically manufactured goods, investing their savings locally (Legrain 2003), and paying taxes to their national government. Indeed, for many economists, the best proof of the continued power of the nation state is the general rise in fiscal revenues in many countries. This is mainly in the industrialized world, however, not in LDCs, where inefficient tax collection systems mean that state power tends to be embodied in tighter regulations. Figure 5.6 measures the tax burden in selected OECD member states as the ratio of fiscal revenues to total GDP. The point here is that, if the state's role in a national economy had diminished, this ratio could be expected to fall.

In actual fact, tax burdens have risen everywhere since 1975—which more or less coincides with the beginning of the era that was supposed to feature the rebirth of small state neo-liberalism. Tax levels fell in a few countries after 2000, but, rather than confirming a loss of state power, this could also be analysed as little more than a modernization of the way in which states intervene (Hibou 2004). In reaction to criticisms of government bureaucracy, nowadays more and more state functions are subcontracted to private intermediaries. States continue to set the framework for such activities. Indirect governance does not mean less governance.

Lastly, it is worth nothing how some politicians blame globalization for unpopular policies they may have to announce, like freezes on wage hikes. In so far as globalization serves as an excuse protecting the politicians in question from criticism, it has the effect of increasing their power (Gritsch 2005).

	1975	1985	1995	2000	2004/5
Mexico	–	17.0	16.7	18.5	19.8
USA	25.6	25.6	27.9	29.9	26.8
Japan	20.9	27.4	26.9	27.1	26.4
Korea	15.1	16.4	19.4	23.6	25.6
France	35.5	42.4	42.9	44.4	44.3
Germany	35.3	37.2	37.2	37.4	34.7
Turkey	16.0	15.4	22.6	32.3	32.3
UK	35.3	37.7	35.0	37.2	37.2
OECD total	29.7	32.9	35.1	36.6	35.9

Figure 5.6
Total tax revenues as a percentage of GDP (OECD 2008: 19; reprinted with the kind permission of the OECD).

Economic patriotism

The resurgence of economic patriotism is the clearest sign of the 'reluctance of people to be ruled by politicians and bureaucrats from the other side of the world, over whom they have no democratic or other control' (Friedman 2000: 205). The fact that there are so many examples of this attitude, at a time when globalized thinking is supposed to be so dominant, indicates how premature it is to talk about the geography no longer being important (Bauman 1998). Borders still count in this world.

Recent cases of economic patriotism include:

+ **Economic patriotism**
Idea that a society might show loyalty to domestic firms by purchasing their products and/or preventing foreign ownership.

- *2005*. The French government lists fourteen 'strategic' sectors in which foreign interests are not allowed to take a majority stake. Not only was the Italian energy company ENEL prevented from taking over the French consortium Suez (only a few years after France's public-sector utilities firm EDF had acquired Montedison, a private sector Italian company) but Pepsico, the American soft drinks maker, was also deterred from acquiring the Danone drinks company.

- *2006*. The American government prevents British firm P&O from selling its six ports in the USA to the Dubai-based company Ports World because of generally negative sentiments locally towards Middle Eastern countries at a time of international tension.

- *2007*. The Spanish government keeps EON, a German energy firm, from acquiring Endesa, a local energy provider—even though Germany is a fellow EU member state.

- *2008*. The Russian government places unusual pressure on BP's joint venture with local oil firm TNK, visibly to reassert national control over a strategic sector (Wachman 2008).

- *2008*. In Italy, Silvio Berlusconi's supposedly neo-liberal administration fights to keep foreign companies from taking over troubled airliner Alitalia.

- *2009*. Renault shifts production from Slovenia back to France after receiving loans from the French government to help it survive the financial crisis.

Economic patriotism is sometimes confused with the discretionary application of state power for strategic purposes. One example is the Chinese government's continued use of FDI regulations (see Chapter 8) to restrict foreign ownership of domestic banks. This assertion of national sovereignty was mirrored in the US government's opposition in 2005 to efforts by the Chinese National Offshore Oil Corporation to acquire a stake in California energy company Unocal. Note that, just two years later, the Bush administration reacted to the eruption of the credit crunch by letting Middle Eastern investment funds take an equity stake in US banking giant Citigroup. Governments may say they favour a policy of economic patriotism, but when it is in their national interest to deal with foreign interests, they will do so. In international business, patriotism is a multi-layered concept and variable.

The argument against economic patriotism is that it constitutes, in the words of a recent British politician, a return to outright 'protectionism' (Giles et al. 2007), and is therefore a grave danger to a world that has benefited greatly from free trade. Some commentators view economic patriotism as a new form of mercantilism—the old trade theory that Adam Smith and his classical successors worked so hard to discredit (see Chapter 4). In the UK, for instance, there is general acceptance of the fact that foreign interests run many if not most national industries, even though this has turned the country into a kind of 'aircraft carrier' (Gribben 2007). The term commonly used for this process is 'Wimbledonization', in reference to the tennis tournament that the British host but (almost) never win. This rejection of narrowly patriotic reasoning is exemplified by the decision that Barclays Bank took at the time of the 2008 financial crisis to refuse the UK government's offer of additional capital and opt for funding from Middle East sovereign wealth funds. At the same time, another British institution, the Royal Bank of Scotland, took the opposing view and submitted to the authority of the national government (in exchange for desperately needed capital). What is significant is that British analysts discussed these decisions solely in terms of whether the two banks could afford to reject state funding and avoid public ownership. At no point did either institution's 'patriotism' come into question.

Advocates of an economic-patriotism approach tend to stress, on the other hand, that foreign shareholders lacking personal ties to a country are likely to be less sensitive to local populations' needs (jobs, reinvestment of profits) or domestic politicians' social influence (Matelly and Nies 2006). There was an outcry in January 2009, for instance, when the foreign owner of a refinery located in the English county of Lincolnshire tried to bring relatively cheaper Italian and Portuguese labourers to the UK at a time of rising domestic unemployment. Like all theories, internationalism has its limitations. Even the most hardened internationalists would accept that governments have a duty to protect certain national interests. US authorities generally argue against protectionism but fund American space, military, and energy research projects in which US companies alone can participate. Japanese governments support open international markets as a matter of general policy but fight to ensure food autonomy by protecting domestic rice farmers. A nation state can accept certain aspects of global deregulation without abandoning all of its powers to protect domestic constituents.

Thinking point

What difference, if any, is there between economic patriotism and mercantilism?

Case Study 5.2

States and their protective role: *Vive la différence*

France's reputation as a protectionist country is not statistically accurate: 'foreign ownership of French firms rose from 15 per cent in the early 1990s to an estimated 35 per cent by 2006, one of the highest percentages in the world; and by 2004, one-seventh of all French workers were employed by foreign-owned firms, a higher proportion than in Germany or the UK' (Dietsch 2006). Moreover, an increasing number of French companies have actively developed or acquired of foreign subsidiaries. Many French people would not agree with the perception that theirs is a particularly chauvinistic society.

Yet this reputation exists and is not entirely without justification. French voices have long taken exception to 'turbo globalization', accusing the global trading

European farmers demanding better market conditions (European Community).

regime, with its neo-liberal agenda, of being a secret US attempt to advance American interests. It is this attitude that drove Culture Minister Jack Lang in the early 1990s successfully to negotiate a 'cultural exception' (*exception culturelle*) regime that exempted French cinema, music, and TV production from normal WTO restrictions on state support (see Figure 5.7). A similar logic was at work in 2000, when the French state brokered a merger between two domestic banks (BNP and Paribas) at a time when most other mergers in this sector were between international partners. There is also France's continued unwillingness, despite its policy objective of aiding the developing world, to permit any significant reform of the EU's Common Agricultural Policy, which subsidizes French farmers but is a huge burden on the EU budget. Lastly, some politicians (like Bernard Carayon, a conservative member of France's National Assembly) have built an entire media career around economic patriotism, spreading the idea that economics is a war that governments must wage on constituents' behalf. In this view, it is legitimate for states to adopt any means necessary to advance national economic interests, whether this means bending international trade rules or

engaging in acts of 'economic intelligence' (industrial espionage). This is very distant from classical economists' idea that everyone wins from trade.

In sum, France is full of contradictions. On one hand, many international business sectors feature French companies among their global leaders. On the other, this is a society where a farmer named Jose Bové could blow up a McDonald's restaurant to symbolize his rejection of an American lifestyle yet remain a popular presidential candidate. French attitudes towards the state's role in a globalized world are much more complicated than is commonly understood—xenophobic political parties receive more support than in most other EU countries yet France remains a leading contributor to the European construction process. The French are often accused of 'nationalism'—but it is unclear how this differs from the economic 'patriotism' found in many countries worldwide. It also seems inconsistent to blame France for protecting its farmers at a time when environmentalists are arguing that people should be eat more locally produced food. It is usually a good idea, before criticizing someone else's political ideologies, to look objectively at one's own biases.

Domain	*Exception culturelle* policies
Radio	At least 40 per cent of all songs played must be French in origin
TV	At least 45 per cent of all programmes broadcast must be French in origin
Cinema	Revenues from tax levied on cinema tickets are used to fund domestic productions
Language	French language utilization requirements

Figure 5.7
How the French state protects domestic cultural industries from international competition.

States as tools of international competition

Rather than analysing the rise of IGOs and regional associations as a sign of declining state power, some analysts argue that the shift from traditional bilateral forums (where one state deals directly with another) to multilateral negotiations has actually increased the bargaining power of some governments (Kelly and Grant 2005). This includes small and medium-sized states whose voice is amplified due to their membership in large organizations (for example, Luxembourg in the EU) but also to big countries like the USA, often accused of using international organizations to advance a free trade agenda described as a 'Trojan horse' for American interests (Mathews 2005). When small and/or poor countries are locked in a one-on-one trade dispute with a superpower, they face a disproportionate threat of retaliation, since they are likely to suffer more from a trade war than their counterpart. Conversely, smaller states that join an international organization will be able to leverage this membership to improve their negotiating position. This is one reason why so many LDCs remain members of the WTO, despite receiving what some call an unfair deal from the organization.

Many international negotiations pitting industrialized against developing countries offer forums where nation-states have a chance to exercise power. For OECD country governments, the goal is often to protect domestic producers from relatively cheaper LDC rivals. A prime example is the way that the USA and the EU both subsidize local farmers in a clear breach of the rules of free trade. A similar analysis might be made of the Trade Related Aspects of Intellectual Property Rights (TRIPS) protection agenda for intellectual property rights that the world's wealthier nation-states have tried to push through the WTO. Some describe this agenda as a blatant attempt to protect Western pharmaceutical MNEs' advance over new Indian or Brazilian rivals producing generic substitutes at very competitive prices (Papaioannou 2006). Conversely, LDC states often use international forums as defensive shields, arguing that their countries should be partially exempted from certain aspects of the OECD countries' incessant drive towards greater market liberalization—and justifying this by the way that advanced nations themselves used

+ Intellectual property rights
Exclusive enjoyment of the benefits derived from intangible assets such as trademarks, patents, and copyrights.

Inside business

John Hughes, Former UK diplomat, Ambassador to Argentina (2004–08) and Venezuela (2000–03)

(speaking in a personal capacity)

Historically within the Foreign and Commonwealth Office (FCO) there has been a division between departments dealing with bilateral issues versus those dealing with multilateral/functional ones. The FCO understands full well, however, that many issues are transnational.

This is true for embassies as well. Working in the bilateral section of the British Embassy in Norway, I spent much time dealing with the multilateral issue of Conventional Forces in Europe. In our Embassy in Chile (during the Pinochet regime), I worked on universal human rights.

The FCO and UK Trade and Investment (UKTI) fully recognize the importance of business in the modern world. For SMEs, embassies often provide market sector reports designed to help them decide whether there is a likely market for their goods or services in a particular country. Large British companies do not need that; they are usually in the market themselves. For them the Ambassador provides insights into the 'political realities' of the country and offers assistance in getting access or messages across to key local decision-makers.

In my view, the 'role of the state' is not fixed. It changes over time. During the 1990s, many countries argued in favour of the retreat of the state—sometimes referred to as the Washington Consensus. In the face of the world credit crunch, some of the states which advocated that have given aid to big business in a way that would have seemed inconceivable previously.

The vision of the role of the state can also differ between regions of the world. There were many countries in Latin America that rejected the Washington Consensus theory long before the credit crunch.

Almost universal access to communications is a key characteristic of our globalized world. Prejudicial action by a state or company in one part of the world reverberates everywhere. In part because this is the actors on the world stage are not just states and companies; non-governmental organizations using modern communications techniques are also important in this particular context. In cultural terms also, state borders are no longer the barriers they once were; interest in sport and music is now truly international.

Does this mean that we are moving to a borderless world? Is the nation state withering away? I doubt it.

Even in our increasingly globalized world, governance tends to be based in the nation-state. There are examples, such as the European Union with its twenty-seven member states, deciding to 'pool or share sovereignty' on some issues. There is also a trend towards more trading blocs. And many issues can be dealt with only internationally. Still, in most cases the nation-state remains the essential unit of international relations. It will continue to evolve over time, but it is by no means certain that we will see a truly borderless world.

protectionist approaches at the beginning of their own development trajectories (see Online Resource Centre, extension material 5.4). Examples of this defensive use of state power include Malaysian and Chinese governmental policies that have insulated the two countries' domestic markets from international currency speculators, controlling exchange rates to ensure stability and/or national competitiveness. Other LDC states, such as Singapore and South Korea, are more proactive, pursuing a course of 'guided capitalism' that includes targeted help for certain strategic export industries (Gilpin 2001). Note that it is no coincidence that these examples of competitive state practices all involve Asian countries. Relations between the public and private sectors tend to be less adversarial in this part of the world than they are in the West. The lesson here is that an active and/or powerful state is not necessarily incompatible with a country's pursuit of a market orientation. The example of Japan Incorporated, where many if not most of the country's industries have come together under government coordination to create an export powerhouse, attests to the role that states can play in enhancing national competitiveness.

> Go to the ORC

Thinking point
Are strong global markets necessarily based on weak nation-states?

Last but not least, the most extreme example of states becoming a tool of international competition is 'state capitalism' (Lyons 2007). The two main actors in this category are state-owned enterprises and 'sovereign wealth funds', or government-run pools of national currency reserves seeking to acquire assets worldwide (see Chapter 14). There is nothing new about such funds, but their recent expansion is noteworthy. In 2007, for instance, China launched a fund worth upwards of $300 billion, investing not only in blue chip stocks globally but also (and more controversially) in the African energy sector and US private equity group Blackstone. States in the Arabian Gulf earn trillions of petrodollars from oil production, money that they too are likely to invest in the international capital markets (de Boer et al. 2008). When governments wield such enormous sums, it is hard to argue that the state is in retreat.

	In developed countries	**In developing countries**
Proactive interventions	• Initiatives aimed at prying open LDC service sectors (e.g. 'GATS': see Chapter 6) • Procurement programmes sparking domestic R&D • Regime competition	• State capitalism: pooling of national funds • Industrialization policies: ascending the value chain • Relaxation of regulations
Defensive interventions	• Tariff/non-tariff barriers • Ownership restrictions • Agricultural subsidies	• Administrative obstacles • Performance requirements • WTO/Doha Round oppositions

Figure 5.8
How states affect the international business environment: wealthy and poor country objectives often diverge.

Challenges and choices

→ It can be very difficult for MNE executives to calculate how much leeway they have when negotiating with a host country. The answer largely depends on the extent to which their company needs the country or vice versa. If managers perceive the country as being crucial to their internationalization plans, they will tend to show greater flexibility. Inversely, where a particular location is of lesser importance to them, they might drive a harder bargain to try to get better market entry conditions. Note that this latter approach is often constrained by ethical considerations. It is bad for a company's reputation to be seen as bullying a host government, especially one representing a poor LDC.

→ A related challenge is the possibility that a 'friendly' host country government changes its approach and starts to make extra demands of an MNE that has already set up operations there. Several nation states that used to be dominated by MNEs have gained greatly in self-confidence since their economic emergence. If they resent the way MNEs used to treat them, there is every chance that they will try to get some revenge. A significant political risk exists in many parts of the world.

Chapter Summary

Globalization, neo-liberalism, and MNEs' rising power have all affected state power, but it would be wrong to conclude that states no longer matter. After all, they remain the entities that exercise the most direct control over national territories and populations. A more accurate analysis is that modern politics involve a 'new sovereignty … [one where] nation-states are simply one class of powers and political agencies in a complex system of power from world to local levels' (Hirst and Thompson 1999: 16, 276). As the chapter's first section demonstrated, states still have many reasons to intervene in international business, as well as tools enabling them to do so. Whether they ultimately decide to act depends on different factors: the dominant political economic paradigm at a given moment in time; the extent to which this paradigm has spread; and each country's specific set of circumstances.

The chapter's second and third sections were concerned with the question of whether states have lost their power to affect trade and FDI. After reviewing arguments that some aspects of modern globalization—such as global governance, technology, and deregulated finance—have weakened the nation state, the counter-argument was presented, suggesting that governments still retain significant power. This is based on the continued importance of domestic business, the rise of economic patriotism, and the importance of state power as an instrument of international competition.

The world is growing smaller by the day, so there is little question that state power must increasingly be negotiated outside a country's national borders. 'Enmeshed within horizontal and vertical networks of multiple supra-state, sub-state and non-state actors' (El-Ojeili and Hayden 2006: 97), modern states are not the only actors on the world stage. Chapters 6 and 7 will look at two other categories.

Case Study 5.3

States and industrial support: Cotton candy for Texas farmers

In 2004, an economist named Pietra Rivoli (2006) travelled across the world following the path taken by a T-shirt that she had just bought. Expecting to find proof of rising market power, what she discovered instead was a value chain driven by political and historical factors, where the most successful actors were people who had actually avoided market risks such as price instability and competition. Her story, and specifically her time in the USA, shows the ongoing importance of the state in international business.

Dr Rivoli's initial visit was to the Reinsch family cotton farm in Smyer, Texas. Having analysed that national economic advantages always vary over time, she wondered why American cotton-growers have been successful for so long. Her conclusion was that this dominance largely derives from their ability to get the US government to help them, mainly through subsidies that provide protection from adverse price movements and help farmers to purchase modern equipment. The amounts that the US government distributes to domestic farmers not only contradict its commitment to the WTO's free trade philosophy but exceed the total income of US cotton-growers' competitors from the developing world. In other words, because of this state intervention, American and non-American cotton-growers are in no way operating on a level playing field.

Dr Rivoli also noted that the US government's support for domestic growers restricts American textiles manufacturers' access to cheap foreign cotton. In most countries, a processing industry suffering higher input costs due to this system of domestic preferences would lobby the national government to let in cheaper imports. The US government is wealthy enough, however, to pay subsidies can be paid to cotton-growers and purchasers alike. This kind of action is feasible only in countries with sufficient budgetary resources.

Government influence over the cotton sector goes beyond direct financial aid. One of cotton farmers' main problems is their difficulty in finding cheap labour willing to endure long hours of back-breaking toil, usually under a burning sun. Historically, workers would shun cotton-picking if they had other possibilities, meaning that by harvest time growers are often short of field hands. To complicate matters further, because the cotton harvest is vulnerable to climate conditions (the crop cannot be picked in the rain), it is hard to predict exactly when workers are needed. Growers therefore run the risk of paying a workforce to sit around idly waiting for better weather.

The US government has intervened in the labour market on many occasions to help domestic cotton farmers overcome these labour problems. The first (despicable) intervention was the enslavement of black workers, from the seventeenth century, when the cotton trade was first launched in this part of the world, until the American Civil War was won in 1865. The prohibition of slavery should have created free labour movements, but it is precisely this kind of market uncertainty that farmers feared. Hence the introduction of a new category of workers: 'sharecroppers' tied to a cotton plantation by the fact that they were paid in housing and food instead of cash. The life of a sharecropper was extremely hard, and social reformers campaigned for decades to outlaw this practice. Farmers, correctly guessing that their badly exploited workers would flee the cotton fields if alternatives became available, repeatedly and successfully lobbied governments in the late nineteenth and early twentieth centuries to deny basic worker rights. It was not until the 1933 Agricultural Adjustment Act that the US federal government finally committed itself to recognize sharecroppers' right to seek employment freely.

Just a few years later, however, the US government was again intervening to protect cotton farmers from free-market volatility. In 1942, Congress organized a 'Bracero' programme allowing Mexican workers into the USA to offset the loss of manpower during the Second World War. To keep farmers from bidding up the new workers' services (and increasing labour costs), the government determined that the Mexicans could work for only one employer and would be prevented from leaving whichever farmer had originally hired them, even if another offered better pay. Once again, America's cotton farmers had sought their salvation in government intervention instead of free market mechanisms.

Dr Rivoli's remarkable study also highlighted interventions by the Chinese government, while demonstrating that poor African governments cannot afford to offer anything equivalent. Noting that slavery-like 'indentured' labour systems have operated in many countries other than the USA (for example, India) without producing the same outcomes, she deduced that the Reinsch family's ongoing success stems not only from the support that American cotton farmers have historically received from the US government but also from their entrepreneurial spirit, competency, and willingness to integrate new knowledge. Yet even

Texas cotton farmers' technological strengths have been built on government support. For instance, the Reinsch family farm is located in the vicinity of an excellent R&D facility that is partially state-funded. Former US President George W. Bush, ex-governor of Texas and once a neighbour of the family, used to preach a minimal role for the state in his speeches. The reality is that governments have always played an active part in the American economy. Interventionists may be the only parties to openly support a strong state—but they are not the only ones trying to benefit from it.

Case study questions

1. How do US government subsidies affect the different actors in the world cotton markets?
2. To what extent has government labour policy shaped US cotton production?
3. What arguments might LDC cotton competitors use when negotiating with US trade representatives?

Whereas US farmers can afford advanced cotton-picking technology, their LDC rivals often have no choice but to resort to child labour, a practice vigorously denounced by IGOs like the International Labour Organization (© International Labour Organization).

Discussion questions

1. Is the rising power of international business a good or bad thing for democracy?
2. Advocating united global action to combat the credit crunch, a British prime minister once painted a picture of a 'world without countries' (*Guardian* 2009). Is this an attractive or realistic prospect?
3. To what extent should, and can, a political economic system that succeeds in one country become a model for another?
4. Buckman (2004) has alleged that globalization is similar to communism in so far as it concentrates power in fewer hands. Is this a reasonable assertion?
5. Which sectors of business activity might national governments find easier or less easy to control? Why?

References

Anderlini, J. (2009). 'Beijing in Call to Boost State Sector', *Financial Times*, 4 Mar., p. 4.

Bauman, Z. (1998). *Globalization: The Human Consequences*. New York: Columbia University Press.

Bogdanich, W., and Hooker, J. (2007). 'The Poisoning of Chinese Trade: From China to Panama, a Trail of Toxic Medicines', 13 May, www.iht.com (accessed 12 Dec. 2007).

Buckman, G. (2004). *Globalization: Tame it or Scrap it* (London: Zed Books).

Chaffin, J., and Tighe, C. (2009). 'EU Slaps Tariffs on US Biodiesel', *Financial Times*, 4 Mar., p. 8.

Davies, H. (2009). 'French Lessons on the State's New Role', *Financial Times*, 4 Mar., p. 15.

de Boer, K., Farrell, D., and Lund, S. (2008). 'Investing the Gulf's Oil Profits Windfall', May, www.mckinseyquarterly.com (accessed 3 July 2008).

Dietsch, M. (2006). 'Mondialisation et recomposition du capital des enterprises européennes', *La Revue internationale et stratégique*, 62 (Paris: Dalloz).

El-Ojeili, C., and Hayden, P. (2006). *Critical Theories of Globalization*. Basingstoke: Palgrave Macmillan.

Friedman, T. (2000). *The Lexus and the Olive Tree*. New York: Anchor Books.

Fukuyama, F. (1993). *The End of History and the Last Man*. New York: Harper Perennial.

Giles, C., Blitz, J. and Barber, L. (2007). 'Darling Rules out Private Equity Clampdown', 3 July, www.ft.com (accessed 12 Dec. 2007).

Gilpin, R. (2001). *Global Political Economy: Understanding the International Economic Order*. Princeton: Princeton University Press.

Gribben, R. (2007). 'Britain Struggles to Take on the Foreign Invaders', 16 Feb., www.telegraph.co.uk (accessed 14 Dec. 2007).

Gritsch, M. (2005). 'The Nation-State and Economic Globalization: Soft Geo-Politics and Increased State Autonomy', *Review of International Political Economy*, 12/1.

Guardian (2009). 'Globalization: Parallel Worlds', *Guardian*, 31 Jan., p. 34.

Held, D., and McGrew, A. (2002). *Globalization/Anti-Globalization*. Cambridge: Polity Press.

Hibou, B. (2004). *Privatising the State*. London: Hurst and Company.

Hirst, P., and Thompson, G. (1999). *Globalization in Question*. Cambridge: Polity Press.

Hoekman, B., and Kostecki, M. (2001). *The Political Economy of the World Trading System*. 2nd edn. New York: Oxford University Press.

IMF (2007). '*World Economic Outlook Database*', Apr., www.imf.org (accessed 11 Mar. 2009).

Kelly, D., and Grant, W. (2005). 'Introduction: Trade Politics in Context', in Kelly and Grant (eds.), *The Politics of International Trade in the Twenty-First Century: Actors, Issues and Regional Dynamics*. Basingstoke: Palgrave Macmillan.

Lal, D. (2003). 'Free Trade and Laissez Faire: Has the Wheel Come Full Circle', www.econ.ucla.edu (accessed 17 Oct. 2008).

Legrain, P. (2003). *Open World: The Truth about Globalization*. London: Abacus.

Loveridge, R. (2002). 'Incorporating the Multinational: Socio-Technical Interfaces between the MNC Affiliate and the Host Country', *Asian Business and Management*, 1/2 (Aug.).

Lyons, G. (2007). 'How State Capitalism Could Change the World', 8 June, www.ft.com (accessed 12 Dec. 2007).

Marcin, K. (March 2008). 'How does FDI Inflow Affect Productivity of Domestic Firms? The Role of Horizontal and Vertical Spillovers, Absorptive Capacity and Competition', *Journal of International Trade and Economic Development*, 17/1 (Mar.).

Matelly, S., and Nies, S. (2006) (eds.). 'La Nationalité des enterprises en Europe', *La Revue internationale et stratégique*, Paris: Dalloz.

Mathews, R. (2005). 'Free Trade and an Emerging Revolutionary Planet', 8 Oct., www.vivelecanada.ca (accessed 14 Dec. 2007).

Monks, R. (2005). 'Governing the Multinational Enterprise: The Emergence of the Global Shareowner', in A. Chandler and B. Mazlish (eds.), *Leviathans: Multinational Corporations and the New Global History*. Cambridge: Cambridge University Press.

OECD (2007). Organization for Economic Cooperation and Development, 'Total Tax Revenue as Percentage of GDP', www.oecd.org (accessed 17 July 2007).

OECD (2008). *Revenue Statistics 1965–2007*. Paris: OECD.

Ohmae, K. (2005). *The Next Global Stage: The Challenges and Opportunities in Our Borderless World*. Upper Saddle River, NJ: Wharton School Publishing.

Ong, A. (2006). *Neoliberalism as Exception: Mutations in Citizenship and Sovereignty*. Durham, NC: Duke University Press.

Papaioannou, T. (2006). Towards a Critique of the Moral Foundations of Intellectual Property Rights, *Journal of Global Ethics*, 2/1 (June).

Perkins, J. (2004). *Confessions of an Economic Hit Man*. San Francisco: Berrett Koehler Publishers.

Rivoli, P. (2006). *The Travels of a Shirt in the Global Economy*. Hoboken, NJ: John Wiley and Son.

Schfer, D., and Milne, R. (2009). BMW Chief Warns against State Aid for Ailing Producers, *Financial Times*, 4 Mar., p. 25.

Strange, S. (1997). *The Retreat of the State: The Diffusion of Power in the World Economy*. Cambridge: Cambridge University Press.

Tobar, H. (2008). Mexican Farmers Protest NAFTA, *Los Angeles Times*, 3 Jan.

WTO (2007). World Trade Organization, 'Share of Goods and Commercial Services in the Total Trade of Selected Regions and Economies, 2005', www.wto.org (accessed 11 Mar. 2009).

Wachman, R. (2008). 'Kremlin Leaves BP Shaken, but it Wont Stir', *Observer*, Business and Media section, 8 June, p. 7.

Williamson, J. (2002). 'What Washington Means by Policy Reform', www.iie.com (accessed 17 July 2008).

Wolf, M. (2004). *Why Globalization Works*. London: Yale University Press.

Wolf, M. (2009). 'To Nationalise or not is the Question', *Financial Times*, 4 Mar., p. 15.

Woods, N. (2004). 'Order, Globalization and Inequality', in D. Held and A. McGrew (eds.), *The Global Transformations Reader: An Introduction to the Globalization Debate*. Cambridge: Polity.

Further research

Castells, M., et al. (2006). *Mobile Communication and Society: A Global Perspective*. Cambridge, MA: MIT Press.

In a series of texts that began with *The Rise of the Network Society* in 2000 and continued through the above publication, Professor Manuel Castells has tried to show how information is replacing energy as the main driver of economic productivity. In this vision, geographic proximity is less important than it used to be, with communications technologies like the Internet decentralizing operations even as global control becomes increasingly centralized. The end effect is that people now live in a world where network arrangements are much more effective and powerful than traditional hierarchies. The implications for the authority of geographically bound nation-states are significant.

For Professor Castells, a good example of network power exerted on a global scale is financial capitalism. Similarly, the rise of networks also explains why an increasing number of MNEs have started to organize their units on a project basis. The ability of economic actors (MNEs, SMEs, individuals, governments, or any other organization) to participate in a network is determined by their ability to contribute to its goals. The new international environment requires skilled flexible workers and is largely defined by their inclusion in (or exclusion from) networks. For people participating in networks, state power *per se* is no longer a prime concern. At the same time, people at the bottom of society with nothing to offer the network and who are therefore most likely to be excluded from it necessarily remain very reliant on the state.

Online Resource Centre

Visit the Online Resource Centre that accompanies this book to read more information relating to states in international business: www.oxfordtextbooks.co.uk/orc/sitkin_bowen/

6 Actors in International Business: Global Governance

Overview

The chapter starts with a discussion of today's leading international organizations (IOs) with global governance responsibilities. The first section covers multi-purpose organizations that try to replicate, internationally, certain functions that nation-states fulfil domestically. This includes the United Nations (UN) and bodies referred to here as regional agreements (RAs). The second section focuses on the three Bretton Woods intergovernmental organizations (IGOs) that are so important to modern international business, first and foremost the World Trade Organization (WTO) but also the World Bank and the International Monetary Fund. The chapter's final section covers single-purpose IGOs, including specialist governance bodies and non-governmental organizations (NGOs).

Section I: Multi-purpose international organizations
    United Nations
    Regional agreements
    G8/G20

Section II: The Bretton Woods organizations
    The World Trade Organization
    The World Bank and the International Monetary Fund

Section III: Single-purpose IGOs
    Specialist organizations
    Non-governmental organizations

Learning Objectives

After reading this chapter, you will be able to:

✦ explain the need for global governance

✦ identify obstacles to international compromise

✦ compare degrees of regional integration

✦ critique the Bretton Woods IGOs' methods and aims

✦ judge the validity of NGOs' world views

Case Study 6.1

Global governance and regional bodies: Polish plumbers

In its biggest enlargement move ever, the European Union (EU) accepted ten new members in 2004, mostly from the Continent's ex-communist East. The path followed by these countries since the Second World War had failed to afford them the standard of living that their Western neighbours enjoyed. Their hope was that joining the EU would help them to catch up. What was less certain was how this integration would affect the older EU states.

The prospect of tens of thousands of young East European immigrants sparked an emotional debate in the West. The French prime minister expressed concern that the EU's proposed Bolkestein Directive, which would have let foreigners operate under their home countries' less stringent labour laws, might put host country workers and contractors at a disadvantage. In France, commentators stoked fears that hordes of 'Polish plumbers' would take up to one million French jobs and undermine the country's long-standing social model, characterized by its generous but expensive welfare system. A media panic erupted, leading in May 2005 to French rejection of a constitutional referendum aimed at modernizing EU operating procedures. The vote was a defeat for European integration and Bolkestein was quietly sidelined.

Organizational enlargement is a difficult process requiring major efforts to satisfy existing members' concerns. In summer 2005, the Polish government sponsored humorous advertisements showing a handsome plumber inviting people to visit Poland. The point was to remind French society that it too might benefit from the new EU members. The situation gradually calmed down, especially once it became clear that mass migration to France was not going to take place. Between May and November 2006, French authorities received a mere 10,165 residency requests from Eastern bloc workers. This was much lower than expected and reflected developments keeping Polish workers at home, like the country's growing role as an outsourcing destination for many multinational banks' administrative operations. There is every chance that initial fears will disappear altogether as Poland continues to develop—especially if many Poles end up returning home in the wake of the 2008–9 recession. This is not the first time that a new accession state has met with hostility, one example being the way that French farmers used to destroy trucks carrying produce from Spain when the country first joined the EU. Today Spanish imports to France no longer encounter any resistance. In the not so distant future, the same should apply to Polish plumbers.

Advertising Poland to the French: a good plumber is hard to find (© ONT Poland).

Introduction

Thinking point

Why was the EU's Eastern enlargement a controversial event?

International organizations (IOs) are created by their members, often nation-states, as debate forums and/or bodies for implementing joint actions in areas of common interest. Growing awareness that many contemporary problems (including security, development, environment, trade, and cross-border investment) cannot be solved by nations working separately means that strong support exists for organizations endowed with cross-border responsibilities. The sum total of the work done by these bodies is called global governance.

When an IO is born, it is given a charter specifying its mission. This can involve a number of functions (Diehl 2005):

+ **Global governance**
Regulatory and supervisory functions fulfilled by authorities whose responsibilities exceed national borders.

- supervising and enforcing an ideological vision (for example, the WTO and free trade);
- setting norms (for example, UN environmental standards);
- protecting members' interests (for example, the EU Common Agricultural Policy);
- coordinating national actions (for example, the G8).

Countries hope that an IO can achieve multilateral agreements more transparently and inexpensively than they can themselves in one-to-one negotiations. Theoretically, the cross-border nature of an IO means that it is better placed than a nation-state to promote international values and regulations, and punish violations. This is not always the case in reality.

Bureaucrats working for IOs generally have some freedom to interpret their missions as they see fit. This often results in a situation where an organization's sense of purpose shifts, in a process that sociologists call 'mission creep' (Barnett and Finnemore 2004). Not only do members' intentions change but IO officials start making independent decisions based on whatever knowledge they have accumulated and the rules and values that the IO itself has developed. As the organization evolves, it retains legitimacy only if enough members approve the new direction it is taking. Some would argue that having so many IOs, with each focused on its own concerns, is an ineffective way of dealing with today's enormous global governance problems (Boughton and Bradford 2007).

+ **Intergovernmental organizations (IGOs)**
International bodies created by nation-states to deal with cross-border issues, often for coordination purposes.

Strictly speaking, IOs are either supranational or intergovernmental in nature. In a supranational IO, power gets transferred to the organization itself, with officials making decisions on a majority basis and all members forced to comply. In an intergovernmental IO, decisions must be unanimous and cannot be forced on unwilling members. Common practice, however, is to refer to all bodies of international governance as intergovernmental organizations (IGOs) when members are states, or as non-governmental organizations (NGOs) when membership is comprised of civil society groups.

+ **Regime**
General system organizing interactions between different groups. The term often refers to a body of regulations and the institutions that formulate and enforce them.

Section I: Multi-purpose international organizations

For clarity's sake, the best way to analyse today's global governance regime is to distinguish between multi- and single-purpose IGOs. The main multi-purpose IGOs are the United Nations (UN) and regional agreements (RAs). These are international organizations that replicate, to a certain extent, nation-states' governance functions.

+ **Regional agreement (RA)**
Treaty between neighbouring nations to develop an institutional platform where issues of mutual interest can be discussed and decided.

United Nations

The United Nations (UN), together with its judicial wing (the International Court of Justice), is the closest thing that the world has to a global government. Every country

Photo 6.1
The UN: a forum for policy debate with few enforcement powers (UN Photo/Eskinder Debebe).

can send a representative to the UN, whose General Assembly acts as a sort of global parliament.

'The UN is famous for its Security Council, which focuses on political and military matters, but it is the UN's Economic and Social Council that has the most influence on international business. Alongside this, the UN also runs numerous autonomous agencies, including the Food and Agriculture Organization (FAO); the World Health Organization (WHO); the UN Educational, Scientific and Cultural Organization (UNESCO); and, above all, the International Labour Organization (ILO). According to its website, the ILO's main goals are to 'promote rights at work, encourage decent employment opportunities, enhance social protection and strengthen dialogue in handling work-related issues'. It tries to achieve this by organizing dialogue between governments, employers, and unions and by drafting and monitoring international labour standards. Like many UN agencies, however, the ILO's success at raising awareness through campaigns, publications, and training is restricted by its inability to enforce its recommendations.

The UN organizes conferences on many topics (see Figure 6.1). These forums exist more to decide international standards than to agree binding resolutions. A formal organization is often created to convince nation-states to comply with any standards set. One recurring event with

Africa	Education
Ageing	Elections
Agriculture	Energy
Aids	Environment
Atomic Energy	Family
Children	Food
Climate Change	Governance
Culture	Health
Decolonization	Human rights
De-mining	Human settlements
Development Cooperation	Humanitarian/disaster aid
Persons with/disabilities	Indigenous people
Disarmament	Information Technology
Drugs and crime	Intellectual property

Figure 6.1
Global issues on the UN agenda, October 2007 (www.un.org/issues).

Figure 6.1
(Continued)

International finance	Science and technology
Iraq	Social development
Labour	Outer space
International law	Statistics
Law of the Sea/Antarctica	Sustainable development
Less-developed countries	Terrorism
Millennium goals	Trade and development
Palestine	Volunteerism
Peace and security	Water
Population	Women
Refugees	Youth

special relevance to international business is the UN Conference on Trade and Development (UNCTAD), a forum and information centre that exists to 'promote the development-friendly integration of developing countries into the world economy' (UNCTAD 2009).

The UN is strongly supported by many nations and individuals who view it as a podium for constructive debate and appreciate its humanitarian values. Yet it has also come under criticism, in part because of its bureaucratic nature, but also because its admirably democratic culture often prevents effective decision-making. The question is whether the UN is too big to manage. This is one of the reasons why nation-states have had to seek global governance solutions at a closer level.

Thinking point

How effective is the UN?

Inside business

Ibrahim Gambari, Under-Secretary-General, United Nations
(speaking in a personal capacity)

Ibrahim Gambari is Under-Secretary-General and Special Adviser to the Secretary-General at the United Nations. He was previously Under-Secretary-General for Political Affairs (2005–7), Under-Secretary-General and Special Adviser on African Affairs (1999–2005), Permanent Representative of Nigeria to the United Nations (1990–9), and Foreign Minister of Nigeria (1984–5).

The United Nations (UN) is an international organization established in 1945 after the Second World War. Since 2006, it has been comprised of 192 member states and is committed to maintaining international peace and security, developing friendly relations among nations, and promoting social progress, better living standards, and human rights. Mr Gambari makes clear that the Secretary-General's responsibilities—and those of international civil servants like himself—are primarily to implement mandates enacted by the UN's legislative bodies—that is, the General Assembly and the Security Council. Where member states are unable to agree, there is 'room' for the Secretary-General to 'take initiatives' or 'to point the way in terms of the fundamental objectives of the Charter'.

Regarding the UN's impact on international companies, it has a positive influence in three ways: (1) agenda setting for international business, (2) encouraging a programme of private and public partnerships, and (3) establishing and promoting the Global Compact. The last of these is a strategic policy initiative for businesses committed to aligning their operations and strategies with ten universally accepted principles in the areas of human rights, labour, environment, and anti-corruption. By doing so, business, as a primary agent driving globalization, can help ensure that markets, commerce, technology, and finance advance in ways that benefit economies and societies everywhere. Companies adhere to Global Compact is by 'voluntary self-assessment'.

The UN attempts to work with international companies whose activities take place in areas of conflict. It encourages them to ensure that their business does 'not exacerbate existing conflicts'. The case of 'blood diamonds' is one where the 'Kimberley process' has created the possibility of a partnership between the diamond industry, the relevant governments, and the UN.

In an era of globalization and interconnectedness, the world faces many challenges that can be resolved only through a 'collective response'. Issues such as the environment, HIV/AIDS, and the financial crisis cannot be addressed seriously, let alone resolved, by one nation. This further emphasizes the importance of regional organizations and their coordination role.

A partnership also exists between the UN and other more business-related international organizations such as the IMF, the World Bank, and the WTO. While all of these institutions have their own specific mandate, the heads of each attend a Chief Executives Board chaired by the UN Secretary-General; this allows for an exchange of views on general and specific challenges facing the world.

Regional agreements

The general term 'regional agreement' (RA), which can refer to anything from countries simply agreeing to debate specific issues to wholesale transfers of sovereignty to a regional body, will be preferred here to the more specific term 'regional trade agreement'.

Forerunners to RAs have existed for centuries. Many earlier versions involved a central power imposing its will on a weaker periphery (for example, Turkey's Ottoman Empire dominating the states it administered or the French dominion in Northern Africa). Friendlier arrangements, like the late nineteenth-century *Zollverein* (Customs Union) between independent German states, were few and far between. It is only recently that the world has witnessed voluntary RAs involving neighbours and trading partners promoting similar values and purposes.

One of the main benefits of such arrangements is that countries willing to integrate their economies in a regional division of labour stand to benefit from efficiency gains. As long as trade diversion effects are not too strong, economies joining an RA should experience higher overall productivity, among other reasons because companies are forced to hone their skills in a larger, and therefore more competitive, environment. Intra-regional competition also enhances learning. At the same time, it puts workers under greater pressure to perform (see Figure 6.2).

Politically speaking, regions constitute an intermediary level of governance between global and national policy-making. This is very advantageous for certain countries, especially smaller ones that might otherwise struggle to be heard. The proliferation of RAs is due partly to the loss of national sovereignty in today's globalized world

+ **Trade diversion**
When imports come from less efficient producers located within an RA instead of from more efficient outside producers.

Advantages of RA membership	Disadvantages of RA membership
Raises efficiency: work allocated in a way reflecting members' different advantages	Possibility of 'trade diversion'
Products sold across larger markets	Increased competition for jobs
Greater currency stability	Loss of national sovereignty
Poorer members' living standards might converge with wealthier neighbours	Division of labour benefits some members but harms others
Peaceful relations	Domination of larger member states

Figure 6.2

Advantages and disadvantages of joining a regional agreement.

Figure 6.3
Regional agreements range from loose pacts to completely integrated unions.

Least integrated

↓

Preferential trading area: where countries decide to eliminate some barriers to trade with one another; implemented via trade pacts (e.g. EU–ACP agreements)

Free trade area: where countries decide to eliminate most barriers to trade with one another; there is no common external tariff, however (e.g. NAFTA)

Customs union: free trade area where members have also adopted a common tariff on goods from outside the region (e.g. ASEAN)

Common market: customs unions where members have also implemented a free movement of capital and labour (e.g. Mercosur)

Single market: common market whose members have also pooled many of their government functions, including tax policies; member states might pursue a joint monetary policy (e.g. European Union)

Currency union: single market whose members also share a single currency and therefore coordinate monetary policy (e.g. Eurozone)

↓

Most integrated

(see Chapter 5). With multinational enterprises (MNEs) increasingly integrating their global supply chains, and given the power of international finance, national borders are penetrated more easily than ever. What happens abroad (industry consolidation, crime, pollution, and so on) can have a strong impact domestically. Nation-states therefore need to carry out many of their traditional governance activities on a wider, more regional scale.

Regions also offer a more manageable level of action than global IGOs such as the UN or the WTO, which are more distant and therefore less accountable. In addition, belonging to an RA gives national politicians an opportunity to blame it for policies (like open borders) that, as Chapter 4 discussed, will benefit some constituents but harm others. Lastly, RA membership keeps countries from being locked out of fellow members' markets by preventing protectionist barriers to trade, or, in the case of a currency union like the Eurozone (see below), by stopping member states from competing via currency devaluations.

RAs vary in terms of the extent to which each requires members to transfer power—that is, to 'integrate' national sovereignty into the regional body (see Figure 6.3).

It should be remembered that, in some parts of the world, a country can belong to more than one RA at a time. In addition, many RAs have evolved over time, generally moving from a less to a more integrated arrangement.

RAs in Europe

The European Union (EU)

The world's most politically and economically integrated RA was born in the 1950s as the European Economic Community (EEC). Its six founder members—France, Germany, Belgium, Holland, Luxemburg, Italy—were trying to rebuild their economies after the Second World War while counterbalancing US and Soviet Russian power. Their ambition to avoid future wars explains European nations' desire for an RA that is as tightly knit as possible. The EU's philosophy has always been that peace requires regional loyalties above and beyond national patriotism. Its remit is, therefore, much wider than a purely economic RA, and many of its bodies are endowed with supranational powers. One example is the kind of initiative that the EU advanced in 2009 in response to the credit crunch, creating a regional watchdog to 'name and shame' countries whose regulatory authorities had been ineffective (Barker and Tait 2009). This activism often leads to accusations that the EU's Brussels headquarters has become a giant, unaccountable bureaucracy. At the same time, it is precisely because so many citizens support European construction that the EU has been allowed to expand. Indeed, for some observers the main concern is that the EU's broadening agenda will dilute what is, at heart, its deeply ethical culture (Leconte 2008).

Thinking point
Is the EU anti-democratic?

The EU has gone through many phases. One of the most crucial was its transformation from the EC common market to the more integrated EU single market. This happened in 1992 with the signing of the Maastricht treaty, which paved the way for the 2002 introduction of a single currency throughout most of the region (called the Eurozone). Since its enlargement on 1 January 2007 to twenty-seven member states, the EU has been home to nearly 500 million consumers. It is a huge organization with a wide range of bodies and total budget of around €100 billion. It is the biggest RA in the world (see Figure 6.4).

The EU represents member states' interests at many global forums. This can involve negotiations with other OECD nations, like the dispute with the USA over the subsidies that the two powers have been paying to aeroplane manufacturers Airbus and Boeing, respectively. Other negotiations are with emerging powers like Russia, whose summer 2008 intervention in Georgia received sharp criticism from the EU, or China, often rebuked by Brussels for trying to gain European market share by 'dumping' products at below-market prices (see Chapter 5). In addition, the EU often features at multilateral forums like the WTO, presenting a powerful, united front on behalf of its member states. Lastly, the EU regularly engages directly with non-European MNEs operating on its territory, one example being the €1.06 billion fine it levied on Intel in May 2009 after accusing the company of paying other intermediaries to use its chips instead of products made by its rival Advanced Micro Devices (BBC 2009b).

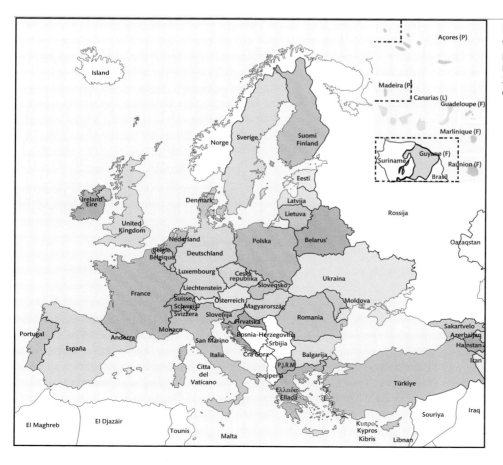

Figure 6.4
Current and prospective EU member states, 2007 (European Commission).

At the same time, given its diversity, the EU cannot please all members all the time. For instance, European farmers have been receiving Common Agricultural Policy (CAP) subsidies for decades. There is widespread agreement that these subsidies could be reduced. Yet France, with its strong farmers' lobby, has successfully opposed cuts in the EU agricultural budget. As a key contributor to the Union, France is fully within its rights to protect its perceived national interests—but its vision is not shared by most of its partners. A similar example was when the UK asked the EU to negotiate greater access to Japan's financial services market, in exchange for further European openness to Japanese car and electronics imports (Pilling 2008). This move would have been good for the UK, with its traditional strengths in banking, but less helpful for fellow EU members, whose manufacturing sectors would have suffered greater competition from Japan. Despite the basic EU principle of regional solidarity, exemplified by the aid package that wealthier members offered their struggling Eastern neighbours during the 2009 recession, it can be extremely difficult for the EU to juggle members' contradictory wishes and interests.

European Free Trade Association (EFTA)

This loose association was comprised, as of June 2009, of Iceland, Liechtenstein, Norway, and Switzerland—European countries that have not sought to join the EU but need a body to organize their relations with it. Since June 1992, the EU and EFTA combined have been referred to as the European Economic Area.

RAs in Asia

Association of Southeast Asian Nations (ASEAN)

The original aim of the newly decolonised less-developed countries (LDCs) that make up ASEAN was to encourage nation building by preventing member states from interfering in each other's sovereign affairs. The mission changed radically over the years, with ASEAN's 'Vision 2020' agenda now targeting full-blown economic integration. One milestone in this transformation was the 1992 launch of the ASEAN Free Trade Area, whose purpose (according to the RA's website) is to enhance 'the region's competitive advantage as a single production unit'. Since 2005, most trade within the core group of ASEAN-6 countries (Brunei, Indonesia, Malaysia, Philippines, Singapore, and Thailand) has been subject to tariffs of 5 per cent or less, with many non-tariff barriers (NTBs) having been eliminated entirely. Unsurprisingly, this has deepened the integration of member states' economies. Moreover, there is every chance that this process will accelerate in the years to come. In February 2009, ASEAN leaders met to discuss their concerns over the particularly sharp fall in member states' industrial output as a result of the credit crunch. This was one consequence of the region's over-reliance on exports to non-ASEAN markets (the West but also China and Japan), all of which had been deeply affected by the crisis. The decision was made to place greater priority on trade within the RA, which up to that point had accounted for only one-quarter of members' exports. What had become apparent was the limits of the Asian tiger economies' decades-long policy of depending on external demand. Clearly, the time had come for a fuller development of their internal markets.

ASEAN+3

ASEAN summits regularly include extra meetings between the original six members and the region's three other economic powerhouses, China, Japan, and South Korea. The ASEAN+3 forum was created in response to the perceived need for a larger body representing regional interests following the 1997 currency crisis, which some Asian governments blamed on Western speculators (see Chapter 13). This is a regional grouping of nations that share certain cultural and philosophical affinities. It also reflects the rise in intra-Asian commerce, which now accounts for more than 50 per cent of all trade in this part of the world—yet another sign that the USA no longer dominates international business to the extent that it once did (Fukuyama 2008). All in all, the purpose of ASEAN+3 is to give greater resonance to Asian ideas and interests. This region may lag behind Europe in terms of political integration, but it is one of the main drivers of the world economy and therefore justified in seeking a louder voice on the world stage.

Asian Pacific Economic Cooperation (APEC)

This is a minimalist forum for voluntary economic cooperation comprised of all major Pacific Rim economies (including the USA, Russia, and Australia), is characterized by informal arrangements rather than strict regulations. In the past, trade liberalization in the Asia–Pacific region was mainly done on a voluntary, unilateral basis, with countries often deciding individually whether to offer one another lower tariffs. APEC members do not have a common tariff on imports from outside the region, and each can negotiate deals with non-members as it sees fit. It is true that APEC's 1996 Bogor declaration committed the grouping's more industrialized members to cut internal tariffs to 5 per cent by the year 2010 (with LDC members doing the same by 2020). However, there is no guarantee that this goal will be reached. In reality, APEC may be little more than a forum to 'promote dialogue amongst the world's most dynamic economies' (Higgott 1998). Some analysts believe that minimalist RAs like APEC contribute little to global trade, especially in higher value-added sectors relatively unaffected by pricing levels (Beattie 2007). After all, tariff policy is just one aspect of the international trade regime.

> **Thinking point**
>
> Are some RAs too insignificant to have a major efffect?

RAs in the Americas

North American Free Trade Agreement (NAFTA)

Founded on 1 January 1994, partly in reaction to the European integration process NAFTA links Canada, Mexico, and the USA in a pact aimed at eliminating intra-regional tariffs on many types of products, especially consumer durables, textiles, and agricultural produce. Other goals include the relaxation of FDI restrictions (see Chapter 5, 'Performance Requirements'); protection of intellectual property such as patents and trademarks; and creation of trade dispute mechanisms. What NAFTA does not seek are single tariffs on imports from outside the region. Nor does it allow the free movement of labour. Above all, it is not trying to become a single market, much less a replacement for national government.

NAFTA has succeeded in so far as intra-regional trade and FDI have risen but it has also had a few less fortunate outcomes. By opening Mexico's food markets up to highly subsidized (and industrialized) American agribusiness interests, NAFTA has made life very difficult for small Mexican farmers. This has had several consequences, including a rise in the number of displaced Mexican agricultural workers seeking employment in the USA. Secondly, many North American industries' supply chains now stretch south of the border to include low-cost Mexican *maquiladora* plants that import American components to assemble them on goods re-exported to the USA. This 'offshoring' and/or outsourcing movement has lowered production costs for many American companies and provided work for people in northern Mexico. At the same time, it has had a negative effect on many local labour markets in the USA and raised concerns that Mexico might become a 'pollution haven' for dirtier US industries (Ederington 2007). This explains why, when President Bill Clinton negotiated the original NAFTA agreement in the 1990s, he also drafted labour and environmental standards to deal with the negative externalities that inevitably arise when production is displaced from a wealthy nation to a poor one. Note that, whereas the consensus used to be that RAs will work only if member states have converged towards a similar level of socio-economic development, NAFTA presents an interesting case of an RA that associates advanced economies (the USA and Canada) with an LDC (Mexico). In this way, it reproduces within a regional framework the kind of cross-border relationships that have come to typify modern globalization. At a certain level, this is comparable to the inter-member hierarchy that now exists within the EU after its incorporation of poorer Eastern Europe transition countries. Unlike the EU, however, NAFTA is not expected to have a major impact on people's lives. Indeed, tensions tend to heighten when this occurs.

Mercosur

In 1991, Brazil, Argentina, Uruguay, and Paraguay signed a treaty promoting free trade in goods and free circulation of persons. This was an attempt to counterbalance repeated US efforts to pry open Latin American markets, most recently via the so-called Free Trade of the Americas initiative. Mercosur has at best made slow progress towards economic integration, although there has been an acceleration over the course of the 2000s with the development of closer trade relations to the Andean Community (Bolivia, Columbia, Ecuador, and Peru), and with the 2004 launch of a South American Community of Nations whose long-term ambition is to grow along EU lines.

Caribbean Community (CARICOM)

Replacing an old free trade agreement, CARICOM has the explicit goal of developing into a single market characterized by harmonized economic legislation and policy. This RA also seeks to fulfil wider, non-economic missions, including actions on sustainability, HIV/AIDS, and security. Given most member states' status as LDCs, CARICOM mainly exists to formulate a 'single development vision'.

RAs in Africa and elsewhere

African Economic Community (AEC)

This is an umbrella organization for the different regional economic communities to which African countries belong, sometimes with overlapping memberships. Driven by principles of unity, decolonization, and development, the AEC aims to advance towards full integration, although frequent conflicts have impeded progress. The most successful grouping at present is probably the Economic Community of West African States (ECOWAS), a common market characterized by harmonized economic policies, single external tariffs and a joint currency, the Central African franc.

African, Caribbean, Pacific states (ACP)

This is a loose confederation of developing countries that have signed joint pacts with the EU (most recently, the 2000 Cotonou Agreement) to create preferential, low-tariff access to European markets for many agricultural and mining products. The ACP also tries to use development aid to foster price stability in the primary goods sectors that are so important to many of its members. Cotonou has come under fire from the WTO for its 'discriminatory' aspect, since it involves preferential treatment (see Online Resource Centre, extension material 6.1) for some but not all of its members, contradicting WTO principles of non-discrimination and reciprocity. The end result has been a series of bilateral negotiations during which some EU representatives have threatened to withdraw ACP countries' special access if they do not sign

> Go to the ORC 🌐

+ Reciprocity
Notion that all parties to a transaction should grant and receive benefits of equivalent value.

'Economic Partnership Agreements' removing barriers to trade (Cobham and Powell 2007). This approach upsets many observers who note the hypocrisy of OECD countries that had themselves applied high barriers to trade during their own development trajectories trying to prevent LDCs from doing the same (Bunning 2007).

G8/G20

Alongside the UN and the RAs, the main multi-purpose IO is the G8, which is not so much an organization as an ad hoc body that exists to call regular meetings between the leaders of the world's most influential countries. In recent years, topics have ranged from debt relief and poverty in Africa to terrorism, climate change, energy, and food. In April 2009, an expanded summit called the G20 convened in London to discuss a coordinated response to the credit crunch. The general consensus was that national responses to the global crisis (fiscal stimulus packages, re-regulation of the global banking system, repression of tax havens) could be effective only if designed and coordinated at the highest level.

Section II: The Bretton Woods organizations

There are hundreds of specialist IGOs today, each focusing on the global governance of a particular issue that cannot be dealt with sufficiently within a national framework. In the field of international business, however, the most important IGOs are the three that came out of the 1944 Bretton Woods conference that set the architecture for today's post-Second World War trading regime. These are the International Monetary Fund (IMF); the International Bank for Reconstruction and Development (IBRD), now known as the World Bank; and, above all, the General Agreement on Tariffs and Trade (GATT), which gave birth to an IO known today as the World Trade Organization (WTO). Figure 6.5 summarizes these three IGOs' main characteristics.

Volumes of research have been written on the motivations underlying the birth of the Bretton Woods IGOs. Analysts usually speak of participant nations' desire to avoid future tensions by creating institutions where cross-border concerns could be discussed and decided in a transparent and friendly manner. This was in reaction to the beggar-thy-neighbour policies that many countries adopted in the 1930s, a protectionism whose negative effects on world trade deepened the Great Depression. By encouraging cooperation and coordination,

+ **Debt relief**
Idea that the poorest borrower nations should not be asked to reimburse debt, either because the borrowings have been misused and did not benefit the recipient country, or because the borrower is too poor to reimburse.

> **Thinking point**
> Why do the IMF, the World Bank, and the WTO have so many critics?

+ **Beggar-thy-neighbour policies**
Where one country purposefully tries to improve its economic position at the expense of its trading partners, by keeping exchange rates artificially low, taxing imports, and so on.

	World Trade Organization	International Monetary Fund	World Bank
Headquarters	Geneva	Washington DC	Washington DC
Director (spring 2009)	Pascal Lamy (France)	Dominique Strauss-Kahn (France)	Robert Zoellick (United States)
Operational decisions made by:	Consensus: one country one vote (in reality, agenda set during 'Green Room' negotiations)	Executive Board: votes weighted to reflect members' 'quotas' (role in world economy)	Boards of Directors: 5 appointed by countries with largest number of shares, 19 others representing national groups
Number of employees	625	2,490	8,600
Key data (2008)	Operating budget: Swiss fr. 185 million	Outstanding loans: $19.4 billion	New commitments: $24.7 billion

Figure 6.5
Overview of the Bretton Woods organizations.

global governance is supposed to prevent countries from turning inwards at times of crisis. Note that this same argument was revived in 2008, in the wake of the global credit crunch.

Other texts have been more critical of these IGOs, attacking them for their role in promoting a hierarchical neo-liberal world order (Kelly and Grant 2005) or accusing them of consolidating the power of the USA (Drezner 2007). Instead of commenting on the validity of these and other criticisms of the Bretton Woods organizations, the analysis below will try to adopt a more neutral approach, highlighting their explicit aims and actions.

The World Trade Organization

The Bretton Woods conference had originally envisaged the creation of a strong International Trade Organization (ITO) with formal links to the IMF, the World Bank, and the International Labour Organization (ILO). When the US Congress decided in 1948 not to approve the ITO, what remained in the trade arena was the less ambitious GATT treaty. Unlike the ITO, the GATT had no links to other IGOs; did not seek to promote full employment (as did the ILO); and had an ineffective dispute settlement mechanism. It did, however, provide a loose framework for a step-by-step reduction in quantitative tariffs on the cross-border flow of goods. Trade ministers from signatory nations would engage in targeted discussions called 'rounds' (see Figure 6.6). Any problems arising between sessions would be dealt with in ad hoc committees, meaning that the GATT did not have much of a permanent oversight function (Wilkinson 2006). On the other hand, this regime balanced the need for an open world economy with the sovereignty concerns that many countries had at the time—GATT had no 'supranational' mandate to interfere in domestic decision-making (Kelly and Grant 2005).

GATT weathered several storms, in particular the protectionist policies (like the wave of NTBs, see Chapter 5) that accompanied the global recession of the 1970s. By the 1980s, supporters of free trade were suggesting that a stronger body was needed. GATT's relatively modest remit meant that it did not cover several key international sectors, such as agriculture and textiles—areas of prime importance for many LDCs. Additionally, it had made so much progress in lowering tariffs that little more could be done. For some, this meant that it was time to move market deregulation on to a wider agenda that would include the trade in services, FDI, and intellectual property.

The Uruguay round of GATT negotiations concluded with the Marrakesh Agreement, which gave birth to the World Trade Organization on 1 January 1995. As Figure 6.4 shows, as an organization the WTO is relatively compact (see Online Resource Centre, extension

Figure 6.6	Year(s)	Name of round	Main features
The main rounds of GATT and, since 1995, WTO meetings (BBC 2009a).	1948	Geneva	45,000 tariff concessions affecting $10 billion (around 20 per cent) of world trade; kick-started liberalization
	1949	Annecy	5,000 tariff concessions
	1951	Torquay	8,700 concessions, cutting 1948 tariff levels by 25 per cent
	1955–56	Geneva	$2.5bn in tariff reductions
	1960–62	Dillon	Concessions worth $4.9bn of world trade; negotiations about birth of European Economic Community
	1964–67	Kennedy	$2.5bn in tariff reductions; anti-dumping agreement
	1973–79	Tokyo	$300bn in tariff reductions; focus on non-tariff barriers
	1986–94	Uruguay	Agricultural subsidies cut, full access for LDC textiles, intellectual property rights extended; birth of WTO
	2001–	Doha	Development agenda; OECD country/LDC conflict

- There should be no discrimination in the world trade system

- A gradual, negotiated move towards open borders is intrinsically beneficial

- Trade decisions should be transparent and not arbitrary

- Competition is desirable as long as it is fair

- Trade should be used to encourage development and economic reform

Figure 6.7
The WTO's
fundamental beliefs.

material 6.2). However, there is no doubting its impact. On its own website, the WTO defines itself as a negotiating forum; the embodiment of a set of rules; and a venue for settling disputes. Its functions are to administer WTO trade agreements; host trade negotiations; handle trade disputes; monitor national trade policies; offer technical assistance and training for developing countries; and cooperate with other international organizations. This is an extremely broad mandate. The WTO is the cornerstone of today's global trading regime.

> Go to the ORC

In more ideological terms, the WTO fights for a generally neo-liberal approach, which it equates with economic progress (see Figure 6.7). It is in no way a neutral body giving equal support to members' free trade and protectionist policies. Quite the contrary: it explicitly encourages the former and opposes the latter—a divide that has caused a fundamental contradiction in its mission statement. On the one hand, the WTO requires consensus amongst members before deciding on policy. On the other, it discourages policies that run contrary to its inclinations. This means that the WTO is often in conflict with some of its own members.

The WTO paradigm materializes in a set of principles that member states are supposed to apply when trading with one another. Just as important, however, is members' acceptance of its authority to judge any trading disputes that may arise. Indeed, the reason why the WTO has greater scope than most other IGOs is its capacity to act simultaneously as lawmaker, judge, and police.

Five principles guide the WTO's actions.

1. *Most-favoured nation (MFN)*. If a WTO member grants favourable treatment (like lower tariffs) to goods made in one member state, it must offer the same preferences to all members. There are exceptions to this rule. First, regional free trade blocs (like the EU Single Market) can favour internal flows over extra-regional trade, even if the latter involves a fellow WTO member. Secondly, under certain circumstances, a country can offer LDC producers special access to its market. Lastly, some discrimination is allowed if the goods in question have suffered from unfair market practices (like 'dumping'). On the whole, however, the MFN arrangement facilitates exports by WTO members. It is usually the main reason why countries want to join this IGO.

2. *National treatment*. The WTO also specifies that members should strive to give similar treatment to all goods, regardless of whether they are produced locally or by a fellow member state. This acceptance of imports is the main price that a country pays to join the WTO and serves as a counterbalance to MFN. Together, the two principles are what cement 'reciprocity' as a key WTO value, the idea being that any pain caused by WTO membership will be offset by gains. Note that some (mainly industrialized) countries have tried to get national treatment to apply also to services and copyrights/patents, the two 'new issues' that became part of the WTO agenda in the mid-1990s when interest rose in a General Agreement on Trade in Services (GATS) and Trade Related Aspects of Intellectual Property Rights (TRIPS).

3. *Fairness*. A common misunderstanding is that the WTO advocates free trade in all circumstances. In reality, there are situations (balance-of-payments crises, temporary surges in imports, unfair competition) in which it does tolerate countries adopting

'safeguard' protections. Conversely, the WTO will object when countries adapt barriers to trade that it considers 'unfair' or market-distorting.

4. *Special and Differentiated Treatment for LDCs*. Various WTO clauses recognize developing countries' special needs. As shown by philosopher Robert Nozick's 'time slices of history' theory (Singer 2004), establishing a single set of rules for everyone neglects the effects that a country's past has on its present capabilities. In this view, it is unfair to LDCs to force them to play by the same rules as the OECD countries, since the former cannot afford 'safety nets' (for example, welfare systems). When citizens of wealthy countries lose their job because of foreign competition, they can expect help until they find new employment—unlike LDC citizens, who risk starvation. In a similar vein, very poor countries cannot even afford the capital equipment and technologies that they need to take advantage of the improved market access that is the main reason for joining the WTO. One of the ways in which Special and Differentiated Treatment materializes for LDCs is in the diffusion of a General System of Preferences (GSP) exempting them from MFN reciprocity requirements. The system's implementation has been patchy, however, with the world's advanced economies often setting up a GSP only in high value-added sectors where LDCs are hardly present, as opposed to the more commoditized sectors (such as steel, shoes, or textiles), where LDCs' price advantage makes them more competitive. It is true that a greater distinction is needed between the treatment of LDCs that are 'emerging' and those that are not. Understandably, OECD countries are 'reluctant to extend to China the special treatment they may grant to Cameroon' (Dadush and Nielson 2007). In general, the least straightforward (and most contentious) aspects of WTO governance are development-related.

5. *Dispute resolution*. WTO members who believe that they have suffered from unfair trade practices can make use of structured complaints process. The hope is that they will turn to this facility instead of retaliating unilaterally against trading partners whom they believe have treated them badly. Parties are encouraged to come to out-of-court settlements, with only about one-third of all cases completing the Dispute Settlement panel process. For those cases (see Figure 6.8) that are judged, however, the panel's ruling is binding, unless a consensus agreement exists to reject it. Countries are expected to comply with Dispute Settlement rulings by ceasing the practice in question—although some continue and simply compensate the injured party for any damages suffered. For instance, for most of the 2000s the EU in general (and France in particular) preferred to pay a yearly fine of $150 million rather than abandon its ban on US beef with excessive levels of growth hormones.

	Year	Issue	Country launching complaint
Figure 6.8 Some recent disputes brought before the WTO Dispute Settlement Body (www. wto.org).	2006	Countervailing Duties on Dynamic Random Access Memories	Korea (vs Japan)
	2007	Domestic Support and Export Credit Guarantees for Agricultural Products	Brazil (vs USA)
	2007	Measures Affecting the Protection and Enforcement of Intellectual Property Rights	USA (vs China)
	2008	Customs Valuation of Products (inc. alcoholic beverages) from the European Communities	European Communities (vs Thailand)
	2008	Tariff Treatment of Certain Information Technology Products	Japan (vs European Communities)
	2008	Measures Affecting Financial Information Services and Foreign Financial Information Suppliers	Canada (vs China)
	2009	Measures Affecting Poultry Meat	USA (vs European Communities)

At a certain level, the WTO is a very useful tool. Its consensual decision-making process (one nation, one vote) should ensure that all participants, from the largest to the smallest, get a fair hearing. Its transparency commitments should promote good governance practices, shielding member states from powerful lobbies—only governments are authorized to negotiate at the WTO, and they are expected to argue for the interests of the nation as a whole. Lastly, its multilateral nature should mean less bullying by the world's more powerful states—one example being the way that the USA, out of fear of WTO condemnation, has more or less stopped resorting to the 'Special 301' unilateral trade retaliations that its 1974 Trade Act once allowed (Iida 2005).

At the same time, the WTO remains the most disputed, and even disliked, of all the major IGOs. WTO ministerial conferences are usually accompanied by enormous protests. A few demonstrators may oppose all forms of modern capitalism, but, as US President Bill Clinton pointed out in 1999 at the first major anti-WTO riots in Seattle, many critics have well-founded arguments (see Online Resource Centre, extension material 6.3). Like all governance bodies, the WTO must evolve. Some observers argue that the best way to reform it is to empower it to deal with non-trade-related matters. Others would not tamper with its mission and simply argue that the agenda-setting process must be changed. Some call for the WTO's dissolution. The future of this key IGO is anything but clear.

> **Thinking point**
> Should the WTO be kept as is, reformed, or disbanded?

> Go to the ORC

Case Study 6.2

Global governance and IGOs: No cancan in Cancun

The WTO was prevented from reaching an agreement at its 1999 Seattle meeting by boisterous street protests and poorer members' sense that its agenda did not address their concerns. Reconvened in Qatar two years later, the WTO launched the Doha Development Round, a programme given this name because of growing recognition of the need to link trade to LDCs' specific problems. A compromise agenda was found, with all members agreeing to start negotiations and attend a ministerial conference in 2003 at Cancun, Mexico.

It was here that the resentments that had built up over previous years finally exploded. Even as the EU and USA continued to flaunt their free trade principles by subsidizing domestic farmers (effectively closing their home markets to LDC imports and gaining unfair advantage in other markets), the WTO's priority was to get LDCs to accept 'new issue' policies whose adoption would mainly serve the interests of European and American corporations. One of these policies was the GATS service liberalization agenda, which would allow banking or insurance MNEs from advanced countries to enter previously protected LDC markets. Another was TRIPS, whose strong patent protections would,

Many of the world's leading IGOs are highly contested (© iStockphoto).

for instance, keep Brazilian or Indian generic drug producers from making cheaper versions of the anti-AIDS medicines that Western pharmaceutical companies had invented. A third policy proposal (Trade Related Investment Measures, called TRIMs) would have expanded the WTO's oversight remit into areas such as competition, public procurement programmes, and FDI performance requirements. Traditionally, these had been the sole preserve of sovereign nation-states. They are some of the few weapons that weak LDC host governments can use when bargaining with powerful MNEs. The neo-liberal argument that adopting such measures would benefit LDCs was unsurprisingly rejected.

Cancun was a scene of great uproar. The conference centre was surrounded by tens of thousands of NGO protestors, whose numbers were considerably augmented by Mexican farmers dismayed by their country's enforced importation of subsidized, genetically modified corn from the USA. There was the public suicide of the former director of the Korean Advanced Farmers Union, Lee Kyung Hai, who at the moment of his death was holding a sign saying 'The WTO kills farmers' (Ross 2003). The conference itself saw the formation of a new constituency of LDCs called the 'G22', comprised of influential LDCs such as China, India, and Brazil who refused any progress in 'new issue' negotiations until the world's agricultural trading system had regained some fairness—a difficult task given the strength of EU and US agricultural lobbies. The meeting adjourned without any clear sense of how the WTO might recover its liberalization dynamic. Little progress was been made at ministerial conferences organized after Cancun (for instance, Hong Kong in December 2005 or Geneva in September 2007). At the same time, it is not entirely surprising that the WTO would grind to a standstill one day—given the divergence in actors' interests (Devadoss 2006), this outcome was always a possibility.

The International Monetary Fund and the World Bank

The IMF is an IGO specializing in crisis lending. Set up after the Second World War to revive the international financial system, it provides temporary funding, often at concessionary, below-market interest rates, to countries with balance-of-payments problems. Its sister organization, the World Bank, whose original mission was to support European reconstruction, provides long-term funding, mainly to developing countries seeking to build up their infrastructure. Member states are supposed to fund these international financial institutions (IFIs) proportionately to their relative importance in the global economy. Voting rights are distributed along the same lines. The global hegemony of the United States at the time of the IMF birth was reflected in its originally high share quota. By 2007, the US stake had fallen to 17.1 per cent, versus 32.4 per cent for the EU countries. There is widespread recognition that further reforms in governance structures are necessary. A first response was the World Bank's 2008 appointment of a professor from China, Lin Yifu, as its chief economist. However, deeper changes have been slow to materialize (Phillips 2007). Both the IMF and the World Bank are still run out of Washington. They still follow the convention of always choosing a European and an American citizen for their respective CEOs. Above all, they continue to under-represent Asian interests, which totalled a mere 11.5 per cent of all IMF voting rights in 2006. Given Asia's enormous population, rising GDP, and stockpiles of cash reserves, this imbalance of power seriously undermines the IGOs' legitimacy. A few Asian countries did receive increased voting rights in 2006, but the changes were very timid, with China's share advancing fractionally from 2.94 to 3.65 per cent. This is entirely insufficient.

Another frequent criticism of the two Bretton Woods IFIs is that their resident experts tend to suggest policies representing industrialized countries' views and interests. A prime example of this was the requirement, from the mid-1980s onwards, that borrowers agree to engage in 'structural adjustment' programmes and implement Washington Consensus principles (see Chapter 5) before receiving support. Loans often came with the requirement that state spending or social programmes be slashed and domestic financial markets opened up to foreign financiers. The reason given for such 'conditionalities' was that governments forced to seek IMF and World Bank loans had been necessarily at fault for long-term mismanagement, and therefore needed to change their entire economic orientation. The assumed change was the wholesale adoption of 'one-size-fits-all' neo-liberal policies.

In certain instances, this advice had disastrous effects. For example, governments in Tanzania and Kenya, two countries in the throes of an AIDS crisis, were required to charge patients for hospital appointments that used to be free, leading to a sharp fall in the number of patients seeking much needed treatment. The conditions imposed on Ecuador's government for loans offered in the 1990s were that it should stop subsidizing domestic fuel. This led to an 80 per cent rise in retail prices for this vital commodity, a catastrophic outcome for millions of very poor households (Palast 2003). Actions of this kind laid the IMF and the World Bank open to accusations that their real aim was to ensure the 'hegemony of capitalism on a global scale' (Cammack 2003: 170); that they were anti-democratic (Woods 2004); and that, by imposing capital market liberalization (see Chapter 14) on poor countries before their financial institutions were ready, they were contributing to 'global instability [and] political chaos' (Stiglitz 2004). By the early twenty-first century, the IMF and World Bank had become figures of hate for many reformists.

In response, the two IGOs began to alter their approaches. The first shift occurred in 1999, when a number of lending packages were renamed 'Poverty Reduction and Growth Facilities'. This symbolic gesture coincided with a new attitude towards borrowers, who, instead of being forced to adopt policies primarily aimed at solving short-term problems such as capital flows or trade gaps, were now being asked to focus on more structural problems, like finance sector modernization (Gomel 2002). The World Bank also began experimenting in the early 2000s with what it called a more 'holistic' approach to financial intervention, adapting its loan conditions to ensure a better fit with borrowers' specific needs. More emphasis was placed on the two IGOs' secondary but vital role of providing technical advice to improve debtor nations' monetary policies and banking systems. IMF and World Bank forecasts are key inputs in many countries' economic planning process. Even the fiercest critics of these two IGOs accept that they are priceless sources of information.

Between 2000 and 2007, however, a new set of problems arose. Resentful at past interference and sitting on growing piles of cash following years of rapid export growth, the big emerging countries no longer needed IMF or World Bank funding and began to reimburse outstanding debt prematurely. By 2008, the two IFIs had very few customers beyond a circle of highly indebted poor countries (HIPCs) that were largely incapable of making any repayments. Even for these HIPC borrowers, IMF and World Bank funding often paled in comparison with direct government aid (Weisman 2007) or loans from 'sovereign wealth funds'. The IMF lost so much money in 2007 ($103 million) that it had to sell off some of its gold reserves. As for the World Bank, its reputation was deeply damaged that same year by a corruption scandal associated with its then president, Paul Wolfowitz —who had himself campaigned against loans to corrupt regimes. The two organizations were also being sharply criticized by debt relief advocates outraged by the actions of 'vulture funds' who would purchase the IGOs' outstanding loans to the world's poorest countries at a discounted rate and subsequently sue these HIPCs for the full amounts (Seager and Lewis 2007). By early 2008, serious doubts reigned about the future viability of the IMF and the World Bank as cornerstones of the global financial system.

The 2008 credit crunch turned things around for the two bodies, especially the IMF, which found itself in autumn 2008 discussing urgent funding possibilities with countries as varied as Iceland, Belarus, Hungary, and Pakistan. On the one hand, some might say that the crisis further undermined these IFIs' legitimacy by revealing the flaws in the deregulated capital markets model that had been the basis of their policy advice since 1989. At the same time, given many countries' desperation for capital resources wherever they could be found, plus the general need for specialists capable of re-engineering the global financial system, it now seemed clear that the IMF and World Bank would have work to do for many years to come. Whether they will retain their current missions or have their competencies renegotiated under the aegis of a future Bretton Woods II conference (Sachs 2008) remains to be seen. There were reports that IMF loans to Belarus during the 2008 credit crunch came with pressure that the borrower should privatize its banking sector—at a time when many leading IMF member states, starting with the USA and the UK, were taking their own banks into public ownership (Stewart 2008). Similarly, the package that the IMF offered Hungary about the same time came with a demand for drastic budget cuts—despite the fact that most of the Fund's leading member states were themselves running budget deficits because of the global crisis. By laying themselves open to accusations of hypocrisy and blind ideology, the Bretton Woods institutions run a risk of losing legitimacy. A prime example is the predicament that the IMF faced in early 2009, when it started to run out of financial resources after months of crisis lending to struggling LDCs. On the one hand, without getting new resources from cash-rich countries like China, the Fund would be unable to perform its mission. At the same time, it would have been unrealistic to expect China to support the IMF without being given a greater say in the way the organization is run (Beattie 2009). Seen in this light, reforming the Bretton Woods IGOs is not just desirable; it is crucial to their long-term survival.

> **Thinking point**
>
> What future is there for the IMF/ World Bank?

Section III: Single-purpose IGOs

It would be impossible to provide a full list of all the bodies that make up the global governance framework within which MNEs operate. Instead, this final section will offer a brief introduction to a few specialist organizations and to the NGO sector as a whole.

Specialist organizations

One way to categorize single-purpose IGOs is to distinguish between groups that promote particular policies and others representing specific sectors' interests. The former category, comprised of think tanks, advocacy groups, and information centres, is best exemplified by the Organization for Economic Cooperation and Development (OECD). The latter is mainly comprised of IFIs and producer organizations fighting on behalf of specific sectors.

The OECD (www.oecd.org) was created in 1961 to represent the world's advanced economies and support free markets. Working out of its Paris headquarters, this IO uses its enormous data resources to monitor all kinds of economic developments and produce analyses that it hopes will be taken up by policy-makers everywhere (and not just member states). As highlighted throughout this book, ideas are an important part of the international business framework. Thus, despite its lack of formal competencies, OECD wields real authority in so far as it influences people in power. This influence can sometimes be felt in unexpected areas. For instance, in summer 2008, OECD Secretary-General Angel Gurria organized meetings in the City of London and with UK Prime Minister Gordon Brown to emphasize the Organization's conviction that the international business community needed to accelerate its efforts to combat climate change. The OECD has traditionally been very successful at making sure that its voice is heard.

Sector specific organizations include the IFIs that countries establish on a joint basis to conduct a certain number of banking activities. The IMF and the World Bank feature in this category, as do regional development banks like the European Bank for Reconstruction and Development (EBRD), the Inter-American Development Bank (IADB) and the Asian Development Bank (ADB). In recent decades, these entities have often been used to funnel aid or loans to emerging or transition economies—one example being the €32 million package that the EBRD, the European Investment Bank, and other IFIs put together in March 2009 for East European banks caught up in the credit crunch. Also worthy of note is the Bank for International Settlements (www.bis.org), which specializes in providing national central banks with information and coordinating their transactions. The IFI sector has a key role to play in the wider debate about the need for a more coordinated international financial system (Ikhide 2004).

A final category is comprised of international producer organizations representing sectorial interests during trade negotiations. Some of these bodies struggle for legitimacy, accused by policy-makers of behaving as cartels. As Chapter 1 has shown; however, countries specializing in low value-added goods can suffer if they do not improve their terms of trade. One way to do this is by raising the international price for the good(s), either by reducing

> **+ Cartel**
>
> Groups of producers that instead of competing, collaborate with one another on supply quantity and pricing decisions.

supply or by engaging in oligopolistic practices. This explains many African nations' long-standing support for the International Cocoa Association (ICA), which tries to keep cocoa-bean prices at a level that will provide farmers with sufficient income. Other producer organizations have been more successful along these lines, a leading example being the Organization for Petroleum Exporting Countries (OPEC), a key player in the global energy sector. OPEC's remarkable power derives largely from consumer nations' inability to reduce their dependency on this resource (Rose 2004). IGOs representing so-called strategic sectors will always wield more power than ones specializing in marginal activities.

+ Oligopoly
Market dominated by a few sellers, who might therefore have a disproportionate power to collude outside the market framework and fix prices in a non-competitive manner.

Non-governmental organizations

It is difficult to come up with a single definition for the NGO sector, a key component in what is sometimes referred to as the 'global civil society'. The first recognized NGO, founded in the USA in 1839, was the 'Anti-Slavery Society'. At one point, non-profit organizations, ranging from family groups to small advocacy networks, were the main actors offering the kind of 'anti-politics of the powerless' (Kaldor 2004) that typifies this sector. In every nation of the world, there are countless local charities run by good-hearted volunteers seeking to right a perceived wrong. Nowadays, however, civil society actors are just as likely to be huge, professionally run organizations focused on all kinds of global issues, ranging from the environment to war, poverty, and women's rights (see Figure 6.9). Indeed, it is hard to conceive of a major international social, political, economic, cultural, or ecological issue that has not received the attention of an NGO.

No one knows exactly how many NGOs exist today, but the number is assumed to run into tens of thousands. At a time when the Internet has both broadened awareness of global problems and empowered women and men alike to express themselves on all varieties of topics, it is no surprise that like-minded individuals end up joining advocacy groups focused on globalization-related problems. Falling participation in many national elections attests to widespread disillusionment with local politicians' ability to shape events. For many citizens, NGOs offer a substitute platform for action.

NGOs come in all sizes and shapes. Since the 1980s and 1990s there has been a proliferation of loosely organized grassroots networks that the economist Joseph Stiglitz calls the 'discontents of globalization'. These are many of the people seen protesting publicly at major IGO events like WTO trade conferences or G8 annual meetings. They can be contrasted with the big professional NGOs such as Greenpeace or Oxfam, many of whom are now too famous to be ignored by governments and therefore participate regularly in all kinds of policy forums, including ones organized by the WTO or the UN. MNEs are also increasingly willing to listen to civil society actors, if only to gain favour with the general public by proving their ethical credentials (see Chapter 3). Indeed, some transnational NGO alliances have become so adept at manipulating the global media to broadcast their

Names	Focus
Greenpeace; Friends of the Earth	Environment
Oxfam; War on Want	Poverty
Amnesty International; Human Rights Watch	Human rights
Focus on Global South; Trade Justice Movement	Trade
Child Rights Information Network; Save the Children	Child labour
Wateraid; World Wildlife Fund	Conservation

Figure 6.9
Some of the leading globalization-oriented NGOs.

views that it would be impossible for MNEs (or national governments) to ignore them. The importance attached to these organizations' opinions is quite normal—complaints about international business have always been an integral part of international business.

It is relatively easy to generalize about the kinds of things that globalization-critical NGOs believe in. Many oppose radical neo-liberalism, which they accuse of glorifying greed, weakening national governments, creating financial instability, aggravating income disparities, lowering many individuals' standard of living, damaging human health, endangering the environment, and destroying cultural diversity (Wolf 2005). What is harder to ascertain is any consensus about a replacement system. At one level, a distinction might be made between 'alter-globalizers' and 'anti-globalizers'. The former category includes 'egalitarians' who recognize globalization's capacity to create wealth but are disappointed by growing inequalities between the haves and have-nots (Steger 2002; Cohen 2006), as well as 'reformists' who denounce excessive deregulation and seek a more rules-based and/or fairer trading system (Buckman 2004). Anti-globalizers, on the other hand, reject globalized capitalism, demand that power be returned to the local economic level, and denounce what they see as neo-liberalism's 'malign intent' (Bhagwati 2004). Their attitudes range from antipathy towards all MNEs to the rejection of materialism, blind anti-Americanism, and even outright xenophobia. It should be recognized that international business debates are often framed in highly emotive terms—by NGOs but also by their critics (see Online Resource Centre, extension material 6.4). As stated in Chapter 1, it is easy to argue that this discipline has deeper roots in human psychology than in hard science.

> Go to the ORC

Challenges and choices

→ One of the main business justifications for a regional arrangement is that it enables firms from member states to work in a bigger marketplace, thereby enhancing their ability to withstand more robust global competition. The problem is that many leading MNEs are more regional than global in terms of their outlook. The challenge for managers is to avoid the temptation of developing strategies that will prepare their company only for regional rivals, ignoring the benchmarks set by companies strategizing on a more global plane. The feasibility of this choice depends on whether the world is going to start to converge in terms of consumers' purchasing power and the international distribution of wealth.

→ Many reformist NGOs exist to denounce real and/or perceived misconduct by companies. MNEs are not always sure how to deal with civil society actors. On the one hand, they need to listen and react to the public's complaints, make necessary improvements, and consolidate their image as good citizens. On the other, not all NGO criticisms are accurate or realistic. MNE executives must acquire the ability to judge each case on its own merits. This can be difficult, given managers' personal biases.

Chapter Summary

Today's global governance regime first arose because of the growing awareness that many national problems cannot be resolved unless countries transfer certain sovereign prerogatives to IGOs. Such organizations are attractive because they provide a forum for debate and coordination, as well as a way of counterbalancing the rising power of MNEs. At the same time, their legitimacy rises and falls depending on the extent to which their agendas match member states' interests (Gilpin 2001). This contradiction is central to today's system of global governance. To be effective, IGOs must be able to override national governments—but this need for independence also opens them up to criticism.

Above and beyond multi-purpose organizations like the UN or regional arrangements like the EU, ASEAN, and NAFTA, the three IGOs with the greatest impact on international business are the WTO, the IMF, and the World Bank. Each was designed with a specific purpose in mind but has evolved in ways that some observers greet but others criticize. Together with specialist IGOs and reformist NGOs, the bodies of global governance constitute, alongside nation-states, the second pillar of actors determining the politics of international business. Chapter 7 will review the third and final pillar in this trilogy: companies.

Case Study 6.3

Global governance and NGOs: David takes on the Goliaths

In a bid to enhance their overall economic efficiency, a great many countries adopted market-deregulation policies during the 1980s. The new political paradigm culminated in greater wealth for a number of people but also produced negative side effects, including huge income disparities and excessive volatility in the world's financial markets. Many international investors and banks, increasingly freed from supervisory constraints, turned to speculation as a business activity in and of itself. More than ever before, money was being used to make more money, with colossal sums accumulating in the hands of private financiers. Where central banks had once reigned supreme, herds of cash-rich investors now pushed 'hot capital' (very short-term investments and divestments) in and out of local economies, irrespective of a host country's needs. A leading example of this was the attack on the European Monetary System in 1992. The subsequent turmoil, which can be blamed on speculators' greed

and/or on wrong policies by governments and central banks, ended up costing taxpayers billions of pounds.

It is one thing when currency attacks occur in affluent regions like Europe. It is another when they affect poor countries whose populations cannot afford them. Some economists believed that the wave of currency attacks that hit South East Asia in 1997 had beneficial effects, since they revealed to local governments the unsustainable nature of their currency management policies. However, for other observers, ranging from anti-business protestors to globalization-friendly economists like Jagdish Bhagwati, the sight of rich Western financiers breaking LDC central banks was a sign that all is not right in the global currency regime.

The goal for critics of the modern regime became raising public awareness of the devastation that speculative currency attacks can cause. In the 1970s,

Reformist NGOs often accuse globalization of aggravating income disparities (Ingram).

Nobel laureate James Tobin had floated the idea that a 1 per cent tax on foreign exchange transactions would hamper traders who destabilize national currency markets for purely speculative reasons, hopefully by eliminating virtually all transactions unrelated to real trade in goods and services. Reform-minded campaigners, shocked by what had happened in South East Asia in 1997, revived this proposal and decided to convince governments to implement it.

NGOs exist in part so that reformers have a way of expressing their views. Across the world, there are many idealistic NGO professionals who devote their lives to spotting injustices and seeking remedies. One such individual, a veteran of earlier campaigns against apartheid South Africa and the use of landmines in war zones, was the Londoner David Hillman. Like many others, David was dismayed by what had happened in Thailand and Indonesia in 2007 and therefore reacted favourably when asked by the anti-poverty NGO, War on Want, whether he would spearhead a drive to convince world governments to adopt the Tobin Tax proposal and rein in currency speculation. This effort required coordination with like-minded campaigns elsewhere, both in the UK and abroad. Governments can be convinced of the need to change policy, in the international business arena as in many other areas, only if there is widespread support for change. David Hillman set about making this case.

The first step was to marshall all Tobin Tax forces into a single network to ensure that the NGO community was speaking with a single, coherent voice. James Tobin's original idea had been supplemented by the work of a German economist, Paul-Bernd Spahn, who argued for a two-tier tax, based on a second levy aimed at dissuading sustained currency attacks. It was crucial that NGOs, when speaking with politicians, differentiated between the various aspects of the proposal. Many reform campaigns have been fatally weakened by a lack of clarity.

The next step was to drive a multi-pronged communications effort, revolving around participation in public conferences in the UK and abroad; the production of short campaign films mailed to opinion-makers (mostly politicians); and media exposure in the written and online press. This stage began with an explanatory phase, during which time David worked to educate key players about the details of what had become a relatively technical proposition (implementing and enforcing the tax). Then, after about eighteen months and once key figureheads had been brought on board, greater focus was placed on targeting real decision-makers, reaching, in England, as high as the Chancellor of the Exchequer.

Several heads of state and/or government (in France and Brazil, for example) showed interest in what was now known as the currency transaction tax (CTT). To keep the pressure coming, David organized debates, pitting Jim O'Neil, a well-known economist from Goldman Sachs, against a CTT advocate. The purpose of these debates was to convince the public of the proposal's seriousness by showing that it could withstand criticism. David also made a decision to move the CTT effort out of the War on Want NGO and lodge it in a smaller new entity called Stamp Out Poverty. This was to ensure continued focus on this specific effort, which might otherwise have been swamped in broader development campaigns. In 2007, a new video called *Can Pay, Should Pay* was published on You Tube, featuring a number of activist politicians, NGO leaders, and academics. NGOs like Stamp Out Poverty are constantly competing for media attention—the problem of a dysfunctional currency trading regime is only one issue among the many that politicians are asked to address. At the same time, by revealing the dangers of a system that permits unsupervised risk-taking, the 2008 credit crunch reinvigorated David Hillman's fundamental CTT argument. It remains to be seen whether expected government efforts to rein in financial speculation over the next few years will be accompanied by the policy for which he has fought so hard for so long. What is clear is that NGOs like the one he leads will continue to be a factor in international business for many years to come.

Case study questions

1. To what extent can groups of concerned citizens achieve change in the world?
2. What if anything legitimizes NGO efforts to influence policy-makers?
3. How can NGOs avoid 'charity fatigue' on the part of politicians or donors?

Discussion questions

1. Can international organizations remain focused on the issues they were created to handle or do they necessarily assume a life of their own?

2. International organizations give smaller members powers that they would otherwise lack in a bilateral negotiation. Does this mean that IOs will always be contested by larger states?

3. Why has the UN not turned into a world government?

4. Has regionalization led to a convergence in national economic policies?

5. Why should a government hand power over to an IGO such as the WTO or IMF?

References

Archer, C. (2001). *International Organisations*. 3rd edn. London: Routledge.

Barnett, M., and Finnemore, M. (2004). *Rules for the World: International Organizations in Global Politics*. Ithaca, NY: Cornell University Press.

Barker, A., and Tait, N. (2009). 'Darling Backs EU Watchdog', *Financial Times*, 4 Mar., p. 19.

BBC (2009a). 'Timeline: World Trade Organization', 7 Jan., http://news.bbc.co.uk (accessed 1 July 2009).

BBC (2009b). 'EU Slaps a Record Fine on Intel', 13 May, http://news.bbc.co.uk (accessed 27 June 2009).

Beattie, A. (2007). 'Trading Ritual and Reality', *Financial Times*, 19 Sept., p. 15.

Beattie, A. (2009). 'A Gap to Fill', *Financial Times*, 2 Mar., p. 10.

Bhagwati, J. (2004). *In Defense of Globalization*. New York: Oxford University Press.

Boughton, J., and Bradford, C. (2007). 'Global Governance: New Players, New Rules', *IMF: Finance & Development*, Dec.

Buckman, G. (2004). *Globalization: Tame it or Scrap it*, London: Zed Books.

Bunning, M. (2007). 'The EU is Bullying the World's Poor to Rush into a Dubious Deal on Rrade', *Guardian*, 19 Nov., p. 29.

Cammack, P. (2003). 'The Governance of Global Capitalism: A New Materialist Perspective', in R. Wilkinson (ed.), *The Global Governance Reader*. London: Routledge.

Cobham, A., and Powell, S. (2007). 'The EU is Trying to Trick Developing Countries into Poor Trade Deals', *Guardian*, 8 Nov.

Cohen, D. (2006). *Globalization and its Enemies*. Cambridge, MA: MIT Press.

Dadush, U., and Nielson, J. (2007). 'Governing Global Trade', *IMF: Finance & Development*, Dec.

Devadoss, S. (2006). 'Why Do Developing Countries Resist Global Trade Agreements?' *Journal of International Trade and Economic Development*, 15/2 (June).

Diehl, P. (2005). *The Politics of Global Governance: International Organizations in an Interdependent World*. London: Lynne Rienner Publishers.

Drezner, D. (2007). 'The New World Order', www.realclearpolitics.com (accessed 2 May 2007).

Ederington, J. (2007). 'NAFTA and the Pollution Haven Hypothesis', *Policy Studies Journal*, 35/2 (May).

Fukuyama, F. (2008). 'Is America Ready for a Post-American World?', *New Perspectives Quarterly*, 25/4.

Gilpin, R. (2001). *Global Political Economy: Understanding the International Economic Order*. Princeton: Princeton University Press.

Gomel, G. (2002). 'Crisis Prevention and the Role of IMF Conditionality', in M. Fratianni et al. (eds.), *Governing Global Finance: New Challenges, G7 and IMF Contributions*. Aldershot: Ashgate.

Higgott, R. (1998). 'The International Political Economy of Regionalism', in W. D. Coleman and G. R. D. Underhill (eds.), *Regional and Global Economic Integration*. London: Routledge.

Iida, K. (2005). 'Is WTO Dispute Settlement Effective?' in D. Kelly and W. Grant (eds.), *The Politics of International Trade in the Twenty-First Century: Actors, Issues and Regional Dynamics*. Basingstoke: Palgrave Macmillan.

Ikhide, S. (2004). 'Reforming the International Financial System for Effective Aid Delivery', *World Economy*, 27/2 (Feb.).

Kaldor, M. (2004). 'Global Civil Society', in D. Held and A. McGrew (eds.), *The Global Transformations Reader: An Introduction to the Globalization Debate*. Cambridge: Polity Press.

Kaldor, M., et al. (2003). *Global Civil Society*. Oxford: Oxford University Press.

Kelly, D., and Grant, W. (2005). *The Politics of International Trade in the Twenty-First Century: Actors, Issues and Regional Dynamics*. Basingstoke: Palgrave Macmillan.

Leconte, C. (2008). 'Opposing Integration on Matters of Social and Normative Preferences: A New Dimension of Political Contestation in the EU', *Journal of Common Market Studies*, 46/5 (Dec.).

Palast, G. (2003). *The Best Democracy Money Can Buy: The Truth about Corporate Cons, Globalization and High-Finance Fraudsters*, New York: Plume.

Phillips, L. (2007). 'Closing the Deal: IMF Reform in 2007', Overseas Development Institute Briefing Paper, London (Oct.).

Pilling, D. (2008). 'London Pushes EU–Japan Deal on Market Access', *Financial Times*, 7 Apr., p. 7.

Rose, E. (July 2004). 'OPEC's Dominance of the Global Oil Market: The Rise of the World's Dependency on Oil', *Middle East Journal*, 58/3.

Ross, J. (2003). 'Bridging the Distance', 15 Nov., www.sfbg.com (accessed 24 Oct. 2008).

RTL (2006). 'L'invasion du plombier polonais n'a pas eu lieu', 20 Nov., www.rtl.fr (accessed 24 Oct. 2008).

Sachs, J. (2008). 'Amid the Rubble of Global Finance, a Blueprint for Bretton Woods II', *Guardian*, 21 Oct., p. 30.

Seager, A., and Lewis, J. (2007). 'How Top London Law Firms Help Vulture Funds Devour their Prey', *Guardian*, 17 Oct., p. 27.

Singer, P. (2004). *One World: The Ethics of Globalization*. London: Yale University Press.

Steger, M. (2002). *Globalism: The New Market Ideology*. Lanham, MD: Rowman & Littlefield.

Stewart. H. (2008). 'Same Old Medicine for the New Europe', *Observer*, Business and Media section, 2 Nov., p. 6.

Stiglitz, J. (2004). 'The Promise of Global Institutions', in D. Held and A. McGrew (eds.), *The Global Transformations Reader: An Introduction to the Globalization Debate*. Cambridge: Polity Press.

UNCTAD (2009). 'About UNCTAD', www.unctad.org (accessed 1 July 2009).

Weisman, S. (2007). 'Old Guard of Banking Struggles to Adjust to Global Economy', *Observer*, 3 June, *New York Times* insert, p. 5.

Wilkinson, R. (2006). *The WTO: Crisis and the Governance of Global Trade*. Abingdon: Routledge.

Wilkinson, T. L. (2007). 'Eastern Europe Challenges India as Hub for Bank-Office Work', *Wall Street Journal – Europe*, 19 Nov.

Wolf, M. (2005). *Why Globalization Works*. New Haven: Yale Nota Bene.

Woods, N. (2004). 'Order, Globalization and Inequality', in D. Held and A. McGrew (eds.), *The Global Transformations Reader: An Introduction to the Globalization Debate*. Cambridge: Polity Press.

Further research

Matsushita, M. (2006). *The World Trade Organization: Law, Practice and Policy*. 2nd edn. Oxford: Oxford University Press.

Over the years, the WTO has started to accumulate a massive body of institutional law, reflecting its key role in the global trading system. This book contains information on topics like members' tariff, quota, and MFN obligations, while also discussing a wide range of globalization-related issues, including unfair trade, regional trading arrangements, competition, intellectual property, trade in agriculture, and government procurement. Lastly, it takes a polemic view of certain controversial issues, like situations where free trade may be incompatible with human rights, or the special case of trade with LDCs.

Telo, M. (2007) (ed.). *European Union and New Regionalism: Regional Actors and Global Governance in a Post-Hegemonic Era*. 2nd edn. Abingdon: Ashgate.

This broad compilation of texts covers many aspects of European regionalization, identity and governance. It is divided into theoretical perspectives; comparative analysis of regional groupings; 'European Union as a New Civilian Power in the Making'; and a section analysing future scenarios. The focus is as much on governance as on political economy, meaning that this book will be of particular interest to readers who, in addition to international business, are keen to learn more about how power is shaped in, and by, regional arrangements.

Online Resource Centre

Visit the Online Resource Centre that accompanies this book to read more information relating to global governance in international business: www.oxfordtextbooks.co.uk/orc/sitkin_bowen/

7 Actors in International Business: Companies

Overview

The chapter begins by analysing companies in international business, specifically reviewing how multinational enterprises (MNEs) operate abroad in light of the political, economic, and technological constraints they face and the managerial paradigms they apply. One MNE category worthy of special focus is small and medium-sized enterprises (SMEs). The second section analyses how MNEs affect host countries, largely through their foreign direct investment (FDI) and lobbying activities.

Section I: Companies crossing borders
Multinational enterprises
Small and medium-sized enterprises

Section II: How MNEs interact with host countries
Foreign direct investment
Lobbying

Learning Objectives
After reading this chapter, you will be able to:

✦ identify the principles guiding MNEs' historic efforts to shape their international operations

✦ identify SMEs' main international strengths and weaknesses

✦ discuss the rationale underlying FDI

✦ describe the impact of multinationals' FDI operations on host economies

✦ characterize international lobbying

Case Study 7.1

MNEs and international operations: IBM's Indian summer

Since 1991, market liberalization has been a core policy for a succession of Indian governments. The consequence is that a number of MNEs have been reappraising this huge continent-sized country, a land of contrasts where terrible poverty coexists with excellent schools of technology and that educates millions of world-class mathematicians and engineers year in year out. With many multinationals deciding to build up their presence in India, the country has become a major international hub for a variety of activities, ranging from banking administration to pharmaceutical research and information technology (IT). IBM is part of this wave.

IBM's Indian operations employed 53,000 persons in 2007, both in low-cost activities like call centres and in high value-added functions such as research and development, software production, and business process outsourcing. That same year, CEO Sam Palmisano announced plans to invest a further $6 billion in this dynamic economy. He even decided to shift IBM's annual global investor conference to Bangalore, India's IT metropolis.

One of the main reasons behind IBM's decision to raise its profile in India is that competition from emergent local software companies like Infosys have put it under pressure to cut costs. With highly competent Indian programmers earning far less then their US counterparts, one obvious response for IBM has been to undertake

an FDI in Infosys's home market. From an Indian perspective, FDI of this kind is a double-edged sword. It brings funding and management knowledge while offering much needed jobs. At the same time, it drains some of India's human capital away from domestic companies and distorts the national wage structure by widening the gap between workers who earn money from globalization and others who do not. Even though most Indians would probably consider the presence of an MNE like IBM as beneficial, it is worth noting that the victory of the Congress Party in the country's 2004 parliamentary elections was mainly attributed to widespread discontent with the kinds of inequalities that globalization can engender. In India, as elsewhere, foreign firms often meet with mixed reactions.

From IBM's perspective, this FDI embodies the idea that nationality no longer counts. As Mr Palmisano puts it: 'Work flows to the places where it will be done best.' In its early years, IBM was primarily a domestic US company. At a later stage, it began running distinct supply chains in countries across the world. Now, in the late 2000s, IBM's functions are spread all over the world, with its chief procurement officer being located in Shenzen (China) and its international financing back office in Rio de Janeiro (Brazil). IBM may maintain headquarters in New York and many of its executives may still be American, but it is unclear to what extent this remains an American company.

India is capturing a growing share of the global IT market (© iStockphoto).

Introduction

Alongside nation-states and intergovernmental organizations, companies are the main drivers of international business today. With their ability to allocate resources globally, generate new technologies, and affect standards of living everywhere, MNEs have left few societies untouched. Negotiating as equals with governments, multinationals' power often puts them in a position to influence domestic politicians. A clear hierarchy characterized most societies in times past, with politicians sitting on top of the pyramid and companies being forced to adapt to whatever framework they designed. Nowadays, multinationals' revenue streams exceed the gross domestic product (GDP) of some of the countries where they operate. This has altered the balance of power between states and MNEs, especially since companies' mobility allows them to play one government off against another (see Chapter 5). The general public sometimes resents the way supposedly non-political organizations like MNEs dominate a democratically elected government. However powerful multinationals may be, there will always be pressure on them to fit into their local environment.

Section I: Companies crossing borders

Companies with international interests come in many shapes and sizes, ranging from small domestic firms with one-off foreign interests to big firms that are permanently transacting outside their national borders. The actual composition of MNEs' foreign activities depends on political and economic conditions, technological advances, management paradigms, and company size. It is important to note how the relative significance of each of these factors has varied over time. Indeed, a full understanding of MNEs' behaviour requires knowledge

> Go to the ORC ☻

of their history (see Online Resource Centre, extension material 7.1).

Multinational enterprises

MNE behaviour is partially a reaction to external factors (see Figure 7.1). Some of these drivers (funding, political environment, logistics, and communications) were introduced briefly in Chapter 1, but it is useful to keep track of their different manifestations over time, if only to identify the various ways in which MNEs react to the conditions they face. As stressed throughout this book, corporate behaviour is only significant once put into context.

MNE behaviour also reflects internal factors such as managers' personal outlooks and decision-making processes, all of which materialize within the configurations they have chosen. This justifies a brief introduction in the section below to multinational structures—a topic whose theoretical and practical aspects receive greater airing in Chapters 8 and 9.

External drivers of multinational activity

The first external factor affecting multinational operations is *funding*. Logically, servicing remote markets is riskier and more difficult, thus potentially more expensive,

Figure 7.1 Some drivers of multinational activity have remained constant over the years—only their forms have changed.		Pre-twentieth century drivers of globalization drivers	Drivers of globalization in the modern era
	Funding	Companies with publicly traded shares	Globalized financial markets
	Policy framework	Mercantilism, then free trade	Deregulation
	Logistics	Ships, rail	Trucking, planes
	Communications	Telegraph, telephone	Internet

than domestic business. In the distant past, states used to be the prime source of finance for international business. However, as the merchant classes started to accumulate wealth, they gradually assumed this role. An early example is the way that the rise of stock markets and limited liability companies in the seventeenth century led to the creation of the British East India Company, one of the world's first MNEs. Today it would be impossible to analyse MNEs' expansion without referring to the international financial markets where they access much of the capital they need.

The *political environment* is another key factor for MNEs, which, because of their foreign status, have always been subject to the scrutiny of national authorities. Poor relations with host governments can cause enormous problems for companies, leading in some extreme cases to expropriation—one example from 2009 being the way that the Chavez regime in Venezuela seized a rice plant owned by Cargill, the giant US agribusiness company (Carroll 2009). Tensions can also affect MNEs' dealings in certain states—as exemplified by the pressure that former US president George W. Bush put on European MNEs like Siemens and HSBC to scale down their operations in Iran (Gow and MacAskill 2007). Yet another obstacle to international business, as discussed in Chapter 5, is economic patriotism. Recent examples include Spanish government efforts to prevent British Airways from increasing its equity stake in local airliner Iberia (Michaels et al. 2007), or attempts by the US Congress to attach 'buy American' provisions to its 2009 economic stimulus package. In general, MNEs will face a hostile political environment if there are local suspicions that their presence does not advance host country interests. A bad atmosphere can be extremely costly, one example being when the Indian government launched a $2 billion lawsuit against Vodafone in 2008, accusing it of using offshore units to avoid capital gains taxes on a stake it had acquired in local company Hutchison Essar. International business does not exist in a political vacuum.

> **+ Expropriation**
> Where private property is seized by a government, often without compensation.

> **Thinking point**
> How natural is it for host country populations to mistrust foreign MNEs?

The third constant in international business is *logistics*. As explained in Chapter 4, early exploration efforts were often driven by improvements in naval technology. In a similar vein, the Industrial Revolution in the eighteenth century was stimulated by the invention of the steam engine. Early globalization in the late nineteenth century was characterized by great projects like the Suez and Panama canals or the Trans-Siberian railway. This construction work facilitated the movement of goods—and of managers, whose diffusion of corporate knowledge is another important driver of MNE expansion (Jones 2005b; Wilkins 2005). Today, fleets of trucks and aeroplanes help companies to ship components, finished products, and people to foreign locations. In the absence of rapid transportation, global supply chains linking distant sites would be unfeasible. Without cargo planes, for example, there would be no possibility for British supermarket Tesco to import Kenyan roses or New Zealand apples during the European winter. Globalization in its current form is dependent on affordable logistics.

Lastly, MNE operations have always relied heavily on rapid and reliable *communications*. It was only after the telegraph and telephone spread about a century ago that MNEs were able to achieve any real integration or coordination of their worldwide operations (Wilkins 2005). The Internet fulfils a similar function today, helping companies not only to achieve superior intelligence about foreign markets b ut also to coordinate their subsidiaries and form effective global value chains. The intra-firm transfer of knowledge that Internet technology enables is as important to MNEs as the trade in goods.

> **+ Integration**
> Where the activities of different group units are coordinated to the extent that the mission of one unit is defined in the light of the mission of another.

> **+ Intra-firm**
> Activities occurring within the confines of one and the same group.

The kinds of knowledge that MNEs have typically shared relate not only to products and processes but also to multinational management systems. Historically, different principles have dominated thinking about the best way to structure cross-border operations. Paradigms vary in time in the same way that economic conditions do.

Evolution of multinational paradigms

MNEs have tended to develop subsidiaries according to two principles. Much early FDI involved horizontal integration, when companies would open overseas units doing roughly

> **+ Horizontal integration**
> Where a firm establishes a presence in a new market by running activities similar to the ones it manages in its home market.

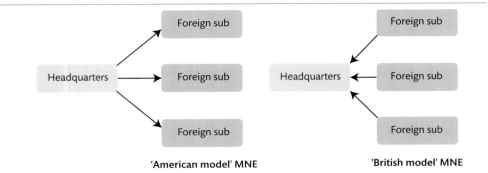

Figure 7.2
MNE models
during the first era
of globalization
(1880–1929). The
arrows indicate the
direction of cross-
border knowledge
flows (Jones 2005a).

the same things abroad as were already being done at home, in countries characterized by roughly the same level of industrial development. These similarities made it easier for companies to internationalize. Examples include the German engineering group Siemens, which launched UK operations in 1852, or the Scottish thread maker Clark, which set up a plant in New Jersey in 1865.

Early MNEs had less information about foreign environments than modern companies do. They also faced greater barriers to entry (partly because of the absence of trade-friendly intergovernmental organizations like the World Trade Organization) and suffered from slower communication and transportation links. All these factors hindered inter-subsidiary relationships and meant that most units had to be managed separately. In actual fact, given how erratic cross-border deliveries were at the time, it would have been inconceivable for one plant's production to rely on components shipped from a distant sister unit. Where one foreign subsidiary traded with another, it was usually only to sell finished products.

From the late eighteenth century until the 1929 Wall Street Crash, the spread of free-trade politics and improvements in transportation and communications deepened many companies' cross-border connections and gave birth to what has become known as the first 'golden era of globalization' (Jones 2005a). Multinationals in this period would generally develop their cross-border networks in one of two ways (see Figure 7.2):

+ **Sister unit**
Two separate corporate entities that share the same parent company.

- 'American' model MNEs. Firms would build up their competencies at home and either export goods or engage in FDI specifically to overcome trade barriers (for example, moves by Ford and General Motors into Europe in the 1920s).

- 'British' model MNEs. Firms would build their subsidiaries depending on local competencies and embed these units into a wider global network (for example, the Jardine trading company in Hong Kong).

Both these models contained the seeds of typical HQ–subsidiary configuration modern MNEs'(see Chapter 9). Furthermore, by accepting that different sites can specialize in different activities depending on their strengths, the British model came one step closer to a direct application of Adam Smith's international division of labour principles (see Chapter 4). Associated with this approach was the question of whether all sites necessarily had to have the same parent company. Companies that ended up owning all units working upstream and downstream from themselves were described as vertically integrated. This approach (see Figure 7.3) remains a common mode of MNE organization. Indeed, by some accounts, intra-firm trade of unfinished goods represents up to 60 per cent of all cross-border trade. Vertical and horizontal integration are topics that lie at the very heart of FDI and internationalization studies.

+ **Vertical integration**
Where a firm controls, and/or moves towards controlling, both upstream and downstream sides of its value chain.

As discussed in Chapter 5, the first era of globalization came to an end in the 1930s and 1940s following the Great Depression, the Second World War, and decolonization. The net effect of these upheavals was that the national governments of the time were generally more interested in protecting their domestic economies than in the benefits of open borders. In turn, this led to a sharp contraction in international trade and FDI, with many

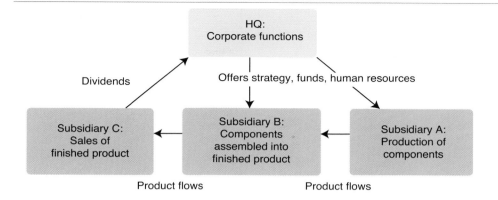

Figure 7.3
Example of a vertically integrated MNE: One key aspect of this configuration is the transfer of components from one subsidiary to another.

firms subsequently deciding to manage their different international units on a standalone, multi-domestic basis (see Online Resource Centre, extension material 7.2). To a certain extent, this revived the horizontal logic that had dominated before the first golden era of globalization.

After the 1944 Bretton Woods conference, a series of global negotiations launched within the framework of the General Agreement on Trade and Tariffs (see Chapter 6) breathed new life into international business. By the 1960s, barriers to trade and FDI were falling again, and a 'big is beautiful' paradigm took root in many boardrooms. This thinking translated into many managers' conviction that, where possible, companies should maximize economies of scale by integrating vertically and expanding globally. This return to a logic of vertical integration prevailed among American MNEs seeking to apply overseas the same mass production logic that they were pursuing in their huge home market. However, it also dominated in Europe, which was rising from the ashes of the Second World War, and whose Western half was moving towards the creation of a common market. Many European MNEs, ranging from financial institutions like Deutsche Bank to industrial firms like Philips or food companies like Danone, expanded up and down their regional value chains in an attempt to achieve the critical mass that would help them serve the increasingly unified market of the European Union (EU). A similar approach was adopted a few years later by textiles firm Hirdaramani, which started out by manufacturing both fabrics and shirts at its original factory in Sri Lanka before opting for an offshoring solution revolving around a specialist fabrics plant in Cambodia, where a particular skill exists for this kind of activity. With the world becoming smaller every day, the new paradigm was that companies must be big enough to service regional and even global markets.

The 1970s was a watershed period in MNE history because of the rise of Japanese firms, whose 'Toyotaist' model came to be seen as better adapted to a world of differentiated global consumers than the existing 'Fordist' model, which had been geared towards the mass production of a limited range of goods (see Chapter 11). With firms that were much more energy-efficient than their US rivals (Glyn 2006) and had positioned themselves cleverly in fast-growing sectors such as consumer electronics (Sony and Matsushita) or computing (Fujitsu and Toshiba), Japan was now an industrial powerhouse. Just as importantly, its management systems became a benchmark for MNEs everywhere.

One of the main characteristics of the Japanese model is that MNEs no longer necessarily had to own the foreign units comprising their value chains (see Figure 7.4) but could instead opt for a model of 'vertical disintegration'. In this approach, a central prime contractor assumes less direct responsibility for operations and organizes instead a network of trusted external partners to whom it can outsource such work. Many household names, like Toyota or Panasonic, have been very successful in applying this 'small is beautiful' paradigm, which has become a dominant feature in multinational thinking today.

Prime contractors view international business differently from vertically integrated firms. Whereas the latter will be concerned mainly with costs, the main factor for companies

> Go to the ORC

+ Multi-domestic
Describes companies whose worldview, thus organization, stresses differentiated national markets rather than one unified global market. The end result is that each subsidiary manages its value chain more or less autonomously, with little if any coordination at the regional or global level.

+ Offshoring
Where a firm moves an activity that it used to run domestically to a subsidiary it owns abroad, usually to cut costs.

Thinking point
Can an MNE ever become too big?

+ Prime contractor
Company at the heart of a network of companies, whose supply orders are the main trigger for other members' own production plans.

Thinking point
How easy is it for Western MNEs to copy Japanese management paradigms?

Figure 7.4
An MNE either covers
the international
value chain with its
own subsidiaries or
contracts overseas
operations with outside
parties.

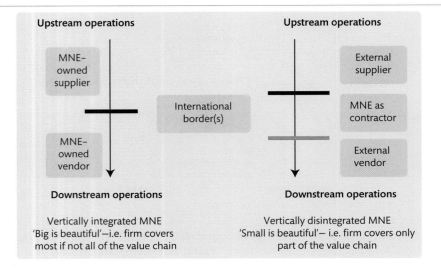

Vertically integrated MNE
'Big is beautiful'—i.e. firm covers
most if not all of the value chain

Vertically disintegrated MNE
'Small is beautiful'— i.e. firm covers only
part of the value chain

operating in a network is coordination and therefore interdependency. This is conditioned by various factors, including partners' relative sizes; who possesses the more valuable technology; and the balance of political power (with companies from desperately poor less developed countries often starting from a weaker bargaining position). Interdependence also reflects partners' corporate cultures, with some firms being more disposed to friendly relations, whereas others are more accustomed to competitive interactions. MNE network relationships (see Figure 7.5) are one of the levels where companies' micro-level strategies intersect most visibly with their macro-level international business environment.

Although this brief review of multinational history has uncovered many commonalities, the reality is that MNEs pursue a variety of behaviours at any given point in time. One way to categorize this diversity is by region of origin. Indeed, most global authorities, including the Organization for Economic Cooperation and Development and the United Nations, specifically classify multinational behaviour on this basis. This is logical, given the many studies showing that the vast majority of MNEs conduct most of their business in their home regions (Rugman 2005). Working in an MNE may require a more cosmopolitan outlook, but the fact is that many individuals retain at least some connection to their culture of origin. This does not mean that everyone working in a particular region behaves similarly, or that companies in one part of the world do not imitate their counterparts elsewhere. There is simply a strong argument supporting the growing consensus in international business that, between the global and national perspectives, the region offers an increasingly fruitful level for analysing MNE behaviour.

Thinking point

To what extent
should MNE
behaviour be
categorized along
regional lines?

Figure 7.5
Prime contractors
at the heart of MNE
networks coordinate
relations among
different tiers of
suppliers.

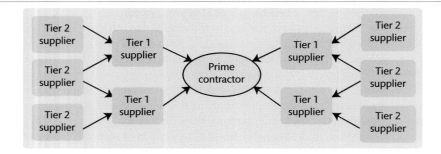

MNEs' regional characteristics

One way in which MNEs from different regions can be compared is in terms of their research efforts (OECD 2007). For instance, North American MNEs in many sectors have benefited greatly in the recent past from fast productivity growth, driven largely by advances in IT. Corporate research spending amounted to a respectable 1.75 per cent of total national GDP in the USA in 2006—a number augmented by a further 0.75 per cent if government-funded research & development (R&D) is included. The continuous development of new products and above all new processes is rooted in US companies' strong connections to universities (see the discussion in Chapter 11 on knowledge spillovers). On the other hand, the financialization ethos that dominates in the USA (Froud et al. 2006) means that American MNEs are also under greater pressure than their foreign counterparts to maximize short-term returns. This tends to create riskier corporate behaviour, which often manifests itself through companies' investment policies and financial or product innovation strategies. Lastly, the North American corporate environment is also noteworthy because of the role that FDI plays in this part of the world. The USA has become the world's leading recipient of FDI, although it is hard to say whether this reflects its financial imbalances or its attractiveness as an FDI destination—probably both.

For European companies, a significant trend in the years since the fall of communism and the advent of a single EU market has been the drive towards greater sectorial consolidation. Many companies that used to dominate their national markets have been forced into transcontinental strategies over the past twenty years, one consequence of which has been a rising number of cross-border merger and acquisition operations. Also noteworthy is the region's strong FDI growth in recent years, driven mainly by West European companies investing in Eastern transition economies. At the same time, many European MNEs remain vulnerable because of the region's relatively mediocre R&D spending, which amounted in 2006 to a mere 0.9 per cent of combined GDP in the EU. Furthermore, the productivity of European labour, measured in GDP per worker, lags far behind the levels achieved by US firms, despite a clear improvement in recent years. The EU's Lisbon agenda, dating from 2000, aims to address some of these weaknesses through the promotion of a more 'knowledge-based' economy.

+ **Financialization**
View that a firm's mission is to maximize financial returns. Often associated with the presence on the Board of Directors of 'active' investors specifically working to ensure that the firm engages in actions that will enhance 'shareholder value'.

+ **Consolidation**
Where producers within a sector join forces via takeovers or mergers in order to reduce over-capacities.

Photo 7.1
Asian MNEs traditionally spend a higher than average percentage of revenues on R&D (Photodisc).

Lastly, Asian MNEs can be divided into two categories. On one hand, there are longer-established companies from Korea and Japan, with their particular strengths in consumer durables and capital goods. On the other, there are younger MNEs from the two emerging giants: China, a global manufacturing centre; and India, more specialized in services but which also has certain industrial strengths (see Chapter 16). Factors such as economic patriotism, the 2008 credit crunch, and ecological constraints may slow Asia's rise, and it is noteworthy that a disproportionate percentage of Western dealings in this part of the world continue to involve trade rather than FDI. Indeed, emerging markets still account for only a small percentage of total global FDI flows. Nevertheless, ever since the 1990s, Asia has been far and away the world's most dynamic region, and it is a safe bet that Asian MNEs will continue to outperform rivals from other regions as their home markets catch up to Western standards of living. Note the above-average R&D spending by firms from this part of the world, as well as the enormous numbers of young engineers being trained in local universities. Such developments bode well for the future of Asian MNEs.

Regions also vary in terms of average company size. Indeed, one global constant is that SMEs account for the majority of all companies. This fact alone justifies their separate study as an international business topic.

Small and medium-sized enterprises

It is almost impossible to estimate how trade and FDI break down exactly among the many different types of companies engaging in such activities. Even within the SME category, there are significant variations between companies whose international dealings are sporadic at best, others that transact abroad regularly, and tiny, start-up 'micro-multinationals' that use the Internet to 'go global' from the very outset (Copeland 2006). Irrespective of these variations, the lack of attention that SMEs receive in much international business analysis is a mistake: in many countries, such companies account for a significant proportion of all trade and FDI.

A prime example is Germany, where *Mittelstand* ('medium-level') companies are responsible for an estimated 30 per cent of all exports (Theopold 2009). The country is home to upwards of 250 SMEs that can be classified as world-class champions in their respective markets. These often operate in niches that are too narrow to be exploited profitably using a larger company's heavier (and thus more expensive) industrial assets, and yet have been profitably mined by SMEs. This can involve finished products (for example, Neumann microphones and Bechstein pianos) as well as the intermediary goods (for example, Zeiss glass lenses and Solar-Fabrik photovoltaic cells) that larger companies subsequently use for their own production processes. Successful *Mittelstand* firms are characterized by their narrow product portfolios (they rarely engage in diversification strategies); constant efforts to realize gradual innovation in their specialist areas; and ambition to dominate their respective markets. A trait common to some companies in this category is their refusal to outsource sales or production to external partners—despite their small size, German SMEs (unlike many of their foreign rivals) strive to control as much of their international value chains as possible. Above all, they are very commercially-oriented, constantly checking on their main customers in different target national markets to stay informed of any changes in preferences.

Such flexibility contrasts with the situation in many larger companies, whose size often creates 'diseconomies of scale', materialized in heavy bureaucracies and procedures. Many large MNEs struggle to develop the responsiveness that they need to keep up in fast-moving international environments. Thus, instead of being rivals, small and large MNEs often complement one another, with each tending to thrive in a different environment.

SMEs generally play a relatively greater role in locations (like Southern Europe or many LDCs) where a lack of equity funding makes it harder for companies to expand.

Inside business

Emil Gigov, Partner, Albion Ventures LLP

Albion Ventures is a venture capital investor, providing debt and equity funding for smaller, entrepreneurial, fast-growing businesses across all sectors. Albion manages over £200 million in seven venture capital trusts. Our typical investment size is between £1 million and £10 million and we always take a minority equity position in the investments we make. Although the companies we back are based in the UK, many of them operate internationally providing their goods and services across the globe.

The majority of companies that we invest in are relatively small but fast growing. Albion is a hands-on investor, working closely with its investee companies at a strategic level. We provide valuable experience of growing smaller businesses as well as useful introductions through our extensive network of senior contacts. We guide our investee companies through further funding rounds and provide the necessary support on the eventual sale or flotation of the company. As a non-executive director I sit on the board of every company that I invest in. Part of my role is to represent the interests of Albion Ventures, but I also have to ensure that the company achieves its business objectives.

The availability of information on smaller companies is typically limited. That is why it is important to understand a particular sector well when looking for investment opportunities. The companies themselves, as SMEs, need our leveraging of past experience and our wide network of contacts across all industries, especially when they are looking to conduct business internationally. Many of these companies sell their products and services internationally, either through their own subsidiaries, or through local partnerships or agents.

Indeed, smaller companies are catalysts for economic progress in many parts of the world. This is particularly true in countries blessed with large numbers of tiny but dynamic micro-multinationals, a new category of SMEs that offer many if not most of the knowledge-related service activities driving much international business today (basic and applied technologies, IT, consulting, or legal advice). Individually, SMEs may not have as much power as their larger counterparts, but their combined impact is substantial.

Nevertheless, it is clear that size can severely handicap smaller firms. This is a topic of great concern for many business economists, to the extent that the UN has organized several conferences devoted specifically to the internationalization difficulties of SMEs (UNECE 2001). As demonstrated by Figures 7.6 and 7.7, such problems have been divided into two categories: external barriers; and internal handicaps.

SMEs and politicians are aware of these problems and constantly seeking to remedy them. At a political level and in recognition of SMEs' contribution to employment (some EU estimates are that smaller companies account for up to 70 per cent of all European jobs), governments often provide this sector with special assistance, including export promotion facilities, financial aid, and international data. Some countries have restructured their corporation tax brackets so that SMEs pay lower marginal rates than large companies do. In more corporate terms, the SME sector as a whole has become a major investor in modern telecommunications systems, which smaller companies hope to use to improve their intelligence of foreign consumers and, potentially, partners (see Chapter 8). Lastly, a number of specialized federations have organized worldwide to represent the diverse interests typifying this sector.

> **Thinking point**
>
> How much should states help SMEs to compete with their larger rivals?

Figure 7.6
Main external
barriers to SME
internationalization.

International problems facing SMEs	Comments
Bureaucracy	Same amount of paperwork as larger firms (i.e. customs forms) but spread over smaller volumes
Product and service range	SMEs' narrower portfolios make it harder to attack diverse international markets
Language/cultural barriers	SMEs have less human capital to cope with differences
Commercialization	SMEs can rarely afford foreign retail outlets yet struggle to control external vendors
Branding	SMEs cannot invest as much as large firms overcoming consumers' home bias
Supply chain pressures	Payment delays, price wars —larger firms' deep pockets allow them to squeeze SMEs
Scale	SMEs do not have same size advantages as larger firms (bulk purchases/scale output)
Government support	Larger firms are more effective than SMEs at lobbying for export assistance
Intellectual property	SMEs have fewer resources to monitor possible infractions

Figure 7.7
Main internal
handicaps for SME
internationalization.

SME handicap	Comment
Lack of entrepreneurial, managerial, and/or marketing skills	Many top graduates go to big name firms.
Difficulties in accessing financial resources	Banks often penalize SME borrowers
Lesser quality management capabilities	SMEs might not have enough spare staff to pursue a quality agenda
Trade documentation (i.e. packaging, labelling requirements)	SMEs might not be able to afford trade specialists to deal with complexities
Insufficient investment in technological assets and know-how	SMEs' size means that they struggle to fund crucial non-productive functions like R&D

Case Study 7.2

Small companies in international business: Green and Black's

In 1991, Josephine Fairley and her husband, Craig Sams, founders of a pioneering organic food company named Whole Earth, set out to develop the world's first organic chocolate bar. Working out of small premises on London's Portobello Road, the couple began by launching a new label called Green and Black's (www.greenandblacks.com) and set out to change their supply network. By 1994, they were ready to market 'Maya Gold', a new product made from Central American cocoa beans whose growers were paid 10 per cent more than they would under normal market conditions. By offering suppliers a 'living wage', Green and Black's was positioning itself in the fast-growing niche of ethical consumer products. Later, it became the first brand in the UK to receive 'fair trade' certification (see Chapter 3). It is worth noting that this SME developed an international dimension from the very start, although more on the purchasing side than on the sales side.

Sainsbury's, a large British supermarket, began selling the Green and Black's label from 1992 onwards. Local market coverage was very patchy, however. Being both owners and managers of their company, Fairley and Sams did not have the resources to fund a bigger distribution network. Outside finance had to be found, so in 1999 the couple sold 80 per cent of their company to an investor group led by a former head of the New Covent Garden Soup Company. This was a successful move, in part because the new partners also had experience in the high-quality foods sector. After 2000, Green and Black's was carried by all UK supermarkets, and its annual revenues grew by 69 per cent on average over the next four years. By the end of 2004, the company was producing revenues of £22.4 million and had thirty employees.

Despite this success, Green and Black's size remained a handicap, both limiting the sums it could distribute through supplier communities in Central America (a crucial part of its brand image) and its market coverage in the UK. Supermarkets account for 80 per cent of the British food market but only 60 per cent of sweets sales. Most confectionery products are impulse purchases made at newsagents and other small retail outlets. Green and Black's needed further capital to attack these channels and just as importantly to explore possible expansion into Australia and the USA. The lengthy supply lines that are part of an international sales network can be prohibitively expensive for an SME—yet, if Green and Black's did not attack certain foreign markets, there was

a good chance that better-funded rivals might invade its niche. Hence Fairley and Sams's decision in 2005 to accept a takeover bid from Cadbury's, a large British MNE with global reach but very different traditions. The couple were highly criticized for this move. They may have felt, however, that they had no choice.

SMEs seek niche markets in a world of giant MNEs (reproduced with the kind permission of Green and Black's).

Having reviewed the different ways in which corporate behaviour is shaped by political, economic, and technological variables, it will be useful to study the reverse effect and see how MNEs affect the host countries where they operate. It is this focus on the two-way interaction between companies and their environments that enriches international business and distinguishes it from narrower management disciplines.

Section II: How MNEs interact with host countries

Whereas trade affects countries once goods cross national borders, FDI and lobbying materialize at the heart of a national economy. This particularity means that they deserve a special mention in the study of companies' international behaviour.

+ Lobbying
Attempts to influence policy-makers, often elected officials.

Foreign direct investment

The OECD defines FDI as a situation where a foreign owner has an equity stake of at least 10 per cent in a company's ordinary shares and aims to establish a 'lasting interest' in the host country. FDI can involve any part of a value chain, from the upstream extraction of raw materials to the downstream retailing of services or finished goods. A distinction is commonly made between horizontal FDI, where the company operates in the foreign country at a similar stage of its international value chain, and vertical FDI, where the cross-border move involves operating at a different stage as it does at home. Horizontal FDI is usually considered 'market-seeking', since it is generally motivated by an MNE's desire to expand sales—although, for some upstream companies, horizontal FDI can be an attempt to acquire resources and/or dominate competitors (for example, the 2007 merger between mining giants Alcan and Rio Tinto, seeking to consolidate their leadership of the global aluminium market). Vertical FDI, on the other hand, is considered more 'efficiency-seeking', since its purpose is to help a company control its value chain more effectively. There are two ways of doing this. In the case of 'backwards' integration, the MNE expands its operations upstream (towards the supply side). This is usually to reduce costs, although here too the goal can be to access resources, as the Swisscom telecommunications company did in 2007 when it bought the Italian Fastweb, which manufactures the broadband equipment required for the acquirer's operations. 'Forward' vertical integration, on the other hand, means that the company is making a downstream FDI, usually to increase sales. This was the purpose, for instance, of Russian energy giant Lukoil's 2006 acquisition of eighty-three JET petrol stations in Poland. Worldwide, the UN Conference on Trade and Development (UNCTAD) counted about 79,000 MNEs with 790,000 foreign subsidiaries in 2007. These entities, with global sales of nearly $31 trillion, accounted that year for 11 per cent of global gross domestic product (GDP) and provided employment for 82 million persons. They were also responsible for close to one-third of global exports. Clearly, FDI is a central topic in international business.

Moreover, FDI can influence home and host countries both positively and negatively. With some studies indicating that vertical and especially horizontal FDI has a more positive effect on growth in developed countries than in LDCs (Beugelsdijk et al. 2008), FDI is as much a political as an economic topic. It will now be discussed from both perspectives.

Assessing FDI from a macro (national) perspective

Supporters of FDI highlight the benefits for a home country of offshoring activities like IT services, business process operations, or simple manufacturing functions. Such actions can save firms money (Blanco et al. 2005) and enable their remaining domestic units to focus on activities where they have a comparative advantage. This was the reasoning applied, for instance, by Italian–French hi-tech company STMicroelectronics when it relieved its home country facilities of the responsibility for producing basic components like silicon wafers, offshoring this activity to Singapore and concentrating its European units on more advanced activities such as smartcards and micro-controllers. Where the concentration on strategic, higher value-added sectors improves a home country's overall macro-economic performance, it can ultimately increase domestic employment, despite the initial loss of jobs.

Criticisms of FDI from the home country perspective, on the other hand, will stress its negative effects on short-term employment. Many OECD economies have suffered from deindustrialization (that is, a shrinking industrial base) because of foreign competition in the manufacturing sector. The social consequences can be particularly devastating because many factory jobs are concentrated in just a few specific regions. Mass closures have destroyed entire communities in France (Lorraine), Germany (Ruhr), and the USA (Ohio/Western Pennsylvania). The call from politicians and economists for worker mobility should not mask the human costs for unemployed factory workers and their families of having to move away from their home towns.

Aggravating this problem is the growing displacement of service sector jobs leaving OECD countries, a trend that has been shown to have a particularly negative effect on public attitudes towards globalization (Coe 2008). There is also the problem of rising disparities between those who benefit from globalization, including shareholders or workers with

Photo 7.2
Communities can
be devastated when
local factories close
(© iStockphoto).

secure jobs, and those who lose their jobs or whose wages are being squeezed (Glyn 2006). One analyst has calculated that, despite rising average earnings in the USA, from the mid-1990s onwards median earnings stagnated—that is, globalization has benefited a few people enormously and most not at all (Altman 2007). Home country governments also lose out on tax revenues when, as studied in Chapter 14, MNEs use FDI to move operations (and declare profits) overseas.

In terms of host country interests, supporters of FDI point out that local firms are likely to benefit from MNEs' intangible competencies, including technological know-how and managerial competencies (Wei and Liu 2006). The knock-on effect for local firms and workers' skills levels can be very positive, especially when the foreign units manufacture intermediary goods and services that domestic firms can put to good use in their own production processes. Examples include the way that the arrival of Western retailers such as Tesco, Carrefour, and Walmart helped to modernize China's retail distribution network. MNEs usually achieve higher productivity than national firms do. This is because their larger size enables them to do more R&D; handle a wider variety of products; and employ more skilled labour (Barba Navaretti and Venables 2004; Bhagwati 2004). Lastly, some studies have shown that national development trajectories are positively affected in those instances when FDI is funded by equity capital rather than debt (Goldin and Reinert 2005). In short, business economists have found many arguments for portraying FDI as a good thing for host countries.

People who see FDI as harming host countries often accuse multinational giants of forcing 'dependency relationships' on local governments (Buckman 2004) strong-armed into looking the other way while MNEs plunder resources and exploit workers (Petras and Veltmeyer 2007). Another criticism is that MNEs tend to transfer little useful technology and often use their units to import expensive components that will worsen the host country's trade deficit. There is also unhappiness in some quarters with the way that big MNEs sometimes overwhelm domestic markets by squeezing out smaller national companies—one example being US giant Starbuck's decision to move into UK neighbourhoods already populated by locally owned coffee shops and diners (Guest 2006). More generally, people may resent the fact that MNEs can use their potential mobility to pressure national governments into offering them tax breaks, 'circumventing national regulations and policies more easily than national firms can' (Barba Navaretti and Venables 2004). In this vision, FDI is an economic process that helps the MNE more than it does the host economy.

Figure 7.8 summarizes the key questions underlying a cost/benefit assessment of FDI's impact on host countries. Like most international business topics, FDI is neither intrinsically good nor intrinsically bad.

> **Thinking point**
>
> To what extent do large MNEs use FDI as a means for bullying weak national governments?

Figure 7.8
Judging MNEs' impact
on host economies
(adapted from Barba
Navaretti and Venables
2004).

Economic aspect	How does FDI affect the host country?
Capital flows	Inflows; outflows Were the funds for the FDI brought into the country or raised locally? How much does the MNE take out in dividends? What policies has the government had to pursue to attract FDI? How easily can foreign investors withdraw funds?
Development	Infrastructure; industrialization; terms of trade Does the FDI involve high or low value-added activities? How does the FDI position the country in terms of the international division of labour? Does it discourage local entrepreneurship? Had the FDI never occurred, could local goods or imports have served the country's needs? What social damage is being caused by the changes to the country's current economic structures?
Competition	Short-term disruptions; long-term productivity effects Has the FDI broken up existing monopolies and injected greater competition into the marketplace? Or is it simply crowding out local producers? Are MNEs competing with one another locally or forming a cartel?
Flow of goods	Imports; exports To what extent does the FDI rely on imports of components or finished products rather than locally sourced inputs? What are the knock-on effects for local firms? To what extent is the MNE exporting its output or selling it locally?
Labour	Job volatility; comparative pay scales; standards Is the FDI creating new jobs or taking staff away from other employers? To what extent does the FDI resort to part-time workers or local contractors? Are workers/unions subjected to added pressures? Is any extra training being offered?
Knowledge spillovers	Technology transfers, new management practices Has the FDI raised local productivity? Have any learning clusters developed? Is the host country capable of absorbing new knowledge or hosting hi-tech activities?
Sustainability	Pollution policies; competition for (and utilization of) resources What pollution mitigation/abatement policies are associated with the FDI? Does it use best practices and clean technology?

It is only through a balanced answer to these questions that the real impact of a given FDI can be accurately assessed. Like many other international business debates, observers tend to generalize wildly in this area. The reality is more of a mixed picture.

Assessing FDI from a micro (corporate) perspective

An MNE's decision to do business in another country via FDI as opposed to another, less capital-intensive mode of entry—such as trade, outsourcing, or licensing (see Chapter 8)—is one of the most important decisions that a firm will make. Because of the extra costs and additional knowledge required to succeed with an FDI, companies will embark upon this course only if they have hope of gaining substantial benefits from it—or if it means that they avoid the disadvantages of not investing abroad.

Proactive reasons for engaging in FDI

Vertical integration. Where companies open specialist production units in different countries to maximize each location's particular advantages, they are also putting themselves in a position to increase economies of scale and develop expertise. As long as intra-firm flows can be coordinated advantageously, the end effect will be a more rational production organization. This kind of 'internalization' (see Dunning's 'Eclectic Paradigm' theory in Chapter 4) means that companies are in a better position to protect and enhance the knowledge that gives them a competitive advantage over rivals, since they retain responsibility for all operations and can therefore control and even monopolize the learning that comes from with this. A good example is the way that Apple owns a direct stake in many of the businesses (chips, software) whose combined output it uses in iPod handsets.

Proximity to resources.　One resource in international production is manual labour. This is often the driver behind FDI, with companies seeking to take advantage of the huge wage differentials that exist across the planet. On other occasions, the resource being sought through FDI is a physical commodity such as oil or minerals. This rationale will become increasingly important as global demand for finite commodities creates supply shortages (see Chapter 16). Lastly, it is not only primary resources that companies seek through FDI but also access to knowledge, a crucial factor in many hi-tech sectors. An example of this was the decision by French computer company Honeywell-Bull to set up a representative office in California's Silicon Valley, thereby increasing its exposure to trendsetters in the world of computing.

Proximity to customers.　Companies often try to locate manufacturing facilities near or in an emerging economy such as China or India for the obvious reason that it increases their chances of gaining a foothold in a dynamic market offering good growth prospects. This is particularly important if the host country government requires its national market to be served via FDI rather than imports, because of the positive impact that inward investment might have on local employment. A second proximity strategy involves replicating the internationalization moves of a customer with whom a company has a long-standing supply relationship. One example is the way that Japanese automotive manufacturer Chuo Spring built a factory in Thailand following the decision by its main customer, Toyota, to undertake an FDI in this country.

International economies of scale.　The critical mass that firms achieve through FDI can occur on the upstream, production side but also on the sales side. This can be useful, for instance, when domestic manufacturing capacities exceed home country demand. One example is the way that big British banks like HSBC have opened branches across continental Europe to sell financial products originating in its London offices.

Government incentives.　Lastly, FDI can also involve opportunistic behaviour by MNEs taking advantage of government measures to encourage inwards investment. Chapter 5 detailed some of these incentives, which include competitively low corporation tax rates, industrial grants, and specific infrastructure outlays maximizing the productivity of new facilities.

Defensive reasons for engaging in FDI

Government interference.　Because of the frequent perception that investment (through the capital, knowledge, and jobs that it provides) is more advantageous to a host country than imports, governments sometimes establish barriers to trade specifically to induce MNEs to enter their markets via FDI rather than through trade. Note that such policies, which during the 1970s motivated FDI decisions by Japanese carmakers in the USA or Volkswagen in Brazil, have become somewhat less prevalent in recent years because of WTO policing.

Lack of domestic capacities.　Given the importance of economies of scale in many price-sensitive sectors, companies from smaller countries might be at a disadvantage unless they create an internationally sized production network. This logic was, for example, one of the reasons underlying the 1994 acquisition by Swedish appliances company Electrolux of facilities owned by the German company AEG.

Foreignness.　A foreign brand will sometimes be penalized by consumers, if not for reasons of xenophobia, then simply because they are more familiar with domestic alternatives. One way for a firm to overcome this obstacle is by engaging in FDI, thereby showing greater commitment to the host country. Foreign firms can show their devotion to a local population through employment policies. Local marketing is another tool that companies can use to the same effect—one example being the way that leading London football club Tottenham Hotspur used to be sponsored by Holsten, a brewery from Hamburg seeking to break into the already crowded UK market.

The need to diversify exposures.   Two risks that companies can reduce via FDI have already been discussed in Chapter 1. One involves foreign exchange—that is, the danger of accumulating costs in countries prone to currency rises and/or revenues in countries prone to currency devaluations. The second involves marketing, with Product Life Cycle theory (see Chapter 12) teaching that a product can grow old and unprofitable in one country yet remain young in another. Indeed, much FDI by food sector companies such as Nestlé or General Foods is specifically aimed at juggling global variations in products' life cycles.

FDI also allows companies to diversify their general macro-economic exposures. At a given moment in time, different countries will find themselves at varying stages of the economic cycle, with some experiencing a period of growth even as others enter recession. An MNE with operations in just one country risks losing out on a boom occurring elsewhere. Global FDI also increases a company's chance of being present as an LDC emerges from poverty.

Undermining competitors.   Lastly, some companies undertake FDI without any great hope of making much money from the venture. Instead, their goal is to create greater competition in a rival's market of origin, undercutting its profits there to prevent it from engaging in price wars elsewhere. This is one explanation for the decision that French tyre company Michelin took in 1988 to engage in FDI in the USA, the home market of its global rival, Goodyear.

Recent trends in FDI

 > Go to the ORC

+ **Mergers and acquisitions**
Mergers occur when two companies agree to combine their operations in a new company where both have more or less equal powers. Acquisitions occur when one company takes over another—either with its approval or on a hostile basis—and becomes the new entity's main shareholder.

As discussed in Chapter 1 (and the Online Resource Centre, extension material 1.3), the credit crunch had some very negative effects on FDI in 2008 and beyond. Preliminary statistics show, for instance, that total cross-border mergers and acquisitions (M&A) activity—one form of FDI (see Chapter 8)—was 29 per cent lower in the first half of 2008 than it had been in the second half of 2007. Other indicators show that FDI (along with trade) declined even more rapidly in 2008 than total economic activity did. This means that international business, unusually, accounted for a smaller percentage of the world economy at the end of the year than it had at the beginning. The possibility that companies and managers turn inwards when conditions are difficult has very interesting theoretical implications.

Nevertheless, it is still very useful to study FDI data for the period immediately preceding the credit crunch, if only because it reveals potential patterns in case FDI reverts to its longer-term trend in years to come. Global inward FDI hit $1.833 trillion in 2007, up strongly for the fourth year running (UNCTAD 2008). $1.248 trillion of these inflows (68 per cent) went to developed countries, with $500 billion (27 per cent) going to LDCs and the rest to the transition economies. Wealthy countries' share of total inflows has slowed in recent years, after the nearly 79 per cent level recorded as recently as 1990 (when the UK alone received about as much FDI as Latin America, Russia, India, and China combined). However, in line with the gravity model discussed in Chapter 4, the vast majority of all FDI flows are still from one industrialized country to another (see Online Resource Centre, extension material 7.3). Despite theories about the extra advantage that multinationals derive from FDI in developing countries (Dietsch 2006), it seems that many MNEs are still more comfortable with moves to countries that they find easier to understand. The ongoing dominance of 'North–North' FDI is partly a response to the problems that many MNEs have faced in the past when entering LDCs characterized by lesser intellectual property rights protections (Lung 2007). It also reflects the growing role that 'private equity' firms from the world's so-called advanced economies have come to play in FDI, particularly in cross-border M&A, increasingly motivated by short-term

 > Go to the ORC

Thinking point

When, if ever, will FDI levels recover from the 2008 credit crunch?

opportunism rather than by long-term wealth creation strategies (Barba Navaretti and Venables 2004). All categories combined, M&A operations (which totalled $1.637 trillion in 2007) are most likely to occur in OECD countries characterized by mature legal systems and financial markets capable of coping with mega-deals that regularly exceed $1 billion (UNCTAD 2008).

As emerging economies' living standards rise and their regulatory systems become more transparent, South–North FDI flows should gain in importance. Some of this will be the effect of cash-rich sovereign wealth funds, as exemplified by Abu Dhabi's 2007 acquisition of an 8.1 per cent stake in Advanced Micro Devices (AMD), America's second largest micro-processor manufacturer. Even more significantly, LDC firms have become increasingly active in acquisitions of OECD country firms. Examples from 2007–8 include takeovers by Indian steelmakers Tata and Mittal of Corus (UK) and Arcelor (Luxemburg), respectively, or the purchase of Jaguar Land Rover by India's Tata Motors. Given that the fastest-growing category of MNEs since the mid-1990s has involved firms from developing and transition economies, and in light of the strong growth being recorded in South–South FDI flows (which now amount to 16 per cent of the global total), there is every chance that today's developed countries will lose their domination of global FDI one day.

In sectorial terms, currently around three-fifths of all FDI is in the service sector (including trade and finance), around one-quarter in manufacturing, and the rest in primary goods. The expectation is that FDI in this latter sector will rise in the future, as energy and commodity prices pick up (after falling temporarily because of the 2008–9 recession). This prediction is based on fundamental demand conditions, partially driven by the rapid industrialization of the developing world, above all China. By some measures, Petrochina became the world's largest oil company in November 2007, following investments in countries such as Sudan, Angola, and Nigeria. The expected growth in primary sector FDI will benefit resource-rich countries like Russia and Brazil, as well as those MNEs that have already secured their global supplies of raw materials. Conversely, downstream processors like China's leading steelmaker, Baoshan Iron and Steel, might struggle to secure the iron ore that they currently import from international mining companies like Australia's BHP. To remedy this vulnerability, and much in the same way as European industrialists acquired foreign mines and oilfields a century ago to fuel the first era of globalization, there is every chance that a large number of industrial MNEs will use FDI in the future as a means towards backwards integration. One effect of this strategy, in a world afflicted by resource depletion, will be to intensify their interactions with host country governments.

> **Thinking point**
>
> Will South–South FDI ever dominate investment global flows?

Lobbying

Negotiations between MNEs and host countries are extremely complicated bargaining situations (Agmon 2003). At a certain level, they derive from different parties' economic interests. The concept of 'obsolescing bargaining', for instance, says that an MNE can put more pressure on a government before it invests in a country than afterwards. The amount of pressure that can be applied depends on how important the MNE is to the country, and vice versa. Logically, a company will have to be more conciliatory when trying to enter a dynamic market such as India or China. Conversely, where the host country is absolutely desperate for the capital, knowledge, and jobs that the FDI can bring, the MNE will be in a stronger bargaining position (Grosse 2005). This is especially true if the host government is aware that the company has a large multinational network enabling it to shift production elsewhere, quickly, and for relatively little cost (Ietto-Gillies 2004). Much depends on whether the MNE is planning to use the FDI to produce goods that will be re-exported, thus earning foreign currency for the host country, or to sell goods and services into the local market, thereby displacing national firms.

MNE–host country relationships are influenced by more subjective factors at other times. These include the host government's general attitude towards foreign interests— for example, whether it pursues more mercantilist or neo-liberal policies. In all

likelihood, governments run by free market friendly politicians will be more welcoming to FDI than ones whose sole priority is to protect the interests of domestic constituents. Trust in a foreign MNE will also depend on its track record. A feeling of mistrust can arise if there is the perception that an MNE has a pattern of trying to take advantage of countries' weaknesses. One reason why so many LDCs still require MNEs to engage in 'joint venture' mixed ownership alliances with local partners is their deep-seated suspicion of the motives and methods of what some critics have come to denounce as the 'corporatocracy' of domineering mega-firms (Buckman 2004). Even globalization-friendly economists can have some sympathy with LDCs' aversion to MNEs' lobbying activities. Jagdish Bhagwati (2004), for instance, has noted the inappropriateness of some US companies' successful lobbying to get Washington to force Mexico into accepting an intellectual property regime specifically tailored towards American interests before agreeing to sign the NAFTA treaty. Another bone of contention is the way that the US government was lobbied by American firms in 1999 to keep Thailand from placing any restrictions on foreign cigarette sales, the argument being that public health measures of this sort were 'GATT-inconsistent'. This kind of aggressive lobbying, which often involves MNEs getting their powerful home country governments to bully weak LDC host countries, unsurprisingly generates feelings of hostility that, in turn, get in the way of harmonious international business relationships. The short-term advantages that an MNE is able to negotiate may be offset over the long run by the negative brand image that the local population will associate with it—or with other companies from the same country of origin.

Nonetheless, there is no doubt that interactions between many MNEs and national governments are friendlier than they were before the 1990s, back when the world was torn between communism and capitalism and subject to greater ideological polarization than is the case today. One explanation for this generally broader acceptance of foreign companies' influence is the cosmopolitan value system advocated in many modern universities, as well as the 'insiderization' effects of several decades of globalization (which has the consequence of making most MNEs seem less foreign). Feelings of economic patriotism may continue to undermine foreign ownership in some countries, but obstacles of this kind can generally be overcome if the MNE is perceived as adding real value to the local economy and not accused of causing cultural, social, or environmental harm. As mentioned in Chapter 3, widespread recognition of the benefits of a positive reputation has changed the nature of international lobbying. Nowadays, MNEs tend to resort to advocacy approaches involving the organization of well-publicized open forums where they try to win the battle for hearts and minds. The focus is no longer on heavy-handed threats behind closed doors but on convincing friendly foreign audiences of the advantages of establishing a partnership relationship—although often on the MNE's terms.

Lobbying is already widespread in many OECD countries. It has come under repeated criticism—for example, during the 2008 US presidential campaign—for providing companies with an unfair advantage to the detriment of other interest groups. This explains the adoption of different codes (like the European Commission's 2001 Green Paper on Governance) aimed at restricting lobbyists' conduct. At the same time, some observers take the opposite view that advocacy lobbying is nothing more than managers' democratic right to influence political decisions in areas of interest to MNEs, such as foreign trade, agriculture, technical standards, and intellectual property rights (Coen and Grant 2005). This is based on the idea that lobbying is not intrinsically unfair as long as everyone has a similar opportunity to employ lobbyists (Hoekman and Kostecki 2001). There is no doubt that, in much of the world, joining an advocacy group (see Online Resource Centre, extension material 7.4) has become a standard way for MNEs to gain the attention of home and host country governments alike.

It is also worth noting international variations in lobbying approaches. The US legislative process, for instance, is marked by so-called pork barrel politics where members of Congress actively seek funds for projects benefiting the constituencies they represent. In a certain sense, this means that power is less centralized here than in Europe, where almost all EU-wide decisions are made in Brussels (Guégen 2007). At the same time, EU member states clearly hold much more power than US federal states. The USA and the EU also have different systems for funding political parties and campaigns. These considerations all affect the ways in which international lobbyists might try to influence local politicians.

Lastly, there is a striking difference between lobbying in the western hemisphere and in Asia, where companies might apply what the Chinese call a *guanxi* approach to construct personal relationships and a sense of social obligation with politicians (see Chapter 2). Government-business relations in this region are deeply rooted in local cultures, meaning that professional lobbying in the US or European styles will be less effective here. Yet Western MNEs also need good relationships with local authorities in Asia, especially in countries like China, where bureaucratic decisions like licensing are not always made in a way that is particularly transparent to foreigners. This explains why so many MNEs retain the services of individuals capable of developing good political connections. In this as in many other areas of international business, 'insiderization' is a key factor of success.

+ **Advocacy**
Speaking out on behalf of a certain constituency in order to influence policy-makers to adopt a friendly stance.

> Go to the ORC

Thinking point
How ethical is (cross-border) lobbying?

Challenges and choices

→ One of the main challenges facing MNEs is how to organize their value chain in a way that will enhance overall efficiency. If managers decide to specialize units worldwide in the different stages of the production process, they will increase unit-level economies of scale but complicate intra-firm coordination, making this more expensive. If they decide instead to configure each site so that it is capable of hosting the full range of value chain operations, they will facilitate co-ordination but also incur extra costs due to the duplication of certain tasks on several sites. It is difficult to calculate the optimal balance between too much and too little international integration.

→ Size is another challenge for many firms, especially during their formative early years. If a company remains small, it will struggle to achieve the critical mass required for certain aspects of international business. This means that it may be condemned to act as a niche player and remains vulnerable to the risk that larger rivals might one day force their way into its sector of activity. Conversely, for various strategic, financial and human resource reasons, rapid growth can be very risky for young companies. Size for size's sake is rarely a reliable internationalization strategy.

Chapter Summary

This final chapter in the trilogy examining the main actors in modern international business has focused on MNEs, the constraints they face, and the impact of their actions on the home and especially host countries where they operate. Multinationals' room to manœuvre across borders is limited by several factors, including the funds available to them, the political support they enjoy, and the logistics and communications obstacles that they face. Size is another key variable affecting companies' performance in the international markets. All these factors vary in time and place, as do MNEs' responses, first and foremost being their FDI actions and relations with host country governments (some times based on lobbying).

At the end of this trilogy of chapters, what remains is a mixed picture of states, IGOs and companies' political power. Each of these actors has its own priorities: governments looking out for constituents' interests; companies protecting shareholders and/or implementing managers' visions; and NGOs pursuing their mission. At the same time, each has tools that it uses to restrict rival actors' room to manœuver. States and IGOs can enact regulations, for instance, while MNEs can decide to invest in (or divest from) certain countries. In the absence of a shared ideological framework providing a common sense of purpose, the actors of international business can easily fall into conflict. Large MNEs' size and international presence is apt to cause resentment that, in turn, can undermine their cross-border possibilities. To remedy this situation, MNEs have begun incorporating broader social considerations into their strategies. This is the link between the economic and ethical topics discussed in Chapters 2, 3 and 4, and the more political topics discussed in Chapters 5, 6, and 7. Altogether, these elements constitute the macro-level framework within which international business is conducted. What remains is the micro-level, corporate perspective – the topic covered in the latter half of this book.

Case Study 7.3

The politics of a Total investment

The French oil giant Total (http://burma.total.com/) has been working since July 1998 with partners Chevron, the Petroleum Authority of Thailand, and the Myanmar Oil and Gas Enterprise to operate a 150 billion cubic metre gas field at Yadana in Myanmar (formerly Burma) (Total 2009a). By 2006, the local military junta, often considered one of the worst dictatorships in the world, was levying an estimated €350 million worth of taxes and fees on this huge thirty-year project, following the founders' very substantial initial investment of $1 billion (Maitre 2007). Essentially, Total and its partners were contending with an authoritarian regime guilty of violating citizens' human rights on a mass scale, as exemplified by the long-standing house arrest of Nobel Peace Prize recipient and democracy campaigner Aung San Suu Kyi and fierce repression of demonstrations by Buddhist monks in 2007. Unsurprisingly, Total was criticized for its presence in Myanmar, with films like Milena Kaneva's

Total Denial (www.totaldenialfilm.com), for instance, scrutinizing the nature of its relationship with this military regime. Total is too big a firm to go unnoticed.

When Christophe de Margerie, Total's Director General, was asked in October 2007 whether his company might withdraw from Myanmar, as demanded by a number of NGOs, he firmly refused, arguing that 'Total, no more than any other company, cannot ask a government what it does with its money' (Bezat and Decamps 2007; author's translation). In this view, as long as an MNE has demonstrated corporate responsibility as Total has done according to de Margerie it cannot and should not be blamed for the misdeeds of the host government of a country where it operates. The implication is that companies have limited powers, and thus limited responsibilities. As Total's website states: 'Unfortunately, the world's oil and gas reserves are not necessarily located in democracies ... To those who ask us to leave the country, we reply that far from solving Myanmar's problems, a forced withdrawal would only lead to our replacement by other operators probably less committed to the ethical principles guiding all our initiatives. Our departure could cause the population even greater hardship and is thus an unacceptable risk' (Total 2009b).

This argument may have some merit but it did not convince everyone, starting with Denmark's Minister for Foreign Affairs Per Stig Moller, who decided to call for EU sanctions on all investments in Myanmar. Moller's demand was taken up by several European pension funds, which withdrew a total of about €150 million in investments from Total. Similarly, in 2008 reformist NGOs planned a series of high-profile protests against Total petrol stations in London.

At stake was the very complicated political issue of whose wishes should predominate when MNEs have dealings with governments of dubious repute. On the one hand, it is in the interests of the Myanmar regime for Total to continue its operations there. Revealingly, the French government has not asked Total to stop trading in Myanmar but merely to freeze future investments. On the other hand, the EU, whose decisions often take precedence over those of its member states, has implemented sanctions such as visa and imports bans against Myanmar—while still allowing Total to do business there. One lesson is that MNEs actually find room to manœuvre when there are conflicts in government policy. This is especially true in a sector as crucial as energy. Firms working in less strategic fields might find it harder to resist the barrage of criticisms that Total has faced.

Despite widespread ethical concerns, it is worth noting that as of July 2009 investors had withdrawn relatively little capital from Total. In fact, one of the world's biggest sovereign wealth funds (and a renowned

ethical investor), the Norwegian Global Government Pension Fund, largely maintained its holdings. Of course, things might change if public opinion were to convince Total shareholders to dump its stock. It would be interesting to determine what sorts of actions have the greatest effect on MNE behaviour.

Case study questions

1. Can Total be held responsible for the Myanmar government's actions?
2. Why has the boycott of Total shares not been more effective?
3. How should Total balance shareholder and government interests?

Exhausted worker in Myanmar; there is much debate about whether companies should undertake FDI in countries with dubious regimes (© iStockphoto).

Discussion questions

1. List concrete examples of the different ways in which FDI by MNEs has had a positive or detrimental effect on host countries.

2. Now that Ford has manufactured and sold cars in Europe for nearly a century, how important is it that the company originally came from the USA?

3. Is SMEs' share of international business destined to rise or fall? Why?

4. How long will the Triad continue to dominate world FDI flows?

5. Which sectors are likely to dominate FDI flows in the future?

6. Is lobbying by international business an example of democracy at work or a case of institutionalized corruption?

References

Agmon, T. (2003). 'Who Gets What: The MNE, the National State and the Distributional Effects of Globalization', *Journal of International Business Studies*, 34/5 (Sept.).

Altman, D. (2007). 'Managing Globalization: Has It Hurt US Workers?', 17 Apr., www.iht.com (accessed 31 Oct. 2008).

BBC (2005). 'Cadbury Gobbles up Organic Rival', 13 May, http://news.bbc.co.uk (accessed 31 Oct. 2008).

Barba Navaretti, G., and Venables, A. (2004). *Multinational Firms in the World Economy*. Princeton: Princeton University Press.

Beugelsdijk, S., et al. (2008). 'The Impact of Horizontal and Vertical FDI on Host's Country Economic Growth', *International Business Review*, 17/4 (Aug.).

Bezat, J.-M., and Decamps, M.-C. (2007). 'Investir aujourd'hui en Birmanie serait une provocation', *Le Monde*, 6 Oct., p. 4.

Bhagwati, J. (2004). *In Defense of Globalization*. New York: Oxford University Press.

Blanco, T., et al. (2005). 'How France can Win from Offshoring', www.mckinseyquarterly.com (accessed 15 Sept. 2007).

Buckman, G. (2004). *Globalization: Tame it or Scrap it*. London: Zed Books.

Carroll, R. (2009). 'Chávez Seizes US Rice Mill and Rails against Price-Cap Dodging', 5 Mar., www.guardian.co.uk (accessed 27 June 2009).

Coe, D. (2008). 'Jobs on Another Shore', *IMF: Finance and Development* (Mar.).

Coen, D., and Grant, W. (2005). 'Business and Government in International Policymaking: The Transatlantic Business Dialogue as an Emerging Style?', in D. Kelly and W. Grant (eds.), *The Politics of International Trade in the Twenty-First Century: Actors, Issues and Regional Dynamics*. Basingstoke: Palgrave Macmillan.

Copeland, M. (2006). 'How Startups Go Global', 29 June, http://money.cnn.com (accessed 7 July 2008).

Dietsch, M. (2006). 'Mondialisation et recomposition du capital des enterprises europénnes', *La Revue internationale et stratégique*, 62 (Summer).

The Economist (2007), 'Hungry Tiger, Dancing Elephant', 7 Apr., pp. 69–71.

Froud, J., Johal, S., Leaver, A., and Williams, K. (2006). *Financialization and Strategy: Narrative and Numbers*. London: Routledge.

Glyn, A. (2006). *Capitalism Unleashed: Finance, Globalization and Welfare*. Oxford: Oxford University Press.

Goldin, I., and Reinert, K. (2005). 'Global Capital Flows and Development: A Survey', *z*, 14/4 (Dec.).

Gow, D., and MacAskill, E. (2007). 'Washington Tells EU Firms: Quit Iran now', *Guardian*, 9 Nov.

Grosse, R. (2005) (ed.). *International Business and Government Relations in the 21st Century*. Cambridge: Cambridge University Press.

Guégen, D. (2007). *European Lobbying*. 2nd edn. Brussels: European Politics.

Guest, K. (2006). 'Small Businesses: Are You Local?', 30 Nov., http://news.independent.co.uk (accessed 31 Oct. 2008).

Hoekman, B., and Kostecki, M. (2001). *The Political Economy of the World Trading System*. 2nd edn. New York: Oxford University Press.

Ietto-Gillies, G. (2004). 'The Nation-State and the Theory of the Transnational Corporation', www.econ.cam.ac.uk (accessed 31 Oct. 2008).

Jeffries, S. (2005). 'I Should Cocoa', 16 May, www.guardian.co.uk (accessed 31 Oct. 2008).

Jones, G. (2005a). *Multinationals and Global Capitalism: From the Nineteenth to the Twenty-First Century*. Oxford: Oxford University Press.

Jones, G. (2005b). 'Multinationals from the 1930s to the 1980s', in A. Chandler and B. Mazlish (eds.), *Leviathans: Multinational Corporations and the New Global History*. Cambridge: Cambridge University Press.

Lung, Y. (2007). 'Une mondialisation à un rythme effrené', *Sud-Ouest*, 30 Mar.

Maitre, M. (2007). 'UPDATE 1-Total CEO says will not withdraw from Myanmar', Reuters, www.reuters.com/article/companyNewsAndPR/idUSL0563017320071005 (accessed July 2009).

Mathiason, N. (2005), 'Activists in Attack on Financiers' Profits from Sudan and Burma', *Observer*, 4 Nov.

Mathiason, N. (2008). 'The Baron who Holds Burma's Purse Strings', *Observer*, 3 Nov., p. 7.

Meyer-Stamer, J., and Wältring, F. (2000). 'Behind the Myth of the Mittelstand Economy', www.meyer-stamer.de (accessed 31 Oct. 2008).

Michaels, D., et al. (2007). 'How National Interests Sank the Iberia Deal', *Wall Street Journal—Europe*, 27 Nov., p. 3.

OECD (2007). 'Main Science and Technology Indicators', www.oecd.org (accessed 31 Oct. 2008).

Palast G. (2003). *The Best Democracy Money Can Buy: The Truth about Corporate Cons, Globalization and High-Finance Fraudsters*. New York: Plume.

Perkins, J. (2005). *Confessions of an Economic Hit Man*. London: Ebury Press.

Petras, J., and Veltmeyer, H. (2007). *Multinationals on Trial: Foreign Investment Matters*. London: Ashgate.

Purvis, A. (2006). 'How a £1.50 Chocolate Bar Saved a Mayan Community from Destruction', 28 May, www.guardian.co.uk (accessed 31 Oct. 2008).

Rugman, A. (2005). *The Regional Multinationals: MNEs and 'Global' Strategic Management*. Cambridge: Cambridge University Press.

Theopold, S. (2009). 'Tomorrow's Champion: Strategies and Growth Patterns of SMEs', 5 Mar. EBSI Madrid forum presentation.

Total (2008). 'Total out of Burma', www.totaloutofburma.blogspot.com (accessed 1 Nov. 2008).

Total (2009a). 'Description of the Yadana Project', http://burma.total.com/en/gazier/p_2_2.htm (accessed 1 July 2009).

Total (2009b). 'The Issue', http://burma.total.com (accessed 1 July 2009).

UNCTAD (2008). 'World Investment Report: Transnational Corporations and the Infrastructure Challenge', www.unctad.org (accessed 6 Feb. 2009).

UNECE (2001). 'Entrepreneurship and SME Development', www.unece.org (accessed 1 Nov. 2007).

Wei, Y., and Liu, X. (2006). 'Productivity Spillovers from R&D, Exports and FDI in China's Manufacturing Sector', *Journal of International Business Studies*, 7/5 (Sept.).

Wilkins, M. (2005). 'Multinational Enterprise to 1930: Discontinuities and Continuities', in A. Chandler and B. Mazlish (eds.), *Leviathans: Multinational Corporations and the New Global History*. Cambridge: Cambridge University Press.

Further research

Brakman, S., and Garretsen, H. (2008). *Foreign Direct Investment and the Multinational Enterprise (CESifo Seminar)*. Cambridge, MA: MIT Press.

FDI's rapid annual growth since the early 1990s, exceeding even the rise in international trade, underlines how crucial this kind of business is to globalization. Since the 1980s, however, relatively little has been added to the body of theory describing this phenomenon. Brakman and Garretsen attempt to remedy this with a multidisciplinary approach that draws from different schools of thought (industrial organizations, game theory, and economic geography). They review many specific FDI topics in great depth, starting with the link between investment location and deregulation trends, mainly in Europe. Their book also studies the net advantages and disadvantages of FDI for host economies. All in all, this is worthwhile reference for readers with a particular interest in FDI.

Online Resource Centre

Visit the Online Resource Centre that accompanies this book to read more information relating to companies in international business: www.oxfordtextbooks.co.uk/orc_/sitkin_bowen/

International Strategy

8 Modes of Internationalization

Overview

The first section reviews the strategic thinking underlying different modes of market entry, ranking them by companies' level of commitment to a host country. This is followed by a comparison of trade and FDI as internationalization choices, analysed in terms of the 'boundaries of the firm' concept and differentiated for vertical and horizontal kinds of FDI.

The second section discusses specific market entry methods. It starts with a look at MNEs' decision whether to build new facilities abroad or to acquire existing assets, and compares full and partial ownership of such assets. The chapter concludes by analysing different kinds of foreign partnerships.

Section I: Leaving home: theories, mindsets, and strategies

Degrees of internationalization

Trade versus FDI: drawing the boundaries of the firm

Vertical versus horizontal internationalization

Section II: Entering foreign markets

Greenfield versus brownfield investments

Equity arrangements

Non-equity arrangements

Learning Objectives

After reading this chapter, you should be able to:

+ identify the factors that motivate managers to commit resources abroad
+ perceive the trade versus FDI choices in terms of its impact on the boundaries of the firm
+ discuss the relative merits of greenfield versus brownfield investments
+ assess the utility of international joint ventures and cross-border mergers and acquisitions
+ compare the costs/benefits of collaborating with foreign partners

Case Study 8.1

Market entry challenges: China and Japan

China and Japan are global leaders in trade, with huge surpluses putting them at the heart of the international financial system. In terms of inward foreign direct investment (FDI), however, they have a much lower profile. Trading in Asia is not as easy as trading with Asia.

Officially Japan may welcome foreign investment, but FDI here in 2007 amounted to a mere 3 per cent of gross domestic product, versus 22 per cent in the USA and 37 per cent in the UK (Pilling 2007). Many multinationals (MNEs) struggle to succeed in Japan. In the late 1990s, for instance, US financial giant Merrill Lynch paid heavily to acquire Yamaichi Securities, hoping to tap into Japan's enormous pool of savings. Business never took off, largely because of a lack of brand recognition—one customer saw Merrill's trademark bull logo and came in to order a barbecue lunch. Within a few years, the company had to close most of its Japanese offices. Then came the example of Vodafone, the British telecommunications giant, which paid £7.9 billion in 2001 to acquire a controlling stake in Japan Telecom. The new company struggled to maintain market share, largely because of consumers' perception that the goods it was offering were overly standardized. French retailer Carrefour suffered for the exact opposite reason, disappointing Japanese consumers by selling local produce instead of the European products they craved. As for American retailer Walmart, its problems stemmed from an inability to source local goods at competitive prices.

Whereas many FDI problems in Japan are market-related, in China the main obstacle is often the state. Despite the loosening of earlier restrictions (like the 1979 Joint Ventures law, which had made FDI conditional on the exporting of output), foreign holdings are still capped in most sectors. This can make things difficult for MNEs, many of which would prefer to enter this complex economy by taking a majority stake in a Chinese company and then acquiring local knowledge. However, Western firms often have problems stabilizing their dealings with Chinese partners, whom they accuse of not respecting

FDI in Asia can be a challenging path (Photodisc).

contractual obligations or intellectual property. Divorces are frequent, with a long list of MNEs (including Volvo, Paribas, Fiat, and Danone) having prematurely terminated their Chinese joint ventures. Other market entrants experience difficulties at the initial authorization stage. For instance, an attempt by Citigroup and UBS to strengthen their Chinese presence in 2006 by acquiring troubled local firm Guangdong Development Bank was thwarted by bureaucratic actions to prevent foreigners from 'buying state assets on the cheap' (McGregor 2006). The WTO has called upon the Chinese government to ease MNE entry processes but progress has been slow. Tensions caused by the credit crunch mean that there is also little hope for significant improvement in the short run.

Introduction

Except for a few 'born-global' firms (Fan and Phan 2007) like the dot.com start-ups that arose around the year 2000, most of the world's leading MNEs were born in a home market where they grew before venturing abroad. The actual decision to internationalize, and the way this is done, is often referred to as a strategic 'mode of entry' choice. Figure 8.1 displays this decision graphically, using terminology that the chapter will study in further detail. The figure represents a decisional ladder showing different levels of corporate commitment to internationalization. The initial decision facing a firm is whether to trade from home or engage in FDI. Where it opts for the latter alternative, the first question becomes whether the FDI should be done on an equity basis. If so, the firm must decide whether to build a new site or to take over another firm's existing operations. Additionally, at every stage of this process it will want to consider whether it should act by itself or with help from a partner, often coming from the host country in question.

After developing an international presence, MNEs must coordinate the cross-border configurations that they have put together (Chapter 9) and manage any cultural challenges that arise (Chapter 10). Altogether, this trilogy of chapters will strengthen the book's argument that international business is not a science but the outcome of a series of decisions that are at least partially subjective in nature. Managers' actions cannot be analysed without regard for their personal psychology.

+ **Internationalize**
Decision to enter foreign markets; involves upstream and/or downstream activities.

+ **Commitment to internationalization**
Depth of a company's engagement of human, physical, and financial resources abroad. This can range from simple import/export activities to running large, wholly-owned foreign subsidiaries.

Figure 8.1
The ladder of internationalization choices.

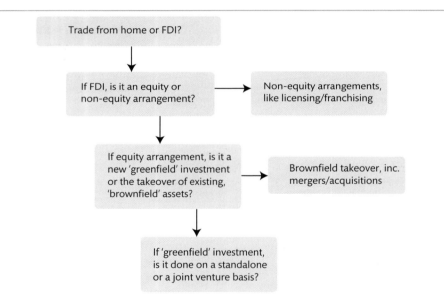

Section I: Leaving home: theories, mindsets, and strategies

Internationalization studies revolved around schools of thought that try to explain why and how companies go abroad. Chapter 4 has already discussed several theories linking such actions to differences in national economies. Chapter 9 will analyse the theoretical links between firms' organizational philosophies and the geographic structures that they set up. The theories underlying the present chapter, on the other hand, focus on the actual decision to enter a foreign market. The main construct used here is called the 'stages of internationalization' approach and derives from the 'Uppsala model' (Johanson and Vahlne 1977). It says that foreign expansion should be viewed as a learning process, with firms committing resources abroad only as they become more comfortable with the environments they discover. The expectation is that firms will usually internationalize first via simple import/export arrangements that become gradually more complex over time (Ruzzier et al. 2006). Then, when they are ready for FDI, they tend to start by entering a neighbouring country and/or culture before going further afield. This means that the key factor in firms' overseas trajectories is the confidence that they have in their internal capabilities and/or accumulated expertise (Tuppura et al. 2008). There might also be a connection between their perception of the degree and type of uncertainty associated with a particular market entry mode and their overall commitment to internationalization (Li and Rugman 2007). It is rare for international managers to have a complete understanding of the foreign environments to which they are thinking of moving. Imperfect knowledge is an integral part of international business.

The Online Resource Centre, extension material 8.1, details other theories with relevancy to market entry, first and foremost being 'transaction cost economics'. It is no surprise that internationalization has attracted so much attention from theorists. Going abroad is one of the most crucial decisions that an executive will ever have to make.

> Go to the ORC

Degrees of internationalization

International business is challenging, with some studies struggling to find evidence that firms with a greater cross-border presence necessarily improve their performance (Contractor et al. 2003). Transferring resources (mainly capital, knowledge, personnel, and materials) overseas is an expensive and difficult process for many companies and creates a host of problems (Nadolska and Barkema 2007). Some problems are industrial in nature, like the difficulties that German carmaker BMW faced in the 1990s after buying Rover, a UK company accustomed to lower-quality standards than its new owners. Others are more financial, like the enormous debt that France's Vivendi incurred to fund its 2000 acquisition of US entertainment company Universal. Others are intellectual property related, as exemplified by the dispute between French food company Danone and its Chinese partner Wahaha, accused of setting up parallel operations to sell the same products as the two firms' joint venture (Dyer 2007). Lastly, some problems are more strategic in nature, one example being when firms seeking a first-mover advantage enter a volatile new economy before it has stabilized and suffer high pioneering costs as a result. Internationalization is always a challenge.

Despite these risks, international operations are clearly a saving grace for many companies struggling in saturated home markets. For example, despite the onset of the credit crunch, German shoemaker Adidas was able to announce a 151 per cent rise in 2008 profits thanks to rapid sales growth in Latin America (up 36 per cent) and Asia (up 18 per cent). This can be compared with a 14 per cent fall in the company's North American sales (*Associated Press* 2009). Similarly, MediaTek, Taiwan's biggest mobile phone chip producer, was able to announce a big rise in its first quarter 2009 sales despite the global recession, thanks to high demand from low-income Chinese citizens benefiting from governmental support packages (Kwong and Hille 2009). Seen in this light, internationalization is no longer a luxury but a necessity for many firms.

Managers' confidence in their firm's ability to internationalize is partly based on rational analysis of its internal capabilities but also on their subjective and cultural reaction to the 'foreignness' of the environment where they are thinking of operating. The conclusions they reach will strongly affect their commitment to internationalization. The more confident a company is that it can succeed abroad, the greater the amount of financial and other capital it will be prepared to invest.

Conversely, companies whose managers have more of a 'domestic mindset' (Nadkarni and Perez 2007) will prefer staying at home and interacting with foreign markets only via import/export activities or, at most, a tiny representative office. Thus, as Figure 8.2 shows, it is possible to rank the main market entry modes by the amount of physical, capital, and human resources that each requires.

Thinking point

To what extent is internationalization based on a company's blind confidence in its abilities to succeed regardless of the location?

+ **Pioneering costs**
Costs of the mistakes that a firm makes when entering a new market featuring unknown parameters.

Thinking point

To what extent is 'foreignness' an objective or subjective perception?

Figure 8.2
Different modes of
market entry require
the internationalization
of different amounts
of financial capital,
human capital, and
knowledge.

Market entry mode	Description	Scale of commitment
Import/export from home	Firm remains domestic but buys from foreign supplier / sells to foreign buyer	Low
Licensing/franchising	Firm gives permission to an agent to manufacture/retail abroad on its behalf	
Joint venture (form of FDI)	Firm makes equity investment abroad in conjunction with a partner	
Wholly-owned subsidiary (FDI)	Firm makes standalone equity investment abroad	High

+ Licensing
Contract where
a licensor grants
permission to
a licensee to use one
of its assets, usually
intellectual property,
as part of a business
process. In return, the
licensor will receive
royalties.

+ Franchising
Contract where
a franchiser grants
permission to
a franchisee to run
a business bearing
its name, often
using supplies that it
provides. In return, the
franchiser will receive
income, often based
on the franchise's
performance.

+ Joint venture
Business unit
specifically created by
different companies
to achieve a particular
mission. Usually
involves pooling
resources such
as equity capital,
knowledge, processes,
and/or personnel.

Thinking point

At what point in
a failed venture
should a company
renounce
internationalization?

Managers' tendency to adopt a 'domestic' or 'global' mindset varies in time and place. One relevant way to analyse this is through Porter's 'Diamond' model (see Chapter 4), according to which firms that have overcome tough challenges at home feel more prepared to deal with difficulties abroad. An example of this might be recent forays by French banks like BNP or Société Générale into North Africa (Parasie 2007) and Russia (Gauthier-Villars 2007)—moves that were not only made in reaction to the companies' overcrowded domestic market but also a sign of their confidence in their ability to deal with interventionist host governments, a skill that they first learned back home in France. There is also a tendency for MNEs to expand more quickly in places that have a culture similar to their own. One example is the ease with which US multinational Starbucks penetrated the English market, compared to the problems it suffered in Israel, where it was forced to close many outlets in 2008 and terminate its relationship with local partner Delek. A distinction might also be made between market entries involving the operational 'exploitation' of relatively familiar capabilities, or the riskier 'exploration' of something unknown (Barkema and Drogendijk 2007). Lastly, attitudes towards internationalization are also conditioned by how well people process the failures of past foreign ventures (Desislava and van Witteloostuijn 2007. The losses that the British retailer Marks & Spencer sustained overseas in the 1990s, for example, did not prevent it from renewing its international ambitions fifteen years later, with varying degrees of success (Davey 2007). Some companies are disheartened if their first internationalization efforts fail but others keep trying.

Lastly, the market entry behaviour of small and medium-sized enterprises (SMEs) is worth a special mention. On the one hand, most SMEs today go abroad at a much earlier stage in their lives than used to be the case (Neupert et al. 2006). On the other, SMEs' internationalization potential continues to suffer from many handicaps, first and foremost being their comparative lack of resources (see Chapter 7). SMEs are often family-owned, a factor that correlates negatively with internationalization (Fernandez and Nieto 2006), if only because a firm lacking corporate shareholders has lesser access to the substantial funding that foreign operations often require. Excluded from costlier opportunities (large company takeovers or big marketing campaigns), family-run SMEs are often restricted to smaller actions in well-defined niches and/or forced to network with other firms to achieve critical mass. One example is the way that many small vineyards in south-west France have tried to optimize their international marketing operations by banding together in an association called the Conseil Interprofessionnel du Vin de Bordeaux (CIVB). Family-run firms may also lack the managerial competencies to attack foreign markets. The end result is that small companies often do not have the means, and/or confidence, that allow larger MNEs to internationalize at the more gradual, stage-by-stage pace that gives them the time they need to learn about a new market.

SMEs can react to this handicap in one of two ways. Some will behave more conservatively than a larger MNE would do in the same situation and choose a less financially committed and faster form of internationalization, such as export or licensing/franchising (Hutchinson et al. 2006). However, others might decide to respond even more radically via 'accelerated internationalization', a process where the SME's entire strategic focus changes specifically to incorporate the new international possibilities (Chetty and Campbell-Hunt 2003). This is very different from the gradual approach envisaged under the Nordic (Uppsala) 'stages' theory. The choice between these two options depends on the strategic attitudes of the SMEs' owner-managers, whose personalities will have a greater impact in a smaller structure than they would in a large MNE (Lloyd-Reason and Mughan 2002). At this level, like so many others, the link between psychology and strategy is crucial to understanding international business.

Trade versus FDI: drawing the boundaries of the firm

As discussed above, for firms reluctant to engage physical or capital resources abroad, entering foreign markets means trading out of their home base. This applies especially if such activities are not overly penalized by high transportation costs or tariffs.

A company with a minimal commitment to internationalization will take delivery of foreign purchases, or transfer ownership of foreign sales, at its 'factory gate'. This is to avoid having to organize logistical responsibilities such as freight, insurance, or customs documentation (see Chapter 11). The priority for firms with little commitment to internationalization is to minimize complications by sticking to tried and tested core competencies. In this sense, trade is a relatively easier way to leverage domestic experience.

Whereas most SMEs necessarily have a limited international presence, there are also big firms that could afford to set up substantial wholly-owned affiliates abroad if they wanted to—but have decided otherwise. As explained in Chapter 7, since the 1980s an increasing number of firms have opted for a 'small is beautiful' mindset, preferring to outsource operations that other companies can do better and/or more cheaply. Designing the boundaries of the firm is one of the main decisions that international managers must make (see Figure 8.3) and the trade versus FDI choice is crucial in this respect. Note that, along with its strategic aspects, this decision is also based on a financial calculation. If the FDI would cost the firm more than the profit margins appropriated by external suppliers or vendors, then using import/export as a prime mode of internationalization makes sense. If, on the other hand, the FDI costs less, then it is worth considering a shift to this approach.

+ Boundaries of the firm
Range of value chain operations that a firm undertakes itself without resorting to outside partners.

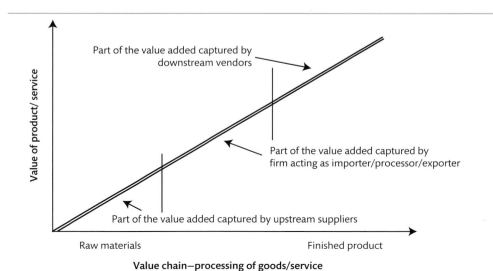

Figure 8.3
Value added in a shared international value chain.

Part of the value added captured by downstream vendors

Part of the value added captured by firm acting as importer/processor/exporter

Part of the value added captured by upstream suppliers

Value of product/ service

Raw materials   Finished product

Value chain—processing of goods/service

> Go to the ORC

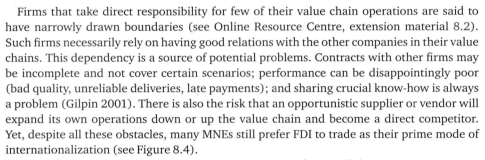

Figure 8.4
Trade is a simpler option than FDI but also creates strategic vulnerabilities.

	Advantages	Disadvantages
Trade only (import/export)	• Easier to manage, requires less knowledge • Engages less capital, thus lower risk • Keeps balance sheet smaller and more flexible, thus more responsive to changing economic situations	• Firm develops less overseas experience • The value added generated during the good's transformation will have to be shared with other companies • Depends on partners; risk of opportunistic behaviour
FDI	• Control/confidentiality • Higher profit potential/visibility • Increases knowledge of/comfort with foreign market	• Harder to manage • Harder to finance • Greater risk of failure

Firms that take direct responsibility for few of their value chain operations are said to have narrowly drawn boundaries (see Online Resource Centre, extension material 8.2). Such firms necessarily rely on having good relations with the other companies in their value chains. This dependency is a source of potential problems. Contracts with other firms may be incomplete and not cover certain scenarios; performance can be disappointingly poor (bad quality, unreliable deliveries, late payments); and sharing crucial know-how is always a problem (Gilpin 2001). There is also the risk that an opportunistic supplier or vendor will expand its own operations down or up the value chain and become a direct competitor. Yet, despite all these obstacles, many MNEs still prefer FDI to trade as their prime mode of internationalization (see Figure 8.4).

Even after opting for internationalization via FDI, firms still have many aspects to consider. The first is whether the FDI is more property-related or knowledge-based, with studies offering evidence that the latter has a more lasting influence on international growth than the former (Tseng et al. 2007). The fast-expanding Indian pharmaceutical sector provides examples of these different FDI orientations. On one hand, there is DRL's 2006 purchase of German company Betapharm, motivated by the acquirer's straightforward desire to expand its commercial networks. On the other, several deals by budding giant Ranbaxy, plus NPIL's purchase of Avecia in the UK, were all undertaken in a bid to acquire new skills (Kale 2007), an outcome that the two companies hope will enable them to cover a more lucrative part of their products' value chains. FDI that is based on a firm developing a new line of business may be riskier than one seeking a straightforward expansion of existing commercial territory (Doukas and Lang 2003), but its potential rewards are also higher.

The most fundamental distinction in FDI analysis is whether a particular action is vertical or horizontal in nature. The cost factors associated with these two modes, first defined in Chapter 7, are worth exploring in greater detail (Barba Navaretti et al. 2004).

Vertical versus horizontal internationalization

As explained previously, the main reason for MNEs to engage in vertical FDI up and down their global value chains is to reduce dealings, thus potential problems, with outside partners. At an extreme, vertical FDI can lead to the building of specialist 'focused factories' in different countries, each engaged in one specific aspect of the overall production process (see Chapter 11). The advantage of this kind of manufacturing organization is

Photo 8.1
Indian pharmaceutical giant Ranbaxy has repeatedly used FDI as a means of acquiring new skills (© Ranbaxy Inc.).

that all units can take advantage of the particular competitive advantages inherent to their locations. In Asia, for example, it is noteworthy how low-skill work like textile weaving has generally moved to countries like Bangladesh, where labour is abundant, whereas more technological work like microprocessor development is centralized in scientifically more advanced countries like Singapore, where capital is abundant. This trend towards focused factories corresponds to the Heckscher–Ohlin factor proportions theory discussed in Chapter 4.

With manufacturing plants relying on sister units to cover the other stages in their global value chains, a focused factories approach (see Chapter 11) means that each plant will produce and/or export a greater quantity of the particular good for which it is responsible. This increases plant-level economies of scale and learning. One example of this is the way that the Swiss–Swedish MNE ABB uses its Ludvika site to manufacture many of the electrical modules (for example, current transformers or voltage transformers) that it sells to customers and/or assembles in more complex products produced by other ABB plants. A second example is the way that banks with London trading rooms set up back offices in India, increasing flows between internal units, each an expert in its own function. A growing proportion of internationalization is based on this kind of intra-firm logic, with MNEs engaging in multiple FDI projects culminating in different in-house units trading with one another up and down the value chain. The separation between MNEs' trade and FDI decisions can be artificial. The two are often complementary.

The downside for MNEs with this sort of configuration is that shipments between different international locations increase 'trade costs' such as packaging, freight, and tariffs, as well as time lost in transit. Some MNEs try to reduce such costs by focusing production on a very few sites, first and foremost locations with good links to the plants where the companies run their final product assembly activities. Examples include components factories that industrialists have set up in northern Mexico near the US border, or the automotive parts plants that German carmakers have built in neighbouring East European countries like Hungary. At a certain point, however, managers may decide that the firm-wide trade costs of the vertical integration approach outweigh its benefits. In this case, they will opt for 'vertical disintegration', drawing the boundaries of their own firm more narrowly and increasing trade with external partners.

Chapter 7 introduced the concept of horizontal FDI, where firms reproduce abroad the same activities as the ones they run at home. This kind of internationalization mode, which is often based on the transfer of knowledge, reflects the relatively significant presence of MNEs (compared to purely domestic firms) in technologically advanced sectors characterized by complex production processes. Where there is value in 'bundling' different manufacturing stages together, an approach that many Japanese hi-tech companies have put to good use over the years, it can make more sense for manufacturers to focus as much of their global production activity as possible on a single manufacturing site, especially since this should help them to preserve confidentiality. Indeed, some companies conclude that the best way to protect their trade secrets is simply to export finished products from their original plant(s) and avoid FDI altogether. However, if international sales expand too quickly, a single site can quickly run into capacity constraints. Horizontal internationalization is the logical response to this limitation.

Of course, horizontal FDI also costs more, since it involves duplicating certain activities on several sites. This can become particularly expensive when each new site is designed to service one specific market rather than customers or sister units worldwide. Moreover, output from an MNE's new horizontal plants will tend to reduce the need for exports from its existing units, affecting their economies of scale. It remains that these are losses felt at the level of each individual plant. On a broader plane, it is possible to develop firm-level economies of scale through horizontal FDI, since many assets will not have to be replicated on each new location. This includes some tangible assets but especially intangible ones such as scientific know-how, patents, or brand reputation. In large MNEs with worldwide sales, shared resources of this kind go a long way towards paying the extra cost of horizontal FDI as opposed to other modes of internationalization.

Figure 8.5 summarizes the advantages and disadvantages of these two modes of market entry.

In short, most large MNEs have a variety of reasons for, and ways of, venturing abroad. The course that they choose will depend on many factors, including whether the expansion is for upstream or downstream purposes, the depth of managers' willingness to commit to internationalization, and the kinds of resources being transferred. Like all international business decisions, there is no optimal solution—just the response that managers feel is most appropriate to a given set of circumstances.

Figure 8.5
The two main FDI strategies.

	Vertical FDI	Horizontal FDI
Purpose	Internalize global value chain	Leverage existing competencies abroad
Facilities	Focused factories	Multi-function facilities
Economies of scale	At the level of the plant	At the level of the firm
Trade	Often intra-firm	Often in host country
Weakness	High trade costs	Duplication of overheads

Case Study 8.2

Driving the Latin way: Fiat builds its South American presence

In 2006, Fiat's plant in Belo Horizonte (Brazil)— responsible for manufacturing almost all of the 500,000 vehicles that the company sells annually in Latin America— received the good news that local capacities would be further expanded by an investment of $1 billion over three years. The Italian carmaker

was looking to build upon its success in Brazil, the region's most dynamic market with 1.7 million new car sales annually, and a country where Fiat already had a 25 per cent market share. The main target for new growth was Mexico, Latin America's second leading market with annual new car sales of 1.1 million. Fiat

had no production facilities in Mexico, so it was likely that the planned growth in regional output would entail imports from Fiat's European plants and/or the reopening of a dormant unit in Cordoba (Argentina). These were both costly solutions that could be justified only if Fiat were to increase its volumes in Latin America's higher margin segments. Unfortunately, in a developing region with relatively few affluent consumers, such segments are few and far between.

To overcome these hurdles, the idea arose that the new Brazilian investment should be used not only to improve production processes but also to strengthen the team of 300 development engineers working for Fiat in Belo Horizonte—the largest concentration of design skill outside the MNE's global headquarters in Turin (Italy). The task of these Brazilian engineers was to ensure that locally produced cars were specifically attractive to Latin America consumers. This would involve, for instance, redesigning a standard global product like the Palio to give it a sportier look. There would also be some engine adaptation work to ensure that Latin American Fiats run on the different fuels used in this region, including Brazil's ethanol-based bio-fuels. By the end of this process, Fiat was hoping to increase market share from 12 to 15 per cent (Marsh 2006), generating sufficient additional revenue to justify the FDI.

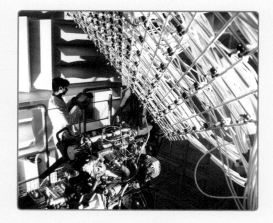

Centro Ricerche Fiat: fully anechoic engine test facility. Part of Fiat's internationalization has involved moving research activities from Italy to Brazil (reproduced with the kind permission of Centro Ricerche FIAT S.C.p.A.).

Fiat had tested the markets in this part of the world and found them to its liking. Early successes locally had given the company the confidence to carry on. Questions about its ability to service the Mexican market were still unresolved, but for the time being, the Italian carmaker felt pleased about the market entry strategies that it had chosen.

Section II: Entering foreign markets

Even after an MNE has taken the leap and finally decided to develop a foreign presence (in whatever form), it still has a number of options. Many companies, especially SMEs but also larger MNEs uncomfortable with a given location, will enter it via an 'intermediate step' like a representative office, possibly staffed by one or two persons only. The purpose of starting with a few local representatives is to increase organizational learning about a destination before risking greater resources there. Representative offices are places where company executives travelling to the country can stop off to get their bearings when first visiting. This was a common practice, for instance, for Western banks entering China in the 1990s.

Where companies opt for full-blown FDI, an initial decision is whether to build new greenfield facilities (alone or with a partner) or take over existing assets via a brownfield strategy. This choice is often referred to as the 'build or buy' dilemma.

+ Greenfield investment
When a firm enters a new market by building new facilities

+ Brownfield investment
When a firm enters a new market by buying existing facilities.

Inside business

Rodney Turtle, Strategic Marketing Director, Schneider Electric

Schneider Electric is a large MNE, operating worldwide with about 114,000 employees in more than 100 countries and with a third of its revenue coming from emerging countries. Its headquarters are just outside Paris, France, and its 2008 sales amounted to €18.3 billion. Part of Schneider's growth, especially in recent years, has come from a process of organic growth and a policy of acquiring companies—it doubled in size between 2004 and 2008 through such acquisitions.

Schneider's revenue from emerging economies rose 14 per cent and its acquisitions increased by 3.1 per cent, particularly through Pelco, the world leader in video security systems, and Xantrex Technology, a major player in renewable energies. As the company's CEO, Jean-Pascal Tricoire, said, 'Against the backdrop of the global crisis, Schneider Electric has proved that its fundamentals and business model are sound, with 6.6 per cent organic growth in 2008 and an operating margin of 15 per cent.'

Rodney Turtle (Strategic Marketing Director, Schneider Electric Ltd.) commented on the company's pragmatic approach to internationalization. One of the features of Schneider is the drive to standardize global processes and competencies across the world, without compromising their preference for trusting local intelligence in helping them to develop local operations. The company seeks to have an important local commercial presence while adapting Schneider's worldwide offers to the local market. The company has to balance its marketing and sales of different products and services between local, regional and worldwide offers. In general, the Schneider group sets the overall strategy and framework for financial planning with the locally operating companies establishing strategic targets on a contingent and rolling basis.

One of the 'win-win' operations is Schneider's joint venture with Toshiba in creating variable speed drives based on the two companies' complementary geographic coverage and sales channels. The two companies have worked together since 1988 with subsequent joint ventures for development, manufacture and marketing.

Schneider's programme for progress for 2009–2011, One Schneider Electric, consists of three main initiatives:

- *One solution provider*: accelerating the company's drive to become a leading solution with strong energy efficiency benefits to end users

- *One leader in new economies*: further boosting its global footprint by reinforcing its presence in new economies as drivers for long term growth and cost competitiveness.

- *One global company*: simplification and globalization of support functions (Finance, HR, Marketing, IT) and boosting industrial productivity in its supply chain.

Greenfield versus brownfield investments

There are several reasons why an MNE might opt for a greenfield or a brownfield investment as its mode of market entry. At a strategic level, greenfield investments are preferred when the purpose for the expansion is to exploit technologies, whereas brownfield investments are preferred when the purpose is to acquire downstream capabilities and service the local market (Anand and Delios 2002). This largely reflects the fact that, with a greenfield mode, it is easier to preserve the confidential nature of a company's technological knowledge, since this can be transferred internally from the MNE's existing sites to its new locations. For example, Intel's chosen method for growing its operations in Costa Rica has been to construct greenfield 'campuses' hosting research and other functions on sites located 12 miles outside the nation's capital. On the other hand, where commercial knowledge is the key factor of success, a brownfield entry will usually be deemed more appropriate. An example is the decision made by Indian conglomerate Tata to (re-)enter the British market in 2008 by acquiring local brands Jaguar and Land Rover instead of developing its own facilities. Among other reasons, it was felt that the target companies' long-standing relationships with car dealerships would have taken too long to replace.

In practical terms, MNEs facing this 'build or buy' dilemma have different variables to consider. One advantage of the greenfield approach is that it saves it firm from having to spend time and effort on identifying and acquiring an appropriate target—assuming that one even exists. An example was when German retailer Metro realized that, to develop a functional supply chain in India, it needed to build its own facilities—refrigerated transportation is a key capability for modern supermarkets, and the relative lack of local agents capable of this function forced Metro to create it from scratch (Bellman and Rohwedder 2007). A greenfield entry also means avoiding

the goodwill costs associated with the purchase of an existing asset. At times when stock market valuations are high, this can be very expensive.

The advantages of brownfield entry, on the other hand, include the fact that the approach avoids the start-up problems inherent in any new venture. One example is the decision by American retailer Walmart to enter the Indian market through a partnership with a local firm, Bharti—possibly in reaction to its disastrous entry in Germany in the 1990s, when it lost considerable sums because of insufficient knowledge of the local environment. Another advantage of the brownfield approach is the possibility of benefiting from the target company's brand image. This explains why target firms are often allowed to keep their old name. Examples include Swiss International Airlines after its 2005 acquisition by Lufthansa, or the Japanese retailer Seiyu, bought by Walmart that same year. Brownfield expansion also means that a company is taking over an existing producer instead of adding to the sector's total production capacities and increasing global supply—the effect of which would be to drive down market prices, something that is not in the company's interest as a producer. In addition, rising environmental constraints argue against the unlimited construction of new assets on previously undeveloped green fields. In a similar vein and with the notable exception of primary sectors such as agriculture or mining, many areas of economic activity already suffer from excessive productive capacities.

Lastly, it is worth mentioning that the preference for a greenfield or brownfield entry will also depend on how foreign a particular market feels to the manager making the decision. People sense different levels of (dis)comfort when entering a particular market. Research has revealed some MNEs' tendency to prefer brownfield investments when expanding into countries that are culturally very different from their home market. This is especially true if the firm lacks significant previous international experience or plans to allow the new affiliate to develop its own marketing strategy and therefore needs to acquire good customer relationship skills (Slangen and Hennart 2008). Once again, there is an apparent link between managers' willingness to commit resources abroad and their confidence in their ability to cope with foreign environments and cultures.

+ Goodwill
Difference between the price at which a company can be purchased and the break-up value of its assets.

Thinking point

To what extent is MNEs' greenfield expansion to blame for ecological devastation?

Equity arrangements

Greenfield investments are often motivated by managers' conviction that they can acquire a first-mover advantage in a foreign market. Chapter 9 offers a fuller explanation of this proactive, 'push' orientation. For the moment, it suffices to note that, in the absence of local knowledge, companies are usually assuming greater risk when starting a foreign operation from zero—they simply will not know as much about the host market as home country professionals do. One example is the 2007 decision of UK retailer Tesco to bring its innovative express grocery outlet concept to the USA (see Chapter 12). By building stores in the Western United States without sufficient understanding of regional variations, and without a local partner to teach it, the MNE struggled to expand its American customer base (Ascenzi 2008). Radically new visions developed by distant corporate executives may not be very appropriate to local conditions. In many cases, it is safer simply to try to fit into a country's existing economic fabric. This is one of the reasons why brownfield investments are the prime vehicle for modern equity-based internationalization arrangements.

International mergers and acquisitions

One of the leading categories of equity-based market entry is international mergers and acquisitions (M&A). This form of brownfield entry is usually driven either by downstream motives like the search for new markets, upstream motives such as the search for resources or the strategic sense that the sector is suffering from over-capacity and needs to consolidate. M&A tends to occur in waves, often because managers in a given line of business have come to similar conclusions about which strategies are most appropriate at a particular moment in time. Different waves of international M&A can have different causes, but the net effect is often to concentrate a sector in the hands of a few enormous MNEs. This is what makes M&A such a controversial topic for many critics of globalization.

For example, waves of M&A hit international banking in 1999 and 2000; tele-communications in 2005; and various primary sectors (including oil, cereals, and metals) in 2008—a year that also saw a renewed wave of international M&A in the international finance sector. This time around, however, it was less a case of managers making positive expansion decisions and more a question of banks with strong finances taking advantage of victims of the credit crunch. Examples include Barclays and Paribas's acquisition of units belonging to Lehman Brothers and Fortis, respectively. Indeed, historically many international M&A operations have been overtly motivated by isolated stock market opportunities—one case being HSBC's 2008 takeover of Indonesia's Bank Ekonomi. Opportunism has always had a role to play in international business.

Figure 8.6 provides data on cross-border M&A since 1994. The first notable aspect is its cyclical nature. Activity levels have exploded upwards during boom years but collapsed completely at times of crisis, as after the 9/11 attacks on New York. Complete statistics for the period following the 2008–9 financial crisis were not yet available by the time of publication, but initial indications are that M&A activity plummeted, in part because the credit crunch meant that MNEs could not source the large amounts of capital that are an absolute necessity for this mode of internationalization. At the same time, falling stock markets mean that a number of worthwhile companies are suddenly trading at affordable prices. This could spark a renewal of opportunistic M&A in the not so distant future.

Figure 8.6
Key M&A figures, in US$ billion (adapted from UNCTAD 2007, 2008; reproduced with the kind permission of the Department of Public Information, United Nations).

	1994	1997	2000	2003	2006	2007
World	127	305	1,144	296	1,118	1,637
Developed economies (purchases)	113	272	1,100	257	930	1,411
as percentage of world total	89%	89.2%	96.1%	86.8%	83.2%	86.2%
Primary sector M&As (purchases)	7.9	17.9	17.1	23.6	94.3	130.9
as percentage of world total	6.2%	5.9%	1.5%	7.8%	8.4%	8.0%
Manufacturing M&As (purchases)	69.3	121.8	294.1	93.2	241.1	370.3
as percentage of world total	54.6%	39.9%	25.7%	31.5%	21.6%	22.6%
Service M&As (purchases)	49.9	165.1	832.6	180.2	782.6	1,135.2
as percentage of world total	39.3%	54.1%	72.8%	60.9%	70%	69.3%

Type of international acquisition	Example
Upstream: (backward integration) Acquisition of inputs	Purchases of mines in Africa and elsewhere by Chinese mining company Minmetals
Downstream: (forward integration) Acquisition of market share	Acquisitions made by France Télécom in Africa to offset slowdown in domestic market (Mullen 2007)
Complementarities: • Geographic (former companies had strengths in different parts of the world)	Nestlé's 2008 acquisition of Gerber baby foods, raising its profile in the USA
• Product (former companies had strengths in different product ranges)	Mittal's 2007 takeover of Arcelor, fitting its strengths in commodity steels with its target's strengths in hi-tech products
Efficiency savings: Synergies	Italian utility Enel's acquisition of Endesa to save €1 billion per year by 2012 on R&D, operations, administration and procurement

Figure 8.7
Different kinds of M&A. The importance of each depends on the business environment.

A secondary noteworthy trend is that industrialized countries continue to dominate M&A worldwide, still accounting for 86.2 per cent of all such transactions in 2007 despite some emerging countries' strong capital position. This can be largely explained by the hyperactive stock markets that have come to typify the OECD countries, often driven by speculative interests like private equity funds (see Chapter 14). Lastly, the sectorial breakdown of international M&A is also interesting, with the sharp fall in industrial sector operations being matched by a rise in service sector activity. In time, rising commodity prices are likely to increase the proportion of international M&A involving raw materials-related primary-sector activities.

International M&A can be studied at many levels. The main macro-economic issue here is whether a particular country is a net provider or receiver of M&A-related capital flows. Cross-border M&A operations are more widespread in the absence of capital market controls (see Chapter 14) and/or when a host country government tolerates foreign ownership of national companies. Inversely, M&A will not flourish in countries where there is resistance to foreign ownership or suspicion that international oligopolies are trying to undermine competition or limit consumer choice. High stock market valuations can also be an obstacle to M&A.

At a micro level, M&A offers two main advantages as a mode of expansion. On the one hand and as demonstrated by Figure 8.7, by bringing together companies with complementary capabilities, cross-border M&A enables significant synergies. On the other hand, it can also be a relatively quick way to build an international presence. This is not always the case, however. For instance, when European airliners BA and Iberia tried to negotiate a merger in 2008, despite the urgency of the situation (passenger numbers were falling sharply owing to higher fuel prices and the credit crunch), negotiations were to last for nearly one year.

+ Synergy
Idea that the value of a newly combined company will be greater than the separate value of its constituents.

Once a cross-border M&A has been concluded, often after a high-profile stock market battle, managers will still have a great deal of work to do to ensure the new entity's success. This area of international business is explored in Chapter 9's discussion of MNEs' 'change-management' strategies, but it is already worth noting that screening and choosing partners who will be trustworthy and offer a good strategic fit constitutes a major challenge for all cross-border collaborative arrangements. Of course, there are many success stories in this area. One was the 2005 merger between Unicredit, an Italian bank, and HVB, from Germany. The new combined entity was able to benefit from partners' ability to rationalize existing computer systems and branch networks, and from their complementary presence in several growth markets, including Poland and Croatia. Another success story is the way that Renault was able to learn frugal, labour-intensive low-cost manufacturing methods from its Indian joint-venture partner Mahindra and Mahindra and put these techniques to good use at Dacia, the company it had acquired in Romania. Finding a suitable foreign partner is a real concern for MNE executives. Where no such partner exists, they may be forced to resort to risky organic growth or even turn down overseas opportunities from which their competitors might then be able to profit.

+ Organic growth
Where a company expands by growing its internal capabilities instead of through external acquisitions.

International Joint Ventures

> Go to the ORC ●

Most MNEs that want to enter a foreign market via an equity arrangement but are unwilling (or not permitted by the host country government) to do so on a standalone or M&A basis will end up opting for a strategic alliance with another company. This general term (see see Online Resource Centre, extension material 8.3) refers to anything from a limited one-off cooperation in a specific function (research, transportation) to something as significant as a fully-fledged merger. An international joint venture (IJV) is when the strategic alliance involves an equity arrangement in which the MNE and its partner each take a percentage stake in a new company, often built on a greenfield basis. Some IJVs feature 50–50 joint ownership, but in others one of the partners will have at least a 51 per cent share to ensure overall control.

IJVs are an interesting as a market entry mode, largely because of the nature of partners' relationships. By putting up equity capital, an MNE entering a joint venture is making a strong commitment to internationalization even as it seeks outside help. At the same time, this partnership aspect creates certain complications. Depending on the IJV's stage of maturity, if partners come from countries that are culturally very dissimilar, their relationship is likely to be unstable (Meschi and Riccio 2008). The question then becomes whether the IJV is worth the aggravation.

Thinking point

Are IJVs a positive decision or the sign that a firm is afraid of going it alone?

Some IJVs are mandatory, occurring because the host country (often an LDC) requires incoming multinationals to enter partnerships with local firms. Such requirements are often motivated by host countries' desire to engineer a more extensive transfer of technology, taking advantage of the R&D-intensive nature of many IJVs, particularly export-oriented ones (Zhang et al. 2007). At other times, host governments impose an IJV arrangement on incoming MNEs for more defensive reasons, because they fear the domination of foreign interests. In some countries, there is a real sense that foreign ownership must be tightly controlled in 'strategic' areas. This always includes the defence sector, but, because finance is also crucial to economic policy (hence national sovereignty), most countries tend to classify banking as another strategic activity—especially after the 2008 global financial crisis revealed the impact it can have on the rest of an economy.

> Go to the ORC ●

Banking sector IJVs are particularly prevalent in countries like China with a strong tradition of government intervention—like China, the leading example of mandatory IJVs. There is no doubt that joint-venture provisions in Chinese FDI legislation (see Online Resource Centre, extension material 8.4) have evolved markedly in recent years. The general trend has been towards greater liberalization, especially since China joined the WTO in 2001. The country's first attempts to harmonize its banking norms with global standards, including with regards to MNEs' market entry conditions, date from 1994. Nevertheless, many restrictions remain in place, depending on the exact kind of banking in question, the branch's location in China, and whether the bank is listed on a local stock market. An additional factor is whether the IJV started out as a new, 'wholly foreign-owned enterprise', or began with the takeover of an existing entity. In the latter case, foreigners' maximum shareholdings are capped at 49, 33, and 20 per cent, respectively, depending on whether the venture is a commercial bank, investment bank, or stockbroker. This patchwork of regulations may be confusing but there is one constant: in most cases, banking MNEs seeking to enter China should expect to work with a local partner. This is a country where IJV tends to be mandatory, not voluntary.

Many firms do not mind this requirement. Indeed, IJVs are an attractive solution for MNEs afraid of having to manage the market entry process and/or subsequent operations without outside help. Liberalization has not been a one-way street in China, and local interests regularly pressure the authorities to place tighter controls on foreign affiliates. Thus, having a local partner who knows how to handle government officials can be of great use to non-Chinese MNEs. Similarly, tax levels can vary markedly in China, depending on how bureaucrats decide to classify a particular venture. There is often a great deal of flexibility in the way such decisions are made. Here too it pays to have a good local lobbyist (see Chapter 7).

This does not mean that all collaborations run smoothly in the Chinese banking sector—there are many examples of Western banks separating from their local partners, like the January 2007 divorce between France's BNP Paribas and Changjiang Securities. Despite the potential for problems, however, the simple fact is that, in complicated foreign environments, it may be impossible for MNEs to succeed on their own.

Local government contacts are only one of several reasons that many multinationals opt for IJV. On the one hand, with this kind of market entry, MNEs have to put up far less equity capital than they would if operating alone. On the other hand, like international M&As, IJVs help companies to achieve synergies, reduce competitive pressures, and implement vertical internationalization strategies—or, often even more profitably, horizontal ones (Slovin et al. 2007).

In terms of choosing local partners, MNEs tend to seek parties capable of fulfilling specific functions in the host country environment. This can involve the recruitment or retention of personnel, supply chain operations, and/or customer relationships. In turn, the incoming MNE is usually expected to offer technological expertise in processes and/or products, provide access to international funding sources, and, where possible, bring a recognizable brand name. The exact breakdown of partners' roles, along with the new venture's legal status (usually a partnership or limited liability company), depends on both sides' bargaining position but also on whether the IJV's aim is to sell into the host country or to use it as a manufacturing base for exports elsewhere.

The great weakness of the IJV structure is the potential for arguments between partners. It has been estimated that anywhere from 30 to 60 per cent of all IJVs fail within five years (Geng 2007). In addition to the difficulties of finding an able and willing partner in the first place, tensions can arise for a number of reasons, including one side's sense that the other is under-performing operationally; changes in either partner's strategic goals; and problems of culture, communications, and above all trust (Anoop 2006; Madhak 2006). A company that loses faith in its partner will often try to limit the scope of their cooperation. An example from the early twenty-first century was when Mitsubishi engineers refused to discuss a new design with their Volvo partners simply because the latter wanted to introduce changes at the last minute. Their idea had been a good one, but, because the working method was jarring to the Japanese culture, tempers flared (Manzoni and Barsoux 2006). Once trust has been lost, it is hard to restore. Managers are human, after all; not all business practices are rational.

<aside>
Thinking point

If so many IJVs are doomed to fail, why should companies risk this kind of structure in the first place?
</aside>

Many IJVs are born out of a desire to split the costs associated with a new activity, but, if the partners are rivals outside their joint venture, neither will want the other to benefit from it disproportionately. An IJV stands a better chance of surviving if partners come from entirely different sectors. One example is the sales promotion partnership between Japanese electronics giant Fujitsu and German software firm SAP, companies that operate in complementary sectors and are therefore not direct rivals. Another promising joint venture founded in 2007, Vivergo Fuels Ltd, will lead to the construction of a bioethanol plant at Hull in north-east England under the shared leadership of BP (offering fuel expertise), British Sugar (offering agricultural know-how), and American chemicals giant Dupont (offering competencies in biotechnology). Conversely, many IJVs are in danger from the start because they associate companies that are rivals in other markets. Examples of companies attempting research collaborations with competitors include Colgate-Palmolive and Nestlé's joint venture to develop dentally hygienic gum, or Michelin and Goodyear's co-development of flat tyre technology. All in all, the tensions that exist within IJVs mean that they are apt to under-perform in other modes of market entry. This is especially true in fast-changing, high-growth environments where shared management can be particularly problematic (Belderbos and Zou 2007). IJVs' high failure rates have sparked much research on how to unwind them if and when they fail. The easiest exit is for one partner to buy the other out, but this is not always feasible and can cause further problems. In those instances where IJVs are too challenging and standalone FDI is too risky and expensive, companies need to consider other, less-committed modes of internationalization.

Non-equity arrangements

Companies that are hesitant about investing their own equity capital in a foreign venture can choose instead to share their intangible assets (knowledge, brand name) with a local partner in exchange for the payment of fees and/or royalties. These kinds of non-equity arrangements, called licensing or franchising contracts, are a common long-term market entry strategy. Other strategic alliances, such as turnkey projects or management contracts, will be devised on a more ad hoc basis.

International licensing

There are basically two ways for firms to enforce private property rights. On the one hand, where they own a particular process or item, they can sue anyone copying their intellectual property without permission to get them to cease such behaviour and, if possible, pay compensation. Conversely, they can proactively authorize another party to borrow their intellectual property rights, specifically because this will allow them to enter a foreign market more quickly and for a lower investment (thus a lesser risk) than if they were acting on their own. The legal term for this kind of authorization is licensing, materializing in a contract between one party granting rights (the 'licensor') and another party (the 'licensee') receiving them, usually in exchange for the payment of licensing fees and/or royalties.

Licensing contracts typically contain many specific clauses, starting of course with a precise definition of the product or process covered in the agreement and including the geographic territory where it applies, its duration, the licensor's remuneration, and any contract termination/renewal terms. International licensing agreements apply in many different areas but are often manufacturing-related. According to the International Licensing Industry Merchandisers' Association (www.licensing.org), the four leading areas of licensing are character and entertainment (replication of figures from movies, television, and so on); corporate trademarks and brands (for example, Coca Cola licenses bottlers worldwide to produce and market its products); fashion licensing (involving the world's biggest names, such as Nike, Louis Vuitton, or Gap); and sports licensing (for example, replications worldwide of Manchester United or David Beckham football shirts). In addition to these headline-grabbing examples, licensing also drives many other international business transactions. A frequent example is when a pharmaceutical MNE makes a discovery and licenses a rival in another country to market it there, partially because the cost of developing the new product means that the innovator no longer has sufficient funds to finance its foreign distribution (see Chapter 11). It is impossible to get an accurate calculation of the total volume of international licensing agreements at a given point in time. For some companies, however, this is clearly an enormous source of income. Disney Corporation, for instance, estimated its 2008 global licensed merchandise sales at $30 billion, up $27 billion from the year before (Fields 2008). By offering a quick and relatively low-risk way of entering new markets, licensing overcomes some of the main obstacles to internationalization.

International franchising

Franchising's rationale and contractual aspects are similar to licensing, but its focus is more on downstream, commercial actions. A 'franchisor' signs a contract ('master licence') with its local agent ('franchisee'), granting the latter the right to operate under the former's trade name and distribute its goods or services in a particular territory. To enable the franchisee to perform this function, the franchisor will typically provide all necessary support, including supplies, training, and advertising. The remuneration it receives in return is based on royalties, usually calculated as a percentage of the franchise's gross sales.

Many famous MNEs, often in the retail and fast-food sectors (Starbucks, McDonald's, Burger King), have internationalized via this mode because it is quick and easy. Indeed, as detailed in Figure 8.8, franchising is used in many sectors of activity worldwide. The advantage for the MNE is that it does not need to invest equity capital in overseas commercial outlets and can take advantage of local partners' experience in operating outlets and attracting in customers. The advantage for local agents is that they can benefit from the brand name and know-how of a company with a tried-and-tested business model.

Advertising

Assisted living

Automotive products/services

Beauty supplies/services

Business consultants

Cheque cashing

Children products and services

Cleaning commercial/domestic

Clothing and shoes

Computer/electronics/Internet

Cosmetics

Financial services

Food

Furniture

Gardening

Handyman services

Health aids

Home — decoration/improvement

Hotels/motels

Photography/Imaging/Printing

Real Estate

Retail

Security systems

Seniors care

Travel

Vending

Weight control

Figure 8.8
Abridged list
of 'Franchise
Opportunities
Worldwide' advertised
on the website www.
franchiseek.com, April
2008.

Running licensing/franchising partnerships

In an ideal scenario, an MNE will sign a collaborative agreement with a local partner and things will run smoothly. Of course, like all foreign ventures, non-equity arrangements have their downsides. First, the royalties that the MNE receives may offer significant returns (especially since it has been able to enter the market without putting up any equity capital) but are necessarily far lower than the unshared potential profit of a wholly-owned subsidiary. Secondly, like all collaborations, licensing/franchising is associated with a number of risks. These include confidentiality (industrial espionage); exclusivity (whether the partner might open up a rival operation one day); and performance (whether the materials that the partner uses or the business practices it implements will harm the MNE's reputation).

The question then becomes how to control one's foreign partners. The contracts linking MNEs and their local agents must reflect legal conditions in the host country and be enforceable. This is easier to achieve if the MNE has a local presence staffed by individuals with knowledge of the local environment. In the UK, for instance, McDonald's has staff members charged with monitoring local franchises' performance. This optimizes contract performance but also represents an additional cost for the company.

Above all, the question is how the MNE is going to find a partner it trusts. In September 2007, for instance, the Ritzio Entertainment Group, Russia's largest gambling company, entered into negotiations with Virgin Megastores for franchising rights in Russia.

On the one hand, this must have seemed like a good opportunity for a UK chain seeking to enter a fast-growing but very different consumer market. On the other hand, it raised several causes for concern, including Ritzio's lack of experience in retailing the kinds of products that Virgin sells, and the MNE's difficulty in controlling the accuracy of Russian accounts. Finding a reliable local partner with useful and compatible business competencies is, in such an instance, an absolute priority for the incoming MNE. At a certain point, however, it might decide that no such partners exist. In this case, consideration will have to be given to the possibility of the company itself taking responsibility for market entry—for example, via greenfield FDI. The net effect would be that the company would revert to doing in-house ('internalizing') the operations that it had hoped to allocate to external partners under a collaborative arrangement. This is an example of how an MNE's market entry possibilities shape its ultimate configuration.

Ad hoc non-equity arrangements

When a public infrastructure project (like the Bangkok public transportation system or the Channel Tunnel) is so huge that no one company has the financial or technical resources to complete it alone, the contractor or order-giver will often organize a 'call for tender' from groups of companies organized into a consortium, inviting them to bid for the contract. Such a consortium will usually have a prime contractor who coordinates the tasks allocated to each participant. Partners in the consortium are contractually allied, in the sense that they work on the same overall project. At the same time, in general their ties are too temporary to justify an investment of equity capital. Once the project is completed, the consortium will be expected to hand over the keys to a fully functional system to the order giver and disband. This explains why such arrangements are known as turnkey projects.

+ Turnkey project
Large projects where a group of companies, called a consortium, bids to win the right to build the asset (plant, infrastructure).

By definition, ventures of this kind are few and far between, if only because of their gigantic size. There is, however, every chance that, as increasing amounts of capital accumulate in the hands of developing countries that, by definition, require significant infrastructure investment, turnkey projects will become a more common mode of market entry. It is already widespread in certain growth sectors, such as water systems and public transportation.

A final category of non-equity arrangements involves 'management contracts', where companies receive payment in exchange for sending competent staff members to foreign organizations on temporary work assignments. This mode of entry is relatively widespread in certain specialist sectors like health care, one example being the way that Johns Hopkins

Medicine International, a subsidiary of a major university in the US state of Maryland, enhances its income by running a large hospital in Abu Dhabi. Similarly, in 2008 another US-based organization (University of Pittsburgh Medical Center) announced plans to run at least twenty-five cancer clinics worldwide within the next ten years, leveraging international contacts signed by its partner General Electric to build relationships with local decision-makers. The details for all such agreements (fees, ownership structure) will vary depending on local circumstances (Glader and Whalen 2008). As an entry mode, management contracts are sufficiently light and flexible to accommodate the diversity required for particular kinds of service activities.

Challenges and choices

→ MNE executives are challenged by market entry more than by any other international business topic. Before they come to a decision in this area, they must overcome the irrational fears (or over-confidence) to which all humans are prone—not an easy thing to do when they know that they are going to be judged on their knowledge of what are often relatively unfamiliar foreign environments. At a certain point, executives have to decide that they have enough knowledge to make their final investment decision. It is difficult knowing when the right time has come.

→ Similarly, managers often find it difficult to judge whether to enter a foreign market on their own or share the risks and costs (but also the profits) with a partner. This choice reflects their ability to make an accurate assessment, both of present and future challenges in the host country, and their MNE's corporate culture. Some firms view all competitors as deadly rivals, whereas others are more focused on doing whatever it takes to get business done. The reality is that some potential partners are more trustworthy than others. International managers do not have a crystal ball enabling them to predict the future with full confidence.

Chapter Summary

The chapter starts by detailing why some MNEs choose to enter foreign markets via trade and others via FDI. One of the main arguments at this level relates to how much of the global value chain a firm wants to occupy by itself and how much it is willing to share with partners—that is, how narrowly it chooses to draw its boundaries. It was demonstrated that SME approaches to this decision will be constrained by a number of size-related factors. This discussion was followed by analysis of international managers' varying levels of comfort with overseas investment. The section concluded with a comparison of vertical and horizontal forms of FDI.

The second section reviewed MNEs' different modalities for entering foreign markets, once they have decided to do so. For those firms with sufficient resources to make substantial equity investments abroad, one of the first decisions is whether to build a new greenfield site or to acquire brownfield operations—for example, via an international merger/acquisition (M&A). A related question for larger MNEs that can potentially afford a wholly-owned subsidiary is whether to follow this course or seek a foreign partner, for example, as part of an international joint venture. The chapter ended with a study of non-equity-based collaborative arrangements such as international licensing and franchising. The point was made that, where companies cannot resolve problems with partners, they might prefer to run their multinational activities in-house. This begs the question of how such operations are to be structured. Chapter 9 will try to provide an answer.

Case Study 8.3

Internationalization as a collaborative effort

This case study describes a real situation involving a Bank and a Broker, whose names have been withheld for reasons of confidentiality.

The prime consideration for the Bank at the heart of this case study was always to protect its excellent credit rating. One way to achieve this was by transacting only with high-quality, 'blue-chip' customers.

The Broker, on the other hand, did not make its own products. It was a pure intermediary, sourcing products from banks and passing them on to customers at a mark-up, realizing small profits on every deal it made. To survive, it needed high volumes.

To expand its clientele, the Broker would deal with just about any customer that wanted to trade—even companies with lower credit ratings. To manage this risk, it had devised a system for calculating and collecting deposits that customers paid up front. This was the Broker's main competency, since it made it safe to deal with the kinds of customers that the Bank would normally not accept.

The Bank was prepared to work with the Broker, whose own credit ratings were satisfactory (largely because of the quality of its deposit collection system). By accepting to work through this intermediary, the Bank was able to achieve safe, albeit indirect, access to customers with whom it would not otherwise have traded. Up until now, this had seemed like a good basis for a collaborative arrangement that largely involved trading between the Banker's and Broker's Zurich offices. It is true that these were deals that the Bank's salespersons had to price these deals very competitively, selling products to the Broker at a wholesale price so that the latter could also profit on the deal. This sometimes irritated the Bank's traders, who were judged by the margins earned on the deals they structured. On the other hand, for the Bank's sales staff, largely judged on market share, such low-margin, high-volume business was perfectly acceptable.

The Bank's salespersons did fear, however, that the Broker might one day try to attack the same blue-chip customers as the ones that the Bank was servicing directly. This had never happened in Switzerland but there was always a possibility that the two companies' commercial targets would overlap in a foreign market. Indeed, the

Broker's market reputation abroad could be boosted if it could deal with the kinds of customers that the Bank was servicing directly back in Zurich. An associated risk for the Bank was that if the Broker got angry because the two companies were competing directly for the same customers in some foreign market, it might decide to source product from other suppliers back home in Zurich.

In short, the challenge for the Bank was to define an appropriate basis for working with the Broker outside the two companies' home market. The question arose one day when the Broker arrived with a proposition from its Copenhagen office, which had recently struck up a promising relationship with two Danish companies that wanted to trade the kinds of products that the Broker usually sourced from the Bank in Zurich. The Broker hid the potential clients' names, but the Bank's Head of Sales soon realized that they were prospects that he was working on himself. Nothing had happened yet, because the Bank's credit officers in Zurich found it difficult to judge the creditworthiness of these Danish prospects— variations in accounting standards are a constant headache in international business. Nevertheless, the Head of Sales still hoped that he could trade directly with the customers one day, charging them the full price that the Bank's end users normally paid. The problem was that he was now being asked by the Broker to facilitate this very same business at a lower, wholesale price.

Despite this disappointment, the Head of Sales was basically prepared to accept the new business through the Broker, since it would be the Bank's first entry into Denmark, a market about which he knew little. He felt that it could be useful to take advantage of whatever relationships the Broker would develop.

The Bank's Head of Trading, on the other hand, was not happy at the prospect of adding to the business already being transacted with the Broker. For him, the Danish customers were worth servicing only on a direct basis, thus at the full end-user price. He was also concerned that the Broker had no exclusivity contract with the Bank and might pressure it into lowering its prices even further by threatening to source product from competitors. For the Bank's externally-oriented sales staff,

In the end, the Bank department responsible for the products in question was taken over by a woman with a background in sales. Her decision was to service the Broker in Copenhagen. This angered her production-side colleagues, to the extent that they intentionally inflated the prices being offered to the Broker on deals back in Zurich. As a result, the Bank's global volumes with the Broker suffered—before the Danish business had even had a chance to get off the ground.

Case study questions

1. Should the Bank have treated the Broker as a rival in the Danish market or as a partner?
2. What other market entry strategies might the Bank have considered in Denmark?
3. What personal motivations influenced different managers' mode of entry strategies?

MNEs compete strenuously for the same customers in stable markets like Scandinavia (© iStock photo).

international collaboration was a good thing. For their internally-oriented production colleagues, it was not.

Discussion questions

1. Is a 'global' mindset necessarily riskier than a 'domestic' one?
2. What determines the speed at which a company internationalizes?
3. Can SMEs ever be as comfortable with internationalization as large MNEs?

4. What effect will future environmental constraints have on the choice of greenfield versus brownfield expansion?
5. When do the risks of international partnerships outweigh the advantages?

References

Anand, J., and Delios, A. (2002). 'Absolute and Relative Resources as Determinants of International Acquisitions', *Strategic Management Journal*, 23: 119–34.

Anoop, M. (2006). 'How much does Ownership really Matter? Equity and Trust Relations in Joint Venture Relationships', *Journal of International Business Studies*, 37/1 (Jan.).

Ascenzi, J. (2008). 'Tesco Struggles in US Debut', 23 Mar., www.thebizpress.com (accessed 8 Nov. 2008).

Associated Press (2009). 'Adidas Profit Gets Lift from Asia and Latin America', *International Herald Tribune*, 5 Mar., p. 13.

Barba Navaretti , G., Venables, Anthony J., et al. (2004). *Multinational Firms in the World Economy*. Princeton: Princeton University Press.

Barkema, H., and Drogendijk, R. (2007). 'Internationalizing in Small, Incremental or Larger Steps?', *Journal of International Business Studies*, 38/7 (Dec.).

Belderbos, R., and Zou, J. (2007). 'On the Growth of Foreign Affiliates: Multinational Plant Networks, Joint Ventures and Flexibility', *Journal of International Business Studies*, 38/7 (Dec.).

Bellman, E., and Rohwedder, C. (2007). 'Metro Cultivates System to Grow in India', *Wall Street Journal-Europe*, 28 Nov., p. 4.

Chetty, S., and Campbell-Hunt, C. (2003). 'Paths to Internationalization among Small to Medium-Sized Firms', *European Journal of Marketing*, 37/5–6.

Contractor, F., Kundu, S., and Hsu, C.-C. (2003). 'A Three-Stage Theory of International Expansion: The Link between Multinationality and Performance in the Service Sector', *Journal of International Business Studies*, 34/1 (Jan.).

Davey, J. (2007). 'M&S Prepares to Go Global – Again', *Sunday Times*, 4 Nov., p. 9.

Desislava, K., and van Witteloostuijn, A. (2007). 'Foreign Direct Investment Mode Choice: Entry and Establishment Modes in Transition Economies', *Journal of International Business Studies*, 38/6 (Nov.).

Doukas, J., and Lang, L. (2003). 'Foreign Direct Investment, Diversification and Firm Performance', *Journal of International Business Studies*, 34/2 (Mar.).

Dyer, G. (2007). 'Danone and Wahaha Dispute Intensifies', 14 Apr., www.ft.com (accessed 1 Apr. 2008).

Fan, T., and Phan, P. (2007). 'International New Venture: Revisiting the Influences behind the "Born-Global" Firm', *Journal of International Business Studies*, 38/7 (Dec.).

Fernandez, Z., and Nieto, M. (2006). 'Impact of Ownership on the International Involvement of SMEs', *Journal of International Business Studies*, 37/3 (May).

Fields, M. (2008). 'Disney Licensed Merchandise Sales to Hit $30 Billion', 11 June, www.brandweek.com (accessed 8 Nov. 2008).

Franchiseek International (2008). www.franchiseek.com (accessed Apr. 2008).

Gauthier-Villars, D. (2007). 'French Bank Looks to Russia for Growth', *Wall Street Journal-Europe*, 21–3 Dec., p. 1.

Geng, L. (2007). 'To Be or Not To Be: The Fate of International Business Ventures', Mar–Apr., http://agora.lakeheadu.ca (accessed 11 Apr. 2008).

Gilpin, R. (2001). *Global Political Economy: Understanding the International Economic Order*. Princeton: Princeton University Press.

Glader, P., and Whalen, J. (2008). 'GE in Cancer Clinic Deal', *Wall Street Journal-Europe*, 13 Nov., p. 6.

Hutchinson, K., Quinn, B., and Alexander, N. (2006). 'SME Retailer Internationalization: Case Study Evidence from British Retailers', *International Marketing Review*, 23/1.

Johanson, J., and Vahlne, J.-E. (1977). 'The Internationalization Process of the Firm: A Model of Knowledge Development and Increasing Foreign Commitments', *Journal of International Business Studies*, 8/1.

Kale, D. (2007). 'Internationalization of Indian Pharmaceutical Firms', www.brunel.ac.uk (accessed 6 Apr. 2007).

Kwong, R., and Hille, K. (2009). 'Surprise Vigour of China Demand Lifts MediaTek', *Financial Times*, 4 Mar., p. 27.

Li, J., and Rugman, A. (2007). 'Real Options and the Theory of Foreign Direct Investment', *International Business Review*, 16/6 (Dec.).

Lloyd-Reason, L., and Mughan, T. (2002). 'Strategies for Internationalization within SMEs: The Key Role of the Owner-Manager', *Journal of Small Business and Enterprise Development*, 9/2.

McGregor, R. (2006). 'Backlash Puts China Finance Deal on Hold', 15 Mar., www.ft.com (accessed 1 Apr. 2008).

Madhak, A. (2006). 'How Much Does Ownership Really Matter? Equity and Trust Relations in Joint Venture Relationships', *Journal of International Business Studies*, 37/3 (May).

Manzoni, J.-F. and Barsoux, J.-L. (2006). 'Untangling Alliances and Joint Ventures', 19 Oct., www.ft.com (accessed 11 Apr. 2008).

Marsh, P. (2006). 'Fiat Shifts up a Gear in Latin America', 24 Oct., www.ft.com (accessed 1 Apr. 2008).

Meschi, P., and Riccio, E. (2008). 'Country Risk, National Cultural Differences between Partners and Survival of International Joint Ventures in Brazil', *International Business Review*, 17/3 (June).

Mullen, J. (2007). 'France Télécom Looks to Africa for Growth', *Wall Street Journal-Europe*, 21–3 Dec., p. 4.

Nadolska, A., and Barkema, H. (2007). 'Learning to Internationalise: The Pace and Success of Foreign Acquisitions', *Journal of International Business Studies*, 38/7 (Dec.).

Nadkarni, S., and Perez, P. (2007). 'Prior Conditions and Early International Commitment: The Mediating Role of Domestic Mindset', *Journal of International Business Studies*, 38/1 (Jan.).

Neupert, K., Baughn, C., Lam Dao, T., and Neupert, K. (2006). 'SME Exporting Challenges in Transitional and Developed Economies', *Journal of Small Business and Enterprise Development*, 13/4.

Parasie, N. (2007). 'French Banks Seek Assets in North Africa', *Wall Street Journal-Europe*, 26 Nov.

Pilling, D. (2007). '*Investing in Japan: A Tough Nut to Crack*', 13 Mar., www.ft.com (accessed 1 Apr. 2008).

Ruzzier, M., Hisrich, R., and Antoncic, B. (2006). 'SME Internationalization Research: Past, Present, and Future', *Journal of Small Business and Enterprise Development*, 13/4.

Slangen, A., and Hennart, J.-F. (2008). 'Do Multinationals Really Prefer to Enter Culturally Distant Countries through Greenfields rather than through Acquisitions?', *Journal of International Business Studies*, 39/3.

Slovin, M., Sushka, M., and Mantecon, T. (2007). 'Analyzing Joint Ventures as Corporate Control Activity', *Journal of Banking & Finance*, 31/8 (Aug.).

Tseng, C.-H., Tansuhaj, P., Hallagan, W., and McCullough, J., Tseng, C.-H. (2007). 'Effects of Firm Resources on Growth in Multinationality', *Journal of International Business Studies*, 38/6 (Nov.).

Tuppura, A., Saarenketo, S., Puumalainen, K., Jantunen, J., and Kyläheiko, K. (2008). 'Linking Knowledge, Entry Timing and Internationalization Strategy', *International Business Review*, 17/4 (Aug.).

UNCTAD (2007). 'World Investment Report', http://stats.unctad.org (accessed 10 Apr. 2008).

UNCTAD (2008). 'World Investment Report', www.unctad.org (accessed 17 Mar. 2009).

Zhang, Y., Haiyang, L., Hitt, M., and Cui, G. (2007). 'R&D Intensity and International Joint Venture Performance in an Emerging Market: Moderating Effects of Market Focus and Ownership Structure', *Journal of International Business Studies*, 38/7 (Dec.).

Further research

Readers will note that this chapter contains more references than usual from a single source: *Journal of International Business Studies* (*JIBS*), published by the Academy of International Business (AIA), a leading association of scholars and specialists in this discipline. This was intentional. Not only has *JIBS* been a benchmark review since the 1970s, but the 'modes of internationalization' topic treated here is a key topic for international business authors publishing in this journal.

Similar to *JIBS* is the *International Business Review* (*IBR*), a publication by the European International Business Academy (EIBA), which was founded in 1974 under the auspices of the European

Foundation for Management Development. Both AIA and EIBA are active associations that, in addition to publishing reviews, organize regular events and themed conferences.

Lastly, for readers with more of a background interest in the macro-framework surrounding MNEs' internationalization drives, great value is to be found in Oxford University Press's *Journal of Economic Geography* (*JEG*). This review offers higher-level thinking at the intersection between the two disciplines mentioned in its title.

Online Resource Centre

Visit the Online Resource Centre that accompanies this book to read more information relating to modes of internationalization: www.oxfordtextbooks.co.uk/orc/sitken_bowen/

9　Multinational Structure and Control

Overview

The chapter's first section reviews the main organizational theories and structures characterizing MNE control systems. The underlying idea is that, at any point in time, an MNE will organize a worldwide configuration of units reflecting its specific strategic intent. Analysis will be divided into three main organizational configurations (multi-domestic, global, and transnational) and five structures (international, functional, product, geographic, and matrix). The chapter's second section discusses MNE structures' interpersonal aspects, highlighting sociological principles of organization such as control, specialization, and coordination. This is followed by analysis of how firms integrate new teams into their existing international structures. The attitudes underlying such efforts reflect MNEs' 'push' and 'pull' orientations, concepts discussed in the chapter's final section and further enriched in the book's next three chapters.

Section I: Multinational theories and structures

    Historical MNE configurations

    Global versus regional focus

    Glocalization: juggling global and local perspectives

Section II: Managing people across borders

    Principles of organization

    Integrating international teams

    Push versus pull paradigms

Learning Objectives

After reading this chapter, you should be able to:

✦ monitor historical changes in MNEs' dominant organizational logic

✦ assess how MNEs organize themselves in relation to their circumstances

✦ apply sociological principles to MNE structures

✦ link the location of power within an MNE to its strategic purpose

✦ identify the change management problems that arise when new units join an MNE network

Case Study 9.1

MNE restructuring: Unilever united

When a company has survived for as long as Unilever (www.unilever.com) has, it knows that new challenges often necessitate new strategies and structures. This grand old name in European consumer goods—the manufacturer of famous household brands such as Lipton tea, Knorr soup, Lux soap, and Vaseline—has traditionally run a decentralized organization, reflecting in part its dual Dutch and British origins. Moreover, like most companies in the fast-moving consumer goods sector, it has long considered adaptation to be its key factor of success, even before consumer markets began to globalize. This vision remains central to Unilever's self-image, with the company continuing to claim a 'multi-local' focus even as it tries to coordinate operations in nearly 100 countries worldwide.

The problem in the hyper-competitive environment of the early twenty-first century is that multinationals running similar operations in several countries at once are not very cost-effective. With Unilever achieving lower operating profits than its great rival, Proctor and Gamble in the early 2000s, CEO Patrick Cescau sensed the need to streamline his group's organization and launched an initiative called 'One Unilever'. The first step of this restructuring process involved thinning out Unilever's top ranks, with half of all 1,200 executives worldwide losing their job by the end of 2005. A new senior team was set up, consisting of three Regional Presidents (for Europe, the Americas, and Asia/Africa), two Product Category Heads, one Chief Financial Officer, and one Chief Human Resources Officer. This compact but diverse committee, pooling competencies in functional, product, and geographic areas, set the tone for leaner management structures at lower, more operational levels. A case in point was the change made to the European Foods research and development (R&D) centre that, having once employed 1,160 persons on 60 sites stretching across Europe, was now asked to run only 29 sites, leading to a loss of 240 jobs. In this simpler and tighter R&D structure, new product development would be run out of six European 'Centres of Excellence', sized to both ensure a concentration of technical capabilities across all categories and encompass all global, regional, and local innovations. A decision was also made to consolidate and amalgamate different country and factory teams, making each more diverse and adapted to local circumstances; a key factor—in the implementation of food innovation. Unilever's new look is very different from its traditional model of autonomous national subsidiaries. The focus nowadays is on cross-border coordination and cost-effectiveness—priority challenges in the modern world.

Unilever's broad international product portfolio requires an adapted organization (Unilever).

Introduction

Whereas Chapter 8 highlighted the decision to enter foreign markets, Chapter 9 reviews how MNEs manage existing operations. The two topics are not entirely unrelated, since many internationalization decisions are specifically taken because an MNE wants to assume a particular cross-border shape ('configuration'). There is no doubt, however, that international structure deserves its own analysis, if only because of the difficulties that MNEs can face when coordinating the activities and objectives of subsidiaries that can be geographically and culturally very diverse.

There are several reasons why MNEs are so difficult to configure. First, as shown by Figure 9.1, organizations are living bodies and therefore susceptible to change. The structures that a group executive establishes to achieve certain goals are likely to affect employees' world views and future behaviour. What cannot be predicted with certainty is the feedback effect that these new attitudes and actions will have on the structures in which they materialize. Secondly, with executives' organizational efforts often focusing on internal objectives, there is always the risk that MNE configurations will be ill-adapted to the diverse and sometimes contradictory environments in which they work. Sociologists like Talcott Parsons (1964) have studied how a system's efforts to adapt to its settings can be at odds with its need to ensure internal coherency. In international business as in other social sciences, structures and mindsets influence one another. When examining the succession of structures and modes of control that MNEs have implemented over time, it is worth remembering that philosophies fall in and out of fashion.

Section I: Multinational theories and structures

Over the years, many theorists have tried to build models explaining companies' international behaviour. One example, discussed in Chapter 4, was Vernon's Product Life Cycle theory, which specified that firms tend to locate their global production units depending on the stage of maturity reached by the product in question. The Uppsala 'stages' model described in Chapter 8 stresses the role played by learning as firms gradually enter new markets. All these theories, and others still, including George Yip's vision of 'global strategic transformations' where companies change their business model in anticipation of crises (see Online Resource Centre, extension material 9.1), bear some relationship to the current chapter's discussion of MNE structures and control.

> Go to the ORC

In terms of the specific way in which MNEs manage their existing operations, however, the theories that stand out most are the ones that try to unveil the connection between companies' ambitions and the systems they create to achieve their goals. MNE organizational theories are based on different conceptions of the location of power within an international group. Broadly speaking, these range from a simple nation-by-nation orientation where

Figure 9.1
The interactions underlying collective action; intent, structure, circumstances, and performance are mutually connected.

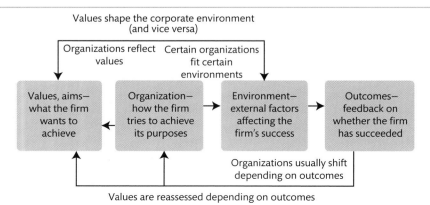

Values shape the corporate environment
(and vice versa)

Organizations reflect values   Certain organizations fit certain environments

| Values, aims— what the firm wants to achieve | Organization— how the firm tries to achieve its purposes | Environment— external factors affecting the firm's success | Outcomes— feedback on whether the firm has succeeded |

Organizations usually shift depending on outcomes

Values are reassessed depending on outcomes

subsidiaries enjoy maximum autonomy to a globalized orientation characterized by an all-powerful headquarters. This spectrum typifies the core distinction that Chapter 1 makes between international business and globalization.

Historical MNE configurations

Firms have long sought to build configurations allowing them to benefit from the international business opportunities they encounter. In 1960, a young economist named Stephen Hymer wrote a seminal text analysing how firms shape their international operations (Hymer 1976). One of the many outcomes of the FDI studies that Hymer conducted was to divide MNE organizational history into three distinct stages, each characterized by a dominant logic (Ietto-Gillies 2005). This is a good starting point for tracking how MNE structures have evolved over time.

According to Hymer, most companies that later became world leaders began life under the tight control of a few key managers working on a single product out of a single location. At this early stage of development, managers tend to view their first foreign operations as mere 'appendages to dominant domestic operation' (Bartlett and Ghoshal 2002: 5). Thus, a company's first foreign moves often involve separating overseas activities from the bulk of their business and grouping them into an international division comprised of specifically offshore activities such as trade documentation or international funding (see Figure 9.2). This type of structure might seem appropriate to firms that do most of their business domestically and consider their home market a priority. But it is also deeply flawed, since it tends to create a mindset where the group executive underestimates national specificities. As a result, few MNEs opt for this structure nowadays.

Hymer considered that one of the main drivers behind internationalization is companies' desire to exploit their 'monopoly advantages', meaning the unique capabilities that often materialize in the way they manage their value chains. As discussed in Chapter 7, many firms at the time of Hymer's writing (in the 1960s and 1970s) tried to internationalize along vertically integrated lines, largely because the general managerial paradigm at the time held that it was in companies' interest to control as much of their global value chains as possible. Usually this meant that the group executive would take direct responsibility for the cross-border implementation of strategy. In turn, this often resulted in a division-based structure known as the 'Unitary (U-form)', illustrated in Figure 9.3. For Hymer, this was the second organizational stage that most MNEs were destined to experience once their capabilities had reached a certain level.

One of the configurations typifying second-stage MNEs is the functional organization, a U-form in which each division is defined by a corporate function (such as manufacturing, marketing, or finance). Here, it is the 'centre' (head office) that controls the 'periphery' (the foreign subsidiaries), whose mission is to implement strategies and technologies that have been handed down from the top. The focus in such an organization is on the different value chain operations that a company performs, irrespective of product or location. This approach is mostly applicable in MNEs (like oil companies) featuring relatively undifferentiated product ranges or that operate within a relatively new sector of activity still characterized by narrow product portfolios. The first examples of functional organizations

Thinking point
When, if ever, does it make sense for a company to lodge activities in an 'international' division?

+ **International organization**
Structure based on the idea that all foreign environments share certain characteristics that differ from the firm's dominant domestic market and should therefore be combined in a specific division.

+ **Functional organization**
Structure where power is centralized, based on the idea that a firm's key factors of organization are its internal capabilities.

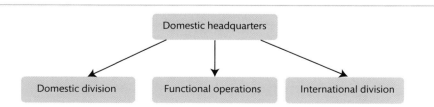

Figure 9.2 'International' organization.

go all the way back to the early twentieth century when this configuration was first applied by trailblazing MNEs such as General Motors, Shell, Standard Oil, and, above all, Ford, whose early internationalization efforts generally involved transferring the same 'methods of organization and production as [those] developed in the parent company' (Bélis-Bergouignan et al. 2000). An MNE's main priority in a structure of this kind is to ensure headquarters' operational control.

As the international business environment evolved over the course of the twentieth century, Hymer detected the rise of a third organizational stage, one he called the 'multi-divisional (M-form)'. To respond to global consumers' increasingly differentiated demands, MNEs began to need structures that were more flexible than the U-form. For some, this meant adopting a 'product' organization, with each division being set up as an independent profit centre (see Figure 9.4). The purpose in a structure of this kind is to ensure that decisions made by one division have little or no effect on sister units, which should remain free to pursue their own product policies, in line with local market conditions. This is especially important in conglomerates (such as Westinghouse, General Electric, but also some Japanese *keiretsus*—see Chapter 11) characterized by the lack of any real overlap between product lines. It is no use focusing an MNE's efforts on its internal functions when each of its product lines requires entirely different capabilities.

Another variant of the multi-divisional M-form structure—and one that became very popular among MNEs that view responsiveness as their priority—is the 'geographic' organization (see Figure 9.5). Where consumer attributes (or production conditions) vary widely from one country to another, structuring efforts along 'functional' or 'product' lines makes less sense than empowering those front-line units that have most knowledge about local circumstances—the national subsidiaries. The emphasis here is on international differentiation instead of global strategy. As a result, power in this kind of MNE shifts from the centre to the periphery, with group headquarters performing little more than resource allocation, performance control, and strategic coordination missions. A leading example of an MNE promoting this kind of structure is the food giant Nestlé (www.nestle.com, see in particular the organizational chart on the website). This company has traditionally given each of its national subsidiaries a great deal of autonomy to make key product portfolio decisions. In geographically organized MNEs, being a country manager is a very desirable position.

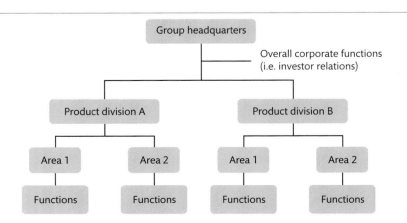

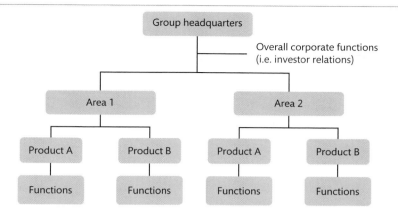

Figure 9.5
'Geographic'
organization.

By stressing local autonomy over central power, a geographic organization is a key configuration in the multi-domestic philosophy that highlights subsidiaries' differences as opposed to their similarities. To a certain degree, this is a conception where MNEs are viewed as little more than the sum of very different parts.

Power in multi-domestic firms is therefore very fragmented. Greater responsiveness to local circumstances is a strength but also a weakness, since it can involve a wasteful duplication of certain functions (such as R&D or manufacturing) across several countries. This increases overheads, making it harder to achieve group-wide economies of scale. It is one of the reasons why Unilever ended up refocusing its global research efforts, as discussed in Case Study 9.1. The role of the head office can also be confusing in a multi-domestic firm, especially when the group executive is asked to make both investment and operational decisions instead of focusing only on the former and leaving the latter to local managers (Rugman and D'Cruz 2000). Lastly, multi-domestic organizations are disappointing in terms of the amount of knowledge that gets transferred between national subsidiaries. The reason is because employees in this type of configuration often communicate solely within the confines of their immediate geographic unit and ignore colleagues from other regions. This is a crucial shortcoming in a world where reduced barriers to trade have intensified global competition, forcing MNEs to seek advantage anywhere they can find it. One key source of competitiveness is a group's ability to ensure that the knowledge developed by one unit located in one country can be shared with a sister unit located elsewhere. This is particularly crucial when ground-breaking technological progress and generic innovations are involved. Conversely, anything that causes poor intra-firm communications or coordination is counterproductive. This explains why so many MNEs abandoned the multi-domestic approach in the latter half of the twentieth century.

Photo 9.1
The way that firms
organize themselves
often reflects their
vision of the world
(Photodisc).

Global versus regional focus

As Chapter 12 will discuss, by 1983 renowned observers like Theodore Levitt were already proclaiming the convergence of many international markets, particularly ones involving branded consumer goods. This meant that, for MNEs in many sectors, what mattered was no longer differentiation along national lines (the main focus in a multi-domestic logic) but the ability to service global customers. Facing rivals who were increasingly sized to do battle on a planetary scale, firms needed to organize their operations in a way that would maximize their own economies of scale. The new goal of achieving a global reach and efficiency called for appropriate organizational configurations.

The rationale for global MNEs

The key objective for firms pursuing a global strategy is to increase interdependency and achieve efficiency by coordinating the performances of subsidiaries in one part of the world with sister units located elsewhere. One aspect of this approach is that units might have to subsidize one another from time to time (Hamel and Prahalad 1985). This will occur only if the group executive has sufficient authority over local managers to force them to share surpluses with fellow subsidiaries as need be. Thus, the rise of global structures in the late twentieth century was to a certain extent the reassertion of headquarters' power over subsidiaries. Emphasizing standardization and economies of scale, global firms would tend to organize production around highly coordinated specialist plants scattered strategically across the planet (see Chapters 7 and 11). On the marketing side, they would wage global advertising and branding campaigns, promoting a few gigantic brand names to consumers, often from a very young age onwards (Klein 2000). Above all, throughout the 1980s and 1990s, they could rely on a growing intellectual consensus that the global perspective was destined to dominate future organizational thinking. The publicity attached to a given paradigm is crucial to its acceptance. This is because managers risk their careers if their actions are at odds with what everyone else is thinking. After all, if the decisions they make correspond to received wisdom at a certain point in time and things then go wrong, they can always escape personal blame by pointing out that everyone else committed the same mistake. It is harder for them to defend themselves, on the other hand, if their original decision was unusual. In international business as in other disciplines, mavericks are always likely to stand out—for better or worse.

The shortcomings of the global approach

In recent years, a rising number of observers have started to take a negative view of the global approach. One criticism is that little room remains for independent thinking at the local level when headquarters executives who are interested only in a group's overall activity portfolio are the ones deciding subsidiaries' missions (Dicken 2007). An associated worry is that local units might suffer from de-skilling as headquarters shift competencies from one subsidiary to another in a game of global chess that ignores each unit's specific ambitions. In a similar vein, subsidiary employees may feel resentment at having to follow the orders of foreign decision-makers working out of a distant global head office. In more psychological terms, they can be confused by the global organization's 'de-territorialized' business network (Held and McGrew 2002), one where physical proximity has little to do with human relations or the location of power. After all, working right next to one's boss usually allows for better interactions than reporting to someone situated thousands of miles away. Note also the risk in a global company that knowledge will be transmitted only vertically, from headquarters to subsidiary or vice versa, undermining the possibility of subsidiary–subsidiary information flows. Lastly, in more economic terms and as described in Chapter 8, when global organizations serve local markets from distant central manufacturing locations, they tend to suffer higher 'trade costs'.

+ **De-skilling**
Where a reduced level of competencies is required from a business unit, often because it has been asked to specialize in one or just a few value chain operation(s).

	Function	Rationale
Functions that are likely to be centralized, thus lodged in MNE headquarters	R&D	Confidentiality
	Manufacturing, logistics	Economies of scale, coordination
	Finance, IT	Shared platforms
Functions that are likely to be decentralized, thus lodged in MNE subsidiaries	Design	Market intelligence
	Sales	Customization
	Human resources	Personal culture

Figure 9.6
Certain functions, by their very nature, tend to be run out of an MNE's centre, others out of its periphery.

Thus, after having been so popular in the late twentieth century, global configurations are now viewed as quite imperfect. Like other international business solutions, they are applicable in certain situations but not in all. As Figure 9.6 shows, in some cases it makes sense to centralize particular functions, like supply chain management, because this helps an MNE to 'achieve worldwide optimisation, monitor supplier performance, check alternatives and monitor demand throughout all of the pipeline' (Christopher 2005). On the other hand, it is often just as good an idea for operations like customer service to be run locally, if only because this will strengthen the interpersonal relations that are a key factor of success in a downstream function. An example of this is the way that major international airliners like British Airways (BA) run representative offices in many of the countries they serve. BA could save money by fielding all the phone calls it receives worldwide out of just one site. However, a centralizing solution of this sort would have run counter to the marketing approach preferred by customers in this sector. An MNE's decision about where to locate its functions will vary depending on whether the priority is internal cohesion or external adaptation. Indeed, MNEs must often simultaneously juggle global and multi-domestic orientations, the two opposite ends of the spectrum of possible organizational logics. Of course, having extremes also hints at the existence of intermediary solutions. One is the figure of the regional MNE.

The rise of regional MNEs

Some leading observers have expressed doubts about how many truly global firms really exist today. Their contention is that most MNEs focus on their region of origin (almost always one of the three Triad zones), which usually accounts for at least 70 per cent of total revenues (Rugman 2005). In other words, most companies derive their main economies of scope and scale from services or products that they produce within their home region. Thus, there is little advantage, and hence incentive, for them to venture further abroad. As discussed in Chapter 8, managers tend to feel more comfortable with a regulatory environment and general business culture that is more familiar to them. Conversely, running units on a global basis often means spreading managerial resources too thinly. Lastly, firms with global operations often face higher transaction costs in the form of economic, political, and social barriers to entry (ranging from import tariffs to xenophobic reactions).

The reality is that many firms still apply an at least partially global logic to their upstream activities—especially in sectors (like pharmaceuticals) where the cost of transporting goods is low in comparison with the cost of building multiple production facilities. At the same time, much of the so-called global production in sectors like automobiles or chemicals actually takes place in 'clusters' (see Chapter 11) that have been organized along regional lines. Similarly, many MNEs situate their R&D activities close to the home country headquarters, if only because it is easier for them to register patents in the legal environment that they know best.

Thinking point

How global can an MNE ever truly become?

+ Economies of scope
Production efficiencies that firms achieve because they can manage their product portfolio in a way that creates synergies. This occurs, for instance, when a given marketing initiative can be used to sell more than one item at a time.

As for downstream activities, with the exception of a few sectors like consumer electronics, it is questionable whether Levitt's prediction of a mass global convergence in consumer preferences has actually come true. Indeed, many MNEs expand regionally via horizontal integration (see Chapter 8) precisely because it is easier for them to cater to populations that share their existing customers' social, economic, and cultural attributes—and because nearby foreign markets usually have a better chance of possessing at least some similarities with their home market. This explains why so many MNEs nowadays configure operations along regional lines. In these cases, the global headquarters' role is usually little more than ensuring inter-regional transfers of assets and knowledge.

Some analysts disagree with this idea that international business is dominated by MNEs' home regions, offering evidence that many do sell goods elsewhere and operate regularly on a bi-regional and/or global basis (Osegowitsch and Sammartino 2008). Moreover, the growing number of MNEs that come from emerging economies like China and India but sell into the world's wealthier regions means that at least some companies have been drawn into a global configuration. Over the next few years, it will be worth monitoring the breakdown in MNEs' global and regional volumes, in part to assess the impact that this has on MNE configurations. One very good source of information is UNCTAD's World Investment Report, whose 'Transnationality Index' assesses the geographic distribution of sales and assets for the world's largest companies. It is notable that, whereas UNCTAD's 2005 report had highlighted an ongoing home bias, the main trend in 2007 was Western MNEs' accelerated interest in Asia for both manufacturing and commercial purposes. The increasing attraction of the Far East for MNEs worldwide could work against the regional thesis and strengthen the idea that a more global outlook will dominate in the future. On the other hand, the 2008–9 financial crisis had the opposite effect, increasing the share of total global activity accounted for by purely regional (and even national) transactions.

Notwithstanding these macro-economic factors, there are other reasons why the total number of regional MNEs has risen in recent years. In the European Union, where many countries have moved to liberalize sectors (such as banking or utilities) that provide services to both individuals and to businesses, customers often need or want to have a sense of proximity to the company they are dealing with. This is one explanation for the 'nearshoring' trend noted in Chapter 11. Another explanation for the resurgence of proximity as a factor in international business is the pressure that MNEs will face to shorten their supply chains as environmental constraints translate into higher fuel prices. Globalization clearly exists, but it may not be as widespread as its supporters contend.

Glocalization: juggling global and local perspectives

During the 1980s, recognition of different multi-domestic, regional, and global MNE models gave birth to so-called parenting theory, which states that companies will adopt the specific organization that they think suits their strategic purpose best at a particular point in their internationalization trajectory (Goold and Campbell 1987). In this view, whereas some MNEs see long-term strategy as a key factor of success and therefore centralize planning activities, others consider it more effective for subsidiaries to take fuller responsibility for budget performance and therefore favour decentralization.

The risk here is that, if companies focus too much on the fit between their structure and strategy, to the exclusion of other considerations, they risk becoming imprisoned in a rigid and bureaucratic mindset of their own making. As noted by Jack Welch, CEO of General Electric (GE) during the 1980s and 1990s, managers will be discouraged from showing much needed initiative if they are asked to strategize (and/or communicate) only within the narrow boundaries of the official role they have been allocated within a particular structure (Byrne 1998). In other words, MNEs should not be forced to choose between global integration and local adaptation, since both are necessary to succeed in today's international business environment. The question then became how to configure a multinational so that it can achieve these two apparently contradictory goals. This search gave birth to the figure of the transnational firm (Bartlett 1986).

Managers' mentality can be just as important as MNE structures

Transnational theorists argue that attitudes and relationships are just as crucial to an MNE's success as official reporting lines. The idea here is that companies need to develop a 'multi-dimensional' mindset (Levy et al. 2007) that will nudge people into looking beyond their 'administrative heritage' and culture of origin and get them to accept ideas originating elsewhere. In truth, it does not matter whether a useful procedural innovation starts in a firm's headquarters or subsidiaries—all that counts is that it spreads throughout an organization. In Bartlett's opinion, this is best achieved by encouraging two-way flows between headquarters and subsidiaries, and/or multilateral flows among subsidiaries.

One of the aims of this approach is to avoid the kinds of problems that often arise when a head office tries to force foreign subsidiaries to reproduce its strong home country culture. An example of this from the early 2000s was when Toyota executives brought Japanese working methods to the Valenciennes plant in northern France. Many staff members (thus unions) were angry because of the pressures they were made to feel following the implementation of an ambitious new performance system. In today's world, it is rare that an MNE's centre can simply dictate to its periphery. According to the 'knowledge-based theory of the firm' (Kogut and Zander 1992), the main driver of corporate organization is knowledge, but, because this is deeply embedded in a unit's local culture and practices, it is almost impossible to replicate it anywhere else. Hence the need for staff members to develop a wide range of capabilities that they can apply in varying circumstances.

In short, the transnational approach is meant to replace the one-way, top-down, or bottom-up information flows characterizing, respectively, global and multi-domestic MNEs. One expression used to describe the new vision is 'glocalization'. Many companies use this terminology nowadays, one of the best-known examples being the advertising campaign that the British banking giant HSBC ran in the 2000s to publicize itself as an organization that is local everywhere (see Chapter 12). A similar construct (see Unilever example in Case Study 9.1) involves 'multi-local' firms ready to manage challenges at the national, regional, and global levels simultaneously, depending on whether a given situation is driven by domestic or international factors (Ghislanzoni et al. 2008). MNEs that are capable of alternating paradigms have reached an advanced level of organizational flexibility.

A transnational approach is a useful compromise, but it can also create a serious organizational dilemma. One cause is the kind of transnational working arrangements where people are asked to assume a leadership role in some situations but not in others. This mixing of roles raises questions about the permanency of multinational structures and has spawned a corpus of management literature devoted to concepts such as 'management by projects' and 'flexible working teams' (see Online Resource Centre, extension material 9.2). On other occasions, the dilemma derives from people's sense of self-interest. In a structure like an MNE, certain selfless actions are always necessary for the common good. Examples include the need to share an innovation or to prospect customers that a sister unit will subsequently serve. Where subsidiary managers focus exclusively on their local unit's competitiveness or if they are not rewarded sufficiently for contributions to other teams, they may be less motivated by the overall group interest (Ghoshal and Gratton 2002). Even worse, group and subsidiary interests are sometimes in direct conflict. The two levels may disagree, for instance, about a product's pricing or whether it should have simple or advanced technological attributes—possibly because it is at a different stage of its life cycle in the subsidiary's territory than in most of the other segments where the MNE is competing. Such conflicts of interest mean that transnational reporting lines can be very confusing.

Other problems associated with a transnational approach are more cultural in nature. It has been shown, for instance, that colleagues working in a company's headquarters and subsidiaries will tend to interact more positively, and exchange more information, when

+ **Transnational firm**
Company whose aims, and therefore organization, will alternatively highlight global efficiency, local flexibility, and shared learning.

+ **Organizational dilemma**
Where employees are confused by the contradictory interests that they are asked to represent at different levels within their organization.

> Go to the ORC

they possess similar national, cultural, and/or linguistic backgrounds (Makela et al. 2007). Conversely, when people's backgrounds are very different, the information exchanges upon which a transnational company relies can be difficult to achieve. Note that this obstacle can be overcome if employees learn to recognize the value of different cultural practices, however foreign they may seem. The Japanese business culture is just as foreign to US workers as it is to Europeans, yet, unlike their Valenciennes counterparts, employees at the Toyota plant in Huntsville (Alabama) had relatively few problems adopting Japanese 'quality circle' working practices, an HRM approach in which ideas are shared from the bottom up. In essence, this tolerance for foreign thought processes meant that the company's US workers were closer to a transnational mentality than their French colleagues. Flexible structures are difficult to implement in the absence of flexible mindsets.

Creating the conditions for a transnational MNE

+ Matrix organization
Structure based on the idea that multiple reporting lines broaden employees' vision of the business and can create synergies.

Thinking point

How can MNEs optimize information exchanges without suffering from overload?

Thus, the transnational company seeks to maximize vertical (hierarchical) and horizontal (geographical) exchanges between all units—a principle embodied in a relatively recent structure called the 'matrix' organization (see Figure 9.7). The idea here is that, irrespective of people's unit of origin, there are many occasions when they should be temporarily allocated to ad hoc structures specifically created to fulfil a particular task. This so-called matrix logic became especially popular during the 1990s, where it was applied by several leading MNEs, most notably the Swedish–Swiss engineering company Asea Brown Boveri (ABB). The hope was that, by encouraging multiple reporting lines and developing forums for information sharing, new synergies would arise, benefiting all product, function, and geographic divisions. The main goal was to ensure that the whole of a company would be able to use the knowledge held 'explicitly' (openly) or 'tacitly' by any one of its units (Davenport and Prusak 1998). Indeed, many large MNEs struggle to analyse data and knowledge stored in different departments and sites. Getting useful information to the right people at the right time is a major concern for international managers. Most MNEs have organized a range of systems and roles to achieve this (newsletters, multi-site videoconferencing, internal communications specialists, and/or peer visits). At a deeper, more personal level, the issue here is how much trust colleagues need in one another before they are willing to share knowledge.

Because of its multiple reporting lines and potential for information overload, a matrix organization is often confusing to members and will really succeed only if certain individuals within the organization are capable and willing to act as traffic controllers. These key staff members will have the job of identifying and redirecting colleagues' competencies. This is no easy task, seeing as the knowledge that a company holds is often very compartmentalized. In many cases, this traffic controller's role will be played by national subsidiary (country) managers, who are once again starting to receive the kind of attention that they used to enjoy back in the days when multi-domestic structures were dominant. At the same time, because it is considered very complex to manage, the matrix organization is starting to lose some of its popularity.

Figure 9.7
A 'matrix' organization. Everyone shares knowledge, with variable teams comprised of people from different departments.

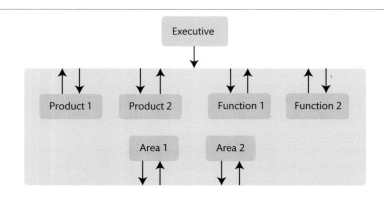

MNEs as alliances of equals

Since national subsidiaries, on the one hand, and regional or global headquarters, on the other, are all capable of contributing to an MNE's collective welfare, there is a strong argument to make that the only accurate way of representing a group's different constituencies is to view them as equal members in a network of diverse interests (Birkinshaw 2000). This concept can be visualized in Figure 9.8. In some cases (for example, US construction and mining equipment manufacturer Caterpillar or Japanese electronics firm Matsushita), a strong headquarters culture means that group technology and strategies tend to be determined by the MNE's centre. In other cases, it is the periphery that sets the pace—one example being the way that competencies developed by Fuji Xerox's Japanese marketing subsidiary in reaction to local standards helped it to become the group's lead R&D centre. Contrary to the general organizational principle of top-down authority, the key to international success today may be a more balanced relationship between head offices and subsidiaries, or what Hedlund (1986) has called the heterarchy of an organization that combines diverse and equal power bases. What head offices provide are overview and the ability to coordinate. What subsidiaries offer are alertness to global opportunities and, depending on their size, a certain capacity for driving initiatives in domestic or international markets (and within the firm itself). Because they are in constant touch with suppliers and customers, subsidiary managers are fertile sources of information, thus useful drivers of change. They deserve as much credit as head office strategists do.

By hypothesizing that a firm is just as likely to accumulate advantages abroad as at home, the transnational logic is at odds with transaction cost theory (see Online Resource Centre, extension material 8.1), which assumes that most firm-specific advantages are generated in the firm's home country. It also contradicts resource-based theories (see Online Resource Centre, extension material 11.3), rooted in the idea that resources and capabilities develop at the level of the firm as a whole. What it recognizes instead is that different units contribute in different ways to overall performance. This is an important advance in general understanding of how MNEs work.

If power and knowledge can both be created at the subsidiary level, the real challenge is ensuring that these factors are disseminated through the MNE's internal market. In turn, this raises the issue of which mission should be assigned to which unit. Things can get complicated if subsidiaries are empowered to show too much initiative, since they might compete with one another for whatever 'good' jobs will increase their usefulness to the rest of the group. In this case, the centre's main authority over the periphery is to ensure fair competition among subsidiary managers competing to extend their missions. What remains after this is a model of modern MNEs as federative organizations in which headquarters and subsidiaries compete constantly over their respective competencies (Andersson et al. 2007).

+ **Heterarchy**
Organizational principle that corporate units are allies and therefore equals in the management of their joint enterprise. In an MNE, this signifies that no one unit should take a global lead.

Thinking point

Should an MNE's headquarters necessarily have more power than its subsidiaries?

+ **Internal market**
Where related corporate units deal with one another as buyers and sellers of resources. Associated with 'intrapreneurship', which is the notion that individuals can act as entrepreneurs within large organizations.

> Go to the ORC 🌐

+ **Federative organizations**
Structures whose subunits are recognized both as autonomous entities with freedom to manœuvre and as members of a unified group.

Figure 9.8
Power, strategy, and information flows in different kinds of multinational configurations.

Global flows: top-down

Multi-domestic flows: bottom-up

Transnational flows: bilateral and multilateral

In the end, the suitability of a multi-domestic, global, or transnational configuration depends on subsidiaries' assigned mission and degree of autonomy, which is itself a reflection of their size (Johnston and Bulent 2007). If subsidiaries' role is to respond to specific local market needs, coordinating their marketing and/or production processes with fellow subsidiaries becomes somewhat less useful and a multi-domestic logic more feasible. On the other hand, in some MNEs subsidiaries exist only to contribute inputs to the rest of the regional or global value chain, or to provide customers worldwide with one standardized product. Under these circumstances, a global logic might make more sense. Lastly, in hybrid situations where subsidiaries serve both domestic and global purposes and where managers live in a world of 'semi-globalization' (Ghemawat 2007), a more useful approach might be a transnational decision-making system, which does not obey a rigid organizational chart as much as it tries to let human initiative flourish at all levels.

Case Study 9.2

MNE controls: Tata no longer in tatters

In its early days, the giant Indian conglomerate Tata Enterprises (www.tata.com) would export any products for which it could find an overseas market, ranging from rice, jewellery, and castor oil to cars, marine products, and pharmaceuticals. As with many firms, an initial exploration of foreign markets through exports was followed by a series of foreign direct investments (FDI). The problem was that, with such a wide product range, there was little coherency between Tata's overseas subsidiaries. Coordinating this vast empire became very difficult for the group's Indian headquarters. As the twenty-first century dawned, Managing Director Sudhir Deoras felt a need for change.

The first decision taken by Deoras was to abandon less strategic activities and leverage his company's internal strengths by regrouping remaining product lines into eight strategic business units (SBUs)—leather, steel, minerals, power projects, engineering (including automotive and chemical products), textiles, commodities, and information technology. The next step was to create an atmosphere in which knowledge, capital, expertise, products, and processes could flow easily between all units. It was decided that a good way to start this process would be to organize an International Synergy Meeting. This was held in Mumbai in December 2001.

The meeting, attended by senior and middle management executives from India and overseas, created a platform that would allow Tata's overseas

entities and SBUs to 'develop and evolve an aligned corporate strategy and to share a common vision'. Finding a unity of purpose was crucial at a time when the company was trying to implement a new organization. Henceforth, industry experts located in different countries would report not only, as previously, to local country heads but also to global SBU chiefs. These dual reporting lines were specifically set up in recognition of the dual local–global identity that has become a feature of many modern MNEs. For the organization to succeed and gain acceptance from Tata's international managers, however, it was crucial that more transnational attitudes take root. This is where the Synergy agenda set by Mr Deoras came in.

Things continued to evolve over the years, and by 2008 the conglomerate had organized its ninety-eight companies into a group of 'promoter operations' (such as Tata Financial Services or Tata Interactive Systems) and seven actual business sectors (engineering, materials, energy, chemicals, services, consumer products, and information systems and communications). With a long-standing presence in countries as diverse as South Africa, Bangladesh, the Emirates, China, Thailand, and the USA, Tata has always benefited from strong differentiation capabilities. Now, in the early twenty-first century, key employees are being asked to think along more integrated, cross-border lines. One way to achieve this has involved reconfiguring Tata's organizational chart. The other involved reconfiguring employees' mindsets.

Tata: an international conglomerate's lack of synergies makes it hard to
develop a cohesive structure (© 2009 Tat Sons Ltd).

Section II: Managing people across borders

Irrespective of whether an MNE has implemented a local, global, or transnational configuration, international managers will try to run it according to a set of sociological principles that are themselves worth studying in greater depth. A century ago, eminent sociologists like Max Weber (1921) had analysed the nature of bureaucratic procedures to monitor their effects on employee behaviour. Group dynamics constitutes a special branch of management studies. It is no coincidence that, in many languages, a 'firm' or 'enterprise' is often referred to by a word that translates in English to 'company', and thus to an activity undertaken by a group of persons working in society and not by one individual acting alone. Business is a highly social profession.

Principles of organization

When MNE executives reflect on the types of structures that will help them to achieve their goals, they are generally guided by a set of overriding principles.

Centralization

This principle refers to the extent to which power is exercised by an MNE's head office (centre) instead of its subsidiaries (periphery). Figure 9.6 offers business reasons why various corporate functions might be run out of different parts of an MNE, but the fact is that centralization is also a psychological, human resource issue (see Chapter 15). Companies that concentrate power in the centre must find a way to motivate subsidiary managers so that they feel valued. If subsidiary employees are supposed to focus on their host country alone, it is important that they feel at home in this environment. Otherwise, they will need to have more of a regional and/or global outlook. An associated issue is how employees see the role that they have been assigned as a result of their MNE's (de)centralization policies. People's satisfaction with the particular assignment they are given will depend on their psychological make-up, specifically their openness, attitude towards risk, and ability to compromise (Roth 1992). It is one thing drawing organizational charts, but quite another finding people who want to fit into the slots.

Studies have detected a connection between employee performance and the different ways in which MNEs coordinate and control their business worldwide (Kim, Park, and Prescott 2003). It was no surprise, for example, when Walmart announced in 2008 that it was hiring a German national—Dr Stephan Fanderl, who had previous experience helping Metro AG enter Poland—to lead its expansion into Russia and other emerging markets. Working out of its headquarters in the state of Arkansas, this relatively centralized American MNE had had many problems during past internationalization drives. This was partially due to its having placed too much power in the hands of headquarters executives who were relatively unfamiliar with the foreign environments that they were being asked to manage. Turning to a manager who was not Russian and could therefore keep his emotional distance from the host country— but who had experience in entering Eastern European markets—seemed a good solution. In addition to the need for appropriate structures, international business also means getting people with a balanced vision of the requirements of particular cross-border situations.

Hierarchy

This organizational principle is rooted in the recognition of authority. In corporate environments, which are more or less undemocratic and have often been compared to military organizations, this would appear to be a relatively straightforward principle. In reality, reporting lines can be very confusing in MNEs. Whereas employees in a domestic company usually work in proximity to their boss, (and are therefore clear about who determines their objectives and judges their performance), MNE employees often have two bosses: their local-country manager; and the person in charge of their product or functional area. Things can get particularly complicated when this latter manager works out of a different time zone. Dual

+ Strategic business unit
Identifiable entity within a corporation that is large enough to plan strategy and organize resources on its own.

reporting lines, as witnessed in the Tata case study, have the advantage of ensuring greater coordination of local and global strategies, but if a person has two bosses pursuing two different business philosophies (with regards, for instance, to pricing, product adaptation, or customer segmentation), it can also be very hard knowing whom to please. It is true that this kind of confusion can be quite empowering, since it enables employees to play one boss against another. At the same time, it is often a source of a great deal of tension.

Specialization

One solution to the confusion over people's multiple roles within an MNE is specialization. Implementing this principle can be quite difficult, however. For instance, defining narrow missions is not always appropriate in small and medium-sized enterprises (SMEs), where, by definition, fewer people are working, meaning that each may have to fulfil several roles. There are many cases of SMEs where the person in charge of marketing also has to assume legal responsibilities like international contracts. The advantage for large MNEs of having specialized staff members is that everyone can accumulate greater expertise in their particular area of competency. On the other hand, it is harder in specialized MNEs to ensure that knowledge circulates adequately. The challenge that people face here is avoiding 'tunnel vision', which occurs when they cannot see how their personal mission fits in with what colleagues in other departments or locations are doing. Indeed, unless a company pursues an active policy of lifelong learning or career enrichment (see Chapter 15), specialists normally only get a chance to really broaden their competencies once they have been promoted up the management ladder. Generalists, on the other hand, may find it easier to develop a broader overview, but the cost will be shallower knowledge.

Coordination

The more specialized the missions within an organization, the harder it is to coordinate them. A good way to visualize this is by imagining that each employee has a 'territory' to manage. This territory can be defined along functional lines (a stage in the firm's value chain) but also in terms of products or geographic area. The company needs to ensure that all these territories fit together in a cost-efficient manner and in a way that they are defined minimizes any duplication of efforts while maximizing speed of action. This can be achieved through organizational planning and design and by getting different territories to adopt similar 'language systems', thereby enhancing knowledge-sharing (Luo and Shenkar 2006). This latter factor is one of the reasons why so many non-English-language MNEs (such as Switzerland's Credit Suisse or Germany's Deutsche Post World) use English as the corporate language at management meetings.

Photo 9.2
Tunnel vision means not being able to see how one's own objectives fit in with everyone else (Photodisc).

Problems can arise when boundaries change between employees' territories: because the company perceives a need for greater coordination; because one employee has the ambition of taking over another's territory; or due to external circumstances. However carefully an organization is designed, the human nature of business means that things do not always go as planned.

Control

> Go to the ORC

Companies spend considerable resources on control—or 'organizational performance' (see Online Resource Centre, extension material 9.3). In widely dispersed MNEs whose executives are physically remote from the teams they are supposed to monitor, getting feedback on whether performance matches expectations can be difficult. Multinational managers constantly visit their foreign teams, but, by definition, these will be sporadic occurrences. MNEs all establish global (or at least regional) reporting systems to compensate for this deficiency. However, information transmitted over long distances does not always paint a full picture of what is happening in far off national subsidiaries. On the one hand, country managers have a vested interest in protecting their local units from head office interference and therefore may not communicate all relevant facts. On the other hand, head office executives suffering from information overload may not have the time to cope with anything more than a short and necessarily incomplete document. It is common, for example, for a manager seeking permission to enter a new market to be asked to describe the opportunity on a single sheet of paper. Indeed, this is what happened to one of the book's authors when he began prospecting in Sweden. He returned from Stockholm with a seven-page report on the local economy only to be told by his manager that this was too long. One constant in international business today is that people are incredibly busy. The ensuing need for abbreviated communications necessarily undermines their control, however.

Learning

> Go to the ORC

The difficulties in communicating complete information in a busy MNE environment explain why a new element has been added in recent years to the traditional list of key organizational principles—learning. There have been many studies on this and related phenomena, like 'organizational learning' (see Online Resource Centre, extension material 9.4) or 'knowledge management' (see Chapter 11). Some observers have even taken to portraying companies as bodies of learning characterized by almost lifelike qualities (Morgan 1986). At a practical level, MNEs often hire international corporate communications professionals to publish internal newsletters and run regularly scheduled (video) conferences. They invest huge sums in information systems enabling a multi-site sharing of information—relating, for instance, to customer preferences. MNEs like Nestlé have also historically incurred huge travel bills flying managers to sister units worldwide so as to enhance information exchanges. Getting colleagues from one time zone to service customers working out of another is a great source of commercial synergies for a company, since it extends the number of hours in a day when a group-wide commercial relationship can be mined. Learning is a very real profit source for MNEs.

Note that not all learning is internal. As discussed in Chapter 8, one key element in modern international business is the kind of relationship that companies entertain with their (foreign) suppliers. After all, it is only by accessing relevant knowledge held by external value chain partners that an MNE can achieve true global reach and efficiency. This was the specific route followed, for instance, by the British telecommunications giant Vodafone (Ibbott 2007), which worked hard to bring outside suppliers into what it called a 'virtual global network organization' built around the goals of shared knowledge and data.

Photo 9.3
Engaging in change
management: change
has different effects on
different people within
a unit (© BPI).

It is a conception where knowledge flows are elevated to the main principle of multinational organization.

Integrating international teams

The section above detailed the different principles underlying human interactions within MNEs. Organizing such relationships when creating a new unit is difficult enough, but it can be even harder to achieve the necessary levels of cohesion when the company is trying to integrate a foreign unit that it has just acquired. Work environments revolve around organizational routines and cultural affinities, and anything upsetting this balance, like being taken over by a foreign owner, can be very damaging to employee performance and motivation. This is one of the reasons why international change management deserves a special mention in discussions of MNE structure and control.

Change is a constant in corporate life and managing change a key task for international managers. Most analysts agree that the first step towards successful organizational change is to establish and communicate objectives that are understandable to everyone involved. Studies have indicated that companies whose managers are closely involved in the change process, whether on a domestic or an international scale, have a better chance of succeeding (Meaney and Pung 2008).

Organizational change processes are often divided into a succession of phases, including recognition of the need for incremental or discontinuous change; communication of upcoming changes; training; motivation; implementation; and review (Hayes 2006; Hughes 2006). At the best of times, this will be a very slow process, especially where an international merger is involved, in part because of the psychological impact of the new owner's foreignness. Some of the resentment that people feel when the foreign owner forces change upon them results from xenophobia. More generally, the problem stems from the lack of any relationship, trust, and/or shared values between the party imposing the change and the parties on whom it is being imposed (Olie 1990). This has led to the birth of a whole industry in international change management. Consultants like BPI (www.bpi-group.com) offer advice on how MNEs might redeploy personnel when acquiring firms abroad. It is a competency that is especially important in countries like France, where strong legislation (and even stronger sentiments) come into play whenever a foreign MNE takes over a local company—especially if people get fired in the aftermath. To soothe negative feelings that can be very damaging to the future company's brand reputation and productivity, many takeover operations, like Mittal's 2006 acquisition of European steelmaker Arcelor, have come with an assurance from the acquirer that firings will be minimized.

Inside business

Philippe Pascual, Director of International Sales and Marketing, BPI—Management Consultancy

BPI is an HR-oriented management consultancy focusing on three main activities: (1) outplacement, (2) management—recruitment and training, and (3) change management, including restructuring. The company operates globally, with its main focus in Europe and North America.

BPI can be involved before a merger/acquisition, giving specific and general advice, including a survey of the economic situation or labour laws. It can also intervene during the course of an acquisition, helping a company to communicate effectively with a takeover target and advising on a whole range of human resource (HR) issues. The industrial aspects of the national culture in France can be crucial for the success of a takeover. In France, for example, there are many regulations relating to the social aspects of business, including many companies' complex relationships with French trade unions.

The acquisition of a French company by a foreign investor raises a number of key questions. For employees, the main concern is jobs. For managers, the question is more what sort of adaptation they may have to make in carrying out their operational duties.

In terms of BPI's role in relation to the development of corporate social responsibility in the companies with which it works, the goal is not only to help the company as a whole but to enhance employees' security and general position. Employees' perceptions of the main changes and the rationales for the acquired company's new structure and operations are crucial. Changes to financial reporting within the new company, or to job contracts and pay, are also crucial. The simpler parts of the acquisition are often those concerned with production, since these tend to be technical.

Skills development and transfers to all parts of the acquired company are a key element of a merger or acquisition. A crucial aspect is ensuring that, through BPI's global IT system, communications between different parts of the company are effective and clearly understood. Although much of this can be achieved through an international communications system, face-to-face contacts and personal interactions are always important in business.

International takeovers are a good example of the kinds of problems that MNEs face when trying to bridge national cultural differences. To successfully integrate new units and gain employees' commitment to a combined structure, MNEs must first allocate resources to prepare and implement the change process. In the absence of 'tight integration', the operation can destroy value (Lees 2003). Key employees might be upset with the difficulty of reconnecting their function into a new web of relations and could leave, taking their competencies with them. The scale of the challenges faced in such situations varies depending on several factors. One is the extent to which the merging of structures affects people's current assignments and reporting lines. The greater the changes and/or number of people affected by them, the harder the adjustment. Another difficulty is integrating the two companies' technologies, starting with their computer systems. Full mergers, where all operational and managerial aspects must be combined, are extremely challenging (Haspelagh and Jemison 1991). In this case, because of the likely duplication of certain roles, new colleagues end up being seen as rivals. This is exactly the wrong start if the operation is to avoid the kind of 'us versus them' atmosphere that has damaged so many international (joint) ventures over the years. An example of operations failing for cultural reasons includes the Daimler/Chrysler merger, when conflicts between new German and American colleagues led to allegations that the operation had destroyed value (Deutsche Welle 2007). This occurs when a new combined group creates less value than the old companies would have done separately, based on their pre-merger performances. Of course, there is also an argument that, where the acquirer is the more successful firm, it makes sense for its well-worked routines to be brought in, since they will be an improvement over the target company's former systems. In 2007, the Korean *chaebol* (conglomerate) Doosan bought the US company Bobcat, a huge construction equipment manufacturer, but, instead of sending its own managers to direct the new acquisition, it simply concentrated on communicating its successful management practices (Barton and Deutsch 2008). The argument here was that displaying confidence in existing staff members is better than forcing foreign managers on them. In difficult situations, (like the integration of two international workforces), anything that can be done to calm people's emotions is useful.

Push versus pull paradigms

Thus, a crucial factor in an MNE's efforts to consolidate its overseas presence is the organizational paradigm guiding its efforts. As explained above, a key divide in international business is whether the company seeking to develop a new configuration is pursuing a headquarters-oriented vision, or if it starts with a local subsidiary perspective. This fundamental choice plays out at the level of individual managers' cultural mindsets (see Chapter 10) but also in regards to companies' strategic choices.

To simplify, for the rest of this book, direct and indirect references for this philosophical arbitrage, which some have called the 'integration–responsiveness' dilemma (Prahalad and Doz 1987), will talk about 'push' versus 'pull' choices. 'Push' multinationals consider that internationalization should be an extension, and sometimes a direct reproduction, of the strategies, configurations, and mindsets that they developed back home. They tend to be more focused on their organization's internal strengths than on whether it suits different national environments. Their preference will be to centralize power in headquarters and allocate to foreign subsidiaries the task of rolling out, with as little adaptation as possible, existing products and processes. Fully confident in their upstream capabilities and technological prowess, market studies may seem less crucial to them. In general, they will be animated by the idea that theirs is a new and better product or service that should be able to command a high price everywhere.

If they are right, 'push' MNEs can achieve fantastic first-mover advantages. The best success stories for such firms usually occur in innovative hi-tech sectors. Microsoft's success, for instance, clearly derives more from its invention and diffusion of top performance software than from its cultural adaptability. It remains that the potentially higher rewards of a 'push' approach are associated with much greater risks, mainly because firms operating thusly this approach are never entirely certain of foreign demand for their brand new product. Nor can they ever be certain, when importing new knowledge into a country, that local workers and suppliers will be able to take full advantage of the associated learning (Chung et al. 2003). A 'push' approach is always a shot in the dark.

'Pull' firms, on the other hand, specifically start by checking demand in foreign markets before working backwards and calculating how they might be able to satisfy it. They will often decentralize power to subsidiaries and empower them to accumulate local knowledge. In turn, this helps to determine the product portfolio that the MNE will offer in each location. Using market signals as a starting point is safer, since it gives the company the certainty that the goods it produces are what customers actually want. At the same time, this lesser risk is associated with lower returns. On the one hand, to please an international clientele,

> **Thinking point**
>
> Are 'push' firms necessarily arrogant? Do 'pull' firms lack a strong identity?

'pull' companies tend to have wider product ranges and will therefore standardize less and achieve lower economies of scale than more specialized companies will. On the other, the signals to which they respond are also heard by rivals, who might rush in to satisfy the very same demand. Since no one operating in a 'pull' market achieves first-mover advantage, there is no possibility of imposing premium pricing.

Despite these limitations, with sectors such as food or clothing that are deeply embedded in national cultural differences, success usually depends on the adoption of a 'pull' approach. 'Pull' MNEs might try to gain some competitive space by developing new niches, as French baker Brioche Dorée did in the USA with its croissant fast-food concept, taking an existing product and positioning it in a novel manner. Ultimately, however, firms in 'pull' markets are forced to adapt. They cannot ignore local specificities in the same way as 'push' organizations can in the new markets or segments that they create. Of course, this also means that locals are less likely to resent 'pull' MNEs as foreign invaders. The key to success, as so often in international business, lies in determining which approach balances an MNE's internal needs with its external environment.

Challenges and choices

→ A dangerous moment for a young MNE is deciding at what point in its internationalization trajectory it needs to focus less on existing competencies and more on the specificities of the new markets that it is trying to enter. If focus is prematurely shifted from internal functions like production, there is the risk that existing capabilities will be diminished. If managers wait too long before focusing on consumer preferences, they run a risk of being seen as providing of uninteresting standardized goods and services. Moreover, where customers have contradictory interests (alternatively seeking commodity or specialist products), there is the additional difficulty for companies of identifying which demand to satisfy as a priority.

→ International recruitment is a second strategic challenge for MNEs. If they hire people who are deeply rooted in a host country culture, they can benefit from new employees' specific knowledge but must also work to ensure their identification with group values. Where MNEs hire cosmopolitan managers, there is a greater risk that the corporate strategy will, at some point, run afoul of host country interests. For many companies, the 'glocalization mindset' is more of an ideal than a reality.

Chapter Summary

The chapter began with an analysis of three main business configurations that have historically guided international managers' efforts to shape their cross-border activities. Each of these approaches (multi-domestic, transnational, and global) varies in terms of subsidiary autonomy, production process fragmentation, and product standardization. At different points in history, and depending on whether the MNEs involved focused mainly on internal capabilities, local responsiveness, or information circulation, they have tended to adopt varying international, functional, product, geographic, and matrix structures. Each has its strengths and weaknesses.

The chapter's second section showed that however coherent an MNE's organization is, it can only succeed if people agree with the goals being pursued. Collective enterprise is guided by a number of basic principles, including centralization, hierarchy, coordination, specialization, control, and learning. Work groups develop routines integrating these factors, and anything upsetting their habits, like a foreign takeover, creates severe change management problems to which companies must attend. International managers' approaches to these kinds of challenges tend to break down into 'push' versus 'pull' orientations. The chapter concluded with an introduction to these concepts, to be studied in further detail over the upcoming chapters.

Case Study 9.3

MNE structures: When books and education don't mix

This case study describes a real situation, but names have been changed for reasons of confidentiality.

'Democracy' is a company with two separate but related product lines: academic texts manufactured and sold by the 'Books' department; and learning packages (texts associated with Online Resource Centres and external seminars) run out of the 'Education' department. The headquarters and main office are in Toronto, but a substantial European operation is also run out of Edinburgh. Both centres have a 'Books' team and an 'Education' team. The global Head of Books is Scottish, and, as the most senior manager in the UK subsidiary, she also acts as country head. The global Head of Education works out of Toronto in proximity to the CEO, a fellow Greek with whom her family has a long-standing personal relationship and whom she sees as an uncle.

The 'Education' team is widely, and justifiably, seen as possessing greater technical competency than the 'Books' department. 'Education' professionals are also better paid, since their high-margin, low-volume product potentially offers more value added than books, which is more of a commodity business. This difference in status has caused some resentment between the departments. There are other sources of conflict as well.

Because the 'Books' Department sells more of a standardized product, it has a wider range of customers than the 'Education' department does. Many of these customers purchase books alone, making it clear which of the two departments has responsibility for servicing the account. Other customers, however, buy both books and education packages, and the two departments then have to fight over who should take credit for the business. Similar disputes have erupted regarding which department should be allowed to make initial contact with attractive prospects, many of whom are organized differently from Democracy. Clearly, because they want to build up their own department's bonus pools, 'Books' and 'Education' specialists both want to take the lead role in developing potentially lucrative customers, without having to share any of the glory (or profits) that come from a new account. One solution would be to have 'Books' and 'Education' salespersons make separate visits to the same customers, each marketing a different

Problems can arise when MNEs run complementary products out of different departments (Photodisc).

product. This is not very realistic, however, since it would waste customers' time and irritate them—outsiders have no interest in Democracy's internal rivalries. Another solution would be to get a single salesperson from one department to sell both products during customer visits. In reality, however, 'Books' employees are incapable of selling complicated 'Education' packages, and 'Education' employees have little interest in selling books when their annual bonuses are determined solely by the profits made by their own department.

The battle over marketing territories has gone on for years. The tensions are particularly poignant for Edinburgh 'Education' professionals doing early morning deals before their product boss gets to the office at 7 a.m. Toronto time (1 p.m. in Scotland). Above and beyond a certain deal size, all Democracy managers have to get executive approval before they can finalize the transaction. In the UK morning, this means asking the Head of Books, since she is also the local country head. The problem is that she will often take advantage of this situation to get 'Education' professionals to do things that are in her interest but not theirs, specifically forcing them to lower prices on hi-tech packages almost below cost, in an attempt to get customers to purchase more books, thereby enhancing the profits of her own department. The Head of Books justifies this stance with the argument that the entire company benefits from this increased turnover. But she is thinking along the lines of a low-margin business in which volume is everything. In a hi-tech business like 'Education', each deal comes with specific after-sales service costs and is only worth it if margins are big enough. When

UK 'Education' staff members protest because of the policies that the Head of Books is forcing on them in the UK morning before the Head of Education gets to the Toronto office, they are accused of being selfish and thinking only of their own narrow interests rather than the company as a whole. They are also criticized for not agreeing to spend time accompanying 'Books' salespersons on courtesy calls to major book customers whose interest in educational packages is at best vague and therefore not worth their while.

Complaints from the UK team have filtered up to the Head of Education in Toronto, who is not entirely sure how to deal with them. On the one hand, if she goes to the CEO to argue her department's case, she will be suspected of misusing family connections to gain favourable treatment within the company. On the other hand, there is no doubt that the current structure is being abused by the Head of Books seeking to manipulate Edinburgh Education department personnel for her own purposes. After lengthy reflection, the Head of Education has decided that the best step forward is to offer the CEO a review of alternative forms of organization.

Case study questions

1. What are the strengths and weaknesses of Democracy's current product organization?
2. List and justify the alternative organizations that Democracy's CEO might consider adopting.
3. How would Democracy's current managers and employees react to each of these alternatives?

Discussion questions

1. Why is an MNE better advised to adopt a global strategy in certain sectors of activity, and a local strategy in others?
2. What are the different ways in which MNEs coordinate subsidiaries' actions?
3. Is there anything significant about the location of an MNE's headquarters?
4. What mechanisms can MNEs use to optimize knowledge flows?
5. What are the obstacles faced by managers running teams on foreign sites?

References

Andersson, U., Forsgren, M., and Holm, U. (2007). 'Balancing Subsidiary Influence in the Federative MNC: A Business Network View', *Journal of International Business Studies*, 38/5 (Sept.).

Ball, D., and Patrick, A. (2007), *How a Unilever Executive is Thinning the Ranks*, 26 Nov., http://online.wsj.com (accessed 23 May 2008).

Bartlett, C. A. (1986). 'Building and Managing the Transnational: The New Organizational Challenge', in M. Porter (ed.), *Competition in Global Industries*. Boston: Harvard Business School Press.

Bartlett, C., and Ghoshal, S. (2002). *Managing across Borders: The Transnational Solution*. Boston: Harvard Business School Press.

Barton, D., and Deutsch, C. (2008). 'Transforming a South Korean Chaebol: An Interview with Doosan's Yongmaan Park', Sept., www.mckinseyquarterly.com (accessed 20 Mar. 2009).

Bélis-Bergouignan, M.-C., Bordenave, G., and Lung, Y. (2000). 'Global Strategies in the Automobile Industry', *Regional Studies*, 34/1.

Birkinshaw, J. (2000). *Entrepreneurship in the Global Firm*. London: Sage Publications.

Byrne, J. (1998). 'How Jack Welch Runs GE', www.businessweek.com (accessed 2 July 2008).

Christopher, M. (2005). *Logistics and Supply Chain Management: Creating Value-Added Networks*. 3rd edn. Harlow: Prentice-Hall.

Chung, W., Mitchell, W., and Yeung, B. (2003). 'Foreign Direct Investment and Host Country Productivity: The American Automotive Component Industry in the 1980s', *Journal of International Business Studies*, 34/2 (Mar.).

Davenport, T., and Prusak, L. (1998). *Working Knowledge: How Organizations Manage What They Know*. Boston: Harvard Business School.

Deutsche Welle (2007). 'Daimler Chrysler Boss Confirms Talks on Chrysler Sale', 4 Apr., www.dw-world.de (accessed 4 July 2009).

Dicken, P. (2007). *Global Shift: Mapping the Changing Contours of the World Economy*. London: Sage.

Ghemawat, P. (2007). 'The Hard Reality of Semiglobalization and how to Profit from it', 14 Nov., http://changthis.com (accessed 19 May 2008).

Ghislanzoni, G., Penttinen, R., and Turnbull, D. (2008). 'The Multilocal Challenge: Managing Cross-Border Functions', Mar., www.mckinseyquarterly.com (accessed 19 May 2008).

Ghoshal, S., and Gratton, L. (2002). 'Integrating the Enterprise', *MIT Sloan Management Review*, 44/1.

Goold, M., and Campbell, A. (1987). *Strategies and Styles*. Oxford: Blackwell.

Hamel, G., and Prahalad, C. (1985). 'Do You Really Have a Global Strategy', *Harvard Business Review* (July–Aug.).

Haspelagh, P., and Jemison, D. (1991). *Managing Acquisitions*. New York: Free Press.

Hayes, J. (2006). *The Theory and Practice of Change Management*. 2nd edn. Basingstoke: Palgrave MacMillan.

Hedlund, G. (1986). 'The Hypermodern MNC: A Heterarchy?', *Human Resource Management*, 25/1.

Held, D., and McGrew, A. (2002). *Globalization/Anti-Globalization*. Cambridge: Polity.

Hughes, M. (2006). *Change Management: A Critical Perspective*. Trowbridge: Cromwell Press.

Hymer, S. H. (1976). *The International Operations of National Firms: A Study of Direct Foreign Investment*. Cambridge, MA: MIT Press (originally a Ph.D. thesis, 1960).

Ibbott, C. (2007). *Global Networks: The Vodafone–Ericsson Journey to Globalization and the Inception of the Requisite Organization*. Basingtoke: Palgrave Macmillan.

Ietto-Gillies, G. (2005). *Transnational Corporations and International Production: Concepts, Theories and Effects*. Cheltenham: Edward Elgar.

Johnston, S., and Bulent, M. (2007). 'Subsidiary Size and the Level of Subsidiary Autonomy in Multinational Corporations: A Quadratic Model Investigation of Australian Subsidiaries', *Journal of International Business Studies*, 38/5 (Sept.).

Kim, K., Park, J.-H., and Prescott, J. (2003). 'The Global Integration of Business Functions: A Study of Multinational Business Units in Global Industries', *Journal of International Business Strategy*, 34/4 (July).

Klein, N. (2000). *No Logo*. Toronto: Knopf.

Kogut, B., and Zander, U. (1992). 'Knowledge of the Firm, Combinative Capabilities, and the Replication of Technology', *Organization Science*, 3/3.

Lees, S. (2003). *Global Acquisitions: Strategic Integration and the Human Factor*. Basingstoke: Palgrave MacMillan.

Levitt, T. (1983). 'The Globalization of Markets', *Harvard Business Review*, 61/3.

Levy, O., Beechler, S., Taylor, S., and Boyacigiller, N. (2007). 'What we Talk about when we Talk about "Global Mindset": Managerial Cognition in Multinational Corporations', *Journal of International Business Studies*, 38/2 (Mar.).

Luo, Y., and Shenkar, O. (2006). 'The Multinational Organization as a Multilingual Community: Language and Organization in a Global Context', *Journal of International Business Studies*, 37/3 (May).

Makela, K., Kalla, H., and Piekkari, R. (2007). 'Interpersonal Similarity as a Driver of Knowledge Sharing within Multinational Corporations', *International Business Review*, 16/1 (Feb.).

Meaney, M., and Pung, C. (2008). 'Creating Organizational Transformations: McKinsey Global Survey Results', Aug., www.mckinseyquarterly.com (accessed 16 Nov. 2008).

Morgan, G. (1986). *Images of Organization*, Newbury Park, CA: Sage Publications.

Olie, R. (1990). 'Culture and Integration Problems in International Mergers and Acquisitions', *European Management Journal*, 8/2 (June).

Osegowitsch, T., and Sammartino, A. (2008). 'Reassessing (Home-) Regionalization', *Journal of International Business Studies*, 39/2 (Mar.).

Parsons, T. (1964). *The Social System*. New York: Free Press.

Prahalad, C., and Doz, Y. (1987). *The Multinational Mission: Balancing Local Demand and Global Vision*. New York: Free Press.

Roth, K. (1992). 'Implementing International Strategy at the Business Unit Level: The Role of Managerial Decision-Making Characteristics', *Journal of Management*, 18/4.

Rugman, A. (2005). *The Regional Multinationals: MNEs and 'Global' Strategic Management*. Cambridge: Cambridge University Press.

Rugman, A., and D'Cruz, J. (2000). *Multinationals as Flagship Firms: Regional Business Networks*. New York: Oxford University Press.

UNCTAD (2007). 'World Investment Report: Transnational Corporations, Extractive Industries and Development', www.unctad.org (accessed 14 May 2008).

Weber, M. (1921). *Economy and Society*. Berkeley and Los Angeles: University of California Press.

Further research

Roberts, J. (2007). *The Modern Firm: Organizational Design for Performance and Growth*. Oxford: Oxford University Press.

For companies operating in a fast-changing world, adaptation is a never-ending process. International managers are constantly reworking their organizational architectures to achieve the corporate structure and control systems that they feel are most likely to perform optimally in light of the circumstances that they face at a given moment in time and in a particular country. Redesign efforts usually focus on the location of decision-making authority and the shape of employee incentive mechanisms, but they can also spill over into broader strategic considerations, such as the boundaries of the firm, knowledge management, and, more generally, the value systems that company employees are encouraged to accept. Drawing from both historical and contemporary examples of MNE organizational design, the book argues that efforts in this field are likely to succeed only if they are conceived of holistically and fit a company's overall competitive strategy and external environment.

Online Resource Centre

 Visit the Online Resource Centre that accompanies this book to read more information relating to multinational structure and culture: www.oxfordtextbooks.co.uk/orc/sitkin_bowen/

10 International Corporate Cultures

Overview

The first section discusses a range of analytical models that enable managers to understand the corporate culture of their competitors and partners. It presents the key factors that need to be considered when assessing the possibilities of planning and implementing strategies for corporate change.

The second section reviews the external and internal contexts that have an impact on corporate cultures. It looks at the values and ethos of different types of companies and the importance of understanding these within different national economic structures.

Section I: Understanding corporate culture and change

Models for understanding corporate culture

Organizations and culture change

Section II: Corporate values and ethos

Visions, missions, and values

External contexts for international corporate culture

Cultural differences

Internal contexts for MNEs

Strategic change in MNEs

Learning Objectives

After reading this chapter, you should be able to:

+ understand the significance of MNEs' values and ethos

+ assess the importance of corporate culture models in analysing MNEs

+ understand the key factors in variations in corporate culture

+ evaluate rationales and methods of corporate change

+ appreciate the international manager's role in the process of change

Case Study 10.1

Olayan: Corporate culture in a privately-owned group

The Olayan Group was founded in Saudi Arabia in 1947 as a trucking and supply company (the General Contracting Company) working on the Trans-Arabian Pipeline. It has grown into one of the world's largest privately owned companies, with an increasingly global reach and offices in Athens, London, New York, and Vienna, as well as in Saudi Arabia. The Group is a multinational enterprise with about fifty wholly owned companies, joint ventures, and affiliated businesses and just under 9,000 employees. In the Middle East, Olayan has numerous operating companies and substantial equity holdings. Among the partners and principals connected to Olayan in the region are Kimberly-Clark, Toshiba, Colgate-Palmolive, Burger King, Coca-Cola, Nestlé, and Cardinal Health.

Like many privately-owned international groups, Olayan is able to take decisions quickly, change direction, be closer to the customer, and make new investments in ways that publicly owned companies that have Stock Exchange listings sometimes find more difficult. The advantages to being privately owned include being able to take a longer-term view of the business because the company is not tied to concerns about its share price, the interests of stockholders, and the sometimes hostile views of market analysts. This flexibility has not, however, prevented the Group from restructuring itself so that its divisions reflect its multinational development. It has done this while retaining an element of family focus and contact with its regional origins.

One reflection of the Olayan Group's ability to combine the operations of an MNE with its Middle Eastern and family orientation has been the range of its philanthropic activities, from its contribution to the establishment of renal-care training centres in Saudi Arabia to pioneering recruitment policies in non-traditional job opportunities for women. The new generation of Olayan directors and managers have continued to emphasize that 'good

The Riyadh headquarters of the Olayan Group's Middle East Operations (reproduced courtesy of The Olayan Group).

deeds mean good business' and that companies such as Olayan need to 'become good corporate citizens with a keen awareness of social responsibility'.

The contribution of the Olayan Group and its charismatic founder, Suliman S. Olayan, to international business throughout the Middle East has been recognized in many ways, but none more profound than the decision in 2003 of the American University of Beirut to name its Business School the Suliman S. Olayan School of Business. The University's trustees hailed Mr Olayan (who died in 2002) as 'one of the world's most astute and highly trusted private investors ... a valuable bridge between cultures and economies ... a man with vision and unimpeachable integrity, and ... an eminent role model for younger generations'. Olayan's growth illustrates the ability of companies to grow organically, take on different roles, and to adopt a new corporate culture that is suitable to its stage of development. It demonstrates that it is possible for a small company to grow into an MNE, with a range of international activities and achievements that permit it to be measured alongside other MNEs, both public and private, from around the world.

Introduction

This chapter focuses on the corporate cultures of firms that operate internationally, primarily MNEs. As was seen in Chapter 2 on national cultures, such companies operate in an environment where they have to face and adapt to an external culture or several external cultures. To be successful, they must get the business basics right—reducing costs, devising the right product, setting the right price, managing people, operating efficiently, and so on—and to adapt to the national cultures where they are carrying out their activities. Some firms are more successful at international business than others, and this can sometimes be because of another key factor: their internal culture.

The factors in firms' internal cultures are closely linked to the corporate structures they adopt (Chapter 9), to their roles in the business world (Chapter 7), to their modes of internationalization (Chapter 8) and to their functional operations (Chapters 11–15). Beyond these aspects of corporate culture, there is also the driving ethos of the organization—its reason for being—that marks it out as unique in its field. This ethos is often displayed in some version of the company's written statement about itself: a set of values, a slogan, or a motto.

The rationales for companies to cross their own borders and engage in international business have been defined in Chapter 9 as deriving from push and/or pull factors. In essence, companies can receive their initial impetus towards internationalization as a result of the push from the development and saturation of their domestic activities and/or the pull of the opportunities afforded by the international market. This theme re-emerges here as the corporate cultural models for understanding MNEs are analysed.

Section I: Understanding corporate culture and change

Many analytical models have been proposed by academics and practitioners to understand corporate culture. These models range from those that are deliberately limited in scope, with a simple set of categories, to others that construct an analysis of many dimensions. Many of the models are equally applicable to domestic companies as to MNEs.

The international business scene is constantly changing, and some of the models put forward are designed to assist managers in assessing the degrees to which change will be accepted or rejected within an organization. An understanding of strategies for business change is essential for managers as they progress through their corporate careers.

+ **Corporate culture**
Common values shared by employees at all levels of the business. This can sometimes form an implicit or explicit control mechanism within the company.

Models for understanding corporate culture

To understand both domestic and international corporate cultures, it is essential to access a variety of useful models. A straightforward and simple guide to organizational culture is that of the British management writer Charles Handy (1993), who classified it by the power of individuals' roles and functions and identified four archetypes: those of Power, Role, Task, and Person). Handy also attached the names of Greek gods to the four different cultures (see Figure 10.1).

The first of these, the Power culture (Zeus), emphasizes the concentration of power in the hands of one individual, the boss. The lines of control are exercised by the priority of personal contacts over procedures; the most powerful person dominates the decision-making process. This sort of organizational culture is typical of companies where ownership is private or held by

Power	Zeus	(spider's web)
Role	Apollo	(temple)
Task	Athena	(matrix/net)
Person	Dionysius	(amoeba)

Figure 10.1
The four cultures
Handy (1993).

a single family, led by a charismatic leader or the founder. Examples of this sort of international company and corporate style include the Virgin Group, led by Sir Richard Branson, the Olayan Group (see Case Study 10.1), and the Really Useful Group, run by the musician and theatrical impresario Lord Andrew Lloyd Webber. International investment banks and brokerage firms are also often organized on the lines of a dominant Power culture. Proximity to the boss is vitally important and key decisions are made quickly. The company's administration is small, and costs are kept low.

Order and efficiency are valued most highly within the Role culture (Apollo). Decision-making takes place at the top, and power is derived from the hierarchical structure of the company. Responsibilities and powers are clearly defined in the job descriptions for each company employee. Examples of this are large MNEs such as Shell, IBM, Nestlé, and General Motors, as well as former 'public-sector' corporations such as the French utilities and energy company EDF (Chapter 1) and the British Broadcasting Corporation (BBC). The size and structure of the international company can mean that such organizations are slow in responding to changes, often relying on their existing routines and trying to ignore changed circumstances. Some of the large life insurance companies that offer wider financial services, such as Allianz, Axa, and Fortis, have displayed this form of organization and, in some cases in the 2008–9 financial crisis, have been slow to react to external change.

Handy's third model of corporate culture is the Task culture (Athena). Power comes from the expertise required to complete a task or project, with decision-making occurring through meritocracy. Key emphases in this model are coordination, organization into groups and teams, and tasks based on specific projects; all are vital for MNEs and their multinational structures and teamwork. It fosters a high level of adaptation and innovation by emphasizing talent, youth, and team problem-solving. For many international pharmaceutical companies, advertising agencies, management and technical consultancies, and technologically innovative companies, such as Microsoft and Apple, this Task culture tends to be dominant. Task cultures require highly paid experts who are driven to analyse organizational problems in depth. Because of the high costs incurred, such companies often construct more formal routines and move towards the more hierarchical culture of the Role model.

The fourth organizational format is the Person culture (Dionysius), which is highly individualistic. Accordingly, this model is often adopted by universities and professional service firms, such as partnerships of architects, doctors, or lawyers. Employees see themselves as independent professionals who are keen to exercise independent and individual judgement in finding solutions and making decisions. The phrase often used about trying to manage academic members of staff in universities—'it's like trying to herd cats'—summarizes the independent nature of employees in this model. The person culture can lead to strong ideological conflict among its professionals, because they see themselves as having hired out their services or skills to the organization.

The four models set out by Handy enable managers to be aware of the different cultures within a variety of businesses. While it is rare for these models to be seen in their pure form in practice, it is possible to locate any company as being closer to one model rather than

+ Meritocracy
Form of social organization in which the leaders have achieved their status by their own efforts—on merit.

Thinking point

To what extent are Handy's four cultures oversimplified and overgeneralized?

another. This is essential when managers are viewing their own organizations and any that they have to work with.

Organizations and culture change

The idea of corporate culture is a contentious area and there is little agreement on its nature, structure, and influence. In the main, however, that there are both external and internal influences. Each organization has its own culture, consisting of its set of beliefs, values, 'learned ways of managing' (Lynch 2006), systems and structures, approach to strategy, and ability to change. The organizational culture is the 'filter and shaper' through which all levels within the business—workers, managers, leaders, CEOs—understand, develop, and implement strategies and any changes or adaptations to the direction of the company (Lynch 2006).

The principal external influences on corporate culture include factors such as demographics (age profile, socio-economic groups, gender roles), language and communication, religion and beliefs, and governments' policies on social developments. These factors are very complex within a single country; in international business, the complexities are multiplied many times. For example, as shown in Chapter 2, countries vary widely in terms of their social attitudes towards religion and the relative equality of men and women. For international companies, the impact of these external influences may be on their approaches to the shape and structure of their own workforce, the kinds of products that suit the market, the advertising and media that can be used, and the effect on the relationship between the company and the community.

A key model, devised by Trompenaars (1993), Trompenaars and Hampden-Turner (1997), and Hampden-Turner and Trompenaars (2000) for the organization of international corporations is called the four diversity cultures (see Figure 10.2). This assumes the major dimensions of person versus task and of centralization (which is also assumed to be hierarchical) versus decentralization (which is assumed to be more egalitarian). Both dimensions are very common measures and can often be easily determined.

The four diversity cultures derived from this model were named by Trompenaars, as noted in Figure 10.2. The key factors of the four different types—Incubator, Guided Missile, Family, and Eiffel Tower—are outlined below. Some of the implications for managing international businesses involve employee relations, attitude to authority, ways of thinking and learning, attitudes to people, and managing change.

Figure 10.2
Four diversity cultures models, derived from Trompenaars (1993), Trompenaars and Hampden-Turner (1997: ch. 11), and Hampden-Turner and Trompenaars (2000: app. 4) (Nicholas Brealey Publishing/ NB Ltd).

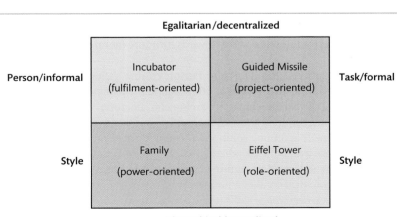

As far as relationships between employees are concerned, the Eiffel Tower model suggests that the employee has a specific role in a mechanical system of required interactions, whereas the Incubator model features more diffused and spontaneous relationships which grow out of shared creative processes. Thus, the Eiffel Tower model can be applied to the workings of a large hierarchical and formal MNE such as Shell or IBM; the Incubator model describes more accurately the close relations that exist in a small, creative business such as an IT consultancy or an advertising agency.

For the dimension of attitude to authority, the Family model ascribes status to parent figures who are close to each other and are all powerful within the company, whether international or domestic; this is true, for example, of the family-run businesses like the Olayan Group (see Case Study 10.1) and the Hirdaramani Group (see Chapter 3). By contrast, the achievement of status in the Guided Missile model is earned by project group members who work together and contribute to the targeted goal.

With respect to thinking and learning and attitudes to people, the models operate as set out in Figure 10.3

As far as the final factor is concerned, and one that is often crucial to the development of international corporations, the different models in relation to managing change indicate that, in the Family model, the 'Father' changes course, whereas in the Eiffel Tower model, the organization has to change rules and procedures. In the Guided Missile model, the company has to shift aim as the target moves, whereas in the Incubator model, the imperative is to improvise and attune. When applied to specific MNEs, the ability of the 'family-oriented' businesses to take the lead in change management from the 'boss' is contrasted with the more hierarchical, publicly quoted, profits-driven companies such as Unilever (Case Study 9.1), where the organization has to undertake major changes in its rules, procedures, and operations.

A further model that is useful for analysing and understanding MNEs' corporate culture is the Cultural Web, which identifies six interrelated elements, as originally devised by Gerry Johnson (1987, 1992) and used in *Exploring Corporate Strategy* by Johnson et al. (2007). These help to make up the 'paradigm'—the pattern or model—of the work environment. Analysing the factors in each, reveals the bigger picture of the company's culture: what is working, what is not working, and what needs to be changed. In addition to monitoring change, Johnson's view of strategic management suggested that executives had to be able to signal changes in corporate culture. Planning change is required to alter the everyday routines that affect the behaviour of those who work in the MNE.

	Family	Eiffel Tower
Ways of thinking and learning	Intuitive, holistic, lateral, and error-correcting	Logical, analytical, vertical, and rationally efficient
Attitudes to people	As family members	Human resources
	Guided Missile	**Incubator**
Ways of thinking and learning	Problem-centred, professional, practical, and cross-disciplinary	Process oriented, creative, ad hoc, and inspirational
Attitudes to people	Specialists and experts	Co-creators

Figure 10.3
Ways of thinking and learning, and attitudes to people (adapted from Trompenaars 1997; Hampden-Turner and Trompenaars 2000).

There are six elements in Johnson's cultural web.

Stories

Stories refer to the past events and people that are talked about inside and outside the company. The focus here is on what matters in the organization and what the company chooses to emphasize. The stories told and the examples used are good indicators of what the MNE values and what is perceived as appropriate behaviour. The emphasis is also on what constitutes success or failure.

This is often revealed in the statements made in the history or the background of a company, such as the attention paid to the character and life story of Suliman S. Olayan, the founder of the Olayan Group (see Case Study 10.1).

Symbols

Symbols are the visual representations of the company, including logos, the standard of the offices and other facilities, and formal or informal dress codes. Symbols can also include whether there are separate restaurants for different levels of employees, and how managers and workers are rewarded through fringe benefits, including travel, health insurance, and gym membership.

Throughout this book, there are a number of images and other pictorial representations of the MNEs that have contributed to it. They can be viewed as the first symbols of how the company wants to visualize itself. Some companies spend a vast amount of money on changing logos and corporate colours in order to signal shifts in corporate intentions and strategy.

Power structures

This refers to the location of real power in the company. It may involve one and two key senior executives, a group of executives (the inner circle, as mentioned by Handy's Power Culture above), or even a department. The most significant aspect is identifying those people who have the greatest amount of influence on decisions, operations, and strategic direction.

As with the organizational structures below, the existence of key decision-makers may not be obvious from the external representation of the structure. For example, stereotypically, but also with some basis in reality, decision-making in some American and Japanese companies may still be significantly determined on the golf course.

Photo 10.1
Decisions aren't always made in the boardroom (© iStockphoto).

Organizational structure

This includes both the structure defined by the organization chart, and the unwritten lines of power and influence that indicate whose contributions are most valued, as suggested through rituals and routines.

The organizational structures adopted by MNEs and other companies were explored in depth in Chapter 9. For some managers, it is important to understand that, particularly in some 'high-context cultures' (see Chapter 2), the key decisions will be made in ways that are not always evident from the highly intricate chart of how the company works internationally.

Control systems

The ways that the organization is controlled include financial systems, quality systems, and the measurement and distribution of rewards.

An important element within the control system can be decisions made over the type of pay rewards. In MNEs in some countries, it is automatic that employees can take a reasonable proportion of their pay in overtime; for others, such as Nordic or Scandinavian workers, there is both a social inhibition on working beyond the set hours and a belief that, if work is carried out efficiently, it can be accomplished within the working day.

Rituals and routines

These include the daily actions of people that signal acceptable behaviour. The emphasis in this element is on the normal ways of doing things and normal procedures. In some cases, the guide to these acceptable procedures is not written down but still regulates what is expected to happen in given situations, and what is valued by management, including such things as long service, quality standards, innovation, and sales achievements. These elements can really only be learnt 'on the job'—when people are working in a company, they realize what they have to do under the special circumstances they find there. Such rituals and routines also vary between offices and factories within the same MNE but located in different countries.

All these models help to explain how companies operate internationally. What is even more crucial for MNEs are the intersecting forms of national culture and corporate culture that impact on each other and on how the MNE is viewed. Companies with a particular national base have developed differently. from others with a different national origin. For example, although it was rare for successful MNEs to have joint national origins, one can say that the achievements of Unilever and Shell proved that Anglo-Dutch companies could work well. For many decades, these two MNEs' maintained joint management boards with decisions being made in both the Netherlands and the UK. For some companies, their national origins have been retained regardless of how large and global they have become. It is impossible to think of MNEs such as Coca-Cola and Ford as being anything other than American, or of BA being anything other than British. At a simpler level, there is a company such as ArcelorMittal, which as a result of the merger in 2006, has combined Asian and European operations under the strong control of the Mittal family.

Another topic in internatonal corporate culture is the rise of multicultural teams. Such teams demonstrate the complexity of how different cultures fit together (see Online Resource Centre, extension material 10.1). A key factor is the conjunction of each team member's personal and national background within the company's own organizational culture. To what extent is it possible for the corporate culture to overcome each individual's personal or national culture? How strongly does each person retain his or her national characteristics?

> Go to the ORC ⬤

Section II: Corporate values and ethos

Visions, missions, and values

All MNEs (and most other organizations in the world, whether business related or not) have adopted some form of words that are intended to encapsulate their *raison d'être* (their reason for being). These words usually form the organization's vision, its mission statement, or set of values (Mission Statements 2008). The mission statement is designed to provide a focus for the attention, activities, and purposes of the organization, its employees, and all other stakeholders. Although these wordings may appear rather simple and open to internal or external criticism, they often express clearly and directly what the company stands for and why it is successful.

The vision or mission statement is usually supported by a slogan or motto (sometimes called a strapline) that will be used throughout trade and promotional literature and on its website as a regular reminder of what it stands for.

One of the world's largest facility and project management corporations, Johnson Controls, has 140,000 employees worldwide in more than 1,300 locations. The company is engaged in the sectors of automotive experience, building efficiency, and power solutions. It has a very straightforward vision: 'A more comfortable, safe and sustainable world', supported by five values: integrity, customer satisfaction, employee engagement, innovation, and sustainability (Johnson Controls 2009). Johnson Controls' international presence is emphasized by its being world leader in integrated facility management for Fortune 500 companies, managing more than one billion square feet worldwide. However, the simple message of its vision is maintained throughout the MNE.

The Olayan Group (see Case Study 10.1) has a complex set of statements indicating its *raison d'être*: four paragraphs setting out its mission statement (Olayan 2004); four core values focusing on customers, business partners, people and shareholders; seven operating principles, including integrity, excellence and accountability; and its vision consists of five areas (opportunity, alliances, impact, strength, and vision). By contrast, the Hirdaramani Group has a single sentence each for its vision ('To offer quality customer service through innovation, leadership and excellence and to be responsive to change in a competitive world') and Mission ('To instil professionalism by embracing a positive spirit of enterprise within the group, with the aim of gaining a global market share') (Hirdaramani 2009).

Nestlé expresses Corporate Business Principles in a long statement, noting that these principles will be adapted and changed over time as the world changes, and a reminder that it still stands for 'basic ideas of fairness, honesty, and a general concern for people'. Its motto/slogan is 'Good Food, Good Life' (Nestlé 2008). Similarly, Nokia (see Chapter 14) has a lengthy statement called Vision and Strategy, the strapline of 'Connecting People' and the more formal statement that 'Nokia is the world leader in mobility, driving the transformation and growth of the converging Internet and communications industries' (Nokia 2008).

As can be seen from the small selection above, the international nature of these statements usually consists of stressing the movement of the company into the international arena, either as a player seeking 'a global market share' or as a 'world leader'. They can provide a solid clue as to the international achievements and aspirations of MNEs and they are sometimes a reflection of whether the company's main motivation to internationalize is 'push' or 'pull' (see Chapters 7 and 8). Companies such as Olayan and Hirdaramani have started on a small scale from a national base and expanded onto the global scene in a mix of push and pull: the push from the development and saturation of their domestic activities; and the pull of the opportunities afforded by the international market.

+ **Mission statement**
Defines in a few words or sentences the reason for existence of any entity or organization. It embodies its philosophies, goals, ambitions, and values.

Thinking point

Are mission statements of any use to company directors, employees, investors, or other stakeholders?

Global corporate ethos

Each company has its own way of doing things. As people move from one job to another and from one company to another, they are able to notice visible and more intangible things that define the working environment and the working practices of each. Visible characteristics include the structure as defined by the MNE's organization chart, the nature of the factory or office building, the corporate logo, the layout of the rooms and offices, and the type of clothing that staff are required to wear. The more intangible factors include the values and mission, the reporting and control systems, and the global corporate ethos.

There are three broad types of global corporate ethos, each related to a particular form of identification that a firm has sought, or by which it is known internationally. These types are identification with values, brand, and sector. For each ethos, there is an overall justification as to why this has been designated, although, as many company people and analysts would suggest, it is rare for any single company to claim to be identified with only one theme.

A good example of a values ethos is the BBC, which prides itself on being 'objective'. Its large team of reporters across the world and its extensive range of radio, television, and Internet broadcast outlets are its attempt to guarantee comprehensive and objective news coverage, as well as providing a full service of programming in other areas. Behind the strapline banner of 'Inform, Educate, Entertain', its set of values is led by 'Trust is the foundation of the BBC: we are independent, impartial and honest' (BBC 2009).

Examples of the brand ethos are those companies that are identifiable on a worldwide basis by their names and their brands; these are MNEs such as Toyota, McDonald's, Sony, Coca-Cola. For these companies, the identification as a brand can derive from their view of themselves and/or from the view held by others, whether competitors, consumers, or observers (see Chapter 12 on marketing and brands).

The sector ethos MNEs are those that, regardless of brand and/or values, see themselves most significantly as identifiable by the sector of business in which they operate. Major firms in the capital markets—banks, investment houses, private equity firms—may identify themselves primarily by their function—that they are in business to make money. Such companies include Deutsche Bank (see Chapter 13, Inside business), Morgan Stanley, Nomura, HSBC, and Goldman Sachs. Despite the dramatic events of the financial crisis of 2008–9 (see Chapter 14), the companies that survived have an even stronger identification with the sector as the defining factor in their corporate ethos.

It is rare, of course, for MNEs to associate themselves with only one type of identity. Not only do they normally have a more complex view of themselves but they are also very competitive within each industrial sector as to who has the right to regard themselves as the pioneer or the innovator, or as the leading brand.

> **+ Global corporate ethos**
> Essential set of characteristics that define the ways in which the MNE is organized and has its staff operate and behave.

> **Thinking point**
> What international advantages are gained by MNEs identified by brand?

International business negotiations

An important feature of corporate culture—and national culture (see Chapter 2)—is that companies need to be able to negotiate successfully with each other, with national governments, and with international institutions. The distinctive culture of each firm has, therefore, an impact on the stance that it may take in such negotiations. Increasingly, employees of many companies are operating internationally; in the 1990s it was already estimated that about 50 per cent of an international manager's time might be spent on negotiations (Hendon et al. 1996). These managers need to be trained in sensitivity towards the differing national cultures in which they operate and in understanding how culture can affect the negotiating position of their own business and other organization(s) in deal.

As with domestic negotiations, managers must look at the balance between their competitive and collaborative approaches, the framework for the negotiation, including strategy, tactics, and implementation, the phases of preparation, interaction, and post-negotiation, and key issues such as communication, price, timing, and legal agreements. The success of international business negotiations can bring the massive financial and cost-cutting benefits associated with cross-national mergers and acquisitions but just as often do not work.

The case of the short-lived Daimler–Chrysler marriage is a recent instance of a linkage where the correct fit was not negotiated. The merger of 1998 was rapidly dissolved in 2007. Alongside the more long-term failure of the merged business to build the right vehicles were the misunderstandings that had arisen in the original negotiations between the German and American corporations. The charismatic leadership of Jürgen Schremp, the German boss, managed to persuade the management and shareholders of Daimler–Benz that the merger with Chrysler was the right move in trying to create a global corporation. From the American perspective, the merger was immediately contentious, with many investors contesting in the law courts whether the transaction was the 'merger of equals' or a straightforward German acquisition. From the beginning, the growing pains of a marriage of opposites were evident: the formality and hierarchy of the German conglomerate did not match well with a Chrysler method of operation that was informal, with cross-functional teams and free-flowing discussions (Vlasic and Stertz 2000). There were also financial and legal issues involved in the inability to get the two sides to fit together, but at the heart of the failure was a mismatch in corporate culture.

External contexts for international corporate culture

The corporate culture of a firm is derived from internal and external factors. External factors are drawn from the widest aspects of society such as national culture, art and literature, language, spiritual and religious beliefs—as discussed in Chapter 2. Others are more specific but still drawn from the economic and business philosophies that prevail within the country and their implementation within industry and commerce. The impact of the country of origin of an MNE is sometimes more long-lasting and prevalent than might be imagined. However international certain companies become, they also remain rooted in their original culture. Despite the adoption of abbreviations and acronyms by many companies (BP, BA, BT, BG), it is clear that the 'B' stands for British and that these large MNEs remain British in their corporate cultures.

For MNEs and other companies operating across the globe, their corporate culture becomes even more complex. There is the human dimension of having many people from so many different cultures interacting in such complex ways around the world; the architectural complexity of MNEs' structures of geographical divisions and functional departments; and the strategic challenge of maintaining control over a massive organization and ensuring that it retains its single purpose and direction. The culture of a successful MNE is multifaceted and exceptionally complicated.

A key development for workers and managers is the change that has come about in some countries and that is forecast for others: the arrival of the post-industrial society. Heralded by a number of social commentators, as early as the 1960s and 1970s, the key features of the post-industrial society were identified, particularly by Daniel Bell (1974), as being related not only to economic and social structures but also to norms and values. Bell's seminal work, *The Coming of Post-Industrial Society*, emphasized a shift from manufacturing to services; the centrality of industries based on new scientific developments; an emphasis on rationality and efficiency; the rise of new technical elites; and the advent of new principles of social stratification. Bell's concern about the post-industrial society was that its new values might cause a disconnection between socio-economic structures and culture, such as the domination of free market regimes, the growth of economic inequality, the outsourcing

+ **Post-industrial society**
Defines the development of a late capitalist society with such features as the growth of free markets, greater mass consumption and, ultimately, more leisure time.

of domestic jobs, and a surge in mass consumption (see Online Resource Centre, extension material 10.2).

> Go to the ORC

The positive aspects of the post-industrial society are intended to be greater leisure, a better work–life balance, and the greater availability of consumer products and services for more and more consumers. Whereas some of this has been achieved in certain countries—especially the developed, Western industrialized societies (the OECD countries) and the oil-rich countries of the Middle East—the post-industrial or leisure society has sometimes come at the social cost of a loss of job security, higher structural unemployment and the fragility of economic interdependence. All these developments have an impact on the external business environment in which international companies operate in the twenty-first century and on their corporate cultures. In the post-industrial society, companies make choices about work–life balance for their employees, structural and hierarchical arrangements within the company, and the extent to which the offering of products and services may change.

A step beyond the post-industrial or leisure society has been the beginnings of the emergence of a virtual society and economy (see Online Resource Centre, extension material 10.3). This is predominantly a feature of the Internet and the movement of consumers towards accessing information, products, and services via this medium. One of the key features of online advertising and purchasing has been the massive growth of the medium itself and many associated developments: social networking, blogging, podcasting, and texting. Beyond the virtual economy, there has been the idea of using gaming and virtual worlds in order to model the real economy in a way that, it is hoped, will provide simulated predictors of future development (see Further Research).

> Go to the ORC

Cultural differences

As can be seen throughout this book, a prime consideration for all present and future managers is not only their personal attitudes and responses to cultural differences but how they influence their company's attitudes towards the countries they work in and from which they originate. The impetus for the company to do business internationally is a 'push' or a 'pull' factor. For some companies, their prime reaction to carrying out international business is to prioritize the home country (where they originate) over their host country; this is known as an 'ethnocentric' policy. Other companies adopt a policy in which the company responds more directly to local considerations—that is, those of the host country; this is generally known as polycentric or indeed geocentric, where the policy is to act regardless of national origins (see Chapter 12).

At a personal level, managers of MNEs need not only to be aware of cultural differences but be able to act and respond appropriately in a range of different national and cultural situations. In some cases, particularly in 'high-context' cultures (see Chapter 2), many of

Photo 10.2
Virtual worlds and gaming are becoming increasingly important in business (© iStockphoto).

> Go to the ORC ◉

the cultural signals are subliminal, consisting of forms of social behaviour, of expressions of language used, and of body language, including gestures (see Online Resource Centre, extension material 10.3). Whereas participation in drinking after work and karaoke evenings is commonly expected in Japan, it would be unexpected and unacceptable in most countries of the Middle East. For many Europeans and Americans, it would not be unusual behaviour but would be seen as an additional part of the need to do business, rather than an essential component.

For those doing business in the Middle East and in many parts of Asia, it is essential to understand the need to build long-lasting relationships. It is not acceptable in such cultures to fly in, do the business, and fly out; it is necessary to get to know business counterparts and build the deal from the viewpoint of successful personal relationships.

Language

Thinking point

Do successful business people really need to speak more than one language?

Language can be a true source of cultural difficulty. Not only is it courteous to learn and understand the language of business counterparts; it is sensible and smart to do so. Those who are limited to their own language can be at a real disadvantage either in the formal meetings, or in the variety of social settings in which business is conducted. Although it is often thought that the language of international business is English, a number of reports in English-speaking countries, such as Australia, the USA, and the UK, have indicated that this is often no guarantee of success. In a 2005 report, 20 per cent of British companies surveyed reported that they had lost business as a result of language and cultural barriers to international trade. It is accepted that a cultural barrier can be as significant an obstacle as language in international business and what is even more worrying is that only 11 per cent of British companies say that they have systems in place for dealing with such barriers (Hagen 2005).

A poll conducted by Harris/Decima for Berlitz Canada showed that 'bilingual and multilingual Canadians have more career options, build stronger relationships with colleagues and clients and get promoted and move up the pay scale faster than their one-language colleagues' (Bitti 2008). In the survey, 66 per cent of respondents said they had a greater range of job options within their field; 62 per cent said being bilingual or multilingual afforded them more flexibility in terms of where they could work; 48 per cent said speaking another language accelerated their career rise; and 44 per cent said speaking more than one language helped them earn more money and more quickly. The higher the tax bracket that respondents were in, the truer this was.

In conjunction with the survey, William H. Osborne, president of Ford Motor Co. of Australia and former president of Ford Canada (who learned French while working there), noted that it was 'imperative that today's executive be multilingual' and that, since the 'business world is global and these days, with instant communications and global networks, there are very few businesses that have strictly a local focus' (Bitti 2008).

For people who understand certain languages, there are clues about meaning that are very difficult for those who have no knowledge or ability in that language. English, for example, makes no distinction between the use of a plural/singular or formal/informal when speaking to another person; the word used is 'you' in all instances. In many other languages, both European and non-European, this is not the case, and clear differences are indicated in the language used when addressing other people. French, Spanish, German, and Italian, for example, all have a formal and an informal form of 'you'. Using the wrong from can create serious problems.

For many companies in the twenty-first century, there is a real choice to be made about which languages should be used for internal communications. This can be of real benefit to those individuals who are multilingual and multicultural. Even more crucially for the development of corporate culture, some companies deliberately recruit from the widest range of nationalities to ensure that they gain competitive advantage from internationally adaptable and flexible workforces.

Some of the simplest gestures and other aspects of body language can be easily misunderstood in the wrong cultural context. In most countries, a nod of the head means 'yes'. In Greece and Bulgaria, a nod has the opposite meaning. Such a fundamental difference in non-verbal communication between cultures can easily lead to misunderstandings. There are also significant cultural differences at the moment of greeting: for most Northern Europeans and Northern Americans, a firm handshake between men would be entirely appropriate; not extending the hand and touching one's chest, as is common in parts of Asia and the Middle East. Neither method of greeting is better than another, but all managers in international business need to be aware of what is appropriate.

Other aspects of cultural difference at this personal and interactional level include expressions of courtesy and respect, the ways in which people indicate agreement and disagreement, methods of showing interest, the role of silence, and the appropriateness of giving and receiving gifts. Managers should make the effort to be aware of others and be self-aware. In some cultures, it is always appropriate to bring a corporate gift when undertaking a business trip. The nature of the gift may need to be tailored correctly to the status of the business counterpart. For some cultures, too, the colour of the gift may be crucially important; in China, for example, red is a positive colour denoting happiness and positive feelings.

Finally, it is often necessary for international managers, both as representatives of their MNEs and as socially concerned individuals, to take a stance on various major issues of the day. This means that managers may need to have a view on business ethics, on their approach towards environmental protection and climate change, and on service to the community and society. The relative importance of this will also depend on the policies of the home country from which the MNE originates and of the host country where business is being conducted. This is a difficult tightrope to walk. For example, what it may be appropriate to say and do in Myanmar with its military government may be more restricted than in Mauritius.

Photo 10.3
Gestures and body language vary significantly between cultures (© iStockphoto).

Inside business

Michelle Cherfan, Account Manager (Soft Drinks & Home Appliances),
Haggar Holding Company

Haggar Holding Company produces and manufactures various products in the Sudan, including soft drinks, refrigeration, and tobacco; it also supplies telecommunications and oilfield services to the Sudanese market and operates as agents for Samsung Electronics and consumer products like Cadbury's chocolates and has liaison offices with a number of activities in Europe. The company's main values are derived from Ms Cherfan's grandfather, who pioneered the business, which was set up over 100 years ago. The company has focused on the people who are involved as employees and as stakeholders in the business. The Sudanese brands of the company are recognized as well-known domestic products.

Family is a very important factor in Haggar Holding Company's corporate culture, as is often common within businesses in Africa and the Middle East. The company has a Code of Conduct that is incorporated in a booklet given to all employees, who then feel that they also contribute to the work of the company. The company also gives a percentage of its profits every year to the Haggar charitable foundation.

Corporate social responsibility is embedded within the company. This stems from the values that originally led Haggar to assist in the building of local communities and thus the establishment of medical clinics and schools. The creation of these communities also meant that the people who were supported in this way were able to purchase Haggar's various products. The group has over 300 students on university scholarships and runs an internship programme for university students during the long summer holidays.

The company has needed to adapt to the complexities of Sudanese culture, since the North is Muslim and governed by Sharia law, whereas the South is Christian or animist. The company maintains close relations with the relevant government ministries and with think-tanks and universities, so that Haggar is able to keep up to date with policies and trends within the country. The current Chairman sits on a number of national committees and University Councils, and the members of the company behave and operate as part of a global business.

Internal contexts for MNEs

The many factors related to external culture for companies are virtually matched by the internal ones. The different layers of a company in terms of, for example, hierarchy, structure, control systems, responsibilities, and tasks are sufficient to create very individual cultures for each firm. When the variations of personality, attitude towards work, team or individualist orientation, and national and ethnic background are added, the complexity of internal dimensions creates a further set of considerations. To attempt to uncover and explain the internal cultures of MNEs, the following sections explore departmental issues, interpersonal relationships, and social aspects of corporate culture.

Departmental cultures

Within industries and business sectors, there are different types of departmental or divisional cultures. These are obvious to anybody who visits offices, factories, or production facilities around the world. Without wishing to uphold stereotypes, it is possible to distinguish a number of cultures that can exist within the same firm or, where a company is predominantly focused on a particular activity, that permeates the whole operation. These different cultures can be represented by the way in which people dress and behave.

There is a tendency for the focus in the research departments to be on their scientific and professional nature, thus represented by white coats. The demeanour of the staff in such an operation tends towards engagement with serious enquiry, intellectual debate, and attention to testing and results. This tends to be less the case with the high-technology companies, especially those in the computer and IT industry. Here the research side of the company is often composed of mavericks with a casual sense of dress but a hard-driving outlook to getting the work done. This has been exemplified at CEO level by the hard-working but casual demeanour and dress of such leaders as Steve Jobs (Apple, NeXT, and Pixar) and Bill Gates (Microsoft).

Within the manufacturing and production sections of the firm, the focus is on work on the assembly line, hard manual labour, or the manipulation of technical equipment, such as fork-lift trucks. Such members of staff are characterized by their working uniforms and are still traditionally known as 'blue collar' workers. Any visitor to an international logistics, transport, or delivery firm, such as DHL, TNT, Fedex, and UPS, will witness their massive operations, which, though highly technical, are still based on labour-intensive and mechanized activity.

For those people within departments such as marketing, including advertising and public relations, there is often a more relaxed dress style. This may be reflected in the permission for members of staff to dress down more than they would in other areas of the business, perhaps even to the point for men of unusual hair styles, such as ponytails, or of earrings or other piercings. This apparently more casual corporate culture, including the adoption of less formal dress, has been shown in very market-oriented MNEs by leaders such as Sir Richard Branson (Virgin) and Charles Dunstone (Carphone Warehouse). The most formal corporate culture has tended to be within finance departments or among staff who are predominantly concerned with accounting and finance functions. In terms of dress, this is exemplified by the wearing of formal suits, including pinstripes, and of white shirts—hence the common terminology of 'white collars'. This most formal culture is exemplified among CEOs by the style and dress of leaders, such as almost all bankers and many others from so-called blue chip companies. Women managers in these companies are also inclined to wear the same uniform of dark suits and white shirts.

Thinking point

Does dress-down Friday appear in all corporate cultures?

Interpersonal relationships at work

Among MNEs across the world, there is a range of differences that derive from both national and corporate cultures. There are a number of examples of this within industrialized countries, so that personal relations at work are directly affected by the national conceptions and habits within employment. At one extreme, there was Japan. The life of the Japanese salaryman was arduous and hard-working, with a dedication to the office and the business that was thought in other cultures to be far too serious. Typically, Japanese salarymen often worked very long hours, including late evenings and weekends (Mead 2005).

The socializing side of business was regarded as an essential part of working life, with bouts of excessive drinking and wild karaoke. The flip side of this extensive commitment of the managerial class to this kind of business life was that they were then guaranteed jobs for life and the 'cradle to grave' security of the company (Mead 2005: 63). The era of this commitment on both sides of the corporation began to diminish in the last decade or so of the twentieth century. The converging lines in Figure 10.4 show that the trend away from the permanent worker in Japan began in the 1980s and has continued, so that, by 2007, part-time, contingent, and contract workers constituted nearly 40 per cent of the working population, nearly twice the proportion in the 1980s. The permanent workforce, among which were the salarymen, has now declined from over 80 per cent to only just over 60 per cent.

Thus, as the economic conditions changed in Japan in the 1990s, the matching values of staff loyalty to the company and the company's guarantee of life-time employment were

+ Salaryman
White-collar worker (based on a Japanese model) who works in the large bureaucracy of a business (or government office). The salaryman has long working hours, low prestige in the corporate hierarchy, and an absence of significant sources of income other than salary; the term is almost always used only for male employees.

Figure 10.4
Permanent and
temporary workers
in Japan (taken from
Japan's Ministry of
Internal Affairs and
Communication).

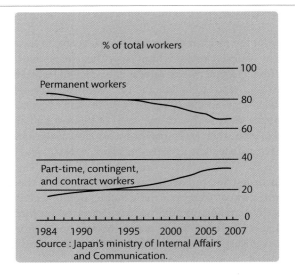

no longer viable. More serious and worrying was the response among the more established Japanese middle-managers: the disastrous effect of a doubling of suicides—to nearly 10,000 in 1998 (Mead 2005: 63).

There are further indicators of the differences that can be shown in the working relationships within MNEs. An interesting—and physical—manifestation of this comes from the ways in which North Americans and Japanese organize their office and other working spaces, as shown in Figure 10.5. The individualist nature of the American layout is dramatically different from the more collectivist set-up of the Japanese office. The emphasis in the latter is on team work rather than on individual endeavour.

Social aspects of corporate culture

Many people spend a substantial amount of their life at work, rather than at home. Even the modern developments of computer access from home, wireless-free facilities, hot-desking,

Figure 10.5
American and
Japanese organization
of working (adapted
from JB Intercultural
Consulting 2009).

American organization of working

Large spaces, with large desks and distance between desks/offices.
Workers have separate cubicles, separate offices.
Sit with backs to others—work requires privacy, concentration.
Each employee has a set of his own papers, information, PC, etc., in his office.
To communicate with someone, use phone, or get up and walk to his desk.
Work spaces are personalized (photos, art, etc.).
Windows mean status.

Japanese organization of working

Compact use of space, with small desks, closely spaced.
Desks of a work unit are put together to form one large table.
Everyone faces each other.
Not much room for papers, etc. Must be very neat; use collective supplies.
Supervisor sits at the head, the most junior sits at the foot.
You work on projects with those who sit nearest you.
Communication is continuous because you talk to or overhear everyone else's business.
Workspaces are for work only; only a few personal touches are allowed, if any.
Window seat means exile from active working group.

video conferencing, and teleworking have not significantly reduced the amount of time that most workers and managers have to spend in the office or the factory. The quantity of international business conducted by video conferencing, sometimes as much as 3–4 hour conferences or a series of such conferences spread over a couple of days (GSK 2008), has not prevented managers from having to be physically in the office most of their working life. Given the continuing centrality of working time, it is not surprising that a key factor of corporate life is the bringing together of business and social lives within MNE activities.

A great development in modern business life is team building through corporate events. Such activities are designed to help companies develop their business and ensure that managers and workers from the same company understand the strengths of the people they work with on a day-to-day basis. Organizers of corporate events offer a range of physical and mental challenges that are designed to tackle some of the issues in the workplace such as time management, delegation, and communication. Beyond the team-building activities, there are MNE events such as conference organizing, motivational days, themed evening events, corporate entertainment, and corporate hospitality.

In the USA, a significant feature of business life is the celebration within companies of certain American holidays, especially the 4th of July. In many US companies, there will be a company picnic on Independence Day, with a series of sports and games played (usually touch football and softball) and a barbecue. The purpose of the company's 4th of July picnic is both social and corporate. On the social side, it is an opportunity for managers and workers to meet with their families and friends; and, on the corporate side, it provides an opportunity to encourage teamwork and bonding between members of staff.

By contrast, for French companies, there is considerable focus on permitting a separation between private life (*la vie privée*) and company life. It is assumed that these two aspects of a worker's life are separate and should be kept so. There is some reluctance, therefore, to engage in team building through corporate events or to arrange for business and private life to coexist.

Case Study 10.2

Bombardier: From snowmobiles to energy-efficient travel

Bombardier is a world-leading manufacturer of innovative transportation solutions and operates under two broad manufacturing segments—aerospace and transportation—with revenues of US$19.7 billion in 2008. It is headquartered in Montreal, Canada, and has 60 production and engineering sites in 23 countries, and a worldwide network of over 45 service centres.

Bombardier has a global workforce of 62,500 employees, representing 75 nationalities, who speak 20 different languages. Its main businesses are aerospace and rail industries.

Bombardier Transportation is reputed to be the global leader in rail equipment and system manufacturing and a provider of related services. In the first part of the twenty-first century, millions of people travel every day on Bombardier transports (subway cars (underground trains), automated metros, commuter and intercity trains) in Mexico City, Toronto, Chicago, New York, and Kuala Lumpur. Bombardier Aerospace is a world leader in the design and manufacture of innovative aviation products and a provider of related services. Thousands fly in Learjet, Challenger, and Global Express business jets.

There are three main reasons why Bombardier is significant for any study of corporate culture: the move from a single area of technology on a relatively small scale into an MNE that has developed a wide range of products; the development from a Canadian base to one where Bombardier operates in twenty-three countries; and the adoption of environmentally sound policies and practices.

In the 1970s and 1980s, Bombardier made acquisitions in the aircraft and rail industries (including Learjet Inc. in the United States, Canadair in Canada, and Shorts Brothers in Northern Ireland). Bombardier has become the world's undisputed leader in business aircraft and regional jets. In July 2008, the company launched the CSeries aircraft (including CS100 aircraft and CS300 airliners) with the latest environmental, performance, and passenger-oriented features so that it will be 'the greenest single-aisle aircraft in its class, scheduled to enter service in 2013'. As with its aircraft, the company has also introduced new rail technology: the train manufacturing systems emphasize flexibility, the use of standardized components, reduction in operating and maintenance costs, and a high resale value.

Bombardier's core values of integrity, commitment to excellence, customer orientation, and shareholder value have characterized its corporate commitment to innovation and entrepreneurialism. The company's emphasis on managing its business in a sustainable manner has permeated its corporate culture since it was founded in 1942 by Joseph-Armand Bombardier.

The culture changes have been in the structure of the company, its product offering, its global reach, and its

need for different ways of thinking and working as it has grown. Perhaps the most significant changes were the growth of Bombardier through major acquisitions and deals (including a $1 billion deal in the 1980s for subway cars in the New York City system). The corporate changes have been brought about through the internationalization and professionalization of the company, turning it into a genuine MNE.

Bombardier's corporate culture has evolved during its shift from concentrating on a single area of technology to offering a very wide range of products (image supplied by BRP Recreational Products UK Ltd).

Strategic change in MNEs

+ **Strategic change**
Radical reorganization and restructuring of the direction and operation of a company.

Making a strategic change and the means for its execution and implementation is one of the fundamental activities that an MNE can undertake. Although MNEs are continuously changing, albeit at a gradual and incremental pace, the strategic change that really matters is the one that can be identified as 'the proactive management of change ... to achieve clearly identified strategic objectives' (Lynch 2003). This often includes a high degree of risk and uncertainty, both for the organization as a whole and for many of the employees. Among the many different academic and professional views of what causes change and how it should be implemented, it is useful to focus on the following three reasons for strategic change in MNEs, as proposed by Kanter, Stein, and Jick (1992).

- *Response to changes in the business environment.* An MNE's strengths and weaknesses need to be constantly evaluated in relation to the external world.
- *Life-cycle differences.* Changes in one division or department of an MNE require a change of emphasis or funding. For example, the development of the interface between mobile telephony and the Internet has brought about internal changes to companies such as Sony and Apple. The issues of change in these areas include the relative size, shape, and power of one division compared to others, and the need for reallocation and coordination of resources.

- *Power changes within an MNE.* Various individuals and teams within an organization struggle for control and power on a regular basis, but, when a strategic change is being proposed, implemented, or concluded, the struggle for influence and benefits is intensified.

Once the change managers within an MNE understand some or all of the motives for strategic change, they need to be able to shape and control the process. This requires a clear plan, a determination to stick to the plan, and an intelligent management of the people involved as both winners and losers in the process of change. This is a sufficiently difficult task within a domestic company operating within a single national culture. It is even more complex in a large multinational enterprise with a range of subsidiaries, competing regional bases, and the involvement of external influences, including national governments and official international bodies. At BP for instance, between 1995 and 2007, John Browne led a strategic change that transformed the company from a key UK-based energy player, with some American connections, to the world's third largest global energy company. This was done partially through the setting of strong strategic goals and determined adherence to them, as well as through some bold acquisitions: Amoco (1998), ARCO (2000), and Burmah Castrol (2000), and a Russian joint venture, TNK–BP (2003).

As with any major strategic corporate change, there is normally and inevitably some resistance. In order to overcome this, the MNE's management team needs to create the major conditions for change (recognizing the need, setting standards, monitoring performance), to identify and support those individuals and groups who will help them to lead the change, and also to promote those individuals and groups on the basis of their commitment and contribution to the new strategic direction. Only in this way can MNEs bring about changes to their corporate culture.

The most dramatic changes to corporate culture will come from the massive expansion by the new developments within the Internet, gaming, and social networking as applied to corporate ventures. The unpredictable outcome of these developments does not mean that they should be ignored, and there are indications that throughout the world the younger generations are on the brink of changing many ways of viewing and understanding economies, business structures, and corporate cultures. The move in many economies in the 1980s and 1990s from large state-run corporations to privately owned and operated ones was not fully foreseen; the trend in 2008–9 to massive state intervention in the highly capitalistic financial and banking sector was also not predicted. Both of these changes brought about—or will bring about—deeply significant changes to the corporate structures and cultures of major companies.

Challenges and choices

→ Internationally operating managers face the challenges of assessing not only their own companies in terms of corporate structure but also their overseas partners and competitors. Particularly with competing companies, managers need to have analytical models that assist them in working out the real threats that such companies may pose. Their rivals' corporate culture is a key factor that can aid them in working out the appropriate strategy for challenging them in a way that is likely to be successful.

→ Companies' choice of local partner can be vital to their success. Their knowledge and understanding of which other companies might be best suited to a joint venture, or other partnership, depends on many factors. A vital factor is whether the values, missions, and corporate cultures of the partners are going to be a good fit. As the business world moves into the relatively unknown and unpredictable exploitation of the Internet, gaming, and social networking, the challenges and choices can only be expected to be even more dramatic.

Chapter Summary

The first section of this chapter set out the key determinants and models for understanding corporate culture and assessing how change takes place within the world of international companies. It is difficult to encapsulate the complex interplay of internal and external influences into a simple model. However, the different examples of MNE image and activity illustrate the factors that may have a bearing on the culture and the way it may be changed.

The attempts to change structures, direction, or strategy are usually conducted within the framework of the prevailing culture of the company; such changes are often relatively minor and incremental. From time to time, however, the managers of change, usually a new CEO supported by outside consultants, think that a radical alteration is required. Such was the case with British Airways (see Case Study 10.3) and with many other public-sector privatizations, whether in Britain, Bulgaria, or Brazil.

The second section of the chapter outlined the factors underlying existing international corporate cultures. This helps the drivers of change to know where they will find points of resistance and where they will be able to enlist allies for the new direction of the organization. It is not an exaggeration to say that changing an MNE's corporate culture is a task that is similar to turning a large cargo ship around. It takes a great deal of effort, patience, communication, and time but also means that the captain or CEO must not deviate from the changed strategy.

The culture of multinational corporations is the context in which their structures, systems, and operations take place. To understand these is the first step towards being able to manage MNEs and direct them along routes that lead to greater success, market share and profitability.

Case Study 10.3

BA: Successfully changing an international corporate culture

Part of the business landscape throughout most of the twentieth century was the existence of national leading this sector. airlines, the flag carriers. All developed countries had a national airline leading this sector. In the UK, for example, it was clearly BOAC (British Overseas Airways Corporation) and BEA (British European Airlines) that were the flag carriers, representing Britain in all parts of Europe and the wider world. For Germany, it was Lufthansa; for the Netherlands, KLM; for Italy, Alitalia; for Belgium, Sabena; for Japan, Air Japan; for France, Air France. In all these national airlines, the government held a large share participation or was directly in control through other forms of ownership or a 'public corporation'. The ethos and values of these companies were solidly public: they were designed to be a public service rather than competitive and profit-seeking.

In newly decolonized countries one of the essential symbols of independence—alongside the flag, national anthem, the new currency, and armed forces—was a national airline. The last half of the twentieth century saw the rise of airlines such as Air India, Iran Air, Syrian Arab Airlines, Royal Air Maroc, Air Burundi, and EgyptAir. In general, the national airlines were advertised and designated as the favoured carrier for all nationals, and the principal airline for all business people travelling abroad. For all government members and officials, it was virtually forbidden for them to fly on any other airline.

State-owned national carriers were reputed to be generally inefficient and badly managed. In particular, they were known, among other things, for 'the rudeness, the dirt, the revolting food, the lack of any kind of service ethos' (Hensher 2008). This view seemed to prevail among the passengers not only of the new flag carriers but also of the larger, older airlines of European countries.

In the 1980s and the 1990s, the wave of privatization and airline deregulation meant that the dominance of the national carriers diminished. For some such as Sabena and Swissair; this meant rapid or slow death to the point where, by the early part of the twenty-first century, they had disappeared. For others, they remained much as they were and continued to receive large government subsidies. Others gained immensely as privately run, better-managed, efficient, and profit-seeking airlines. One of the great examples of this was the transformation of the British state-run airlines that became BA (British Airways). As a private company, operating principally out of London's Heathrow airport, it carries the colours of the national flag and, from time to time, behaves like a national carrier, but it has undergone a massive cultural change from public to private.

The change in BA's corporate culture has occurred over the three decades since its privatization in 1982. On a regular basis and under successive CEOs and Chairmen, the company has undergone cost-cutting through reductions in staffing levels, reorganization of its flight operations, the creation of profit centres, and the development of a streamlined IT system (Shibata 1994; Orlov 2008). New subdivisions were created, and each manager was tasked with certain profit objectives. Within this new structure, there was greater delegation of authority and a focus on management by objectives. In the first decade of the twenty-first century, the development of an information management division and the creation of the Single IT Solution (SITS) system enabled BA to save about £100 million per year 'just from a little process re-engineering and a new focus on ... [the] interface with the customer' (Orlov 2008).

At various times since the 1980s it has been acknowledged that BA has transformed itself from 'a loss-making state-owned carrier to the world's most profitable airline'. The airline was widely recognized as 'a world-class customer-focused organization' (Manzoni and Barsoux 2002). More recently, BA appears to have survived the rapidly changing nature of aviation, airport ownership, and airline restructuring. In September 2008, *Condé Nast Traveller*

BA still carries the national flag, but its corporate culture has undergone significant changes (supplied by British Airways plc).

magazine named BA as the 'Best Business Airline' at its annual awards. So, BA has managed to enter—and then exit—the world of budget airlines (with its short-lived venture with GO), to retain its hold on flight slots at major airports, including its base at Heathrow, to undergo further cost-cutting under successive CEOs, and retain its position as one of the world's major carriers. In contrast to many of its competitors, whether private or state owned, it has undergone many adjustments to its corporate culture, and has emerged successfully as one of the world's major airlines.

Case study questions

1. What changes to corporate culture stemmed from the decisions to privatize BA (or other national carriers)?
2. Why did newly independent countries want their own national airline?
3. What resistance to cultural change might the change drivers have faced?

Discussion questions

1. How do MNEs try to guarantee adherence to their vision, values, and mission? How does this vary in different parts of the business and in different regions of the world where companies operate?

2. What efforts do MNEs make in order to establish a corporate culture that allows for 'work–life' balance?

3. What conclusions can be drawn about corporate culture from the ways in which MNEs organize their working space?

4. Is corporate change within international business more complex now than it was in the 1980s?

5. In 2009–10, has the world achieved a post-industrial or a leisure society?

References

Adler, N. J., with Gundersen, A. (2008). *International Dimensions of Organizational Behavior*. 5th edn. Mason, OH: Thomson South-Western.

BBC (2009). www.bbc.co.uk/info/purpose (accessed 29 Apr. 2009).

Bell, D. (1974). *The Coming of Post-Industrial Society*. New York: Harper Colophon Books.

Bitti, M. T. (2008). 'Language of Business: Multilingual Canadians have More Career Options,' *Financial Post*, 6 Aug., www.financialpost.com (accessed 27 Apr. 2009).

Brown, A. D. (1998). *Organisational Culture*. 2nd edn. London: F. T. Pitman.

The Economist (2008), 'Sayonara, Salaryman', 3 Jan.

Ghauri, P. N., and Usunier, J.-C. (2003). *International Business Negotiations*. 2nd edn. Oxford: Pergamon.

GSK (2008). GSK employees, confidential information.

Guirdham, M. (2005). *Communicating across Cultures at Work*. 2nd edn. Basingstoke: Palgrave Macmillan.

Hagen, S. (2005). *Language and Culture in British Business*. London: CILT.

Hampden-Turner, C., and Trompenaars, F. (2000). *Building Cross-Cultural Competence: How to Create Wealth from Conflicting Values*. Chichester: John Wiley.

Handy, C. (1993). *Understanding Organizations*. London: Penguin.

Hayes, J. (2007). *The Theory and Practice of Change Management*. 2nd edn. Basingstoke: Palgrave Macmillan.

Hendon, D. W., Hendon, R. A., and Herbig, P. (1996). *Cross-Cultural Business Negotiations*. London: Quorum.

Hensher, P. (2008). 'Alitalia Flies into the Sunset, and not before Time', *Independent*, 16 Sept.

Hofstede, G. (1984). *Cultures Consequences: International Differences in Work-Related Values*. London: Sage.

Hofstede, G., and Hofstede, G. J. (2005). *Cultures and Organizations: Software of the Mind*. 2nd edn. London: McGraw-Hill.

JB Intercultural Consulting (2009). www.culture-at-work (accessed 25 Apr. 2009).

Johnson, G. (1987). *Strategic Change and the Management Process*. Oxford: Blackwell.

Johnson, G. (1992). 'Managing Strategic Change: Strategy, Culture and Action', *Long Range Planning*, 25.

Johnson, G., Scholes, K., and Whittington, R. (2007). *Exploring Corporate Strategy*. 8th edn. Harlow: FT/Prentice Hall.

Johnson Controls (2009). www.johnsoncontrols.com (accessed 25 Apr. 2009).

Kanter, R. M., Stein, B., and Jick, T. (1992). *The Challenge of Organizational Change*. New York: Free Press.

Kay, J. (2002). 'Twenty Years of Privatisation', *Prospect*, 1 June.

Lechner, F. J., and Boli, J. (2007) (eds.). *The Globalization Reader*. 3rd edn. Oxford: Blackwell.

Lynch, R. (2003). *Corporate Strategy*. 3rd edn. Harlow: FT Prentice Hall.

Lynch, R. (2006). *Corporate Strategy*. 4th edn. Harlow: FT Prentice Hall.

MacDonald, L. (2001). *The Bombardier Story: Planes, Trains and Snowmobiles*. Toronto: J. Wiley & Sons.

Manzoni, J.-F., and Barsoux, J.-L. (2002). 'Flying into a Storm: The Bob Ayling Era at British Airways', *Management Today*, 1 Jan.

Mead, R. (2005). *International Management: Cross-Cultural Dimensions*. 3rd edn. Oxford: Blackwell.

Mission Statements (2008). www.missionstatements.com (accessed 2 Oct. 2008).

Mole, J. (1995). *Mind Your Manners: Managing Business Cultures in Europe*. London: Nicholas Brealey.

Nestlé (2008). www.nestle.com (accessed 2 Oct. 2008).

Nokia (2008). www.nokia.com (accessed 2 Oct. 2008).

Olayan (2004). The Olayan Group in Saudi Arabia and the Middle East (Corporate Profile 2004), www.olayangroup.com (accessed 29 Apr. 2009).

Orlov, L. (2008). 'British Airways: A Case Study in "Lean IT"', *CIO Update*, www.cioupdate.com/insights/article.php/3767846 (accessed 6 Oct. 2008).

Peters, T., and Waterman, R. H. (1995). *In Search of Excellence*. London: HarperCollins.

Schneider, S. C., and Barsoux, J.-L. (2003). *Managing across Cultures*. 2nd edn. Harlow: FT Prentice Hall.

Shibata, K. (1994). 'Privatisation of British Airways: Its Management and Politics, 1982–1987', *EUI Working Paper EPU No. 93/9*, Florence: European University Institute.

Trompenaars, F. (1993). *Riding the Waves of Culture: Understanding Cultural Diversity in Business*. London: Nicholas Brealey.

Trompenaars, F., and Hampden-Turner, C. (1997). *Riding the Waves of Culture: Understanding Cultural Diversity in Business*. 2nd edn. London: Nicholas Brealey.

Vlasic, B., and Stertz, B. (2000). *Taken for a Ride: How Daimler-Benz Drove Off with Chrysler*. Chichester: John Wiley.

Walker, D. M., and Walker, T. (2003). *Doing Business Internationally: The Guide to Cross-Cultural Success*. 2nd edn. London: McGraw-Hill.

Further research

Castronova, E. (2005). *Synthetic Worlds: The Business and Culture of Online Games.* Chicago: University of Chicago Press.

Guomundsson, E. (2008). 'An Economist on the Virtual Economy', *Business Week*, www. businessweek.com (accessed 24 Mar. 2009).

Woolgar, S. (2002) (ed.). *Virtual Society? Technology, Cyberbole, Reality.* Oxford: Oxford University Press.

The role of corporate culture and change in a post-industrial or leisure society is likely to be affected in the next few years by the radical developments taking place on the Internet. In particular, the blurring of the line between virtual and real world has come from the growth in people's Internet use. People now rely on the Internet not only for information but for the purchasing of services and goods.

Steve Woolgar, Edward Castronova, and Eyjolfur Guomundsson are among the leading commentators on gaming, virtual societies, and virtual economies, and their impact on the development of international business. One of the key features of online gaming and virtual (or synthetic) worlds is that the growth rates are exponential; the number of new games doubles every twelve to eighteen months. Demand growth has persisted, although it seemed almost certain that there would be too much supply, too many new games, and too rapid a growth in capacity.

Online Resource Centre

Visit the Online Resource Centre that accompanies this book to read more information relating to international corporate cultures: www.oxfordtextbooks.co.uk/orc/sitkin_bowen/

part

4

International Functions

11

International Production

Overview

This chapter studies the upstream side of the international value chain, specifically focusing on what multinational companies (MNEs) do to create the products and services that they offer worldwide. The first section deals with MNEs' accumulation of knowledge through research and development (R&D). The second section discusses global supply chain management, with special focus on outsourcing. Note the difference between the term 'supply chain' and the broader concept of 'value chain' that refers to all operations from raw materials through to the sale of finished products or services. The final section looks at international manufacturing, defining the concept of industrial models before concluding with an overview of logistics and operations.

Section I: Knowledge accumulation
National research efforts
Multinational R&D

Section II: Global supply chain management
International outsourcing
Macro-level trends affecting international outsourcing
Supply relationships

Section III: International manufacturing
Industrial models
Logistics and physical operations

Learning Objectives

After reading this chapter, you will be able to:

+ perceive the role that knowledge plays in international production
+ link different stages in supply chain management
+ apprehend the strategic aspects of supplier relationships
+ compare manufacturing orientations
+ analyse upstream operations within a broader value chain context

Case Study 11.1

Michelin: From rubber trees to tyre plants

Dut to the large-scale outsourcing that is a key feature of modern globalization, industrial sectors in many OECD countries were already experiencing severe job losses eve n before the credit crunch erupted in 2008. Like many people, Richard Puech was disturbed by the devastation that mass unemployment wreaks on a local community. A particularly troublesome case in his native France was when giant tyre-maker Michelin, long considered a 'national champion', decided to transfer otherwise profitable operations from its historic plant in Montluçon to factories in Asia, where workers earn much lower wages. The main purpose of this move was to satisfy demands for greater profitability from shareholders, many of whom were not French. As a documentary journalist, Richard Puech was in position to explore the 'Affaire Michelin' and set out to make a film called One Day in the Life of a Tyre (2001).

What he discovered is that tyres are produced using sap harvested from rubber trees grown in small plantations in Thailand and Malaysia. Despite their hard work and near monopoly at this stage of the process, rubber producers barely earn enough to survive. This is because rubber trades at very low prices in New York commodity markets that farmers have no power to influence. The reality is that the fair trade principles described in Chapter 3 have spread to very few sectors.

Michelin is one of the world's leading purchasers of rubber sap. To access supplies, the company runs operations in Singapore, whose convenient location and financial power make it the world's gateway for rubber exports. This site is used to carry out elementary transformation activities, like drying raw sap and cutting it into rubber sheaths for transportation. Just as important is the Singapore financial desk, where staff use modern communications networks to track rubber prices on a minute-by-minute basis. Michelin calculates how much it can pay farmers by working backwards from the market price. Severe global competition (and the need to pay institutional investors healthy dividends) means that it has very little room to increase payments to suppliers—or to the workers back in France who are responsible for the semi-processed rubber's final transformation. Quite the contrary, as a rival CEO explains in the film, companies operating in saturated global markets are under so much pressure nowadays that their main priority is often pure cost-cutting, regardless of the strains that this places on the production process.

Like many companies in this situation, Michelin has innovated to create a niche (puncture-proof tyres) where comparative production costs are less important. Nevertheless, with so many parties interested in the rubber/tyre business, it is difficult to see how the value chain can produce enough profits to satisfy everyone. Future solutions are just as likely to be determined by politicians as by managers.

Rubber-tree farmers receive a tiny proportion of the total value created in the tyre sector (Corbis).

Introduction

One of the most crucial value chain decisions that an international manager will make is how wide a product range should be offered. At one extreme, companies can emphasize standardization and high-volume production of a narrow range of goods. At the other, they can emphasize adaptation and the ability to offer a wide range to an international clientele. Generally speaking, production specialists are interested in standardizing, since this enables economies of scale and helps them to achieve their operational goal of manufacturing goods cheaply and efficiently. Their downstream colleagues, on the other hand, tend to support a wider and more customized product range, since this makes it easier for them to sell into different national markets. The tension caused by these contradictory outlooks forms a key part of the 'push' versus 'pull' model of MNE paradigms introduced in Chapter 9.

Because upstream and downstream functions are so closely intertwined, it is useful to view the present chapter in conjunction with Chapter 12's presentation of international marketing. There is also a close connection to the corporate responsibility issues raised in Chapter 3, given that the main ethical problems associated with globalization today (environmental fallout, labour standards, regime shopping) often materialize at the level of a firm's manufacturing function. Lastly, there are also ties to Chapter 8's discussion on the 'boundaries of the firm' or the extent to which MNEs handle their own operations management (Sako 2006). Intersecting all these debates, international production is too important a topic to be overlooked, even by persons not planning to work in manufacturing.

To visualize a value chain's different upstream stages, readers may wish to revisit Figure 1.1. Generally speaking, production is defined as all the steps taken to create a product or service. Unprocessed inputs (raw materials) are transformed into components (or parts) that are combined into modules and subsequently assembled into the final goods sold in the market. The good increases in value at each of these stages, which is why the whole process is called a 'value chain'. It is crucial for readers' understanding of international production that they envisage the final outcome as the sum of all the intermediary transformations. A complex machine like a computer, for example, is made out of many different modules (microprocessor, motherboard, hard drive), themselves comprised of many components. An example from the service sector would be an insurance policy, built on the foundation of an administrative infrastructure (customer call centres, claim processors) on top of which advanced mathematical and financial models are applied. The skill of producing a good or service often means piecing together different constituents.

Section I: Knowledge accumulation

As shown in Chapter 2, classical analyses of economic advantage by theorists like Adam Smith or David Ricardo have traditionally been formulated in terms of factor inputs like capital, labour, or physical resources. Over time, however, it has become apparent that differences in economic performance reflect another factor as well—knowledge, or the sum total of people's experience, ability to handle complexity, judgement, intuition, values, and beliefs (Davenport and Prusak 1998). Much work has been done on how knowledge management (KM) increases 'organizational learning' (Nonaka and Takeuchi 1995). This analysis is relevant, for instance, to the Uppsala 'stages of internationalization' model discussed in Chapter 8. KM has become an increasingly important production factor since the 1980s, because of advances in information technology, the rise of the so-called knowledge economy, and the growing share of global wealth produced by knowledge-intensive service sectors like biotechnology.

+ **Modules**
When components are assembled into a unit that fulfils a particular function in a system. Such units can be plugged without alteration into the rest of the system. Groups of modules are known as 'subassemblies'.

+ **Knowledge management**
Systems that companies use to maximize the benefits of knowledge accessed internally and externally. Mainly comprised of research and development (R&D) but also refers to data and information systems.

+ **Knowledge economy**
Sum total of markets that help actors to acquire knowledge, viewed as a product/ service in and of itself.

Knowledge management is not only an upstream phenomenon. Marketing specialists will have their own knowledge to manage (customer lists, consumer preferences), as will financial professionals (currency regulations, capital controls, etc.). Nevertheless, many of the world's best-known MNEs have built their success on production advantages specifically derived from transforming knowledge into new products or services. Examples include Microsoft operating systems, the Toyota Prius (a hybrid car running on both petrol and electricity) and Nokia's market-leading mobile telephone technology. KM becomes a particularly important aspect of production when goods or services are conceived as 'bundles' not only of tangible materials but also of intangible inputs like technology and know-how (Ietto-Gillies 2005).

There are two ways to apprehend knowledge creation: at the national level; and in terms of MNEs' research and development (R&D) activities.

National research efforts

An economy's level of technological advancement is one result of the relationship between the different actors involved in producing and disseminating knowledge—firms, universities, research centres, and government agents. In some analysts' view, these actors work together in 'national innovation systems' (see Online Resource Centre, extension material 11.1).

National R&D environments vary greatly. Figure 11.1 offers statistics on different economies' R&D intensity, or the percentage of GDP spent on R&D. There are also differences in knowledge spillover possibilities for MNEs. Most companies fund their own R&D but want to benefit as well from breakthroughs by fellow researchers. Many set up operations in places like Silicon Valley in California, Sophia-Antipolis in France, or Bangalore in India, specifically because a hi-tech cluster already exists there. By working more closely with other firms, often cutting-edge local SMEs (Prashantham and McNaughton 2006), MNEs hope to achieve synergies in the knowledge accumulation process. Note that host governments tend to actively welcome such moves because they facilitate the inward transfer of technology.

+ **Knowledge spillover**
Where companies gain knowledge through proximity to external sources such as universities, research centres, or other companies.

> Go to the ORC

+ **Cluster**
Where firms in similar lines of business operate in close physical proximity to one another, reflecting historical factors or strategic intent and building close ties.

Photo 11.1
How does knowledge get from the classroom to the factory floor? (Corel)

Figure 11.1
Variations in national
and corporate R&D
spending (Eurostat
2007; © European
Communities,
1995–2009).

	R&D intensity - spending as percentage of GDP	Corporate R&D spending as percentage of national R&D spending
1. EU-25	1.85	54.9
including Sweden	3.86 (2005)	65
UK	1.73	44.2
France	2.14	51.7
Germany	2.5	66.8
2. United States	2.68	63.7
3. Japan	3.18	74.8
4. China	1.23	65.7

Thinking point

How likely is it
that current OECD
economies will
maintain their
advance over
the rest of the
world in terms of
controlling global
knowledge?

This is often realized by getting the foreign MNE to enter a joint venture with local partners (Phan et al. 2006) and/or by establishing helpful institutional and legal frameworks, such as the European Research Area or the World Intellectual Property Organization.

Statistics show wide variations in national research outputs. Despite the rapid rise in total research spending in emerging economies like China and India, about 99 per cent of all patents registered in the world are from Triad countries. Even in this zone, innovativeness can vary greatly. For example, EU countries, with a few noteworthy exceptions like Sweden, invest comparatively little in research. The EU is also where non-business actors (like state-subsidized research centres) account for the highest percentage of national R&D efforts. Japan, on the other hand, devotes almost twice as much of its GDP to R&D as Europe does. As tends to be the case throughout Asia, much of this spending comes from the corporate sector, albeit under government guidance. The USA has a middle position in terms of both the percentage of GDP spent on research and the importance of the corporate sector (OECD 2006a; b).

In absolute terms, with outlays of $330 billion the USA was world leader in 2006, accounting for about 42 per cent of all R&D spending in OECD countries, in front of the EU-15 with $230 billion. Just as interesting was the rise in Chinese R&D spending, which surpassed Japan's $130 billion to reach $136 billion. Between 1995 and 2004, the number of researchers in China rose by 77 per cent to 926,000, making this the world's second largest pool for R&D employees, just after the USA, which had 1.3 million researchers (OECD 2006a). China's growing R&D effort will have great economic impact, especially since much of this research is by domestic firms, something that has been shown to have a larger effect on national productivity than spillover from foreign MNEs' research (Unel 2008). Ultimately, this will influence the kinds of products that MNEs produce in China. Much of the country's recent industrialization has been based on low value-added goods, but the abundance of researchers being trained and/or working in China means that things are destined to change. Contrary to the 1990s, when global outsourcing mainly involved MNEs seeking lower-cost manufacturing locations, today's emphasis is more on sourcing whatever low-cost inputs a country has to offer. Given the ever-increasing number of researchers from developing countries, such inputs are just as likely nowadays to be intellectual as physical (Hill 2006).

Multinational R&D

Knowledge management involves more than pure R&D, also referring in a corporate setting to data and information transfers (see Chapter 9). Nonetheless, most MNEs view research as the cornerstone of their KM efforts and indeed their entire upstream activity.

Rank	MNE / country of origin	Main sector	R&D spending (€ bn)
1	Pfizer (USA)	Pharmaceuticals	5.76
2	Ford Motor (USA)	Automotive	5.46
3	Johnson & Johnson (USA)	Pharmaceuticals	5.40
4	Microsoft (USA)	IT	5.40
5	Daimler Chrysler (Germany)	Automotive	5.30
6	Toyota Motor (Japan)	Automotive	5.17
7	GlaxoSmithKline (UK)	Pharmaceuticals	5.13
8	Siemens (Germany)	Engineering	5.02
9	General Motors (USA)	Automotive	5.00
10	Samsung (S. Korea)	Electronics	4.66
11	Intel (USA)	IT	4.45
12	Sanofi-Aventis (France)	Pharmaceuticals	4.40

Figure 11.2
MNEs ranked by global R&D investment, European Commission (2006).

As shown in Figure 11.2, one of R&D's main characteristics is its costliness. There is rarely any certainty that a product innovation will sell well enough globally to justify initial R&D outlays, which can be enormous. In 2007, for instance, research spending as a percentage of sales ('technological intensity') reached 15.9 per cent in the pharmaceutical/biotechnology sectors, the world's leading R&D investors (ahead of hardware equipment and automotive fields). It is true that these three fields account for around two-thirds of total global corporate spending on research, with normal R&D/revenue ratios in other sectors staying in the 2–8 per cent range (Jaruzelski et al. 2006). Many MNEs spend so much on R&D that they cannot afford the commercial networks needed to distribute their innovations worldwide—even though global sales are their only hope of recouping initial costs. Thus, many international alliances between rival MNEs have been based on a need to share R&D. Examples from the year 2007 included UK giant GlaxoSmithKline's pharmaceuticals collaboration with India's Ranbaxy, or the link-up between IBM (USA) and Toshiba (Japan). Note that R&D's cost factor is a particular constraint for SMEs, whose smaller size means that they are often unable to achieve sufficient global sales to justify major research investments.

Since knowledge is key to international competitiveness, MNEs strive to protect the confidentiality of their secrets. A distinction is commonly made between whether a particular type of knowledge constitutes a public good or not. Firms will try to maximize their knowledge advantage by extending any exclusivity rights they have—one example being pharmaceutical companies' efforts during the 1990s and 2000s to control the production of AIDS medicine (WHO 2006). Confidentiality is difficult to maintain during a company's internationalization process, however, and MNEs may choose to transfer only less strategic categories of knowledge, relating, for instance, to management practices instead of product characteristics. The choice may also reflect the MNE's nationality of origin, with studies showing, for instance, that Japanese and US companies entering a country like China tend to implement different levels of technological transfer when entering a country like China (Duanmu 2006).

Lastly, as summarized in Figure 11.3, the same 'pull' versus 'push' concepts that Chapters 9 and 10 used to analyse MNE organizations and cultures, respectively, are also key to international R&D.

- *'Push' R&D*. In this orientation, the MNE imposes its new idea on the market instead of starting out by reacting to signals. Push MNEs often concentrate R&D activities on a single site, usually global headquarters, to maximize confidentiality and cost control. This means, however, that researchers are not working in proximity

Thinking point

Is the duration of an international patent more of an economic or a political debate?

+ Public good
Good that is 'non-exclusive' (i.e. available to everyone), and whose use by some does not decrease its availability for others.

Figure 11.3
Arguments for and
against centralizing
MNE research.

Pro-centralization (push approach)	Anti-centralization (pull approach)
Assemble critical mass of scientists	Mobilize diverse teams of scientists
Better chance of protecting secrets	Possibility of alliances
Lower overhead costs	Greater customer focus
ICT used for scientific communications	More opportunities for knowledge spillover

to the different markets that their new product will affect. Less concerned with international variations in consumer preferences, they may be tempted to seek a single global standard. The example of Microsoft, with its powerful R&D unit in Redmond (Washington State, USA), springs to mind. Where a new standard (like Windows Operating System) is a superior innovation, 'push' R&D can be very successful and create first-mover advantage. But problems will also arise when researchers' distance from their markets means that their research focus is irrelevant to consumers' preoccupations.

- *'Pull R&D'.* 'Pull' MNEs see their business as starting with customer signals and therefore try to maximize researchers' exposure to the outside world. The idea is that innovators are more likely to develop commercially viable goods or services when they react to market demand instead of following personal inclinations. A 2008 example of this orientation was when British pharmaceuticals company GlaxoSmithKline asked government agencies worldwide to specify exactly which therapies it should focus on before committing to further innovation efforts.

A similar debate on the applicability of 'push' or 'pull' approaches applies to international design, which can be defined as KM's physical modelling stage. In the hope of achieving economies of scale, an MNE might try to 'push' a single design onto all its foreign markets. A famous example from the 1990s was when Ford spent $6 billion designing a 'world car' (known in its first version as the Mondeo in Europe and the Contour in North America). In the end, global sales were uneven and disappointing. Conversely, other MNEs' design efforts are driven by a 'pull' orientation that tries to put staff members in touch with various market preferences. Towards the late 1980s, for example, US toolmaker Black and Decker ran design centres in more than twenty countries. This was a good idea in so far as the appliances that the company built were adapted and sold well. However, duplicating design centre overheads was so expensive that it became untenable, with Black and Decker ultimately changing course in the 1990s and locating its design efforts on few sites only.

It is impossible to overstate the importance of knowledge management as an international production function. Decisions taken at the very beginning of a value chain will have crucial knock-on effects as products or services evolve towards their final shape. For instance, Dell's original decision to offer IBM PCs instead of Apple Macs has clearly affected many other supply decisions relating to components that are compatible with one standard but not the other. Upstream decisions are almost never taken without managers considering their ripple effects.

+ Design
Activities aimed at
defining a product's
final shape and
attributes.

+ Supply chain
management
Ways of directing
the transformation
of a physical good.
Includes purchasing
supplies and stocks;
coordinating and
training of suppliers
and sub-suppliers;
and overseeing the
logistical flow of goods
and information.

Section II: Global supply chain management

Supply chain management (SCM) refers to all the operations involved in sourcing, producing, transporting, assembling, and finalizing a product or service. Global SCM occurs when firms are in a position to purchase and take delivery of raw materials, components, and modules anywhere in the world. As Chapter 7 discussed, to a certain extent these are macro-level phenomena that can be analysed in political, economic, social, and ecological terms. They can also be studied from a more micro-level, corporate perspective. It is this latter focus that the 'International outsourcing' section below will highlight.

The first dividing line in global SCM is whether an MNE sources raw materials and components from an external provider or from a foreign unit that it owns. The latter solution, is the 'offshoring' configuration that MNEs often implement when pursuing a vertical integration strategy (see Chapter 5), raises a number of logistics and production location issues. This includes international outsourcing, a leading driver of international business today.

International outsourcing

There are several explanations for MNEs' growing tendency to focus on core competencies and outsource certain value chain functions to other companies. As Chapter 7 showed, financialization means that many MNEs now prioritize financial performance indicators like return on equity (ROE) over traditional corporate objectives like market share. One way that companies can increase their ROE is by 'shrinking the balance sheet'. This is because they will have fewer assets to finance if they run fewer functions in-house. The strategy has the added benefit of increasing flexibility, a key factor of success in an era of global competition and rapidly changing in consumer demand. After all, during periods of economic downturn, it is easier and cheaper to renegotiate supplier contracts than to shut down factories. A good example of this was the speed with which companies from the USA and Europe cut orders to their Asian suppliers following the 2008–9 crisis.

Companies are also no longer frightened by the kind of coordination problems that occur when outside partners are brought into the production process. Inter-firm communications have been greatly enhanced by the development of electronic data interchanges (EDI) and Internet-based applications such as vendor managed inventory, collaborative planning forecasting, and replenishment or efficient consumer response (Naim et al. 2004)—all of which optimize the inter-firm flow of goods. It is easier than ever for a company to work hand in hand with its suppliers to monitor key parameters such as inventory levels, delivery times, and standards. This has had enormous consequences for MNEs' international value chain strategies. Many of the world's best-known names (carmakers like Volkswagen but also computer-makers like Dell or TV-makers like Sony) manufacture only a small percentage of the final products they sell. In one extreme example of outsourcing, 'hollow firms' like Nike have almost no physical production activities at all (and run few if any retail outlets). Nike's main activity is branding—and, above all, coordinating the different firms comprising its network.

For simpler goods, outsourcing often involves companies trying to take advantage of suppliers' cost advantages and/or economies of scale by acquiring inputs externally for less than it costs to produce them in-house. For more complex goods, there is the added advantage of being able indirectly to access whatever technology the supplier uses to make an input. In both cases, by outsourcing non-essential functions, firms are freeing themselves to focus on those areas of activity where they can be most productive (see Online Resource Centre, extension material 11.2, for the 'resource-based view' of the firm).

> Go to the ORC

However, as Figure 11.4 shows, outsourcing also has its shortcomings. The company purchasing the inputs (the 'prime contractor') becomes dependent on suppliers, losing the ability to produce inputs and the specialist knowledge that comes from this. It can also be dangerous, for example, if adverse currency or raw-material price movements increase the component's price and the buyer cannot find a substitute. The same applies when workers' wages rise rapidly in those countries where the company has developed its main outsourcing relationships—as was the case in 2007 when manufacturers in some areas of China and India struggled to find enough recruits to cope with rapid demand growth. Many MNEs today have become entirely reliant on their supply chain, to such an extent that, when the 2008 financial crisis erupted, a priority for a company like German engineering giant Siemens was to use part

Figure 11.4
Corporate advantages/
disadvantages
of international
outsourcing.

Advantages	Disadvantages
Lower costs	Will not develop knowledge/experience
Access to supplier technology	Dependent on supplier
Productive flexibility	Potential quality problems
Higher return on equity	Delivery risks

of its cash surplus to strengthen suppliers' treasury position by offering them credit that they were no longer getting from banks (Mortished 2008). This kind of joint financial planning is a sign of how crucial supply chain collaboration has become in many sectors of activity.

There is also the strategic risk that suppliers might adopt a forward integration strategy (see Chapter 7) and expand their own operations down the value chain, ultimately becoming competitors to their customers. One example is Russia's Lukoil company, which not only owns major Siberian oil reserves that it sells in the wholesale markets but in 2006 also began acquiring ConocoPhillips petrol stations throughout Europe, rivalling its own customers. The US small aircraft producer Cessna faced a similar risk following its 2007 decision to outsource the production of complete models to China's Shenyang Aircraft Corporation. Whereas Boeing, the giant US airplane manufacturer, outsources only parts production, Cessna's strategy of empowering suppliers to build products in their entirety has put it in danger of being crowded out of this value chain one day.

Another problem arises when suppliers, particularly ones operating in emerging countries marked by lax regulations, deliver poor-quality goods. This is why quality controls have become a key part of negotiations between order-givers and suppliers. An example of what can happen when quality goes wrong is the uproar faced by US toy-maker Mattel after selling unsafe products it had bought from suppliers in China. Indeed, as Chapter 3 showed, outsourcing has been linked with very serious ethical problems since the 1980s. If labour standards are low in the country to which production has been moved, the MNE might be accused of ignoring the exploitation of its supplier's workforce. For instance, some NGOs, like the Clean Clothes Campaign, have expressed their concerns about the ethics of sporting goods specialist Adidas outsourcing football production to Pakistan, a country where factories employ children to work extremely long hours for little pay in extremely difficult conditions. Similarly, by moving production to locations with low pollution standards, international outsourcing can be harmful to the environment, as witnessed by the terrible air quality in many Chinese factory towns. The fuel consumption and emissions caused by the long-distance transportation of components and finished products also contributes to global warming. Recent analysis suggests that 'for consumer goods makers, hi-tech players, and other manufacturers, between 40 and 60 percent of a company's carbon footprint resides upstream in its supply chain—from raw materials, transport, and packaging to the energy consumed in manufacturing processes. For retailers, the figure can be 80 percent' (Brickman and Ungerman 2008). In short, like other upstream activities, outsourcing lends itself to both macro- and micro-level debates over MNE behaviour.

Lastly, outsourcing can contradict the lean production principles that many firms have adopted in recent years, one of which highlights the need to reduce inventory costs by delivering components 'just in time' before they are required on the customer's assembly line. It can be risky for a company to source materials from the other side of the world, since the necessarily longer lead times increase the likelihood of late arrivals undermining production schedules. In February 2008, for instance, damage to undersea cables disrupted Internet connections between Europe and India, hindering some of the data transfer processes that are an important activity in international outsourcing. Indeed, to counter the risk of uncertain long-distance deliveries, some firms are starting to feel the need to hold larger inventories—thereby defeating the very purpose of a just-in-time organization (Tabrizi and Tseng 2007).

Thinking point
International outsourcing helps the suppliers involved but what impact does it have on the host society as a whole?

+ Lean production
Production philosophy that emphasizes saving resources through less waste, better inventory management, better-quality, and shorter industrial cycles. Largely derived from the 'Toyota Production System'.

+ Lead time
Time it takes, once an order has been placed, to deliver a good to the order-giver's premises.

Solutions exist for many of these distance-related problems, but they can be expensive. For example, a real-time tracking and inventory management software called radio frequency identification technology (RFID) helps contractors to monitor components' location. In turn, this helps them to forecast deliveries and manage inventories more accurately. On a more structural level, some component-makers have taken to building 'supplier's parks' immediately adjacent to contractors' overseas plants (for example, the 'Blue Macaw' project near Volkswagen's Gravatai factory in Brazil). Such initiatives strengthen the argument that it is better to analyse MNEs' actions as network members than to focus on what each does separately.

A fuller understanding of modern outsourcing means looking at current macro-trends and different kinds of supplier relationships.

Macro-level trends affecting international outsourcing

Outsourcing has evolved significantly in recent decades. The main driver used to be the procurement of low-cost components or finished products from the world's poorer regions like South East Asia, which tended to specialize in textiles and basic semiconductors; or Latin America, particularly after US automakers began buying parts from North Mexican *maquiladora* factories. Protests against manufacturing job losses in the industrialized world were often met with the argument that less developed countries (LDCs) are incapable of entering higher value-added segments, which will therefore be dominated by OECD countries. The concept here was that countries' relative advantages would necessarily lead to an international division of labour.

However, with leading LDCs demonstrating their ability to engage in increasingly sophisticated activities, Western MNEs have started to outsource entirely different kinds of

+ **Procurement**
Act of purchasing resources or inputs.

Thinking point

Are any jobs in the developed world immune to the risk of being outsourced to LDCs?

Photo 11.2
An Indian call centre: service sector jobs are being outsourced too (Corbis).

production. This does not mean that traditional, manufacturing-oriented outsourcing will disappear. In late 2007, for example, General Motor's Vice-President for Global Purchasing was predicting a 25 per cent rise in GM's purchase of components from China, in addition to the twenty million items that the company was already sourcing from Chinese suppliers monthly to supply its plants worldwide (Fairclough 2007). But outsourcing is just as likely to involve knowledge-related, administrative, and R&D activities. Examples can be found in the world's three leading outsourcing destinations: India, where suppliers run customer call centres and assume responsibility for many MNEs' business processes, including invoicing and accounting; the Philippines, which dominates the global market for medical transcriptions; and the ex-Soviet Union (Russia and Ukraine), which accounts for a rising share of global software development. It was always wrong to imagine that partners located in LDCs or transition economies would be unable to compete in the knowledge economy.

MNEs' outsourcing strategies have changed in other ways as well. Whereas earlier models often involved dealings with a single partner, some firms have taken to breaking up their outsourcing needs into smaller contracts with different companies (called 'multi-sourcing'). This affords the prime contractor extra security in case the supply chain is disrupted. In addition, it forces suppliers to compete with one another on price and innovativeness (Thomas 2007). Modern MNEs also try to improve their bargaining position with global suppliers by centralizing global purchasing for all subsidiaries, thereby enabling bulk buying. This requires a high performance communications and logistics system.

+ Bulk buying
Where goods or services are purchased in large quantities, there is a greater chance of negotiating a lower per unit price, since the seller will achieve economies of scale that it can pass on to the buyer.

Case Study 11.2

Dellism: A new model value chain?

Figure 11.5
The Dell supply chain involves a full integration of communications, manufacturing, logistics, and assembly functions.

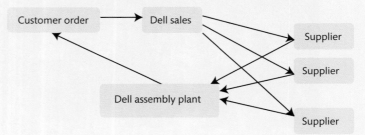

When a customer buys a personal computer from a Dell (www.dell.com) salesperson, the order is transmitted immediately to one of the company's 'manufacturing facilities' as soon as payment has been verified. The decision as to which facility should fill the order depends on geographical proximity and/or the particular product. For example, most laptop notebooks that Dell sells worldwide are made in Asia.

What Dell calls its 'manufacturing facilities' could more accurately be described as 'assembly plants'. The company manufactures few if any of the components used in its computers. When notification of a laptop notebook purchased in the USA reaches Dell's Malaysian plant, for instance, the

parts will be immediately ordered from a 'supplier logistics centre' comprised of the many supply chain partners running operations immediately adjacent to every Dell plant worldwide. Each supplier is in constant communication with the company, determining future delivery quantities and tracking current parts. As illustrated in Figure 11.5, communications are at the heart of the Dell system.

Dell's supplier system is what allows it to meet the three commitments it makes. The first promise is a customized system, which becomes feasible because of Dell's ability to vary the sub-systems that it orders from suppliers. The second is quick delivery, enabled by the company's ultra-rapid communications and efficient suppliers' parks. Lastly, Dell can offer low prices thanks to the volume discounts it demands from suppliers but also because its just-in-time delivery system cuts inventory costs, largely borne by the suppliers themselves.

The whole arrangement serves to shift industrial burdens to suppliers, who are also squeezed by Dell's policy of multi-sourcing certain products to enhance delivery security. The question then becomes why should they work with such a demanding customer. The answer lies in the sheer volume of orders from Dell. Having one the world's biggest computer retailers as a customer enables companies to achieve economies of scale that they would otherwise struggle to attain. Largely specialized in upstream functions, many of Dell's rivals lack its commercial competencies, infrastructure, and brand recognition.

Clearly there is great value for Dell in using modern communications and logistics to link the different threads comprising its international production process. Dell's own industrial competency involves relatively simple assembly operations and is not enough to explain its profitability. At the same time, the company's lack of manufacturing experience could become a weakness. Dell depends on suppliers for its product features. The risk is that the suppliers will try to bypass it one day to deal directly with consumers.

Dell provides information technology but also puts IT at the centre of its own processes (Dell).

There are signs that the rapid growth in outsourcing is slowing and even reversing. In service industries (like banking) where customers have strong cultural sensitivities, there has been a move to bring call centres back to prime contractors' countries of origin (for example, in 2006–7, Abbey, NatWest, Lloyds TSB, Aviva, and Powergen all repatriated their call centres to the UK from India). In the textile sector, where fashion changes quickly and time to market is key, some MNEs now believe that the delays inherent in long-distance supply chains no longer justify the cost advantage. This explains the rise of nearshoring solutions, exemplified by the recent decision by European clothing companies like Mango to source product from Eastern Europe or Turkey instead of China (*The Economist* 2005). As the costs of long-distance outsourcing rise (because of higher *wages, fuel bills*, and inflation or a rising currency in the host country), MNEs will have to reassess their supply chains. There is no guarantee that the conditions that made a strategy viable in the past will apply in the future.

Some companies have been so disappointed by outsourcing (poor-quality goods, irregular deliveries) that they have turned to the opposite strategy of 'in-sourcing', bringing

+ **Time to market**
Lag between a product's design and/or value chain transformation and its being made available to end users.

+ **Nearshoring**
Where operations are outsourced to a low-cost location relatively close to the company's country of origin.

Figure 11.6
Different ways
of organizing
international supply
chains.

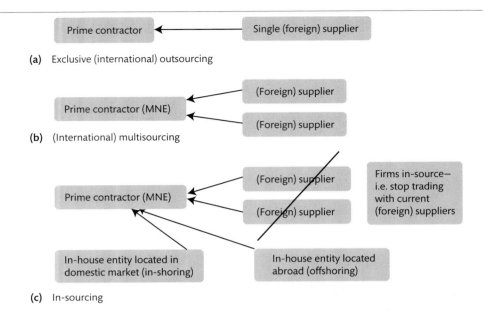

(a) Exclusive (international) outsourcing

(b) (International) multisourcing

(c) In-sourcing

+ **Externalization**
Where a firm gives
an outside party
responsibility for
some of its business
functions. The opposite
of internalization.

+ **Vertical** *keiretsu*
Japanese
business network based
on a principle of
long-term inter-firm
cooperation. A vertical
keiretsu is comprised of
companies specializing
in different value chain
activities and will
generally include a bank
for funding purposes.

+ **Horizontal** *keiretsu*
Japanese
business network based
on a principle of
long-term inter-
firm cooperation.
A horizontal *keiretsu* is
comprised of similar
firms allying with trading
companies to ensure the
widest possible market
coverage.

Thinking point

How strict should
an MNE be with its
suppliers?

back in-house functions that used to be sourced externally (see Figure 11.6). This makes most sense in hi-tech sectors where cost is less of a crucial factor. One example from 2005 was the decision by British telecommunications giant Cable and Wireless to cancel many of its existing externalization agreements. Companies from less hi-tech sectors, like UK lawnmower manufacturer Hayter, have also turned to in-sourcing because of adverse currency movements, rising wages in some LDCs, and falling global demand (Webb 2009). The benefits of outsourcing, including productivity gains, must constantly be weighed against its disadvantages.

Supply relationships

Depending on their strategy and corporate culture, prime contractors can establish different kinds of supplier relationships (Harland et al. 2004). Examples include the 'integrated hierarchy' of single product firms that depend heavily on specific suppliers, or the 'semi-hierarchy' of multidivisional firms characterized by a lesser degree of dependency. Other suppliers' relationships include the 'coordinated revenues links' that typify licensing/franchising arrangements and the 'medium-term trading commitments' of companies that prefer to work with shortlists of suppliers.

A simpler way to categorize supplier relationships is to differentiate between the short-term, so-called American model; the longer-term Asian model; and the compromise 'flagship' model.

In the short-term model, subcontractors are asked to bid anew every time a contractor tries to replenish its supplies. As such, they will only be as good as their latest bid and are constantly at risk of losing business if they slip on quality and/or price. There is little room for loyalty or joint planning in this kind of relationship, but it does force suppliers to remain competitive. An interesting case is the Covisint online auction platform that Ford and General Motors developed to force potential suppliers worldwide to compete for contracts. Covisint has grown over the years to cover different kinds of inputs, including information-technology (IT) services. It is a way for prime contractors to pass on to their upstream partners the competitive pressures that they face themselves.

The focus in longer-term supply models is on collaboration up and down the supply chain. Encapsulated in Japanese vertical or horizontal *keiretsus* but also in Korean *chaebols* and Chinese *guanxi* networks with their roots in close, long-term relationships, these supply systems are prime examples of business being embedded in a cultural context. In the above examples, they reflect the Asian emphasis on social harmony as opposed to individual success (see Figure 11.7). In a *keiretsu*, for instance, a prime contractor will lend its name (for example, Mitsubishi, Mitsui, Sumitomo) to a network of companies that work together to cover all the upstream operations needed to bring a good to market. Firms typically take an equity stake in one another and plan investments, research, and product design together. This is a comfortable arrangement based on extremely stable contracts that are usually renewed without non-*keiretsu* members having any opportunity to compete. Even in cases of 'follow sourcing' where subcontractors build factories abroad to service their prime contractor's overseas operations, Japanese *keiretsu* suppliers can still count on winning most contracts, whether or not an explicit *keiretsu* agreement exists (Solis 2003). Predictability of this kind is priceless, since it helps suppliers' industrial planners to decide between small capacities that cost less but cannot accommodate peaks in demand, and large capacities that can cope with bigger orders but cost more. Being able to size plant capacities correctly is an advantage translating ultimately into lower costs that the supplier can then share with the contractor.

Asian supply networks are not without their faults. For instance, the difficult recession that Japan experienced during the 1990s has often been blamed on *keiretsu* members' tolerance for partners' poor investment decisions. Over-dependence on external partners can also be dangerous, as Toyota itself discovered when the 1995 Osaka earthquake flattened many of its suppliers' facilities, causing enormous disruption to its just-in-time system. At the same time, there is no doubt that Asia's rise as a centre of international manufacturing is partially rooted in the success of its supply chain organization. This has drawn the attention of many Western MNEs. In international production, as in other areas of international business, success breeds imitation.

A number of Western MNEs have also moved over the years to establish similarly collaborative supply chains, possibly in an attempt to imitate the success of Japanese *keiretsus*. This approach, described as the 'flagship' concept (Rugman and D'Cruz 2000), is often pursued by prime contractors who compete in markets under their own name while leading networks of dedicated suppliers that are usually organized into clusters. The benefits for the network's flagship leader is that it can count on reliable sourcing and faces a lesser risk that suppliers might take advantage of tight supply conditions to raise prices. Flagship leaders can also internationalize more quickly because they do not have to build their own manufacturing facilities. One example cited by Rugman and D'Cruz is Ikea, the Swedish furniture retailer. Confident that centralized control over subcontractors' product design and quality operations will guarantee adequate sourcing and protect its brand name, this MNE has been free to focus resources on opening stores in Europe and elsewhere. The extra management costs that Ikea has incurred because of the need to supervise its suppliers

+ *Chaebol*
South Korean equivalent of Japanese *keiretsu*, but, instead of companies holding shares in one another, shareholder equity remains largely in the hands of the lead firm's founding family.

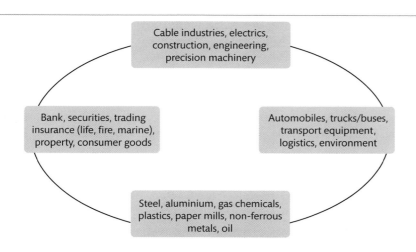

Figure 11.7
Close links between partners in Japan's collaborative supply chains.

have been more than offset by the savings it achieves by sticking to its core competencies. In a sense, the flagship arrangement is a microcosm of the division of labour concept.

Flagship suppliers, on the other hand, benefit from the prime contractor's expertise in production and materials planning, quality control, and technical assistance. On occasion, suppliers can piggyback the leader's ability to buy raw materials in bulk, thus cheaply. Above all, flagship suppliers benefit from greater stability, with guaranteed sales volumes allowing them to size their production capacities more accurately. This is the kind of umbrella that Italian clothing-maker Benetton, for example, offers the different companies that produce the wool it processes.

At the same time, flagship suppliers also incur extra costs. New suppliers are often forced to build expensive, capital-intensive facilities to manufacture the components they are expected to provide. Indeed, one analysis of the flagship arrangement is that it involves prime contractors passing on to their suppliers some of the performance pressures that they themselves face. This is particularly true in sectors characterized by very demanding customers, such as mass retail and fast food, although it also applied in the Dell example.

Not all pressures are cost-based, however. For many suppliers, it is just as important to offer technological competencies—one being the ability, as discussed above, to share all kinds of supply chain information. Many flagship leaders are interested in 'concurrent engineering', or the possibility for upstream and downstream partners to design in parallel the different value chain stages for which each is responsible (Nassimbeni 2004). Nowadays, industrial collaboration often starts as early as a product's pre-production phase, with suppliers and contractor cooperating openly ('tacitly') on basic component designs to ensure that they fit into modules seamlessly (Kotabe et al. 2007). The priority in this 'fractal production' approach is to ensure coherency between the different sub-systems that, when combined, comprise the final product. To the extent that such operations reflect a group effort, it is clear that international production is shaped by the way that a company draws the boundaries between its own operations and its partner's. Like most aspects of international business, manufacturing must be analysed in conjunction with managers' strategic paradigms.

Inside business

Arve Thorvik, Thorvik International Consulting AS, Formerly Vice President for European Affairs, Statoil Hydro (speaking in a personal capacity)

Arve Thorvik is an independent consultant in the oil and gas business, working on energy and environment issues with companies including Statoil Hydro, where he was most recently Vice President for European Affairs, based in Brussels. Originally, Statoil Hydro was formed in Norway as a fully-owned state oil company. It has now become an international oil and gas company, rather than a Norwegian one. Statoil Hydro operates in more than forty countries around the world, mostly in upstream activities. It concentrates on producing oil and gas and letting others bring these commodities to market. Years ago, it had its own fleet of ships, but now like many other companies in the business, it no longer owns or operates its own logistical capability. Logistics are carried out by service companies that are contracted specifically for this purpose.

The oil industry has a particular business configuration, featuring a separation of functions between exploring and surveying companies, drillers and producers, refiners, and final downstream players that market the products to other businesses or individual consumers. The energy industry is one where competitors often work together. For example, in the exploitation of an oil and gas field, there will be a lead company working closely with others servicing and subcontracting the activities. Each will own a piece of the action. The industry is also built on long-term rather than short-term relationships, since from the moment of exploration until the emergence of products can take anything from seven to fifteen years.

A crucial relationship is with the host country where the oil and gas has been discovered. Natural resources are usually owned not by private citizens but by the state. Therefore, it is absolutely vital to have a close and comfortable relationship with the government, otherwise, the company will not be able to obtain a licence to operate. 'You have to play by the rules, you have to adapt to the situation ... and you have to be willing to share your knowledge and your competence.'

Section III: International manufacturing

The only way that an MNE can satisfy consumer demand for a timely delivery of different goods to different locations worldwide is if it has an efficient manufacturing and logistics network. Companies have had varying ideas at different times about the most efficient way of devising such networks. The principle of this book, as set out in Chapter 1, is that no one best way exists. This means that there is value in analysing the range of industrial models that firms have pursued over the years.

+ Industrial models
Manufacturing systems determining the sequencing of operations within factories. Also refers to flow of goods before and after industrial transformation, and to the distribution of any income generated.

Industrial models

Readers interested in exploring the concept of industrial models can consult the Online Resource Centre, extension material 11.3. A good starting place in modern industry is the mass production system that Henry Ford first implemented in the early twentieth century. This model offered the advantage of standardization and efficiency, featuring specialized workers stationed along an assembly line and completing a succession of tasks and productions for assembly in the final product. By enabling economies of scale, Ford's system cut costs, leading to lower retail prices and, in turn, expanded sales. One of the first applications of this logic was the Ford Model T car, a trailblazer among mass-manufactured and mass-consumed products. For much of the twentieth century, this industrial model was the starting point for many managers' economic vision.

> Go to the ORC

As powerful as Henry Ford's approach was, it had several flaws. First and foremost was its emphasis on uniformity. This may have been acceptable in the early stages of a new product, but as markets mature, consumers tend to require greater diversity. This was problematic for Fordist manufacturers. Offering a broad product range is expensive, both because it takes time to switch factory equipment from one production line to another, and because shortening a production run reduces economies of scale.

To solve this problem while continuing to reap the benefits of mass production, Ford's great rival at General Motors during the 1920s, Alfred Sloan, devised a strategy that has been described as a 'volume and diversity' approach (Boyer and Freyssenet 2002). Sloan's idea was that manufacturers can achieve economies of scale by making invisible sub-assemblies using the same components, even as they give consumers a sense of customization by differentiating the visible parts bolted onto the product at the end of the manufacturing process (see Figure 11.8). Car buyers can see, for example, whether a particular vehicle comes with a sunroof, but the brand name of its carburettor (for example, Holley or Edelbrock) will not be immediately apparent to them. The practice of standardizing for as long as possible before differentiating as late as possible has at various times been referred to as deferred differentiation, 'platform strategy', or 'postponement' (Kumar and Wilson 2007). The advantage of this approach is that it allows manufacturers to combine scale with

+ Deferred differentiation
Manufacturing strategy that combines economies of scale and product diversity by standardizing inputs for as long as possible in the production process before introducing adaptations as late as possible.

diversity. Moreover, it is easier for companies to manage stocks if their production system is based a deferred differentiation logic where generic modules are being stored instead of sub-assemblies that are specific to just one model (Christopher 2005). Indeed, the only real problem with this approach is how hard it can be to balance factory workloads when lines are not being differentiated at the same stage of their respective production processes (Ko and Hu 2008). The production engineers who overcome such mathematical challenges are the quiet heroes of international production.

Sloan's ideas drove many of the consolidations that have marked international business since the 1920s. His platform strategy would become particularly widespread in the automotive industry, where famous takeovers such as Volkswagen's purchase of Spain's SEAT Motor Company in the 1970s or Renault's more recent acquisition of Nissan were designed to save money by rationalizing factories that had previously manufactured different chassis (platforms). On the surface, VW and SEAT cars, like Renault and Nissan cars, continued to look different, satisfying consumers' desire for choice. Most shared the same platform underneath, however, enabling manufacturers to achieve economies of scale.

The Fordist mass production model also had problems because of its assembly line organization. First, disruptions to operations anywhere along the line (for example, if a workstation ran out of parts) would shut down the whole process. To offset this risk, Fordist manufacturers tended to carry large inventories of parts, an expensive undertaking. Secondly, the Fordist factory's lack of flexibility meant that it was not particularly suited to a world where MNEs were increasingly expected to serve diverse customer bases. It was largely in reaction to these challenges that a new industrial model, called 'Toyotaism', became the dominant international manufacturing paradigm from the 1970s onwards.

The Toyota Production System was built on the idea that, contrary to received wisdom, volume manufacturing can coincide with product flexibility—as long as there is minimal uncertainty about the level and timing of factory flows ('throughput'). The goal is for assembly lines to develop the ability to 'handle different models and specifications without missing a beat' (Caulkin 2007). This was achieved by getting staff members to adopt what the Japanese call a *kaizen* (continuous improvement) attitude, based on a search for a 'permanent reduction in costs' (Boyer and Freyssenet 2002). The Toyotaist approach was bottom up, the idea being that the people actually responsible for productio n operations were the ones in the best position to figure out how to increase efficiency. Employees would meet regularly in 'quality circles' to discuss process improvements. In a world featuring increasingly knowledgeable consumers, quality became a factor in all industrial models— but none more so than Toyotaism, dominated by a Total Quality Management (TQM) philosophy targeting zero output defects.

TQM was an ambitious goal that firms usually achieved only through a combination of approaches. The first was that contractors needed to audit themselves and/or their

Figure 11.8
Deferred differentiation in a Chinese restaurant kitchen. Customers get different dishes but the restaurant owner also achieves some economies of scale.

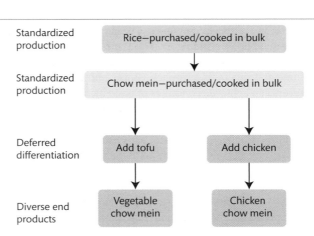

suppliers. One of the leading systems in this area is 'Six Sigmas'. First developed by Motorola in the 1980s, it involves asking strong managers to improve business processes by establishing thresholds for quantitative defects and keeping statistics on performance. Corporate controls of this kind can be relatively difficult to implement, however. For cultural reasons, not everyone cooperates with quality controls as readily as Japanese employees traditionally have done. An inspector may not always be fully welcomed in the workplace, since it might not be in people's interest to share all the information that they have about how their roles are designed. Inspections are also expensive to run, and in some cases (i.e. where a TQM approach is supposed to be implemented throughout a supply chain), it is unclear whether the contractor or the supplier is supposed to bear the extra cost. Lastly, internal inspectors may be incompetent or subject to a conflict of interests.

One solution has been the creation of autonomous quality assessment organizations. The leader in this area is the Geneva-based International Organization for Standardization (www.iso.org), often referred to as the ISO. This international organization has determined a total of more than 16,500 standards covering all aspects of quality, notably relating to management systems (covered in ISO 9001) and environmental performance (ISO 14001). Nowadays, most MNEs are prepared to enact the changes they need to receive ISO certification because they want to show stakeholders and customers that they are truly committed to quality. ISO's success is a sign of how quality attitudes have spread since the 1970s, when leading Japanese MNEs first began marketing quality as a key feature of their international profile.

Aside from quality and in addition to the 'just-in-time' and 'lean' principles discussed above, another noteworthy aspect of the Toyota Production System was its revolutionary inventory management process. Instead of ordering supplies based on predictions of future demand, a Toyotaist prime contractor would ask subcontractors to replenish stocks at a rate defined by real customer demand. In this *kanban* (automatic signalling) logic, supplies to each level of the value chain are 'pulled' by the next level downstream, and ultimately by orders from end users. The system can be opposed to one where replenishment is 'pushed' by factory schedules, which are poor predictors of flows in firms serving volatile global markets. *Kanban* prevents the distortions ('bullwhip effects') that Fordist supply chains cause when factory production volumes are misjudged. This happened, for instance, during the 2008–9 crisis (Glatzel et al. 2009) when the world was treated to the spectacle of thousands of unsold new cars being warehoused in ports from Long Beach (California) to Malmo (Sweden). By stopping surplus production from piling up, *kanban* keeps inventory costs down. Conversely, in those instances where supplies run short, *kanban* reduces bottlenecks and delays. Much of Japanese companies' international success has been attributed to their ability to run 'lean' supply chains.

Despite Toyotaism's success since the 1980s, it would be wrong to assume that this is the only successful industrial model possible. Depending on a company's objectives, other models will succeed in other circumstances. The Dell case study shows a firm that has been extremely successful replacing a traditional manufacturing function with an assembly/logistics focus. Also noteworthy is the industrial model developed by the Swedish carmaker Volvo, which specializes in top-of-the-range products and stresses worker knowledge more than output volumes or product diversity. Against the backdrop of Sweden's commitment to lifelong adult learning, the company created a hybrid production system called 'Volvoism'. The idea here is to combine a standard 'platform strategy', in which Volvo vehicles largely share the same chassis as their Ford group counterparts, with an enrichment of tasks. Workers are encouraged to raise their general skill levels by doing a range of jobs over the course of the year—a polyvalent approach that is the exact opposite of Fordist (and to a lesser extent, Toyotaist) specialization. As long as they are accompanied by efficient sourcing and logistics strategies, different industrial models can be implemented in response to many of today's international manufacturing challenges.

<aside>
Thinking point

Is quality a cultural topic?
</aside>

<aside>
Thinking point

Is there ever just one best way of organizing an international supply chain at a given point in time?
</aside>

<aside>
+ Polyvalent
Ability to perform many different functions—i.e. the opposite of specialization.
</aside>

Logistics and physical operations

Clearly, a vertically integrated company that makes all its own components faces different pressures from one that outsources everything and whose only real physical activity involves assembling or simply branding finished products built by other companies. For many MNEs, the reality lies between these two extremes, since they will run some strategic operations in-house and outsource the rest. The ability to link the whole physical process via logistics is therefore crucial.

Logistics features at all levels of the supply chain, from initial inputs to the recycling of used packaging ('reverse logistics'). Global competition means that deliveries of raw materials, components, and finished products must be quicker and more flexible than ever. This puts enormous pressure on logistics professionals. Sometimes the demands are commercial in nature, coming from retailers who require their suppliers to replenish outlets that might be scattered worldwide, or from knowledgeable online shoppers who force companies to compete on delivery performance. On other occasions, the problem that logistics is being asked to resolve is production-related. This can involve the replenishment of globally dispersed assembly operations; the vulnerability of many supply chains to political risk or natural catastrophes; and the unfortunate way that inventory often accumulates in the form of finished products, where it is the most expensive (Christopher 2005). It is only through top logistics performance that international manufacturers can meet these challenges.

Most MNEs are not capable of this, however. Logistics requires not only physical capabilities but also a great deal of specific knowledge, about geography and infrastructure but also about documentary and regulatory requirements, customs administration, and banking practices. Sometimes a company will take responsibility for a shipment on a cost, insurance, and freight (CIF) basis. On other occasions, it will leave these tasks to its counterpart and simply make or take delivery of the goods on a free on board (FOB) basis. This is an important distinction, not only because it reflects a firm's confidence in its ability to organize logistics but because each of these formats (CIF or FOB) implies different legal rights and obligations. Documents like 'bills of lading' have evolved to convey information about the nature of goods in transit, carriage details, and above all transfer of ownership procedures. Specialist customs house brokers and freight forwarders 'clear' goods through border controls on MNEs' account, paying duties where required and organizing further transportation from the point of arrival to final destination. Bank 'trade finance' departments offer an array of financial instruments, one example being 'letters of credit' reassuring sellers that they will be paid once buyers or their agents receive the ownership documents for the goods in question. Logistics in the broadest sense of the term refers to a very wide range of 'trade operations' (see Online Resource Centre, extension material 11.4) that are just as important as the physical movement of goods. This explains, for instance, the attention paid to reviving trade finance at the April 2009 G20 summit in London. At a very basic level, international business would be impossible without the vast number of trade intermediaries exercising their professions worldwide.

> Go to the ORC 🌐

Indeed, it is precisely because logistics are so complicated that MNEs increasingly outsource their needs in this area to specialist 'third party logistics providers'. The largest of these '3PLs' (German firms DHL Logistics and Schenker along with Japan's Nippon Express) offer a full range of logistics services (see Case Study 11.3). With their ability to consolidate different parties' shipments, they can transport larger volumes, thereby achieving economies of scale that an MNE working alone could not match. Moreover, patchy transportation infrastructure in some of the regions currently experiencing the fastest growth in trade (China and Eastern Europe) requires specialist knowledge that few companies possess (Rushton and Walker 2007).

Logistics affect MNEs' upstream organization in different ways. One is by enabling 'centralized inventories'. Many companies have taken to storing their global stocks of semi-finished and finished products in just a few key regional distribution centres. Examples include German chemicals firm BASF's central staging platform for Asia in Singapore, or US office equipment-maker Katun's centre for South American operations in the Uruguayan free trade zone. This system has the advantage of saving on overheads, but it also increases the distance between the MNE's storage facilities and consumer markets, potentially slowing delivery times. To compensate, many companies have organized with their customers the same kinds of joint information systems that they operate with their suppliers. This too is a logistics solution.

An analogous development is the rise of 'focused factories', where companies specialize each of their plants worldwide in a specific production. One example is the climate control plant that automotive supplier Visteon has built at Dubnica in Slovakia, the only unit in the group producing this kind of sub-assembly. As Chapter 8 explained, the advantage of this approach is much higher economies of scale at the factory level. On the other hand, it also causes longer lead times and complicates packaging and communications. This is particularly problematic when the MNE is trying to serve a global customer making large consolidated orders for goods manufactured in different focused factories located worldwide (see Figure 11.9). In this case, the rationale for the MNE's plant location decisions must be juggled against the logistics constraints that they create.

Whereas plant locations used to be determined solely by factors like proximity to resources or markets, and by the various considerations that Vernon described in his Product Life Cycle theory (see Chapter 4), companies now situate their units in light of a whole range of strategic criteria, including knowledge spillover possibilities, host government attitudes, but most importantly the size and importance of the market(s) that a plant is being asked to service. To a certain extent, the mission that an MNE attributes to a particular production unit will depend on where its output is sold. Some plants serve only the countries or regions where they are located. Others send their output globally, either to sister MNE units or directly to customers (Dicken 2007). A key distinction must also be made between plants that merely assemble modules produced elsewhere, and others that manufacture their own generic goods. The former are cheaper and less capital intensive, and can therefore be dispersed relatively easily. This differs from big manufacturing plants, which by their very nature cost more and are therefore less likely to be replicated worldwide. The terms 'manufacturing' or 'production' are often applied wrongly in so far as they refer to different things. Precise use of terminology is always a crucial skill for an international manager.

+ **Free trade zone**
Tariff-free 'export processing zones' that many countries have set up to attract industrial activity. Little or no taxes are paid as long as the items being assembled or temporarily stored here are re-exported.

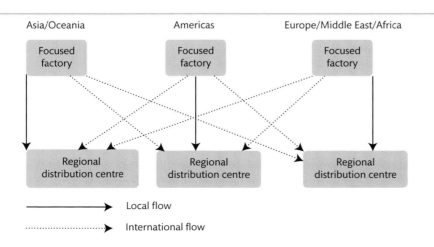

Figure 11.9
Complicated logistics in modern manufacturing.

Challenges and choices

→ Nowhere in international business is the contradiction between global and local viewpoints more apparent than in MNEs' supply chain management. A company's financial health can be severely compromised or substantially improved by its production location decisions. Clearly, it is an advantage for such activities to be situated in places where factor inputs (labour, resources) are comparatively inexpensive. Other considerations can be just as important, including a site's logistics, government relations, knowledge management, or coordination problems. Because MNEs incur most of their costs upstream, getting the location decision right is crucial.

→ Another major challenge for companies is determining to what extent they should skew their international value chain to suit the strategic needs of their upstream or downstream departments. The two areas have fundamentally opposing orientations (standardization versus adaptation) and in most MNEs the group executive must spend an enormous amount of time juggling their interests. It is impossible to overstate the amount of tension that exists in most companies between production and marketing specialists.

Chapter Summary

The chapter divided the international value chain's upstream portion into three sections. The importance of the first topic, knowledge management, reflects the realization that the success of many MNEs and national economies derives from their innovation efforts. The second section focused on supply chain management, specifically international outsourcing and different kinds of supplier relations. The final section explored international manufacturing, starting with varying industrial models, each of which emphasizes different principles (like specialization for Fordism or quality for Toyotaism). The chapter concluded with an overview of physical operations, drawing a connection between companies' logistics possibilities and plant location decisions.

Case Study 11.3

International transportation

The handling and/or delivery of goods and services is both a key driver of international business and a mirror of general macro-economic conditions at a particular time. Before the 2008–9 global crisis, liberalized trade regimes, along with fragmented global supply chains and the trend towards focused factories, had led to an explosion in the physical trade of both finished goods and components. This state of affairs strained many countries' transportation capacities, owing in part to the fact that many goods manufactured in Asia are consumed in the USA and the EU. To carry greater loads, shippers needed ever-larger vessels. In turn, this saturated the

loading and unloading capacities of ports worldwide. Governments invested heavily in infrastructure to address a problem that manifested, for instance, in delays at many Chinese harbours. Similar congestion was experienced at the US–Canada border, where increased security measures by the Americans slowed border crossings. Convinced that the main challenge they faced was congestion, transporters reacted by major productivity and capacity investments, purchasing, for instance, bigger and better cranes to roll containers on and off ocean freighters as quickly as possible. With hindsight, this turned out to be the wrong analysis.

The recession exposed the tremendous over-capacity that had built up in the transportation sector, as it had in so many others. Trading volumes plummeted, leading within a few short months to the spectacle of rows of enormous cargo ships lying dormant in English rivers (Milner 2008) and off Singapore harbour. Vessel charter rates crumbled on London's Baltic Exchange, the market where global bulk freight is priced. In turn, this brought many ship-owners to the brink of bankruptcy. Expensive loading equipment recently installed in ports from Hamburg to Shanghai lay dormant. Some feared that the optimism that had animated the transportation sector for more than a decade was just another example of an economic bubble.

Nor was the recession the only problem that transporters faced. Most transportation modes are extremely vulnerable to fuel prices, which fell during the recession but are likely to rise again over the long term due to the effects of resource depletion. Logistics companies have tried to meet this challenge in different ways. One example is UPS's development of a 'green fleet' of delivery vans, some of which are expected to run on hydrogen fuel cell technology or hybrid electricity systems. Another is Maersk's installation of waste heat recovery systems on its ships to save engine power. Much greater technological innovation will be necessary in the future, however, particularly for the least fuel-efficient of all transportation modes—air cargo. Irrespective of its immediate prospects, this sector is predicted to suffer over the longer term due to the knock-on effects of the credit crunch and higher fuel prices. Even the International Air Transport Association (IATA) accepts that air cargo will experience slower future growth than its rival, ocean container freight. Airliners will try to save costs by easing the burdensome paperwork associated with air cargo (up to thirty-eight documents per shipment), but this is a marginal step. For routine port-to-port transportation, ships and trains have a much brighter future than planes.

The future for road haulage is mixed. On the one hand, costs are high and expected to rise further because of fuel and tax increases. On the other hand, trucks are a flexible means of transportation and can be used to satisfy the growing demand from the main transportation customers (international manufacturers and large retailers) for integrated, end-to-end solutions. As such, they often figure in the product portfolio of dedicated third party logistics specialists, who, above and beyond the full range of transportation modes, are usually expected to provide a number of additional trade services. These usually include warehousing, customs house brokerage, freight forwarding, order tracking, and consolidation/deconsolidation facilities. Only the largest companies can afford to be present in all these areas. This explains the succession of synergy-seeking mergers and acquisitions that the transportation sector experienced over the past decade—one headline example being Deutsche Post's £3.7 billion acquisition of British giant Exel in 2005. At the same time, the sector remains highly fragmented, not only for historical reasons (states' historically strong presence in this area) but also because the necessary competencies vary widely worldwide.

It bears repeating that before the 2008 credit crunch, most of the growth in international trade occurred in emerging or transition economies, where the transportation infrastructure is of variable quality. In China, for instance, initial industrial expansion in coastal cities offering easy access to modern ports has been followed by growth in inland regions that are much harder to reach. Accessing more remote destinations requires adapted modes (like barges) and good relations with government officials. In this most globalized of industries, local knowledge remains crucial.

Case study questions

1. How might rising fuel costs and climate change issues affect the future of international transportation?
2. What will the long-term effects of the credit crunch be on the transportation sector? How, in turn, will this affect MNEs' organization of their upstream operations?
3. How much further consolidation can be expected from third party logistics specialists?

Ports overloaded by the explosion in trade during the early 2000s suffered from overcapacities in the wake of the credit crunch (Photodisc).

Discussion questions

1. What can governments do to encourage national research and development?

2. To what extent is global outsourcing sustainable in its current form?

3. Can Japanese *keiretsu* supply chains be replicated in other business cultures?

4. How has the 2008–9 crisis affected international manufacturing?

5. What are the strategic dangers facing a company like Dell whose entire production system relies on logistics performance?

References

Boyer, R. and Freyssenet, M. (2002). *Productive Models: The Conditions of Profitability*. Basingstoke: Palgrave Macmillan.

Brickman, C., and Ungerman, D. (2008). 'Climate Change and Supply Chain Management', July, www.mckinseyquarterly.com (accessed 28 Nov. 2008).

Caulkin, S. (2007). 'Toyota's Never-to-be-Repeated All-Star Production', 2 Dec., www.guardian.co.uk (accessed 20 June 2008).

Christopher, M. (2005). *Logistics and Supply Chain Management: Creating Value-Added Networks*. 3rd edn. Harlow: Prentice-Hall.

Das, A., and Jayaram, J. (2007). 'A Socio-Technical Perspective on Manufacturing System Synergies', *International Journal of Production Research*, 45/1.

Davenport, T., and Prusak, L. (1998). *Working Knowledge: How Organizations Manage what they Know*. Boston: Harvard Business School.

Dicken, P. (2007). *Global Shift: Mapping the Changing Contours of the World*. 5th edn. London: Sage Publications.

Duanmu, J.-L. (2006). 'Country of Origin Effects on Knowledge Transfers from MNEs to their Country Suppliers: An Exploratory Investigation', in F. Fai and E. Morgan (eds.), *Managerial Issues in International Business*. Basingstoke: Palgrave MacMillan.

The Economist (2005). 'The Rise of Nearshoring', 1 Dec., www.economist.com (accessed 9 June 2009).

European Commission (2007). 'Monitoring Industrial Research: The 2007 EU Industrial R&D Investment Scorecard', http://iri.jrc.ec.europa.eu (accessed 20 June 2008).

Eurostat (2007). 'Research & Development in the EU: Preliminary Results', 12 Jan., http://ec.europa.eu/eurostat (accessed 20 June 2008).

Fairclough, G. (2007). 'Fueling China Auto Parts', *Wall Street Journal-Europe*, 5 Dec., p. 20.

Financial Times (2007). 'Transport and Logistics', insert, 27 Mar.

Friedman, T. (2005). 'Global is Good', *Guardian*, 21 Apr.

Glatzel, C., Helmcke, S., and Wine, J. (2009). 'Building a Flexible Supply Chain for Uncertain Times', Mar., www.mckinsey.quarterly.com (accessed 22 Mar. 2009).

Harland, C., Knight, L. and Cousins, P. (2004). 'Supply Chain Relationships', in S. New and R. Westbrook (eds.), *Understanding Supply Chains: Concepts, Critiques and Futures*. London: Oxford University Press.

Hill, A. (2006). 'A Theory of Evolution for Outsourcers', 26 June, www.ft.com (accessed 19 Nov. 2008).

Ietto-Gillies, G. (2005). *Transnational Corporations and International Production: Concepts, Theories and Effects*. Cheltenham: Edward Elgar.

Jaruzelski, B., Dehoff, K. and Bordia, R. (2006). 'Smart Spenders: The Global Innovation 1000, Strategy + Business', www.strategy-business.com (accessed 20 June 2008).

Ko, J., and Hu, S. (2008). 'Balancing of Manufacturing Systems with Complex Configurations for Delayed Product Differentiation', *International Journal of Production Research*, 46/15 (Aug.).

Kotabe, M., Parente, R., and Murray, J. (2007). 'Antecedents and Outcomes of Modular Production in the Brazilian Automobile Industry: A Grounded Theory Approach', *Journal of International Business Studies*, 38/1 (Jan.).

Kumar, S., and Wilson, J. (2007). 'A Manufacturing Decision Framework for Minimizing Inventory Costs of a Configurable Off-Shored Product Using Postponement', *International Journal of Production Research*, 45/17 (Sept.).

Milner, M. (2008). 'Price of Sending Freight by Sea Sinks under Weight of Slowdown', *Guardian*, 27 Nov.

Mortished, C. (2008). 'In a Supply Chain, even the Smallest Parts Matter', *The Times*, 19 Nov., p. 63.

Naim, M., Disney, S. and Towill, D. (2004). 'Supply Chain Dynamics', in S. New and R. Westbrook (eds.), *Understanding Supply Chains: Concepts, Critiques and Futures*. London: Oxford University Press.

Nassimbeni, G. (2004). 'Supply Chains: A Network Perspective', in S. New and R. Westbrook (eds.), *Understanding Supply Chains: Concepts, Critiques and Futures*. London: Oxford University Press.

Nonaka, I., and Takeuchi, H. (1995). *The Knowledge Creating Company*. New York: Oxford University Press.

OECD (2006a). 'China will Become the World's Second Highest Investor in R&D by the End of 2006', www.oecd.org (accessed 19 Nov. 2008).

OECD (2006b). 'OECD Science, Technology and Industry, Outlook 2006, Highlights', www.oecd.org (accessed 19 Nov. 2008).

OECD (2007). 'Science, Technology and Industry Scoreboard 2007: Briefing Note on the United States', www.oecd.org (accessed 19 Nov. 2008).

Phan, T., Baughn, C., Ngo, M., Neupert, K. (2006). 'Knowledge Acquisition from Foreign Parents to International Joint Ventures: An Empirical Study in Vietnam', *International Business Review*, 15/5 (Oct.).

Prashantham, S., and McNaughton, R. (2006). 'Facilitation of Links between Multinational Subsidiaries and SMEs: The STAC Initiative', *International Business Review*, 15/5 (Oct.).

Puech, R. (2001). *One Day in the Life of a Tyre (Un jour dans la vie d'un pneu)*, Paris: Capa Presse TV.

Rugman, A., and D'Cruz, J. (2000). *Multinationals as Flagship Firms: Regional Business Networks*. London: Oxford University Press.

Rushton, A., and Walker, S. (2007). *International Logistics and Supply Chain Outsourcing: From Local to Global*. London: Kogan Page.

Sako, M. (2006). *Shifting Boundaries of the Company: Japanese Company—Japanese Labour*. Oxford: Oxford University Press.

Solis, M. (2003). 'On the Myth of the Keiretsu Network: Japanese Electronics in North America', *Business and Politics*, 5/3.

Tabrizi, B., and Tseng, M. (2007). *Transformation through Global Value Chains: Taking Advantage of Business Synergies in the United States and China*. Stanford, CA: Stanford University Press.

Thomas, K. (2007). 'Outsourcing is More than just Saving Money', 9 May, www.ft.com (accessed 19 Nov. 2008).

Unel, B. (2008). 'R&D Spillovers through Trade in a Panel of OECD Industries', *International Trade and Economic Development*, 17/1 (Mar.).

Wadhwa, S., Saxena, A., and Chan, F. T. S. (2008). 'Framework for Flexibility in Dynamic Supply Chain Management', *International Journal of Production Research*, 46/6 (Mar.).

Webb, T. (2009). 'Grass of Home Grows Greener as UK Firms Discover "In-sourcing", *Observer*, Business and Media section, 8 Mar., p. 6.

WHO (2006). World Health Organization, 'Access to AIDS Medicine Stumbles on Trade Rules', *Bulletin of the World Health Organization*, 84/5 (May).

Further research

McKinsey Quarterly online review, 'Operations' section, www.mckinseyquarterly.com/Operations.

McKinsey is a leading consultancy firm that operates an Internet journal featuring articles of great value to readers interested in issues such as international outsourcing, manufacturing performance, product development, purchasing, supply chain and logistics. For example, a September 2006 article entitled 'Understanding International Supply Chain Risk' reproduced a survey of 3,712 executives from a worldwide sample of companies, providing a detailed ranking of participants' various upstream concerns. An August 2008 article entitled 'Managing Global Supply Chains' detailed the rising international risks that MNEs face upstream (first and foremost being the complexity of products/services), as well as their problems in dealing with them. A more macro-level article from September 2008 entitled 'Time to Rethink Offshoring' gave a well-documented argument that rising wage costs in some emerging economies, combined with higher energy prices, has eroded the advantages of offshoring for many MNEs. New items are uploaded frequently, and there is also a large archive on hand. Readers should consult McKinsey about registration possibilities.

Braunerhjelm, P., and Feldman, M. (2006). *Cluster Genesis: Technology-Based Industrial Development*. Oxford: Oxford University Press.

Academics increasingly recognize regional clusters of related firms and organizations as a leading driver of economic growth and innovation. However, there is relatively little understanding of how such clusters first come into existence. The book focuses on the origins of clusters, including Silicon Valley in California with its focus on computing and more recently green technology; biotechnology in China; and information and communications technology in Ireland.

Online Resource Centre

Visit the Online Resource Centre that accompanies this book to read more information relating to international production: www.oxfordtextbooks.co.uk/orc/sitkin_bowen/

12 International Marketing

Overview

The chapter focuses on the issues for international companies of pull and push marketing, on how and when companies decide on the standardization or adaptation of their products, and on issues of growing importance, including ethical and green marketing, business-to-business marketing, branding, and Internet marketing. It details the factors that can lead to success and failure in international expansion and international marketing and indicates the challenges and choices for an MNE in its value chain. The influence and impact of some of these factors can be predicted and optimized if the MNE takes a measured and considered approach to its international marketing strategy.

Section I: International marketing choices

Pull versus push marketing

International marketing strategy and marketing mix

Seven types of cultural adaptation

Section II: Issues in international marketing

Business-to-business (B2B) marketing

Ethical or green marketing

International branding

Internet marketing

Learning Objectives

After reading this chapter, you should be able to:

✦ understand a range of key issues related to international marketing

✦ recognize the strategies and phases for marketing overseas by MNEs

✦ assess standardization and adaptation in international marketing

✦ understand the impact of culture on international marketing and advertising

✦ evaluate key developments in international marketing, including Internet marketing

Case Study 12.1

Honda advertising in India

For MNEs aspiring to achieve global reach, a real challenge is choosing whether or not to adapt their products to local circumstances and markets. One of the least expensive ways of doing this is by adjusting the product's image through advertising.

Honda has an innovative approach to advertising, especially on television. Behind its keynote slogan 'The Power of Dreams', it has launched many products, starting originally with motorbikes, before moving to standard automobiles like other carmakers (cars, trucks, sports utility vehicles, and people carriers) and extending to jet aircraft. Consumers worldwide recognize the company as much for its advertising as for the goods it advertises; it has strong international images for its brands.

The 'Choir' advertisements launched in 2006 to publicize the Honda Civic, a small city car, were innovative because of the way they associated a relaxing mode of cultural expression—a choir—with the sounds made by an automobile, thus reducing its more mechanical aspects. The advertisements were reported to have been downloaded internationally three million times in the month following the launch; the iPod version even got into iTunes' Top 50 chart (Adlab 2006). As for the micro-site, a record 679,000 unique visitors were reported—an exposure that led to Honda's highest ever test-drive bookings.

Honda's extensive range of products includes, at the less expensive end, a series of scooters. Clearly market conditions and consumer demand for scooters vary around the world; Honda's approach to this product marketing is equally varied. For the European market in 2002–3, there was a much greater emphasis on high-grade technical specifications, with Honda's 125cc scooter emphasizing the fact that it was outfitted with fuel-injection equipment, designed to improve fuel efficiency.

Honda has taken a different approach to the selling of very colourful motor scooters, the Hero Honda, into the Indian market. Among the range of about six different scooters, one was branded as 'Hero Honda Pleasure', aimed directly at young female customers. The advert emphasized weddings, children playing in a park, and the independence of women and hooked into the slogan: 'Why should boys have all the fun?'

There is no doubting the success of this range of motor scooters: in 2009 Hero Honda had about 56 per cent market share in India, with sales of over 3.3 million per year, and high monthly sales growth—for February 2009, it was 12 per cent. These successful sales figures are partly accounted for by the advertising campaign that demonstrated a clever approach to a particular segment of the Indian market. Large MNEs, such as Honda, are capable of targeting a range of markets and segments through the massive purchasing power that they wield in their international marketing strategies.

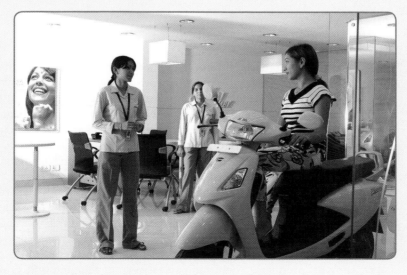

Hero Honda advertisement. The clever marketing campaign for Hero Honda scooters resulted in strong sales (reproduced with the kind permission of Honda).

Introduction

For many companies, the new markets for their goods are international so their corporate marketing strategies have to consider the implications of moving from their original domestic markets to developments beyond their own borders. International marketing is as vital for smaller companies as for massive MNEs. For all of these, their international expansion strategies will be driven by pull or push marketing.

The concepts of pull and push marketing are extensions of views introduced in Chapter 9 where companies' structures and operations are seen as being developed from different approaches to internationalization. The pull or push orientation reflects the attitude of the company as the consumer demand for products and services has expanded on a global scale. International marketing is designed to ensure that global consumers' needs and desires are met and satisfied.

Part of the international expansion of the marketing function of companies is related to the development of and fascination with brands. Brands are global assets used by marketers to differentiate their products, services, and images from their competitors. In the scramble for international market share, companies seek to maximize their advantages from the economies of standardization and the specificities of adaptation; branding, ethical trading, and use of the Internet are the most recent differentiators.

The first section explores the challenges and choices that international companies make in relation to the marketing imperatives of pull and push approaches, standardization and adaptation. These choices are made by managers who consciously seek to maximize their companies' advantages internationally, as well as domestically.

Section I: International marketing choices

When managers market internationally, they face a spectrum of strategic choices. They take decisions within the context of the key forces that shape the international corporate environment: the expansion of world trade, the growth and enlargement of trading blocs, and the staggeringly rapid development of new communications networks (including the Internet and IT communications). The way in which these choices are made helps to identify different kinds of international marketing effort.

Pull versus push marketing

The overriding approach taken in this chapter is to consider the marketing of goods and services from the perspective of where each international company locates itself on the spectrum of pull marketing or push marketing, as shown in Figure 12.1. These concepts relate in part to the pull and push corporate structures discussed in Chapter 9.

Pull marketing is when a company reacts to signals from the market. Companies that undertake pull marketing are generally more accurate in the methods they use to carry out market research, are likely to face more competition, tend to offer lower prices, and are unlikely to benefit from any first-mover advantage. By contrast, push marketing is generally more risky internationally. It occurs when a company sells goods that are relatively unheard of and usually undertakes less accurate market research. If the new product is right for the market, it can be launched at a premium price and, hopefully, has the potential to gain very large market share.

In the 1950s and 1960s, the Japanese were considered to be the key producers of 'copycat' products. Their companies were developing and growing beneath the shadows of US industry and were known as imitators of whatever was produced in the Western world. In general, Japanese companies produced copies of already

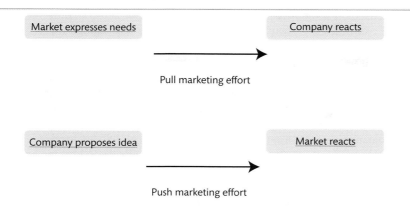

Figure 12.1
Pull versus push
marketing.

Market expresses needs → Company reacts

Pull marketing effort

Company proposes idea → Market reacts

Push marketing effort

established items, including motorbikes and cars, electrical equipment, and plastic products. This was very much the era of pull marketing for Japanese industry. Later in the twentieth century, Japanese companies moved towards push marketing as they became great innovators, particularly in the area of electronics, with products such as the most successful format for video recorders (VCRs)—JVC's VHS system—and the Sony Walkman.

An example of push marketing is the highly innovative approach taken by Apple in developing cutting-edge products in the i-range, e.g. iPod, iTunes, iMusic, and iPhones. Although Apple was not necessarily the absolute first into these developments or products, its approach to the customer was such that it was thought to be a key innovator. Apple always emphasizes style and innovation, and this has often paid dividends in its niche sales. With the launch of the iPhone, for example, Apple was not only innovative but managed to secure massive sales in the USA and in subsequent markets. In July 2007 in the USA, the iPhone was reputed to have sold nearly 500,000 units in the first weekend and 1 million within three months. (By 2009, worldwide sales had reached 3.79 million in 81 countries but had started to slow (Davies 2008; Keen 2009).) In the UK and Germany, as the iPhone was launched in the autumn of 2007, there were changes to Apple's international strategy, in particular locking customers into one phone network provider. The customer response to this, however, was to complain and then to subvert the changed strategy; a small industry for 'unlocking iPhones' was born. The risk of international push marketing is that companies are unsure of the likely outcomes.

Standardization versus adaptation

Few companies operate entirely at one end of the spectrum of standardization (most closely related to the push imperative) or adaptation (most closely related to pull marketing). Part of what differentiates each choice is the extent to which a company seeks to sell the same product or service worldwide or adapts its products or services to the local market. The implications of the standardization versus adaptation approach have also been explored in previous chapters.

Within the marketing function, this same dilemma must also be faced. For example, the standardization of products refers to the extent to which a company can sell the same product in its domestic and international markets, whatever their location and size. Among the prime advocates of such an approach has been Microsoft, which has endeavoured to capitalize on economies of scale and to ensure that only one system is used on personal computers (PCs). Although Microsoft has faced a number of challenges to its top position in the world as far as PC and operating systems are concerned, its intention to dominate the computing world has been clear since the late 1980s (Coyle 1998).

+ Deferred
differentiation
Manufacturing
strategy that combines
economies of scale and
product diversity by
standardizing inputs for
as long as possible in
the production process
before introducing
adaptations as late as
possible.

Thinking point

Why are
cars usually
standardized as
much as possible
in the production
process?

MNEs focused on standardization apply the principle of deferred differentiation (see Chapter 11) so that they postpone as long as possible any change from a globalized standard product (or service) to the various local adaptations that may be recommended at the regional or local level. The countervailing trend to standardization is adaptation (or customization). This approach requires that products and services are adapted for each market, meeting the particular needs of customers. The previous chapter referred to deferred differentiation as the way in which MNEs' production function attempts to address the scale/scope dilemma; glocalization is the downstream version of this international management approach: the idea of 'think global, act local'.

In the early years of the twenty-first century, 'glocalization' became the claim of a worldwide bank, HSBC. Using the tag line 'the world's local bank', HSBC stressed its global reach simultaneously with its understanding of local and national norms and cultural behaviour. Its advertising played on the dangers of bank representatives who did not fully understand local cultures and were liable to offend local business people. Obviously, the HSBC representatives were seen as being sensitive to national cultures so that the bank and possessing local knowledge. Similarly, Danone, the French food products MNE, stressed their 'worldwide business with a local presence' (*Outlook Journal* 2003). This meant that the company was prepared to have its products marketed as national rather than French brands, even to the extent of Americanizing its name in the USA to Dannon. The MNE stressed that its international marketing strategy was driven not by the French headquarters but by the needs of local markets and the inventiveness of subsidiaries (*Outlook Journal* 2003).

Another that helps to determine a company's approach to the standardization–adaptation issue the Boston Consulting Group's growth share international marketing matrix explaining why companies market products differently in different countries, depending on their stage of development. Whereas Vernon's 'Product Life Cycle' theory (see Chapter 4) has noted that an MNE will move its main focus of production from more developed to the less developed countries, as the product itself moves from being a new to an older product, this chapter looks at the role of the product depending on the state of the market. The Boston Consulting Group's (BCG) matrix— see Figure 12.2—is applied to international marketing as the MNE's products reach different lifecycle stages in national markets around the world.

A modern example of the use of the growth share matrix is in the communications revolution led by mobile phone developments. For a company such as Apple, its 'standard products'—computers, laptops, music players—are located in the 'cash cows' box, generating major proportions of revenue from the established OECD markets; such products are classified as 'stars' in the growing Asian markets and as 'question marks' in the more slowly developing markets of Africa. For Apple, the 'dogs' category will be achieved in the OECD markets when its older products are being run down or possibly got rid of completely. The growth share matrix provides a way of understanding that well-established MNEs will permit certain products, and sometimes entire product divisions, to be sold off once they have moved from the 'cash cow' box towards the 'dogs' category. An MNE can also find that its misunderstanding of the market for a particular product can undermine its international marketing strategy.

Marketing errors and failures

+ Ethnocentric
Company's replication
in the international
market of the way
in which it markets
its products and
services in its domestic
market—this approach
has worked well at
home so it does not
need to be changed.

The successes and failures of international marketing strategies are likely to be more expensive than domestic ones. There are a number of ways in which MNEs can make poor decisions when addressing their international marketing dilemmas. There can be such errors as misinterpretation of signals, whether cultural, social, or economic, MNE managers' projection of their own tastes, and an ethnocentric view of consumers' product preferences.

Inside business

Robert Dennis, Advisory Board Member, Zafesoft

Zafesoft, a small hi-tech company operating in the field of digital information security, faces particular challenges in the international marketing of its security solutions. As a niche vertical player, it needs to make decisions on how it generates leads and how it delivers solutions to customers of different sizes. Zafesoft has to be tough in its approach in order to be competitive with its larger rivals.

Zafesoft is a software start-up company focused on the security of digital information in office documents. Zafesoft targets companies that deal with health care information, financial information, other proprietary and commercially valuable information, where the loss or compromise of this information can result in the loss of privacy and/or illegal financial transactions (credit cards, and so on) or loss of competitive advantag e. Companies that outsource their operations, for example, to Asia, Eastern Europe, or countries in the Middle East, are especially vulnerable to these risks. Zafesoft markets its software solutions through personal contacts, by directly approaching and getting face time with chief security officers, chief technology officers, or chief administrative officers, and through vendor partnerships.

The company has dedicated teams that cover a particular region or set of accounts, and, while there are clear divisions between sales and account management in terms of the job function, the overall goal is the same. Marketing efforts are global and vertical, the goal being to generate warm leads that can be funnelled to the appropriate sales channel. Each team is separately responsible for prospecting for business; once a new account has been won and a solution implemented, it is the responsibility of a designated account manager to maintain the relationship and keep the customer happy. Any problems raised by the customer are resolved by Zafesoft as a whole.

The staff work very closely together to ensure that the functionality within the solution meets the needs of the customer base. In a dynamic company of this size the corporate structure is relatively flat, and as a result there is no real division between employees working in development, product management, or sales, other than their natural expertise. The company adapts to its different markets in a variety of ways. For example, the approach to the Japanese market requires Zafesoft to have a local Japanese company acting on its behalf to help build relationships and navigate local bureaucracy, and as a result there is usually a much longer sales cycle; this is also true for the other Asian markets. In some cases, there is resistance to the approaches of new and foreign companies such as Zafesoft, particularly if there are similar home-grown solutions and services.

The size and demands of its customers often dictate the Zafesoft development roadmap. In addition, market research coupled with continuous customer feedback mean that Zafesoft will often adapt its offering to the needs of its largest customers. Currently Zafesoft is not large enough to offer multiple solutions, so this allows it to focus on specific products and services; and because of its small size Zafesoft is very agile and is able to respond very quickly to its customers' demands usually within days and weeks rather than months, as in the case of larger organizations.

The Internet has really opened up the world for companies such as Zafesoft. Similarly, while the company gains access to the market, it also accesses a wealth of information through the industry's technical and business sources.

Figure 12.2
The BCG portfolio
matrix from the
product portfolio
matrix (© Boston
Consulting Group,
1970).

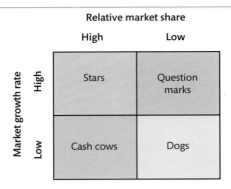

+ **Geocentric**
Company adopts
the most suitable
marketing strategy,
taking into account the
values of the company
and those of the target
market.

+ **Polycentric**
Company adapts its
marketing and sales
strategy as closely
as possible to the
target country—that
is, the market that it is
entering is so particular
that the marketing
strategy and the
products themselves
must be adapted to the
local conditions.

MNEs follow three basic approaches as to how they face the issue of standardizing or adapting their products or services internationally: ethnocentric, geocentric, and polycentric.

The two contrasting management approaches (ethnocentricism and polycentricism), as well as the mid-point of geocentrism, have been touched upon in earlier chapters and are discussed in further detail below from the perspective of international marketing. These approaches are fundamentally derived from business arrogance (ethnocentric) or corporate accommodation to the specific nature of individual local markets (polycentric).

Some of the world's largest retailers have found that foreign markets can be very difficult. The giant US retailer Walmart failed to do well in the German market for a variety of reasons, including its acquisition of the wrong chain of stores in the wrong locations. Many of Walmart's failings were to do with its inability to adapt culturally to the many different needs of German employees and the demands of German customers, attempting to treat German employees in the same way as American workers, and arranging the store layout in a way that was favourable in the USA but not at all suited to the German market (Knorr and Arndt 2003). This demonstrates the crucial importance of understanding the particular nature of any market where a foreign company intends to operate.

Similarly, Marks & Spencer discovered, as have many other British companies, that the American market is very different from the UK and, after nearly twenty years of activities in the USA, if finally admitted that its acquisitions and attempts to operate across the Atlantic had failed. Although such large retailers engage in a considerable amount of preliminary survey work and undertake detailed plans for entry into the US market, they appear to be misled by the apparent similarities of language, culture and style. Marks & Spencer's purchase (and subsequent sale) of Brooks Brothers was shorter lived and less successful than its operation of King's supermarkets, but even the latter were finally sold off in 2006 (Cope 2001; Finch 2006). It will be interesting to observe in 2009–10 the fate of Sir Philip Green's venture into the US market with his British clothing retailer Topshop (BBC News 2009).

Even for Starbucks, a few markets have proved resistant to the normally worldwide marketing success of the North American coffee company. Notably, in Israel in 2003, Starbucks decided that it had failed to understand the existing coffee culture of the country, including its need for security, and pulled out of its six coffee houses in Tel Aviv (Marino 2003; Starbucks 2009). Starbucks had erred on a number of counts relating to the choice of partner (the Delek Group) and the type of market entry mode, and to a misunderstanding about the extent and type of competition in the market for coffee drinking.

In the media sector, there is the interesting case of the launch of the Russian edition of the Condé Nast magazine *Vogue* in 1998 (BBC Education 1999). Apart from the major financial and economic impact of the crash of the rouble in August of that year, there was cultural ignorance in the company's approach to a Russian version of the magazine. This was compounded by the misguided assumption that there was no need to research a new

Upstream focus Ethnocentric	Geocentric	Downsteam focus Polycentric
Standardized product		Locally adapted product
Advantages of scale		Benefits of scope
Market is identical		Market is dissimilar
Customers are the same		Customers are different
High specialization		Maximum variety

Figure 12.3
Competing logics of upstream ethnocentrism versus downstream polycentrism.

market in any great depth. Ironically, it was the son of the publisher/owner, Jonathan Newhouse, Jr., who assumed that his own Russian-origin background (his grandfather was born Solomon Neuhaus in Russia) and the expert Americans he had assigned to the Moscow office could put together a version of the magazine that would meet the needs of the Russian market. This was a failure, and, after the first few issues, *Vogue* was restyled with more Russian themes and covers and Russian (or Russian-looking) models (BBC Education 1999).

Kodak also failed to adapt when it showed over-confidence in its own brand name on first entering the Japanese market in the 1980s, although its difficulties have also been attributed to technological challenges from Fuji and its own mismanagement (Hopkins 1990; Finnerty 2000). Kodak assumed it could trade on its well-established name in the USA and Europe without fully realizing the power of existing rivals in the Japanese market, especially Fuji, which had an established position and a better name for the Japanese consumer. It took Kodak a few years to adapt its original strategy to a more positive position within Japan.

International marketing strategy and marketing mix

The international marketing department of an MNE needs to devise and carry out a full and proper international strategy, which is classically based on its decisions on the marketing mix, referred to as the 4 Ps or the extended version of 7 Ps. The corporate strategy is designed to market the product or service devised by the company in the best way possible.

+ Marketing mix
Different phases of a corporate marketing strategy—product, price, promotion, and place.

Phases and 4 Ps

The basic elements of an international marketing mix are reflected in the phases of the marketing strategy, whether international or domestic: *product, price, promotion, and place*; the extended version adds *process, physical evidence*, and *people*. The first steps in devising such a strategy relate to establishing the nature of the product and its price. This process takes the product from its creation, research, and design through to final production and sale in the marketplace. Increasingly, international marketers need to consider the growing focus on products suitable to consumers' lifestyles and modern ways of living. Marketing research can uncover knowledge about consumer preferences so as to enhance product development and satisfy the preferences that are based on expectations about both the functional and experiential benefits of a new product see Online Resource Centre, extension material 12.1 on consumer behaviour).

> Go to the ORC

International product

These phases of strategy definition and implementation are at the heart of success or failure in bringing goods to market. One of the central debates within international marketing is determining whether increasingly global markets are ready for truly global goods that, as has been discussed above, require little or no adaptation of the product (or service) itself.

Thinking point

Does the 2008–9 economic crisis herald the end of global products?

Were this to be the case, the global good would have the same characteristics wherever it was sold; the only variations would be in relation to pricing, methods of promotion, and location or place of sale/purchase. In certain cases—such as, for example, perfumes and drinks—this appears to be the way the product is sold, with even the advertising and promotion, and often the place, being the same across the world.

The reasons for *product adaptation* range from the cultural to the technological. In some circumstances, companies have to adapt their products because the countries in which they are being marketed and sold have specific laws and requirements.

In India, Australia, New Zealand, Kenya, Ireland, and the UK, for example, all road vehicles drive on the left and most are thus designed as right-hand drive. However, the majority (about two-thirds) of the world's drivers are in left-hand drive markets. This means that car manufacturers seeking to sell worldwide have to be prepared to adapt their designs and production for both left-hand and right-hand drive markets. This requires certain marketing decisions that have an impact on the technological make-up of their production systems.

Another cultural product adaptation based on legal reasons is the German purity law (the Reinheitsgebot of 1516) related to the production and sale of beer. German breweries adhere to these regulations (amended in 1993 as the Biergesetz) and use their compliance as a valuable marketing tool, so that German consumers continue to give enormous credence and loyalty to beers that are 'pure'. The Germans have followed European Union (EU) requirements and allowed the importation of foreign beer brewed with added ingredients such as rice, corn, and other un-Germanic additives. Since the EU ruling and the introduction of foreign beers to the market, however, such beers have not made dramatic inroads into the German market (see Beverage Testings Institute (www.tastings.com/beer/germany.html)). In a sense, therefore, foreign brewing companies trading their own beers into the German beer market are inclined to follow the lead set by German breweries.

Thinking point

Are 'quality' laws used by OECD countries simply modern methods of protectionism?

The German purity law is one of the best worldwide examples of marketing seeking to exploit its identification with positive attributes of a so-called leading country. It would be assumed, for example, that the best pasta comes from Italy, that Japan sets the standard for electronic goods, that the best steak is from Argentina, and that the highest-quality vodka is from Russia.

Companies follow different competitive strategies in different markets to maximize their impact, whether in terms of price or product. Rather like the increasing adoption of air conditioning in cars as standard, this kind of marketing strategy changes over time. Whereas Northern European car purchasers of the 1970s would have regarded air conditioning as an unnecessary luxury, the clientele of the 2000s think of it as essential for their lifestyle. Within each national market, as well as in the world as a whole, different messages have different resonances at different times. To some extent, this is a reflection of changes in advertising literacy, as products become more complex, advertising becomes more subtle and consumers more sophisticated.

Within the standardization and adaptation spectrum, most companies operating internationally endeavour to optimize their ability to target as many segments as possible with a single product or service; more specialized companies tend to target only a selection of segments. The success of global products such as Levis, Coca-Cola, Pepsi-Cola, and McDonald's demonstrates that broad market segments can be reached internationally. Even on a more restricted basis, there are other products, including film series such as *Harry Potter* and *The Lord of the Rings* that have been successfully marketed into a wide range of sectors, thus bypassing 'the filter of national cultures' (Usunier and Lee 2005).

International pricing

As with domestic pricing decisions, the key choices to be made by international managers depend on the overall corporate strategy for the market, product, or service. Companies may decide to stick with the cost basis for pricing by ensuring that the price fixed is in line with the costs of producing the good; this may also be a decision to adhere to a price floor—the minimum price that can be afforded—or to a price ceiling—the maximum price that the market can tolerate. MNEs also base pricing decisions on the international distribution costs.

An MNE can opt for standard or adaptive pricing. Standard pricing means that the product is offered at the same basic price throughout the world, whereas adaptive pricing gives greater decision-making power to managers in subsidiaries, so that they can adapt the price to the local market (Hollensen 2007). In any MNE, there are pricing specialists located in different divisions, and their separate inputs need to be coordinated in such a way as to produce a coherent pricing strategy. For initial entry into a new market, an MNE decides whether it will adapt its normal strategy and opt for an artificially low price (penetration pricing), as was used by Sky TV in establishing large market share in competition with terrestrial television channels in many OECD countries. The marketing of luxury products usually requires the opposite strategy of maintaining the brand image with a high price (premium pricing); this choice usually applies to 5-star hotel chains, first-class airline tickets, high-quality pens, watches, and jewellery. In some cases, the MNE that is first into the market can raise its prices to benefit from its temporary competitive advantage (skimming strategy). Many electronic goods when first sold in new international markets are priced in this way until such time as the competitive advantage is lost.

In general, international costs will almost always be significantly higher than domestic ones. The additional factors that impact on the international marketing of products are the need for labelling and packaging that may be country specific, the tariffs, taxes, customs duties, or other charges related to importing and exporting, possible administration fees, and the extra costs of logistics and transportation (Hollensen 2007). Sometimes a simple change in the exchange rate between the producing country and the importing country can overturn the careful working-out of costing and pricing so that very quickly the price in one currency is no longer feasible in another (see Chapter 13).

International promotion

The international promotion of products and services still relies on a range of methods designed to place goods in front of consumers. The challenges of international promotion are that MNEs are unsure whether the methods of communicating the message of their products or services in the domestic market can be replicated in the international arena. The use of marketing budget, media, and sales forces may be entirely different. Advertising via television, billboards, magazines, or websites is subject to different rules and regulations as well as to different consumer reaction.

Some of the problems of international promotion, including advertising, are covered in Section 2. A key factor for the international marketing division of a company is the accessibility of media in which the products and services will be promoted and the level of 'advertising literacy' in different countries. Advertising needs to be pitched appropriately, and, as Goodyear (1991) suggested, five different levels can be identified. At the most basic level, advertising is focused on repetitive, factual messages about the product. The next two levels reflect a shift from the product's attributes towards the brand and the benefits that consumers will obtain from purchase and use of the product. At the fourth level, the advertiser is engaged in very little selling of the product, as the emphasis is on reinforcing the consumer's identification with the brand. The fifth and most sophisticated level is where the emphasis is virtually on the advertising itself; the advertisement makes little or no direct reference to the product (or even the brand) but simply provides stimulation and entertainment to the consumer. In the international market, these levels mean that, in general, the most advanced and complex consumer societies of the OECD countries will accept promotion and advertising towards the more sophisticated end of the spectrum. In the same countries, however, there are some restrictions on other forms of promotion. For example, in Germany there are considerable restrictions on promotions such as cold calling, mail shots, prizes, and promotional draws (Yeshin 2006).

There are other differences, too, in the use of print media within OECD countries. Loose inserts in newspapers and other printed materials are more common in the UK and Germany than in France and Spain. Perhaps as a result of the use of this form of promotion, inserts are commonly ignored by Germans and Britons, whereas the French and Spanish public pay more attention to them (Elms 2001).

The international communications revolution has brought the promotion of global products to the world through the use of satellite and cable television, evident by the worldwide reach of magazines such as *Vogue* and *Cosmopolitan*, and the Internet. The growth of the web can bring globalized messages to consumers; and is sophisticated enough to permit the transmission of localized messages with the international promotion strategy of an MNE. The new medium of company websites has increasingly become the main method of promotion for MNEs in the developed world, but it needs to be remembered that less than 25 per cent of the world's population has access to the Internet, so much international marketing must still be conducted in some of the more traditional ways (see Internet World Stats (www.internetworldstats.com)). The promotion of products and services is constrained by the budgets of MNEs or their international marketing departments, and the issue of pricing is, therefore, crucial. The tension between the marketers and the accountants can have a major impact on international marketing strategies.

International place

MNEs pay particular attention to place within their marketing strategy. This involves channel management—that is, the control of the systems by which the product is brought to market: logistics, transportation, distribution, delivery, and the locations for sales of the products. For most companies, their products are sold through a variety of outlets: hypermarkets, supermarkets, shopping malls, discount stores, open-air markets, boutiques, department stores, and so on. Some new methods of distribution rely primarily or solely on the Internet.

Some MNE retailers, such as Carrefour, Walmart, and Tesco, have established such a predominant position in the marketplace that they have great influence with their producers, suppliers, and distributors. Their dominance of the supply chain reinforces their ability to establish ever larger super- and hyper markets, as shown by the massive growth of hypermarkets in the Shanghai area of China.

The purpose of the international marketing mix and the strategy adopted by companies is to demonstrate how the MNE is meeting the needs and desires of consumers throughout the world. To succeed in this, the company must ensure that it prepares and plans its marketing operations in the most thorough manner.

Market research, marketing information, and market position

+ Segmentation
Identification of customers with similar characteristics so that a commercially viable marketing strategy can be devised and implemented.

+ Targeting
Designing and aiming of a message at specific types of customers within markets that have been selected as the focus for a company's offering.

Chief among the many reasons for success and failure in international market entry and marketing are the collection of marketing data, the research into market segmentation, the targeting of customers, the methods for getting close to consumers, and the ways in which companies can ensure customer loyalty to goods and services. Far-sighted MNEs with sufficient financial power are able to spend a significant proportion of time and money on attracting and retaining customers.

A key example of apparently good market research was demonstrated in 2007–8 by the large UK-based supermarket Tesco with the launch in parts of south-west USA of its Fresh and Easy stores. These outlets were designed as stores for healthy foods at good value—neither at the top end of the market nor attempting to match Walmart's 'rock-bottom prices'. In its domestic market (the UK) and others, Tesco had established a loyalty card (the Tesco Clubcard) to give it an exceptionally rich source of customer data.

Before creating the new stores in California and other states, Tesco undertook an extensive process of research that included a number of Tesco executives and anthropologists living with sixty families in an attempt to understand their eating, drinking, and buying habits and the use of a mocked-up store to track the movement of customers. Despite this thorough work, Tesco's expansion plans have slowed and it has realized that it may have misjudged the habits

Photo 12.1
Tesco Fresh and Easy
store in California
(reproduced with the
kind permission of
Tesco).

of American consumers (Finch 2009). The head of Tesco's operations in the USA was reported as having to admit, for example, that it had 'underestimated the number of customers who stockpile discounted products, such as meats, in their freezers' (*Independent* 2009).

Despite the temporary blip in the USA, Tesco's activities in relation to the establishment and marketing of its Fresh and Easy stores indicated a continuing commitment to this kind of investigation and understanding of its markets and customers. As Townsend (2007) has commented, 'Tesco has long relied on in-depth research to inform its international growth; cash-and-carry aisles were introduced to its Thai stores, for example, as a direct response to local competition'. According to a Lehman Brothers analysis, 'Tesco's international business has a depth of management which is sector-leading among its peer group ... Each country is run as a stand-alone business, with predominantly local management coupled with ex-pat specialists' (Townsend 2007).

It is not only large MNEs that can undertake successful international marketing into unexpected markets; the possibility also applies to small and medium-sized enterprises (SMEs). An interesting case of international expansion by a medium-sized firm is PAUL bakery, which was established in 1889 in Lille, France. Domestically, the expansion of PAUL began in the 1950s and 1960s, to the point where the company had 330 outlets in 2007. In the last few years, PAUL has expanded extensively into new markets from Bahrain and Qatar, Japan and Turkey, to Spain and Holland. In the UK in 2009 there were twenty-eight shops/restaurants, mostly in and around London, but also at Edinburgh airport. The supposed unique selling proposition (USP) of PAUL is the quality and exclusiveness of its bread and other products (www.PAUL-uk.com). It markets itself as being uniquely French ('L'amour du pain'—or a passion for bread) and has made this a successful proposition in the UK, where there can sometimes be resistance to products that originate in France.

The case of PAUL illustrates the peculiar position and the specificities of international marketing for SMEs: they tend to be too small to run a volume product, so they are either condemned to work as a niche seller or are able to relish this position as long as their international order books are full or their international expansion continues at a measured and manageable pace. Regardless of the company's own view of its position, any SME operating internationally can be a target of vertical integration for a larger company. This would occur, for example, if a large restaurant chain decided that it should acquire PAUL as part of its extensive provision of a range of restaurant experiences. It would also suit a food and drink MNE that did not have this kind of product/service offering within its range or wanted to purchase a larger share of this market.

> **Thinking point**
>
> Why is PAUL an exception to the view that SMEs often fail internationally?

Photo 12.2
PAUL is an example
of international
expansion and
successful marketing
(reproduced with the
kind permission of
PAUL).

Case Study 12.2

Dasani in the UK

In 2004, the launch of Coca-Cola's bottled water product, Dasani, became a classic case of failing to understand the market and of nearly wrecking the image and product range of a major MNE through the marketing failure of one product (Anderson and Kumar 2004). The growing British market for bottled water (about 10 per cent per year) was dominated by foreign brands such as Perrier, Vittel, and Evian, with strong competition from many UK private-label waters and supermarket brands. Bottled water sales in the UK were dominated by Danone (about 35 per cent of the market) and Nestlé (about 15 per cent of the market). Coca-Cola viewed the market as ripe for entry and exploitation. Its strategy was to use the UK as the springboard for entry and expansion of its non-carbonated beverages within Europe.

Certain market issues might have prevented Coca-Cola's launch of Dasani: a sophisticated market with strong existing consumer identification and loyalty, and increased market competition, which

was squeezing industry profit margins. This might have put off a less powerful MNE, but Coca-Cola persisted in its determination to enter the UK and European markets. Dasani is 'manufactured' rather than taken directly from springs or other natural water sources: it is effectively tap water that undergoes what Coca-Cola calls a highly sophisticated purification system. Most American consumers regarded this as a valid hi-tech way of producing good-quality bottled water. Once this method was known in the UK, British consumers clearly did not regard it as acceptable. Of course, the customers who bought and drank it did not fully understand that it was not natural until a health scare led to the recall of Dasani.

In March 2004, it was discovered that the levels of bromate in Dasani were higher than legal levels and were caused by its manufacturing process. Quite correctly, the company consulted the Food Standards Agency and, although there was no direct threat

Bottled water is an example of a competitive and difficult market (© iStockphoto).

to public health, it agreed to recall the entire stock of 500,000 bottles in the UK within about twenty-four hours. Media coverage of the recall led to a public realization of the manufactured rather than the natural quality of Dasani and to scathing comments about it being 'just tap water'. The public, therefore, felt that they were paying a great deal of money simply to have filtered water that had come out of the normal piped water system.

The nature of the scandal and the massive media coverage not only had an impact on the sales—and existence—of Dasani in the UK market but thwarted any attempt by Coca-Cola to tackle the bottled-water market in the rest of Europe.

Seven types of cultural adaptation

The combination an MNE's location on the push–pull marketing axis and the ethnocentric–polycentric spectrum can be used as a measure of its international marketing strategy and, to some extent, the likelihood of its international success. To consider some of these issues more fully, this section outlines the main cultural factors to be taken into account in international marketing (see Figure 12.4).

The separation of these factors is not always as clear cut as Figure 12.4 might suggest. Some of these factors are related to products themselves and others to the advertising itself, or the form of the advertising.

(a) *National and country-specific* factors often incorporate some of the other listed factors, but some general approaches to life, living, and lifestyles can be identified; these factors are sometimes a reflection of real or perceived national stereotype. The British attitude towards humour, for example, means that products can often be advertised and sold with a touch of fun and comedy. For both print and visual advertising of international brand motor cars, such as Audi or BMW, the stereotypical approach to be taken for the British is far more humorous than it is for other countries such as Italy or France (more inclined to an emphasis on style, luxury, and sex), or Germany (more susceptible to a technical sales message). In a market such as Japan, it is very important to have celebrity endorsements (about 60 per cent of all advertisements), whereas the German market tends to be unimpressed by this (about 6 per cent of all advertisements) (Usunier and Lee 2005).

Figure 12.4
Cultural factors
in international
marketing.

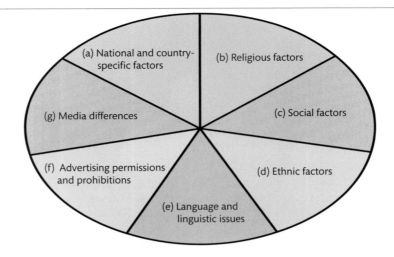

(b) The *religious factor* within international marketing is most evident when comparing countries where Islam, Hinduism, or Christianity are most prominent. Global brands and MNEs realize that they need to tailor their products and messages to fit the dominant religion. For McDonald's, the essential constituent of a burger worldwide is beef but, in India, where Hindus revere cows, this is replaced by chicken or lamb. Similarly, beverage companies operating in Muslim societies need to focus on non-alcoholic products within their portfolio.

(c) Marketers operating across borders have to take into account a vast array of *social factors* as they seek to research, analyse, and segment these international markets. These include the demographic pattern of each country—for example, the age distribution of the population, the degree of urbanization, the structure of families, the extent of education, and the proportion of men to women. Each of these factors, and many others, can have a significant impact on the marketing of certain products and services. For example, where women have equal status to men in a society, they will tend to represent an equally important market for many goods. In Western and industrialized countries in the 1990s and 2000s, a new market has been revealed with the purchasing power of retired people, the so-called grey market: they have well-developed tastes for products such as travel, pensions, or recreational facilities and they wield enormous spending power.

Thinking point

In which countries are woman more targeted as consumers and why?

(d) *Ethnic factors* have a role to play both within countries and between them. Within some countries, there are often groups that have different needs, tastes, and purchasing patterns. In the USA, Americans of Hispanic origin demand food and drink products that remind them of their ethnic/national origins in the Latin American countries from which they come, or with which they identify (Usunier and Lee 2005). Similarly, the high proportion of workers from India (and other parts of the Indian subcontinent) who reside in the United Arab Emirates (about 50 per cent of the population) greatly affects the marketing and sale of products in the UAE.

There are cases, too, where a famous MNE misreads the ethnic messages that it intends to attach to a product and its accompanying advertising. In spring 2009, Burger King launched in the UK and Spain its 'Nuevo Texican Whopper': 'the taste of Texas with a little spicy Mexican'. The TV adverts showed a tall Texan cowboy and a short Mexican wrestler wearing the Mexican flag as a cape. It should not have surprised Burger King that this attracted serious criticism from people such as the Mexican ambassador to Spain, whose complaint was that Burger King 'improperly use the stereotyped image of a Mexican'. The criticism resulted in the adverts being pulled from TV and not being released into the US market with its large Hispanic population, many originally from Mexico (Feldman 2009).

(e) Many countries are not only socially and ethnically diverse but also have *different languages and linguistic* traditions. What appeals to the French speakers of Belgium may not appeal to the Flemish speakers; the same applies, obviously, to other bilingual countries such as Canada, Wales, as well as to the many multilingual societies. In addition to the political and economic consequences of these linguistic splits, MNEs and other firms need to prepare marketing and selling strategies to take account of these differences. For Belgium, advertising agencies usually create advertisements simultaneously in Flemish and French, whereas, for example, in South Africa (which has eleven official languages—though the most used are English and Afrikaans), the agencies usually conceptualize an advertisement in English and then translate it. The translated adverts often fail to take into account the cultural factors that are crucial to selling into that sector of the market. Aside from the inevitability of having marketing campaigns and packaging in different languages—and in a country such as India, with fifteen official languages, including English, there are different shopping patterns to consider. Clearly, these are not solely linguistically determined but are a reflection of the socio-cultural aspects of the different groups (Hollensen 2007).

(*f*) Each country, especially in the industrialized world, has specific laws and regulations in relation to what is *permitted and prohibited in advertising*. For all countries, the regulatory framework for advertising covers a range of areas, such as no use of pornographic or overtly sexual images, regulations banning violent messages, and prohibitions on the exploitation of children. In particular, since the 1990s there has been concern about the obesity of children and the consequent need to restrict (or ban) the advertising of unhealthy products, such as fast food, high-sugar drinks, sweets and chocolates, to children.

In the Western world, the tobacco industry has found that the advertising and marketing of products have been increasingly restricted. This has primarily been a consequence of the evidence of health risks associated with the consumption of tobacco. Progressively, cigarette advertising has been removed from all media in many OECD countries, so that tobacco MNEs have had to move their message to sports sponsorship and many LDCs. In the European Union, the Directive of 2003 related to the approximation of the laws, regulations, and administrative provisions of the EU members states in connection with the 'advertising and sponsorship of tobacco products'. It classified tobacco products and its associated promotion as being cross-border issues that needed to be regulated within the EU as well as by national legislation and restrictions. For example, the UK's law (Tobacco Advertising and Promotion Act of 2002) was then supplemented by 2004 regulations on point of sale and brand-sharing (see the Department of Health (www.dh.gov.uk)). The international marketing consequence of the Western prohibitions on smoking has been increased attention by the tobacco companies on markets in Asia and other parts of the less-developed world.

(*g*) Within the category of *media* (which includes newspapers, magazines, billboards, and online), there are differences such as patterns of television broadcasting, coverage, and viewing (Usunier and Lee 2005). A country like the UK, which has high viewing figures (in 2009 about 75 per cent of the population watched more than twenty-five hours per week), will respond more to high levels of advertising on television and to products that are particularly susceptible to such advertising. TV advertising in the UK includes, for example, massive campaigns tied into children's programmes. These products include the obvious ones such as toys, as well as a whole range of food and drink items. Many are thought to have contributed to the problem of obesity among young people and, as indicated above, have been restricted by law.

This wide range of culture, or culture-related, factors shows how complex the task is for international mangers as they seek to make decisions about what products to market, and where and how. The challenges they face make it very hard for them to take the right decisions and, perhaps above all, to avoid choosing strategies that could lead to embarrassment, failure, or scandal.

Section II: Issues in international marketing

There are four issues of current and growing significance in international marketing: business-to-business (B2B) marketing, ethical or green marketing, international branding, and

> **Thinking point**
>
> In which countries is TV advertising for children intended to make parents spend money unnecessarily?

> **+ Business-to-business (B2B) marketing**
> Marketing of products and services to businesses—i.e. the marketing and sales relationship between one company and those other companies to which it supplies, or from which it receives, products and services.

Internet marketing. There are obviously other issues that could be stressed as being of similar importance to these, such as the complexities of international market segmentation and targeting, international market research, and the role of marketing in the strategic decisions of MNEs considering market entry and the mode(s) of such entry. All these have been mentioned in this chapter—or elsewhere in the book—but here the focus is on four selected issues.

Business-to-business (B2B) marketing

While most of this chapter has been concerned with marketing to final customers or consumers—that is, members of the general public who buy goods and services for their personal consumption, or business-to-consumer (B2C) marketing—it is important to acknowledge the significance of business marketing (B2B), as this accounts for a considerable proportion of international marketing activities.

For companies marketing and selling in the B2C sector, their emphasis is usually on seeking a large target market, being product driven, and maximizing the value of the transaction. Being product-driven they emphasize merchandising and point of sale, and try to create a single-step purchasing process (a short sales cycle), and stress emotional buying decisions (based on price, desire, or status) in the customer. The original distinction between B2C and B2B arose from an attempt to differentiate between those buying 'online' (B2B) and those buying in more traditional ways. The development of Internet availability and access has made this distinction less valid, and the difference is now acknowledged to be between commercial/industrial (B2B) and personal (B2C) purchasers.

The size of the B2B market is difficult to determine with any accuracy, but for the 1990s it has been estimated at more than $10 trillion per year, or about 7–10 per cent of the total amount spent annually on international marketing activities and global sales transactions (Hillebrand 2000). What is not in doubt is the different nature of the B2B market, where,

+ **Business-to-consumer (B2C) marketing**
Marketing of products and services to the end consumers or customers– i.e. members of the general public who consume the products or services directly for themselves.

Photo 12.3
Television advertising during children's programmes has been blamed for increasing the problem of obesity amongst children in many countries (© iStockphoto).

as Minet (2001) has suggested, the nature of the product development is 'linear' (rather than 'cyclical' as in B2C marketing), the driver is 'technology' (not 'fashion'), the customer motivation is 'organizational need' (not 'individual wants or desires'), and the focus is on 'sales and application' (not 'consumer characteristics').

The dimensions of the B2B marketing can be exemplified by an MNE such as IKEA, which requires regular supplies of items that will eventually be sold to the consuming public. For IKEA, this means competition between suppliers of the different types of furniture (and other products). Each supplier will promote its products to the buyers at IKEA, compete on design, quality, manufacturing schedules, and price, and endeavour to secure as large a contract as possible with IKEA. The successful supplier(s) will have achieved substantial sales of its products to a mainstream MNE in the home-furnishings business. IKEA has about 1,800 suppliers in more than 50 countries (Kotler et al. 2008). However, none of the final consumers (the public) will ever know the suppliers' names; the products that are bought will all be under the IKEA brand.

Another instance of the B2B market is the supply to an airline, such as Japan Airlines (JAL), of all the customized components for its aircraft, the provision of catering, the supply of fuels, and so on. Apart from the names of such suppliers as Rolls Royce or Pratt and Whitney for engines, and BP or Esso for fuels, it is unlikely that any flying passengers will know who provided the seats, seat belts, air-conditioning system, or flooring. The main difference involved in such B2B marketing is the scale of the activity: very large budgets but usually involving fewer suppliers and buyers; and more targeted promotional activities, including the building of personal relationships between the professional buyers and sellers in the market.

Ethical or green marketing

This area of marketing demonstrates a company's ethical stance, its sense of corporate responsibility, and its concern about the environment. This includes an interest in where products are sourced, whether products are subject to a large carbon footprint—that is, the distance they have travelled between producer and customer and the transportation costs incurred—whether they subscribe to FairTrade principles and codes, and the degree to which foodstuffs and drinks may be produced organically—that is, without artificial or chemical additives (see Chapter 16). It is clear that this area of marketing is more complex than can be explained in a relatively short section of this chapter.

There is concern in the area of ethical marketing as to whether companies are indulging in this as a cynical and rather insincere ploy to capitalize on a current trend or whether they are developing this form of marketing as a genuine part of their corporate ethos and have it as an integral part of their strategy and operations. A grid for assessing the extent of a company's green credentials was proposed in 2007 in *The Green Marketing Manifesto*, where John Grant proposed three levels of marketing (public, social, and personal) ranked with three types of objective (setting standards, sharing responsibility, and supporting innovation). Grant's purpose was to find ways of evaluating the 'green-ness' of corporations, brands, and products (Grant 2007).

The introduction and use by BP, for example, of the slogan 'beyond petroleum' and the sun/helios symbol in 2001 was a reflection of the change of direction for BP itself—and for energy companies in general. The change was also manifested by BP's universal use of a new lower-case 'bp' for advertising purposes and of the more environmentally friendly colours of green and yellow, though BP had at times used these earlier (Wickham 2009). The new BP logo and slogan also grew out of a series of bold mergers and acquisitions between 1998 and 2002, including Amoco, ARCO, Castrol, ErdolChemie, Vastar, and Veba. As a global operation, BP expanded and developed its operations in photovoltaics (solar), biofuels, carbon capture, and wind power. The new company clearly needed to rebrand an organization that had grown threefold in size and had expanded in its diversity of people and activities.

The new focus on energy and environment had originally been heralded by Lord Browne (CEO of BP, 1995–2007) in a ground-breaking speech at Stanford University in 1997. The speech had controversially acknowledged the link between the responsibility of international oil companies, the extent of fossil-fuel consumption, and global warming. BPs' competitors in the oil and gas business initially criticized this stance (Mouawad 2009). Subsequently, BP's move was acknowledged as being influential in persuading the 'big oil' MNEs to restyle themselves as global energy companies interested in the whole range of energy sources and their more economical uses. The development of BP Alternative Energy in 2005, including solar energy companies around the world, and its renewed international development of energy resources in, for example, China, Vietnam, and Russia reinforced this move to attempt to be as green a leader as possible in the oil and gas sector. Since 2008, under the new CEO (Tony Hayward) and management, the renewable energy activities, though remaining a separate business unit within BP, no longer have divisional status (Mortished 2007). In general, the majority of the environmentally conscious features continue to be developed and the company has retained the 'BP' designation for advertising purposes, the corporate colours, and the sun/helios logo.

There are even more recent developments in relation to carbon footprints, especially for internationally available agricultural products. There is a tension between encouraging producers in LDCs to send their products vast distances to the consumer markets of the OECD countries and encouraging OECD consumers to rely more on locally produced goods. Increasingly, both suppliers and customers are becoming more aware of the environmental costs to the planet—that is, not just the direct but the indirect costs of transportation. Supplying Londoners with flowers from East Africa, rather than Lincolnshire and Holland, is now seen as being environmentally unfriendly and the source of an ethical conflict between trade with the less-developed world and damage to the global environment This relative distance has become a new international marketing argument.

International branding

Over the years, marketers have stressed that it is not so much the product or the service itself that is important in influencing consumers but the branding that is important. The idea of a brand is that the name, image, and symbols of the product or service are equally important. International branding has, therefore, become a key aspect of the marketing of products and services, especially where the brand is perceived to be able to cross borders.

The right branding can be critical for the success of any company's domestic or international business. For MNEs, a well-planned and executed international branding campaign is crucial to expand into new markets, as well as securing and strengthening existing markets. On the international stage, branding has the added complication of trying to ensure that the brand message remains intact in spite of the cultural differences that exist around the world. Brand recognition is created by the accumulation of experiences with the specific product or service, relating to its use and its image, both perceived and real.

The branding of services, as can be seen from Figure 12.5, has been focused on the Internet and computing (Google, Microsoft, IBM, and Apple) and on mobile phones (Apple, China Mobile, and Vodafone). Note the pre-eminence of Apple's brand since the iPhone was added to the computing products of the company. This reflects the centrality of Apple design and products, as the iPhone drives 'the real-time communications revolution'. The iPhone is 'the critical engine of the new media economy … [as it] has swept away the traditional barriers between a mobile telephone, a web browser, a computer, a portable entertainment system and even an e-book reader' (Keen 2009).

Other areas in which successful international branding has occurred involves products such as drinks (alcoholic and non-alcoholic), perfumes and other toiletry products, cars, and luxury products, such as top-range watches. For many successful brands, part of their appeal has been the close relationship between the design of the product and its function or

Rank	Brand	Brand value, ($ m.)
1	Google	100,039
2	Microsoft	76,249
3	Coca-Cola	67,625
4	IBM	66,622
5	McDonald's	66,575
6	Apple	63,113
7	China Mobile	61,283
8	GE (General Electric)	59,793
9	Vodafone	53,727
10	Marlboro	49,480

Figure 12.5
The world's top 10 most powerful brands, 2009 (Millward Brown Optimor 2009).

its image. Design within marketing and design management itself are critical to the impact of the brand and, in some cases, to the enduring longevity and appeal of the product (see Online Resource Centre , extension material 12.2).

> Go to the ORC

Many criticisms of international branding have been broadcast by the popularity of the nologo website (www.naomiklein.org/nologo) and the writings of Naomi Klein. The book, entitled *No Logo*, was originally published in North America and the UK in 2000 and is now available in over twenty-five languages. Klein's principal idea is that big brands (such as McDonald's and its character symbol Ronald McDonald) target young children worldwide in a kind of mass psychological experiment that turns consumers into robots. The more robotic the consumer can be, the smaller the need for product or service differentiation. This means that companies can sell the same thing everywhere, thus saving themselves adaptation costs. This raises the issue of whether international consumers are thought to be converging or diverging. Where they converge, they are more accepting of 'global' brands; where they diverge, they tend to resent the attempted homogenization of their lifestyles.

Thinking point

Are consumers worldwide converging or diverging?

Concerns about the impact of brands can be seen in the mixed responses to international brands that are believed to illustrate the American lifestyle. Resistance to Americanization has been led in France, for example, by José Bové, a farmer and political activist, who has campaigned against the spread of fast-food restaurants, especially McDonalds, against the introduction of genetically modified (GM) foods, and for the international peasant movement, now called 'La Via Campesina' (http://viacampesina.org).

Interestingly, such developments are starting to be combined with the ethical and environment-conscious concerns of consumers, as illustrated above. The more that the world moves towards sourcing products locally, the less likely it is to encourage global brands—unless they are made close to the customer. Therefore, the trend in the first half of the twenty-first century is likely to be towards the encouragement of more FDI and greater closeness of producer and customer.

Internet marketing

One of the most interesting developments within the world of marketing, selling, and purchasing has been the rise since 1995 of the World Wide Web, the Internet. A key issue is whether the Internet represents a dramatic change in the conduct of international business or whether it is simply a different medium and means of getting products to consumers. As discussed in Case Study 12.3, it can be argued that the potential of the Internet has not yet been fully realized and that it does represent a dramatic new phase in business. It is instructive that the UK figures for Internet marketing reflect the uncertain and new nature of its development. As measured

Thinking point

Why would some international consumers not buy products and services on the Internet?

by 'online market size', in 2008 Internet marketing constituted only 6.7 per cent of total retail spending, but grew annually by about 30 per cent between 2003 and 2008 (Verdict Research in Thompson 2008).

The question of how much Internet services, and the medium itself, are standardized rather than adapted is one that is still to be resolved, as are the issues about how successful these networks will become as international advertising and marketing vehicles. Indeed, the development of social networking has reinforced the view that viral marketing is a key trend for the future of increasing marketing reach and sales in the next few decades.

There is an infinite amount of 'shelf space' on the Internet, even though, as is evident from companies such as Amazon, it still requires vast amounts of warehousing in order to satisfy consumer demand. Anybody who has seen the vast storage depots that supply Amazon customers with their books, DVDs, and CDs realizes that some of what the Internet does is little different from what is provided through the distribution of catalogues and mail-order sales. The key difference between old warehousing and the Amazon system is the ruthless application of technology to the Amazon structures. The Amazon warehouses in the USA were expensive to build (about $50m each) and expensive to operate. They have become, however, models of efficiency because of the high degree of computerization, the interactivity between people and computers (signals to workers, collection of items, weighing and dispatch), and the generation of large amounts of data on factors such as line speed, robot-picking, productivity, conveyor belt blockages, and bottleneck problems. The warehouses have become so efficient that Amazon turns over its inventory about twenty times per year, whereas other retailers are fortunate to achieve a rate of fifteen times.

The successful growth of the Internet in its many forms may be a result of the theory of the Long Tail (see Online Resource Centre, extension material 12.3), which claims that the world's culture and economy are increasingly shifting away from a focus on a relatively small number of 'hits' (mainstream products and markets) and towards a huge number of niches ('the tail'). As the costs of international production and distribution fall, especially online, narrowly targeted goods and services can be as economically attractive as mainstream items.

Of course, the question can be asked as to whether the success of Amazon (worldwide profits continuing to rise on revenue of about $13.5 billion in 2007) is a result of it offering goods on the Internet rather than through older media or a result of the efficiency of its warehousing systems—and the drive and skills of its CEO, Jeff Bezos. This is likely to remain a debatable point until later in the twenty-first century, when there will be some historical perspective on the international marketing of goods via new Internet businesses.

+ **Viral marketing**
Strategy that encourages individuals to pass on marketing messages to others, creating a multiplier effect spreading the message's exposure and influence.

> Go to the ORC

Challenges and choices

→ One key challenge for international marketing over the next few years is the extent to which the use of the Internet and social networking sites becomes the industry norm, and the impact this will have on other methods of marketing.

→ This involves difficult decisions about the information management systems to be purchased, maintained, and extended, the staffing levels required in this new marketing world, and the likely development of affordable, single platform home-entertainment systems that combine the current features of TV, DVD, computer, telephone, gaming, and the purchase of goods and services. One of the key choices for the industry is the extension of online marketing to children. In 2008,

there were about 100 youth-focused virtual worlds, some aimed at children as young as 5 years old. For the industry, the key challenge is to provide 'legitimate reassurance to parents that the sites their children use adhere to strict codes and standards' (Richard Deverell, Controller of BBC Children, cited in Carter 2008).

→ International marketing may also witness further choices regarding the extension of green and ethical marketing to a wider range of products and services and to more segments of the world's population. To be truly effective in securing a sustainable world, the production, distribution, marketing, and sales of such goods and services must become more universal.

Chapter Summary

The coverage of international marketing in this chapter has addressed a range of key issues including strategies for marketing overseas, questions of standardization and adaptation, push and pull marketing, the impact of cultural aspects on marketing and advertising, the key role of branding, the importance of good research and closeness to customers, and the emergence and future of Internet marketing.

The possibilities of expansion outside a company's domestic market are fraught with problems, even for major MNEs, but it is clear that the right strategy and implementation can lead to success. Such positive stories in international expansion are often related to good market research, intelligent understanding of different cultures, sensible advertising and marketing approaches, and a quality product or service being delivered to the right market segment at the right time and in the right way. Although the most significant roles in international marketing are played by large MNEs, it should be clear that SMEs can also take the strategic option of successful international sales, marketing, and distribution.

Case Study 12.3

Facebook: The present and future of international network marketing

The great marketing phenomenon of the early part of the twenty-first century has been the development of advertising and sales through social networking. The main social networks have included Facebook, Twitter, My Space, Bebo, Linkedin, and Flickr. The market leader was Facebook, which made a rapid fortune for its young founder, Mark Zuckerberg—who, at the age of 23, was estimated to be worth $15 billion in September 2007. In a very short time, all these social networks have expanded from their original base (usually the USA) into an international phenomenon. As with most developments on the Internet, the American impetus has remained strong, but, as the networks have expanded, they have become genuinely global—within the communities that are web-connected.

Facebook started in February 2004 and was initially a social networking site restricted to students of Harvard College. It rapidly extended to other Boston colleges and universities, then to all international academic and educational institutions, and finally to anybody anywhere in the world. Facebook's growth rates were astounding, rising from the sixtieth to the seventh most-visited website between September 2006 and September 2007. By September 2007, the website had achieved the largest number of registered users with over 42 million internationally active members; by April 2009, it had

nearly 200 million worldwide. In October 2007, the race between potential purchasers, including Google, was won by Microsoft, which paid $240 million for a minority stake in the company, thus buying the exclusive rights to sell advertising on Facebook and valuing the whole of the company at about $15 billion. These figures were revised in 2008–9 to indicate that the true value of Facebook may be closer to between $2 billion and $3 billion.

Facebook and the other social networks are inevitable developments from the user-generated content feature of the Internet. Whereas earlier developments within the commercial exploitation of the Internet tended to mirror normal sales and marketing patterns, the rise of the social networks threatened to break new ground. The early users of the Internet tended to create cyberspace catalogues—the goods were easily viewed, ordered, and paid for through their websites, but there was still a crucial delivery of a physical product, such as CDs, books, foodstuffs, computer hardware, and other goods. The later users (that is, social networkers) looked at the Internet in an entirely different way. Not only were they looking at the features of cyberspace in the way that Manuel Castells (2001) had foreseen, but they were also able to attract large volumes of advertising onto their websites.

For Facebook, registered members join for no charge, since the idea is for Facebook to make money out of domestic and international advertising. The real battle in the market is for the competing firms, such as Microsoft and Google, to contend for shares of online advertising. The value of Facebook is its extensive and international membership: 'a goldmine waiting to be tapped' (Ashworth and Heath 2007). What has not yet been fully developed is how advertisers will connect with users. As Ashworth and Heath (2007) suggested, any purchaser of Facebook is assuming that each of the 42 million international users is worth about $238 each, and thus able to 'generate that much in advertising and commercial value over their lifetime'. Such spending power—or anything approaching it—represents a gigantic international market over a long period of time.

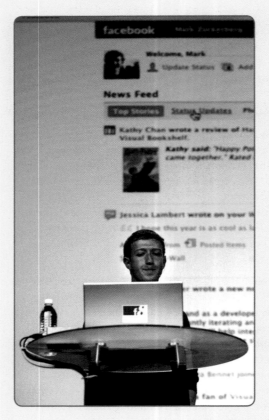

The growth of social networking sites such as Facebook has provided new opportunities for product and service marketing (Corbis).

In 2007, Facebook added free classified advertisements (Facebook Marketplace) to its website, thus competing with established online companies such as Craigslist. An interesting comment on this surprising development related to one of Facebook's chief competitors, MySpace: 'Pundits in the 1990s thought that gigantic sites would offer mainstream films, TV and videos on demand. These may appear one day but, for the moment, the biggest businesses are MySpace, Facebook, Flickr and YouTube: sites that, paradoxically don't feel like businesses because their content is produced by the customers' (Cohen 2007).

The potential of Facebook was seen in the possibilities of international crossover marketing. Facebook's progress over 15-20 years will demonstrate how well social networks have become an integral part of product and service marketing for all generations, not just young people who have grown up with it in the early part of the twenty-first century. Above all, it can be contended that 'the capacity for interactivity is greater on the web than with any other mass media' (Yeshin 2006: 372). This means that customers have far greater control over the way in which they interact with the advertising message, with the marketing of goods and services, and with the manipulation of the content of the medium. The customer has the real possibility of choosing and responding to particular marketing messages that they like—they have become more active consumers than ever before. The interactivity of the World Wide Web as an international marketing medium is reaching its zenith with the rise and success of social networks such as Facebook.

Case study questions

1. For international consumers and MNEs, what are the marketing benefits of social networks and other Internet sites?
2. Why has Facebook spread so quickly across the world?
3. Why is it difficult to agree on the real value of Facebook, and other Internet sites?

Discussion questions

1. What are likely to be the most internationally successful Internet marketing websites by 2015? Why?

2. What are the key benefits for an international retailer of 'loyalty cards'?

3. Why are popular internationally sold bottled waters (such as Perrier, Evian, Dasani, etc.) now thought to be a less ethical purchase than ten years ago?

4. What are the most common reasons for successes and failures in the international marketing of products and services?

5. Why do MNEs so often make cultural mistakes in their product launches and/or advertising?

References

Adlab (2006). 'Honda's "Choir" Hits Three Million Downloads', 23 Mar., http://adverlab.blogspot.com/2006/03/hondas-choir-hits-three-million.html (accessed 21 Nov. 2007).

Anderson, J., and Kumar, N. (2004). 'Dasani UK: Brand under Attack', *European Case Clearing House*, ECCH 504-022-1.

Ashworth, J., and Heath, A. (2007). 'Because He's Worth It: Facebook Hits the Jackpot', *Business*, 29 Sept.

BBC Education (1999), 'To Russia with Vogue', *Trouble at the Top*, Episode 2, Series 3.

BBC News (2009). http//:news.bbc.co.uk (accessed 10 Apr.).

Bradley, F. (2005). *International Marketing Strategy*. 5th edn. Harlow: Pearson Education/FT Prentice Hall.

Brassington, F., and Pettitt, S. (2007), *Essentials of Marketing*. 2nd edn. Harlow: Pearson Education.

Carr, D. (2008). 'You Want It, You Click It (Waiting Is Not an Option)', *Observer*, 13 Apr., *New York Times* insert.

Carroll, E. (2007). 'The Rise of the Social Network Phenomenon', *Independent*, 26 Sept.

Carter, M. (2008). 'Is this Harmless Child's Play—or Virtual Insanity?' *Independent*, 2 June.

Castells, M. (2001). *The Internet Galaxy: Reflections on the Internet, Business and Society*. Oxford: Oxford University Press.

Chaffey, D., Ellis-Chadwick, F., Johnston, K., and Mayer, R. (2006). *Internet Marketing: Strategy, Implementation and Practice*. 3rd edn. Harlow: Pearson Education/FT Prentice Hall.

Clark, A. (2007). 'Microsoft Stake in Facebook Values Site at $15bn', *Guardian*, 25 Oct.

Cohen, N. (2007). 'Stand up for Tila, an Unlikely Web Warrior', *Observer*, 30 Sept.

Cope, N. (2001). 'Marks & Spencer Disposes of Brooks Brothers for a Knock-Down $225m', *Independent*, 24 Nov.

Coyle, D. (1998). 'The Simple Idea that Lies behind Microsoft's Aim to Rule the World', *Independent*, 19 Feb.

Davies, C. (2008). 'iPhone Sales Figures Prompt Stockpile Questions', *iPhone Buzz*, 25 Jan., www.iphonebuzz.com (accessed 7 Apr. 2009).

Department of Health (2009). 'Tobacco Publications', www.dh.gov.uk (accessed 19 Apr.).

Elms, S. (2001). 'Multi-Country Communication Planning', *Admap*, Jan.

Feldman, C. (2009). 'Burger King's Whopper of an Ad', *Houston Chronicle*, 16 Apr.

Fill, C., and Fill, E. (2004). *Business-to-business Marketing: Relationships, Systems and Communications*. 4th edn. Harlow: Pearson Education/FT Prentice Hall.

Finch, J. (2006), 'M&S Quits America with Sale of Supermarkets', *Guardian*, 1 Apr.

Finch, J. (2009). 'Tesco Feels US Downturn as Fresh & Easy Turns Stale,' *Guardian*, 20 Apr.

Finnerty, T. C. (2000). 'Kodak vs Fuji: The Battle for Global Market Share', Lubin School of Business, Pace University (paper written under the supervision of Dr Warren J. Keegan).

Goodyear, M. (1991). 'Global Advertising: The Five Stages of Advertising Literacy', *Admap*, Mar.

Grant, J. (2007). *The Green Marketing Manifesto*. Chichester: John Wiley.

Hillebrand, M. (2000). 'Forecasters Fuel Feeding Frenzy on B2B Projections', *E-Commerce Times*, 27 Jan.

Hollensen,S. (2007). Global Marketing: A decision-oriented approach. 4th edn. Harlow: Pearson Education/FT Prentice Hall.

Hopkins, H. D. (1990). 'Kodak vs Fuji: A Case of Japanese–American Strategic Intervention', paper, Temple University.

Hopkins, H. D. (2003). 'The Response Strategies of Dominant US Firms to Japanese Challengers', *Journal of Management*, 29/1: 5–25.

Independent (2009). 'Tesco Admits it Misjudged US Shopper', 23 Feb.

Keen, A. (2009). 'Why Apple Isn't Feeling the Bite even as other Tech Titans Tumble', *Independent*, 27 Apr.

Klein, N. (2000). *No Logo*. London: Flamingo.

Knorr, A., and Arndt, A. (2003). 'Why did Wal-Mart Fail in Germany?' *Materialien des Wissenschsftsscherpunktes 'Globalisierung der Welwirtschaft'*, Instituts für Weltwirtschaft und Internationales Management (IWIM), Universitat Bremen, 24 (June).

Kotler, P., Armstrong, G., Wong, V. and Saunders, J. (2008). *Principles of Marketing*. 5th European edn. Harlow: Pearson Education.

Marino, V. (2003). 'Starbucks Closes Shops in Israel', *New York Times*, 6 Apr.

Millward Brown Optimor (2009). 'BrandZ Top 100 Most Valuable Global Brands 2009', www.millwardbrown.com (accessed July 2009).

Minett, S. (2001). *B2B Marketing: Different Audience, Different Strategies, It's a Different World*. Harlow: Pearson Education/FT Prentice Hall.

Mortished, C. (2007). 'New BP Executive to Join Lord Browne at Riverstone', *The Times*, 19 Nov.

Mouawad, J. (2009). 'Going Green? Maybe after this Barrel ...', *Observer*, 19 Apr., *New York Times* insert.

Outlook Journal (2003). 'Think Global, Act Local', interview with Chairman and CEO, Accenture, Oct., www.accenture.com/Global (accessed 30 Apr. 2009).

Schiffman, L. G., and Kanuk, L. L. (2007). *Consumer Behavior*. 9th edn. Upper Saddle River, NJ: Pearson Prentice Hall.

Starbucks (2009). 'Facts about Starbucks in the Middle East', www.starbucks.com/aboutus/pressdec, 16 Jan. (accessed 26 Jan. 2009).

Stone, B. (2009). '200 Million and Counting', *Observer*, 5 Apr., *New York Times* insert.

Thompson, J. (2008). 'Crunch, what Crunch?' *Independent*, 4 June.

Townsend, A. (2007). 'Coming to America', *Business*, 6 Oct.

Usunier, J.-C., and Lee, J. A. (2005). *Marketing across Cultures*. 4th edn. Harlow: Pearson Education/FT Prentice Hall.

Wickham, T. (2009). 'The Art of Advertising', *BP Magazine Centenary Special*, 2.

Yeshin, Tony (2006). *Advertising*. London: Thomson Learning.

Further research

Moen, O., Madsen, T. K., and Aspelund, A. (2008). 'The Importance of the Internet in International Business-to-Business Markets', *International Marketing Review*, 25/5.

The purpose of the article, based on survey data from 635 Danish and Norwegian firms, is to provide evidence on the uses and market performance effects of information and communication technology (ICT) on international business-to-business (B2B) marketing activities of SMEs. The authors' findings are that there are serious limitations to the use of ICT in international B2B marketing, that ICT is used primarily for the accumulation of new market knowledge, and that ICT for sales purposes is rather limited and sometimes viewed negatively. The authors suggest that the development of long-term customer relationships and the importance of face-to-face interactions are essential for the establishment of commitment and trust between businesses; ICT can assist in these goals but cannot supplant the achievement of the goals through interactions between people within the B2B organizations.

Online Resource Centre

Visit the Online Resource Centre   that accompanies this book to read more information relating to international marketing: www.oxfordtextbooks.co.uk/orc/sitkin_bowen/

13 Foreign Exchange Management

Overview

The chapter starts by clarifying the origins of the risks facing companies that operate in a multi-currency environment. The main distinction is between foreign exchange (FX) risks associated with the regular value chain activities of a multinational enterprise (MNE) and other categories of risk. This is followed by analysis of the different ways that companies try to minimize currency risk, distinguishing between short-term 'hedging' and the in-depth restructuring of an MNE's international configuration. The final section offers a brief overview of banks' currency dealings before examining the different instruments that companies use to manage their FX exposures and the currency markets in general.

Section I: Identifying foreign exchange risk
The concept of exposure
Sources of FX exposure

Section II: Managing foreign exchange risk
Long-term 'natural' hedging
Short-term financial hedging

Section III: Currency trading
Dealing in the FX markets
Foreign exchange markets and regimes

Learning Objectives

After reading this chapter, you should be able to:

✦ analyse the different corporate activities that create foreign exchange risk

✦ compare possible strategies for managing their exposures

✦ assess MNEs' appetite for FX risk and any possible effects

✦ evaluate the shifting balance of power within the global FX market

✦ determine whether the FX market fulfils its assigned role

Case Study 13.1

Multinational currency dealings: Heineken handles its risk

With a network of 115 breweries and countless distributors in more than 65 countries worldwide, Heineken faces foreign exchange (FX) risk on a daily basis. The main currencies it trades, alongside its home currency (the euro), are the US dollar (USD), Chilean peso, Singapore dollar, Nigerian naira, Russian rouble, and Polish zloty. Heineken's strategy for the currencies that its global units trade on a daily basis is to smooth out the effects of any short-term volatility. It does not cover the risks incurred when translating foreign operations' net asset values onto its consolidated balance sheet, however. This latter risk will, therefore, affect its earnings and is always specified in the annual report.

In terms of short-term ex posures, Heineken's policy is to eliminate up to 90 per cent of all currency risks, largely comprised of intra-group USD cash flows. The main instruments used are currency options or forwards with maturities of less than one year. Both are categorized as 'cash-flow hedges' and calculated at fair value in line with the 'hedge accounting' principles that Heineken uses to ensure the transparency and general effectiveness of its currency management operations. At yearend 2006, the company estimated that an overall rise of one percentage point in the euro's value would have reduced total pre-tax earnings by approximately €4 million for fiscal year 2006. This was minimal compared to Heineken's consolidated profit of €1.345 billion that year. Clearly, the group was keeping a tight rein on its currency exposure.

Looking ahead on 31 December 2006, Heineken did not expect foreign exchange movements to have any major effect on earnings. A large proportion of the dollars that the company expected to receive in the near term had already been sold, at rates that were only slightly lower than the 2006 average rate of $1.2543 per euro. With hindsight, Heineken's prudent policy of always protecting itself against a weaker dollar turned out to be a good thing. The USD would weaken further over the next eighteen months, falling as low as $1.59 to the euro in July 2008. Fortunately, the negative effects of exchange rate movements totalled a mere €171 million in 2007, or just 1.4 per cent of the €12.6 billion company's revenues of that year. Of course, had the dollar recovered earlier, Heineken would have lost money from its forward sales at 2006's lower levels. It could not have known this at the time, however. The past is always easier to predict than the future.

Heineken's global sales create mutiple exposures (© Heineken International).

Introduction

Thinking point

Is a single global currency realistic or desirable?

One of the main consequences of the European Union's decision to adopt the euro in 1999 was that firms operating in this part of the world were finally freed from some of the complicated and expensive foreign exchange market operations that used to be necessary under the previous regime of fluctuating regional currencies. A secondary benefit was that it became easier for managers to assess economic realities in different EU countries, which could no longer use currency devaluation as an artificial way of altering national competitiveness. This had the effect of forcing politicians to deal with economic problems more directly. On the face of things, international business would be much simplified if the world traded in just one currency.

+ **Foreign exchange (FX) market**
Virtual marketplace(s) where currency prices are set through market supply and demand. The market is the sum total of the prices quoted and traded by all participants, nowadays almost always using electronic means of communication.

This kind of 'currency internationalization' (see Online Resource Centre, extension material 13.1) is extremely unlikely, however. It is almost impossible for countries with very divergent economic structures and policies to share the same currency. Moreover, the abolition of national currencies would meet too much resistance from the many supporters of a global regime based on sovereign nation-states (Rogoff 2001).

At the same time, because adverse currency moves can wipe out a company's profit margins, foreign exchange is a risk that MNEs cannot afford to neglect. Many spend enormous sums on information systems enabling their treasury function to centralize data about their global currency position at any given time (Myers 2006). For most MNEs, FX is a crucial function.

> Go to the ORC

Section I: Identifying foreign exchange risk

+ **Exposure**
Risk when assets do not match liabilities for a given commodity, like a currency, whose price might fluctuate.

The first task in identifying foreign exchange exposure is to clarify why firms operating in multi-currency environments are at risk when prices move. After this, analysis will explore the main foreign operations that generate FX risk.

The concept of exposure

Thinking point

To what extent does the US dollar's currency status as world reserve give US firms an unfair advantage?

There are many occasions when firms handle currencies other than the one traded in their home country. The US dollar, for example, is the standard currency of transaction in commodity markets such as oil or rubber but also for complex goods like aeroplanes. For non-dollar-based companies, trading in these sectors necessarily entails foreign exchange exposure. Conversely, firms whose entire value chain involves the use of one currency alone can trade with foreign partners without exposing themselves to direct FX risk (although they will still face an indirect 'economic risk', because of the way that currency movements affect other firms' competitiveness).

Managing FX exposure is a costly and difficult process that MNEs like to avoid if at all possible. For this reason, a key aspect of international contract negotiations is the currency of transaction. The party that is in the stronger position (usually the one that is bigger or technologically more advanced) will tend to demand that the deal be denominated in its own currency, forcing the other side to cope with FX exposure.

+ **Denominate**
Specify the currency of transaction.

A firm is exposed to FX risk if the three following conditions are met:

+ **Home currency**
Currency a firm uses to calculate its consolidated global accounts.

1. it has several currencies on its books, whether on the asset side (sums owed by foreign customers) or the liability side (sums owed to foreign suppliers);
2. its assets in any one currency do not match its liabilities in that same currency (creating an 'asset–liability gap');
3. the price of the currency in question varies against the price of its home currency.

+ **Long position**
Owning more of a commodity in the form of assets than the amounts owed in the form of liabilities.

FX management is based on two fundamental risks. Where a firm has a long position and more assets than liabilities in a given currency, the risk is that the currency will fall before the assets can be sold, decreasing their value. Where a firm has a short position and more liabilities than assets in a given currency, the risk is that the currency will rise before the liabilities can be acquired, increasing their cost. To repeat, regardless of a firm's currency of origin, it will be exposed to FX price variations as long as its different currency positions are not equal to zero at all times.

Once the existence of a foreign exchange exposure has been quantified, the next step is to identify what caused this risk, and what impact it might have. The answer will depend on factors like the nature of the company's international operations (trade or foreign direct investment); the volumes in question (different for small and medium-sized enterprises and large MNEs); and the configuration it has set up.

+ Short position
Owing more of a commodity in the form of liabilities than the amounts owned in the form of assets.

Sources of FX exposure

The main sources of FX risk come from the exposures that MNEs incur because of their daily value chain activities and can be described as 'transactional'. These risks are either recurrent in companies like global retailers that deal in foreign currencies all the time or infrequent in ones where currency dealings are more sporadic (for example, construction companies).

Transactional FX risks

The first category is *commercial risk*, which occurs when a company sells goods or services to a customer and receives foreign currency in payment. Sales of this kind increase the exporter's 'long' exposure, and thus the risk that the foreign currencies it receives will fall in value before it can resell them. As Figure 13.1 demonstrates, one example would be a euro-based German SME that exports solar panels to the UK. In so far as the foreign currency in which the exporter denominates its sales (British pound) differs from the domestic currency in which it incurs costs (euro), it is exposed to the risk that the former will fall in value before it can be sold for the latter. The British importer, on the other hand, would be buying foreign goods in its home currency and therefore has no exposure. Conversely, *operational risk* arises when a firm buys goods or services from a supplier and pays in foreign currency. These purchases increase the importer's 'short' exposure, and hence the risk that the foreign currencies in which it pays its liabilities will become more expensive before it gets a chance to acquire them. In the example of Germany–UK solar technology trade, if the UK firm were to pay its German supplier in euros, the deal would expose it to the risk that this currency would rise in value against the British pound, the currency in which the importer manages its accounts. On the other hand, in this case the German exporter's foreign dealings would be in its own home currency, meaning that it would not be exposed to any direct FX risk.

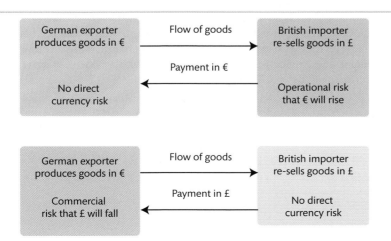

Figure 13.1
FX risk of a German export to the UK depends on currency of transaction.

Figure 13.2
Hypothetical long
versus short currency
exposures.

	Position subsidiary A	Position subsidiary B	Net group exposure	Risk
in USD ($)	+10	–5	Long $: + 5	$ will sink
in yen (¥)	–20	+10	Short ¥: –10	¥ will rise
in euros (€)	+5	–20	Short €: –15	€ will rise
in sterling (£)	0	+5	Long £: + 5	£ will sink

Thus, it is the currency of transaction that determines whether the exporter is going to have to face a commercial risk or the importer an operational risk.

The example above presents a simple situation where one firm faces a single exposure generated by one cross-border deal. This differs greatly from the reality for many MNEs, which operate in a multi-currency environment day in day out, running up costs on many sites and in many currencies across the world, and accumulating revenues in the same way. It is commonplace for an MNE subsidiary in one country, say Switzerland, to accumulate assets and liabilities denominated in euro, USD, yen, and other currencies alongside the Swiss franc, and for a sister unit, say in Japan, to have its own exposures in these currencies and others as well. This is why, as shown in Figure 13.2, almost all international companies calculate their operational exposures on a net basis, not only within each unit but among all units worldwide. Chapter 14 contains a section on the 'netting' process, a key aspect of MNE financial management and organization.

+ Net basis
Remaining exposure
after a firm's short
position in a given
financial category have
been subtracted from
its long positions in the
same category.

Non-transactional FX risks

A third category of FX exposure is *translational* risk, which occurs when currency variations affect a company's efforts to convert foreign assets or liabilities back into its home currency. This includes the dividends that an MNE's foreign subsidiaries send back to its headquarters; the foreign currency loans that the MNE makes or receives; and, above all, the value of foreign assets. Take a Japanese firm that owns a plant in the USA. Figure 13.3 shows how currency variations could affect its yearend results without it having engaged in any new deals. In this example, the value of the firm's assets overseas does not move in host country terms but changes when translated back into the home currency.

Analysts often question whether companies should protect themselves against translational risk, and, if so, how (Hyman 2006). The issue arises because some companies intentionally configure their international operations in such a way as to diversify exposures so that risks faced in one currency zone are offset by risks elsewhere. In this case, hedging any component of the group's FX risk would disturb the overall balance and create new exposures.

A fourth source of FX exposure is *speculative risk*. MNEs are free to decide what percentage of their currency risk they wish to offset. A company might reason that its treasury specialists are as competent at currency trading as the bankers with whom they currently offload

Figure 13.3
Translational
risk. MNEs with
international assets are
automatically exposed
to currency variations.

	Year 1	Year 2
Value of US plant in dollars	$100 million	$100 million (unchanged)
Dollar/yen exchange rate	$1 = ¥110	$1 = ¥100
Value of US plant in yen	¥11 billion (100 million × 110)	¥10 billion (100 million × 100)
Book loss between Year 1 and Year 2	¥1 billion	

their exposures. Porsche was said, for example, to have made more money from 'active' foreign exchange management in 2007 than it did from selling cars (Shipman 2007). At the same time, running FX risk can also be dangerous—as witnessed by the case of European aerospace and defence company EADS, which declared foreign currency translation losses of €153 million over the first nine months of 2007, after suffering similar losses in 2006 (EADS 2007). Whether a firm should (or can) cover all of its risks is a central debate in currency management, one dealt with in greater detail in the section below on short-term financial hedging.

It is worth noting that transactional, translational, and speculative FX exposures involve risks that can be identified, and thus managed, immediately. This differs from *economic risk*, which involves the long-term fortunes of the currencies of the countries where an MNE has interests. A good example of economic risk is the decades-long rise in the Japanese currency's value from a 1949 rate of 360 yen per dollar to an April 1995 peak of 80. In the 1950s and 1960s, Japanese companies, incurring manufacturing costs in their home currency, the yen, began exporting products (like automobiles) in US dollars. Thus, the dollar's long-term downtrend against the yen had the effect of squeezing their profit margins. Japanese exporters could have decided to raise retail prices in dollars to restore earnings, but this would have made them less competitive in the US at a time when they were trying to increase market share. Hence their decision to keep USD retail prices stable and offset the falling margins by improving productivity at home. This is one rationale behind the Toyota Production System (see Chapter 11).

At a certain point, however, the yen had risen so high, and the dollar had fallen so low, that it was no longer possible for Japan-based manufacturers to compete profitably. As shown by Figure 13.4, Japanese MNEs would have understood that the yen's strength was a long-term trend and reacted accordingly. The currency squeeze, in conjunction with the quotas that the US authorities decided to levy on Japanese car imports, explains Toyota's decision to engage in FDI in the United States from the 1970s onwards. Once the company had diversified its production locations, the negative effect of further dollar weaknesses on its US revenues were largely offset by their positive effects on its new US liabilities (production costs). Of course, FDI is a major, structural action that should be undertaken only if a firm believes it is facing a lasting problem.

Indirect economic risk can be when a competitor has production facilities located in a third country characterized by a weak currency, and seeks competitive advantage by exporting goods from this cheap location. One example is the way that many EU carmakers have rushed to build plants in East European transition economies that are relatively inexpensive, not only because of lower wages or taxes but also because their currencies are fragile and not yet part of the Eurozone. MNE strategies for managing currency risk range from the tactical to the strategic. In international business, foreign exchange is much more than a mere treasury function.

+ Hedging
Where a party offsets a risk through a new deal exposing it to the exact opposite risk. The original exposure is called the 'underlying' risk. The new exposure is called the 'hedge'.

Where a limited rise been expected in yen	Japanese MNEs would still manufacture in Japan and offset adverse currency movements through • productivity efforts • short-term financial transactions
Where a durable rise was expected in yen	Japanese MNEs would engage in FDI and manufacture/sell in USA. Costs incurred in USA benefited from weaker dollar. Dividends on US operations were sent home (repatriated) to Japan.

Rising yen: Sinking dollar

Figure 13.4
Historic Japanese responses to dollar weakness.

Section II: Managing foreign exchange risk

As exemplified by Japanese exporters' historic responses to the long-term rise in the yen, whenever a company fears that an adverse currency movement is destined to have lasting effects, reconfiguring its entire global value chain becomes a viable option. Immediate exposures, on the other hand, tend to be dealt with through simpler mechanisms, above all short-term financial hedging.

Long-term 'natural' hedging

As explained in the above discussion on 'economic risk', an MNE is subject to a foreign exchange 'squeeze' if its configuration means that it tends to accumulate assets in a weak currency and/or liabilities in a strong one. The only possible reactions are for it to change the currencies in which it denominates assets and liabilities and/or ensure that its long and short exposures are more evenly matched. Both of these adjustments require major, and costly, shifts in a company's global value chain. The question then becomes when such structural initiatives are worth it.

Take the example of the US dollar's weakness in the early 2000s, largely caused by huge American trade and budget deficits. This trend had the effect of squeezing firms that invoiced customers in dollars but whose own liabilities were denominated in currencies that were stronger at the time, like the British pound. One example was UK semi-conductor designer Arm Holding, whose CEO said: 'The only way you can respond is by matching your cost base. That means jobs going outside the UK. We have gone as far as we can and about 50 per cent of our costs are now overseas' (Hughes 2007). FX is often the driver behind a company's internationalization.

There are two ways to build up this kind of overseas cost base. The quickest and easiest is to source more components from suppliers who invoice in a weak currency. This is one explanation for the explosion in outsourcing witnessed since the 1980s. A more structural but costlier and less flexible way to develop a foreign cost base is through FDI. In the case of offshoring, this usually involves setting up a plant in a country specifically because of its traditionally weak currency. Where the aim is to reduce overall FX exposure, the MNE will locate plants in the markets where it realizes a significant proportion of its global revenues. With this latter approach, sometimes referred to as 'natural hedging', if the currency in question weakens in the future, the company's sales will fall but so will its costs. In this way, FDI helps MNEs to offset their long-term 'long' exposures.

Conversely, to offset long-term 'short' (buy-side) exposures, MNEs can try to increase revenues denominated in the strong currencies in which they pay their suppliers, or in the currencies of the countries where they already run a manufacturing base. A case in point is the situation facing many Western MNEs that source products in China. Given the country's massive export surpluses, its currency, the yuan, is likely to jump if the Beijing government ever allows this to happen (see Case Study 13.3). Until now, most MNEs have used China solely as a cost base, but the prospect of a strengthening yuan, and of Chinese consumers' rising purchasing power, means that many are now looking to develop their retail network here, in the hope that the expected increase in yuan-denominated manufacturing costs will be offset by higher revenues in this currency. There are many examples of companies with operations in China that are currently trying to expand their sales networks there. One is European telecommunications alliance Nokia–Siemens, which signed a network deal in 2007 to service the Wuhan–Guangzhou railway line in southern China and another providing coverage for eleven cities and twelve million subscribers in Yunnan province. Another is American brewer Anheuser-Busch, which in 2007 announced plans to build a new brewery in China and double the number of cities where its signature brand, Budweiser beer, is sold. Of course, it is rarely clear whether a company's motive for increasing sales in a country stems from

a desire to offset currency risk or to take advantage of market growth, since the two often go hand in hand (countries with rising incomes should theoretically have stronger currencies). What is clear is that FX considerations influence many MNE decisions.

Short-term financial hedging

Where companies have no more than a short-term vision of a given foreign exchange risk— that is, where they have no view on the currency's long-term strength—they will often offset any exposures by hedging them through the foreign exchange market. By creating new exposures that are the polar opposite of the normal risks associated with international business transactions, MNEs can offset potentially adverse price movements for as long as the hedge is in effect. Of course, once it matures, a new decision will have to be made about how to cover the underlying risk.

Unlike long-term structural reconfigurations in a company's value chain, short-term hedges do not prevent an exposure from recurring once the hedge runs out, and there is always the possibility that the new coverage will be transacted at a worse rate. Moreover, recurring short-term hedges raise transaction costs (Hughes 2006), usually comprised of bid-offer spreads that market-users pay to market-makers (see Figure 13.8). Of course, it is always possible that, when one hedging transaction matures, the next might be done at a better rate. Lastly, it is worth recalling that short-term financial hedges are quicker and cheaper to organize than huge structural reconfigurations. Aside from exceptional circumstances, like the late 2008 credit crunch, it is usually fairly easy for an MNE to find a counterpart, usually a bank, on which it can offload its exposure.

+ **Market-maker**
Trader who is always prepared to quote other market participants a price to buy ('bid') and sell ('offer') a given commodity.

Managing short-term exposures

A useful example of the kinds of short-term hedging choices that MNEs typically have to make came in 2005 and 2006, when the Korean won rose by a total of 33 per cent against the Japanese yen. This was a painful development for Korean exporters such as Samsung, Hyundai, and Daewoo trying to compete with their Japanese rivals (Fifield 2006). Part of the problem was their uncertainty about how long the won's strength would last, since the currency has historically moved in tandem with the yen. The Korean companies ended up taking the view that the trend was short-term, thus that hedges selling the yen and buying the won would be more appropriate than major reconfigurations in their value chain.

Figure 13.5 Offsetting a long exposure with a short hedge.		Step 1. Novo notes long exposure,—i.e. risk that $ will fall vs. kroner	Step 2. It therefore shorts (sells) $ against Kroner to hedge this risk	Net effect
	Scenario (a). If the $ subsequently falls. . .	the underlying position loses money as feared (–)	the hedge makes money (+)	Zero: the profit on the hedge offsets the underlying loss
	Scenario (b). If the $ subsequently rises. . .	the underlying position makes an unexpected 'windfall' profit (+)	the hedge loses money (–)	Zero: the loss on the hedge offsets the underlying profit

With hindsight, they were right to remain calm—by January 2008 the won had fallen 13 per cent below its December 2006 rate and their plants in Korea had become competitive once again.

A similarly instructive example from about the same time was provided by the Danish pharmaceutical company Novo Nordirsk, which incurs a substantial part of its manufacturing costs in its home currency (the Danish kroner) but accumulates revenues in pounds, dollars, yen, and euros. With its long position in these latter currencies, Novo Nordirsk's risk was that they might fall before it could convert them back to kroners (in fact, that the pound, dollar, and yen would weaken against the euro, the major trading currency that is most correlated to the kroner). The company therefore implemented a short hedge against its long exposures, selling the counter-value of its 'expected net cash flows in relation to US dollars, Japanese yen and British pounds, for 17, 15 and 9 months, respectively' (Novo Nordirsk 2007). When these three currencies did fall over the first nine months of fiscal year 2007, the Danish MNE was able to record a hedging profit of kroner 644 million (*c.* €86 million). This profit went a long way towards offsetting the losses it suffered because of the kroner's subsequent rise.

Figure 13.5 illustrates how hedging can help an exporter (like Novo Nordirsk in the above example) to offset the risk that the currencies in which its invoices are denominated will weaken in the future.

This same principle works the other way around for importers who run the risk that the currency in which their suppliers invoice them might rise before they can pay their bills. Industrialists importing raw materials for use in their production process face a short risk on two different levels, since they are exposed to rising commodity and currency prices. This is a problem in many oil-starved less-developed countries (LDCs). Retailers whose main business involves reselling foreign goods face a similar problem. One example is Trader Joe's, a US company that specializes in marketing imported European wines and is therefore vulnerable to the euro rising against the US dollar (see Figure 13.6).

As these examples show, once a firm has hedged its currency position in full, it cannot experience unexpected (windfall) profits or losses. In other words, hedging reduces volatility but also affects potential returns (Chincarini 2007). Some managers are happier with the prospect of less uncertainty. This includes executives who think that a company

+ Correlation
Extent to which different assets, like two currencies, move in the same direction.

Figure 13.6 Offsetting a short exposure with a long hedge.		Step 1. Trader Joe's notes short exposure i.e. risk that € will rise vs. $	Step 2. It therefore goes long (buys) € to hedge this risk	Net effect
	Scenario (a). If the euro subsequently rises	the underlying position loses money as feared (–)	the hedge makes money (+)	Zero: the profit on the hedge offsets the underlying loss
	Scenario (b). If the euro subsequently falls	the underlying position makes an unexpected 'windfall' profit (+)	the hedge loses money (–)	Zero: the loss on the hedge offsets the underlying profit

should stick to its original mission and not speculate on currencies, or creditors who are reassured when a borrower's earnings are more stable because it has hedged its exposures. Some people dislike this practice, however. Hedging always incurs transaction costs, even if it turns out subsequently that the coverage was unnecessary because the worst-case scenario never materializes. Furthermore, companies who lock in a price through hedging exclude the possibility of windfall profits, unlike their unprotected rivals. There is also the notion in modern portfolio theory that investors may wish to hold a stake in an MNE specifically because the currency risk to which its operations would normally subject shareholders offsets other exposures they may be holding in their portfolios of assets. In short, it is just as possible to criticize MNE treasurers for over-hedging their FX exposure as for the opposite.

Thinking point

Should a non-financial MNE ever speculate in the foreign exchange markets?

Hedging as an expression of attitude towards risk

Decisions regarding the extent to which an MNE should hedge its FX risk are therefore largely a reflection of people's attitude towards the volatility of earnings. As Figure 13.7 shows, the profits of companies who hedge as a matter of course (that is, who refuse any 'speculative risk') are less volatile, since there will be no unexpected FX profits or losses on top of their regular business. At the same time, because of the costs incurred when transacting a hedge (often the bank's 'bid–offer spread', see below), their profits will be slightly lower. This is normal, since hedging reduces risk, an advantage for which the company should expect to have to pay.

MNE policies in this area depend on several factors. The main one is managers' overall attitude towards risk, which can be a deeply cultural variable (see Chapter 2). Also important is the mission attributed to the treasury department—that is, whether it is defined as a profit centre or as a cost centre. The broader question is whether the company itself is viewed as a pure vehicle for profit maximization, or is supposed to always behave safely to ensure long-term survival.

Note that MNEs rarely choose to hedge all their exposures fully or, inversely, to hedge none of them. Usually they decide upon a percentage that they wish to cover. In 2005, for example, the treasurers at Volkswagen (VW) were uncertain whether they should take advantage of a temporary weakness in the currency in which they incurred costs, the euro, in order to buy it forward and increase coverage of their overall short exposure from 70 to 75 per cent (Mackintosh 2005). Their problem was that VW would lose out if they bought too many euros before it weakened further or if they did not buy enough euros before it rose again. With hindsight, VW's managers were right to take advantage of the euro's temporary weakness to add to the cover, since it did recover subsequently. It remains that they could not have known this at the time. The decision to reduce risk is itself risky.

Currency analysts used to talk about 'lead' and 'lag' strategies as a way of managing FX risk. Respectively, this referred to the accelerated collection of currencies expected to rise,

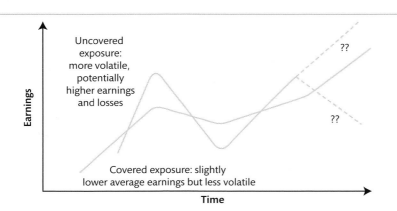

Figure 13.7
Hedging changes a company's earnings patterns.

or disbursement of currencies expected to fall. This was a dangerous basis for corporate decision-making, however, since it implied that treasurers are actually in a position to predict future currency movements with any degree of accuracy. In many cases this is wrong, and the history of international business is full of horror stories of MNEs that have lost money on misplaced FX transactions. The topic of what drives foreign exchange price movements is, therefore, an important one.

Understanding FX price shifts

Explanations in this area are traditionally divided into two categories; 'technical' studies focused on price movements *per se*, and 'fundamental' analyses that try to uncover a link between macro-economic variables and FX prices. Technical analysis generally refers to some FX traders' habit of charting recent price moves to detect trends. In this vision, instead of reflecting reassessments of fair value, changes in prices (of FX or other financial assets) largely depend on traders' evaluation of fellow traders' sentiments, a process that British economist J. M. Keynes referred to as the financial markets' 'beauty contest' aspect. Similarly, studies by Dornbusch (1976) have highlighted currencies' tendency to rise or fall excessively and 'overshoot' their fair value. This can be a headache for companies squeezed between FX volatility and much slower ('stickier') price shifts in product markets driven by a more fundamental economic logic. The FX markets' tendency to overshoot their fair value means that technical analysis is more useful in the short term than in the long run, over which time a currency's real macro-economic quality is likelier to determine its price. This latter vision is key to the second school of currency valuation, called 'fundamental' analysis (Copeland 2005).

Economists mobilize many concepts to explain FX pricing from a fundamental viewpoint. One is the Balassa–Samuelson theory, which states that the currencies of countries experiencing rapid growth should rise, and that wealthy countries should have stronger currencies than weaker ones (Rogoff 2005). Another is the more basic concept that a leading factor in the supply and demand of currencies is an economy's trade balance. The idea here is that a country should have a trade surplus if its currency

+ Fair value
Estimate of what a good is worth objectively, irrespective of potential buyers and sellers' interests or current market price.

Photo 13.2
The US dollar has acted as the world's reserve currency since the 1940s, although there are questions about its future (© iStockphoto).

is too cheap, or a trade deficit if its currency is too high (Batra and Beladi 2008). Another way of expressing this is that, if international consumers purchase increasing amounts of goods from a particular source, 'derived demand' for its currency will rise, in the sense that they need the country's currency to buy its goods. Conversely, if consumers turn away from the country's goods, derived demand will fall. In this way, trade performance should be a reliable indicator of a currency's fair value. This is not always the case, however, as exemplified by the long periods of time during which the USD has been strong despite recurring American trade deficits (a situation explained in part by the dollar's current status as the world's reserve currency). On the whole, however, the idea that FX prices should reflect foreign demand and/or holdings of a currency is a logical one and therefore features regularly among the battery of indicators used by fundamental analysts.

+ **Reserve currency**
Currency that, by consensus is, viewed as the safest vehicle for storing value.

In a similar vein, the concept of *purchasing power parity* means that currencies should be priced so that consumers pay the same to buy the same basket of goods in different countries. This was amusingly translated by the journalist Pam Woodall into something she called the 'Big Mac Index', or the idea that McDonald's famous hamburger should cost the same worldwide once currency translations are taken into account. This is an imperfect measurement, since it excludes many relevant factors (like global variations in labour costs), but it does have the merit of painting a clear picture of what an equilibrium currency price might be. For instance, if a Big Mac costs \$3.30 in the USA and £2.20 in the UK, then the exchange rate between these two currencies should be 3.30/2.20 = 1.5000 dollars per pound. With an early 2009 exchange rate of around 1.4300, this meant that the dollar was about 5 per cent (1.5000/1.4300) above its fair value against the pound, and could therefore be expected to fall by that amount sooner or later.

Another economic concept that is frequently mobilized to predict currency pricing is the *International Fisher Effect* (IFF). This states that future exchange rates can be forecast by differences in countries' interest rates, which should reflect their respective inflation rates as long as real interest rates are held constant. The idea here is that the currency of the country with the highest level of inflation should fall over time. Thus, in early September 2008, the three-month interest rate was 5.75 per cent for the British pound and around 0.89 per cent for the Japanese yen, a difference of 4.86 per cent. At the time, the FX rate was 198 yen per pound. According to IFF, this should have fallen by 198/1.0486 or just below 189 by December 2008. The actual rate in April 2009 was around 140 yen per pound, because the credit crunch had more of a negative effect on the pound than on the yen. This demonstrates that the International Fisher Effect, like all technical or fundamental indicators, is not sufficient in and of itself fully to predict currency movements. In other words, both fundamental and technical analyses are useful but incomplete. There is no such thing as a crystal ball in the FX markets.

+ **Real interest rate**
Nominal interest rate minus inflation rate.

Where technical analysis errs because of its assumption that past price movements tend to repeat in the future, fundamental analysis suffers from a 'disconnect' between the financial markets and the real economy (Rogoff 2001). Thus, because currencies are so unpredictable, most companies are willing to pay for advice. This has given birth to a huge industry in FX forecasting, largely driven by 'sell-side' bankers trying to market their ideas to 'buy-side' customers (like companies or funds). Some of the ideas and innovations that bankers offer are useful: macro-economic information or market news; risk minimization instruments; exposure calculations. Others are less beneficial and potentially dangerous (*Euromoney* 2007c). It is worth remembering that a conflict of interest can always arise when a bank with an existing exposure seeks to convince a customer to trade a certain way. After all, the advice can be biased, since the bank may be trying to offload an unwanted position. The nature of an MNE's relationship to its banks, and to the currency markets in general, is a crucial element in FX risk management.

Case Study 13.2

Currency markets: One day in the life of a London FX specialist

'Got to the office at 7 a.m. to check on the Tokyo afternoon ... the yen fell following that incident off North Korea ... need to share a few charts with a British importer who may want to cover his yen exposure now ... Europe has woken up, Reuters keeps spitting out news releases ... German trade statistics have been announced, the surplus is lower than expected so the euro is down ... quickly ring a few customers ... am now fielding incoming calls, sometimes several phones are going at once and my colleagues have to help out ... one customer is asking for a large deal in dollars versus Swiss, my spot trader asks me whether she is a buyer or a seller ... I know that she's buying dollars but if I tell the trader, he'll raise his price, we might make an extra pip or two but the customer will be angry if she notices ... I say I'm not sure so he makes me a neutral price, I tell the customer who gives me the go-ahead so I shout 'mine' and buy USD on my customer's behalf ... just working out payment details for the customer ... now someone is asking for a sterling–Canadian dollar forward price, the two currencies don't trade directly against one another, so we have to calculate sterling against US dollar (called the 'Cable' rate in slang) then US against Canada ... I get my numbers from the forwards desk, we speak over the intercom, unlike the spot trader who sits within shouting distance ... the back office calls up to check how we should book this latest deal ... Things quiet down over lunch while we wait for New York to open ... I have time to read the research our economist did on the Russian rouble, still a minor currency but it could be big one day if they ever let it float ... now a US customer is asking me to price a dollar–pound option with a strike price of 0.66, I don't recognize that exchange rate ... ah, they're thinking in pounds per dollar, over here we always quote in dollars per pound ... it's easy to convert, 1 divided by 0.6600 equals about 1.5150, a recognizable figure ... it's funny how most of the world agrees on the base currency when making a quote yet a few people still ask for it the other way around ... I get price components from the options traders, plug them into the computer and calculate the premium ... he passes ... that's a shame because the afternoon is pretty dead otherwise ... at least the morning was busy ... it's 5 p.m. now, time to pass the positions over to the night desk in New York.'

Traders track numbers and headlines twenty-four hours a day (© iStockphoto).

Section III: Currency trading

Traditionally, companies seeking to transact FX interests have simply rung their bank and requested a price. This continues to be the case in most treasury departments. At the same time, there have been moves in recent years to give non-bank entities like hedge funds direct access to the same computerized platforms Reuters dealing system or Electronic Broking Services) that are used in inter bank dealing. Generally banks remain essential counterparts to MNE foreign exchange teams, providing advice (particularly important when trading lesser-known, emerging currencies), prices and payment facilities (see Online Resource Centre, extension material 13.2). At the same time, it is worth remembering that banks are profit-making institutions and offer all these services at a price.

> Go to the ORC

Dealing in the FX markets

MNEs will often organize FX dealing relationships with several banks to ensure access to good prices. Inversely, banks' marketing officers are constantly contacting new companies to try to add them to their customer list. One of the most common products that banks offer during such approaches is their market-maker capability.

Inside business

Torquil Wheatley, Director, Client Risk Strategy, Global Foreign Exchange, Deutsche Bank (speaking in a personal capacity)

My job is to oversee the operations in which Deutsche Bank assists companies in handling their foreign currency solutions. We are very customer-driven and have two main areas of activity for companies: providing currency hedging services; and helping companies in dealing with currency as an asset class.

The company carries out about 22 per cent of all currency market flows worldwide, 90 per cent of which are executed electronically. According to the Bank of International Settlements (BIS), daily trading in currencies is about $3.2 trillion. The company operates through primary hubs in Europe (London), North America (New York), and Asia (Singapore, Tokyo, and Australia).

Since 2000 we have seen a trend of currency market specialists being allowed to carry out more of the operations that MNEs used to do for themselves. Although Deutsche Bank still carries out some proprietary operations, it now does much of its business through specialized currency hedge funds. The vast majority of these transactions involve to the G10 currencies, but there is growing interest in emerging market currencies. During the 2008 crisis, heightened volatility and wider spreads made the emerging currencies generally less attractive, and traders returned to the G10 currencies.

In the foreign exchange market, we are usually taught that 90 per cent of trades are speculative and only 10 per cent connected to real business. In fact, from research that Deutsche Bank has conducted, we think that virtually the reverse is true. Only about 10–25 per cent is speculation and 75–90 per cent is connected to real business, like MNEs hedging future receivables.

Companies look to remove unwanted and unrewarded risk, reducing their overall exposure. There will probably be a greater increase in both sides of the market: non-profit-seeking and speculative (profit-seeking). The question for companies is how much of their portfolio should be invested in foreign exchange. Before the 1990s, currency markets lacked the benchmarks that apply in other markets. Researchers in the early 2000s at Deutsche Bank then came up with a transparent, rules-based benchmark that could measure minimum expected returns from currency as an asset class. This can be back-tested over about thirty years. It has generally shown that the volatility of currencies is significantly lower—by about one-third—than equity markets.

As far as electronic trading is concerned, there has been a dramatic increase since the 2000s, with the new systems being applied to forwards and options alongside spot markets.

Banks as FX counterparts

An MNE that uses the FX market will need counterparts willing to quote prices to buy and sell a sufficient quantity of currencies at all times. Finding this kind of 'liquidity' is especially important when markets are erratic or if current trends are disadvantageous. Companies with 'long' dollar exposures, for instance, may want to increase their cover and sell more dollars on days when it is weak. They would, therefore, seek a counterpart willing to take the other side of their new dollar sale—that is, one who is willing to buy dollars precisely on a day when the dollar is dropping. Market-makers' assumption of market-users' risks is the justification that banks use when arguing that they should be rewarded for providing customers with liquidity. The idea here is that bank's trading activities serve all international business since MNEs are more likely to operate globally if they think that they can exit a bad position if need be.

Market-making generates revenues for banks (thus costs for market-users like MNEs) largely due to the spread between the prices at which any one currency will be quoted at a given moment in time. Banks benefit from this spread, selling at the higher price and buying at the lower price, whereas market-users pay for it, selling low and buying high. The wider the spread, the greater the advantage for banks and the higher the cost for users. This is one of the main transaction costs that companies pay to access the foreign exchange market and it helps to support the huge FX trading profits that some banks report every year.

The extent of market-maker remuneration depends on the size of the bid-offer spread, which is relatively narrow for widely traded 'major' currencies (such as the dollar, yen, or euro) when things are quiet but widens during volatile sessions or when more 'exotic' currencies such as the Mexican peso or Brazilian real are involved. Note that market-makers are rarely able to resell immediately and profitably the 'long' or 'short' exposures that they accumulate through their customer dealings. This happens only if the market-maker has enough customers requesting prices at the same time, and then only if there are as many interests on the sell-side as on the buy-side. In this case, the customer transactions would offset one another, letting the market-maker realize the profit from the spread without having any outstanding exposure. Such offsets almost never occur, however, even though, as Figure 13.8 demonstrates, a market-maker will usually adjust its prices to customers to induce them to buy the currencies where it is 'long', or to sell the currencies in which it is currently 'short'. It is at this point that conflicts can arise in banks' FX departments between traders trying to rebalance their positions and salespersons representing customer interests and trying to get a neutral price.

It bears repeating that it is because banks are usually forced to carry long or short positions throughout the course of the day that they will seek remuneration in the form of this bid-offer spread. Of course, many traders are specifically paid to make 'proprietary' decisions for the bank's own account. They derive their opinions from the bank's in-house analysts but also, as often as not, from their observations of the trading behaviour of major market participants, many of whom are their MNE customers. A problem can arise if a bank's traders try to 'front-run' its customers, transacting a deal for themselves at a better price before executing customers' orders at a worse price. There is a whole ethical discussion to be had about MNEs and banks' foreign exchange relationships.

+ Spread

Difference between the market-maker's 'bid' and 'offer' prices. In the FX markets, this is usually calculated in terms of basis points (four digits after the zero, i.e. 0.0001).

Thinking point

Can MNE treasurers ever trust banks to make 'neutral' prices?

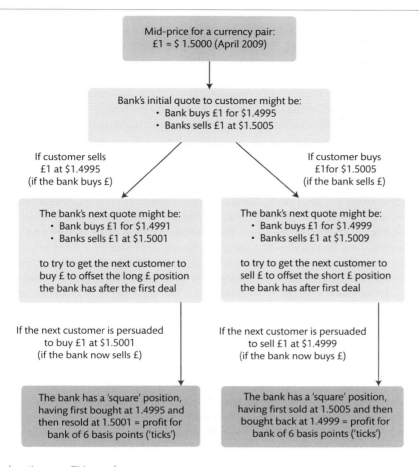

Introduction to FX markets

Some of MNEs' transaction risk would be minimized if they traded their currency needs on organized exchanges. These markets are characterized by more transparent pricing mechanisms. Among other advantages, this prevents the kinds of 'arbitrage' that used to occur in the days before globalized information systems, back when traders could buy a currency in one market and sell it immediately for a higher price elsewhere. Above all, exchanges mean less counterpart risk, since market participants are allowed to trade only if they leave margin deposits covering any probable losses. However, organized exchanges are much more important in the capital or commodity markets than in the FX market, where most trading is done on an 'over the counter' (OTC) basis between two private parties. OTC transactions can be between two banks, in what is known as 'inter bank' dealing, or between a market-user (customer) and a bank. The OTC market offers greater flexibility, with participants being able to adjust transaction specifications (like size or maturity) to their exact needs. On the other hand, lacking a margin deposit system, OTC markets are more prone to the risk of counterpart insolvency and also dependent on participants continuing to offer one another 'trading lines'. Thus it is in the OTC markets (mainly the equity and bond sectors but also in FX) that liquidity evaporated and volatility rose most dramatically during the 2008 credit crunch (Dodd 2008). The markets' inability to perform efficiently when they were most needed raises doubts about their architecture, launching a debate that will last for many years.

According to the Bank for International Settlements (BIS), in April 2007 (thus before the crisis) average daily trading volumes were $1.005 trillion for spot FX, $362 billion for forwards, and $1.714 for foreign exchange swaps, or a total of about $3.1 trillion daily. Moreover, there is anecdotal evidence of a further sharp rise in these volumes through early

2008, before the effects of the credit crunch hit. Trading volumes are up strongly since 2004, largely because new participants, like hedge funds, have started to trade foreign exchange as an investment instrument ('asset class') in and of itself. Some observers predict that the growth in market volumes cannot help but slow down, although the rise of emerging market currencies may lay a foundation for further market expansion in a more distant future (Oliver 2007). Certainly the devastating effects of the 2008 credit crunch on financial market liquidity, including the disbandment of many hedge funds, dampened speculative activity over 2008–9. Whether this was temporary or not remains to be seen.

FX trading instruments

MNEs transact many different currency instruments with banks (Rosenstreich 2005). Most involve an exchange of cash. The leading instrument is 'spot' FX, where two parties agree a price to buy one currency against another for more or less immediate settlement. The second is forward trading, where two parties agree a price to buy one currency against another for settlement at a specified future date and at a price reflecting the currencies' interest rate differential over the period in question (see the International Fischer Effect calculations above). Thirdly, with 'foreign exchange swaps', one party will buy and sell the same amount of a currency for two different dates, while selling and buying varying amounts of another currency for the same dates, again at rates reflecting the two currencies' interest rate differentials. Essentially, swaps' contracted buyback feature means that the parties are using the currency markets to make loans.

However, cash instruments are not the only tools that companies use to create or offset FX exposure. As mentioned above, one of the main weaknesses of a currency hedge is that it excludes windfall profits. This explains the popularity of 'currency options', a flexible derivative that gives the holder the right—but not the obligation—to buy or sell a specified amount of one currency against another on a given date at a specified rate called the 'strike price'. Similar to an insurance policy, options are bought or sold for a 'premium' that one counterpart (for example, a British exporter with a 'long' euro exposure) pays to another, usually a bank. By so doing, the option purchaser will have some protection in place in case an adverse price move occurs (if the euro falls) but can abandon this cover in case a windfall profit becomes possible (if the euro rises). The premium price depends on the market's perceived 'volatility'; the time until maturity; and the distance between the strike price and the current forward price for the maturity date. All these factors affect the likelihood that the option will have intrinsic value (be 'in-the-money') when it expires. Currency options are a widely used derivative, with an average daily volume that, according to BIS statistics, reached $212 billion in April 2007. (See Online Resource Centre, extension material 13.3, for examples of currency forward, swap, and options pricing.)

Many corporate treasurers are unhappy to pay premiums for insurance policies that ultimately are not needed. Such charges seem especially wasteful when foreign exchange markets lack volatility, as they did for most of the 2000s (Ferguson et al. 2007) until the general panic accompanying the 2008 credit crunch led to a flurry of safe haven investments in the USD and downward reassessments other currencies (like the British pound). At the same time, market-maker profits have been negatively affected by the advent of electronic trading systems, which reduce bid-offer spreads by improving price transparency. To maintain profitability, banks have started to make markets in riskier 'emerging' currencies; develop new derivative products (more popular amongst speculators than corporate treasurers); and take generally larger proprietary positions (*Euromoney* 2007a). As crucial as foreign exchange is to MNEs, some critics estimate that only 2–3 per cent of all transactions relate directly to real trade or FDI. In other words, the FX markets are run by financial interest, not by non-financial MNEs. Whether that was the original intention is very doubtful.

+ **Settlement**
Actual moment when one party to an FX transaction transfers the currency it sold to the account of the other party, and receives the currency it bought.

+ **Forward trading**
Trading at a price established immediately for a delivery of assets at a specified future date.

+ **Derivatives**
Instruments whose value is based on underlying cash market prices but where the parties to the transaction do not actually exchange the assets in question.

> Go to the ORC

+ **Safe haven**
Assets that investors tend to purchase to store value in times of crisis. Often include gold, USD, and Swiss francs.

Foreign exchange markets and regimes

Over the years, there have been several different currency regimes. For a long time, countries would prioritize keeping their national currency stable against some external standard, usually gold. Most organized regimes since the Second World War have revolved around the US dollar—although there are signs that it now has competition from the euro (Batavia and Malliaris 2008), the Chinese yuan, and conceivably an International Monetary Fund (IMF) 'basket currency' called Special Drawing Rights.

There are basically three rival regimes governing national currencies today. Where they differ is in terms of the extent to which market participants or state authorities set prices (Caramazza and Aziz 1998). In *fixed* regimes, a country's central bank pegs its national currency to a benchmark—often the US dollar but also baskets of currencies—and ensures that this rate is maintained. Examples include the Kuwaiti or Bahraini dinars, and to some extent the Chinese yuan, which is allowed to move only under strict government supervision. With a *managed float*, a country's central bank sets a target trading range and intervenes in the market as needs be to keep its currency within this range. Prime examples are the Russian rouble and Malaysian ringgit. Lastly, the price for *free floating* currencies (most of the world's 'major' currencies, including euros, yen, and dollars) is determined solely by supply and demand from private interests. Each of these systems is associated with different levels of *convertibility*, or whether authorities will allow transactions in their national currency to be traded without prior administrative authorization.

In line with the neo-liberal paradigm that has dominated since the 1980s (see Chapter 5), the general trend has been towards free-floating currency systems. Some studies view this as a positive trend, having found, for instance, that economic shocks are less likely to damage countries whose exchange rate systems are flexible (Edwards and Levy Yeyati 2005). Yet many countries have maintained their preference for fixed FX regimes, often because this corresponds to their paradigmatic view of how states and private interests should interact. Between these two extremes, managed float systems have lost much of their attraction (Fischer 2001). This is because since the late 1980s, private sector resources have been so much larger than the funds available to central banks that it is almost impossible for the latter to control a national currency once it has been open to speculation. Indeed, in the absence of global coordination, central banks find it almost impossible in the early twenty-first century to impose their will on the FX markets (Ghosh 2008). This means that governments have one less policy weapon at their disposal in times of crisis—as exemplified by the Russian central bank's inability to halt brutal speculative sales of the rouble in the wake of the credit crunch (Hopkins 2009).

It remains to be seen whether the private sector will continue to set the tone in the world's currency markets, and indeed the financial markets in general, or whether governments will regain greater control. Theoretically, currency markets are supposed to fulfil two main functions: price currencies at their fair value so that people have valid information about an economy's real situation and can make appropriate decisions; and provide liquidity to support international business. The problem is that neither fixed nor floating currency regimes fulfil these missions perfectly. Fixed regimes can be criticized, for instance, because of the tendency of central banks and/or politicians to price currencies wrongly by allowing non-currency-related considerations to affect their judgement. If national authorities want their economy to export its way out of a slump, for example, they will be tempted to price its currency at an artificially low rate. This might temporarily make its goods more attractive on the international markets, but it will also stoke inflationary pressures and mask the need for productivity efforts. Indeed, over the years many countries have been accused of these kinds of 'beggar-thy-neighbour' (see Chapter 6) devaluations, most recently the United States with its 'benign-neglect' policy of tolerating and even encouraging a weaker dollar in the mid-2000s. Conversely, if a government's priority is to cut inflation by reducing import costs—as Argentina did in the 1990s, largely under IMF pressure—the authorities might overvalue their currency. One problem then is that consumers' temporarily inflated purchasing power will tempt them to go on a shopping spree for foreign goods. These and other mistakes have sustained neo-liberals thinkers in their conviction that politicians should stay out of the foreign exchange markets.

Yet markets dominated by speculators are just as likely to price currencies wrongly. Traders are often motivated by short-term psychological factors such as 'irrational exuberance' (over-excitement) and 'herd mentality' (imitative behaviour). Such behaviour, which skews pricing mechanisms, is aggravated by the disproportionate power of just a few funds and financial institutions. The world's five leading currency traders in 2007 (Deutsche Bank, Union Bank of Switzerland, Citigroup, Royal Bank of Scotland, and Barclays Capital Markets) had a market share of nearly 60 per cent (*Euromoney* 2007b). Centralization to this degree means that a very few players' trading decisions will have a disproportionate effect, even in the absence of outright collusion. Currencies can spend long periods of time trading at prices that do not reflect a country's true economic situation. The inevitable corrections are painful.

> Go to the ORC

FX prices make sudden sharp jumps for a variety of reasons (see Online Resource Centre, extension material 13.4 for 2008 Nobel Prize winner Paul Krugman's currency crisis analyses). The 1990s, for instance, were a decade of financial turmoil. Concerted speculative attacks in 1992–3 destroyed the European Monetary System and ravaged EU central banks (ultimately leading to the adoption of the euro). Time and time again 'hot capital' would be withdrawn brutally from countries that needed to be able to count on stable sources of FDI for their development needs (Mexico 1995, South East Asia 1997, Russia 1998, Brazil 1999, Argentina 2001).

It is true that there have been few such episodes since the turn of the century. Moreover, not all the crises of the 1990s can be attributed to FX market problems. Europe's 1992 currency system was already strained by higher real interest rates in Germany than in many neighbouring countries, and by investor concerns about mishandled monetary policies across the region (Canale et al. 2008). Several of the Asian economies affected by the 1997 crisis had been prone to 'crony capitalism', where bankers lent money to friends' wasteful projects, undermining local financial stability. However, for many observers, even strong supporters

Photo 13.3
Central banks like the Bank of England are less powerful than they used to be (Photodisc).

of trade globalization, the potential for currency crises is an indicator that all is not right in today's market-driven FX regime. Some observers criticize the domination of small national economies by huge global speculators (Soros 2002). Others fault the excessive power of Washington Consensus advocates like the IMF, which have shown a regrettable tendency to force LDC governments to abandon volatility-constraining currency controls even before they are ready to do so (Bhagwati 2007; Daneshku 2007). Indeed, as discussed in Case Study 6.3, NGOs critical of modern 'casino capitalism' have called on governments worldwide to impose a currency transaction tax (the ex-Tobin tax) to dissuade FX speculation. Following the 2008 financial crisis, bank speculation is not a very popular profession.

Freewheeling modern markets also have their supporters, some of whom consider that the repeated crises of the 1990s actually had a healthy effect, forcing the countries involved to reform their financial systems and paving the way for renewed growth in the 2000s (Rowe 2007). The argument has also been made that occasional FX turmoil is a price worth paying for the advantages derived from greater access to capital (Obstfeld 2005). Like most international business topics, the architecture of the currency market provokes passionate debate.

Irrespective of its causes or the effects it has on economic policy, however, it is clear that currency uncertainty is always a challenge for market-users like MNEs. FX volatility makes it hard for managers to determine a country's true prospects, thus to make the kinds of rational long-term investment decisions upon which international business relies. The currency markets are a prime example of a situation where industrial and financial business interests have problems coexisting.

+ **Currency controls**
Where a government places administrative restrictions on people's ability to buy/sell or lend/borrow assets denominated in the national currency.

Thinking point

Are currency crises an acceptable price for the benefits of having greater access to foreign currency?

Challenges and choices

→ It is crucial for MNEs to have an accurate calculation of their currency exposures. This can be extremely difficult, however, when their business involves millions of transactions in hundreds (and sometimes thousands) of locations worldwide—as is the case for companies like Coca-Cola or McDonald's. Clearly, real-time information on a group's total FX position can be compiled only if a high-performance information system is set up. However, finance executives still have to decide to what extent this data should be centralized, and most importantly, who among the treasury department's different managers is responsible for hedging decisions. Foreign exchange is as much a structural topic for an MNE as a strategic one.

→ Assessing corporate FX traders' performance is difficult. Since most currency exposures are covered, even in MNEs that are relatively more willing to assume risks, one way of judging treasurers is in terms of the overall cost of hedging. Some confusion will remain, however, about which benchmarks to use. Non-financial MNEs that want to trade FX must avoid giving employees an incentive to take undue risks. There is a fine line between acceptable and excessive FX exposure.

Chapter Summary

The chapter began with a definition of foreign exchange exposure before defining different sources of risk: transaction (commercial and operational); translational; speculative; and economic. A distinction was made between risks that can be identified and managed on an immediate basis and those that materialize over the longer term and require more structural adjustments. After comparing MNE reconfiguration and financial hedging strategies, the chapter then looked at currency trading in terms of market participants' varying interests as well as commonly used trading instruments. The final section began with an overview of the foreign exchange markets, defining different currency regimes and concluding with a brief discussion of whether today's FX markets perform as they were designed to.

Case Study 13.3

National currencies: One way for the yuan?

One effect of China having become a global manufacturing powerhouse is its accumulation of a vast pile of foreign exchange reserves. By March 2009, the country was sitting on almost $2 trillion, a vast sum destined to rise even further, given its continued fantastic export performance (Chinability 2008). In 2007, China's trade surplus soared by almost 50 per cent from the year before to reach $262 billion (CNN 2008). Close to $250 billion of China's 2007 export receipts came from the United States and about $135 billion from Europe. Rising energy costs meant that this oil-deprived emerging giant was also spending increasing amounts on imports, but the net effect was one-sided—China had become the world's largest creditor nation, ahead of Japan (which had 2007 foreign exchange reserves of around $1 trillion).

In theory, when a country runs such a strong surplus, its domestic currency should rise in value. In basic supply and demand terms, China has accumulated foreign currencies that are of no use to it in its domestic economy, and that it would therefore normally want to sell against the yuan. By itself, this action should drive down the price of dollars and euros. Similarly, the inflow of so much overseas money into the Chinese economy should stoke up domestic activity levels and accelerated growth in a country whose GDP already rose over the early 2000s at nearly 9 per cent per annum, or three to four times as quickly as its main trading partners. Normally, this growth differential should also lead to a higher yuan.

Yet the yuan has barely moved, for the good reason that it is not really convertible. True to the philosophical tradition of strong state control in a country that remains nominally communist, the Chinese government is not particularly interested in giving foreign speculators the power to set its exchange rate. The Asian crisis of 1997 fuelled the sentiment in China that it would be dangerous for the national government to lose control in this domain. There are also more practical reasons for resisting a floating regime. A higher yuan would undercut the competitiveness of Chinese products at a time when the country is trying to export its way out of poverty. It would also devalue

China's holdings of USD-denominated securities like government Treasury Bonds (Wolf 2007).

In Europe and especially the United States, many politicians have been critical of Chinese currency policies. Their accusation is that China, a new member of the World Trade Organization, wants to take advantage of the possibilities of free trade without opening up its own product and especially capital markets. A cheap yuan also maintains an incentive for MNEs to outsource production to Chinese partners, with many workers across the world suffering from job insecurity as a result. 'Getting tough with China' has become a recurring theme in many Western elections, with both the USA and Europe having enacted symbolic protectionist measures affecting imports of products like paper or brassieres to try to frighten China into revaluing its currency.

Yet there are two sides to this argument. American households' marginal propensity to save fell below zero in 2006–7, meaning that the USA was not only saving nothing but consuming more wealth than it created. This unsustainable behaviour was one of the main reasons why the USA imported so many goods from China—at inflation-busting prices that stayed low because of the yuan's artificial weakness (McCartney 2006). In addition, the lack of American savings meant that the USA needed foreign money to purchase the debts that its government, companies, and households were accumulating. In the end, China had become America's biggest creditor. Moreover, by funding US deficits, precisely with proceeds from its trade surpluses, China has enabled Americans to live beyond their means. If the USA were forced to fund its deficits internally, taxes would rise enormously and households would have much less disposable income to spend. It is tempting to analyse the US–Chinese arrangement as a huge supplier's credit scheme.

Over the course of the 2000s the two countries reached a stalemate, with the USA threatening to levy tariffs on Chinese imports and China threatening to withdraw its savings from the USA and send the dollar crashing. There have been minor gestures of reconciliation, for example, in 2005 when China shifted from a full fixed rate regime, with the yuan set at 8.28 versus the dollar, to a slightly more flexible regime, where the yuan is allowed to move from time to time (reaching 6.84 to the dollar in late 2008). The future remains unclear, however. There is little doubt that a free-floating yuan would rise in value, but for the moment the Chinese authorities do not seem inclined to let this happen. On the other hand, by spring 2009 the possibility of China and its commercial partners dealing in yuans instead of dollars was being frequently evoked, most notably at a May trade meeting between the Brazilian and Chinese heads of state. Whether or not this spells the end of the US dollar as the global reserve currency, such uncertainty makes things difficult for MNEs with a yuan risk to manage.

Case study questions

1. Would a higher yuan resolve US and European trade deficits with China?
2. How does the uncertainty about China's currency affect MNEs' plans for doing business with this country?
3. What kinds of compromises are possible between China and its partners—and what is the worst-case scenario if no compromise is found?

Is the yuan destined to take over from the US dollar as the world's reserve currency? (© iStockphoto)

Discussion questions

1. What kinds of companies are more likely to be exposed to FX risk? Why?

2. When does a short-term transactional risk turn into a long-term economic one?

3. To what extent should a company hedge all, some, or none of its FX exposure?

4. Do banks and non-financial MNEs suffer from a conflict of interests?

5. Do the world's FX markets perform satisfactorily?

References

Bank for International Settlements (2007). 'Triennial Central Bank Survey of Foreign Exchange and Derivatives Market Activity in 2007', Dec., www.bis.org (accessed 16 Feb. 2008).

Batavia, B., and Malliaris, A. (2008). 'The Dollar, the Euro and the Role of Emerging Economies', *International Journal of Indian Culture and Business Management*, 2/1 (30 Nov.).

Batra, R., and Beladi, H. (2008). 'A New Approach to Currency Depreciation', *Review of Development Economics*, 12/4 (Nov.).

Bhagwati, J. (2007). *In Defense of Globalization*. New York: Oxford University Press.

Canale, R.R., Montagnoli, A., and Napolitano, O. (2008). 'Speculation and Monetary Policy Behaviour in the 1992 Currency Crisis: The Italian Case', *International Economic Journal*, 22/3 (Sept.).

Caramazza, F., and Aziz, J. (1998). 'Fixed or Flexible: Getting the Exchange Rate Right in the 1990s', www.imf.org (accessed 3 Dec. 2008).

Chinability (2008). 'Latest News and Statistics on China's Economy and Business Climate', www.chinability.com (accessed 16 Feb. 2008).

Chincarini, L. (2007). 'The Effectiveness of Global Currency Hedging after the Asian Crisis', *Journal of Asset Management*, 8/1 (May).

CNN (2008). 'China's Trade Surplus Soars', Jan., http://edition.cnn.com (accessed 3 Dec. 2008).

Copeland, L. (2005). *Exchange Rates and International Finance*. Harlow: Financial Times-Prentice Hall.

Daneshku, S. (2007). 'IMF Accused of Poor Exchange Rate Guidance', 18 May, www.ft.com (accessed 15 June 2007).

Dodd, R. (2008). 'Over-the-Counter Markets: What Are They?', *IMF: Finance and Development*, 45/2 (June).

Dornbusch, R. (1976), 'Expectations and Exchange Rate Dynamics', *Journal of Political Economy*, 84/6 (Jan.).

EADS (2007). '9m 2007 Report', 7 Nov., www.eads.com (accessed 13 Feb. 2008).

Edwards, S., and Levy Yeyati, E. (2005). 'Flexible Exchange Rates as Shock Absorbers', *European Economic Review*, 49/8 (Nov.).

Euromoney (2007a). 'Alpha Quest Drives FX Market Growth', Jan., 69–76.

Euromoney (2007b). 'FX Poll 2007', May, 170.

Euromoney (2007c). 'How to Keep the Buy Side on-Side', June, 161–8.

Ferguson, R., Hartmann, P., Panetta, F., and Portes, R. (2007). *International Financial Stability*. Geneva: International Centre for Monetary and Banking Statistics.

Fifield, A. (2006). 'Won's Strength against Yen Leaves Korean Exporters Worried', 29 Dec., http://search.ft.com (accessed 15 June 2007).

Fischer, S. (2001). 'Exchange Rate Regimes: Is the Bipolar View

Correct', *IMF: Finance and Development*, 38/2 (June).

Ghosh, A. (2008). 'Turning Currencies around', *IMF: Finance and Development*, 45/2 (June).

Heineken (2006). 'Annual Report', www.annualreport.heineken.com (accessed 12 Nov. 2008).

Hopkins, K. (2009). 'Russian Central Bank is Failing to Stop Decline', *Guardian*, 9 Feb., p. 26.

Hughes, C. (2007). 'Exporters Curse Dollar's Drag on Profits', 13 May, www.ft.com (accessed 15 June 2007).

Hughes, J. (2006). 'Companies too Shortsighted when Hedging', 26 Jan., http://search.ft.com (accessed 15 June 2007).

Hyman, M. (2006). *New Ways for Managing Global Financial Risk: The Next Generation*. Chichester: John Wiley and Sons.

McCartney, J. (2006). 'US–China Meeting Ends without Yuan Agreement', 15 Dec., http://business.timesonline.co.uk (accessed 16 Feb. 2008).

Mackintosh, J. (2005). 'VW Looks to Exploit Euro Fall with New Hedging Plan', 3 June, http://search.ft.com (accessed 15 June 2007).

Myers, R. (2006), 'New Currents in Currency', 1 Dec., www.cfo.com (accessed 13 Feb. 2008).

Novo Nordirsk (2007). 'Stock Exchange Announcement', 31 Oct., www.novonordisk.com (accessed 15 Feb. 2008).

Obstfeld, M. (2005). 'Reflections upon Re-reading "The Capital Myth"', Aug., http://elsa.berkeley.edu (accessed 11 June 2008).

Oliver, L. (2007). 'What it will Take to Stay on Top of the FX Class', *Euromoney*, May, pp. 187–92.

Rogoff, K. (2001). 'On why not a Global Currency', www.economics.harvard.edu (accessed 11 June 2008).

Rogoff, K. (2005). 'Paul Samuelson's Contributions to International Economics', 11 May, www.economics.harvard.edu (accessed 27 Jan. 2009).

Rosenstreich, P. (2005). *Forex Revolution: An Insider's Guide to the Real World of Foreign Exchange Trading*. London: Financial Times-Prentice Hall.

Rowe, J. (2007). 'Countries Take Stock of Financial Soundness Exercise', *IMF Survey*, 36/10 (June).

Shipman, A. (2007). 'Active Currency Management', 3 Dec., www.financeweek.co.uk (accessed 13 Feb. 2008).

Soros, G. (2002). *George Soros on Globalization*. New York: Public Affairs.

Williams, R. (2006). *The Money Changers: A Guided Tour through Global Currency Markets*. Zed Books: London.

Wolf, M. (2007). 'The Right Way to Respond to China's Exploding Surpluses', 30 May, http://blogs.ft.com (accessed 16 Feb. 2008).

Further research

Fenton-O'Creevy, M., Nicholson, N., Soane, E., and Willman, P. (2007). *Traders: Risks, Decisions and Management in Financial Markets*, Oxford: Oxford University Press.

This book, the outcome of a three-year project researching psychological and social influences on the behaviour and performance of 118 traders and managers working in four leading investment banks, discusses their activities, personalities, and value systems; how they perceive the world they inhabit; how they make decisions; and the kinds of risks they take. Similar to past classics like Michael Lewis's *Liar's Poker*, it portrays traders as human beings with very human passions, strengths, and weaknesses.

Taylor, F. (2003). *Mastering Foreign Exchange Currency and Options*. 2nd edn. Harlow: Financial Times Prentice Hall.

Less focused on traders than on markets, the book starts with a historical overview of different currency regimes and notes their impact on FX trading over the years. It goes on to provide an exhaustive discussion of currency products, market players, and the economics underlying their behaviour, before analysing the mechanics of trading and the technological changes that have modified dealing practices since the early 1990s (like the creation of new settlement systems and advent of electronic portals). It also covers technically advanced topics, like the design of 'exotic' currency options. Despite being written in the early 2000s, the book's exhaustive scope means that it is still very topical.

Online Resource Centre

Visit the Online Resource Centre that accompanies this book to read more information relating to foreign exchange management: www.oxfordtextbooks.co.uk/orc/sitkin_bowen/

14 Multinational Finance and Treasury Operations

Overview

The chapter starts with an overview of MNEs' external sources of funding. Debt finance can be accessed through bank loans or the capital markets. Equity finance raises issues relating to investors' appetite for certain securities, leading in turn to a discussion on how well the international capital markets function. The second section looks at internal sources of funding and the movement of surplus cash from one MNE unit to another via netting. The conclusion reviews transfer pricing and ethical aspects of MNE fiscality.

Section I: External sources of finance
> Types of funding
> International capital markets

Section II: Internal sources of finance
> Netting
> Transfer pricing and MNE taxation

Learning Objectives

After reading this chapter, you should be able to:

✦ compare different sources of MNE funding
✦ judge whether the international capital markets function efficiently
✦ explain movements of funds within MNEs
✦ identify some of the tax issues that MNEs face
✦ discuss the ethics of MNE finance

Case Study 14.1

MNEs and capital markets: Keeping Lufthansa afloat

The body in charge of identifying current or potential dangers at German airliner Lufthansa is the company's Risk Management Committee. Several major risks, like terrorism, insurance, overcapacity, protectionism, operating costs, and fuel prices, were noted in the prospectus that accompanied Lufthansa's issuance of €750 million in convertible securities (bonds that can be converted into shares) maturing in 2012. Each risk requires a specific response. To cover its exposure to fuel prices, for instance, Lufthansa runs a structured hedging programme using financial instruments such as forwards and options. This is similar to its currency management system.

In financial strategy terms, the company's long-term objective has been to fund a larger percentage of its fleet maintenance and expansion operations through equity capital. This explains some of its capital market operations, like the convertibles mentioned above or the €750 million in shares that the company issued in June 2004. Lufthansa's Executive Board has also had an authorization, valid until 2011, to issue another €1.5 billion in convertible bonds. As a result, the company's equity-to-asset ratio, which had fallen as low as 16 per cent in 2003, was back to 25.2 per cent by yearend 2006, well on the way to the target of 30 per cent. Just as noteworthy is the way Lufthansa's 'gearing' ratio ('net indebtedness plus retirement benefit obligations/ shareholder's equity') fell from 92.5 per cent in 2004 to 75.7 in 2006. Recognizing its success in reducing debt, Lufthansa was one of only three airliners in the world to be considered 'investment grade' in August 2007, with Moody's ratings agency calling the outlook for its shares as 'positive'.

For its short-term, 'operational' needs, Lufthansa wants to keep a minimum of €2 billion in cash to cope with any unexpected problems. By yearend 2005, the company

had also arranged nearly €2 billion in unused, short-term credit lines, along with a commercial paper programme that could raise a further €1 billion if necessary. Funding facilities of this sort come with a cost but have been worth it. The measures that Lufthansa took during the early and mid-2000s left it better placed than most of its rivals to survive the 2007 fuel crisis and 2008 credit crunch. This is the precautionary tale of an MNE that has benefited from its prudent use of the capital markets.

Capital is the lifeblood of an MNE like Lufthansa (Graficart.net).

Introduction

The foreign exchange risks detailed in Chapter 13 represent only some of the financial challenges that multinationals face. Just as crucial is their ability to access capital. MNEs need funding for both short-term working capital and long-term balance sheet purposes. Having access to funds when times are tough can be crucial to a company's survival. Capital also allows MNEs to acquire strategic assets when opportunities arise. Like labour or materials, it is a key input in the production process.

Companies need to manage the cost of capital. One way of expressing this is the interest paid on borrowings (or on shareholder dividends). Some companies have more cash than they need, so that, using terminology from Chapter 13, they can be described as being 'long' cash. Companies in this position prefer high interest rates, ensuring good returns on their investments. For many more firms, however, especially MNEs seeking to build an international configuration, it is more important that interest rates remain low, to reduce the cost of capital. MNE treasury departments devote substantial resources to managing current and prospective cash needs.

+ **Working capital**
Excess of long-term capital resources over long-term uses of capital. Helps companies avoid bankruptcy by providing a stable source of funds to pay off short-term debts.

Section I: External sources of finance

It bears repeating that one of corporate treasurers' main jobs is to secure the capital that companies need, to acquire assets when an opportunity presents itself, or simply to have a margin of safety in case times get tough. It is hard to conceive of an MNE whose internal cash generation covers all its growth needs, if only because this would indicate that it is not investing enough in productive capacities. Most of the time, MNE finance teams must entertain relationships with external fund providers.

Types of funding

A key decision that companies face is whether to raise capital by borrowing money (debt) or selling shares (equity). The advantage of debt is that the interest a company pays on its borrowings can usually be deducted from taxable income, reducing its tax bill. Moreover, by using borrowed sums to generate profits, the company leverages existing shareholder capital and increases return on equity (ROE). On the other hand, as revealed during the 2008 crisis, MNEs that rely excessively on debt capital to fund their operations are vulnerable to conditions in the credit markets (availability of funds, interest rates). Debt must be reimbursed, and the inability to do so endangers a firm's very existence—as witnessed by the wave of bankruptcies that occurred worldwide in 2008. Thus, the main difference between debt and equity funding is that the latter does not have to be repaid. Indeed, firms are usually under no obligation to pay dividends to shareholders. This advantage is offset by the fact that new investors' purchase of shares in a company 'dilutes' existing shareholders' control over it. This is especially problematic at times when share values are low, since it means that new owners need to inject only small sums before acquiring control (Draho 2008).

Another factor in MNEs' decisions to seek debt or equity funding is whether they are operating in a country that offers greater protection to creditors or to shareholders (Cheng and Shiu 2007). Since each mode has its strengths and weaknesses, MNEs usually try to reduce funding risks by diversifying sources.

Debt funding

Banks offer a wide variety of debt instruments (see Figure 14.1.). Like any commercial enterprise and within the limits of borrowers' creditworthiness, they constantly try to

Type of funding	Examples
Trade finance for import/export transactions	Documentary letters of credit; Bills of exchange
Lines of credit: short-term borrowings	Overdrafts; Commercial paper
Supplier's credits: accelerating collections	Factoring; Bankers' acceptances
Term loans: long-term borrowings	Standby/revolving credit; Project finance

Figure 14.1
MNE funding facilities with banks (see Online Resource Centre, extension material 14.1 for description of each instrument).

> Go to the ORC

expand their customer base. This contrasts with MNEs' growing tendency to work with a shortlist of global banks (plus a few small local banks offering specific services and information that cannot be found elsewhere).

The traditional 'transformation' model of bank funding involves savers depositing short-term funds with banks who then lend them on to borrowers, usually for the longer term. In this model, the bank acts as a screen between providers and users of capital. Its gross margin is the difference between the interest it pays on deposits and receives on the loans it makes.

This traditional model began to reveal weaknesses during the 1980s when several large debtor nations, such as Peru and Brazil, defaulted on their loan repayments, raising fears about the solvency of some of the world's largest banks. To reinforce the global financial system, the Bank for International Settlements (BIS) sponsored a so-called capital adequacy agreement in 1988 called Basel I (supplemented by Basel II two decades later) specifying that banks should have equity capital equivalent to at least 8 per cent of their assets. To meet this so-called Cooke ratio, many banks reduced their direct loans and focused instead on acting as intermediaries between investors and borrowers. The new emphasis became securities issuance of securities in the world's capital markets, with banks receiving commissions for their intermediation services. This process, portrayed in Figure 14.2 as the 'securitization' model, is a key driver behind the explosion in international financial flows since the 1980s.

The first step in this process is for the company seeking funds to get advice on what kinds of securities are currently most attractive to various classes of investors. Large banks have 'originations' specialists who are constantly in touch with MNE treasurers, suggesting different ways of structuring securities (currency of transaction, basis for calculating interest or dividend payments, maturity). Recipients and providers of funds basically have contradictory interests: the former seek to raise as much capital as possible at the lowest cost; and the latter seek maximal returns for minimum risk. A number of sophisticated financial engineering techniques have been developed since the 1980s to bridge the gap between the two. One of

+ Securities issuance
Act of creating tradable capital market instruments (stocks and bonds) that firms sell to investors to raise capital.

+ Capital markets
Sum total of all transactions creating and trading debt and equity securities. Mainly refers to medium and long-term operations.

+ Maturity
Fixed date on which a contract terminates. For a loan, this is usually when the capital borrowed must be repaid.

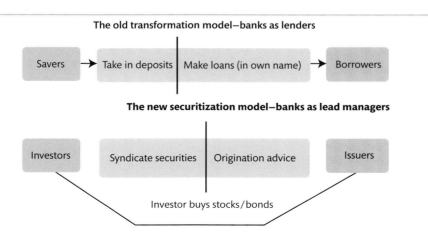

Figure 14.2
Banks become intermediaries in the securitization model.

the most notable inventions is a derivative called a 'swap', where parties to a transaction create exposures that best match their existing needs by exchanging one cash-flow stream against another (for example, fixed versus floating interest rate payments, sometimes in different currencies). Investment banks are paid well for their advice in this area.

Traditionally, the bank originating a security will be its 'lead manager' and 'underwrite' it, providing the borrower immediately with the face value of the issue (minus commissions) before selling most of this initial allocation on to a syndicate of banks and fund managers. In turn, these second-tier investors will either keep the security on their own books or sell it into the 'secondary market', which is where an issuer's existing securities trade until maturity. The secondary market is crucial, since the price at which a company's existing shares and bonds trade helps determine the price it pays on future issuances, and thus the amount of capital it can raise. This is one of the reasons why MNEs are so interested in how the financial markets view their securities.

Growing securitization does not mean that banks no longer lend directly to corporations. Indeed, for SMEs too small to issue securities, banks remain crucial funding sources. All that has happened is that bank credit is now one kind of finance among several.

> **+ Syndication**
> Practice of dividing the risk of a given operation among market professionals.

Yield curves

Cost is a prime concern in the choice of funding vehicles, but debt mathematics can be complicated. A prime distinction here is between loans made on a 'fixed-term' basis, where the interest rate is set when the operation is first arranged, and 'floating-rate' loans, where the interest rate is reset at scheduled intervals, depending on changes in an agreed benchmark. The most widely used short-term benchmark is the London Interbank Offered Rate (LIBOR), calculated from daily money market quotations gathered by the Bank of England. The benchmark for longer-term interest rates—for example, the rate that a borrower pays on its bonds—is usually the 'yield' of government bonds with a similar duration. The difference between short- and long-term interest rates is called the 'yield curve'. This reflects many factors, including liquidity and inflationary expectations (for example, if prices are expected to rise in the future, long-term interest rates will be higher than short-term ones). In turn, the yield curve influences companies' choice between short- and long-term instruments.

Figure 14.3 features yield curves from March 2008—that is, before the credit crunch hit in September of that year. Government and investor reactions to the crisis had abnormal effects on interest rates and especially yield curves. Trying to stimulate activity, national authorities everywhere injected funds into their banking systems, pushing down short-term rates. In a similar vein, most investors predicted a long period of deflation, causing a fall in long-term yields as well. At the same time, other investors feared that rising government debt might revive inflationary pressures one day, renewing interest in alternative investments like gold. All in all, yield curves provide a great deal of information on how policy-makers and investors see an economy's future. In turn, this is very useful to MNE treasurers.

> **+ Money markets**
> Sum total of short-term interbank and commercial lending operations, usually for durations of less than one year.

> **+ Liquidity**
> Volume of funds in a market. Markets are liquid if there are sufficient funds for an asset to be bought or sold without any noticeable impact on price.

Creditworthiness

An MNE's borrowing costs are also affected by perceptions of its creditworthiness. A lender confident of recovering a loan will demand less interest than one worried about the

Figure 14.3
Government bond yield curves from March 2008 (Bloomberg 2008).

In per cent annual yield	2 year	5 year	10 year	30 year
USA	1.65	2.54	3.61	4.50
UK	4.01	4.07	4.41	4.34
Germany	3.19	3.32	3.81	4.44
Japan	0.56	0.84	1.37	2.28

	Rating	Time to maturity in March 2008	Bond yield	Spread above government yield
Oil companies				
Philipps Petrol	A	2 years 3 months	2.17	0.53
Petronas	A−	4 years 3 months	3.46	0.95
Automobile companies				
Toyota Motor	AAA	5 months	3.10	1.34
Daimler/Chrysler	BBB+	1 year 6 months	3.79	2.14
General Motors	B+	23 years 8 months	7.46	2.23
Financial companies				
Bank America	AA−	2 years 10 months	3.64	2.00
Goldman Sachs	AA−	6 years 8 months	5.17	2.67

Figure 14.4
Perceptions of different sectors' creditworthiness are reflected in borrowers paying variable spreads over government yields (*Financial Times* 2008).

borrower's solvency. The standard way of representing confidence is the 'risk premium' (or 'credit spread'). Expressed in basis points, this is the difference between the yields that creditors require from one class of debt as opposed to what a zero-risk borrower (usually the government) pays. In general, the lower the rating and/or the longer the duration, the greater the spread (*Financial Times* 2008).

Much as curves vary, so do credit spreads, as investors reassess borrowers' situations. The 2008 credit crisis, for instance, saw a flood of money pouring out of bank securities into safer government bonds. Effectively, this raised banks' cost of capital. Perceptions of a company's creditworthiness are largely based on the score it receives from a 'ratings' agency, such as Standard and Poor's or Moody's. A highly rated (that is, 'Triple A') company will pay less than another company in the same sector but with a lower rating (that is, 'Triple B'). It is impossible to overstate the importance of credit ratings in multinational

+ **Basis points**
One hundredth of 1 per cent—a common unit in international finance.

Photo 14.1
Disney's local entity—not Disney Corporation itself—was liable for most of the borrowings that the group incurred to build a park near Paris (© Disney).

Thinking point

In light of the 2008 crisis, how much confidence can an investor have in ratings agencies?

finance. Being upgraded or downgraded is a big event in an MNE's life, if only because of the impact on borrowing costs. The downgrading of famous household names (such as General Motors or Citigroup) during the 2008 crisis aggravated their circumstances by causing creditors to withdraw funds at the very moment when they were most needed. The crisis also affected the credit derivative markets that price the yields that investors require from different classes of debt. The data in Figure 14.4 preceded the crisis and therefore reflect more 'normal' credit spreads. It remains to be seen which spreads will apply when the effects of the crisis pass.

There is another way that credit considerations affect corporate borrowings. MNEs often try to record debt in the name of a small subsidiary, sometimes an offshore vehicle specifically established for this purpose. The practice, known as 'ring-fencing', ensures that, if times are tough and loan reimbursements become problematic (as exemplified by the problems faced by Disneyland Paris during the 1990s), creditors can make claims only against the assets of this one subsidiary. From lenders' perspective, of course, it is safer to have loans secured against the assets of the whole of the group. One surprising aspect of an international business career is the amount of time spent negotiating which group entity is responsible for a particular liability.

International equity funding in the traditional sense

The second external source of international funding is equity capital. Chapter 1 introduced this topic by referring to the distinction between 'passive' or 'active' approaches. A key trend since the 1980s has been the rise of active international shareholders seeking to maximize short-term financial returns above any other consideration and ready to pressure CEOs into adopting operational strategies serving this purpose alone. Active shareholders are unwelcome in some financial cultures in so far as they prevent executives from pursuing policies that may benefit more local stakeholders. Other cultures prioritize high share prices, since this helps to protect domestic companies against foreign takeovers. Share performance is also important in societies where people's pension savings are largely invested in the stock market.

Share prices mirror not only general economic conditions but also expectations of future profitability, which depends on many factors. One is the extent to which companies try to increase returns through greater debt and less equity funding (see Figure 14.5). This leverage strategy, also called 'gearing', is more typical of American MNEs, which have historically had higher debt-to-equity ratios than their European and Japanese counterparts. It might be associated with Americans investors' preference for equity investments, contrasting with other regions' greater fondness for bonds. Preference for debt or equity is in part a cultural phenomenon.

Another way that MNEs try to increase their share price is by organizing worldwide 'road shows' to attract potential investors. The trend is towards a concentration of global

---

Figure 14.5
Compared effects of gearing on profitability.

Company A
Equity = 100
Debt = 100
Profits = 20
(10 Per cent of the sum of equity + debt)
Debt to equity ratio 100/100 = 100 per cent
Return on equity = 20/100 = 20 per cent

Company B
Equity = 100
Debt = 150
Profits = 25
(10 Per cent of the sum of equity + debt)
Debt to equity ratio 150/100 = 150 per cent
Return on equity = 25/100 = 25 per cent

equity capital in the hands of relatively few big 'institutional investors' (like CALPERS, the California state employee pension fund). In part, this is because it is increasingly difficult for small private investors to assess a company's prospects in a world where profitability is often determined by distant events. The result has been a rise in cross-border share ownership, to the extent, for example, that non-French investors now hold an estimated 47 per cent of French companies' total stock market capitalization (Norguet 2007). This trend has come under some criticism, owing to fears that, because foreign shareholders have less of a sentimental attachment to the companies they own, they may demand higher returns than domestic owners would while displaying less concern for local stakeholders' welfare. Another concern is that they may make equity decisions based solely on their portfolio's overall risk/return profile (Markowitz 1991) rather than the strategic needs of the company in question. Offshore shareholding is a key element in the financialization logic (see Chapter 7) that characterizes modern international business and has come under increased scrutiny in the wake of the 2008 credit crunch.

+ **Stock market capitalization**
Total number of shares issued times the share prices for all companies listed on a particular exchange.

Other sources of equity funding

One example of the internationalization of equity finance is the rise of sovereign wealth funds (SWFs), enormous pools of capital run by government appointment managers (Figure 14.6). Most SWFs originate from countries with large oil surpluses and/or where the state traditionally has a big economic role (like China). Government involvement in cross-border equity operations has often involved state-owned enterprises (SOEs), one example being when the Industrial & Commercial Bank of China paid $5.5 billion to acquire a 20 per cent stake in the Standard Bank of South Africa (Zhu and Davis 2007). Alongside SOEs, SWFs increasingly serve as conduits for state-driven international equity investments. Examples include the large stake that the Qatar Investment Authority took in British retailer

Thinking point

Do foreign shareholders necessarily have different motives from domestic ones?

Names	Details (with amounts under management as of January 2009)
Abu Dhabi Investment Authority(www.adia.ae)	• Established 1976 • Secures and maintains current and future prosperity of Abu Dhabi via conservative management of investment assets • $875 billion
Government of Singapore Investment Corp.(http://www.gic.com.sg/)	• Established 1981 • Government oversight over diversified long-term investments seeking good returns • $330 billion
Norwegian Government Pension Fund (http://www.regjeringen.no/)	• Established 2006 • Continuation of Petroleum Fund and National Insurance Scheme Fund; implements a 'fundamental social perspective' • $301 billion
China Investment Corporation (http://chinainvestmentcorp.com/)	• Established 2007 • 'Gateway into China through Hong Kong' but also a vehicle for 'conservative' investments abroad • $200 billion
Russian Federation Funds (http://www1.minfin.ru/en/nationalwealthfund/)	• Established 2008 • Includes Reserve Fund (for oil stabilization purposes) and National Wealth Fund • $190 billion

Figure 14.6
Sovereign wealth funds rankings (SWF Institute 2009).

Sainsbury in 2007, or the Abu Dhabi Investment Authority's $7.5 billion investment later that same year in struggling US bank Citigroup. SWFs are predicted to account for a total $4 trillion in capital by the year 2011. As a global investor base, they cannot be ignored.

Some observers lump SWFs and SOEs together, criticizing both for lacking transparency and for making decisions for 'strategic and political purposes' (Traynor 2008) like the acquisition of technology. This is supposedly different from (and somehow worse than) when private foreign investors acquire national companies. Many governments try to handcuff foreign investors via complicated cross-shareholdings where domestic companies take a large enough stake in one another's capital to prevent outsiders from wielding real power. Examples include Japan's *keiretsu* networks and France's *minorité de blocage* legislation (where it suffices that 'friendly' interests accumulate a 33.4 per cent stake to prevent other shareholders from imposing policies that may not serve French interests). Yet aside from standard neo-liberal mistrust of state actors, it is difficult to see why SWFs or SOEs should provoke a greater sense of economic patriotism (see Chapter 5) than other offshore investors do. Nor do all cross-border equity operations provoke similarly xenophobic reactions. Compare the way that the British government allowed a Spanish company, Ferrovial, to take over UK airports operator BAA in 2006 with the bill enacted by Japan's parliament just two years later restricting foreigners' stakes in Japanese airport operating companies to less than 33 per cent of voting rights (Soble 2008). Indeed, capital was so scarce during the 2008 credit crunch that many countries were happy to source funds wherever they could find them. As so often in international business, the requirements of a particular situation count much more than general attitudes.

At this point, it is worth recalling the problems that many small and medium-sized enterprises (SMEs) face in trying to source equity funding. Because most of the larger stock exchanges have minimum size thresholds, many countries try to spark entrepreneurship by creating exchanges specifically for smaller firms, often in hi-tech sectors. Examples include Nasdaq in the USA, Japan's Nippon New Market Hercules, and the UK's Alternative Investment Market. There is some hope that these markets will help to sustain a new sector of activity that holds great promise for the future of international business—namely 'clean technology' (see Chapter 16).

It remains that many start-up companies do not even qualify for these markets and must seek funds elsewhere. Debt funding would be one possibility, but banks often impose harsh conditions on SMEs inducing owners, especially older and more educated entrepreneurs, to turn instead to their personal networks for funding (Vos et al. 2007). Against this background, this most dynamic source of international equity funding for hi-tech SMEs is venture capital, usually provided by small groups of professional investors seeking stakes in firms positioned in growth sectors. This vehicle was the main driver behind the information technology revolution that swept out of California's Silicon Valley in the 1980s, fathering a host of companies that have since grown into household names, including Intel, Google, and Cisco. It is being revived to underpin the new clean technology sector that is Silicon Valley's new priority sector, with $474 million worth of investments having been made in this field during the first nine months of 2006 alone (Richtel 2007). The strength of the venture capital model has been noted worldwide, with many countries enacting measures, often fiscal in nature, to bring local investors and entrepreneurs together. India's burgeoning hi-tech sector, for instance, has become a haven for venture capitalists, recording a total $7.46 billion worth of deals in 2006 (IVCA 2007). This is a textbook example of how free capital markets can facilitate real economic growth.

At the same time, there are many examples of unsupervised international investors wreaking damage on national economies. When large private equity firms like Blackstone, Carlyle, or Kohlberg Kravis Roberts raise enormous sums of capital to acquire viable firms that they subsequently break up—simply because the sum of the parts can be sold for more than the firms cost to buy—clearly there is a problem. This activity, called 'asset stripping', has come under severe criticism in societies where a firm's performance is measured more by its overall contribution to the industrial fabric than by its stock market valuation. An example

+ **Venture capital**
Funds provided by a small group of investors to support the expansion of a new firm, often in a hi-tech sector.

+ **Private equity**
Equity investments in companies that do not involve transactions on an open stock exchange.

is Germany, where leading politicians have openly equated foreign private equity specialists with 'locusts' (Hodkinson 2008). There must be doubts about the incentive mechanisms in a global financial system that induces investors to destroy economically viable companies instead of supporting them.

International capital markets

For most of the 2000s, the debate has been whether the international capital markets in their existing format are the best way of providing the liquidity that enables productive international business to take place—or whether the financialization and deregulation trends of the previous twenty-five years have created a 'global casino economy' benefiting speculators and/or wealthy countries to the detriment of industrialists and/or LDCs (Buckman 2004). In the aftermath of the 2008 credit crunch, a new consensus has emerged. With markets malfunctioning to the extent that they no longer provide or safeguard the capital upon which economic activity relies, it is clearly time for reform. Even traditionally strong supporters of 'financial liberalization' accept this (Wolf 2009). What is uncertain is how the future architecture of the world's financial system will look, and whether this will satisfy MNEs' global financing needs.

Comparing international and domestic markets

The first decision that MNEs make when issuing securities is whether to list them on a domestic exchange or sell them offshore to non-resident investors. Whereas offshore markets feature lower transaction costs and tax advantages, domestic exchanges offer greater transparency and investor protection. Some providers of capital, like fund managers, are required by their statutes only to purchase domestically traded securities. Others do this by choice because of home bias. Despite all the headlines about the globalization of savings, most OECD country savers invest the vast majority of their capital in their home markets. To some extent, this reflects the mistrust that some investors and national authorities still feel about euro-markets (see Online Resource Centre, extension material 14.2. for a brief history).

Thinking point
In the wake of the 2008 financial crisis, could anyone still argue that the international capital markets do not need reform?

+ Home bias
Preference for domestic over foreign activities.

+ Euro-markets
Offshore markets escaping the jurisdiction of national authorities anywhere in the world.

> Go to the ORC

Inside business

Johnny Akerholm, President and CEO, Nordic Investment Bank

Johnny Akerholm was appointed as President and CEO of Nordic Investment Bank (NIB) in 2005. He previously served as Head of the Economics Department, Bank of Finland (1982–95), Under-Secretary of State for Economic Affairs, Ministry of Finance (1995–2003), and Secretary General, European Bank for Reconstruction and Development (2003–5).

Nordic Investment Bank (NIB) is owned by the five Nordic and three Baltic countries. About 80 per cent of NIB's activity takes place in these eight countries, but it is active in more than thirty other countries around the world. When the system had a deal of liquidity, there was not much demand for external finance; however, the situation has been totally different since the financial crisis started in 2007–8. This is an issue related to the economic cycle rather than the demands of different economies, whether emerging or developed.

It is vital that central banks provide liquidity to the economic and financial system in all circumstances and particularly in times of crisis. One of financial institutions' main tasks is 'to turn short-term funding into long-term loans'. The NIB seems to be in a reasonably good position in that it is still able to do this because it has maintained a top rating and good access to the financial markets.

In most cases, investors and speculators work to stabilize the markets, especially when their activities are in accordance with economic fundamentals. It is very difficult to make a distinction between 'good' and 'bad' speculators. Until the crisis, companies found it relatively easy to access financial markets. One positive is that corporate funding is priced more realistically now in terms of risk.

+ Corporate governance
Laws and processes regulating corporate management, including composition of the Board of Directors, protection of minority interests, executive control, and accounting practices.

> Go to the ORC

+ Disclosure
Providing information, often in a specified form, to comply with legal requirements.

Given the uneven global distribution of capital (partially a reflection of variations in national savings rates), the world's financial centres are all very keen to attract foreign investors. One key element in this competition is the degree of regulation characterizing a particular market. The New York Stock Exchange, for example, lost significant securities issuance business to London after the USA adopted the Sarbanes–Oxley Act in 2002, legislation aimed at improving general standards of corporate governance. Enacted in the aftermath of a scandal caused by inaccurate disclosures by rogue Texas energy company Enron, Sarbanes–Oxley requires companies to publish more in-depth information on their activities, an expensive burden that many would like to avoid. Variations in national rules of accounting and governance (see Online Resource Centre, extension material 14.3) are a matter of great strategic concern to MNE finance officers. It will be interesting to see whether the general support for regulatory harmonization expressed at the April 2009 G20 meeting in London extends to international accounting. The implications for MNEs' securities listings could be significant.

In the 1980s and 1990s, many MNEs tended to 'cross-list' their stock on multiple stock exchanges to improve access to different investor bases. This trend reversed somewhat in the early 2000s, as companies realized that increasingly open capital markets, including in the developing world, meant that international cross-listings were less essential now (Dobbs and Goedhart 2008). In the late 2000s MNEs chose to list securities on particular exchanges because of their transaction costs (MacDonald 2007) and, above all, because different markets provided access to different investor bases. Hong Kong, for instance, was seeking to become a hub for Islamic bonds (Cheung 2007) and/or new Chinese investments (Canaves 2007). Similarly, in May 2009 the Chinese government announced its aspiration to allow local markets like the Shanghai exchange to list foreign MNEs' shares at some point in the future. To source capital, MNEs need to know where they will find the international investors with the greatest appetite for their securities.

A vocabulary has developed to differentiate between issuers' nationalities and the location of the financial centres where their securities trade. Specialists distinguish, for example, between a 'Samurai bond' issued in yen and in Tokyo by a non-Japanese company; a 'Shogun bond' issued in Tokyo by a non-Japanese borrower but not denominated in yen; and a 'euroyen' deposit trading in yen outside Japan. The same diversity is found in the international equity markets. It is possible, for instance, for Japanese company shares to trade on the New York Stock Exchange as American depository receipts (ADRs) or for American companies to list their shares in Tokyo to facilitate potential acquisitions in Japan (as Citigroup did in 2007). A wide range of issuance and investment choices is one hallmark of today's internationalized capital markets.

Before the 2008 credit crunch, the net effect of capital market deregulation had been accelerated growth in volumes, especially in the Eurobond markets, which witnessed nearly $2 trillion worth of issues in 2006, compared to nearly $1.5 trillion in the domestic US corporate bond market (Peristiani 2007). Volumes were also exploding, albeit from much lower levels, in emerging markets in Latin America, Eastern Europe, and Asia. By definition, the 2008 credit crunch had the opposite effect, with volumes plummeting worldwide. What remains to be seen is the direction, and amounts, of future cross-border capital flows once the effects of this crisis have passed.

Redesigning the international financial system

Theoretical debate about ideal financial regimes tends to oppose two visions. Everyone agrees that capital flows are supposed to support MNEs' international activities. On the neo-liberal side, a leading principle has been that subjecting executives to investors' judgement is a good way to discipline the former. This is important in big MNEs to ensure that managers' incentives are aligned with the company's overall performance, but also in smaller family-owned firms that might hesitate to take tough but necessary productivity-enhancing decisions. It can also help companies originating from LDCs that may lack a tradition of financial discipline. In this market-oriented worldview, financial capitalism has served companies well precisely because it demands so much from them.

This contrasts with the stakeholder vision that the capital markets should never be anything more than a servant to business. Even before the credit crunch had erupted, numerous economists (and managers) were already bitterly criticizing the way that uncontrolled 'hot capital' can increase the volatility of international finance (Burton and Zanello 2007). Many national economies, especially LDCs, were badly shaken by the currency crises of the 1990s (see Chapter 13). In 1998, the giant US hedge fund Long Term Capital Management went bankrupt owing to over-exposure to Russian risk. The year 2000 saw a mini stock market crash after the dot.com bubble burst. The same happened one year later following the 9/11 attacks on New York. Last but not least, there was the 2008 credit crunch, widely blamed on unsupervised bank sales of complex structured financial products of questionable quality. At a certain point, these recurring crises must be interpreted as being symptomatic of structural flaws requiring major reforms.

One starting point is to monitor crises' international diffusion outwards from the market(s) where they originated, owing in part to the coupling of national economies (Ciner 2007). This phenomenon is based on several linkages. A crisis in one market often has negative effects on investors' capital positions in other markets. Economies for whom a disproportionate percentage of all exports go to one country will suffer if the latter falls into recession. Similarly, economies that depend on overseas funds can suffer from capital flight if investors seek safe havens during a crisis—as happened to many East European transition countries during the 2008 credit crunch (Goodman 2009). If these outflows ended up strengthening the currencies in which their borrowings are denominated, the economy will suffer on two levels: from the withdrawal of much needed capital; and from higher repayment costs in local currency terms. In this view, whereas open capital markets initially benefit countries by offering them access to foreign funds, it often ends up trapping them in a vicious circle of mounting debt.

> **+ Coupling**
> Where countries' economic fortunes are linked owing to the inseparability of their economic and financial interests.

Given these negative by-products of financial globalization, the challenge has become how to 'de-couple' markets to reduce contagion and prevent crises in some economies from affecting others. Opponents to capital market reform would argue that this might undermine the international openness that has generated much wealth over the years. This increasingly appears to be a minority view, however, with a consensus view emerging that the current framework requires major change (MacDonald 2008; Perry 2008). Indeed, fears have grown that, in the absence of deep-seated reform, the world's financial system is destined to produce further catastrophic upheavals, like the potential collapse of the euro in case larger member states like Italy are unable to honour their national debt (Munchau 2009). Given the potential magnitude of such risks, a paradigm shift seems increasingly probable.

By spring 2009, most world leaders were calling for a so-called Bretton Woods II summit to redesign the global financial system. The contours of this agreement have yet to be decided, although several areas of agreement are clear from the outset. There is a need for adequate and coordinated cross-border regulation, and above all for recognition of the growing power wielded by cash-rich emerging countries such as China or India. In reality, this latter reform has been on the cards for several years. Most economists are confident in predicting that emerging economies will account for an even larger share of the global capital markets after the credit crunch than they did before (Böhme et al. 2008). Some even estimate that, by 2025, the larger LDCs will account for nearly half of the world's total stock market capitalization (Bollen 2008). The new geography of international business (see Chapter 16) is certain to be a key factor in a redesigned global financial system. What is less clear is how open the system will be.

On the one hand, open financial markets have enabled the international recycling of surplus capital. Increasingly, since the 1990s, this has often meant moving surplus funds held in Asia and the Middle East to MNEs and indebted countries elsewhere (Stewart and Sunderland 2008)—a facility that many governments have found extremely useful. At the same time, it is partially because the markets were so open that imbalances were able to accumulate in the first place. Thus, the first question in designing a new global financial system is whether capital markets are the reflection or the cause of underlying economic realities.

One element of response may lie in the distinction that economists commonly make between stable FDI flows, where companies take long-term equity stakes in productive projects, and short-term speculative movements. There is a broad consensus that the former flow is a desirable outcome of any global financial system, and that the latter is not. For instance, as demonstrated during the 1997 Asian crisis, when the Thai, Indonesian, and Korean currencies suffered dramatic devaluations, plunging millions of citizens into poverty, 'sudden stops' in capital inflows can destabilize a national economy and destroy real productive assets. Yet it can also be argued that investors invest in an economy in the first place only if they are confident of being able to recoup their funds on demand (Kaminsky 2004). Both neo-liberals and interventionists have valid arguments to contribute to the ongoing debate about the ideal global financial architecture.

Thinking point

Do financial speculators and MNEs have fundamentally opposing interests?

What unites most commentators is their sense that excessive lending by financial institutions, enabled by a surplus of cheap capital in the wholesale markets, has seriously negative effects on economic behaviour. One consequence is over-consumption, as households misjudge their personal wealth. Another is poor investment judgement, as cheap credit encourages companies to expand haphazardly. The lenders themselves usually end up suffering when borrowers are unable to reimburse debt—one frightening example from 2008 being the complete implosion of Iceland's over-extended banking sector. All these problems in the financial system will then have terrible effects on the economy as a whole—a point made by Barack Obama during the 2008 US presidential campaign when he openly questioned whether 'Wall Street' had become more of a threat than a friend to 'Main Street' (that is, non-financial interests). There is widespread consensus today that state authorities require greater visibility of the risks created by the world's top financial institutions—banks but also new players such as private equity interests, hedge funds, and sovereign wealth funds. The exact nature of the new regulations, and specifically whether they will be based on a convergence of current US and European systems (Doran 2009), remains to be seen. One thing is certain, however—in the wake of the credit crunch, complete self-regulation is no longer an option.

Case Study 14.2

Capital markets: How a subprime crisis turned into a major headache

By late 2007, it had already become clear that US lenders were selling too many mortgages to property developers and homeowners, many of whom were struggling to repay the debt they had incurred. Initially, the scale of the problem was not completely recognized. The first thing that people noticed was when a number of

major financial institutions began borrowing increasing amounts of capital from the interbank credit market. This soon led to rumours casting doubt on their solvency. Panic spread and institutions sitting on surplus funds became much less willing to lend them. In the end, this caused a 'credit crunch' affecting other banks whose

relative lack of depositor funds meant that they relied to a greater extent on inter bank lending. By mid-2008, a full-blown crisis had erupted, culminating in the disappearance of powerful investment banks such as Lehman Brothers and Bear Stearns and a loss of independence for household names such as Merrill Lynch and Salomon Brothers.

On the face of things, the problem was purely American in origin. However, the fact that its impact was global shows how international capital markets are interlinked—or, as the expression goes, how when Washington sneezes, everyone catches a cold. There were two main causes for this coupling. Firstly, non-US financial institutions also suffered from the knock-on effects of the tightness in the American money markets. Simply stated, the US squeeze led to a fall in the global supply of capital. Foreign victims of the credit crunch included Britain's Northern Rock building society, which ultimately required government support to survive; Belgium's Fortis bank, which had to be taken over by France's BNP-Paribas; or the UK building society Alliance and Leicester, acquired by Spain's Santander group. Secondly, since US lenders had often repackaged their outstanding mortgage loans and sold them on to non-American banks and funds, investors worldwide were forced to record losses once the value of these assets plummeted. This created further concern about the viability of the world's financial system.

Non-financial companies worldwide were also directly affected by the credit squeeze. Banks became much more concerned about the quality of their outstanding loans, thus more suspicious of borrowers. They withdrew the short-term facilities on which many companies relied to fund current operations, forcing them to burn up internal reserves in order to survive (Kerneis 2008). The long-term debt markets also dried up, with more and more borrowers having to compete for funds, even as investors were taking liquidity out of the markets and turning to safer alternatives such as gold or US treasury bonds. Borrowing costs shot up, since ratings agencies downgraded anything but the safest companies. The 'risk premium' required of lower-quality borrowers also rose. Companies seeking to 'de-leverage' their balance sheets by substituting equity for debt capital struggled because of plummeting share values, which

The subprime US mortgage problems had a devastating effect on MNEs worldwide (© iStockphoto).

fell within a few short months by almost 60 per cent on some Chinese exchanges. Cash became king—a serious problem in an international economy based entirely on the ready availability of long-term investment capital.

Governments worldwide worked hard to solidify their national financial systems (for example, UK Prime Minister Gordon Brown's bank recapitalization scheme) and restimulate their economies (for example, US President Obama's $750 billion fiscal stimulus and infrastructure investment package). Despite drastically lower interest rates, however, the damage was done. As companies starved of funding began to lay off personnel, aggregate demand plummeted worldwide, and the recession became self-fulfilling. Many companies and individuals who had always conducted their financial affairs prudently suffered greatly because of the imprudent behaviour of a small group of financial institutions in relatively few countries. Not only was the credit crunch an economic catastrophe; it was also very unfair.

Photo 14.2
Belgium: Europe's
leading centre for
regional treasury
operations (Oxford
University Press).

Section II: Internal sources of finance

An MNE treasury department undertakes many different tasks. As discussed above, some functions (such as foreign exchange and funding) are more strategic and external in outlook. Others are more tactical and internal. Examples include investment planning, simulation, budgeting, management control, accounting, reporting, cash management, insurance, and tax management. The sum total of these responsibilities gives treasurers a broad overview of all corporate processes. Arguably, finance is the most strategic of an MNE's value chain functions.

MNE treasurers manage not only relationships with external providers of funds, as discussed above, but also the spread of cash throughout their groups. This is a crucial activity for several reasons. First, because of the specialist roles assigned to many MNE subsidiaries nowadays, internal funds tend to be distributed unevenly between units that are 'long' cash and others that are 'short'. Such imbalances require close monitoring. Secondly, as MNEs start to do an increasing percentage of their business in LDCs characterized by comparatively underdeveloped financial markets, internal capital will necessarily assume greater importance as a source of investment capital (Islam and Mozumdar 2007). In this vision, MNE treasurers sometimes need to act as bankers to their own group.

Netting

Banks making markets in tradable credit instruments tend to quote prices with a bid-offer spread (as they do in foreign exchange) and also often charge fees. Thus, companies incur costs every time they transact a funding deal with a bank. It is, therefore, in their interest to reduce the number of operations they do. Towards this end, many MNEs create a 'netting' department that recycles some subsidiaries' surplus cash positions by using it to fund other units' deficits. By internalizing the clearing process, the only amounts transacted with the outside world represent the group's net financial position.

To perform this netting function, MNE treasurers must be able to take an instantaneous snapshot of the different cash positions that each group subsidiary has accumulated in the various currencies it trades. It is a challenging task for firms running global operations, and one that requires a high performance information system. This is the backbone of all global finance. Indeed, with their Reuters screens, piles of spreadsheets, cash-flow simulation models, and economic research papers, some MNE treasury departments resemble bank trading rooms.

As discussed in Chapter 9, finance is one of the corporate functions most likely to be centralized. MNE subsidiaries may have their own accounting and cash teams, but to get a full view of group needs and save on overheads, most companies will lodge their most strategic financial operations, like trading and hedging, in a Regional Treasury Centre (Franck 2005). Such offices are often located in tax jurisdictions that treat MNEs' internal flows favourably. This can involve, for instance, allowing one MNE unit that pays interest on a loan from a sister unit to deduct this payment from its taxable income. A good example of a European country offering this kind of facility is Belgium. This explains why MNEs like Johnson Controls, Procter and Gamble, and General Motors (GMAC) all run major treasury operations and/or netting services near Brussels.

To demonstrate the principle of netting (see Figure 14.7), take the example of an MNE whose Berlin office has a cash surplus of €5 million that it wants to deposit for a period of one month to earn some interest. At the same time, its sister unit in Paris needs to borrow €10 million, also for one month. If at that moment, a bank were to quote 1-month euro deposits at an annual rate of 4.50 to 4.625 per cent (a typical spread in June 2008), and if the two units were to work separately, the Berlin office would lend out its €5 million for one month at the bank's 4.50 per cent borrowing rate—receiving €18,750 in interest—whereas the Paris office would borrow €10 million per cent from the bank at its 1-month, 4.625 per cent borrowing rate—paying €38,542 in interest. In total, the group would pay the difference between these two sums, or €19,795. If, on the other hand, a netting procedure were in place, Berlin would deposit its €5 million surplus with a central netting office, located, for

+ **Clearing**
Process of calculating and paying the net differences between the amounts due to/owed by market participants.

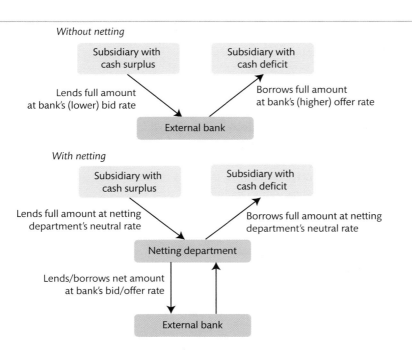

Figure 14.7
Netting based on the establishment of an internal clearing office.

instance, in Brussels, which would then move the funds on to Paris, whose only external transaction would involve borrowing the remaining €5 million it requires at the bank's 4.625 per cent offer rate, for a total 1-month cost of €19,270. By having its subsidiaries grant one another internal loans at a neutral interest rate—and in the absence of any specific tax considerations—the group in this example would have saved €525 just by netting.

As is the case will all intra-MNE capital movements, the price that one unit pays to its sister unit will affect the location where the group declares it profits or losses at the end of the accounting period. Unsurprisingly, this mechanism is of deep interest to MNEs.

Transfer pricing and MNE taxation

With the number of firms operating on a multinational basis having risen from 37,000 in the early 1990s to 64,000 by 2004, and the number of foreign subsidiaries having jumped from 175,000 to 870,000 over the same period, it is no surprise to discover that an estimated 60 per cent of international trade today occurs on an intra-firm basis (*The Economist* 2007). MNE subsidiaries and headquarters deal with one another in a wide range of assets: tangible items such as raw materials, parts, and finished goods; but also capital or intangible items like loans, fees, royalties, trademarks, and dividends. Because such dealings occur between related units, there is a great temptation to manipulate prices for non-economic reasons: so as to clarify each unit's performance assessment; and, above all, to minimize the group's overall tax exposure.

In terms of performance assessment, a decision to transfer capital or goods at a high price will leave more money in the hands of the unit making the transfer, whereas a transfer made at a lower price will favour the receiver. Thus, the transfer price decision being made at this level juggles contradictory interests. Members of the unit benefiting from intra-firm pricing policies will declare higher profits at yearend and feel justified in demanding higher bonuses. The fact that a sister unit was the source of their earnings will not detract from their sense of a job well done. Much time is spent in multi-site MNEs negotiating transfer prices with colleagues from other units. Understandably, international managers often feel greater loyalty to the particular unit employing them than to the MNE as a whole. This is quite human, since, as often as not, it is at the level of this unit that their career (pay, promotion prospects) will be determined. Some firms actually engage in double accounting practices, quantifying employees' contribution to sister units to motivate them to see beyond their own narrow bonus pool. Interdepartmental competition, often occurring up and down the value chain, is ferocious in many MNEs.

Regarding a company's overall tax burden, shareholders' narrow interest is to see profits declared in countries where taxes are low, with losses declared in higher tax regimes. It is important to remember that transfer prices are not the only component of MNEs' fiscal calculations. Countries vary in terms of all kinds of taxes, including customs duties, foreign tax credits, value-added taxes, double taxation measures, and, above all, corporation tax rates. For most MNE tax directors, however, especially in industries like pharmaceuticals that are marked by complex value chains and large transferable profits, transfer prices are considered the most crucial element in their tax-reduction strategies (Ernst and Young 2008). In part, this is because of the flexibility that they are afforded in this area.

Where an MNE's accounting principles comply with national legislations, actions taken to minimize the amount of taxable income it declares are called tax avoidance. If not, the talk is of tax evasion—an illegal and often criminal offence. Note that, even if tax avoidance is legal, many consider it ethically questionable. The practice is enabled by the huge differentials between many countries' corporation tax rates of 25–35 per cent and levels of as low as 10 per cent found elsewhere—most famously in East European transition states pressured by 'regime shopping' MNEs into abandoning much needed fiscal revenues (see Chapter 3). Even more striking are the fiscal policies practised in some of the world's tax havens, like Bermuda, which levies no income tax on foreign earnings, or the British Virgin Islands,

+ **Tax avoidance**
Use of legal means to avoid paying taxes.

+ **Tax evasion**
Use of illegal means to avoid paying taxes.

+ **Tax haven**
Country with particularly low tax rates and regulations.

Thinking point

How tolerable is legal tax avoidance?

	Country A (place of production) Normal tax regime (30% tax rate)	Country B Tax haven (5% tax rate)	Country C (place of sale) Normal tax regime (30% tax rate)
A. Real transaction			
The operation	Return cost €800,000	n.a.	Revenues €900,000
Gross profit	€100,000 (€50,000 declared in Country A, €50,000 in Country C)		
Tax calculation	€50,000 X 30% = €15,000	n.a.	€50,000 X 30% = €15,000
Total tax	€15,000+€15,000 = €30,000		
Net profit	€100,000 (gross profit) - €30,000 (total tax) = €70,000		
B. Tax evasion transaction			
Fictionalized operations	*Declares export to B at €700,000*	Declares export to C at €1 million	Declares payment of €1 million
Profit calculation	*Reminder: Real return cost = €800,000*	Declares payment of €700,000	*Reminder: real sale = €900,000*
Stated profit	(-€100,000)	+ €300,000	(-€100,000)
Tax calculation	(-€100,000) X 0% = €0 (+ tax credit?)	€300,000 X 5% = €15,000	(-€100,000) X 0% = €0 (+ tax credit?)
Total tax	€0 + €15,000 + €0 = €15,000		
Net profit	€100,000 (gross profit) - €15,000 (total tax) = €85,000 (+ tax credits)		

Figure 14.8
Using transfer pricing to locate profits in tax havens and losses in countries with higher tax levels.

which levies no corporation or capital gains tax at all. In the light of such differentials, it is unsurprising that some MNEs are tempted to declare profits in a way that will minimize their overall tax burden.

At the same time, observers worldwide have been shocked by repeated examples of household-name MNEs allegedly abusing transfer pricing mechanisms, accounting loopholes, and/or tax havens to pay little in tax. In the USA, for example, where corporation tax is around 35 per cent, American pharmaceutical giant Eli Lilly ended up paying the government taxes amounting to less than 6 per cent on its 2006 profits of $3.4 billion (Berenson 2007). In the UK, where large corporations would normally expect to pay around 30 per cent, British American Tobacco paid no tax on 2007 gross profits of £3.08 billion (Costello and Pagnamenta 2008). In 2007, British pharmacist Boots paid the UK government £131 million in tax on profits of £455 million. One year later, following a private equity takeover engineered by US venture capitalist KKR, it paid zero tax on pre-interest profits of £535 million (Leigh et al. 2009). Large and vocal NGOs like the Tax Justice Network have sprung up specifically to denounce such practices. They are not the only critics of MNEs' fiscal behaviour. Less revenue means either cutting essential public services or shifting the tax burden to poorer citizens unable to hide their earnings offshore (Christensen 2006). MNE taxation is a social issue as well as a business one.

Figure 14.8 demonstrates how MNEs might use transfer prices to give tax authorities an inaccurate picture of their economic activity. Note that the practices outlined in Figure 14.8 are highly dishonest and therefore completely unacceptable. It bears repeating that this book entreats all international business students always to pursue the highest standards of conduct throughout their careers. However, for analytical purposes, it is useful to visualize the mechanism by means of which a hypothetical MNE might engage in tax evasion.

Ideally, MNEs may not invent unrealistic transfer prices for the express purpose of reducing taxes. Although international standards vary in this area, the measurement favoured by most authorities (including the US Internal Revenue Service and the OECD) is the 'arm's length' principle, where the MNE's subsidiaries price any and all deals as if they are unrelated to their counterparts and a state of perfect competition exists. This is a relatively vague definition, however, leaving MNEs much freedom to set transfer prices—especially if no comparable market exists for the item in question, as is often the case for intangible assets like trademarks. The Online Resource Centre, extension material 14.4, offers further analysis of different pricing methods and how they affect an MNE's overall tax bill. The main categories include:

> Go to the ORC

- 'cost pricing': where the item is transferred without any mark-up;
- 'cost plus pricing': where a defined margin is added to the return price of the item, often a finished product;
- 'profit split' pricing: where the ultimate operating profit realized on an item after it has been sold is split between the manufacturing and sales subsidiaries, after an objective measurement of the contribution made by each.

Calculations can be very complicated in this area. In the absence of transparency and/ or if questionable accounting assumptions are made, companies often face disputes with national tax authorities. These can be very expensive. In 2006, for instance, it cost British pharmaceutical company GlaxoSmithKline $3.4 billion to settle a transfer price dispute with the US tax authorities (*Associated Press* 2006). Note that MNEs can also be at odds with tax authorities for reasons other than transfer pricing. In 2008, for instance, Vodafone went to court to challenge the Indian government's decision to tax a stake it had acquired in a company listed outside India but possessing substantial assets in the country. That same year, ExxonMobil and Shell received a $2 billion tax bill from the Nigerian government for old offshore oilfield contracts. Fiscal disputes are no laughing matter for MNEs.

Because of its cross-border aspects, multinational taxation has become a major global governance issue and is bound to remain so for the foreseeable future. The United Nations now runs a Committee of Experts on International Cooperation in Tax Matters that meets annually to analyse and counter tax evasion. The OECD has also drawn up what it considers a model tax convention that firms are asked to support. One of the main decisions taken at the April 2009 meeting of G20 leaders in London was to put pressure on tax havens. Several national authorities have developed 'advance pricing agreements' to remove uncertainty over corporate transfer pricing policies. There is also a trend towards more active policing of companies and private individuals. In 2008, the German government paid a Liechtenstein bank employee to get the names of German nationals holding secret accounts in that country (Connolly 2008). In 2009, the Paris prosecutor's office said that companies as prestigious as Total, Michelin, and Adidas would be investigated after allegations that they had benefited from Liechtenstein's system (Leigh and Davies 2009). Even Angel Gurria, Secretary General of the OECD and a supporter of free markets, has openly advocated cracking down on tax havens, arguing that the funds hidden there could be used to finance LDC aid commitments. The future of these outlets of secret finance is very much in doubt, and Switzerland's grudging acceptance in early 2009 of the need to alter its 'bank secrecy' laws is a sign of coming changes.

More broadly, there is growing popular concern that MNEs need to bear their fair share of the tax burden that all citizens carry to varying degrees. Indeed, this has become a core topic in many elections worldwide, as witnessed by Barack Obama's argument

during the 2008 US presidential campaign that, beyond a certain level of affluence, people and business need to 'share the wealth'—a very significant statement in the light of the £11 trillion that analysts calculated in 2009 were hidden in the world's tax havens (*Observer* 2009). Some might say that companies who pay significant sums in tax are at a disadvantage to free-riding competitors able to avoid such costs. However, this would be the same as arguing that, because crime pays, companies are justified in acting like criminals—a conception rejected by the authors of this book. A kind of international business where multinationals are encouraged to ignore the legitimate requirements of democratically elected national governments does not hold much promise for the future. One of the changes that is most likely to affect MNEs' operating conditions in the not so distant future (see Chapter 16) is some reassertion of public control over global finance.

Challenges and choices

→ International treasurers in large MNEs are under great pressure to maximize corporate earnings, yet in most non-financial institutions the treasury function is rarely classified as a profit centre. This means that managers are torn between the requirement to manage and minimize costs and personal incentives they may have to make profits. The dilemma plays out at different levels. One involves the funding or investment choices that a treasury makes. Active financial management often produces inconsistent results, especially in economies lacking mature markets. Risk management decisions are in and of themselves risky.

→ Choosing an optimal level of gearing is crucial in all companies, especially in large, globally traded MNEs that must satisfy demanding institutional investors' profitability requirements without taking on too much debt. Excessive leverage increases companies' vulnerability to economic downturns, yet treasurers can be equally criticized if they rely too heavily on equity financing. Different business cultures place varying degrees of emphasis on companies' return on equity (ROE) ratios.

Chapter Summary

The chapter began with a brief comparison of debt versus equity as sources of external finance. Debt funding is largely priced to reflect borrowers' perceived creditworthiness. Equity funding raises questions about where capital can be sourced. MNEs often seek funding in offshore euro markets, which have experienced a rapid growth in liquidity since the early 1990s. At the same time, in the wake of the 2008 credit crunch, serious questions remain about whether these markets aid international business or destabilize it.

The second half of the chapter reviewed internal sources of finance, primarily MNEs' efforts to shift surplus cash from one site to another to achieve wider group objectives and avoid the costs associated with external funding. Above and beyond the performance assessment consequences of such practices, there are also major tax implications. MNEs can alter their overall tax bill depending on the transfer prices they use. In general, the topic of fiscal responsibility has strong ethical overtones.

Case Study 14.3

MNE treasury operations: Nokia knocking on Asia's door

MNEs often organize their treasury function on a regional basis, running teams in the Asian, European, and American time zones. This will cost more than having a single global team. On the other hand, apart from the difficulty of staffing one location on a 24/7 basis, locating finance specialists across the world means that national operations will have a local regional centre to which they can turn for crucial support. There are exceptions to this rule. Payment factories, for instance, tend to be globalized to streamline cash management processes. Moreover, many companies have global units that serve as in-house banks fulfilling a netting function (Beekelar 2008). It remains that many others have decided to handle their funding, risk management, tax, and liquidity needs out of regional centres benefiting from greater access to local information. Nokia, the Finnish telecommunications giant, used to manage all its global treasury needs out of Geneva. Since the mid-1990s, its 55-member-strong global treasury department has been working along more or less regional lines.

Nokia's Singapore centre (comprised of seven employees on this one site and three others working out of Beijing) runs treasury operations on behalf of the group's operating companies in Asia, serving as their in-house bank and helping them to manage their banking and funding relationships. A treasury team accumulates an enormous amount of knowledge that may not be widespread in an

MNE focused on other core competencies. It is therefore crucial that this financial knowledge be shared, although this is easier said than done. For example, MNE treasurers often struggle in an Asian environment, with the region's long tradition of state interventionism having produced a patchwork of national regulations, fiscal constraints, and payment systems that can be difficult to master. Nokia subsidiaries here and elsewhere benefit from the proximity of knowledgeable colleagues possessing an overview of all regional flows of goods and capital. This is especially useful during financial crises, like the one that swept across Asia in the late 1990s. The effects of this 'tsunami' were minimized at Nokia because of its expert treasurers' effective utilization of up to date simulation techniques like Value at Risk (VAR), a process that models future losses on a probabilistic basis. Nokia has so much confidence in its treasury specialists that it has classified their activity as a profit centre. Indeed, working under strict controls, Nokia's treasury staff members are encouraged to engage in speculative trading from time to time. The purpose is to increase their knowledge of how local financial markets work, in the hope that this will improve the advice they offer regional operating companies. This attitude is very different from many other MNEs, which view finance solely as an administrative function.

Jaya Machet, who manages Nokia's Singapore treasury unit along with its global cash management needs

Singapore—the nerve centre of Asian finance (Photodisc).

(including a central 'payments factory' in Geneva), measures her regional centre's usefulness in two ways: on a 'treasury value-added' basis, where Nokia's results are compared before and after her team's contribution; and in terms of the 'incremental value added' that can be attributed to the quality of treasury specialists' advice (Curry 2000; Wood 2006). One example of the latter contribution was when Machet's team helped customers in India to receive goods more quickly by improving the local Nokia subsidiary's collection system through the use of 'Unique Remittance Identifier codes'. Instead of having to devote resources to discovering its own solution, Nokia India was able to leverage the experience of its colleagues from Singapore.

To pool this know-how, the systems used by Nokia's different units need to feature a certain amount of compatibility. One example is the intra-unit transfer of information, a key daily task for all MNEs. This can involve data exchanges between operating companies and the treasury centre(s) responsible for their affairs, or between different treasury centres. Procedures can falter when the units and/or treasury centres operate on different computer platforms. Conversely, harmonization helps to make things run smoothly. Nokia may have decentralized power to its regions, but within each zone the treasury centre reigns supreme.

However, some functions continue to be exercised at a lower, national level. Where a country's financial system or market is particularly complicated and/or favours resident firms, MNEs will tend to empower their national treasury team to oversee particular operations. Along these lines, Nokia Singapore has opened a branch in Beijing specifically because this provides the group with direct access to the growing 'onshore forward yuan–dollar' market. It is also an opportunity to improve relations with Chinese banks, a great advantage in this desirable but complex market.

All in all, Nokia's Singapore treasury centre is destined to retain a key role in the group's global configuration, if only because the work it does enhances Nokia's standing in Asia. In this area of MNE activity, as in so many others, the region offers an optimal compromise between local and global levels of organization.

Case study questions

1. How many tasks does an MNE treasury department perform?
2. What factors dictate where an MNE should locate its treasury operation(s)?
3. To what extent is an MNE treasury team a strategic or an administrative function?

Discussion questions

1. What are the advantages and disadvantages for an MNE of securing funding from banks instead of the capital markets?

2. To what extent should MNEs assume debt to leverage their earnings potential?

3. What factors determine the credit spread that an MNE has to pay at a given point in time?

4. What items might be on the agenda at a Bretton Woods II conference?

5. How tolerable is it for MNEs to use tax havens?

References

Associated Press (2006). 'IRS Settles Biggest Tax Dispute in History', 11 Sept., www.msnbc.msn.com (accessed 3 Dec. 2008).

Beekelar, M. (2008). 'Mitigating Risk through a Centralised Treasury', 7 Oct., www.gtnews.com (accessed 10 Dec. 2008).

Berenson, A. (2007). 'Tax Break Used by Drug Makers Failed to Add Jobs', 24 July, www.nytimes.com (accessed 4 Dec. 2008).

Blair, D. (1999). 'Corporate Treasury in Singapore', www.gtnews.com (accessed 7 Mar. 2008).

Bloomberg (2008). 'Market Data: Rates and Bonds', www.bloomberg.com (accessed 4 Mar. 2008).

Böhme, M., et al. (2008). 'The Growing Opportunity for Investment Banks in Emerging Markets', Aug., www.mckinseyquarterly.com (accessed 3 Dec. 2008).

Bollen, B. (2008). 'A New Economic Leadership Stirs', *Financial Times*, 7 Apr., p. 13.

Buckman, G. (2004). *Globalization: Tame it or Scrap it*. London: Zed Books.

Burton, D., and Zanello, A. (2007). 'Asia Ten Years After', June, www.imf.org (accessed 6 Mar. 2008).

Canaves, S. (2007). 'New Path for Tech IPOs?', *Wall Street Journal–Europe*, 2–4 Nov., p. 19.

Cheng, S., and Shiu, C. (2007). 'Investor Protection and Capital structure: International Evidence', *Journal of Multinational Financial Management*, 17/1 (Feb.).

Cheung, J. (2007). 'Hong Kong Aims to be a Hub for Islamic Bonds', *Wall Street Journal–Europe*, 29 Nov., p. 25.

Christensen (2006). 'Follow the Money: How Tax Havens Facilitate Dirty Money Flows and Distort Global Markets', www.taxjustice.net (accessed 6 Mar. 2008).

Ciner, C. (2007). 'Dynamic Linkages between International Bond Markets', *Journal of Multinational Financial Management*, 17/4 (Oct.).

Connolly, K. (2008). 'Merkel Challenges Liechtenstein over Tax Evasion', 21 Feb., www.guardian.co.uk (accessed 2 July 2008).

Costello, M., and Pagnamenta, R. (2008). 'Old Mutual Mulls Joining the List of Companies Looking for a Foreign Tax Haven', 8 May, www.timesonline.co.uk (accessed 2 July 2008).

Curry, C. (2000). 'A Star Is Born', www.cfoasia.com (accessed 7 Mar. 2008).

Dobbs, R., and Goedhart, M. (2008). 'Why Cross-Listing Shares Doesn't Create Value, Nov., www.mckinseyquarterly.com (accessed 5 Dec. 2008).

Doran, J. (2009). 'US Rejects Global Finance Controls', *Observer*, Business section, 8 Mar., p. 1.

Draho, J. (2008). 'Re-Equitizing Corporate Balance Sheets: Choosing among the Alternatives', *Journal of Applied Corporate Finance*, 20/3 (Summer).

The Economist (February 2007). 'A Place in the Sun: Special Report on Offshore Finance', Feb.

Ernst and Young (2008). 'Precision under Pressure: Global Transfer Pricing Survey 2007–2008', www.ey.com (accessed 10 May 2008).

Financial Times (2008). 'Global Investment Grade', Mar., http://markets.ft.com (accessed 4 Mar. 2008).

Franck, N. (2005). 'Are Regional Treasury Centres Redundant?', 3 May, www.gtnews.com (accessed 6 Mar. 2008).

Goodman, P. (2009). 'The Coveted Currency', *Observer*, 15 Mar., *New York Times* insert, p. 1.

Hodkinson, P. (2008). 'Germany's 'Locust' Controversy Continues', *Wall Street Journal–Europe*, 7 Apr., p. 21.

Islam, S., and Mozumdar, A. (2007). 'Financial Market Development and the Importance of Internal Cash: Evidence from International Data', *Journal of Bank and Finance*, 31/3 (Mar.).

IVCA (2007). 'VC: The Indian Market Scenario', www.indiavca.org (accessed 5 Mar. 2008).

Kaminsky, G. (2004). 'International Capital Flows: A Blessing or a Curse?', www.un.org (accessed 6 Mar. 2008).

Kerneis, A. (2008). 'Managing Corporate Cash Reserves during Turbulent Times', 29 July, www.gtnew.com (accessed 9 Dec. 2008).

Leigh, D., and Davies, L. (2009). 'Liechtenstein Tax Deal Edges Closer as France begins Fraud Inquiry', *Guardian*, 1 Apr., p. 25.

Leigh, D., et al. (2009). 'From the High Street to Tax Haven', *Guardian*, 9 Feb., pp. 16–17.

Lufthansa Investor Relations (2008). www.lufthansa-financials.com (accessed 6 Mar. 2008).

MacDonald, A. (2007). 'Europe Takes Great Leap, Shakes Trading Landscape', *Wall Street Journal–Europe*, 29 Oct., p. 1.

MacDonald, A. (2008). 'Plans to Regulate Banks across Borders Gain Steam', *Wall Street Journal–Europe*, 3 Apr., p. 19.

Markowitz, H. (1991). *Portfolio Selection: Efficient Diversification of Investments*. 2nd edn. New York: Wiley.

Morgan Stanley (2008). 'Asset-Backed Insecurity', quoted in *The Economist*, 17 Jan., www.economist.com (accessed 5 Mar. 2008).

Munchau, W. (2009). ICES European Business School London conference, discussion with author, 17 Feb.

Norguet, D. (2007). 'Une action = une voix', www.etudes.ccip.fr (accessed 4 Mar. 2008).

Observer (2009). 'It's Hypocrisy to Leave British Tax Havens Open', 8 Mar., p. 32.

Peristiani, S. (2007). 'US Corporate Bond Market Losing Dominance—NY Fed', 30 July, quoted in Reuters, www.reuters.com (accessed 4 Dec. 2008).

Perry, J. (2008). 'Retooling of Global Market Oversight Urged', *Wall Street Journal–Europe*, 7 Apr., p. 3.

Richtel, M. (2007). 'Start-up Fervor Shifts to Energy in Silicon Valley', 14 Mar., www.nytimes.com (accessed 4 Mar. 2008).

Soble, J. (2008). 'Tokyo Rethinks its Limits on Foreign Stakes in Airports', *Financial Times*, 5 Feb., p. 7.

Stewart, H., and Sunderland, R. (2008). 'As American Crash Lands, the World Looks East', *Observer*, 27 Jan., pp. 4–5.

SWF Institute (2009). 'Fund Rankings', www.swfinstitute.org (accessed 10 Jan. 2009).

Traynor, I. (2008). 'Sovereign Wealth Funds Likened to Gazprom as Brussels Calls for Rules', *Guardian*, 28 Feb., p. 28.

Vos, E., Yeh, A., Carter, S., and Tagg, S. (2007). 'The Happy Story of Small Business Financing', *Journal of Banking & Finance*, 31/9 (Sept.).

Wolf, M. (2009). 'Seeds of its own Destruction', *Financial Times*, 8 Mar.

Wood, J. (2006). 'Remote Control Treasury?', www.cfoasia.com (accessed 7 Mar. 2008).

Zhu, E., and Davis, B. (2007). 'ICBC Invests in South Africa Bank', *Wall Street Journal–Europe*, 26–28 Oct., p. 17.

Further research

Bonner, W., and Addison, W. (2005). *Empire of Debt: The Rise of an Epic Financial Crisis*. Hoboken, NJ: John Wiley & Sons.

This book describes the addiction to debt that has characterized US consumers, companies, and governments for the past century as being a crucial driver behind an imperial expansion founded on America's ability to access cheap credit abroad. Adopting a deeply cynical tone, the authors offer a detailed history of US reliance on the international capital markets, highlighting the problematic use of debt to avoid normal economic constraints. Despite being written before the 2008 crisis, it is a useful (albeit polemic) tool for discussing the financial imbalances that helped to spark the credit crunch.

Alexander, K., et al. (2006). *Global Governance of Financial Systems: The International Regulation of Systemic Risk*. New York: Oxford University Press.

This is a criticism of the way externalities from financial activities 'impose costs on society at large that exceed the losses incurred by investors'. A prime example is a bank failure. The idea here is that the time has come to develop a system where national macro-economic policies play a greater role in minimizing the risks that entire economies suffer as a result of financial speculation.

Ocampo, J., and Stiglitz, J. (2008). *Capital Market Liberalization and Development*. New York: Oxford University Press.

For decades, capital market liberalization has been a key battlefield in debates about globalization. debates. Many LDCs have liberalized their financial markets, often at the request of international financial institutions like the IMF. By so doing, they have exposed their economies to increased risk and volatility. This book explores the design of international capital markets from LDCs' perspective.

Online Resource Centre

Visit the Online Resource Centre that accompanies this book to read more information relating to multinational finance and treasury operations: www.oxfordtextbooks.co.uk/orc/sitkin_bowen/

15 International Human Resource Management

Overview

The first section of this chapter explores the general principles behind international human resource management (IHRM), with a focus on three basic orientations: (*ethnocentric*, *polycentric*, and *geocentric*) and a consideration of expatriation. In particular, it is argued that the nature of international work in the twenty-first century is undergoing significant changes in working patterns and modes of working, and in the emphasis on local education, training, and hiring.

The second section considers a number of issues crucial to managing international workforces, such as cross-cultural training, performance management, pay for top executives, the position of women in global business, and stress in international jobs. It also examines some of the key changes taking place within the world of employment, including legal aspects, and fundamental developments changing the ways in which people work.

Overall, the chapter relates IHRM issues to the cultural factors that are intrinsic to the conduct of international business and the management of people within multinational enterprise (MNEs).

Section I: Strategic development of IHRM
   Ethnocentric, polycentric, and geocentric orientations
   Expatriation
   International assignments

Section II: Managing international workforces
   Cross-cultural training
   Performance management
   Women in international business
   Stress in international jobs
   Changes in employment and the workplace

Learning Objectives

After reading this chapter, you should be able to

+ understand a range of issues related to IHRM

+ identify and analyse the key strategic problems of international assignments, including changes to twenty-first century jobs

+ assess the advantages and disadvantages of expatriation

+ understand the main issues related to the role of women in international business, to diversity in workforces, and to issues of executive pay

+ identify the key tasks that managers face when managing international workforces

Case Study 15.1

Ericsson and human resource management in India

Ericsson, the large Swedish telecommunications company, is the world leader in this field and has operated in India since it supplied manual switchboards to India in 1903. By 2009, Ericsson was operating half the country's telecommunications networks, had about 4,000 employees across twenty-four offices, and a wireless market share of about 34 per cent. The company offers a full range of telecom services from 'basic telephony, intelligent networks, datacom and the most advanced telecom integration and services to mobile office applications and multimedia applications' (Maki and Soudakova 2008).

Given the size of its Indian operation, Ericsson decided to establish a full Human Resource (HR) Department at its headquarters at Gurgaon in the state of Haryana, just south of New Delhi. Recognizing the irreplaceable importance of staff, Ericsson set up People and Culture (P&C) within the Indian operation. P&C was designed to bring together and nurture competent employees, combining global HR philosophy and practices with local flavour and content. A number of significant features typify Ericsson's operations in India, particularly the policies on staffing, appraisal, compensation packages, and training.

Ericsson's approach to staffing in India is to encourage both internal (Indian) and external (Swedish and global) recruitment. The company prides itself on its culture and values: perseverance, respect, and professionalism. It encourages staff to understand, appreciate, and practise these as 'ways of working' (WoW) when dealing with internal and external customers. Ericsson has a positive attitude towards its Swedish employees working in India and stresses the need for them to be open-minded and culturally aware. Employees selected for international assignments are managed in a uniform and professional manner by Global International Assignments (GIA), which acts as a competency centre within the global HR function. When work appraisals are conducted, individual performance is assessed in the same way in India as elsewhere. As far as compensation packages are concerned, the policy is to give a small amount of additional benefit (supplementary payments for a car, living costs, and additional salary) to employees working abroad—for example, Swedes in India.

The most interesting aspect of Ericsson's human resource management (HRM) operations in India is cross-cultural training, which is seen as preparation for employees working outside their home country. Ericsson focuses on three provisions: meetings with the HRM department on the practical aspects of working in India; meetings for new employees with members of staff who have served there; and a guide or mentor to assist new employees when they work in India. Ericsson's approach to the induction of employees into their new working environments treats them all the same and appears to be very successful. The company sees no reason to adopt a 'third culture' between the Indian and the Swedish: both sets of managers need to adapt to one another on an equal basis.

Good conditions for living and working in India.

Introduction

Firms that operate on an international level face major people challenges in all aspects of their activities. MNEs' key tasks are whether they can (*a*) facilitate effective integration across their many locations and operations and (*b*) take advantage of local differences in culture. Part of the IHRM aspect stems from the essential decisions taken regarding structure. The formal structure of the firm can only hint at the complexity of the international linkages that need to be managed. Indeed, many MNEs have developed such complicated international structures and reporting systems that the effective running of the business is often conducted as much through informal linkages as through a formal organizational chart. The main issues for IHRM departments relate to their role in the strategic direction of the MNE, the development of new international assignments, the nature of cross-cultural training, performance management, and equality of opportunity.

A key factor for firms operating internationally is the need, therefore, to apply integrative management development skills or what Paul Evans (1992) called 'glue technology'. At the start of the twenty-first century, 'multi-domestic operations, joint ventures and strategic alliances were increasingly common forms of business structures across regions or across the world' (Grainger and Nankervis 2001: 83). To ensure maximum effectiveness in very complex organizations, the crucial areas that need to be faced and resolved are the roles of people within these organizations and the management of all levels of people—from assembly line workers to top corporate executives.

Section I: Strategic development of IHRM

IHRM has increasingly been incorporated within the strategic direction of the vast majority of MNEs. There is a clear recognition that IHRM has to take its place on an equal footing with other main functions like production, operations, finance and marketing. Corporations have realized that the management of their human resource is at least as crucial for their success as the management of their capital and sales. In addition to the need to recruit, retain, train, and develop the best managers, firms acknowledge that they must adopt an overall— or holistic—approach to people within the firm: they must participate fully at all stages, such as the creation of the vision, the devising and implementation of the strategy, and the organization of managerial and working structures. This is not just a matter of managing the people once they have been hired but of fully contributing to the direction of the company. Certain firms, such as W. L. Gore, the makers of Gore-Tex (a water-proof material), have not only created excellent products but have maintained a reputation for excellence in their standards and practices of good employee relations. In 2009, for the twelfth successive year, W. L. Gore (www.gore.com) was named as one of the top employers by Fortune magazine; it was ranked fifteenth among US companies.

The essential purpose of the IHRM department is to ensure that the MNE is competitive throughout the world, that it operates efficiently, that it is flexible, adaptable, and locally responsive, and that it is capable of transferring knowledge and learning throughout the MNE's globally organized business units (Schuler et al. 2002). In order to carry out these functions, the IHRM department can be structured in three different ways: decentralized (small), transition (medium-sized), and centralized (large) (Scullion and Starkey 2000). The model of small, decentralized departments in all companies within the group may lead to limited resources for training and preparation of staff for international assignments, possible shortages of well-qualified international managers, and the downsizing of central operations in the HRM area. With the medium-sized transition departments, each business unit or company within the MNE's group has a moderately resourced and staffed operation.

The problem with this size department is often that it does not carry sufficient influence to ensure that the best people are released from their existing duties in order to undertake international assignments. Divisional managers hold onto their best staff, and the battle between the IHRM department and the division is usually resolved in favour of the latter. As the MNE grows, it often attempts to resolve the problems that have been noted above by creating a large centralized IHRM department. The key roles of this department are to carry out comprehensive and sophisticated planning across the group, to engage in strategic staffing under centralized control, and to establish and maintain control over all high-grade international jobs, usually with an emphasis on jobs being given to managers from the MNE's home country. This centralized department will be well resourced, highly regarded within the MNE, and able to implement its overall IHRM strategies (Scullion and Starkey 2000).

Ethnocentric, polycentric, and geocentric orientations

As discussed in earlier chapters and in Chapter 12 in relation to international marketing, one of the key approaches to the behaviour of MNEs derives from Perlmutter's classic study in 1969 on the three different international orientations within IHRM of ethnocentric, polycentric, and geocentric. These orientations play out at the human-resource level as well as from structural, cultural, production, and marketing perspectives. Perlmutter (1969) made a distinction between the different ways in which companies organize themselves.

Within these three overall views there is a range of international models for different firms' engagement in IHRM. The place of IHRM within business organizations can be considered at the strategic, managerial, and workforce levels.

Once the importance of IHRM has been established at the strategic level, it is essential that the crucial nature of its role be transmitted through the organization to both managers and workforce. The advantages spelt out at the top—in the boardroom and among directors and senior managers—can filter down to the rest of the firm's employees at all managerial levels and throughout the workforce. While this cascading operation is normal in all good firms, it is even more crucial in firms with major international activities. The management of other members of staff—both white collar and blue collar—becomes more complex when such people come from different countries, are located overseas, working in cross-cultural teams, and/or globally mobile. The next sections deal with the issues of expatriation and managing workers in foreign locations.

Expatriation

Increasingly, less importance is attached to some of the classic issues concerned with the expatriate role in international workforces, the balance between staff members of different national origins, and the treatment of managerial staff in international jobs. Historically, MNEs and other organizations operating internationally were always concerned with ensuring that they could establish, maintain, and retain international workforces and, in particular, accommodate overseas or expatriate staff carrying out specialized functions or roles in senior management. IHRM literature is full of concern about staffing policies

+ **Expatriate**
Employees working outside their home country.

Headquarters Orientation		
Ethnocentric	**Polycentric**	**Geocentric**
Recruit and develop people from *home country*	Develop *local nationals*	Develop *the best people* everywhere in world

Figure 15.1
Ethnocentric, polycentric, and geocentric orientations (adapted from Harzing 2004; Morris 2004).

+ Expatriation

Process of international transfer of managers, often used as a strategic tool to achieve specific organizational goals.

+ Thinking point

Why do parent country nationals often hold most middle and senior managerial jobs?

relating to parent country nationals (PCNs), host country nationals (HCNs), and third country nationals (TCNs). To some extent, this concern is still relevant and applied within IHRM policies, but it is increasingly common in the twenty-first century for workforces at managerial and specialized levels to become truly international. For example, the staffing of major banks, industrial companies, and computing software firms around the world are increasingly very similar in composition, regardless of where they are located.

Inside business

Mary Durham, Vice President, Finance & HR, OnPATH Technologies Inc.

OnPATH Technologies Inc. is a small private company operating out of the southern part of New Jersey in the USA. It engineers and manufactures data-centre IT physical layer-switching equipment that allows managers in data centres and test labs to interconnect all their equipment through one platform. Once connected to an OnPATH switch, data centre managers can reconfigure networks using software instead of having to rewire their data centre.

The requirements of the job combine the finance functions and HRM. Both sides of the job are subject to the many technology-driven changes to the working environment by technology.

My recent experience and perception of expatriate jobs is that there are fewer of them these days. Expatriation tends to focus on shorter jobs and projects that give people the experience of going abroad without the more permanent moves that used to prevail. International assignments are very useful for understanding international differences and for observing other people's adaptation to different cultures.

In a small company like OnPATH, the recent introduction of a performance management system has encountered similar problems and challenges as elsewhere. You have to ask the questions of what you want to measure and how you are going to measure it. The key challenge is to ensure that appraisals of performance are carried out consistently and at the appropriate time. The overall HRM job requires us to focus on priorities: whom to recruit, how to get new employees 'acclimated' to the company, and, where necessary, how to terminate employees for non-performance.

A key response to the issue of stress in modern working life is that stress levels are different for different people. In general, new and changing technologies mean that people are expected to know more and be 'connected' all the time. The work–life balance is important. A key to this balance is giving employees time off. OnPATH recognizes this need for balance and has instituted a fairly generous vacation policy for a company of our size. However, some people deal with stress by being 'workaholics' and liking these pressures; others need to take breaks and benefit from having a balance between work and their social and family life.

I have not perceived the glass ceiling as being an issue for me personally, because of the choices I have made with respect to my work and personal life. I believe for many women it is still very much an issue. The reality is that business is still a man's world. However, more women are mentoring and helping younger women in business, and lots of women are now becoming CEOs.

To illustrate the current situation and recent changes in IHRM staffing strategies, it is essential to consider studies from the start of the twenty-first century (e.g., Harzing 2004; Morris 2004) that have identified MNE trends. Harzing's survey of 2,689 subsidiaries of nearly 250 MNEs indicated that about 40 per cent of the subsidiaries had a parent country

Advantages	Disadvantages
Familiarity with socio-economic, political, & legal environment and business practices	Communication difficulties with home-office (headquarters) staff
Lower cost of hiring people	Difficulties in exercising control of fellow local nationals
Effective response to demands for localization	Perceived problems of authority and seniority in dealing with headquarters
Familiarity with MNEs' subsidiary operations	Need for fluency in language of parent country
Fluency in language and customs of host country	

Figure 15.2
Possible advantages and disadvantages of employing host country nationals (adapted from Harzing 2004; Morris 2004).

national in the position of managing director. Within this survey, Japanese and Italian companies were the most likely to have parent country nationals in top positions, and Danish companies the least likely. There are clearly advantages and disadvantages to the employment of nationals of different origins in senior and middle positions, as set out in Figure 15.2.

Varied approaches to the employment of nationals of different origins will probably continue to expand during the twenty-first century. If the globalization of business continues, it is likely that the patterns of employment established since the mid-nineteenth century may change quite dramatically. However, there may still be some established rationales for corporate motives in organizing and arranging international postings and transfers. Based on the pioneering work of Edstrom and Galbraith (1977), and developed by a succession of other writers (mentioned below), the three main categories for international transfers are thought to be:

- position filling (transfer of technical and managerial knowledge),
- management development (enhance the manager's international experience), and
- coordination and control (to further the development of the organization).

It is worth commenting on some of the main variations in the rationales of large firms of different national origins. Harzing (2004) has suggested that position filling is more important in British and American MNEs than in other firms. By contrast, and perhaps because they are historically more established and developed MNEs, it appears that British and American companies tend to use international transfers much less frequently as a matter for coordination and control. For Swiss, Dutch, and German MNEs, there is a 'higher than average use of international management training (as a control mechanism)' (Harzing 2004: 263).

The main trend apparent within IHRM at the beginning of the twenty-first century is that MNEs will witness a continued diminution of the traditional role of the expatriate. Not only is the prevalence of expatriates in the management of MNEs likely to decline, but the rise of the truly global CEO, manager, working team, and project group will rewrite the traditional concerns about staff members' national, ethnic, or perceived allegiance. The possible march towards globalization, especially within international business, has ensured that the management of MNEs is increasingly in the hands of the best talent, regardless of origin. As Grainger and Nankervis (2001: 90) pointed out at the start of the century: 'Traditional approaches to expatriation and IHRM are increasingly out of step with contemporary global business realities. Essentially, a new approach to IHRM should recognize that for many companies, international operations are increasingly "normal"; reflect the reality that globalization is making international assignments more common, more frequent and shorter term in duration, and will be based on the understanding that into the future, those who work for international corporations will be increasingly recruited offshore from a wide variety of labour markets.'

Case Study 15.2
Duelling expats

This case study describes a real situation, but the names have been withheld for reasons of confidentiality.

In the 1990s, John rose to the top of his company, one of the largest brokerages in New England in the USA. Starting out as a young trader, John began to drive the company's involvement in the development of a computerized trading software that soon became an industry standard. The company made good money out of this product, both by using it to manage its own positions and also by selling it to other market players. John was quickly promoted to department head, overseeing both the trading and the sales units.

In 2000 newer software came out to eclipse this product, which, despite continued sales, was no longer a cash cow for the company. John's personal position was further undermined by the fact that he began to focus mostly on trading. Shortly after this, the company decided to send John over to be Head of Products at the branch office in Amsterdam. John was not very excited about the prospects of going abroad but was left with little choice and realized that the move might help him to re-energize his sales management skills.

The Amsterdam office was 90 per cent staffed by Dutch nationals, who, as expected in their 'reserve' culture paid little attention to the new boss and got on with business. This irritated John, who saw this as arrogance; he missed the American culture that tended to celebrate stardom loudly. John's hostility was increased by what he saw as his local sales teams' excessive complicity with their customers. He felt that, even though 'his' software was no longer state of the art in the USA, it remained new for Europeans. He also thought that European customers should be happy to pay premium prices for the product. When local staff members disagreed, he construed this as another sign of their 'pride', indicating that, if the local sales force were 'any good', it would be able to apply his desired pricing policy.

John decided to show who was boss and, in particular, to make an example of Lance, an American sales officer who had been hired locally in Amsterdam. Lance had left the USA many years before, finished his university studies in Europe, married a European, and raised a family in the Netherlands. His sales relationships were based on his understanding of local customers' personal needs and culture, and of the competition. His target market consisted of second-tier European wholesalers, a segment that the company was happy to continue prioritizing.

Lance exceeded his sales volume targets but argued frequently with the product manufacturing teams back in the USA about the internal transfer prices at which product should be sold. Lance argued that he could not be expected to charge European wholesalers more than he would their US counterparts and argued he should receive the product at a mid-market rate.

John had no complaints about Lance's performance, but was irritated by his ongoing policy disagreements with Group HQ in New England. Despite having only just arrived in Amsterdam, John decided to insist that Lance offer product versions to customers only at an inflated premium price. Lance tried to arrange meetings between his major customers and John to get the latter to realize that the European market was no longer in its infant stage, but this further angered John. The conflict became intense, with John loudly accusing Lance of 'having gone native' and ordering him to return to HQ to sit in the office for a month and reacclimatize himself.

This clash of cultures—American forcefulness against traditional of Dutch reserve—should have been resolved by the application of a sensible HRM policy, but the conflict was allowed to run out of control.

IHRM policies should take into account different cultures and potential conflicts (© iStockphoto).

International assignments

As MNEs use fewer expatriates there are new types of international assignment, as set out in Figure 15.3. The advantages of the more 'distant' assignments, especially in the 'frequent-flyer' and 'virtual' categories, are that they provide flexibility, reduce costs, and avoid staff resistance to moving. Modern assignments are not only common at the highest levels—where CEOs and chairmen have always employed the latest means of communication and can combine flights around the world with teleconferencing—but have increasingly been

Type of assignment	Characteristics of assignment
Long-term or expatriate	Over one year Family accompany staff Residential accommodation
Short-term	Specific duration (months) Family may accompany staff
International commuter	Weekly or bi-weekly trips Occasional temporary relocation Family stays at home
Frequent-flyer	Regular international trips No relocation
Virtual	Senior managerial responsibility at home and abroad 'Frequent-flyer' combined with email, video conferencing, telephoning

Figure 15.3
New international assignments (based on categories adapted from research by M. Fenwick, cited in Harzing and Van Ruysseveldt 2004).

established at lower managerial levels. Marketing and finance managers, for example, have taken to this newer kind of assignment. The advent of communications systems such as the Blackberry and iPhone has meant that many lower-level employees can mimic the working patterns of their superiors.

Global staff postings used to distinguish between normal and hardship postings. The latter clearly identified with less-developed countries and consequently attracted additional allowances, extra holiday, special arrangements, and more pay. Increasingly, this has changed, as it is now difficult to argue, for example, that a posting to Sao Paulo, Singapore, Shanghai, or other modern metropolises can be regarded as hardship. Clearly there remains a distinction between being posted to office jobs in major cities or to production facilities or mining areas in 'up-country' regions.

+ Hardship posting
Traditional overseas assignment (or posting) that was thought to be undertaken in worse conditions than assignments at home and was thus rewarded with additional allowances, special arrangements, and increased remuneration.

Even though the trend in IHRM may be away from expatriates or PCNs towards the truly global or TCN, there is still a relatively strong impetus within large MNEs for some of their key staffing abroad to consist of expatriates. In order to operate this sort of staffing policy, the MNE needs to be able to reward or compensate the member of staff who will be working outside his or her home country. The compensation package is at the heart of international staffing, whether it is a Swede working in India, an Indian in the UK, or a Chinese manager in Argentina. The linkage that is made within the compensation arrangements is between performance on the international assignment and the pay and benefits that are associated with it. There is also a cultural aspect to pay related to the different ways in which people choose to be paid. Depending on the national culture, there will be a greater or a lesser tendency to prefer the security of a higher fixed salary (even if this means a lower bonus). Inversely, other people prefer to accept a lower fixed salary in the hope of possibly earning a large bonus. The latter system is preferred by a person who is more willing to take risks, and is likely to be more receptive to innovative but unproven ideas or products. In cultures that are less bonus-oriented, the greater preference for stability may create greater receptivity to well-established ideas and products.

The 2008–9 financial crisis led to many employees being made redundant and to higher levels of uncertainty in employment. In particular, this affected the financial and banking sectors, where the payment traditions, especially in North American and British institutions, had developed to the point where a high proportion of staff were paid large bonuses, either as a reward for very good performance or as a guaranteed amount paid at the end of the year. This bonus culture encouraged risk taking and a degree of irresponsibility in personal expenditure. By contrast, people from countries cited in Chapter 2 as being less comfortable

Photo 15.1
A posting to Shanghai is no longer seen as a hardship (© iStockphoto).

with uncertainty are more likely to want a higher proportion of their pay to be guaranteed in a fixed salary. This example of a direct link between corporate culture in particular business sectors, the culture of a host country, and pay structures may also have an impact on the staffing decisions taken by MNEs, including when the company is looking at overseas pay packages.

There are commonly three types of package: home-based, headquarters, and host-based. In the home-based method, the expatriate receives similar pay (and other benefits) as would be given for the equivalent position in his or her home country—that is, a Swede working for an Italian company in India receives a similar package to his or her Swedish counterparts. This method tends to be the most common among large international firms, with about 60 per cent of them using this method for long-term assignments and about 75 per cent for short-term jobs. The headquarters method means that the expatriate receives the same package as for a comparable job in the city or country where the MNE has its headquarters, so that the Swedish manager would get the same as equivalent managers in Italy. Effectively, this method means that the Italian salary package is the standard throughout the world for managers in jobs of similar rank. The third method is where the expatriate receives the local or host country salary; this is sometimes called localization or destination pricing. Depending on various factors, such as the manager's home country, negotiations with the IHRM department and the status of the post, the expatriate may also receive additional benefits (extra allowances, taxation compensation, international assignment premiums, and so on) to adjust the package upwards. In the end, the IHRM department has to ensure that its expatriates are not being penalized for taking on international assignments but also that employees in equivalent posts around the world are not being awarded very different compensation packages.

For many overseas postings, there may still be financial, linguistic, and cultural difficulties associated with certain locations for some potential expatriates. However, it has become an integral responsibility of IHRM professionals to ensure that 'internationally assigned employees are chosen, and appropriately supported, in ways which reflect not only their managerial and technical abilities, but also their capacity and willingness to undertake such positions' (Grainger and Nankervis 2001: 81).

In this context, there are important IHRM functions that are activated so that staff are properly prepared and supported; such functions include: language and cultural training, advice on legal matters, performance management, personal and family assistance, and help with relocation. Many of these factors are considered in Section 2.

The increasingly strategic role and operations of IHRM departments within MNEs was emphasized in the aftermath of the 2008–9 credit and financial crisis when thousands of relatively well-paid and highly trained employees lost their jobs. The speed and depth of the crisis meant that IHRM managers were over-burdened with the consequences of such a massive number of redundancies—more than 120,000 financial jobs lost between spring 2008 and spring 2009 with 16,000 within the UBS (Union Bank of Switzerland) group and 9,000 in the Royal Bank of Scotland (Croft 2009; Simonian 2009). Ironically, some analysts blamed the previous practices of the IHRM departments for inflating salaries and benefits for employees in the financial sector, as well as in other sectors. For many IHRM departments, too, the consequence of the financial crisis was that, at the same time as they were having to handle job cuts and redundancies, they were no longer in a position to continue with normal levels of recruitment. For most companies in the financial sector, it is unlikely that there will be a return to pre-2008 staffing levels nor any upturn in new recruitment until 2010 and beyond.

A further consequence of the financial crisis was that certain elements of the IHRM departments' own budgets were being reduced. One report, focused on central and East European employers, noted that the key cuts within firms were changes in benefits (34 per cent of firms surveyed), freezing of recruitment (28 per cent), layoffs (28 per cent), reduced travelling costs (15 per cent) and, specifically for the HR departments, a reduction in their own costs (13 per cent) (Anderson Willinger 2009).

The changing face of IHRM rides on the impacts of the 2008–9 economic and financial crisis and on the general international trends within work practices. The perceived reduction in the use of expatriates and the increasing variety of international assignments indicate that the role of international human resource management will remain central to the strategic operation of MNEs in the twenty-first century.

Section II: Managing international workforces

In modern international business, international workforces are made up of a variety of employees from a range of countries. Whatever the mixture of PCNs, HCNs, and TCNs, and at whatever level of management, it is essential that the workforce is effectively and efficiently managed. A key component of the management of international workforces is the preparation, training, and development of staff, followed by a system of thorough performance management. The majority of MNEs operating globally, as well as smaller firms, undertake programmes of cross-cultural training (CCT). Increasingly, such programmes have come to be delivered at distance or electronically and are known as e-CCT programmes.

The rationale for these programmes is that well-prepared individuals will be able to work more effectively with the employees they meet on their overseas assignments. They will learn about the language and local customs and the different cultural expectations of the host country, thus enabling them to integrate more smoothly with the HCNs who make up the bulk of the firm that they are joining.

Cross-cultural training

The key elements within CCT (or e-CCT) programmes are:

- identifying the types of global assignments for which CCT is required;
- determining any specific CCT needs;
- establishing the goals and measures for determining the effectiveness of CCT;
- developing and delivering CCT; and
- evaluating the effectiveness of the programme.

The design and implementation of an effective CCT programme must usually match the degree of participant involvement with the rigour of the training. There are various elements for these two parameters, as can be seen in Figure 15.4.

There are broadly considered to be four types of global assignment (a typology devised by Caliguri and Lazarova, as set out in Harzing 2004), each requiring a different amount of CCT work. The first global assignment is *technical*, which is considered to be similar in content

Figure 15.4
Parameters for effective CCT (adapted from Black et al. 1999, reproduced with kind permission).

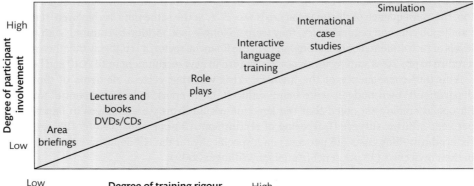

to the domestic activities already carried out by the member of staff. These assignments include staff in the oil and gas business involved in drilling and refining, technicians such as quantity surveyors in construction projects, systems engineers, and analysts interfacing with computer systems. The member of staff is being employed primarily for his or her technical skills; it is these that will largely determine the outcome of the assignment, and, therefore, a minimal amount of CCT is required. The second—and most common—global assignment is described as *functional/tactical*. In this, the essential requirement is a high level of interaction between the member of staff being assigned and the locally employed nationals: a good CCT programme is vital. For some MNEs, the third type of assignment is part of a broader IHRM strategy in which the main purpose is *developmental/high potential*. One of the primary goals is the individual development of the manager being deployed; this may, of course, be the designation of a younger HCN to take on a task in his own country, as well as assigning a rising executive to work abroad. Finally, there are global assignments that are very high profile and at the level of general managers, vice presidents, managing directors, and so on. These *strategic/executive* assignments are often at the core of the competitive development of the MNEs' strategies around the world. The tasks of these top people will include masterminding entry into new markets, turning around failing companies or subsidiaries, establishing a new joint venture, and developing a market base in certain countries.

Thinking point

Why do most technical assignments not require CCT?

Clearly the extent and content of the CCT programme will depend on the type of assignment, the personal characteristics and existing skills of the manager(s), and the short- and long-term goals of the assignment. There will be an emphasis in most CCT programmes on pre-departure training, a selection of language and culture-specific elements, and a balance between one-off or continuous training. Whether the training is delivered within an e-CCT system or by a more traditional method, it needs to be evaluated in terms of a number of key factors, which include the following.

- How effectively was the assignment carried out?
- How far did the CCT contribute to the success of the assignment?
- How well were new cultural values explained, learnt, absorbed, and applied?
- What form of assessment (and self-assessment) was provided for the member of staff and his or her family?
- How well did the member of staff respond to the challenges of the global assignment, in terms of personal development, career goals, adjustment to the host country, and so on?

The international skills required include a broad knowledge of human resource management environments and practices in different countries, including not only knowledge of HRM and industrial relations systems, but also of the effects of national culture and values on work ethics and customary workplace behaviour. Other elements of a CCT programme may include the use of structured mentoring for all kinds of international employees, and corporate initiatives to seek appropriate work for spouses and partners in host countries. Issues related to the adaptation of the spouse as well as the employee may become even more urgent if, as some authors have suggested, 25 per cent of these 'trailing partners' will be male in the near future (Grainger and Nankervis 2001).

One of the aspects of CCT that is sometimes neglected is the training or counselling that is required when a manager's international assignment finishes. It might be assumed that, for anybody going 'home', there is no need for any help; after all, the manager and his or her family are going back to an environment with which they are entirely familiar: their own house, town, and country. However, there are a number of key problems that can be associated with repatriation or reverse culture shock (see Online Resource Centre, extension material 15.1). These are often very dependent on the length of time that the employee and family have been abroad. The main changes are readjustments to the corporate structure and life at the MNE's headquarters, changes (usually a reduction) in the employee's financial package, changes in the home country that have not been fully understood after years of

> Go to the ORC

service abroad, and readjustment to life at home where the family may be living in a smaller house, children are having to settle into another school, and all of them are having to relearn some of what they took for granted. The process of repatriation requires as much careful planning and preparation as CCT for employees embarking on international assignments.

The relationship between effective CCT and business success is taken for granted, but there are still cases in which large companies fail to understand this. The failure of the American retailer Walmart to understand and accept national employment practices and labour conditions, including a reluctance to appoint German managers for its 1998 takeover of the Wertkauf and Interspar stores in Germany, has—quite rightly—been held out as a classic example of this. More of these cases were explored in earlier chapters on the importance of culture in international business.

Performance management

An interesting aspect of IHRM relates to the management of international performance throughout an organization. There are extensive systems of performance management that are explored in traditional HRM textbooks and manuals; they comprise the key steps of recruitment, retention of staff, including appraisal and rewards, and training and staff development. The best companies are usually praised for their successes in nurturing and retaining good staff, and for their ability to combine good human resource relations with the maximization of profit and value.

A very visible aspect of IHRM relates to the payment and overall remuneration packages of the highest-paid and most prominent executives, particularly the worldwide CEOs. Even though much has changed in international business since the 1980s, it is still true that the dominance of US-origin MNEs within the world of international business is reflected in the continuing **pay gap** between American CEOs and other CEOs. As Professor Randall S. Thomas noted in his 2003 study of this phenomenon, it is perhaps most likely that the pay gaps exist because of market forces (Thomas 2003). In 2008–9, the average overall compensation package (pay plus other benefits and shares) for CEOs in the top 300 Standard & Poor's companies was $7.6 million, with the largest package of $104 million being paid to the boss of Motorola, the Indian-born, Sanjay K. Jha.

Historically, it has been argued that top managers of non-American firms had not enjoyed the same increase in bargaining power in relation to pay. The structures of their firms, the shareholdings, and the management meant that 'foreign' (non-American) CEOs were not in a position to benefit from large takeovers in the earlier years of MNE growth, and perhaps until the 1990s this imbalance remained a significant factor. By contrast, American CEOs (or CEOs of US origin or US-based firms) were able to 'capture' their boards of directors and/or their passive and widely dispersed shareholders so as to overpay themselves excessively.

Randall Thomas put forward four arguments related to market-driven forces that may have accounted for this traditional pay difference. Thomas's first argument rested on 'the marginal revenue product of executive labour'. He noted that American CEOs should be paid more, on average, than foreign CEOs, because American CEOs contributed more to their firms' value. American firms had greater growth opportunities and had greater resources to be deployed because they were bigger American CEOs played a much larger role in the decision-making process at their firms than CEOs at foreign firms. They also received more of their pay in the form of stock options, and might hold more of their wealth in company stock than foreign CEOs, and therefore their pay would reflect a risk premium (Thomas 2003).

His second argument on the international pay gap came from an examination of the workings of corporations' internal labour markets and the competition to become CEO. In this view, American firms were different because their CEOs had so much more power than foreign counterparts. After all, in the USA, the CEO was (and is) normally also the Chairman of the Board, whereas in other countries this was rarely the case. For example, in the early part of the twenty-first century, there were significant difficulties for

Sir Stuart Rose, CEO at Marks & Spencer, and for Lakshmi Mittal, CEO at Arcelor Mittal, when they tried to persuade their boards and shareholders to permit them to combine the two top jobs. American CEOs' power was further enhanced compared to those of their biggest foreign rivals, such as Japan and Germany, because boards of directors were smaller in the USA than in Japan, and had only one tier, instead of the two-tier structure in Germany.

Thomas's third point was to note the differences in the opportunity costs for American and 'foreign' CEOs. The opening-up of financial markets since the early 1980s gave US CEOs better access to capital markets for financing their own start-up businesses, raising the value of their alternative opportunities. This occurred first through the use of the Leveraged Buyout (LBO) or Management Buyout (MBO) as a method of financing a new firm, then with the tremendous growth in venture capital financing, and later on (at least for a period of years) when the technology boom made available massive amounts of capital to finance start-ups. Established American businesses that wished to compete for managerial talent were thereby forced to offer executives larger pay packages.

By comparison, non-US CEOs did not have nearly the same access to financial markets to launch their own businesses. Only recently has there been an expansion of executive job opportunities with the deregulation of some capital markets and increased managerial migration. These changes have increased pressure on foreign companies to pay their executives more, but in general they have yet to catch up.

Thomas's final point related to the differential bargaining power that American CEOs had compared to that of foreign CEOs. This different level of power derived from two important forces at work in the USA: first, the shift in the 1980s in the relative bargaining strength of American CEOs in vetoing takeovers of their corporations; and, second, the concurrent acceptance of the idea of pay-for-performance by domestic institutional investors. These changes gave American CEOs tremendous power to stop a hostile takeover unless the sale of the firm was perceived as being in that executive's personal best interests.

Since the 1990s, there has been a more significant change to the dominance of 'American' CEOs. This has come from two contrasting developments: the rise of global corporations and their CEOs, and the scandals associated with certain US MNEs. MNEs have been hit by scandals and allegedly connected to failed corporate governance, accounting abuses, and/or straightforward corporate and CEO greed. This has affected CEOs and senior executives such as Bernie Ebbers at WorldCom, Gary Winnick of Global Crossing, Dennis Koslowski of Tyco, and Andy Fastow, Jeff Skilling, and Kenneth Lay at Enron (Harvard Law School 2000).

Photo 15.2
Carlos Ghosn, CEO of Renault–Nissan (reproduced with the kind permission of Nissan).

Thinking point

What accounts for the success of Indian businesses and top executives of Indian origin and/or nationality?

Perhaps more significantly, there has been the rise of global/international corporations from all over the world, so that their CEOs are neither European nor American. Key examples from 2008–9 of these top people are the Indian business people: Vijay Mallya, CEO of the Indian United Breweries group (which was originally founded by a Scotsman), Lakshmi Mittal, CEO of the global steel giant, Arcelor Mittal (half of which is based in Europe), Sunil Bharti Mittal (no relation), CEO of the telecommunications Bharti Group, and (as already mentioned) Sanjay K. Jha of Motorola.

Beyond these examples, there are CEOs/senior executives whose worldwide experience has been regarded as more important than their original nationality in their rise to the top jobs. Examples from 2008–9 of this type of CEO are Indra Nooyi, the Indian-born CEO of Pepsico; Carlo Radicati, an Italian in charge of Russian Standard vodka; Willie Walsh, an Irishman as CEO at BA, following on from Rod Eddington, an Australian who was CEO from 2000 to 2005; Andrea Jung, a Canadian of Chinese origin who is CEO of Avon Products; Andre Navarri, a Frenchman in charge of the Canadian transportation company, Bombardier; and Carlos Ghosn, a Brazilian-born Lebanese who is now a French citizen and runs Renault–Nissan as CEO. In these two ways, there has been a greater smoothing out of US and non-US pay for CEOs and other leading corporate executives.

Women in international business

A related issue in the world of leadership in international business has been the move towards a greater role for women as CEOs and senior managers in MNEs, This involves reducing the gaps between men and women in the posts they hold, as well as in their pay. It is evident that women have begun to achieve top positions in MNEs, most notably Indra Nooyi and Andrea Jung, as noted above. There are also women in charge of other large corporations: Marjorie Scardino (Pearsons), Anne Mulcahy (Xerox), Irene Rosenfeld (Kraft Foods), and Patricia Russo (Alcatel-Lucent).

It might be expected that MNEs and other business organizations in the developed world, including Europe, would be more advanced in establishing equality of treatment, pay, and seniority for women. Whereas the picture is reasonably positive in certain areas (see Figure 15.5), it is also evident that progress has not been as great as anticipated. In 2007, 'far from powering through the glass ceiling, women take up just 8.5 per cent of seats in corporate boardrooms in Europe's biggest 300 companies' (Attwood 2007). As can be seen from Figure 15.5, there is a wide difference across Europe, with the most advanced and favourable companies being in the four Scandinavian countries and the least favourable being from southern Europe, particularly Italy, Spain, and Greece.

One of the consequences of women's lack of success in getting senior jobs in international business has been the growth in the number of businesses set up and led by women.

Figure 15.5
Women in top jobs: how Europe compares (Independent, 7 Dec. 2007).

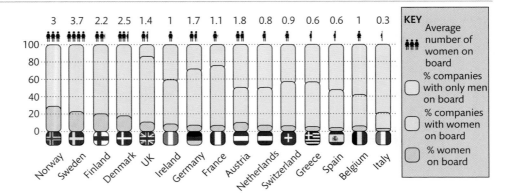

Photo 15.3
Indra Nooyi is CEO of
Pepsico.

This is true both in less-developed countries (LDCs), with the growth of micro-finance, and in the more developed OECD countries. In the UK, for example, it is 'estimated that between 34 and 42 per cent of the UK small business stock is owned or co-owned by women' (Attwood 2007). Part of the reason for this expansion in the creation of women-led businesses is that, in all sizes of company, there is a perceived and real degree of inflexibility in the working regime imposed on members of staff. This often means that these companies perform poorly in allowing staff to achieve a proper work–life balance.

Much of the excellent work on the role of gender in the IHRM aspect of businesses has been carried out by female researchers, academics, and practitioners, especially Professor Nancy Adler. For many women in international business, the key factor that has been described as most limiting to their careers is the glass ceiling. The term implies that the actual level to which women can rise in business is lower than that of men, even though it is not stated explicitly—that is, the real ceiling for women is invisible or transparent, like glass (Glass Ceiling Commission 1991–6).

In 1995 the Glass Ceiling Commission said that the barrier was continuing 'to deny untold numbers of qualified people the opportunity to compete for and hold executive level positions in the private sector'. It found that women had 45.7 per cent of America's jobs and more than half of master's degrees being awarded. Yet 95 per cent of senior managers were men, and female managers' earnings were on average a mere 68 per cent of those of their male counterparts (Glass Ceiling Commission 1991–6).

By 2005 women accounted for 46.5 per cent of America's workforce but still less than 8 per cent of its top managers, although at *Fortune* 500 companies the figure is somewhat higher. Female managers' earnings in 2007 averaged 72 per cent of those of their male colleagues. Booz Allen Hamilton, a consulting firm that monitors departing chief executives in America, found that 0.7 per cent of them were women in 1998, and 0.7 per cent of them were women in 2004. In between, the figure fluctuated. But the firm says that one thing is clear: the number is 'very low and not getting higher' (*The Economist* 2005).

+ Glass ceiling
Artificial barriers based on bias that prevent qualified individuals from advancing upward in their organization into management-level positions.

There are certain factors that indicate continuing discrimination against women in international business, as established by the Professional Women's Network (PWN) of Europe in 2006–7. These factors include the following.

- Women lack visibility: women's public profiles are significantly lower than men's; 28 per cent of the top 100 businesswomen cannot be 'googled'.
- Only 8 per cent of women are heads of committees, against 27 per cent of men; for example, audit committees are almost exclusively headed by men.
- In non-executive board positions, men had 84 per cent of line management positions against women's positions, which are reported as only 57 per cent.
- Only 9.5 per cent of women hold Ph.D.'s against 33 per cent of men; most Ph.D.'s received by businessmen are honorary, whereas women have generally studied in order to achieve their status. PWN's researchers wonder whether this indicates that men 'work smart and women work hard'.

In their research, PWN have also established certain other key differences between women and men. For example, women executives have significantly more social science degrees; women dominate as employee representatives (28 per cent versus less than 1 per cent for men); men tend to retire, whereas it is usual that women serve until they reach the end of their tenure; female executive board members have fewer expatriate assignments than their male counterparts (in general 0.8 versus 2.4 over the course of their career); and, in the accumulation of other posts, executive board women hold more corporate board positions than men, but male non-executives hold more corporate and not-for-profit board positions than women.

According to PWN, there are also a number of key similarities between men and women on international boards, where all executive board members tend to hold a low proportion of MBA degrees (only 12 per cent of women and 15 per cent of men) and a similar number of not-for-profit board positions (that is, 2.5 positions per person).

The European PWN's advice to women in international business, based clearly on the elements set out above, is extensive and mirrors in many respects the view of other professionals and academics, concerned about the gaps between men and women. Because women often lack visibility, PWN advises companies that they can make women aware of the importance and difficulties of these issues and proposes that each woman needs to design a strategic plan for self-promotion. Similarly, women need to be aware of the importance of networking to gain access to and flourish in the topmost levels of MNEs. As women lag behind in expatriate assignments, which often are still a requirement for getting to the top, companies tend proactively to include women in their expatriate planning. Since significant differences in profiles at non-executive level (age, staff/line, expatriate assignments, accumulation of posts) may place women in a disadvantageous position, this requires a strong and inclusive chairperson of the board to take counterbalancing action. Companies that experience an under-representation of women executives but an over-representation of women in staff positions should develop strategic action plans to maximize the promotion of female talent to a higher level.

Above all, consideration of the position of women within international business requires a focus not only on the 'glass ceiling', but on other factors that inhibit the mobility and career development of women. Various other factors are described by terminology such as 'off- and on-ramps', 'glass walls versus class accelerator', the labyrinth, the 'glass shoe', and the 'glass cliff'. Of these many other terms that can be applied to the difficulties facing all sorts of employees, but are most associated with those facing women, the most significant is perhaps the concept of the glass cliff. This suggests that, once a woman has overcome the difficulties of the glass ceiling, she may then be given an exceptionally risky and complicated assignment in which she is likely to fail, and thus to fall over the cliff edge.

In contrast with the study and practice of women in international management, there has been less work on the role of different ethnic backgrounds within MNEs. There are a number of international organizations trying to rectify this situation, such as the International Society

Thinking point

What other limitations or hindrances can confront women in international business?

for Diversity Management, established in Germany, and TCO—International Diversity Management, based in Italy and the UK. Part of the relative neglect of this area derived from the fact that people have tended to focus on the PCN, HCN, and TCN issues (see above) and partly because non-white men appear to have succeeded in achieving top positions within MNEs in a way that has not yet been possible for women. Examples of these include many of the Indian men cited earlier in the chapter as well as the African-Americans Stanley O'Neal (CEO of Merrill Lynch, 2003–7) and Oprah Winfrey (Chairman of Harpo Inc.).

There are genuine benefits to diversity, as it helps to ensure that companies mirror the market, encourage innovation, improve decision-making, enforce ethics, attract talent, and raise the bottom line. It seems that international business is heading towards the position where all managers can share equally in the ups and downs of corporate life.

Stress in international jobs

One of the most serious impacts of international management at all levels is work-related stress. It is clear that modern corporate thinking considers stress to be a potential hindrance to the smooth functioning of international operations. There is far greater concern with assisting employees to achieve a better work–life balance than has been the case in the past (Lightfoot 2008). Some sectors of MNE activity, including work in the financial and market-trading operations, may still favour and reward punishing work schedules, long anti-social hours, and a 'macho' working atmosphere. In some cases this environment is made even worse by the way in which such tensions reflect a considerable degree of political manœuvring within the workplace—the impact of office politics (see Online Resource Centre, extension material 15.2). However, in general, there is a greater understanding of, and proactive attempts to overcome, stress in the workplace. With modern developments such as the Blackberry, many globally operating employees are always 'at work' or 'on platform'. Managers who travel the world are expected to be in touch with the office at all times and to be on call 24–7 (a modern phrase denoting round-the-clock working for the whole week). For such international employees, the lines between work-time and social life, or 'down time', have become increasingly blurred.

> Go to the ORC

There is a strong view among the IHRM professionals that stress at work can be a massively negative factor in the productivity of a company. Excessive stress can be extremely expensive for employers leading to greater absenteeism, lower performance, and a higher rate of employee turnover. The impact of this on business productivity can be significant and is starting to be taken more seriously by MNEs. The evidence for this is demonstrated by the increase in activities such as mentoring and coaching, stress-relieving workshops, and a general call for a more holistic approach to the needs of all corporate workers.

A number of MNEs have established programmes designed to assist employees with stress, including GSK and PWC. The giant British–American MNE GlaxoSmithKline (GSK) combines health assessments, discussion groups, and follow-up evaluations in a programme called 'Team Resilience' that is intended to deal with workplace stress. Various groups within GSK have undergone this process, completing questionnaires about workplace stress and then participating in workshop discussions within their functional areas. The programme has produced proposals for improving conditions within the workplace, including desire for more flexibility in how work is organized (GSK 2006–8; Holland 2008). In a similar fashion, PriceWaterhouseCoopers (PWC) has addressed the issue of stress through annual surveys, the provision of more coaching and greater opportunities to connect with experienced colleagues throughout the firm's worldwide operations. The creation of 'market teams' has led to higher satisfaction levels and lower employee turnover within PWC. The managing director for People Strategy at PWC, Michael J. Fenlon, was reported as noting the successful achievement of creating 'an environment where there's openness and a sense of mutual support' (Holland 2008).

Changes in employment and the workplace

There are three key factors that are beginning to have a large impact on IHRM for the twenty-first century: these are (1) the changing roles, varying from country to country, of trade unions and workers' associations in the operations of businesses around the world, (2) changes in employment legislation in different parts of the world, with particular emphasis on laws relating to a range of forms of discrimination in the workplace, and (3) greater emphasis on flexible working and improving the work–life balance.

+ Work–life balance
Life choices that many people make in order to balance the demands of work with other important areas of their lives such as family, friends, and hobbies.

> Go to the ORC 🌐

Traditionally, battle lines within domestic and international business are drawn up between employer (the company) and employees, often gathered together and represented by a workers' association or a trade union (see Online Resource Centre, extension material 15.3). The hard-line employer was, and still is, keen to get as much work out of its employees at the same time as paying as little as possible and providing the minimum in the way of good working conditions. This may well still be true for many employers, whether in the developed or the developing world. On the other side of the employer–employee divide, there have always been more enlightened employers who have been convinced that the best way of getting the maximum effort from their workforce is to ensure that employees have good pay and good working conditions. A classic example of this is the German concept and practice of co-determination (*Mitbestimmung*), which provides two levels of employee participation in work decisions. Co-determination is established through representation of workers on two 'boards': a works council; and the company's supervisory board. This principle is now in the process of being extended to the formation of the 'European Company', which will be a form of co-determination derived from German, Dutch, or French variants of this principle.

One of the key impacts on international business is the MNE's relations with the workforce and its representatives. Much of the data on these relations is collected and analysed by the International Labour Organization (ILO). In addition to the official facts, figures, and interpretations, it is evident from the authors' experience and that of their business contacts that some national governments and MNEs that are more hostile to fair employee status than others. Certain governments, such as Saudi Arabia and Indonesia, are perceived as being particularly hostile to good relations with trade unions and, on occasion, even to their existence. Trade unions are perceived by many regimes as 'socialist' or 'communist' and condemned by the political elites as subversive and opposed to the safety and ongoing operations of the state. The use of repressive legislation permits such regimes, often with the connivance of the national business class, local companies, and MNEs, to deny workers some of the most basic human rights. In such situations, workers may have to work for longer hours than normally permitted, carry out successive work shifts, be denied the appropriate number of breaks for drinks or meals, be forced to work in excessive temperatures, and even not be paid or compensated properly for their work.

It is essential for future international business managers that they analyse and understand the labour relations of any country in which they operate. They will be involved in the position that their company adopts regarding the nexus of business–labour relations, employment laws, the legal position of trade unions, and the social and legal framework for workers and working conditions.

At a further stage of FDI strategy, or any other form of involvement abroad (see Chapter 7), the MNE will make a detailed assessment of the relative attractiveness of target countries in terms of factors, such as employment laws and customs. For many MNEs, this an assessment of the business environment and range of risks connected with the associated legislation, including laws relating to contracts, pay, and conditions, and job discrimination.

In the countries of the European Union (EU), the development of employment legislation has produced major changes in legislation. Some of the key developments have been in the area of employment discrimination, relating in particular to gender and sexual identity, racial and ethnic origin, and varying types of disability. In the most advanced applications of this legislation, the new framework is founded on the principles and interpretations of

European Human Rights. In a country such as the UK, for example, employee rights were enhanced by the British acceptance of European rights as from October 2000. The new legislation in the UK includes laws on Equal Pay, Ageism, Civil Partnerships, Racial Equality, and Disability Discrimination.

The increasing burden on employers, whether domestic companies or MNEs operating in the UK, is aggravated by the fact that there is greater responsibility on the employer to show positive action has been taken in relation to these varying laws. Some critics complain that such legislation harms business and typifies 'discredited 1970s feminist ideology' (Ruth Lea, former Head of Policy at the Institute of Directors, quoted in Lightfoot 2008). The new laws impose, for example, a burden of proof on both sides in any disputes, but the employer increasingly has to show that it has a full set of policies and procedures; all employees have been informed; full records are kept on all matters related to employment; and decision-making is transparent.

For MNEs it is essential that both the legal department and the human resource specialists understand all the legal requirements of employment, the frequent changes that occur, the impact of EU directives and regulations, the rulings of the European Court of Justice, and the implications of forthcoming legislation.

The final aspect for IHR managers to deal with in some of the more advanced workplaces in the twenty-first century is the extension of modes of flexible working (see Case Study 15.3) and the emphasis placed on establishing a work–life balance. The importance of flexible working is that it helps companies to address and solve skills shortages, open up new markets of talent, and retain workers who would otherwise leave the organization.

One of the outcomes of the legislative changes mentioned above has been the increased legal right to request flexible working arrangements. Whereas employers, in the UK, for example, are not bound to grant the employee's request, they are required to consider it. In 2008 the giant telecommunications MNE BT (formerly British Telecom) had about 12 per cent of its 100,000 employees in the UK working full-time from home, using broadband connections to log into BT's system. As the regional manager for Yorkshire and the Humber, Trevor Higgins, noted in 2008: 'Flexible working is the right thing to do. It's about balancing the firm's needs with those of the employees and deciding what is best for both' (Lightfoot 2008). Within most OECD countries, there has been a general trend towards more of these flexible arrangements. The 2008–9 credit crunch has, in some cases, further encouraged companies to adopt this form of employment as 'many of them start to choose the flexible working ... policy to optimize their human resources and save cost' (Antal International 2009).

A further feature of flexible working is the creation of job-sharing, where usually two employees fulfil the functions of one job. This often occurs more frequently among women employees than men. Although job-sharing is most common at lower levels of work within MNEs, it has also happened at relatively senior management levels. For example, in 2007–8, two very senior female managers at Credit Suisse successfully shared their working week and two women departmental and branch managers at NatWest (since 2008 part of the RBS Group) operated successfully in a similar fashion (Lightfoot 2008).

The developments in flexible working have frequently been expected to affect international managers more rapidly and thoroughly, but it is apparent that people at all levels of work still value the traditions of personal and face-to-face contact. Managers still do not view communicating by email and video conferencing in the same light as knowing exactly with whom they are doing business across the world.

The many changes in international workforces' management have posed key challenges for IHRM departments within MNEs. The adoption of cross-cultural training, extension of diversity within the international workforce, and greater emphasis on the work–life balance are hallmarks of the most enlightened IHRM professionals. Within the context of technological and economic uncertainty, these are real challenges to the managers of the twenty-first century.

Thinking point

What international variations exist in terms of flexible working hours?

Challenges and choices

→ Managers engaged in international human resource management (IHRM) in the twenty-first century face choices that are strategic level in nature. What sort of national staffing composition best suits the company? What sorts of performance management systems are best for the highest-paid executives? How different are these for other levels of managers and workers? How far are certain employees held back by workplace discrimination or different legal structures? The range of issues is immense and central to international business development.

→ The greatest challenge will possibly be the need to develop more sophisticated and permanent forms of flexible working for a higher proportion of the workforce. In 2009, a very small percentage of people worldwide can work flexibly, mainly professionals, hi-tech workers, and job-sharers. In an increasingly international world of work, it is ironic that most workers have little choice about how they work and are still restricted to shifts and 9 to 5 office jobs.

Chapter Summary

This chapter has set out a number of key issues of international human resource management (IHRM) and focused on some of the major developments of the twenty-first century in relation to the world of work. The principal arguments have shown a move away from 'foreign' domination of international work to increasing participation and management by host country nationals (HCNs) in the affairs of MNEs. This reflects the relative decline in the role and influence of expatriates, although cross-cultural training of employees on international assignments remains important.

On completing the chapter, students should appreciate and understand the importance of the development of IHRM at the strategic level within MNEs. Modern IHRM attempts to establish greater diversity and equality in the international workforce, better work–life balance, and the reduction of stress among managers. Organizations that take care of their people are likely to be successful, both in the short term and in the long run.

Case Study 15.3

Cisco: Remote workers and greater security

Cisco (www.cisco.com) is a worldwide leader in networking that transforms how people connect, communicate and collaborate. Cisco's annual global study in February 2008 offered some key findings on remote workers' security awareness and online behaviour. The study indicated how they could inadvertently heighten risks for themselves and their companies. The study's findings prompted Cisco security executives to offer recommendations to information technology (IT) professionals on how to protect their companies against threats and maximize the business benefits of distributed and mobile workforces. The conclusions of the study also highlighted the way in which IHR departments and managers could bring themselves and their companies into closer contact with their more distant employees.

The significance and importance of the study is emphasized by the growing number of remote workers worldwide. According to a 2007 report, 'the worldwide corporate teleworking population of individuals that spend at least one day a month teleworking from home is expected to show a compound annual growth rate (CAGR) of 4.3 percent between 2007 and 2011 ... In the same period, the worldwide corporate teleworking population of individuals that spend at least one day a week teleworking from home is expected to show a CAGR of 4.4 per cent. This population will likely reach 46.6 million by the end of 2011' (Jones 2007).

The 2008 study involved surveys of more than 2,000 remote workers and IT professionals from various

Remote employees are becoming less disciplined in their online behaviour (© iStockphoto).

industries and company sizes in ten countries: the United States, the United Kingdom, France, Germany, Italy, Japan, China, India, Australia, and Brazil. The ten countries were chosen because they represent a diverse set of social and business cultures, stable and emerging network-dependent economies, and varied lengths of Internet adoption.

One of the more important findings is that remote workers feel less urgency to be vigilant in their online behaviour. While most believe that they are more vulnerable outside the office than inside, their perceptions of security threats are softening. In just one year, the number of remote workers who believe the Internet is safer increased by 8 per cent, from just under half (48 per cent) to more than half (56 per cent). This trend is especially prevalent in Brazil (71 per cent), India (68 per cent), and China (64 per cent), three of the world's fastest-growing economies whose workforces are depending more and more on the Internet and corporate networks.

According to the study, IT respondents believe that remote employees are becoming less disciplined in their online behaviour. More than half of the companies (55 per cent) believe that their remote workers are becoming less diligent towards security awareness, an 11 percentage point increase from the year before. Some of the key findings and reasons for risky behaviour include:

- *Opening emails and attachments from unknown or suspicious sources.* China (62%) is the worst

offender. It is arguably more disturbing that this is a growing trend in entrenched Internet-adopter countries like the United Kingdom (48%), Japan (42%), Australia (34%), and the United States (27%).

- *Using work computers and devices for personal use.* A 3 percentage point increase year-on-year shows that more remote workers use corporate devices for personal use, such as Internet shopping, downloading music, and visiting social networking sites. This trend occurs in eight of the ten countries, with the highest year-to-year increase occurring in France (27–50%). In Brazil, this trend rose 16% despite an increasing number of respondents agreeing that this was unacceptable behaviour (37% to 52% year-over-year). Reasons offered: 'My company doesn't mind me doing so', 'I'm alone and have spare time', 'My boss isn't around', 'My IT department will support me if something goes wrong'."

- *Accessing work files with personal, non-IT-protected devices.* Accessing corporate networks and files with devices that are not protected by an employee's IT team presents security risks to the company, its information, and its employees. As the number of remote workers grows, the study reveals an annual rise (45% in 2006 to 49% in 2007) in this behaviour. It is widespread in many countries, especially China (76%), the United States (55%), Brazil (52%), and France (48%).

The 2008 Cisco study contained a number of strategic recommendations for protecting this increasingly dispersed workforce. It is imperative for any company's IT department (including Cisco's) to reassess how it is perceived by employees and how it can proactively influence corporate security. As part of an overall company's IHRM strategy, the IT department can spearhead a consultative engagement with employees.

In the 2008 study Cisco's John Stewart stressed: 'How you communicate and educate employees about essential security practices and policies will be different in Japan than in the United States. It will be different in China than in France. Security awareness and education requires an understanding of your audience's culture. You have to relate to them and earn their trust. Through trust comes respect and cooperation.'

Case study questions

1. For employees who work in an MNE like Cisco, what are the greatest temptations of the IT systems?
2. What security measures can be taken to protect both employees and companies in an increasingly 'porous' global information age?
3. What needs to be done to ensure that IT systems continue to develop in line with changes in the international workplace?

Discussion questions

1. What performance management systems would be most suitable for the highest-paid executives or expatriate middle-level managers in MNEs?

2. How far are women held back by workplace discrimination or by legal structures in different countries?

3. Why are expatriates less in demand at the highest levels of international management in the twenty-first century?

4. What common characteristics are held by CEOs of international companies?

5. What causes stress for international business people? How can IHRM processes assist staff in getting the correct work–life balance?

References

Adler, N. J., and Izraeli, D. N. (1988). *Women in Management Worldwide*. Armonk, NY: M. E. Sharpe.

Adler, N. J., and Izraeli, D. N. (1994). *Competitive Frontiers: Women Managers in a Global Economy*. Oxford: Blackwell.

Adler, N. J., with Gundersen, A. (2008). *International Dimensions of Organizational Behavior*. 5th edn. Mason, OH: Thomson South-Western.

Anderson Willinger (2009). 'What Employers Think about Effects of the Financial Crisis on their Companies', 13 Jan., www.andersonwillinger.com (accessed 21 Apr. 2009).

Antal International (2009). 'Global Survey Finds out Companies Chose Flexible Working Hour for Cost Saving', www.antal.com.cn (accessed 1 May 2009).

Attwood, K. (2007). 'Business Misses the Female Touch', *Independent*, 7 Dec.

Babcock, L. (2008). 'To Get what they Want, Women Need to Learn to Ask', *Observer*, 20 Apr., *New York Times* insert.

Batson, A. (2008). 'Help Wanted: Managers (for US Companies: Top Hurdle in China is Recruiting Talent)', *Wall Street Journal*, 29 Apr.

Benson, R. (2008). 'Take our Jobs', *Financial Times Magazine*, 19–20 Jan.

Black, J. S., Gregersen, H. B., Mendenhall, M., and Stroh, L. K. (1999). *Globalizing People through International Assignments*. Harlow: Addison-Wesley.

Bolino, M. C. (2007). 'Expatriate Assignments and Intra-Organizational Career Success: Implications for Individuals and Organizations', *Journal of International Business Studies*, 38/5 (Sept.).

Briscoe, D. R., Schuler, R. S., and Claus, L. (2008). *International Human Resource Management: Policy and Practice for the Global Enterprise*. 3rd edn. Abingdon: Routledge.

Croft, J. (2009). 'RBS to Cut up to 9,000 Jobs across Globe,' *Financial Times*, 7 Apr.

The Economist (2005). 'Women in Business', 21 July.

Edstrom, A., and Galbraith, J. R. (1977). 'Transfer of Managers as a Co-ordination and Control Strategy in Multinational Organizations', *Administrative Science Quarterly*, 22 (June), 248–63, cited in Harzing and Van Ruysseveldt (2004).

Evans, P. (1992). 'Management Development as Glue Technology', *Human Resource Planning*, 15/1: 85–106.

Glass Ceiling Commission (1991–6). US Department of Labor, various reports at www.dol.gov.

Grainger, R. J., and Nankervis, A. R. (2001). 'Expatriation Practices in the Global Business Environment', *Research and Practice in Human Resource Management*, 9/2: 77–92.

GSK (2006–8). GlaxoSmithKline, interviews with employees.

Harvard Law School (2000). The Harvard Law School Forum on Corporate Governance and Financial Regulation, http://blogs.law.harvard.edu/corpgov.

Harzing, A.-W. (2004). 'Composing an International Staff', in Harzing and Van Ruysseveldt (2004).

Harzing, A.-W., and Van Ruysseveldt (2004). *International Human Resource Management*. 2nd edn. London: Sage.

Holland, Kelley (2008). 'The Tension Builds', *New York Times*, 23 Mar.

Jackson, T. (2002). *International HRM: A Cross-Cultural Approach*. London: Sage.

Jones, C. (2007). 'Teleworking, The Quiet Revolution', dataquest insight: update 14 May, Gartner, Inc., www.gartner.com (accessed 21 Apr. 2009).

Kamenou, N. (2007). 'Methodological Considerations in Conducting Research across Gender, "Race", Ethnicity and Culture: A Challenge to Context Specificity in Diversity Research Methods', Special Issue on Global Diversity Management, *International Journal of Human Resource Management*, Nov.

Kamenou, N. (2008). 'Reconsidering Work–Life Balance Debates: Challenging Limited Understandings of the "Life" Component in the Context of Ethnic Minority Women's Experiences', Special Issue on Gender in Management: New Theoretical Perspectives, *British Journal of Management*, Mar.

Lauring, J. (2007). 'Language and Ethnicity in International Management', *Corporate Communications: An International Journal*, 12/3: 255–66.

Lee, K., Yang, G., and Graham, J. L. (2006). 'Tension and Trust in International Business Negotiations: American Executives Negotiating with Chinese Executives', *Journal of International Business Studies*, 37/5 (Sept.).

Lightfoot, L. (2008). 'How to Improve Work–Life Balance', *Independent*, 10 Apr.

Maki, D., and Soudakova, V. (2008). 'MNCs' Management of Human Resources in India: Case Studies of Two Swedish Companies', unpublished Masters thesis, Lulea University of Technology.

Mendenhall, M. E., Oddou, G. R., and Stahl, G. K. (2007). *Readings and Cases in International Human Resource Management*. 4th edn. Abingdon: Routledge.

Morris, K. (2004). 'Expatriate Training in the Corporate and Non-Corporate Sector', unpublished M.Sc. dissertation, Sheffield Hallam University.

Newbury, W., Gardberg, N., Belkin, A., and Liuba, Y. (2006). 'Organizational Attractiveness is in the Eye of the Beholder: The Interaction of Demographic Characteristics with Foreignness', *Journal of International Business Studies*, 37/5 (Sept.).

Ozbilgin, M. F., and Tatli, A. (2008). *Global Diversity Management*. Basingstoke: Palgrave Macmillan.

Palmer, M. (2005). 'Retail Multinational Learning: A Case Study of Tesco', *International Journal of Retail and Distribution Management*, 33/1: 23–48.

Perlmutter, H. V. (1969). 'The Tortuous Evolution of the Multinational Company', *Columbia Journal of World Business* (Jan./Feb.), 9–18.

Schneider, S. C., and Barsoux, J.-L. (2003). *Managing across Cultures*. 2nd edn. Harlow: Pearson/FT Prentice Hall.

Schuler, R., Budhwar, P., and Florkowski, G. (2002). 'International Human Resource Management: Review and Critique', *International Journal of Management Reviews*, 4/1 (Mar.), 41–71.

Scullion, H., and Starkey, K. (2000). 'In Search of the Changing Role of the Corporate Human Resource Function in the International Firm', *International Journal of Human Resource Management*, 11/6 (Dec.), 1061–81.

Simonian, H. (2009). 'UBS to Cut 11% of Global Work Force', *Financial Times*, 15 Apr.

Stewart, H. (2008). 'The Glass Ceiling isn't Broken – in Fact, it's Getting Thicker', *Observer*, 3 Feb.

Thomas, R. S. (2003). 'Explaining the International CEO Pay Gap: Board Capture or Market Driven?', *Vanderbilt Law Review*, at SSRN: http://ssrn.com/abstract=407600 or DOI: 10.2139/ssrn.407600.

Further research

Visser, M., and Gigante, A. (2007). *Women on Boards: Moving Mountains.* European Professional Women's Network (PWN).

European PWN launched 'Women on Boards' on 6 December 2007 (www.europeanpwn.net). This book presented up-to-date information and statistics on female and international board members in Europe, and discussed the key issues concerning board diversity and how it adds value to corporations.

European Professional Women's Network (PWN) provides compelling evidence for the need to promote more women board members to European companies. The European PWN

Board Women monitor, conducted by Egon Zehnder in 2006, showed that only 8.5 per cent of corporate boardroom seats in the top 300 European companies were held by women. In *Women on Boards*, EuropeanPWN analysed the profiles of the 100 top women compared with their male counterparts and provided advice for both companies and women on board diversity.

Online Resource Centre

Visit the Online Resource Centre that accompanies this book to read more information relating to international human resource management: www.oxfordtextbooks.co.uk/orc/sitkin_bowen/

part
5

Looking Ahead

16 Future Trends in International Business

Overview

The chapter considers two trends expected to have a major impact on the future of international business. After an introduction discussing multinational enterprise (MNE) forecasting, the bulk of the chapter focuses on two issues identified in a survey concluded in April 2008: the rise of certain emerging economies; and the ecological constraint. The first trend is an opportunity for some firms but a danger for others. The second is a serious challenge for everyone, although it will be argued that a bright future awaits MNEs that embrace environmentalist solutions.

Chapter 11 covered a third trend (technological innovation) widely expected to affect MNEs' future prospects. It appears again here as a background variable that enables MNEs to entertain closer relations with distant (emerging) markets, and also as a key component in corporate sustainability. Lastly, the devastating effects of the 2008 credit crunch may not be specified separately, but, as noted throughout this book, it is likely dramatically to alter the context within which MNEs operate. The length of the recession, and the different structural measures that MNEs, governments, and individuals will adopt in response, remains to be seen.

Section I: The shifting geography of international business

> The BRICs' emergence
>
> New rivals and new paradigms

Section II: The ecological constraint on international business

> Environmental Challenges facing MNEs
>
> Choosing an environmentalist future

Learning Objectives

After reading this chapter, you will be able to:

+ appreciate the difficulties inherent to international planning
+ reflect upon the trends affecting the short-, medium-, and long-term future of international business
+ calculate how the changing geography of international business might redirect MNEs' future internationalization efforts
+ identify the new agents and paradigms likely to arise as emerging economies enter the international business stage
+ reassess the relationship between MNEs and the natural environment

Case Study 16.1

Cottoning on to tomorrow's fashions

One of the consumer markets that globalization has affected most is clothing. Young people everywhere wear New York Yankees baseball caps, shirts bearing the image of Argentinean revolutionary Che Guevara, or Palestinian *keefiyeh* scarves. Europeans and Americans imitate each other's preference for skinny or baggy jeans; Japanese students buy Brazilian football shirts; and gossip columnists publicize celebrity fashion everywhere. To succeed, clothing companies have to keep a close eye on international trends.

For MNEs with global sales, it is worth paying for market studies that identify the many different economic, cultural, and demographic factors shaping today's fashions. Take the growing number of middle-class consumers in the world's emerging economies. Maslow's hierarchy of needs concept states that changes in people's level of income leads to shifts in their consumption behaviour—which is, in turn, a key variable in MNEs' internationalization decisions. Thus, luxury clothes-maker Versace has recently targeted Asia because it expects rising incomes in this part of the world to translate into more demand for its top-of-the-range

products. As stressed previously, analysing companies' actions means understanding managers' worldview.

A number of consultancies make a living spotting short-term trends and selling their findings to manufacturers and retailers. One is Cotton Incorporated (www.cottoninc.com), an American SME that arms forecasters with cameras and laptops and sends them across the world to study street fashion and other cultural indicators. Information is compiled and analysed in light of a country's political and economic situation and developments in areas such as food, music, or design. A cultural translation is then made to determine the significance of trends detected and whether they might become fashionable elsewhere. Cotton Incorporated analysts quickly understood, for instance, that rising global interest in sustainability was likely to affect the clothing sector. The company's 2007 annual report announced that environmentally-friendly manufacturing processes were destined to become the 'next frontier of eco-consciousness', implying that companies could adopt such practices to gain favour with consumers. This would be a major adjustment for clothing MNEs, and one that forecasters have to get right.

Clothing fashion travels easily (Robert Mullan).

Introduction

+ Competitive intelligence
Firm's compilation and analysis of information on the outside world. Generally used as a guide for future action.

> Go to the ORC

MNEs always have one eye to the future, employing qualified staff specifically to detect and plan for political, economic, social, technological, and/or ecological trends that may have a significant impact on future operations. The goal of this competitive intelligence or 'watch' function is to help the company to position itself so as to take advantage of any opportunities and/or protect itself from future rivals and adverse conditions. Such efforts are based on the notion that companies can derive as much advantage from competitive intelligence (CI) as from other management functions. Analysing trends' relative significance can be very difficult, however—especially when it is unfamiliar foreign environments that are being scanned (see Online Resource Centre , extension material 16.1).

MNEs' strategic watch capabilities are often, but not always, centralized (Blenkhorn and Fleisher 2005). As explained in Chapter 9, managers working in a company's subsidiaries may have a better understanding of local circumstances but can lack a global overview. Conversely, headquarters staff members are likelier to see the big picture but cannot necessarily break it down. This is a crucial shortcoming, given evidence that it is only at the level of small micro-markets that many trends' real impact will be felt (Proverbio et al. 2008). One way to resolve this dilemma is to empower strategic planners throughout the MNE. This raises questions, however, about the circulation of information within a company. The effects will be negative if subsidiary managers are unwilling to share their real intuitions about the future and simply reformulate headquarters' vision. From a career perspective, the safest option is usually to agree with received wisdom, but this very human reaction can also damage the quality of the forecasting process.

Thus, human capital is a key factor in international forecasting. Generally, the employees most adept at this function are cosmopolitan individuals possessing a 'global mindset' as well as the ability to analyse complex and multidimensional situations (Levy et al. 2007). These qualities are not as widespread in MNEs as might be expected. Studies have revealed that perceptions of the importance of having a global mindset vary from one MNE to another, depending on factors like the spread of nationalities within a company's workforce or the relative importance of international operations (Kedia et al. 2008). Above all, there is a manager's ability to look beyond his or her personal world view and feel what other people are experiencing. Worldliness and empathy have always been key assets in international business.

Inside business

Tom Glocer, CEO, Thomson Reuters

Thomson Reuters is an international business providing professional grade information in areas such as finance, law, tax and accounting, science and health care. As CEO since 2001, I am  responsible to the Board of Directors for the company's performance and strategic direction. For me, the more interesting aspects of being CEO are in the less definable areas, where each CEO seeks to add whatever he or she decides is of long-term sustainable value to the company.

The company does not have a classic industrial supply chain, since its main activity is in digital content. Thomson Reuters' business is generated by the people who are creating news or information or software. The major suppliers are, therefore, stock exchanges, banks, scientists, hospitals, dealer firms, courts, and governments. With regards to decision-making, the company is organized so that the HQ makes the big strategic choices, with other decisions made by eight global strategic business units (SBUs) grouped into a professional and a markets division.

The company does not use terms like outsourcing and offshoring, since it has been established for a long time in countries such as India (since 1866) and China (since 1871). Thomson Reuters identifies different parts of the world where, due to the local skill sets, it will locate operations. For example, the risk management business is centred in Paris, where there is a large number of highly trained, mathematically-oriented financial engineers. This has historically been 'a very smart place' for the company to develop highly sophisticated risk management software.

As far as corporate social responsibility (CSR) is concerned, this should be interwoven into the company's natural operation. In general, a publisher like Thomson Reuters starts off by being environmentally-friendly, since it delivers information in electronic format around the world. The company is concerned with issues such as where we locate our data centres, how we source our energy responsibly, and how we ensure that the data centres are cooled efficiently. However, we feel that it is wrong to take a 'cookie cutter' approach to CSR or to the metrics used to judge it.

Section I: The shifting geography of international business

At any given moment, MNE strategic planners will highlight a particular set of international trends. An in-depth survey that the McKinsey consultancy group published in April 2008 (just before the credit crunch broke out) stated that international executives' main concerns were, in order: emerging economies; ecological sustainability; technological innovation; the globalization of labour; ethical business; powerful capital markets; advances in knowledge management; and socio-economic or demographic changes (Stephenson and Pandit 2008). Not every MNE thinks it will be affected to the same extent by each of these trends. There is a strong consensus, however, that almost all MNEs can expect to experience a 'global remix' due to the rise of the BRICs (Brazil, Russia, India, and China) especially the last two (Scase 2007). It is important to state that the authors of this book are not arguing that the shifting geography of international business necessarily indicates a decline in the OECD economies' fortunes (Bello and Engelhardt 2005). The industrialized world retains technological, institutional, and financial resources that will continue to serve it well. Nor are the BRICs the only less-developed countries (LDCs) emerging onto the global stage. For instance, the huge quantity of petrodollars that the Middle Eastern OPEC states hold will also increase these countries' power. There is little doubt, however, that the BRICs' rise constitutes an important change in the geographic centre of international business, and one well worth exploring in detail.

+ BRICs
Term first developed by US investment bank Goldman Sachs, referring to Brazil, Russia, India, and China as a block to highlight the emergence of these continent-sized countries.

The BRICs' emergence

Despite industrialized countries' ongoing dominance of world trade and investment, statistics reveal a clear rise in the proportion of international business conducted by the developing world (see Chapter 1), particularly the BRICs. Analytically speaking, it is wrong to view these four countries as a single unit (Jain 2006). Russia and Brazil both have extensive natural resources, but, as a 'transition' ex-communist European country, Russia has a very different institutional heritage from Brazil, the former Portugese colony. China and India lack many of the natural resources they need, but each has a population of more than one billion citizens, versus 185 million and 143 million only for Brazil and Russia, respectively.

China and India may both be low-wage economies, but their trajectories are quite different, with China using its labour cost advantage to become a global manufacturing centre and India concentrating more on services. MNEs pursuing interests in the BRICs need to take a differentiated view of each.

Business conditions in the BRICs

Nevertheless, Brazil, Russia, India, and China do have several characteristics in common. First and foremost, since the 1990s each has placed greater emphasis on market economics. Unlike Russia, China continues to call itself communist, but both countries have taken steps to encourage private enterprise and international trade. Like Brazil, India is an ex-colony that first pursued import substitution policies after independence but has steadily reduced its barriers to trade since joining the World Trade Organization (WTO)—which China has also done, unlike Russia. Since the mid-1990s the behaviour of the BRICs, all of which used to be outspoken opponents of free market capitalism and theatres of communism, mercantilism and/or (neo-)colonialism, has gone a long way towards consolidating global neo-liberalism. Without their participation, trade and cross-border investments would be much less widespread today and MNE configurations much more localized.

This is not to say that business conditions in the BRICs are the same as in OECD countries. Levels of corruption are certainly higher, with Brazil, India, and China tied in 72nd place in Transparency International's 2007 'Corruption Perceptions Index' (see Chapter 3). Brazil can be a difficult place to work because of the high levels of criminality associated with income disparities. Stories abound about alleged difficulties in dealing with India's bureaucracy. The lack of transparency in Chinese authorities' decision-making practices forces MNEs operating there to develop a whole range of 'non-market strategies' (Gao 2008). As for Russia, which ranked only 143 on the same corruption score, many MNEs find it hard dealing with a government whose sense of economic patriotism sometimes conflicts with strict interpretations of international commercial law. There is no doubt that success in the BRICs requires specific managerial competencies that may not always be widely available throughout an MNE.

The adaptation is clearly worth the effort, however. In 2006, Goldman Sachs economist Jim O'Neill estimated that more than 25 per cent of world growth over the previous five years had come from the BRICs. Whereas annual GDP rises during most of the 2000s tended to average between 1 and 4 per cent in the OECD countries, the BRICs economies, with the exception of Brazil, regularly experienced an annual rate of 5–6 per cent (and often well above, in the case of China). Of course, growth rates plummeted after the 2008 global financial crisis. In China, for example, the loss of Western export markets meant the closure of more than 67,000 plants, many located in the country's manufacturing heartlands, the Pearl River Delta (Wong 2008). In turn, lower growth in the BRICs damaged Western MNEs that had come to rely on exports to these destinations—one example being steel producer ArcelorMittal, which suffered its first quarterly loss ever in late 2008, mainly because of the fall in Chinese demand. Nevertheless, prospects for long-term growth remain better in the BRICs (see Figure 16.1) than in the developed world. For example, despite the onset of the credit crunch, China, unlike many OECD countries, was able to fund a major stimulus package to sustain domestic activity levels. Thus, over the first four months of 2009, the country's imports of grains rose by 70.1 per cent, iron by 51.3 per cent, and oil by 251 per cent over the same period in 2008, before the outbreak of the crisis (Duffy 2009). Just as noteworthy is the fact that an increasing percentage of rising Chinese imports came from Brazil, which by spring 2009 had displaced the USA as China's biggest trading partner. Add to this the Indian economy's continued strength, and it appears likely that the BRICs' international rankings after the recession will be even stronger than they were before, bolstered by their strong responses to the crisis.

Country	2050 GDP in $ billion (in constant 2003 dollars)
China	44,453
USA	35,165
India	27,803
Japan	6,673
Brazil	6,074
Russia	5,870
UK	3,782
Germany	3,603
France	3,148
Italy	2,061

Figure 16.1
Goldman Sachs
GDP projections,
2050 (Wilson and
Purushothaman 2003;
reproduced with the
kind permission of
Goldman Sachs).

The BRICs as production locations

Growth in the BRICs can be divided between 'exogenous' (external) drivers like exports, and 'endogenous' internal dynamics. The latter category is comprised mainly of domestic demand and investment—including FDI by foreign firms that use these countries as manufacturing platforms for products and services that may be re-exported elsewhere. One driver for FDI is the enormous number of young engineers and scientists currently being trained in Chinese, Russian, and particularly Indian universities. As discussed in Chapter 11, there are many examples of innovative activities such as pharmaceutical research or software development being conducted out of emerging economies. Technological knowledge, always a key driver of international business, is much more widespread than it used to be. In addition, modern communications technologies and infrastructure investment have resolved many earlier problems associated with long-distance production networks linking developed and developing countries. The rapid acceleration of Japanese-built Internet switches creating a direct link between China and India, without transit via the USA as they used to do, also confirms the BRICs' emergence (Markoff 2008). There is no longer any doubt that they have the technological capabilities to engage in high value-added production.

The BRICS' expanding consumer markets further strengthen their role as production sites. Whereas earlier sales to these countries often involved exports from plants located elsewhere, MNEs are now more likely to produce goods locally on an FDI basis. By adopting this 'insiderization' approach, they stand to gain political (and, above all, commercial) goodwill. This is important in a country like China, where studies have shown that consumers are less interested than Westerners in trendy brands, preferring familiar goods that offer value for money (St-Maurice et al. 2008). Localization counts in these emerging economies.

However, this does not mean that an irreversible tide of investments should be expected into the BRICs. The sharp withdrawal of international funds from Russia's stock markets following its military action in Georgia in summer 2008 exemplifies the ongoing concerns that many Western investors feel. Similarly, the credit crunch had very negative effects on global flows into the emerging world, with many investors seeking to move funds to safe-haven destinations. It remains that, as consumption rises in the BRICs, multinationals are likely to develop a more holistic view of their potential as production locations and no longer treat them as mere outsourcing locations.

The BRICs as target markets

Rising wages in the BRICs has led to a rapid expansion in their middle classes, defined as individuals with an annual per capita income of $3,000 or more, expressed in constant (that is, unadjusted for inflation) 2003 dollars. Many MNEs, especially ones whose existing markets are saturated, monitor this trend in the hope that it means solvent new consumer demand for their goods and services. In all likelihood, the BRICs will remain poorer than their Western counterparts on a per capita basis, largely for demographic reasons (see Figure 16.2). Nevertheless, if O'Neill is right in his calculation that the BRICs are likely to experience a fourfold increase to 1 billion middle-class consumers by the year 2015 (and then doubling to 2 billion by 2025), the outlook for growth remains phenomenal.

The expansion of the BRICs' middle classes is also significant because of the kinds of products that households purchase when they shift out of poverty. As income rises, people spend in areas (entertainment, consumer durables, leisure) that were once beyond their reach. This is a great opportunity for firms in the sectors concerned. Analytically, a distinction can be made between markets going through their 'first equipment' and their 'product renewal' stages. The latter refers to older markets where consumers purchase items to replace obsolescent existing goods. The former involves products being bought for the first time. Recent examples of products making this kind of initial breakthrough include DVD players in Europe or the USA (driven by new technologies) and refrigerators in India or China (based on rising purchasing power). This latter example, involving the sale of tried-and-tested goods in new markets, is attractive to MNEs, since it involves items that they already know how to make. The decisions required in this case (manufacturing location, product adaptation, funding) are complicated but less so than if new technologies were involved. This is one reason why the world's leading MNEs are so interested in accelerating sales into the BRICs.

Emerging market demand already sets the tone in a number of global sectors. One is the energy market. Another is telecommunications. Paradoxically enough, in this latter area it is the BRICs' lack of infrastructure that gives them an advantage. Instead of having to lay modern systems on top of older ones, they are free to purchase more up-to-date technology. Thus, with 350 million subscribers by the end of 2007, China had already become the world's biggest mobile phone market, with India expected to hit the 300 million mark in 2010 (Engardio 2007). The result has been a mini-boom, not only for established MNEs but also (and increasingly) for local BRICs firms seeking to address growing local demand for hi-tech consumer goods.

The BRICs have also become crucial to a number of low-tech sectors. At the high end of the scale, nouveau riche customers from Moscow to Delhi and Shanghai are reinvigorating many luxury segments. For mid-scale fast-moving consumer goods, rising demand from the BRICs' new middle classes has been a great opportunity for global retailers such as Walmart,

+ Nouveau riche French expression referring to a population that has recently come into wealth and whose consumption behaviour is changing.

Figure 16.2	Country	2050 per capita GDP in $ billion (in constant 2003 dollars)
Goldman Sachs GDP per capita projections for 2050 (Wilson and Purushothaman 2003; reproduced with the kind permission of Goldman Sachs).	USA	83,710
	Japan	66,805
	UK	59,122
	France	51,594
	Russia	49,646
	Germany	48,952
	Italy	40,901
	China	31,357
	Brazil	26,592
	India	17,366

Carrefour, and Tesco. Above all, the BRICs have provided a much needed boost for global carmakers and their components manufacturers (such as Delphi from the USA or Valeo from France). Goldman Sachs economist O'Neill has predicted that with 200 million car-owners projected by the year 2025, the Chinese automobile market is destined to become the biggest in the world. This explains why many MNEs have invested so heavily in this country, as exemplified by the corporate campus that General Motors built near Shanghai to house R&D activities developing environmentally-friendly technologies targeting the local market (Blumenstein 2007). Brazil is another attractive car market, having grown by 28 per cent between 2006 and 2007 (*Guardian* 2008). As for Russia, this became Europe's second-largest car market in 2008, after experiencing a 65 per cent rise in foreign car brand sales over the previous year (Rauwald and Power 2007). Lastly, the southern Indian city of Chennai has recently hosted new factories built by leading carmakers like Nissan, Toyota, BMW, and Ford, all enthusiastic to enter this market (Fackler 2008). With the BRICs' vast expanses, large populations, and comparatively low levels of car ownership, it is no wonder that they have become a centre of attention for global automotive interests.

New rivals and new paradigms

Entering the BRICs can be very costly, however, as they are complex societies characterized by enormous regional variations. Demand emanating from rural Western China, for instance, differs from typical demand in the country's industrial Eastern coast. Such variations can be cultural in nature and/or reflect big disparities in purchasing power between that part of the population that has achieved a relatively comfortable standard of living and another that is still extremely poor—an inequality that characterizes many emerging nations. Because the BRICs remain poor, the products that MNEs sell there must usually be cheaper and/or offer different functionalities than their ranges sold elsewhere. As discussed in Chapter 11, this kind of adaptation can be very expensive.

The question is whether it is worth the expense. With their much higher cost bases and despite all of their cost-saving outsourcing and FDI initiatives, MNEs originating from OECD countries will struggle to make a profit selling washing machines for $37, personal computers for $200, or cars for $2,000. Yet these are typical of the low prices that firms such as China's Haier and Lenovo (Engardio 2007) or India's Tata were practising in their home markets around 2006–8. In a similar vein, when European conglomerate Unilever entered Africa in the early 2000s, it decided that the only way to satisfy the pent-up demand of the continent's many impoverished households was to sell smaller detergent packages at much lower prices. Of course, this meant tiny per unit profit margins and was probably justifiable only if it helped Unilever gain durable brand loyalty. It is true that the outlook for Africa's short-term emergence is not as promising as it is in the BRICs. What Africa and the BRICs do have in common, however, is that both require a long-term strategic approach. MNEs with the resources to be patient should be able to benefit from their emergence as commercial magnets. Others will struggle.

Multinationals from the BRICs as new players on the world stage

Companies originating in the BRICs are more accustomed to environments characterized by low costs, low prices, and (sometimes) lower quality. Indeed, the rise of MNEs born in the 'Global South' is a significant trend and one that is likely to have a strong impact on the future of international business. Many BRICs multinationals have yet to become household names in the developed world, but their strong competitive advantages mean that this is destined to change by the mid-2010s at the latest (see Figure 16.3). First, these companies tend to have lower cost bases, if only because employees are paid much less than their 'Northern' counterparts. Junior engineers at Chery, a dynamic Chinese small carmaker preparing to enter the North and South American markets, earn just $6,000 a year and sleep in 'bunk beds with four to a room in company dormitories' (Fairclough 2007). It is unlikely that their

Figure 16.3
BRICs companies
likely to become
global leaders and
household names by
the mid-2010s.

Sector	Country	Companies (main activity)
Primary (energy, mining, agriculture)	Brazil	Petrobras (oil), Vale (mining)
	Russia	Gazprom (gas), Lukoil (oil), Severstal (mining)
	India	Indian Oil, ArcelorMittal (steel)
	China	Sinopec (oil), Baoshan Iron and Steel (metals)
Secondary (inc. industrial manufacturing)	Brazil	Braskem (petrochemicals), WEG (motors)
	Russia	Avtovaz (automotive), Gaz (automotive)
	India	Tata (automotive), Bharti Airtel (telecom)
	China	Haier (appliances), Chery (automotive)
Tertiary (inc. hi-tech manufacturing)	Brazil	Embraer (aerospace), TV Globo (media)
	Russia	Rosnanotech (nanotechnology), RSCC (satellites)
	India	Ranbaxy (pharmaceuticals), Infosys (software)
	China	Lenovo (computers), China Life Insurance Company
Tertiary (banks)	Brazil	Banco Itau, Banco do Brasil
	Russia	Sberbank, Vneshtorgbank
	India	State Bank of India, ICICI Bank
	China	Bank of China, CITIC Bank

US, European, or Japanese rivals would make similar concessions. Secondly, increasing numbers of Russian and especially Indian computer companies (such as Infosys and Satyam) can match their OECD competitors qualitatively even as they continue to produce at much lower costs. Chinese technology has also made great strides, with Lenovo becoming a new giant in the global computing sector and the country as a whole now seen as world leader in satellite launches. Lastly, energy companies from Brazil (Petrobras) and above all Russia (Gazprom, Lukoil) benefit from the two countries' wealth of natural resources. The leading BRICs multinationals have advantages that can be mobilized across the world.

BRICs multinationals also enjoy strengths that are particularly advantageous in their home markets, where attitudes towards foreignness can be quite complicated.

On the one hand, real attraction exists for foreign products associated until recently with a lifestyle and standard of living that few consumers could access. Long queues in front of McDonald's restaurants in Russia, at a time when the company was enduring saturation in other markets, confirm this fascination. Yet BRICs populations' strong country-of-origin preferences, as revealed in recent studies of Chinese consumers' lasting affection for food products bearing a local label (Ehmke et al. 2008), shows that they can be just as ethnocentric as their counterparts from the developed world. Companies originating in the BRICs seem aware of this effect, with one study revealing that Chinese companies building brand recognition in OECD countries tend to acquire already established brand names while continuing to publicize their own brand names when entering fellow LDCs (Fetscherin and Marc 2008). As discussed throughout this book, international business is permeated by national loyalty issues, and occasionally by the uglier undercurrents of xenophobia sometimes associated with such phenomena. This is especially true during times of crisis, like the 2008 credit crunch, when some citizens worldwide were demanding that their governments prioritize domestic interests over the more abstract benefits of foreign trade. A home bias exists in the BRICs as it does elsewhere. This will be an advantage for companies originating in these societies as they emerge.

Thinking point

Is BRICs citizens' patriotism different from their OECD counterparts?

A greater role for the state?

Although there is no doubt that the BRICs have adopted numerous free market policies since the mid-1990s, these are countries where neo-liberalism is a relatively new paradigm lacking deep roots. Nor do the four BRICs pursue the exact same orientations in this respect. Brazil, for example, features relatively few nationalized companies any more and has implemented a laissez-faire financial system allowing more or less free capital flows. There has been a similar loosening of financial controls in India, although FDI here remains highly restricted in certain sectors (like retailing) because of fears that large foreign MNEs could enter the market and displace millions of local shopkeepers. This emphasis on protecting small entrepreneurs contrasts with China and Russia, where much power remains in the hands of large, state-owned enterprises. As stated throughout this book, neo-liberalism (like interventionism) assumes different shapes everywhere.

One thing that the BRICs do have in common is economic emergence (and political recognition, as witnessed by their regular inclusion nowadays in the new and expanded version of the old G8 summit system). This will have several effects, first and foremost being the impact on the global financial system. There is a general consensus that the BRICs currencies are destined to strengthen over time, with most analysts also predicting that companies from these countries are destined to account for a greater proportion of the world's total stock market capitalization. Above all, China has become the global creditor upon whom all debtor nations, led by the USA, rely for funding. This fact alone gives the Beijing government, more than any of its BRICs counterparts, a pre-eminent global role.

A second consequence of the BRICs' emergence is that the particular political philosophies of these countries will be given greater airing in future decisions about global trading and investment systems. Despite the relative decline in old-fashioned state power, these are societies where political elites retain as much if not more power than business leaders. During the 2008 credit crunch, for instance, there was a clear contrast between the failure of banking regulators in more neo-liberal countries such as the USA and the UK, and the success of more prudent and interventionist authorities in countries like India in avoiding the kinds of speculative bubbles that uncontrolled free markets can often generate (Nocera 2008). Indeed, decisions taken in the wake of the crisis at the April 2009 G20 summit in London revealed broad political agreement about the need for more state control, at least over global financial flows.

It is too early to predict whether international business, under the influence of the BRICs and in reaction to the 2008 crisis, is about to go through a full-scale paradigm shift similar to the ones that it experienced in the 1930s and 1970s (see Chapter 5). More likely is that, much as they are already asked to do in the BRICs, international managers will need to learn how to incorporate non-market-related considerations into their strategic vision. One such consideration is detailed in Section 2 below.

Case Study 16.2

Brazil emerges with a beat

Brazil was once synonymous with economic instability. For years, this South American giant would experience triple-digit inflation and a current account deficit that left it incapable of repaying international bank loans. Things got so bad that the former national currency (the old cruzeiro) had to be scrapped entirely in 1994—the sign of an economy that was anything but emerging.

Bringing in a new currency had a positive effect, however, mainly because of associated measures calming the inflationary expectations that had caused so many of Brazil's earlier problems. One such policy was the Cardoso administration's firm commitment to balance the national budget. Although economically necessary, this approach meant that fewer social programmes would be engaged to address the poverty afflicting millions of Brazilians, a root cause of the country's high crime rate. The 2002 election of ex-union leader Lula was useful in this respect. The new president steered an even course between a business-friendly environment encouraging investment and entrepreneurship and a sensitivity to poverty reflecting his socialist sensitivities. The rich may have got richer in Brazil but many of the poor have become noticeably less poor, due to jobs created in the private sector but also because of the Bolsa Familia, a generous benefit that the Lula government created in 2003, which eleven million disadvantaged families receive every month. The ensuing social harmony means that, for the first time in decades, Brazil can focus on economic emergence. It has done so to great effect.

Despite lagging a few percentage points behind its fellow BRICs in terms of GDP growth, Brazil clocked up excellent performances in the mid-2000s, creating an average of 1.4 million jobs annually, keeping yearly inflation to a manageable 4.7 per cent, and accumulating $100 billion in foreign exchange reserves—a sum exceeding its national debt. Unsurprisingly, international investors have flocked to its equity markets, which rose by 60 per cent in 2007. Like everywhere else, stocks were hit badly by the 2008 crisis, but the country's prospects remain promising.

Brazil's economic diversity helps to bolster business confidence. The fuel sector features a well-developed ethanol industry and has benefited from the discovery of new oil fields offshore. Traditional strengths in agribusiness and mining have been useful in an era when world commodity prices are on the rise. The construction and banking sectors have taken advantage of the general growth dynamic, as have other industries like aerospace. It would be wrong to forget the problems that Brazil continues to face now, in the early 2010s: the terrible conditions in which millions of favela ghetto inhabitants still live; and the destruction of the Amazon forest, with disastrous effects for local communities and the environment as a whole. Nevertheless, for the first time in living memory, Brazilians have many reasons besides football and samba to dance.

Brazil's emergence is due to both political and economic factors (Photodisc).

Section II: The ecological constraint on international business

Chapter 3 briefly treated sustainability as an element of corporate responsibility, but MNEs' environmental interests clearly go much further. On the one hand, there is the damage caused by the pollution that they can generate. On the other, there is resource depletion, or the exhaustion of the global stocks of the physical commodities that companies need for their production processes. There is an almost unanimous opinion among governments, business leaders, and academics that the future will be characterized by an ever-tightening ecological constraint. This scenario has many negative aspects but also presents exciting opportunities. Indeed, there is a strong argument for regarding environmentalism as an essential strategic function that deserves as much attention as more traditional core functions such as production or marketing (Bresciani and Oliveira 2007).

+ Resource depletion
Consumption of raw materials that cannot be replaced.

+ Environmentalism
Attitude that ecological sustainability should be a priority factor in personal and organizational decision-making.

Environmental challenges facing MNEs

Historically, the business world has given insufficient recognition to the ecological constraint (Hofstra 2007; Monbiot 2007), but this is no longer the case. The conclusions of the UN's 2007 Intergovernmental Panel on Climate Change (IPCC) report, which asserts that global warming is almost entirely a man-made phenomenon, have given much credibility to the environmentalist vision of Planet Earth as a limited, 'finite' system dependent on a delicate and vulnerable biosphere. Sustainability has become a mainstream concern.

+ Biosphere
Sum total of elements on Planet Earth that make it possible to sustain life.

Pollution

Production processes consume inputs and create outputs comprised of the goods or services that a company wants to sell but also the unwanted waste that it generates (see Figure 16.4). Foundries make steel but produce smog and pollutant heavy metals. Paper mills make stationery but use chemicals that infiltrate the water table. Farmers raise crops but spray them with noxious pesticides. Service industries use electricity sourced from power stations that generate radioactive waste (nuclear plants) or carbon dioxide (coal-powered plants). All these unwanted emissions are directly associated with economic activity. They circulate in the biosphere in a way that depends on natural factors (winds, ocean currents, geological formations) and takes no notice of national borders. By definition, pollution is an international problem.

In truth, it is difficult to say who is more responsible for pollution: companies; or private individuals consuming products purchased from companies. Passenger cars emit smog; household heating aggravates global warming; and the inadequate disposal of the trillions of plastic shopping bags has created a several hundred square kilometre island of rubbish in the middle of the Pacific Ocean. At one level, some might argue that business cannot be held accountable for the waste generated by household activities, although the opposite argument is just as strong, since consumers can use only the goods that companies make. Households seeking to reduce their environmental footprint are increasingly asking companies to provide them with products and services that will help them to live more sustainably. It is consumer demand for low-emission, fuel-efficient cars that has driven carmakers such as Toyota, Honda, and General Motors to invest in hybrid automotive technology. It is consumers' desire to buy from firms with an ethical reputation (see Chapter 3) that has sparked a host of sustainable practices, like when supermarkets phase out plastic shopping bags or reduce the food miles of the products they offer. Sustainability can be achieved only if a holistic view is taken of environmental problems instead of allocating blame arbitrarily. The battle against pollution is waged by consumers and companies together. Environmentalism does not conflict with international business but guides it.

+ Emissions
Outflows following an industrial transformation process. Include air-borne gases and water-borne sewage, also known as 'effluents'.

+ Food miles
Distance travelled by a foodstuff between its place of production and consumption.

Figure 16.4
Examples of industrial pollutants (Citepa 2009).

Type	Sources include
Gaseous pollutants	
- Solid particles (inc. asbestos)	Mineral extraction, cement / steel / glass works.
- SO$_2$ Sulphur dioxide	Power stations, refineries, large combustion plants
- Nox Nitrogen oxides	International combustion engines, forest fires
- CO Carbon monoxide	Motor vehicle exhaust fumes
- CO$_2$ Carbon dioxide	Fossil energy
- CH$_4$ Methane	Coal mine, landfill sites, livestock
Heavy metals	
- As Arsenic	Glass-making, metalworking
- Cd Cadmium	Burning solid mineral fuels, heavy fuel oil
- Cr Chromium	Production of glass, cement, ferrous metals
- Hg Mercury	Chlorine production, waste incineration
- Pb Lead	Fusion of lead, manufacture of batteries
- Se Selenium	Glass production, use of heavy fuel oil
Other pollutants	
- NH$_3$ Ammonia	Agricultural activities
- PCDD-F Dioxins	Incineration, fuel combusion

With MNEs having accepted that they bear responsibility alongside other actors in reducing pollution, the question for them then becomes how to achieve this goal. Clearly it is no longer feasible for manufacturers to 'externalize' the costs of their activities, leaving the rest of society the burden of cleaning up their pollution. In the past, when population and industrialization levels were much lower than today, the effects of factory pollution may have been harmful at a local scale (consider the so-called satanic mills of Victorian England), but there was a good chance that nature could dilute their effects (Hardin 1968). This is no longer the case, due to the massive increase in global population, industrial production, and dangerous accumulation of pollution inherited from past generations. Consequently, in many areas, the only sustainable option is for companies to adopt an 'abatement' approach, reducing the total amount of pollution created in the first place. Abatement can be expensive, however, because of the relatively high costs of designing and implementing industrial systems that generate less pollution, and because historically companies have had insufficient economic incentives not to pollute (Goodin 1999). The extent to which

Photo 16.1
Handing out bags made from recycled materials is one way for retailers like the UK's Sainsbury's to respond to ecological constraints (© Sainsbury plc).

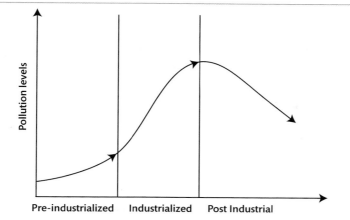

Pre-industrialized   Industrialized   Post Industrial

Figure 16.5
The Kuznets curve links a society's phase of development with its pollution behaviour.

abatement's higher costs are passed on to consumers or subtracted from profits is a key strategic question for international managers.

International variations in environmental sensitivity

Pollution is not dealt with uniformly across the world. Many countries' development trajectory has followed a three-step process known as the 'Kuznets curve' (see Figure 16.5). In this model, undeveloped countries generate little waste but then start to pollute enormously as they industrialize. It is only once they have reached a certain stage of development that they can afford pollution mitigation. There is a consensus that, with the world's most populous nations (China and India) now entering the second Kuznets phase, total global pollution is destined to rise sharply over the 2010s.

Environmentalists feel that this scenario justifies strict global regulation of corporate behaviour. At the same time, some observers would argue that it is unfair to hamper growth in LDCs, since this makes it harder for them to catch up with the standards of living enjoyed in the older industrialized countries, whose own wealth comes at the cost of centuries of environmental damage. At some level, there is a degree of conflict between the global development and environment agendas. IGOs active in sustainability, like the United Nations Environment Programme (UNEP), have tried to resolve this by developing the concept of 'common but differentiated responsibilities' (Elliott 2004). Note that many LDCs are just as worried about environmental degradation as their wealthier counterparts. An example is China, which, with millions of citizens suffering ill health because of rising pollution levels generated by export-driven industries, has moved to promote its environmental regulatory agency to the status of a ministry (Oster and Batson 2008). Environmental quality is as much a measurement of global justice as other, more material, indicators.

If compromises can be found and regulations harmonized worldwide, MNEs will have less cause to locate operations based on some countries possessing less stringent environmental legislation than others. Even if practices will always vary in time and place (see Online Resource Centre , extension material 16.2), public awareness and disapproval of ecological misconduct anywhere in the world should mean that environmental regime shopping will become less frequent in the future than it has been in the past. Given the magnitude of the ecological challenges that the world faces, international cooperation is a precondition for finding effective solutions.

> **Thinking point**
> Should LDCs be expected to assume the same environmental responsibilities as OECD countries?

> Go to the ORC

International environmental governance

Air pollution, or the uncontrolled emission of noxious gases and/or hydrocarbons into the atmosphere, is probably the greatest area of concern that Planet Earth faces today. The main sources of this kind of pollution are cars, factories, biomass, agriculture—and deforestation, which occurs today on a mass scale in Brazil, Indonesia, and Malaysia, as it once did in

Europe and North America. Air quality is poor in many major cities, causing countless early deaths from respiratory illness and damaging the health (thus productivity) of millions of workers worldwide. Polluted air knows few boundaries, with emissions from one country affecting many others. One example is the way that smoke from factories in the north-east United States creates 'acid rain' devastating forests throughout the Canadian provinces of Ontario and Quebec. This underscores the need for intergovernmental organizations to supervise cross-border pollution, much in the same way as the WTO supervises trade.

Along these lines, it is worth analysing MNEs' responses to international variations in air-quality standards. In 2009, for instance, California mandated an increase in the number of zero-emission vehicles running in the state by the year 2020. To meet this standard, companies know that they must invest substantial sums in research. The question then becomes whether the Californian market justifies this expense. Of course, if legislation were harmonized globally, there would be no choice.

+ **Climate change**
Lasting variation in the average temperature of a given location.

The most worrying consequence of decades of air pollution is climate change. Whereas the effects of certain kinds of pollution are felt only locally, by definition global warming is universal. Clearly, as a problem whose consequences are potentially lethal on a mass scale, it is something that MNEs cannot ignore.

Following the 2007 UN-sponsored Bali Conference and 2008 election of Barack Obama in the USA, the global consensus now is that the total concentration of CO_2 particles in the atmosphere should be kept below a threshold specified by the UK's Stern Review as 450 parts per million (ppm), compared with 2005 levels of 380 ppm and pre-Industrial Revolution levels of 280 ppm. Failure to achieve this would probably make it impossible to keep average temperature rises below the 2-degree level beyond which irreversible damage will hit the world's ecosystems. Many analysts fear that the polar icecaps could melt entirely, raising sea levels and flooding coastal regions, including international financial centres such as New York and Tokyo. Others fear raging storms causing catastrophic damage to persons and property, similar to the havoc that Hurricane Katrina caused the residents of New Orleans in 2005, not to mention the oil platforms situated in the Gulf of Mexico. This would bankrupt the global insurance industry. There are also fears that repeated drought could lead to massive crop failures of the kind witnessed over the 2000s in Australia, which had been one of the world's leading wheat producers. Irrespective of government policy, it is certainly in the interest of international business to do everything it can to prevent the worst-case scenario for climate change.

Thinking point
Should MNEs be forced through regulations to cut carbon emissions or merely given incentives to achieve this goal?

Photo 16.2
Smog is a serious public health issue in California and has led to a demand for higher fuel-efficiency standards (Photodisc).

As in other areas of corporate responsibility (see Chapter 3), there is an ongoing debate about the extent to which company efforts to reduce carbon emissions should be voluntary or government-enforced. On the one hand, there is the attitude of businessmen like Michael O'Leary, the CEO of discount airliner Ryannair, who tries to denounce 'environmental headbangers' (Thomson 2007). On the other, many executives have voluntarily joined bodies like the World Business Council for Sustainable Development (WBCSD) and fully accept the need for measures forcing companies to modify the status quo. This can range from outright legislation to green taxes aimed at modifying behaviour (convincing people to fly less, for example) or cap and trade carbon finance markets (Labatt and White 2007). Like many other areas of international business, the environment is a highly political topic.

The cap and trade system is controversial (see Online Resource Centre, extension material 16.3) because it uses market incentives to attack a problem that many environmentalists blame on the excesses of a market economy in the first place. Depending on a sector's specific carbon abatement needs, the cost and speed of developing new technology, and the cost of distributing renewable energies (Enkvist et al. 2007), companies are given CO_2 allocations and incentivized to reduce their carbon footprint over time. Whether this mechanism will work or not remains to be seen. The bigger picture is the extent to which companies are prepared to pay the full cost of implementing a low-carbon economy. This depends on factors like the short-term profitability demands placed upon them by shareholders, the value they can hope to get from an environmentally-friendly brand image, and managers' personal value systems. Above all, many companies are lulled into inaction because the effects of climate change are not always immediately visible.

The same cannot be said of another ecological constraint that MNEs face today—the competition for natural resources. This has a direct effect on companies' bottom line and therefore receives a great deal of attention. It is one thing to expect managers to behave sustainably when they are not convinced that they will benefit from this directly; it is another when profits are in danger. Resource depletion is one level where environmental awareness goes hand in hand with profit-seeking.

Depletion of non-renewable natural resources

In classical economics, greater demand for a good is supposed to increase its price, thus the supply. This model becomes problematic when the supply cannot rise because the good is non-renewable. A prime example is oil, the commodity upon which almost all modern industry relies. As Figure 16.6 demonstrates, rising global demand for this finite resource, fuelled by unsustainable per capita consumption in the world's advanced economies and increased demand from the newly industrialized countries, means that oil reserves are destined to run out sooner rather than later (Shelley 2005). Another way to express this is that Planet Earth is close to peak oil, as witnessed by major oil fields' falling output (Chazan 2008). Thus, irrespective of productivity gains and the speed with which alternative energy sources are adopted, it is clear that energy costs will rise over time for almost all MNEs. Companies in the power generation, petrochemicals, and transportation sectors will be directly hit, as will companies with globally dispersed value chains. By definition, international production systems organized along global lines incur higher logistics costs than ones based on locally produced inputs. In a world of high oil prices, fragmented configurations can be very expensive.

A similar scenario applies with most of the minerals, such as nickel, tin, and copper, that companies use in their production processes. Most commodities moved sharply higher in 2007 and early 2008, boosting prices for many intermediary goods derived from them. One example is hot-rolled steel, a generic product that manufacturers use to make cars, appliances, and other equipment. Its price rose from $650–$700 per metric tonne in early 2007 to $1,000 a year later. An immediate concern for MNEs at the time was whether they could pass such rises on to customers. In April 2008, for instance, steel giant ArcelorMittal was planning a surcharge for its US customers to help soften the impact of the rising cost of

+ Green taxes
Taxes creating a disincentive for firms to behave in an environmentally unfriendly manner.

> Go to the ORC

+ Cap and trade
Scheme that starts with a central authority distributing permits that allow members to engage in a given behaviour (like the emission of CO_2) within certain limits. Initial allocations can be exceeded only by purchasing unused allocations from other scheme members.

Thinking point
Why have many MNEs not prepared fully for a post-oil future?

+ Peak oil
Point at which half of the world's oil reserves have been consumed.

Figure 16.6
World primary energy
demand, 1980–2030
(million tonnes of oil
equivalent (mtoe))
(IEA 2006: 67; 2008: 2;
© OECD/IEA).

Energy	1980 (mtoe)	2008 (estimated) (mtoe)	2030 (estimated) (mtoe)	2008–2030 (estimated percentage rise)
Coal	1,785	3,300	4,441	35
Oil	3,107	4,000	5,575	39
Gas	1,237	2,700	3,869	43
Nuclear	186	625	861	38
Hydro	148	275	408	48
Biomass/waste	765	1,100	1,645	50
Other renewables	33	100	296	296
Total	7,261	12,100	17,095	

the iron ore and other raw materials that it uses to make steel. Given the poor health of some of its customers, such as Ford and General Motors, it was not immediately obvious that this policy would work (Mathews 2008). Price pressures at the early upstream level of a global value chain have negative consequences further downstream. This is one of the reasons why, after decades during which many MNEs tended to ignore the natural environment, there is a growing realization of its importance. A company that cannot pass on rising costs is by definition in trouble.

It is true that raw material prices plummeted after the credit crunch hit in late 2008. For instance, oil fell from a high of $147 per barrel in July to around $40 by December, and iron ore fell from $200 a tonne in February 2008 to $70 in November. This price fall was not the good news that it seemed to be, however. First, it mainly reflected a devastating collapse in global demand in most sectors of activity—bad news that had a far greater effect on company profits than the benefits derived from lower commodities prices. Secondly, the lower costs of traditional fuel sources (and reduction in available capital because of the credit crunch) took away many entrepreneurs' incentive to invest in alternative energy sources such as wind and solar power. This delayed the urgent shift towards a more sustainable industrial economy. Lastly, it is unlikely that MNE planners can count on low commodity prices for long. The deep trend is towards higher prices for raw materials, if only because of global population growth and rising demand from emerging nations embarked upon a course of rapid industrialization and urbanization. A prime case is China, which has shifted from being a net exporter to a net importer of coal (Oster and Davis 2008) and which between 2000 and 2006 became responsible for around 90 per cent of the growth in world demand for copper, a widely used mineral in the construction sector (Helbling et al. 2008). Similarly, initiatives aimed at turning crops into biofuels have contributed to food price inflation and had a knock-on effect on consumer budgets and international agribusiness (see Online Resource Centre, extension material 16.4). The days when MNE planners could ignore natural resources to concentrate on industrial or service activities are long gone.

> Go to the ORC ◉

Choosing an environmentalist future

Usually it is only after a serious ecological need receives negative publicity that people are motivated to seek a solution and the problem becomes a business opportunity (see Figure 16.7). As stressed throughout this book, international managers should always consider the perspectives and insights of those who reject the status quo.

Ecological problem	Opportunities for MNEs
CFC depleting the ozone layer	Arkema (USA) producing less harmful HCFCs
Lack of drinking water	One (UK) funding African irrigation projects
CO_2 emissions	Cosan (Brazil) processing ethanol fuel; Vattenfall (Sweden) developing carbon capture and storage technologies
High energy prices	Toshiba (Japan) selling energy saving TVs; BYD (China) manufacturing battery-run cars
Clean–up operations	SEDA (Germany) building 'end of life' vehicle depollution systems; Veolia (France) offering waste disposal services to municipalities worldwide

Figure 16.7
Environmental problems that have become international business opportunities.

The ecological constraint as an opportunity for MNEs

There have been a few business successes in the fight against pollution, one being improvements in the ozone layer after harmful CFC chemical compounds were phased out from refrigerators and replaced by less damaging compounds. Biodiversity and water-pollution problems, on the other hand, remain as prevalent as ever and therefore constitute real opportunities for MNEs. A prime example is water management, a growing issue due to recurrent droughts caused by global warming and aggravated by unsustainable urbanization patterns. The UN has called for a doubling of water infrastructure investment from current annual levels of $80 billion—engineering projects that will create international jobs for years to come (Jowit 2008).

A second opportunity stems from the growing realization among many urban planners that land is a finite resource whose physical and urban usage requires greater stewardship (Dobereiner 2006). Changes in zoning laws, the trend towards brownfield developments, the construction of public transportation systems, and the growth in urban regeneration projects will keep the global construction sector busy for many decades. This will affect MNEs (such as Bechtel or Deutsche Babcock) that compete for mega-projects worldwide but also SMEs whose technical advice or project management skills implement World Green Building Council principles (Lockwood 2007). Similarly, the disposal, recycling, and transformation of waste is a good opportunity. There is a global market for waste treatement, with most leading companies in this sector (as in Waste Management) operating on a cross-border basis.

+ Stewardship
Concept that one party has a practical if not moral obligation to take responsibility for another.

A noteworthy aspect of all these opportunities is the frequency of public/private arrangements. Since most of the world's clean-up efforts are directed by state authorities, companies seeking environmental contracts overseas will normally be asked to negotiate with government officials. Given public and private sector professionals' different value systems, this is an important consideration for international marketing in this sector. It is also another example of the fact that the borders between the economic and political spheres are less important in international and/or environmental business than they are in most other areas of business.

Towards greener multinationals?

The first step for MNEs serious about making their operations more ecologically sustainable is to undertake an environmental audit. Different reporting metrics (quantitative measures) have been developed, and it would help MNEs, especially ones committed to sustainable FDI, if harmonized cross-border parameters were agreed (Kallio 2008). Greater transparency would also reduce the possibility of 'greenwashing' (see Chapter 3), while keeping consumers and policy-makers informed about companies' real environmental performance. Figure 16.8 exemplifies the kind of environmental data that RATP (the Paris Transport Authority) shares with counterparts, for instance, when bidding on international contracts.

Figure 16.8
Environmental
indicators, 2008 (RATP,
the Paris Transport
Authority).

Air quality: average emissions, broken down by category
Breakdown of bus fleet by fuel source (inc. clean energy)
Noise pollution: complaints, actions taken
Water usage: total consumption, industrial wastewater, disposal
Physical waste: number of collection/sorting sites, types of waste, ultimate disposal
Energy: total usage of electricity, fossil fuels, renewable sources
Environmental innovation: research efforts
ISO 14001 certification: number of sites and employees involved in the process

One of the main purposes of this accounting is to quantify (thus promote) year-on-year improvements in 'eco-efficiency'. From management's perspective, this should translate into leaner operations producing less waste and better resource use (Esty and Winston 2006). It is another level where environmentalism and profitability mesh perfectly.

An even more dynamic way to face the ecological constraint is by embracing a paradigm that has come to be known as 'natural capitalism' (Lovins et al. 2007). The idea here is that companies' main priority should be the management (conservation, re-utilization, re-investment) of resources. The scenario for a 'post-oil' world will be grim unless there is a fourth industrial revolution driven by clean technology. The sooner companies embrace this orientation, the more they will prosper. Ethical activists used to be the only parties demanding that MNEs act sustainably; nowadays, shareholders are likely to do the same.

The move towards clean technology should not be overstated. It is true that much capital is being mobilized towards this end. Numerous MNEs have developed in-house renewables divisions or acquired innovative SMEs; sustainability funds are attracting stock market investors worldwide; and venture capitalists in California's Silicon Valley and elsewhere are pouring funds into clean energy start-ups. Yet most alternative energy sources remain more expensive than traditional sources in kilowatt-hour energy equivalent terms. This slows the sector's growth and largely explains, for example, why by spring 2009 British energy giant BP had decided to cut 620 jobs from its solar activities, imitating the partial withdrawal of other leading MNEs such as Siemens, Iberdrola, and Shell (Macalister 2009). Like any infant industry, short-term returns in this new sector are hampered by high start-up costs, an absence of economies of scale, and immature technology. Following the 2008 credit crunch, there were also doubts about how much capital was available to companies to finance their green transformation, and how much of an incentive they had to embark upon this path as traditional fuel prices fell back again. Some political leaders, like US President Barack Obama and UK Prime Minister Gordon Brown, stipulated that part of the fiscal stimulus packages that they designed in reaction to the crisis should be spent on energy-efficient green infrastructure projects such as 'smart' electricity grids or public transportation. Some doubts remain, however, on how quickly consumers will migrate to new products like electric cars, which remain comparatively expensive and technologically risky due to the lack of (recharging) infrastructure (see Case Study 16.3).

At the same time, MNEs' adoption of environmentalist solutions would benefit not only them but society as a whole. Global competition for finite energy supplies has intensified. Because of the accelerated industrialization of emerging economies active in energy-intensive manufacturing, and as a result of increased automotive and aviation usage as more and more people can afford such modes of transportation, global demand for energy is due to grow by more than one-third by the year 2030, from 11.20 billion tons in 2004 to 15.41 billion tons (IEA 2006). Much depends on the extent to which LDCs' future growth incorporates the use of energy-efficiency technologies, with some calculations discovering that, if the developing world can keep the annual rise in its energy demand to 1.4 per cent

+ Clean technology
Know-how associated
with products and
services that are
powered by renewable
energy sources and/or
can be used to reduce
waste and pollution.

Thinking point

Is clean technology
destined to
become a
fourth industrial
revolution?

Photo 16.3
Waste collected in one
country is increasingly
processed in a second
before being reused in
a third (© iStockphoto).

a year, its total will be 25 per cent lower in 2020 than would otherwise be the case (Farrell and Remes 2009). This is helpful but does not detract from the big picture that the overall demand for energy is on a sharp upward path.

Global energy MNEs will satisfy some of this demand, since higher energy prices justify increased exploration and exploitation of existing oil, gas, or coal fields that are uneconomic at lower prices. Another area destined for expansion is nuclear energy—itself a major international business sector. Despite these efforts, however, there is little hope of conventional energy sources being able to satisfy the world's energy needs in the long run (Shelley 2005). As the years go by, it will become increasingly apparent that going green is not a choice but a necessity.

To summarize, in the future MNEs will need to manage resources more efficiently and promote alternative energy sources through technological innovation. These changes will affect all international managers. The associated need to reorganize cross-border supply chains will affect the global transportation of goods—thus the missions that MNEs give their different units. Renewed localization will affect product definition and marketing. Logistics constraints will change human dynamics by increasing the use of video-conferencing and promoting long-term overseas assignments as opposed to short-term travel. International managers who integrate these ecological constraints into their business planning will have a competitive advantage over everyone else.

Challenges and choices

→ The BRICs' emergence may be an opportunity for OECD country MNEs but it will also challenge their long-standing domination. Because these countries are politically and culturally so different from most OECD societies, managers often feel uncomfortable about entering them without a local partner. Yet where an MNE opts for an alliance with a BRICs partner, there is always a risk that it is arming a future competitor. It is difficult to determine when the benefits of increased exposure to emerging markets justify the extra costs and risks.

→ There is broad international consensus that the ecological constraint amounts to one of the greatest challenges that humankind has ever faced. What is less certain is how MNEs are going to react. Companies that invest heavily in the environment should be able to improve both their operational efficiency and their brand image. On the other hand, the process of adaptation is expensive and may not be justified at current price levels. The real question is to what extent international managers prefer to manage the future proactively rather than simply maintaining the status quo. Like many other decisions, change is a matter of timing.

Chapter Summary

Given the complications inherent in today's rapidly shifting and increasingly globalized markets, it is difficult for MNEs to detect which events are likely to bring them future success or failure. Different paradigms, and thus forecasts, tend to dominate at different points in time. In part, this is because it is often less dangerous for managers to follow an inaccurate consensus opinion than to deviate from it. MNEs try to overcome this conservatism by building multi-pronged global information and communications systems. Their hope is that colleagues will feel comfortable enough with one another to analyse different scenarios as objectively as possible.

Two of the main trends that have focused international managers' attention since the year 2000 are the rise of new economic powerhouses and the growing ecological constraint. In terms of the former, the chapter discussed the BRICs' evolving political economic orientations and identified their manufacturing and commercial advantages for MNEs. At the same time, their emergence is a challenge for existing MNEs, since it gives rise to new global competitors and because the paradigms that have historically dominated in the BRICs differ from the dominant philosophies in the developed world.

Regarding the second trend—pollution and resource depletion—it is safe to predict that, as ecological constraints tighten, environmentalism will be viewed not as a marginal concern but as an integral aspect of international business. This means that there is every chance that MNEs' sustainability functions will become fully-fledged, standalone corporate departments, as crucial to business organizations as marketing or finance already are. Of course, tomorrow's managers will also have to contend with other, as yet undetected phenomena—like the political effects of the financial crisis that erupted in 2008. By definition, the future is never written in stone. A person with a broad international overview will always be a desirable asset for an MNE.

Case Study 16.3

BYD charges ahead

Founded in 1995, BYD (www.byd.com) is a dynamic young Chinese company that has cleverly positioned itself to take advantage of two major international business trends: the rising demand for household durables in Asia (specifically in China); and the need for MNEs to develop solutions to growing environmental problems. BYD started out as a specialist in rechargeable battery technology, building technological competencies (and achieving International Organization for Standardization certification) that helped to earn it a strong reputation in the global IT industry and win the trust of leading telecommunications MNEs such as Nokia, Motorola, and Samsung. The company's initial IT and electronic parts business was very successful, with its nickel and lithium ion batteries becoming global benchmarks and giving BYD a significant share of the world market for mobile phone batteries. The real strategic innovation, however, was when the company took this initial competency and applied it in a growth area—environmentally friendly cars.

With capital partially generated from its successful 2002 entry on the Hong Kong Stock Exchange, 2003 was a crucial year for BYD's diversification strategy. It began with the takeover of Shaanxi Qinchuan Auto Company Limited, a small Chinese automotive company, before going on to build a 1 million m² plant in the Xi'an Hi-tech Development Zone in Central Western China. BYD then acquired Beijing Jichi Car Module Company Limited, built a 560,000m² plant in Shanghai, and moved its car sales headquarter to Shenzhen. Having established a geographic configuration that gave it a presence across

Offering different driving systems, new Chinese carmaker BYD is well positioned for the future (BYD).

China (without forgetting the representative offices that it had previously established in Japan, Korea and the USA), BYD began to work on a new automobile model, called the F3. This ultimately led in June 2006 to the F3e, a small electrical vehicle powered by Fe batteries. Publicized as creating 'zero pollution, zero emission and zero noise', the F3e had a range of 350 km per charge—much further than previous battery-run car prototypes. This would become a crucial sales argument. The success of a technological innovation depends not only on a product's own performance but also on the 'supporting industries' without which it cannot survive. The internal combustion car, for instance, broke through only because of the proliferation of petrol stations providing drivers with fuel. The current lack of stations offering electrical charges for battery-driven 'plug-in' cars has made it difficult for this new technology to emerge. Indeed, insufficient range is one reason why the EV1 electric car that General Motors first launched in the USA during the 1990s failed to take off. By developing a model that does not need to be refuelled more often than traditional cars, BYD makes it easier for customers across the world to migrate to the new standard, which is expected to take hold once the infrastructure is built (see Better Place at www.betterplace.com for more information on recharging stations).

BYD has complemented this technological approach with an industrial strategy aimed at making its electric cars accessible to the lower income middle-class households that are a key feature of the emerging markets offering automotive MNEs the most growth potential. Devising products priced to be internationally competitive is an ongoing policy at BYD. For example, hybrid battery petrol models developed by Japanese MNEs Honda and especially Toyota were retailing in China in late 2008 at remnibi 250,000 or around $36,500, a sum well beyond the reach of most emerging country families. BYD's F3DM hybrid, on the other hand, was selling at about remnibi 150,000, or $21,900 (Ash 2008). As for its pure electric car, known by spring 2009 as the E6, BYD was looking at a retail price of just above $20,000 per unit. This made it much more competitive than rival producers, who had gone for a risky strategy of marketing electric cars as sports vehicles on the other hand, BYD, had positioned its products to broaden their appeal.

The competency that BYD has accumulated in integrating different kinds of technology has also helped it to increase the efficiency of its manufacturing operations. In turn, this has had a positive impact on the company's design and assembly capabilities and also on the different driving systems it offers—a diversity that is crucial for a company targeting varying international markets. Now that BYD has sized its operations to achieve economies of scale, it is well placed to rise up the ranks of international carmakers. Indeed, it has expressed hopes of becoming the world's number one carmaker by the year 2025 (Day 2009). BYD's growing reputation was further strengthened when global investor Warren Buffett took at 10 per cent stake in the company, paying the sum of $230 million. Newspaper headlines in 2009 publicizing the woes of older MNEs such as General Motors or Chrysler do not provide a full picture of conditions in the global automotive sector. The outlook for companies like BYD, with their Asian and environmental focus, remains bright.

Case study questions

1. What specific international obstacles does an emerging MNE like BYD face?
2. How much extra are consumers willing to pay for a product that is environmentally efficient? How might this vary from country to country?
3. Will Asian firms dominate the global automotive sector within a few decades?

Discussion questions

1. Can strategic planning ever be objective or is it always culturally determined?

2. How quickly can MNEs be expected to shift their product ranges to meet the specific demands of emerging market consumers?

3. What implications does Asia's rise as a centre of international business have for the neo-liberal paradigm?

4. Is the environment a constraint or an opportunity for MNEs?

5. To what extent will the new clean energy sectors need state help to succeed?

References

Ash (2008). 'BYD F3 DM: The Chinese Hybrid Revolution Begins Right Now!', 15 Dec., www.chinacartimes.com (accessed 25 Dec. 2008).

Bello, W., and Engelhardt, T. (2005). *Dilemmas of Domination: The Unmaking of the American Empire*. New York: Metropolitan Books.

Blenkhorn, D., and Fleisher, C. (2005). *Competitive Intelligence and Global Business*. Westport, CT: Praeger.

Blumenstein, R. (2007). 'GM to Take Green Road in China', *Wall Street Journal–Europe*, 30 Oct., p. 3.

Bresciani, S., and Oliveira, N. (2007). 'Corporate Environmental Strategy: A Must in the New Millennium', *International Journal of Business Environment*, 1/4 (July).

Chazan, G. (2008). 'Oil-Field Production Drops are Accelerating', *Wall Street Journal–Europe*, 13 Nov., p. 10.

Citepa (2009). 'Air Pollution in Brief', www.citepa.org/pollution/sources_en.htm (accessed 10 July 2009).

Day, P. (2009). *In Business*, BBC Radio 4, 16 Apr.

Dobereiner, D. (2006). *The End of the Street: Sustainable Growth within Natural Limits*. London: Black Rose Books.

Duffy, G. (2009). 'Brazil and China Forge Closer Trade Links', 19 May, http://news.bbc.co.uk (accessed 21 July 2009).

Ehmke, M., et al. (2008). 'Measuring the Relative Importance of Preferences for Country of Origin in China, France, Niger, and the United States', *Agricultural Economics*, 38/3 (May).

Elliott, L. (2004). *The Global Politics of the Environment*. 2nd edn. Basingstoke: Palgrave Macmillan.

Engardio, P. (2007). *Chindia: How China and India are Revolutionizing Global Business*. New York: McGraw-Hill.

Enkvist, P.-A., Nauclér, T., and Rosander, J. (2007). 'A Cost Curve for Greenhouse Gas Reduction', www.mckinseyquarterly.com (accessed 26 Sept. 2008).

Esty, D., and Winston, A. (2006). *Green to Gold: How Smart Companies Use Environmental Strategy to Innovate, Create Value and Build Competitive Advantage*. London: Yale University Press.

Fackler, M. (2008). 'Building a New Detroit in India', *Observer*, 20 July, *New York Times* insert.

Fairclough, G. (2007). 'Accelerating Growth: In China, Chery Automobile Drives an Industry Shift', 4 Dec., http://online.wsj.com (accessed 10 July 2009).

Farrell, D., and Remes, J. (2009). 'Promoting Energy Efficiency in the Developing World', Feb., www.mckinseyquarterly.com (accessed 4 Apr. 2009).

Fetscherin, M., and Marc, S. (2008). 'Chinese Brands: The Build or Buy Considerations', *International Journal of Chinese Culture and Management*, 1/4 (Aug.).

Gao, Y. (2008). 'Nonmarket Strategies and Behaviours for MNEs to Build a Congenial Political Economic environment in Mainland China', *International Journal of Business Environment*, 2/1 (Jan.).

Goodin, R. (1999). 'Selling Environmental Indulgences', in J. Dryzek and D. Schlosberg (eds), *Debating the Earth: The Environmental Politics Reader*. Oxford: Oxford University Press.

Guardian (2008). 'Inside Brazil: A New Future', special report produced in association with Think Link, 14 Mar.

Hardin, G. (1968). 'The Tragedy of the Commons', *Science Magazine*, 162/3859.

Helbling, T., Mercer-Blackman, V., and Cheng, K. (2008). 'Commodities Boom: Riding a Wave', *IMF: Finance and Development*, Mar.

Hofstra, N. (2007). 'Sustainable Entrepreneurship in Dialogue', *Progress in Industrial Ecology: An International Journal*, 4/6 (Dec.).

IEA (2006). International Energy Agency, 'World Energy Outlook', www.worldenergyoutlook.org (accessed 26 Sept. 2008).

IEA (2008). International Energy Agency, 'World Energy Outlook', 2, www.worldenergyoutlook.org/ key_graphs_08/WEO_2008_Key_Graphs.pdf (accessed 11 July 2009).

Jain, S. (2006). *Emerging Economies and the Transformation of International Business: Brazil, Russia, India and China (BRIC)*. Cheltenham: Edward Elgar.

Jowit, J. (2008). 'Huge Increase in Spending on Water Urged to Avert Global Catastrophe', *Guardian*, 11 Sept., p. 25.

Kallio, T. (2008). 'The Janus Face of Sustainable Foreign Direct Investments', *Progress in Industrial Ecology: An International Journal*, 5/3 (June).

Kedia, B., Perez-Nordtvedt, L., Chen, J.-S., Kedia, B. (2008). 'Importance of International Skills for International Business', *Journal for Global Business Advancement*, 1/2–3 (May).

Keeley, G. (2008), 'GM Installs World's Biggest Rooftop Solar Panels', *Guardian*, 9 July, p. 27.

Labatt, S., and White, R. (2007) *Carbon Finance: The Financial Implications of Climate Change*. Hoboken, NJ: Wiley Finance.

Levy, O., Taylor, S., Boyacigiller, N. A., and Beechler, S., (2007). 'What we Talk about when we Talk about "Global Mindset": Managerial Cognition in Multinational Corporations', *Journal of International Business Studies*, 38/2 (Mar.).

Lockwood, C. (2007). 'Building the Green Way', *Harvard Business Review: Green Business Strategy*. Boston: Harvard Business School Press.

Lovins, A., Lovins, L., and Hawken, P. (2007). 'A Road Map for Natural Capitalism', *Harvard Business Review: Green Business Strategy*. Boston: Harvard Business School Press.

Macalister, T. (2009). 'BP Sheds 620 Jobs at Solar Power Business', *Guardian*, 2 Apr., p. 26.

Markoff, J. (2008). 'Global Dispersion of Internet Traffic Shifts Control away from US', *Observer*, 28 Sept., *New York Times*, insert, p. 5.

Mathews, R. (2008). 'Arcelor Plans Surcharge for US Customers', *Wall Street Journal–Europe*, 28 Apr., p. 5.

Monbiot, G. (2007). *Heat: How to Stop the Planet Burning*. London: Penguin.

Nocera, J. (2008). 'Tough Rules Kept Indian Banks Sound', *International Herald Tribune*, 20–1 Dec., p. 11.

Oster. S., and Batson, A. (2008). 'Beijing Revamp Boosts Environment Agency', *Wall Street Journal–Europe*, 12 Mar., p. 10.

Oster, S., and Davis, A. (2008). 'China's Demand for Coal Reverberates across Globe', *Wall Street Journal–Europe*, 12 Feb., p. 1.

Proverbio, S., Smit, S., and Viguerie, S.P. (2008). 'Dissecting Global Trends: An Example from Italy', Mar., www.mckinseyquarterly.com (accessed 26 Sept. 2008).

Rauwald, C., and Power, S. (2007). 'Race to Russia Revs up as VW Opens factory', *Wall Street Journal-Europe*, 29 Nov., p. 1.

Scase, R. (2007). *Global Remix: The Fight for Competitive Advantage*. London and Philadelphia: Kogan Page.

Shelley, T. (2005). *Oil: Politics, Poverty and the Planet*. London: Zed Books.

St-Maurice, I., Süssmuth-Dyckerhoff, C., and Tsai, H. (2008). 'What's New with the Chinese Consumer', Sept., www.mckinseyquarterly.com (accessed 26 Sept. 2008).

Stephenson, E., and Pandit, A. (2008). 'How Companies Act on Global Trends', Apr., www.mckinseyquarterly.com (accessed 26 Sept. 2008).

Thomson, A. (2007). 'You Can't Change the World by Wearing Sandals', 17 Mar., www.telegraph.co.uk (accessed 27 Apr. 2009).

Wilson, D., and Purushothaman, R. (2003). 'Dreaming with BRICs: The Path to 2050', 1 Oct., www2.goldmansachs.com (accessed on 4 Apr. 2009).

Wong, E. (2008). 'Once Engines of Growth, China's Factories at Standstill', *Observer*, 23 Nov., *New York Times* insert, p. 6.

Zachary, G. (2008). 'Silicon Valley Turns its Face to the Sun', *Observer*, 2 Mar., *New York Times* insert, p. 5.

Zimmerman, E. (2008). 'Roaming the World, Hunting for Trends', *Observer*, 8 June, *New York Times*, insert, p. 8.

Further research

Ho, P. (2008). *Leapfrogging Development in Emerging Asia: Caught Between Greening and Pollution*. New York: Nova Science Publishers Inc.

Asia's rapid growth has been accompanied by severe environmental degradation, largely as a result of the pollution that usually comes with rapid industrialization, urbanization, and rising consumption. The book explores to what extent it is possible for certain countries (China, Vietnam, Taiwan, and Singapore) to adjust rapidly to the ecological constraint, for example, by implementing cleaner technologies and strict environmental regulation earlier in their development trajectory than Western countries did. The idea is that this 'leapfrogging' will be possible only if the newly industrialized Asian countries develop an institutional capacity for incorporating sustainable thinking into their economic planning. The book provides an interesting example of an international business topic in which business, politics, ecology, and culture all interact.

Online Resource Centre

Visit the Online Resource Centre that accompanies this book to read more information relating to future trends in international business: www.oxfordtextbooks.co.uk/orc/sitkin_bowen/

Glossary

Absolute advantage Where one country, offering the same amount of input as another, achieves greater output of a good and therefore can be said to produce it more cheaply.

Accountability Idea that actors must take responsibility for their actions.

Adaptation Extent to which a company's products and services are adapted for each market, meeting the particular needs of the customers.

Advocacy Speaking out on behalf of a certain constituency in order to influence policy-makers to adopt a friendly stance.

Autarky Where an entity operates self-sufficiently and in isolation.

Autocratic management Management style that is domineering and dictatorial, sometimes with the exercise of unrestricted authority.

Barriers to entry Regulatory, competitive, financial, and other obstacles that make it difficult for a firm to enter a particular market.

Basis points One hundredth of 1 per cent—a common unit in international finance.

Beggar-thy-neighbour policies Where one country purposefully tries to improve its economic position at the expense of its trading partners, by keeping exchange rates artificially low, taxing imports, and so on.

Biosphere Sum total of elements on Planet Earth that make it possible to sustain life.

Boundaries of the firm Range of value chain operations that a firm undertakes itself without resorting to outside partners.

Brand Collection of images and ideas representing a company or other organization or economic producer; it can refer to specific symbols such as a name, logo, slogan, and design scheme.

BRICs Term first developed by US investment bank Goldman Sachs, referring to Brazil, Russia, India, and China as a block to highlight the emergence of these continent-sized countries.

Brownfield investment When a firm enters a new market by buying existing facilities.

Bulk buying Where goods or services are purchased in large quantities, there is a greater chance of negotiating a lower per-unit price, since the seller will achieve economies of scale that it can pass on to the buyer.

Business cycle Period during which the economy alternates between boom and bust.

Business-to-business (B2B) marketing Marketing of products and services to businesses—i.e. the marketing and sales relationship between one company and those other companies to which it supplies, or from which it receives, products and services.

Business-to-consumer (B2C) marketing Marketing of products and services to the end consumers or customers— i.e. members of the general public who consume the products or services directly for themselves.

Cap and trade Scheme that starts with a central authority distributing permits that allow members to engage in a given behaviour (like the emission of CO_2) within certain limits. Initial allocations can be exceeded only by purchasing unused allocations from other scheme members.

Capital flight A situation when investors or savers transfer large amounts of money out of a country because of fears about local risks or policies.

Capital markets Sum total of all transactions creating and trading debt and equity securities. Mainly refers to medium and long-term operations.

Cartel Groups of producers that instead of competing collaborate with one another on supply quantity and pricing decisions.

Chaebol South Korean equivalent of Japanese *keiretsu*, but, instead of companies holding shares in one another, shareholder equity remains largely in the hands of the lead firm's founding family.

Clean technology Know-how associated with products and services that are powered by renewable energy sources and/or can be used to reduce waste and pollution.

Clearing Process of calculating and paying the net differences between the amounts due to/owed by market participants.

Climate change Lasting variation in the average temperature of a given location.

Cluster Where firms in similar lines of business operate in close physical proximity to one another, reflecting historical factors or strategic intent and building close ties.

Code of conduct List of rules detailing accepted behaviour within an organization.

Commitment to internationalization Depth of a company's engagement of human, physical, and financial resources abroad. This can range from simple import/export activities to running large, wholly-owned foreign subsidiaries.

Comparative advantage Where one country produces all goods more efficiently than another but agrees not to produce, and therefore to import, the good whose production makes the least efficient use of its resources.

Competitive intelligence Firm's compilation and analysis of information on the outside world. Generally used as a guide for future action.

Configuration How a company designs and locates different corporate functions such as research, production, marketing, and finance.

Consolidation Where producers within a sector join forces via takeovers or mergers in order to reduce over-capacities.

Conspicuous consumption Extravagant purchase and use of expensive goods and services usually by a leisure class, in order to demonstrate status and wealth.

Corporate culture Common values shared by employees at all levels of the business. This can sometimes form an implicit or explicit control mechanism within the company.

Corporate governance Laws and processes regulating corporate management, including composition of the Board of Directors, protection of minority interests, executive control, and accounting practices.

Corporate responsibility Idea that a company should ensure that all its actions are both legal and ethical.

Correlation Extent to which different assets, like two currencies, move in the same direction.

Coupling Where countries' economic fortunes are linked owing to the inseparability of their economic and financial interests.

Critical mass Minimum threshold beyond which positive, size-related benefits arise.

Cultural context (high and low) Definition of the situational framework by which it is possible to distinguish the degree a special code is needed to understand the signals and communications of a culture.

Culture Broad term that covers many patterns of human activity that exemplify the ways of life of a certain population.

Currency controls Where a government places administrative restrictions on people's ability to buy/sell or lend/borrow assets denominated in the national currency.

Current account Country's 'balance of trade' (exports minus imports) plus or minus its financial flows from abroad (interest or dividend payments, cash transfers).

Debt relief Idea that the poorest borrower nations should not be asked to reimburse debt, either because the borrowings have been misused and did not benefit the recipient country; or because the borrower is too poor to reimburse.

Deferred differentiation Manufacturing strategy that combines economies of scale and product diversity by standardizing inputs for as long as possible in the production process before introducing adaptations as late as possible.

Demography Statistical study of all populations and the specific features of such populations related to their size, structure, and distribution.

Denominate Specify the currency of transaction.

Derivatives Instruments whose value is based on underlying cash market prices but where the parties to the transaction do not actually exchange the assets in question.

Design Activities aimed at defining a product's final shape and attributes.

De-skilling Where a reduced level of competencies is required from a business unit, often because it has been asked to specialize in one or just a few value-chain operation(s).

Disclosure Providing information, often in a specified form, to comply with legal requirements.

Downstream Later value-chain activities relating to the interface between a company and its customers.

Dumping When exporters sell goods at a loss or below the normal price specifically to gain market share and put rivals out of business.

Economic patriotism Idea that a society might show loyalty to domestic firms by purchasing their products and/or preventing foreign ownership.

Economies of scale When a company increases output using the same equipment, its per-unit production costs fall.

Economies of scope Production efficiencies that firms achieve because they can manage their product portfolio in a way that creates synergies. This occurs, for instance, when a given marketing initiative can be used to sell more than one item at a time.

Emissions Outflow following an industrial transformation process. Include air-borne gases and water-borne sewage, also known as 'effluents'.

Environmental footprint Ecological impact of a human activity.

Environmentalism Attitude that ecological sustainability should be a priority factor in personal and organizational decision-making.

Ergonomics Analysis breaking physical human activities down scientifically into a series of micro-tasks. Also called time and motion studies.

Ethical reporting group Associations of companies and other organizations promising to respect certain ethical standards.

Ethics Study of moral values. For the purposes of this chapter, behaviour will be considered ethical when it is characterized by an intention not to cause harm.

Ethnocentric Company's replication in the international market of the way in which it markets its products and services in its domestic market—this approach has worked well at home so it does not need to be changed.

Euro-markets Offshore markets escaping the jurisdiction of national authorities anywhere in the world.

Expatriate Employees working outside their home country.

Expatriation Process of international transfer of managers, often used as a strategic tool to achieve specific organizational goals.

Exposure Risk when assets do not match liabilities for a given commodity, like a currency, whose price might fluctuate.

Expropriation Where private property is seized by a government, often without compensation.

Externalities When an economic action affects parties not directly involved in it. This effect can be positive or negative.

Externalization Where a firm gives an outside party responsibility for some of its business functions. The opposite of internalization.

Factor endowments Human, financial, and physical assets that an economic entity (often a country) can use in its production process.

Fair trade Trade where profits are distributed fairly along the value chain so that upstream producers receive a decent 'living' wage.

Fair value Estimate of what a good is worth objectively, irrespective of potential buyers and sellers' interests or current market price.

Federative organizations Structures whose subunits are recognized both as autonomous entities with freedom to manœuvre and as members of a unified group.

Financial globalization Deregulation of world capital markets and the associated acceleration in cross-border capital movements of funds.

Financialization View that a firm's mission is to maximize financial returns. Often associated with the presence on the Board of Directors of 'active' investors specifically working to ensure that the firm engages in actions that will enhance 'shareholder value'.

First mover advantage Benefit of being the first party to move into a market segment in a certain location.

Food miles Distance travelled by a foodstuff between its place of production and consumption.

Foodshed The conception of a food system as stretching from its original rural source to its urban marketplace.

Foreign direct investment (FDI) Where a firm funds a permanent or semi-permanent physical unit abroad. One definition is that this involves a company taking a minimum 10 per cent stake in a foreign entity.

Foreign exchange (FX) markets Virtual marketplace(s) where currency prices are set through market supply and demand. The market is the sum total of the prices quoted and traded by all participants, nowadays almost always using electronic means of communication.

Forward trading Trading at a price established immediately for a delivery of assets at a specified future date.

Franchising Contract where a franchiser grants permission to a franchisee to run a business bearing its name, often using supplies that it provides. In return, the franchiser will receive income, often based on the franchise's performance.

Free riders Parties who benefit more from an economic activity than their contribution to it entitles them to.

Free trade Belief that goods and services should be negotiated on foreign markets without any government interference.

Free trade zone Tariff-free 'export processing zones' that many countries have set up to attract industrial activity. Little or no taxes are paid as long as the items being assembled or temporarily stored here are re-exported.

Frictional Refers to the problems that can arise when changes like new technology cause an existing economic sector to disappear and a new one to arise. Friction exists when the process of transition between the two sectors is not smooth—that is, where it takes a long time for people who lose their old jobs to find new ones.

Functional organization Structure where power is centralized, based on the idea that a firm's key factors of organization are its internal capabilities.

Generic Item that is not differentiated for a specific use but has a variety of applications.

Geocentric Company adopts the most suitable marketing strategy, taking into account the values of the company and those of the target market.

Geographic organization Structure based on the idea that an MNE's overriding organizational aim must be to ensure maximum adaptation to local circumstances.

Glass ceiling Artificial barriers based on bias that prevent qualified individuals from advancing upward in their organization into management-level positions

Global corporate ethos Essential set of characteristics that define the ways in which the MNE is organized and has its staff operate and behave.

Global firm Company that is conceived of as serving a unified world market rather than differentiated national markets.

Global governance Regulatory and supervisory functions fulfilled by authorities whose responsibilities exceed national borders.

Globalization Process whereby the world becomes increasingly interconnected at an economic, political and social level.

Goodwill Difference between the price at which a company can be purchased and the break-up value of its assets.

Green taxes Taxes creating a disincentive for firms to behave in an environmentally unfriendly manner.

Greenfield investment When a firm enters a new market by building new facilities.

Gross domestic product (GDP) Country's income, defined by national consumption +/− investment +/− government spending +/− trade balance.

Guanxi Chinese concept in which personal relations and the establishment of mutual trust and obligations are seen as essential for the conduct of business.

Hardship posting Traditional overseas assignment (or posting) that was thought to be undertaken in worse conditions than assignments at home and was thus rewarded with additional allowances, special arrangements, and increased remuneration.

Hedging Where a party offsets a risk through a new deal exposing it to the exact opposite risk. The original exposure is called the 'underlying' risk. The new exposure is called the 'hedge'.

Heterarchy Organizational principle that corporate units are allies and therefore equals in the management of their joint enterprise. In an MNE, this signifies that no one unit should take a global lead.

Hierarchy of needs Maslow's concept sets out a pyramid of layers of human need, from basic needs such as food, water and shelter to the realization of personal potential and self-fulfilment.

Home bias Preference for domestic over foreign activities.

Home currency Currency a firm uses to calculate its consolidated global accounts.

Home/host country People/companies originate from a 'home country'. When they operate abroad, they are working in a 'host country'.

Horizontal integration Where a firm establishes a presence in a new market by running activities similar to the ones it manages in its home market.

Horizontal *keiretsu* Japanese business network based on a principle of long-term inter-firm cooperation. A horizontal *keiretsu* is comprised of similar firms allying with trading companies to ensure the widest possible market coverage.

Import substitution Trade policy of supporting the domestic production of goods that would otherwise be imported.

Industrial models Manufacturing systems determining the sequencing of operations within factories. Also refers to flow of goods before and after industrial transformation, and to the distribution of any income generated.

Industrialization policies Concerted state efforts to increase manufacturing's proportion of national economic output, or to support industrial sectors considered strategic.

Infant industry Sector of activity that has developed only recently in a particular country and whose prospects for survival are uncertain because the sector lacks the capital and experience to compete with existing (foreign) producers.

Insiderization When people or companies are so deeply integrated into a local society that their foreign origins are forgotten.

Integration Where the activities of different group units are coordinated to the extent that the mission of one unit is defined in the light of the mission of another.

Intellectual property rights Exclusive enjoyment of the benefits derived from intangible assets such as trademarks, patents, and copyrights.

Intergovernmental organizations (IGOs) International bodies created by nation-states to deal with cross-border issues, often for coordination purposes.

Internal market Where related corporate units deal with one another as buyers and sellers of resources. Associated with 'intrapreneurship', which is the notion that individuals can act as entrepreneurs within large organizations.

Internalization When a company decides to run a particular function itself (using its own employees) instead of delegating it to an external partner.

International organization Structure based on the idea that all foreign environments share certain characteristics that differ from the firm's dominant domestic market and should therefore be combined in a specific division.

International tax competition Where a country tries to attract offshore funds by offering investors lower tax rates than they can find elsewhere.

Internationalize Decision to enter foreign markets; involves upstream and/or downstream activities.

Interventionism Belief that the state has some role to play in ensuring a fair distribution of wealth and that market mechanisms perform well.

Intra-firm Activities occurring within the confines of one and the same group.

Joint venture Business unit specifically created by different companies to achieve a particular mission. Usually involves pooling resources such as equity capital, knowledge, processes, and/or personnel.

Knowledge economy Sum total of markets that help actors to acquire knowledge, viewed as a product/service in and of itself.

Knowledge management Systems that companies use to maximize the benefits of knowledge accessed internally and externally. Mainly comprised of research and development (R&D) but also refers to data and information systems.

Knowledge spillover Where companies gain knowledge through proximity to external sources such as universities, research centres, or other companies.

Lead time Time it takes, once an order has been placed, to deliver a good to the order-giver's premises.

Lean production Production philosophy that emphasizes saving resources through less waste, better inventory management, better-quality, and shorter industrial cycles. Largely derived from the 'Toyota Production System'.

Learning effects Added production efficiency and lower costs that companies gain from accumulating experience in a particular activity.

Less-developed countries (LDCs) Countries where the industrial base and general level of human welfare do not enable most citizens to achieve a decent living standard. This is an umbrella term covering a vast range of economic, social and demographic situations, ranging from 'emerging' or 'newly industrialized' countries that are on a clear industrialization trajectory to 'failed states' with very poor growth prospects.

Leverage Organizing operations in a way that maximizes output without increasing inputs.

Licensing Contract where a licensor grants permission to a licensee to use one of its assets, usually intellectual property, as part of a business process. In return, the licensor will receive royalties.

Liquidity Volume of funds in a market. Markets are liquid if there are sufficient funds for an asset to be bought or sold without any noticeable impact on price.

Lobbying Attempts to influence policy-makers, often elected officials.

Long position Owning more of a commodity in the form of assets than the amounts owed in the form of liabilities.

Luddism Term used to characterize any resistance to change and innovation in technology. It is derived from the actions of the Luddites, who campaigned against the introduction of textile machinery in the early nineteenth century.

Market failure Where a market performs inefficiently by not allocating resources optimally. Reasons include non-transparent price formation, insufficient competition or rampant externalities.

Marketing mix Different phases of a corporate marketing strategy—product, price, place, and promotion.

Market-maker Trader who is always prepared to quote other market participants a price to buy ('bid') and sell ('offer') a given commodity.

Matrix organization Structure based on the idea that multiple reporting lines broaden employees' vision of the business and can create synergies.

Maturity Fixed date on which a contract terminates. For a loan, this is usually when the capital borrowed must be repaid.

Mergers and acquisitions Mergers occur when two companies agree to combine their operations in a new company where both have more or less equal powers. Acquisitions occur when one company takes over another—either with its approval or on a hostile basis—and has become the new entity's main shareholder.

Meritocracy Form of social organization in which the leaders have achieved their status by their own efforts—on merit.

Mission statement Defines in a few words or sentences the reason for existence of any entity or organization. It embodies its philosophies, goals, ambitions, and values.

Modules When components are assembled into a unit that fulfils a particular function in a system. Such units can be plugged without alteration into the rest of the system. Groups of modules are known as 'subassemblies'.

Money markets Sum total of short-term interbank and commercial lending operations, usually for durations of less than one year.

Multi-domestic Describes companies whose worldview, thus organization, stresses differentiated national markets rather than one unified global market. The end result is that each subsidiary manages its value chain more or less autonomously, with little if any coordination at the regional or global level.

Multinational enterprises Firms whose regular activities cause them to engage with and/or operate in more than one country at a time.

Nearshoring Where operations are outsourced to a low-cost location relatively close to the company's country of origin.

Neo-liberalism Belief in a minimal interference of government in the economy. Often associated with classical economics.

Net basis Remaining exposure after a firm's short position in a given financial category have been subtracted from its long positions in the same category.

Non-governmental organizations (NGOs) Associations created by members of the general public to deal with specific issues or to promote an overall ethos or policy. International NGOs usually focus on cross-border problems.

Nouveau riche French expression referring to a population that has recently come into wealth and whose consumption behaviour is changing.

Offshore Transactions or actors over which national regulators have no authority.

Offshoring Where a firm moves an activity that it used to run domestically to a subsidiary it owns abroad, usually to cut costs.

Oligopoly Market dominated by a few sellers, who might therefore have a disproportionate power to collude outside of the market framework and fix prices in a non-competitive manner.

Opportunity cost Cost of doing something in a certain way, thus not receiving the benefits of doing it another way.

Organic growth Where a company expands by growing its internal capabilities instead of through external acquisitions.

Organizational dilemma Where employees are confused by the contradictory interests that they are asked to represent at different levels within their organization.

Outsourcing Where a company buys supplies that it needs for its products or services from an outside company instead of making them itself.

Paradigm A world view—that is, a vision of how things are and/or should be organized.

Pay gap Different levels of payment between the top CEOs (or other employees) and those at other levels, or between male and female employees.

Peak oil Point at which half the world's oil reserves have been consumed.

Philanthropy Long-term charitable donations to worthy causes.

Pioneering costs Costs of the mistakes that a firm makes when entering a new market featuring unknown parameters.

Polycentric Company adapts its marketing and sales strategy as closely as possible to the target country—that is, the market that it is entering is so particular that the marketing strategy and the products themselves must be adapted to the local conditions.

Polyvalent Ability to perform many different functions—i.e. the opposite of specialization.

Post-industrial society Defines the development of a late capitalist society with such features as the growth of free markets, greater mass consumption and, ultimately, more leisure time.

Prime contractor Company at the heart of a network of companies, whose supply orders are the main trigger for other members' own production plans.

Private equity Equity investments in companies that do not involve transactions on an open stock exchange.

Procurement Act of purchasing resources or inputs.

Product organization Structure based on the idea that each product division should be run as an autonomous business.

Protectionism General policy where a national government adopts policies restricting foreign producers' access to its domestic market.

Public good Good that is 'non-exclusive' (i.e. available to everyone), and whose use by some does not decrease its availability for others.

Pull marketing Form of marketing reflecting the way in which a company is 'pulled' into the market by reacting to demand from the market.

Push marketing Form of marketing characterized by the way company 'pushes' itself into the market by providing and selling goods that are new and relatively unknown.

Race to the bottom Where competition among disadvantaged producers forces them to accept lower remuneration for their services.

Real interest rate Nominal interest rate minus inflation rate.

Reciprocity Notion that all parties to a transaction should grant and receive benefits of equivalent value.

Regime General system organizing interactions between different groups. The term often refers to a body of regulations and the institutions that formulate and enforce them.

Regime shopping Decision to locate an MNE's activities based on the relative laxness of a host country's requirements (taxes, regulations).

Regional agreement (RA) Treaty between neighbouring nations to develop an institutional platform where issues of mutual interest can be discussed and decided.

Reserve currency Currency that, by consensus is, viewed as the safest vehicle for storing value.

Resource depletion Consumption of raw materials that cannot be replaced.

Responsiveness Ability to react quickly to the perceived needs of a situation.

Safe haven Assets that investors tend to purchase to store value in times of crisis. Often include gold, USD, and Swiss francs.

Salaryman White-collar worker (based on a Japanese model) who works in the large bureaucracy of a business (or government office). The salaryman has long working hours, low prestige in the corporate hierarchy, and an absence of significant sources of income other than salary; the term is almost always used only for male employees.

Securities issuance Act of creating tradable capital market instruments (stocks and bonds) that firms sell to investors to raise capital.

Segmentation Identification of customers with similar characteristics so that a commercially viable marketing strategy can be devised and implemented.

Settlement Actual moment when one party to an FX transaction transfers the currency it sold to the account of the other party, and receives the currency it bought.

Shareholder value Idea that the purpose of a company is to maximize returns to shareholders.

Short position Owing more of a commodity in the form of liabilities than the amounts owned in the form of assets.

Sister unit Two separate corporate entities that share the same parent company.

Small and medium-sized enterprises 'Enterprises which employ fewer than 250 persons and which have an annual turnover not exceeding 50 million euros, and/or an annual balance sheet total not exceeding 43 million euros' (Extract of Article 2 of the Annex of Recommendation 2003/361/EC).

Social contract Idea that people will hand some of their rights over to an authority that offers them order in return.

Solvent Having sufficient funds to pay for goods.

Spread Difference between the market-maker's 'bid' and 'offer' prices. In the FX markets, this is usually calculated in terms of basis points (four digits after the zero, i.e. 0.0001).

Stakeholder Anyone affected, however indirectly, by an organization's actions. The term is often understood to include employees, local governments, suppliers, consumers, and host communities.

Standardization Extent to which a company sells exactly the same product in its domestic and international markets.

Stereotype Simplified and/or standardized conception or image with specific meaning, often held in common by people about another group.

Stewardship Concept that one party has a practical if not moral obligation to take responsibility for another.

Stock-market capitalization Total number of shares issued times the share prices for all companies listed on a particular exchange.

Strategic business unit Identifiable entity within a corporation that is large enough to plan strategy and organize resources on its own.

Strategic change Radical reorganization and restructuring of the direction and operation of a company.

Strategic trade policies Trade policy of strengthening local firms' export competitiveness in specific sectors.

Subsidiary (Foreign) unit belonging to a company's head office.

Supply chain management Ways of directing the transformation of a physical good. Includes purchasing supplies and stocks; coordinating and training of suppliers and sub-suppliers; and overseeing the logistical flow of goods and information.

Sustainability Search for societal solutions providing long-term human and environmental outcomes.

Syndication Practice of dividing the risk of a given operation among market professionals.

Synergy Idea that the value of a newly combined company will be greater than the separate value of its constituents.

Targeting Designing and aiming of a message at specific types of customers within markets that have been selected as the focus for a company's offering.

Tariffs Taxes that governments levy on goods (usually imports) when they cross national borders.

Tax avoidance Use of legal means to avoid paying taxes.

Tax evasion Use of illegal means to avoid paying taxes.

Tax haven Country with particularly low tax rates and regulations.

Technology transfer Where technology belonging to one country or company is shared with another under a formal partnership arrangement.

Terms of trade Relationship between the value added inherent to the goods/services that a country imports, on one hand, and that it exports, on the other.

Time to market Lag between a product's design and/or value-chain transformation and its being made available to end users.

Trade balance Relationship between the value of a country's exports and imports. When exports exceed imports, the country has a trade surplus. When imports exceed exports, it has a trade deficit.

Trade diversion When imports come from less efficient producers located within an RA instead of from more efficient outside producers.

Trade liberalization Loosening of regulations in a bid to reduce government influence on a country's import/export performance.

Transnational firm Company whose aims, and therefore organization, will alternatively highlight global efficiency, local flexibility, and shared learning.

Triad/OECD countries World's more affluent and industrialized nations. Triad refers to the three regions of Western Europe, North America, and Japan/Oceania. The Organization for Economic Cooperation and Development (OECD) is a Paris-based association whose membership is comprised of the world's leading economies.

Trickle-down economics The idea that it is acceptable for those at the top of society to be the prime beneficiaries of certain economic policies if their gains ultimately benefit the rest of society. Often used as a justification for low tax regimes.

Triple bottom line Idea that firms should report not only financial but also social and environmental outcomes.

Turnkey project Large projects where a group of companies, called a consortium, bids to win the right to build the asset (plant, infrastructure).

Upstream Early value chain activities undertaken when processing or transforming a product or service.

Value chain Succession of acts that successfully add value to an item as it is transformed from a raw material or input stage to a finished product or service.

Venture capital Funds provided by a small group of investors to support the expansion of a new firm, often in a high-tech sector.

Vertical integration Where a firm controls, and/or moves towards controlling, both the upstream and downstream sides of its value chain.

Vertical *keiretsu* Japanese business network based on a principle of long-term inter-firm cooperation. A vertical *keiretsu* is comprised of companies specializing in different value chain activities and will generally include a bank for funding purposes.

Viral marketing Strategy that encourages individuals to pass on marketing messages to others, creating a multiplier effect spreading the message's exposure and influence.

Welfare systems Provisions made alongside the productive economy to support vulnerable members of society. Usually government-sponsored.

Working capital Excess of long-term capital resources over long-term uses of capital. Helps companies avoid bankruptcy by providing a stable source of funds to pay off short-term debts.

Work–life balance Life choices that many people make in order to balance the demands of work with other important areas of their lives such as family, friends, and hobbies.

World culture Growing concept of a universal culture that rises above national cultures and emphasizes global events and world organizations.

Xenophobia Fear of things that are foreign.

Index